HOW to USE THIS BOOK

- **If you're skeptical of the value of *PLS*, read these first—**

  The Testimonial Essays (the addendum to Chapter 15), and Chapters 8 & 9 (in Part II) and 14 & 15 (in Part III).

- **If you're *not* a skeptic, but do *not* have much time before starting Law School:**

  Read the Opening Statement and Part I.
  Then skip to Chapter 16 (in Part III) and its first addendum, and start following through on "The *PLS* Approach" ASAP.

  Read Chapters 11-13 (in Part III) and Chapter 30 (in Part IX) just before classes start.

  Read Part VI after your first semester, and Part VII after your second.

  Read Chapter 10 (in Part II), Parts V & VIII, the rest of Part IX, and the Closing Argument, when you get the chance.

  * * *

For now, updates, and Falcon's advice column (forthcoming and revived), can be found at **www.planetlawschool.com**

There is also a Yahoo message board/discussion group, "Planet Law School," at **http://groups.yahoo.com/group/planetlawschool/**

Falcon's main e-mail address is **atticus@fineprintpress.com.**
The alternate address is atticusfalcon@pdq.net.
And if all else fails, e-mail him through the Themis Institute (see the addendum to Chapter 10), at themisinstitute@pdq.net.

Snail mail:
Atticus Falcon
c/o The Themis Institute
3112 Windsor Road - Suite A-103
Austin, Texas 78703 - 2350

For information, please contact:

The Fine Print Press, Ltd.
350 Ward Avenue - Suite 106
Honolulu, Hawaii 96814 - 4091
web site: www.fineprintpress.com
e-mail: info@fineprintpress.com

Cover Artwork by Dlorah DeVore.

ISBN: 978-1-888960-50-1

ISBN: 1-888960-50-7

Falcon, Atticus (pseudonym)
    Planet Law School II: What You Need to Know (*Before* You Go)
    —but Didn't Know to Ask...and No One Else Will Tell You

    Includes bibliographical references and index.
    1. Law students—United States—Handbooks, Manuals, etc.
    2. Law—study and teaching—United States
    3. Law schools—United States
    I. Title

    832 p.   22.86 cm.

    KF283.F181 2003   340.071173   CIP 2003103509

Printed in the United States of America
08   10 9 8 7 6 5 4

Table
of
Contents

What You Need to Know (*Before* You Go)—but

SCHOOL II

Didn't Know to Ask...and No One Else Will Tell You

Other Books From
The Fine Print Press

Also for the Law Student

Later-in-Life Lawyers: Tips for the Non-Traditional
Law Student

Law School: Getting In, Getting Good, Getting the Gold

For the Summer and New Associate

Jagged Rocks of Wisdom: Professional Advice for the
New Attorney

The Young Lawyer's Jungle Book: A Survival Guide

Non-Law Adventures

Grains of Golden Sand: Adventures in War-Torn Africa

Training Wheels for Student Leaders: A Junior Counseling
Program in Action

PLANET LAW SCHOOL II:

What You Need to Know
(Before You Go)
—but Didn't Know to Ask
...and No One Else Will Tell You

THE THEMIS INSTITUTE
Austin, Texas

by arrangement with

THE FINE PRINT PRESS, LTD.
Honolulu, Hawaii

Dedicated

to

Thane Josef Messinger, Esq.

—for cajoling me into
writing the original edition
and also this new one.

Thank you, Sir.*

* I think.

THANKS

Six people read part or all of this new edition in manuscript. They caught mistakes (both typographical and otherwise), and suggested changes that made *"PLSII"* a much better work than it would otherwise have been:

Stephen Marsh, Esq., of Dallas, is a member of the Themis Institute's Board of Trustees. (Although I've neither met him nor even talked with him on the phone, I think it's safe to say this guy is proof that it's possible for a real-life lawyer to be as noble as Atticus Finch.)

Thane Messinger, Esq., of Boston, is another Trustee of the Themis Institute...and this book is dedicated to him.

Maureen David just finished (spring 2003) her second year at the University of Cincinnati's Law School (which, by the way, is the oldest law school west of the Alleghenies).

Cynthia Ferebee has now completed her first year at Cornell University's law school. (It was she who suggested the addition of the phrase "*...and No One Else Will Tell You*" to the subtitle of this book for this new edition.)

Philip Rosmarin is at the University of Denver, where his first year of law school just ended. (And his writing is among the most powerful I've ever seen.)

"Naturally Native" (as she is known to readers of The Princeton Review's message board), is someone about whom I dare say nothing further.

* * *

Vincent Eleutherius is my research assistant. He did the drudgework of accessing and copying law review articles and other materials and then sending them to me, looked up web sites and product numbers on recommended books, and called to my attention various conferences on legal education and the legal profession that I would not otherwise have been aware of and thus would not have attended.

David Ronin served as both my "outside" editor and agent (on the first edition as well as this one).

Dlorah DeVore, a professional graphics artist, did the cover of this new edition, and graciously accommodated so many requests for changes that I lost count of them.

Alihaider Kanpurwala, a computer whiz, provided the template for the typesetting of this book. And because I am inept at these things, his telephone "hotline" and "cyberspace fix-its" made all the difference when it came to getting the text ready for the printers.

Opening
Statement

Law School "Lite" v. Doing It *Right*

> *Legal education is unlike* any *academic experience* you've ever had before.

Law school is a world unto itself. Its atmosphere and gravity are different from Earth's. Hence this book's title. And once you've touched down, you can't radio Ground Control for help, saying "Houston, we've got a problem." Not only will *Planet Law School II* be your life support system; it will help you return to Earth safe and sound.

The memorize-and-regurgitate approach that worked so well for you before will not work now. In fact, it will prove counter-productive. It is self-sabotaging. Nearly all law students have to learn that lesson the hard way. And tragically, most don't until after they've finished that all-important first year of law school.

But by far the hardest thing for students to do is to *change* their way of thinking, and studying, from what they did in all their previous years of schooling. Old habits die hard. And the habits of your academic life to date will, in law school, die hardest of all. Although there are a few lucky students who just naturally "think like a lawyer," for the vast majority it requires a conscious effort, and a lot of self-discipline to "re-pattern." That's what this book is for. That's what "The *PLS* Approach" is all about.

I wrote the original edition of *PLS* because the other books for prospective law students provided only generalities, not the *crucial* specifics. Potential future attorneys weren't told what they needed to know to comprehend the law and to do well in law school. Instead, they only got clichés ("take notes," "study a lot," "brief the cases"). Such platitudes are useless; sometimes they're harmful.

Those books are all still on the market, and over two dozen others have joined them—with more on the way—as publishers crank out more "quickie" books to try to cash in on the bumper crop of new law students.

But now, in addition to the nearly worthless *generalities,* there are books with nearly worthless *specifics.* ("Buy a good bed," "Get a pet.")

The books in both groups are what I call "Law School *Lite*." If you go by what they say, you're likely to get washed away—not washed *out,* but certainly swept into a backwater. (In fact, most law students—and new lawyers, too—circle aimlessly in a fog. Either that, or they rush full-steam ahead...onto the rocks.)

But law school isn't brain surgery or rocket science. In fact, *it's actually quite simple.* (But that's not to say it's *easy.*) It's just that you're not told, beforehand, how the system works....And by the time you've figured it out (if, indeed, you ever do), it's too late.

This is something the other books don't want to admit, apparently. In this way, they contribute to the "macho mystique" of law school—which flatters the authors, of course. (This is especially true of those "how to succeed in law school" books written by law *professors.*) I—and many others—took them at face value before starting law school. Don't you.

The original *PLS* was published in May, 1998. In the nearly five years since, I've received thousands of questions, comments, criticisms, and suggestions from present and future law students, from attorneys, and even from law professors and deans. *PLSII* incorporates or otherwise responds to virtually all of them.

This is a lengthy book, because there's a lot you need to know—and you won't find it anywhere else. Perhaps you think this book is too much for you to go through. If so, you'd better forget about law school—now. If it's just too much trouble for you to read *this* book, you will have trouble in law school. Period.

Planet Law School was written for a self-selective group of highly motivated, conscientious students, not mere browsers. Nor is it for those looking for a quick and easy path to success. (There's no such thing in law school.) To shift metaphors: this is for those who want to carefully look before they leap, and who want to get the highest marks from the judges after taking the plunge.

As the page "How to Use This Book" (facing the inside front cover) indicates, though, you do not need to read it straight through before you start law school. (In fact, much of it becomes important only as your first year of law school is winding down.)

Even if you're about to *start* law school or are already *in* it, what's in here can prove life-saving...as you will see. As a general rule, though, *the earlier you read this book, the better.* (But if *all* you do is *read* it, you're kidding yourself as to your sincerity.)

I assume you will read this book, if you do read it, because you want to avoid mistakes. (As the sage put it, "Mistakes are often stepping stones to failure.") This book will help you to avoid mistakes, both major and minor. "Even a *fool* can learn from his *own* mistakes. A *wise* man learns from the mistakes of *others.*" *Planet Law School II* will help you go into law school with the same sort of "inside knowledge" that normally only comes with experience.

> **It isn't enough to work hard.**
> **Nor is it enough to *be* smart.**
> **You have to "*work* smart," too:**
> acquire a sense of what's important
> what's not; and set your priorities.
> This is especially so that all-important
> first year of law school.
> **You can't know *everything*—but**
> **you *can* know what really *counts*.**
> **That's what this book is for.**

Lewis H. Lapham is the editor of *Harper's* Magazine. In his "Notebook" column for the June 2002 issue, he said:

> Among all the American political virtues,
> candor is probably the one most necessary
> to the success of our mutual democratic enterprise,
> and if we amuse ourselves with the pleasure of
> telling welcome lies...we speak to our fears
> and our weaknesses instead of to our
> courage and our strengths.

It is particularly important for future lawyers who, as lawyers, will play such an important role in our mutual democratic enterprise, that they not amuse themselves with the pleasure of *hearing* "welcome lies" regarding the law school *academic* experience, *à la* the Law School "Lite" books.

Planet Law School II, in contrast, speaks to your (well founded) fears—and to weaknesses of which you yourself are as yet unaware. But it seeks to help you convert those fears to courage, those weaknesses to strengths. The final decision, though, is yours.

Atticus Falcon
Member of the Bar
State of the Art
"Law Day, USA,"* 2003

---

* May 1. "Law Day, USA" was first declared in 1957, by the American Bar Association, as America's answer to the annual "May Day" parades in the then-communist and socialist world. From 1958 on, it has been observed by Presidential Proclamation.

For Those Who will *Not* be
Full-Time Law Students

If you'll be attending evening classes, part-time, nearly all of what's here is still valid for you. —In fact, whereas for a full-time student *PLS II* might "only" mean the difference between surviving and *thriving,* for those who are juggling a full-time day job *and* night school, it could mean the difference between "life" and "death."

An Apology

This new edition was supposed to have been published...well, quite awhile ago. As it finally goes to the printers, it's obvious that it will not be available until most students who are starting law school in the fall of 2003 will already be in law school. I am very, very sorry about that—especially because the delay is entirely my own fault.

The only consolations for those who are starting law school in the fall of '03 are: (1) the "How to Use This Book" page will help you find the most important parts immediately—and the first addendum to Chapter 16 will help you to quickly get your hands on the recommended materials; and (2) the book is far better than it would have been had it been completed by any of the—many—deadlines the publisher set.

There will probably be a third edition of *PLS,* but this new edition should hold up well until then. This one almost "killed" me, and I wanted it to be good enough to last awhile.

And for Those Just THINKING
about Law School (or BUSINESS School)...

Now that *PLSII* is *finally* done, I'm supposed to get back to a work-in-progress for those who are just *thinking* about going to law school (or *business* school), but who don't yet need to take the LSAT or GMAT and start on their applications.

The working title is *Destination: Planet Law School (or Business School)? Where, When, How—and Whether—to Go.* It will include information on making the right moves while you're still in college, to improve your chances of getting into your target school. It will also discuss what your target schools should be, how to choose among schools when several comparable schools accept you, and how to get the best financial aid package possible. It should be out by late spring, 2004. (But given how long it took to finish *PLSII,* no guarantees.)

Part I:

From Mystery to Mastery

Chapter 1 - Landing in a Strange, Little World: Courses, Materials, Methods

The Law Degree

The degree nearly all future attorneys get in law school is the J.D. That stands for "Juris Doctor" or "Doctor of Jurisprudence," depending on the school.

Until a few decades ago, the basic law degree was the LL.B, Bachelor of Law. The name was changed in a bid to give lawyers more status, similar to *real* doctors with the M.D., D.D.S, or other medical degree. (However, the term "doctoral degree" generally refers only to the Ph.D.)

Now that the basic law degree is supposedly a "doctorate," it's paradoxical that the next higher degree is still called only a master's. The LL.M. (Master of Law) arose during the days when the basic degree in the law was the bachelor's. Other—less common—names for master's law degrees are J.M. (Juris Master or Master of Jurisprudence), and S.J.M.—Master of Juridical (or Juristic) Science.

There are other law degrees more properly designated as being at the doctoral level, which you can get with or without the LL.M.. But few do.

A big reason for this odd set-up is that, when hiring new law faculty, what the schools look at are (1) where the person got his or her *first* law degree, and (2) whether or not that person Made Law Review (discussed in Chapter 18). Those factors are far more important than what the degree itself is.

That All-Important First-Year

There is no "Introduction to the Law" course for first-year students, no course in "The Western Legal Tradition." You'll immediately find yourself in the thick of things—with assignments to prepare for your very first day of classes. Ironically, if you want an Introduction to the Law or to the Western Legal Tradition, you'd better have already gotten that before law school. Otherwise, you'll have to wait until the dust settles from your first year. Even then, such courses are only electives (if they're offered at all), and you might have a schedule conflict with something that, given your hopes for a career, is a must-take.

Virtually all first-year courses are required, and cannot be deferred. The "Big Six" are:

1. Property
2. Contracts
3. Torts
4. Civil Procedure
5. Criminal Law
6. Constitutional Law

Those, along with Legal Research and Legal Writing, comprise the nearly universal first-year curriculum (although, at many schools— including Harvard—Constitutional Law is an elective). Some are year-long, others one semester. Contracts and Civil Procedure normally last a year. Criminal Law is always just one semester. Property, Torts, and Constitutional Law can go either way, depending on the school. (There's an accelerating trend to cut full-year courses down to just one semester.)

Perhaps you are now expecting a survey of each. If you got that, here's what just two of them would cover:

Property—Seisin; Freehold v. Non-Freehold Estates; Absolute v. Qualified (a.k.a Defeasible) Estates—including Fee Simple Determinable, Fee Simple on Condition Subsequent, and Fee Simple on Executory Limitation; Present Possessory v. Future Interests—including Vested Remainders, Vested Remainders Subject to Divestment, Vested Remainders Subject to Open, Contingent Remainders, Springing Executory Interests, Shifting Executory Interests, the Rule Against Perpetuities, the Rule of Convenience, the Rule in Shelly's Case, the Rule in Clobberie's Case, and the Doctrine of Worthier Title; Concurrent Estates—including Joint Tenancy, Tenancy in Common, and Tenancy of the Entirety; Equitable Interests in Land; Rights Incident to Possession—including the Rights of Lateral and Sub-Adjacent Support; Fixtures; Easements—including Appurtenant Easements v. Easements in Gross, Quasi-Easements, and Easements by Prescription, Necessity, and Express Reservation; Profits —including Mesne Profits, *Profit à Prendre,* and the Doctrine of Emblements; Covenants Running with the Land at Law (including Vertical and Horizontal Privity) v. Equitable Servitudes; Present v. Future Covenants of Title; the Doctrine of Shelter, the Equity of Redemption, and the Doctrine of Equitable Conversion; Race v. Notice v. Race/Notice Recording Systems; and Usufructory v. Proprietary Rights...among other things.

Contracts—Offer and Acceptance, Bargained-for Legal Detriment, and Aleatory Contracts; Unilateral v. Bilateral Contracts; Constructive Conditions; the Statute of Frauds; Merger Clauses and Parol Evidence; Reliance v. Restitution v. Expectancy Interest; Rescission, Repudiation, Anticipatory Breach, and Novation; the Uniform Commercial Code—including the Perfect Tender Rule, Cure, and Replevin...

Enough. Now, do you really want a discussion of these things? Let me guess. Besides, in your first-year courses in these subjects it's highly likely that some (and perhaps most) of the topics listed will not be covered, even though nearly all of them *ought* to be. Unfortunately, you will hear about many of them for the very first time only during your bar "review" course, after graduation. Also, right now, it really isn't important for you to read about all these things—as though I could even put them in a nutshell for you. This isn't the book for that. (Yet, I strongly recommend that you find out about them *before you start law school,* to give yourself an edge. That's what Chapters 2 and 16, especially, are for.)

* * *

Law school isn't like college, where one credit or one year counts as much as another. *First-year* law school grades determine your future, both within law school and as to your job prospects. First-year is (almost) *everything.* Pulling your grades up later is nearly always too little, too late.

First-year courses are of two kinds:

1. The ones that count (now).
2. The ones that don't.

"The ones that count (now)" are those graded other than pass/fail, especially the Big Six. If none of your first-year courses is pass/fail, the ones that count are those used to compute your first-year gpa and class standing. (Some schools have adopted a "High Pass-Pass-Fail" grading system, even for the Big Six.) These are what (usually) determine whether or not you Make Law Review after year one, and whether or not you get Prestigious Summer Clerkships. (Chapter 18 discusses both.) These things, in turn, are (almost always) the key determinants of your job options as you approach graduation.

Yet, ironically, it's the courses that *don't* count (now) that can make or break your career in the Law. Go figure.

The Ones That Count (Now)

1. PROPERTY

Odd as it might sound, "property" is—ultimately—only what the courts are willing to recognize as "property." Granted, some things have "always" been property...but not necessarily.

Perhaps the easiest example of how this works is distinctive characters in the mass media. When radio (and movies with sound) were first proliferating, the people who'd developed distinctive characters had no property rights in those characters. Anyone could copy either the voice or the appearance for commercial purposes, without permission and without paying a fee—even if the imitation was meant to take business away from the original. A few decades ago, a new trend started, recognizing the property right. Today, for someone living, it's acknowledged in all jurisdictions. But only in the *very* recent past have courts—and legislative bodies—allowed the right to continue after the person's death. So today, when you see a television commercial with someone who looks and moves just like Charlie Chaplin, you know the "Little Tramp's" estate signed a contract allowing the portrayal, for a fee. (Either that, or someone's about to get sued for copyright infringement.)

A thousand years ago the English property system regarding real estate was the same as under communism, of all things: the Sovereign owned it all. The only difference was that the King, rather than the State (or "the People") was the Sovereign. He owned it all by right of conquest, as a result of the Battle of Hastings. To the victor go the spoils. And in 1066, William (as in "The Conqueror") took title to every building and every piece of land in England. More than half a millennium passed before the law developed to where "a man's home is *his* castle."*

2. CONTRACTS

Odd as it might sound, as with property, a "contract" is—ultimately—only what the courts are willing to recognize as a "contract."

Contracts are made regarding property, whether realty or personalty (the latter being legal jargon for "personal property"). Money is a form of property, and most contracts involve the exchange of money.

Granted, historically, some things have "obviously" been contracts—

---

* A married couple's house was under the husband's sole control. Nearly another half-millennium passed before the *wife's* right to a say-so, even in her *own* property, was recognized, or before an *un*married woman's home became *her* "castle."

ATTICUS FALCON, ESQ.

but not necessarily. For example, say a 15-year-old aspiring rock star signs a contract with a recording company. The deal isn't binding on the kid—but it *is* binding on the recording company. Unless the star agrees to the contract anew upon reaching "the age of majority" (18, now), he or she is free to walk away from the deal and make a better arrangement elsewhere. Bob Dylan was at one time a very big "folk-rock" star. He was discovered and promoted by John Hammond of Columbia Records in the 1960s. At the time, the age of majority, everywhere, was 21. Dylan (actually, Robert Zimmerman) was 20. In gratitude to Hammond, personally, Dylan insisted that even though he was a minor, he would honor the deal he'd made with Columbia. So, after Dylan turned 21, Hammond didn't ask him to sign a new contract. Sure enough, in his 21st year, Dylan repudiated their deal.

First Lesson in Contracts (and everything else): Sometimes the Liar Wins.

—Or rather, Dylan *tried* to repudiate their deal. Unfortunately for him, either he'd waited too long to talk with a lawyer about changing record companies, or the lawyer at the record company he wanted to switch to was not very good. Dylan had continued to use Columbia's studios for recording his music after his 21st birthday. Ergo, Bingo: through his actions, Dylan had made a "constructive ratification" of the otherwise-voidable contract. He could not repudiate it.

Second Lesson in Contracts (and everything else): it helps to know the law (and to find out all the significant facts in the case).

3. TORTS

The seeming oddities continue: a "tort" is—ultimately—only what the courts are willing to recognize as a "tort."

The word is from the Latin, meaning something like "twist" (and is probably related to "torque," the engineering term). The term became part of the English legal system when the Normans (French) took over after 1066 (see Property, above). Today, it might be better understood as meaning "screw"—because if there's a tort, it's because someone screwed up, causing someone else to *get* screwed up.

A tort is "an actionable civil wrong" other than breach of contract. "Civil" means non-criminal. (With few exceptions, litigation has to be either civil or criminal.) "Wrong" means...wrong, as in "She done him wrong." "Actionable" means...whatever the courts decide, which in practice means you can sue someone for it and maybe win. (You can sue anyone for *anything,* by the way. But that doesn't mean your case won't be tossed out immediately; you might even find yourself being fined by the judge for bringing a frivolous suit. And if what you brought suit for isn't a "cause of action" recognized by the courts, your case is already in trouble.)

What's a tort today might not have been a tort yesterday, and vice versa.

First example: a century ago, a previously-unmarried female of "marriageable age" in "respectable society" had to be vitally concerned about her reputation for chastity. If she was not a virgin, and this fact was known, she was said to be "ruined." Then she would have to either a) marry *outside* respectable society, or b) resign herself to becoming an "old maid" (and "old" meant over 25).

So, any man who claimed to have what was euphemistically called "carnal knowledge" of that woman could be sued in tort for defamation (in this case, slander). If a medical examination proved his alleged lover was in fact still a virgin, the man would have to pay her "damages" (and would himself be excluded from respectable society henceforth). Originally, though, her adult male relatives—one after another—would have just challenged him to a duel until the man was killed. Trial by combat. If and when he died in a duel, her honor, and thus her marriage prospects, were (perhaps) restored. After dueling was outlawed, the woman's only recourse regarding the alleged sexual intercourse was to court, for redress of her alleged undress.

Surprisingly, almost all jurisdictions still have such a defamation law on the books (under "slander *per se*"), even if it's only in the case law rather than statutory. But it's rarely a basis for a lawsuit, for obvious reasons. And in Massachusetts, "chastity" plays a role in the *criminal* law: it's a criminal offense to have sex with a girl who's between the ages of 16 and 18...unless she is no longer "chaste"—i.e., a virgin. (Keep that in mind, you male students at the Bay State's law schools. Remember that scene in *Legally Blonde,* where the HLS guy was trying to simultaneously pick up *two* young females?)

Second example: a century ago, there was no such thing as casualty insurance—at least, not for ordinary people, and maybe not for anyone. If a man held a dangerous job (as, say, a coal miner, a steel-plant operative, or a construction worker), and got injured on the job, there was no system of worker's compensation. And if the injury resulted from unsafe working conditions, the injured employee (by then an injured *ex*-employee) could not successfully sue his employer.

The courts, snugly in the pockets of Big Business, gave three reasons for ruling against him:

(a) the employee "assumed the risk" by taking the job in the first place;

(b) while the *ultimate* cause of the injury was (perhaps) unsafe working conditions, the *immediate* cause was usually the action of a fellow employee—who was just doing what he was supposed to be doing, granted, but accidents do happen; and

(c) —this one's my favorite—to *force* Big Business to provide safe working conditions (by allowing workers to sue for on-the-job injuries) would be to interfere with the prospective employees' "freedom" to "negotiate," for themselves, the terms of their employment (contract)...which takes us back to (a).

Today, of course, workers are protected by statute *and* by the ability to sue. (But then again, this protection, in practice, usually only extends to the right to recover damages *after the fact*. Workers' safety in all but a few industries is still woefully underprotected. —And no, I don't handle this type of litigation, so I'm not grinding my own axe here.)

4. CIVIL PROCEDURE

And, of course, as with everything else, a "civil procedure" is—ultimately—only what the courts are willing to recognize as a "civil procedure."

Granted, Congress and the States can enact codes of procedure, criminal as well as civil. But these given procedures can be invalidated by the courts. Because civil procedure regulates the conduct of litigation itself, the courts usually take the lead in this matter: Judicial Conferences (assemblies of judges) often recommend specific rules to the (other) "law-makers," who then adopt these rules—sometimes with changes.

In your first-year Civil Procedure course you'll study this only at the federal level. You will pore over a mere handful of the Federal Rules of Civil Procedure. But they're easy compared to the case law that pre-dated the FRCP—and you'll definitely be poring over (and maybe crying over) that. For most first-year students, Civ Pro is a nine-month nightmare.

This is not the place to explain why it's a nightmare. You'll just have to take me at my word. (However, Chapters 2-7 will explain how to cope with this course, as with your other first-year subjects.) The following is an example of Civ Pro in action:

You are a lawyer at a firm in New York City. Your firm represents the American interests of a Mexican multinational corporation headquartered in Monterrey. One day, you get a call from there. Seems your client has been sued in a state court in Kansas. The president of the company, a Mexican, was on a flight from Mexico City to Taipei, Taiwan (the Republic of China). The plane had made a brief stop in

Honolulu. While it was on the ground, a process-server handed the legal papers to the executive. The exec sent the documents back to Mexico by overnight courier after he got to Taiwan. Then they were faxed to New York, and the originals followed overnight.

Your first questions, though, concern more than just the nature of the complaint. You want to also see if you can throw a monkey wrench into the legal machinery your client's opponent has set in motion. Whose airline was the executive on? If it was Aero Mexico, that plane is regarded as Mexican territory, even while it's on the ground in the States. Therefore, service of process is subject to *Mexican* law, or the Hague Convention on it. You need to find out from your Mexican counterpart what the rules are South of the Border. But what if the president stepped off the plane while it was on the ground? If he entered onto American soil, the other side might have him.

But usually, foreign citizens in transit are restricted to the customs area of U.S. airports. They're not regarded as having officially entered onto American soil...you hope. You need to check that out. It just might be that the service of process was invalid. In that case, your client does not have official notice of the suit. And without giving valid, official notice of suit, the opposition is already in trouble: the due process requirement of the Fifth Amendment kicks in (as interpreted by the U.S. Supreme Court).

Then you have a second set of questions. All revolve around this one: why in a *state* court in *Kansas?* Regardless of what the dispute is about, you will check to see if you can have this case moved elsewhere. For one thing, you (being a New Yorker) absolutely do not want to set foot in the boondocks, and especially not what you regard as a Godforsaken place like Kansas. Second, you know perfectly well that whoever filed this suit figured they'd have home court advantage. If it's to be a jury trial, they want the edge of having local folks deciding the case against foreigners. So, you have to check out the Kansas law regarding "forum non conveniens." You invoke this to argue that it's really not convenient for your client to have to go to Kansas to defend this suit, and it would be more appropriate for the Mexican multinational to be sued elsewhere. You also check out the possibility of "removing" the case to federal court—preferably a federal court in, say, Manhattan (or at least to Delaware's state Chancery Court: no jury).

And so on. It's fun, fun, fun. (And once you get the hang of it, it really *is* fun.)

Civ Pro is "the rules of the game." As with other games, if you break the rules (and get caught at it), you get penalized (usually). But as with all areas of the Law, if you know Civil Procedure better than the other side does, you can sometimes nip a problem in the bud. This is especially so if the lawyer for the other side isn't a Civ Pro "pro."

5. CRIMINAL LAW

Even a "crime" is—ultimately—only what the courts are willing to recognize as a "crime."

Granted, some things have always "obviously" been crimes...but not necessarily. For example, "homicide" is the killing of one human being by another. But homicide is just the name of a fact situation; it isn't a crime in and of itself. Given the right circumstances, though, homicide does indeed become a crime: murder, manslaughter, etc.

Homicide occurring as part of an accident is usually no crime—although sometimes it's a tort ("wrongful death"). And as the notorious O.J. Simpson saga (1995-98) demonstrated, the State can prosecute an alleged act as a crime, and private parties can sometimes also file suit, in tort, against the accused.

Years ago, causing the death of a child within the womb was both a crime and a tort. Believe it or not, it often still is—as long as the person who caused the death is someone other than the woman whose womb the child is in. Example: the "life in being" is to be a substantial beneficiary under a will, but another person will inherit if that life is never born, and that other person deliberately contrives the death of the unborn.*

Take it a step further: what if there is a fertilized egg—but no womb? Here's the scenario:

a) a young married couple

b) the prospective father had suffered an injury, leaving him impotent, but

c) his sperm is still capable of fertilizing an egg, so

d) he'd had some removed, surgically.

Then add these facts:

e) the prospective mother, because of a medical condition of her own, would be putting her life at risk to get pregnant and carry a child to term, but

f) her eggs are intact and fertile, so

g) she'd had some eggs removed, surgically, and

h) his sperm had been mixed with her egg, in a test tube, and

i) the fertilized egg (now a conceived human being) was about to

---

* Regardless of your position on the abortion issue, you see why I am not using the term "fetus."

be implanted in the womb of a woman who'd been hired to be a surrogate mother.

Now add to that:

j) the prospective mother and father had been told by a moneybags relative that if they had a child, Moneybags would leave his entire (and vast) estate to that child, in his will, but

k) if there were no child, Moneybags would leave his estate to Nasty Nephew, and

l) the will has already been drafted accordingly, and

m) prospective mother and father, and Nasty Nephew, are aware of this.

Finale:

n) Nasty Nephew rushes into the medical facility just after the sperm has been united with the egg in the test tube and knocks it to the floor and stomps on it, destroying the fertilized egg.

Has there been a murder?

Would it make any difference if

o) during the attack, Nasty Nephew also destroyed all the rest of the sperm, and all the rest of the eggs, that had been removed, respectively, from the prospective father and mother, and

p) before further surgery could be scheduled to remove additional sperm and eggs, the couple was killed in an automobile accident?

From the perspective of Crim Law, (p) is irrelevant, and (o) is relevant only on the issue of intent.

But has there been a *murder?* No. That would almost certainly require a threshold test of the viability of the fetus, which is not present here.

Criminal law is divided into two parts: **substantive** and **procedural**. The substantive part concerns what is defined as a crime. The procedural part mostly concerns protecting the rights of the accused, especially regarding "due process of law." Although "substantive due process" is an oxymoron, and "procedural due process" is redundant, that distinction is important.

(*Civil* procedure also makes a distinction between substance and procedure with regard to due process of law, such as when repossessing property, or foreclosing on a mortgage.)

6. CONSTITUTIONAL LAW

All the preceding sections started by emphasizing that *x* exists in the law only if the courts are willing to recognize it. That's the way law is in America, because our English legal heritage is of the Common Law. Most countries (France and Japan, for examples) have Civil Law systems. (This is not "civil" as in civil vs. criminal proceedings, mentioned above. In a civil law system, the legislators and bureaucrats make the laws and rules, respectively. The courts typically have almost no power to do so; nor can they invalidate the laws and rules the others make.)

In our system, in contrast, "interpreting" a law is how judges make new law. This "case law" is every bit as binding as any statute, ordinance, or regulation. (And if the new "case law" is one made by the U.S. Supreme Court, it's even *more* binding than any of the others.) Hence lawyers and courts are vastly more important in the USA and other common law countries than in civil law nations. However, in recent years American law has moved toward more statutes and regulations, both to reduce the courts' dockets and to reduce the disparity in the common law among the states. (For example, a significant part of the law on inheritance now consists of the Uniform Probate Code. There are several more Uniform Codes, on other subjects.) Meanwhile, the civil law countries have moved more toward judicial review—the most important part of the (American) common law.

> "[W]e are under a Constitution, but the
> Constitution is what the judges say it is[.]"
>
> Charles Evans Hughes

Talk about *power*. Note the implication—a reality that Hughes, as Chief Justice of the U.S. Supreme Court, chose to dissemble. As you know, one uppity judge, all by him- or herself, can overturn the action of all 535 members of both houses of Congress *and* the President, for example. And if the Supremes vote to back that judge up, only a Constitutional Amendment (or a change in the Court's membership to produce a new decision, overturning the earlier one) can cancel the negation. Con Law is all about the history of what the Supreme Court says the Constitution is—and what it should be.

As Justice Robert Jackson of the Supreme Court once said, "We are not final because we are infallible. We are infallible because we are final." The similarity between Jackson's declaration and the doctrine of Papal Infallibility is unmistakable. Both are political tools disguised as theology—although in the case of Con Law, the theology is secular.

A bare majority of that committee of lawyers exploited this secular theology to make the final selection of the 43rd President of the United States by themselves. They did this by issuing an injunction that made a mockery of the legal requirements for "injunctive relief." The argument continues even now on the results of the Florida recounts—as to those that were held and those that might have been held. It's argued that the five justices made the correct decision by cutting short a process that would have led to the same result. That is fortunate for the Court's reputation.

Regardless, however, that does not disguise that by insisting on having the last word on the matter, the Court made an unprecedented grab for power to declare itself "final" in matters previously reserved to the electorate. And as the final arbiter of all matters Constitutional, the Court's action was particularly...interesting.

When "Con Law" is one of two courses on the subject (especially when Con Law is a first-year course), it covers the Articles of the original Constitution, plus the 14th Amendment. Con Law "II" then usually just covers one of the Amendments within the Bill of Rights.

* * *

This brings us to the two *most* important courses in law school. Perversely, they're the two courses law schools regard as *least* important: Legal Research, and Legal Writing. (Sometimes they're combined, as "Legal Methods," "Legal Analysis," "Case Analysis," etc.)

The Courses That "Don't Count" (Now) —But Which Can Make or Break Your Career in the Law

The discussion of the Big Six first-year courses emphasized that law changes over time.

Sometimes the pace is glacial, sometimes almost hectic. Yet, if and when you practice law, it will be rare for you to have anything whatso- ever to do with those changes. This is not meant as an insult to you. It's just the way the Law is, for 99.9% of those who are in it. It's safe to say that will include you. It certainly includes me.

In fact, the *weakest* argument you can make to a court is to merely say, "The law ought to be changed." That's tantamount to merely making the child's plaint, "It's not fair!" This is a favorite argument of law school students—and if that's all you can come up with, it's nearly *guaranteed* to get you *low* marks, whether from a professor, a supervising attorney, or a judge. If you can't think of anything better than the nebulous concept of "fairness" (or "justice"), you will nearly always lose. (This is not to say that fairness and justice aren't important. *Most* judges want to "do the right thing"—even though their idea of what's "right" is sometimes bizarre.) You need something more substantial than that. (General discussions of "fairness" that are part of official statutes or adopted in case law, as background to resolving specific issues, are called "**Public Policy**." You need to be aware of the Public Policy behind specific rules, to understand the rules better—and to know whether or not a given rule of law is truly appropriate for the facts at hand. But public policy is neither the meat of the law nor the potatoes of legal analysis.)

A. LEGAL RESEARCH

Legal research has two purposes. The first is to bring yourself up to speed on a new subject. (Because many lawyers specialize, that first purpose for doing legal research is infrequent, except in your first few years of practice.) The second purpose is to "find authority" for your position.

It isn't much of an exaggeration to say the courts don't care what *you* think; courts only care what other *courts* think, especially higher courts.

"**Finding authority**" means proving that some court (or, at the very least, a mere legislative body) has already made a law that fits your fact situation enough that the judge/s before whom you're appearing should rule in your favor. At minimum, you want something that's similar ("**on point**"—not to be confused with going "on point" as a ballet *danseuse*...although, come to think of it, litigation is—sometimes—like a ballet). And if you're real lucky, you'll find something that fits perfectly ("**on all fours**"). Legal Research shows you how to do that.

However, as part of your research, you will—almost always—also find authority that goes *against* you; it might even be *most* of what you find. So, if you can't "**distinguish**" that contrary law (i.e., make a distinction between that and the way *you* want the case to come out), you do want the law to change. Either way, you then practice the art of advocacy.

(Part V—the "Coda" to Parts I-IV—will walk you through a real-world case and its fact pattern, discussing the relevance of various cases that each side said were authority for its position.)

B. LEGAL WRITING

Advocacy takes two forms: oral and written. It's heresy for a trial lawyer to say this, but as between the oral and written, written is the more important...by far.

In dealing with a court, the written precedes the oral—both in time and importance. Even if you're going into a hearing or trial, you first will have submitted your arguments (which reflect your research) in writing to the court. With respect to "finding authority" that's both pro and con, your writings will argue to the judge/s that the authority favoring your position outweighs the authority that goes against you, and why.

Virtually everything you'll write as a lawyer will take a position. However, if what you're writing is strictly for use within your law firm, or strictly for your client's use, you want to be less assertive. Instead, here you're presenting options, and evaluating them. While you can make recommendations, the final decision is for your boss, or your client, to make.

Legal Writing shows you how to handle both situations. However, with the latter type of writing—when you're objectively presenting *both* possible sides of the story—legal writing is probably unlike anything you've ever written before in your entire life. It's hard to master this skill. But it's an important one...in part because *it's what's required on virtually every essay exam you'll take in law school, regardless of the subject.*

The reasons legal research and legal writing can make or break your career as an attorney should already be at least somewhat apparent. They're so important that much of Chapter 17 concerns them. Chapter 19 discusses, in part, why I believe these subjects are given the least attention in law school. (But after reading the next few chapters, you'll probably figure it out yourself.)

*** * ****

Prospective law school students are seldom—if ever—told that the *work* load in Year One is far heavier than in Years Two and Three, despite what the official credit load is. And of course, for nearly all beginning law school students, the subject matter is completely new. First-year is the worst year of law school. For many, it is one of the worst years of their lives. *This* book, however, intends to change that, at least for you.

Materials

REPORTERS

The most common law books are the books that contain the original written opinions of judges, explaining why they decided the cases the way they did. These aren't called "casebooks," though. Instead, they're "reporters." They got this name because, originally, the *court* reporters (humans) prepared summaries of the arguments the attorneys for each side had presented to the court, and stated which argument the judge/s had agreed with, why, and to what extent. (Back then, the judges themselves usually didn't put their opinions in writing.) You will rarely be using reporters in law school, especially in first-year, except as part of the process of familiarizing you with them in your Legal Research and Legal Writing courses.

Most of these are appellate cases. Unlike trial courts, in appellate courts more than one judge hears the case. For each case, there's a winner and a loser. And unless the court's decision is unanimous, there's also a winning side and a losing side within the court itself. The decision is by majority vote. One member of the winning side then writes the official opinion of the "court," stating who won and why. Other members of the majority can write individual opinions; each is a "concurring opinion." Sometimes members of the court who'd voted in favor of the loser then write individual opinions, too. These "dissenting opinions" explain why the majority is supposedly wrong.

Almost every reporter, state or federal, is published by West. (West is the Goliath of legal publishing; the reporters are the main reason it's Goliath.*) Case reporters aren't sold in law school bookstores. You don't buy any: you couldn't afford them, because they're in collections of *hundreds* of volumes. Case reporters are the main purpose of law libraries. (Now, though, case reporters are also on CDs, of course.)

---

* In February, 1996, The Thompson Corporation (officially headquartered in America, but actually a Canadian firm) bought West Publishing (which had been a privately owned firm, not publicly traded) for $3.43 *billion...in cash.* West's annual sales then were said to be $825 million, and its pre-tax profit margin, 25%. That margin would be good for any firm, but for a publishing company it was *awesome.* West was said to employ *7,000* people. That isn't much when compared to General Motors. But for a publishing firm, it's staggering. (Thompson already owned most of the other major legal publishing firms, such as such as Bancroft-Whitney, plus Clark, Boardman, Callaghan, and Lawyer's Cooperative Publishing, and Foundation Press. So now it's like Goliath on *steroids.*)

CASEBOOKS

Not "textbooks." There are virtually no textbooks in law school. Instead, you'll have "casebooks." There's a required casebook for each course. As the name implies, it's full of cases. The law professor/s who put the book together selected and edited each case.

COMMERCIAL OUTLINES

Originally, commercial outlines were to the first year of law school what *Monarch Notes*® and *CliffsNotes*™ are to lower schools. To use an archaic academic term, they were "ponies." They provided canned briefs, summaries of key points. (Regarding "briefs," see Chapter 3.) Today, the brief-in-a-can is the least important part of it. Instead, commercial outlines provide what the professors and the casebooks should but don't: knowledge of the law—what it is, and (sometimes) why. They are wonderful. Chapter 4 discusses them.

OTHER MATERIALS

The most numerous are the paperback Nutshell™ series, published by West. (Sample title: *Secured Transactions in a Nutshell.*) These books vary enormously in quality, as each is written by a different author. West has a "Nutshell" title for almost every standard law school course.

Some other books available are "hornbooks," digests, Shephard's®, and legal encyclopedias such as *American Law Reports.** They're in the library. You'll find out what you need to know about them—which is very little, in law school—once you're in law school (although Chapter 4 discusses hornbooks). You'll *use* them only when you're *out* of law school—unless you do a summer clerkship or legal internship (see Chapter 18), or get involved in Moot Court (see Chapter 19). The last major set of materials consists of the *Restatements* of the Law. Chapter 4 discusses them at length.

---

* If you've ever watched re-runs of the old (black-and-white) *Perry Mason* Show, you might have noticed the still-shot of a small stack of law books while the credits roll. All are volumes of *Corpus Juris Secundum*. With all those Latin words, it looks quite impressive, even intimidating. *CJS* is a legal encyclopedia.

Methods of Instruction

Do you know how to play chess? If so, you probably remember how you were taught, regardless of whether by a tutor or a book: you learned the names of all the pieces, their respective home squares, the method of movement unique to each piece, special rules (queen on color, castling, pawn promotion, *en passant* capture), and all the rest. Then you began to play. Gradually, you got better at it.

Even if you don't know how to play chess, imagine what it would be like if you sat down at a chessboard with none of the pieces set up—and you had previously received none of the instruction mentioned above. However, you were still expected to arrange the pieces properly and then play.

You would not be entirely helpless, though. To continue with this chess analogy: perhaps you've noticed "chess problems" in your daily newspaper. *The New York Times*, for example, regularly runs such a column. It presents a diagram showing the situation on a chess board after *x* moves by each side. Beneath the diagram is a list of those moves. Perhaps there's even a heading, something like "Nimzo-Indian." The problem then asks what White's (or Black's) next move should be. Or else it says something like "Mate in 3," and the problem consists of figuring out how that happens. There's a brief commentary.

Now, imagine that each day's chess problem is the *only* instruction you got. Yet, you were expected to gradually figure out what all the pieces are, how they move, and everything else discussed above. And you were expected not only to *quickly* learn how to play a decent game—but to eventually become a Master.

As you can appreciate, such daily columns really wouldn't be much help at all. In fact, they might just make things more confusing. (For example, the list of moves is written in "chess notation," not English.)

But that's how law is taught, even though it's vastly more complicated than chess. The "teaching" materials are something like a series of these chess problems, from completely different games. And just as in the chess problem, your adversary (here, the professor) says "Your turn."

Welcome to law school.

If you've ever studied a foreign language, you know the teacher and the textbook try to make it as easy as possible for you—because no matter how much help you get, it's still hard to master a foreign tongue. However, the new words are always presented just as a different way of communicating something you already know how to communicate in English. If the new language has a different way of organizing a sentence than English does, you're shown what it is and how it works. Gradually, you expand your vocabulary and your comprehension of the syntax. You create more complicated sentences using more new words. In short, you get more sophisticated, and perhaps eventually become fluent.

Even in "total immersion" courses, where the teacher speaks only in the foreign language and expects you to join in, the sentences are simplistic, just above the level of "baby talk." The instructor uses various approaches to help you realize the meaning of the words. And, of course, you often have a textbook that "lays it all out" for you.

In law school, the material is made as *difficult* as possible for you, on *purpose*. In first-year, you aren't even necessarily *told* the new words. (They're in the text. But when ordinary English words are used as legal terms, and have a different meaning as legal terms, you cannot even tell that they're legal terms.) And you certainly aren't told the concepts the words apply to. The words, and often even the concepts, are completely new.

Yet, even though this is a "total immersion environment," you are completely on your own. And instead of hearing and speaking sentences at the level of "baby talk," you are expected to join in a conversation that's the legal equivalent of a discussion of foreign policy, or art, or the sciences.

THE CASE/SOCRATIC METHOD

Legal education is built on the Case/Socratic Method. Hence the casebook. As mentioned, judicial opinions in casebooks have been edited down. Students read several for each class, and should be prepared to discuss them in a sophisticated manner.

The cases are just the starting point for a discussion usually consisting entirely of "hypotheticals." You have the set of facts presented in the case. The professor then begins a series of "what if" questions. Then he or she changes the facts. Should the decision be the same?

For example, under "Criminal Law" earlier in this chapter, there was a long hypothetical involving the *in vitro* fertilization of a human egg. Change the facts: say Nasty Nephew didn't invade the medical lab and destroy everything. Instead, the egg was implanted into the womb of a surrogate mother. Seven months pass. Everything's proceeding normally. But Nasty Nephew has heard about what's going on—and he's learned the name and address of the surrogate mother. One day he accosts her and gives her a *very* hard punch to the stomach. This causes her to have a miscarriage in a matter of hours. *Now* has there been a murder?

This is the so-called Socratic Method.

But it isn't.

That label was chosen as an act of vanity, to make it appear that law school profs are the modern successors of those pre-eminent ancient Greek philosophers, Socrates and Plato. Because there are those who—understandably—are not familiar with the genuine, original Socratic Method, an explanation is in order.

In Plato's books featuring Socrates, Socrates and his interlocutors would start out with opposite opinions. And just as Erle Stanley Gardner, as a novelist, made Perry Mason the perfect questioner who always triumphs in the end despite the steady resistance of his opponents, so Plato made his Socrates, twenty-four-hundred years ago. Through skillful questioning, Socrates brought the others around to admitting that their assumptions or analysis had been all wrong. If you believe such things really happen—whether in ancient Athens or a modern courtroom— you should consider another career besides Law.

Never mind that in all of history, Socrates is the only *real-life* person who *allegedly* ever used the Socratic Method successfully. American legal education not only pretends it really happened that way, but tacitly adopts the even grander pretension that law professors are the equal of Socrates.

Not so. For one thing, Socrates (actually Plato, who was largely putting his own words into Socrates' mouth) believed that each and every one of us, deep inside, *already knows* all the fundamentally important principles of everything: art, science, justice, you name it. For Socrates/Plato, education consists merely of clearing away the mental clutter that keeps us from realizing and acknowledging these fundamental principles. These principles are the Platonic Ideas, which supposedly have an independent, objective, unchanging existence some-where in the cosmos. And each of us is somehow connected to these Ideas. (Notice the similarity to the belief of the worlds' religions that everyone is somehow connected to that religion's Ultimate Being.)

Law schools insist that, as with Socrates himself, their method is designed to *reveal* principles, to make us aware of what *already* exists. However, the grand principles of the law are really just *rules of thumb* that have developed through the centuries (or sometimes, within just a few years) to guide courts in resolving disputes.

Disputes ("cases and controversies," in the language of the Constitution) are what the Law is all about. Yet, in general, the Law is supposed to be predictable. People can plan their activities, make their investments, etc., with reasonable assurance that what they're going to do is okay—and will *remain* okay. Over time, the rules of thumb change. But they should be recognizably the same over time—especially regarding the fundamentals. The guiding principle, however, is a consensus as to what's fair. (So, "fundamental fairness" *is* important.)

There's nothing wrong with this. Indeed, it's hard to imagine any other way of proceeding. But it ain't no set of Platonic Ideas. In fact, from time to time the U.S. Supreme Court has completely upset the applecart of the law in one area or another. (Abortion, affirmative action, and the meaning of the Fourth Amendment being the most recent—and controversial—examples.)

The professor's hypotheticals are the core of the Socratic Method. As just mentioned, legal principles are really just rules of thumb. Students are supposed to figure out those rules of thumb for themselves. The prof gives a hypothetical fact situation. The prof then calls on a student to create a legal rule of thumb, to be used as a basis for deciding the outcome of the "hypo." Every time a student announces what he or she thinks would be a good rule, the professor changes the facts in the hypothetical. Cleverly, the prof changes the facts in such a way that, if the student's proposal were applied to this new situation, the result would be absurd. So, the student must back off and start again. Through trial-and-error, the students eventually begin to formulate legal principles that seem to work well in most situations. No legal principle is complete without exceptions, of course.

For some in the class, there comes an "Aha!" moment. The future lawyer has suddenly discovered a combination of rule-and-exceptions that seems to fit almost *every* situation. (No such combination exists, however. That's why judges have discretion in deciding cases. The most important legal principle of all is...the judge's "fudge factor," more formally known as "judicial discretion.") Eventually, students discover there are exceptions to the *exceptions*.

* * *

There's a delicious irony to the Case/Socratic Method: *not even Socrates himself had worked things through on his own.* He had a teacher, a woman named Diotima. She was a mystic who had been admitted into a realm of knowledge far above our own. After spending his youth in a fruitless search for enlightenment, Socrates went to Diotima. Apparently impressed by his intelligence and earnestness, she tutored him. (Doubters are free to check Plato's *Symposium*—which, as it turns out, is not so much about love as it is about the love of wisdom, and its meaning, i.e., a philosophy of philosophy: "meta-philosophy.")

Defenders of the Socratic Method would say "So what? Socrates simply questioned others the way Diotima had questioned him." But Diotima did not merely *question* Socrates. True, as Socrates subsequently did, she used her questions to make him realize that his understanding was badly flawed. But once he had accepted that he really understood very little after all, she *instructed* him. Further, in an effort to comprehend her teachings, Socrates asked *her* questions. *Neither the instruction nor the counter-questioning occurs in law school.*

To return to the chess analogy: chess is complex, for those who play it well. Yet, the *basics* of chess aren't much more complicated than the basics of poker, and probably less complicated than those of bridge. The basics of chess are taught in a straightforward manner. Law isn't.

So the moral is:

> *You're going to have to rely on yourself— to a greater extent than you thought possible.*

You, being a perceptive person, are probably now thinking, "Yeah, yeah, I know: 'You get out of it what you put into it,' 'No pain, no gain,' yeah, yeah."

Well, all I can say is, "You'll see."

Christopher Columbus
Langdell's
(Alleged) Discovery

The Case Method and the Socratic Method are actually two sides of the same coin. The Case Method provides the body of material with which students work; the Socratic Method is the prod professors use to compel students to do the work.

In the early 19th century, there were virtually no law schools in America. (Most law schools that claim to have been founded long ago base their claim on the presence of one or two professors who taught only law, as part of a college curriculum. Eventually, these departments were "spun off" as new schools, of law.)

Students were assigned some reading material, often a treatise. It's said that those who taught law in the 19th century used the lecture method. At best, they would "hit the highlights" of the assigned material, in much the same manner as most teachers in college, high school, etc., today. But at worst, the law profs would merely read aloud to students in class, from the assigned work. Apparently neither the students nor the professors asked questions in class. Nor were there any tests of the students' mastery of the material.

The Case/Socratic Method changed that. It was allegedly created at the Harvard Law School, by Christopher C. Langdell, in 1870. ("Langdell" is pronounced "LANG-d'l.") It was the basis of Harvard's emergence as the pre-eminent law school in America.

Langdell was a law student at Harvard for three semesters in 1851 to 1853. Then he went to New York City, and tried to make it as a sole practitioner. (In those days, a "big" law firm had perhaps six attorneys.) He apparently did not have a good rapport with clients. And he apparently also had no ability as a courtroom lawyer. He soon was making his living by doing legal research for other attorneys and ghost-writing legal documents for them. In 1858, his main customer brought him in as a "partner"—but wisely kept him in the law library and a back office, away from clients and courtrooms.

In 1870, he was invited to join the Harvard faculty. The story is that the new president of Harvard University, Charles W. Eliot, had never forgotten a chance encounter he'd had with Langdell at the university when the two were there together as students. Supposedly, they'd never been in contact after that. However, Eliot allegedly remembered Langdell's brilliance, and had tracked him down and offered him the teaching job at Harvard.

So the story goes. Yet, whatever early brilliance Langdell had supposedly shown, he'd never followed through on it. There were many legal publications, even then. (This was before the rise of the academic law journal.) But Langdell never contributed any writing to any of them. In fact, it's hard to find *anything* Langdell is known to have written between 1854 and 1870, though in 1870 he'd reached his 44th birthday.

There appears to be more to the story than meets the eye, though. Eliot was a professional academic, a chemist. He'd absented himself from America during most of the Civil War, to "study European educational methods." At the time, the technological breakthroughs of the industrial revolution had led to more than half-a-century's stunning material progress. This gave science enormous prestige. Science was a means not only of understanding the world but of controlling it. (The 18th-century Enlightenment had championed science even before the technological breakthroughs had begun to occur. For example, George Washington had urged a "science" of government. The modern term "political science," as a college department, is a legacy of that early enthusiasm.)

Thanks to their stunning advances in the sciences, the Germans were already overtaking Britain industrially. Germany's educational system was (and still is) based on the idea that education is a science. Eliot came to believe likewise.

When the civil war ended, he returned to America. He then taught chemistry and mathematics at M.I.T. In 1869, he was tapped to become president of Harvard University.

His appointment was part of a movement to take control of American education away from the Christian ministers who'd dominated it for centuries. This movement sought to replace their other-worldly approach with that of what today is called a "real world" approach. Science, whether natural or "social," was the foundation.

Eliot was one of many who wanted to re-make all of American education in the German image. They succeeded. The modern American university is the result (although there has been a great deal of back-sliding of late).

Christopher Columbus Langdell (coincidentally?) saw *law* as a science. The in-class Case Method was part of a much larger Case Method, a schema that classified cases into various types and then compared/contrasted "like cases." In this way, it mimicked the scientific method, with its emphasis on categories and analysis.

For example, the system of "law digests" (which you'll learn about in your Legal Research course) is based on the system of indices and "headnotes" (created by West). These are very much like biology—

complete with families, genera, and species (although they are not called that in the Law). The most obvious mimicry of all, however is that (as you'll shall see in the next chapter) the Law does not speak of "definitions" of concepts. Rather, it speaks of "elements"—just like a chemist's "periodic table." I do not know (yet) if it was Langdell who first used the term "elements" this way. But it would not surprise me at all, given that the man who rescued him in middle age from a life of obscurity was a chemist.

The claim that Langdell invented the Case/Socratic Method arises from his 1871 casebook, *Selections of Cases in the Law of Contracts*. But that claim to his fame is at least half-wrong. For one thing, there had been other casebooks published before his. However, it is unclear whether they were used as the basis of a Case/Socratic Method in class.

More important regarding the "Langdellians'" claim: the first known use of the Case Method was at New York University's law school, not Harvard's. John Norton Pomeroy, a law professor there, regularly employed it at least as early as 1865. And as mentioned, Langdell was working as a back-room lawyer in New York City throughout the 1860s. I have yet to locate a document establishing that Langdell either knew Pomeroy or at least knew of his Case Method, but this is too much of a coincidence to be a coincidence: the world of the Law in New York City in the 1860s was just too small. I believe the document exists, and that it will surface someday.

As to whether Pomeroy also invented the Socratic Method, I do not know. It is virtually certain, however, that Pomeroy did not see the law as a science. A comment from Grant Gilmore is apt:

> Langdell seems to have been an essentially stupid man who, early in his life, hit on one great idea to which, thereafter, he clung with the tenacity of genius. Langdell's idea evidently responded to the felt necessities of the time. However absurd, however mischievous, however deeply rooted in error it may have been, Langdell's idea shaped our legal thinking...
>
> Langdell's idea was that law is a science.

Gilmore (who died in 1982) was an esteemed and scholarly professor at Yale's law school. He was the principal drafter of Article 9 (on secured transactions) of the Uniform Commercial Code, and the author of two classics for the general legal audience: *The Death of Contract*, and *The Ages of American Law*. (The quotation comes from the latter.)

It's unknown whether Pomeroy, at NYU, sought to remake legal education according to his vision. But that's certainly what Langdell, backed by Eliot, did. At the time Langdell joined the faculty, Harvard had only two other law professors. One of them had been one of two profs who'd dominated the law department for decades (the second dominant faculty member had departed just two years before Langdell's appointment). The two incumbent faculty whom Langdell joined both rejected Langdell's pedagogy. To strengthen Langdell's hand, Eliot named him the first dean of the law school, in 1871. Within a short time thereafter, both the other law profs left Harvard's faculty. Langdell and Eliot replaced them with new, young professors who were Langdell's *protégés*. Nearly all of them went straight from the role of law school student to law school professor. That pattern has spread, and persisted, to this day. (Now, however, future law profs serve a one- to two-year judicial clerkship first, and then often "get their ticket punched" by serving as an entry-level associate at a major law firm for a year or two after the judicial clerkship.)

The Common Law had progressed through fact-specific cases. Gradually, patterns had arisen, giving rise to general principles of law to guide particular types of disputes. The glory of the Common Law is that it proceeds in a bottom-up fashion, rather than in the top-down manner of the Civil Law.

But the American public had become hostile to professional lawyers and jurists. In many states, even judges had no experience or training in the law before taking the bench. Throughout much of the country, one could become a lawyer as easily as one could become a tradesman or merchant. No one bothered to read judicial opinions, to maintain consistency in the law and the rule of reason as the basis for legitimacy of court decisions. So the cases were helter-skelter. In America, the Common Law was becoming no longer common. A handful of eminent jurists wrote treatises to try to bring some understanding and uniformity to the Law, but they were largely ignored.

Langdell invoked the prestige of "science" to overcome the hodge-podge jurisprudence of the time. That was good. But he perpetrated an act of intellectual fraud. For Langdell understood neither the nature of the scientific method *nor* the Common Law.

Both use the inductive approach in formulating rules, but the similarity ends there. The Case/Socratic Method is anything *but* scientific. It was *Aristotle* who championed the inductive method, which is the essence of science. So he and Plato were almost polar opposites. Thus, Langdell was truly audacious in concocting his so-called "Scientific Study of the Law." He had no patience for the painstaking study of the law that a scientific approach would have required even if it were possible (which it is not). As Langdell himself explained in the preface to his casebook (as quoted by Gilmore):

> [T]he cases which are useful and necessary for [the purpose of mastering legal principles or doctrines] bear an exceedingly small proportion to all that have been reported. The vast majority are useless, worse than useless, for any purpose of systematic study.

But in *science*, that is impossible: samples might be *duplicative*, but never "worthless, worse than useless."

So Langdell snuck his own Platonic Ideas of the Common Law into jurisprudence, in the name of Aristotle's inductive method.

As Gilmore describes it:

> The jurisprudential premise of Langdell and his followers was that there is such a thing as the one true rule of law which, being discovered, will endure, without change, forever. This strange idea colored, explicitly or implictly, all the vast literature which the Langdellians produced. That is to say the doctrine—the one true rule of law—does not in any way emerge from the study of real cases in the real world. *The doctrine tests the cases, not the other way around.* (Emphasis added.)

Having decided what the doctrine should be, the Langdellians then searched for cases that illustrated the doctrine in the real world, and proclaimed them to be the "leading" cases on the subject—as though Langdell & Co. were merely following what the courts were doing. He wanted students to believe—wrongly—that there was "*a* right answer" to any question in the Law...and the professors always knew what it was. More important, Langdell's approach made the *academic* legal scholar the arbiter of just what *are* the valid legal principles or doctrines.

Langdell imposed his regimen on the students at Harvard Law School. Again with Eliot's backing, he also (successfully) sought to have Langdell-trained HLS grads become deans of the new law schools that were springing up around the country. Thus he effectively propagated his new legal theology. And throughout the country, professors sought to (and largely did) become the intellectual power behind the judicial "throne," in part because students (including the future judges, of course) were subtly encouraged to view their professors with awe. (The novel and film *The Paper Chase,* and even *Legally Blonde,* perpetuate this sense of awe.)

But by imposing his own narrow views, he only created more divisions within the Law. Not having been successful as a practicing attorney, he disdained the messiness of fact-specific cases. (That's one reason why, to this day, the Case Method relies almost exclusively on *appellate* opinions.) But lawyers and judges at the *trial* level had to deal with the messiness of fact-specific cases.

By the early 1920s, Langdell's approach had been in use for more than half-a-century. It had trained generations of highly influential lawyers, jurists, and professors. But it had failed to transform American law. In 1923, the—prestigious—Committee on the Establishment of a Permanent Organization for the Improvement of the Law issued a report. (Its name alone says much.) The report condemned the "uncertainty" of American law. It said this resulted from *"a lack of agreement among members of the profession on the fundamental principles of the common law."*

If law were really a science, could such pervasive uncertainty have existed? It was only when the successor organization to the Committee for the Improvement of the Law began its work that a truly *common* law was (re-)established. (The Langdellians, however, had a major influence over what was finally promulgated as the "common" law. Yet, even now, there are many ongoing struggles among jurists—as reflected in majority v. dissenting opinions in the courts, including the Supreme Court.)

But the professoriat refuses to consider any alternative intellectual approach to the study of the Law. To this day, the Case/Socratic Method blissfully lives on in the ivory towers of the law schools, despite the fact that its underlying intellectual rationale is just a watered-down version of what has long since been rejected by the academy, the bench, and the bar as mere "formalism."

Staying "Inside the Box"

Who cares? Well, if there's no such thing as a "science" of Law, then perhaps we should reconsider the value of the Case/Socratic Method as a "scientific" study of the Law. With the (major) exception of Richard Posner—*doyen* of "Law & Economics"—the very idea of law as a science has been thoroughly discredited among American legal scholars. Yet, even now, the highest earned degree in the law is the J.S.D., "Doctor of Juristic Science."*

It was the same prestige of science—and the same desire for control—that led Karl Marx to call his own brand of communism *"scientific* socialism." It wasn't until 34 years after his death that his system even began to be implemented. Yet, it's nearly extinct already. But Langdell's triumphed almost immediately, and is still going strong. It's a toss-up as to which "scientific" system will have done more harm, in the aggregate, by the time the Case/Socratic Method follows communism into the dustbin of history.

* * *

With apologies to Polonius (in Shakespeare's *Hamlet*), "Though this be method, yet there is madness in't."

The next six chapters are about how to keep the methodical madness from driving you crazy. A major purpose of *Planet Law School* is to help you—in the words of Rudyard Kipling's poem, *If*—

"Keep your head, when all about you are losing theirs..."

---

* At some schools, it's the "S.J.D.," "Doctor of Juridical Science." The S.J.M degree was mentioned earlier in this chapter. (The LL.D.—"Doctor of Laws"—is nearly always just an honorary degree.)

Chapter 2 -
Laying the Foundation for Your Success

In 1984, the Teaching Methods Section of the Association of American Law Schools published a two-volume report, *Learning and Evaluation in Law School.* Its author was Michael Josephson, then a professor at the Loyola Law School, Loyola Marymount University, in Los Angeles.

In Volume 1, *Principles of Testing & Grading / Learning Theory / Instructional Objectives*, he presents "the law school learning pyramid."*

The "Law School Learning Pyramid" — Level 1

"Knowledge" is the base. Josephson subdivides it. One subdivision is "specifics." This in turn is further subdivided. Two of its parts are important here: "terminology," and "rules and principles."

"Terminology" consists of legal jargon. Says Josephson:

> Knowledge of terminology is rarely tested directly but it is **invariably tested implicitly** since **the terms will be used in the test items themselves.**
>
> [Boldface added.]

—And regardless of whether they're used in the "test items" themselves (i.e., the problems posed), you'd better use the right terms in your answer, and in a way that shows you know what they mean.

As for "rules and principles," he says this:

> A law student should be able **to recognize and state definitions of the fundamental rules and principles** of each course, including alternative formulations such as minority rules, model rules, and significant state variations. Whether tested directly or not, **knowledge of this sort is essential on most law school exams** because it is the basis of many analytical problems."   [Boldface added.]

* His schema is adapted from Benjamin Bloom, *Taxonomy of Instructional Objectives: Handbook I: Cognitive Domain* (1956).

In other words, you don't have short-answer questions such as "state the rule regarding X," or "define the following terms." Nor do you get the type of question that has a series of terms in one column, and a series of definitions or statements of principles in the other column, where you have to match the corresponding items. No fill-in-the-blanks, either.

Later, Josephson comments:

> [L]aw students are expected to "learn" a vast amount of knowledge in each law school class...
>
> Yet, in spite of the foundational importance of this level of learning, **relevant knowledge is rarely taught**...Instead, teachers tend to **assume** that the student will **intuitively sense** what he/she must know **and find a way to learn it.**
>
> ...**[B]asic knowledge is presumed to exist at the time of an exam (***regardless*** of whether the desired information has been made *accessible* or whether the student has been *told* of its importance)...
>
> A teacher who plays "hide-the-ball" with critical knowledge in order to force the student to concentrate on analysis, unintentionally places an extremely high premium on the ability of the **student** to **discover** information **independently.**
> [Ellipses supplied, boldface and italics added.]

Josephson's statement about how professors assume that a student has to "intuitively sense what he/she must know and find a way to learn it" is what I call the professoriat's theory of the "natural-born genius of the law." As one law prof coyly put it, success in law school "appears to involve a substantial degree of natural talent or 'vision.'"* In other words, "Either you have what it takes, or you don't."

Although Josephson says the professor who plays hide-the-ball "*un*-intentionally [emphasis added] places an extremely high premium on the ability of the student to discover information independently,"

---

* Layperson's reference: Kissam, Philip C., "Law School Examinations," *Vanderbilt Law Review,* March, 1989, page 459. Legal citation: Philip C. Kissam, Law School Examinations, 42 VAND. L. REV. 433, 459 (1989).

I disagree. "Hiding the ball" is at the *heart* of the test of a student's ability to "intuitively sense what he/she must know and find a way to learn it." Those who can are presumed to have "a substantial degree of natural talent or 'vision.'" That's what the law professors presume they themselves have, of course.

Never mind that this is a perfect example of the informal logical fallacy known as "begging the question." ("I did well, so I have a substantial degree of natural talent or vision. Students who have a substantial degree of natural or talent or vision will do well.") More important, it means that, by playing "hide the ball," the entire law school experience is designed solely to identify those few students who supposedly do have "a substantial degree of natural talent or vision." As for the rest...well, too bad for them. They obviously don't have what it takes. Maybe they'll eventually catch on—such as when they're out in the real world, as attorneys.

If you think I am exaggerating here, skip ahead to Chapter 8, "The Walrus & the Carpenter." Nothing has changed since Josephson's 1984 report. He *opposed* "hiding the ball." But in the two recent articles reviewed in Chapter 8, the law professors who wrote them are *proud* of it. As you will discover, *they* represent what has always been the vast majority of the law school professoriat. They know exactly what they are doing, and why. And it has nothing to do with helping you to learn anything about the law.

Josephson continues:

> Ironically, *the more concerned a teacher is with the development of high level intellectual skills, the more conscious he/she* should be to *either "lay out" the basic law or see that it is easily accessible.*
>
> [Emphasis added.]

This, of course, is the way it was in your previous schooling. Your textbooks tried desperately to tell you everything you needed to know about the subject, and to be *clear*. Your teachers then lectured in class, ideally to dispel any remaining confusion. They would take questions from students, either in class or out, and try to give *helpful* answers. But this does not happen in law school. Quite the contrary.

> **The problem caused by *unarticulated knowledge objectives* is significantly enhanced by the fact that, instead of *reducing* the importance of information by simply *giving* it to the student, *many law school teachers do just the reverse.* As a means of stressing the importance of "analysis," of "thinking like a lawyer," *these teachers expressly demean the value of learning "blackletter" rules and definitions,* thereby *misleading* many conscientious students to scrupulously avoid trying to find and learn *the very principles the exam will implicitly test.* Similarly, *expressed disdain for all secondary sources (without any attempt to distinguish among them on the basis of quality) can effectively discourage students from efficiently supplementing* case readings and class discussion with *materials better suited to teach the informational level of the course.***
>
> [Boldface and Italics added.]

"Unarticulated knowledge objectives" is what law school is all about—not among the students, but among those who are supposed to be teaching them. You do *not* "get what you pay for." This is why the Opening Statement, and the back cover of this book, said *"Legal education is unlike any academic experience you've ever had before."*

Imagine if medical schools merely gave each new student a cadaver, a bag full of human bones and organs, a microscope, a scalpel, and a book filled with diagnoses of patients. And then the medical schools expected students to figure everything out for themselves—in time for their final exams. A handful each year might succeed. The vast majority would not.

But suppose, further, that *all* the students then took a "medical review" cram course after they graduted, which gave them just enough knowledge to pass their "medical boards" (licensing exams). Clearly, while most students would be able to cram for their boards and pass them, they would not be *prepared* for practice. They would merely be licensed to practice. That's different. All of them—whether or not they were successful in med school—would still have to learn through trial-and-error how to actually practice medicine. The American public would quickly detect severe shortcomings in its medical care, and would be up in arms.

Unfortunately, shortcomings in legal care are not so readily discernable—and even now, the courts and legislatures tend to look out for the interests of their fellow attorneys. So the "system" continues, despite the fact that what happens in law school is like what happens in the bizarre, fanciful medical schools described above. (The Josephson Report, of roughly 20 years ago, for example, soon died a quiet death...as have all reports that are critical of legal "education." And there have been a lot of them, spanning nearly a century now—commissioned by the Carnegie Foundation, or the ABA, or sometimes the law schools themselves...as with the Josephson Report.)

Running the Gauntlet

American Indians in the northeast had a custom whereby they formed two lines of warriors, facing each other, holding clubs. Captives were put at one end of the rows and then told to run to the other end. As they ran, the warriors clubbed them. If a captive made it to the end, he was allowed to live. If he fell before then, he was clubbed to death...unless he managed to crawl the rest of the way.

Law schools don't (metaphorically speaking) beat students to death. But they do club the hell out of them. All but a handful of students are crawling when they finish first year—grateful to still be "alive."

To change the metaphor: law schools engage in a perverse, academic form of Social Darwinism, "survival of the fittest." Their sole interest is in those who do well despite the fact that the school has tried its best to keep them in the dark. Yet, the idea behind Social Darwinism was that the fittest, having survived and triumphed, would propagate, and eventually populate the social landscape. The losers would die out.

With law schools, the *losers* populate the social landscape of the practice of law, as incompetents. And there is no *propagation* of the *fittest,* because the professoriat sees itself as an elite, based on its "natural talent or vision." As an elite, they want to keep their number small. So the interests of the many (including nearly all future clients) are sacrificed to the narrow interests of the few, each generation.

But the law profs overlook a different formulation of Darwinism. It's from T.H. Huxley, Darwin's contemporary: "Rather than survival of the fittest, the purpose is to fit as many as possible to survive." As with the law schools, other professional schools know that few of their graduates are destined for greatness. But unlike law school, *all* the others—engineering, business, medicine, dentistry, architecture, etc.—make an effort to ensure that *all* their graduates are at least *competent* to serve their future employers and clients.

If you are heading for law school (or are now in it), no doubt you got very good grades in your previous higher education. No doubt you believe that, with respect to the Law, you have "substantial natural talent or vision." ("After all, I've wanted to be a lawyer ever since I was twelve years old!")

However, given the fact that your law professors will do their very best to *thwart* your "intuitive sense of what you must know" and your efforts to "find a way to learn it," do you really want to take your chances? —Or would you rather hedge the bet you'd otherwise place on your own "brilliance," and find and use sources of information regarding the terminology, and the rules and principles, that Josephson spoke of as the *foundational* level of the "law school learning pyramid"? Your choice.

But before you make your decision, take a look at the list of topics covered under Property and Contracts, on pages 14 and 15 in Chapter 1. See how you feel about starting law school without a clue as to what any of them mean, or how they interact. Add to that feeling an advance awareness that not one of these things will be explained to you when you're *in* law school—not by your casebooks, not by your professors, not at all.

So, Just What IS Black Letter Law?

Josephson's report referred to "blackletter law," and it's sometimes spelled that way (including in *Black's*, which is "the" legal dictionary). But it can also be written "black letter law," or, as I prefer, "Black Letter Law." It's the real foundation of Josephson's "law school learning pyramid" (even though he does not expressly say so). The various parts of Black Letter Law comprise the building blocks of the law.

Black's defines it as, in part, "One or more legal principles that are old, fundamental, and well settled. The term refers to law set in Gothic type, which is very bold and black." That's a good start. But it's just the bare bones.

Nearly *all* of Law is a matter of *definitions*. You have something you want to define—say it's the legal equivalent of the word "duck." That's the starting point of what might be called the Black Letter Law regarding ducks. The law then works this way: "If it *looks* like a duck, and it *walks* like a duck, and it *quacks* like a duck...it's a duck." Each of these is what in the law is called an "**element**" of *defining* "duckness."

Ah, but what does it mean to "look like" a duck? To "walk" like a duck? To "quack" like a duck?

Then there are the variations. A *duckling* is a duck, but it doesn't look like a duck. Or does it? Ducks are white, or brown or other dark colors. Ducklings are yellow (I think). And what about ducklings that are dyed blue or green or pink, for Easter? Ducks have a flat bill instead of a beak, and so do ducklings. But so do platypi. Further, a duckling goes "peep, peep." It doesn't quack. And ducklings move quickly, more like normal birds, whereas ducks waddle slowly. But a duckling is a type of duck. And what about swans? Or geese? (Or cygnets or goslings, which are—respectively—baby swans and baby geese.) We need to distinguish these from ducks, and from each other.

This is what the "**case law**" is all about...here, the case law on "duckness."

The same thing applies to actions. What does it mean "to love"? I'm not even going to get started on all the possibilities. Suffice it to say we distinguish all kinds of love. Yet, there is more-or-less general agreement about what we mean when we refer to "loving" or "being in love" or "being loved." That is what might be called the Black Letter Law of love: "old, fundamental, and well settled," to again quote *Black's*. True, hardly anyone can come up with a specific definition of "to love," or "loving," or so on, that's universally acceptable. But we all "know it when we see it"...or, at least, we think so. The "case law" of our personal experience is how we work out the particulars. To some extent, that's the way the law works, too.

Legal educators still pretend that the law is "scientific," but it is not. It's a lot closer to philosophy, and sometimes even to poetry.

Getting into the law itself now...

In ancient days, the Ruler had almost nothing to do with criminal law. If someone was the victim of a crime, that person had to seek justice (which usually meant "revenge") privately. Hence the family, and the clan, were crucial. Even Hammurabi's Code and the Jewish talionic law were meant to serve only as guides for private resolution of disputes—in much the same manner as the worker's compensation laws of today. ("You do X, you pay *x* shekels," or whatever.) So, crimes were dealt with as civil matters, similar to torts today.

The 4 *"Meta-Elements"* of the Law

The Basic Four Concepts that cut across the law are **"Duty - Breach - Cause - Harm."** In the *real* world, you start with the Harm. "No harm, no foul." Or in contracts, "No damages, no breach." In the absence of major harm, you (usually) don't bother with it, because it isn't worthwhile. (But in law school, you do bother with it, as a learning exercise.) You have the harm (or rather, your client does). So you go looking for someone to blame, *other* than your client. You work it backwards, really, going from Harm to Cause, then to Duty and finally to Breach. (In Contracts, "duty" occurs, by definition, *if* there *is* a contract. The duty or duties of each party are the essence of the contract.) Although criminal law and tort law have been separate for several hundred years now, it's only been within the past 150 years that contracts and torts have parted ways. Neither existed in anything like its present form until the Industrial Revolution. Until then, there were no lawsuits in contract or tort. ("Trespass and case" were the ancestors of tort law. "Assumpsit" was the ancestor of contract law. The term "contract" existed only in political theory, as "The Social Contract." It was not a legal term.)

These four "elements" are the *major* elements ("meta-elements"—not a term you'll hear in law school, by the way) of *all* areas of the law. (However, only *Torts* normally *uses* these terms.)

"Cause" deserves special attention before proceeding further. It has two sub-elements of its own. The first is **"cause in fact."** It's based on the **"but for"** test: "But for *that*, would *this* have happened?" (There is also the **"substantial factor"** test, when more than one factual cause is involved.) This is what the common understanding of "cause" is.

However, "causation" in the law includes **"proximate cause"** (a.k.a. **"legal cause"**). It asks whether or not, to a **"reasonable person,"** in *these circumstances*, the potential harm was **foreseeable** (i.e., was the risk apparent?). And it asks whether or not a reasonable person would say that the connection between the respondent's act or omission is close enough to the resulting harm that it would be fair to say that the respondent was *really* the cause.

Example: a boss fires someone, who drives home while distressed and deliberately or accidentally runs someone else off the road. No proximate cause, if the other driver then sues the *boss*. It passes the "but for" test, but not that of proximate cause: the connection is too **"remote."**

These four meta-elements of duty-breach-causation-harm even spill over into Crim Pro and Civ Pro. For example, allegations of inadequate "due process" arise from the harm suffered—based on a duty on the part of the State (in the criminal action), or the other party to the lawsuit (in a civil action), as the case may be, and the breach of duty is alleged to have "proximately caused" the alleged harm.

These meta-elements also have a role to play in Constitutional Law. For example, the Constitution both grants and restricts governmental power. Often, there is an explicit duty *not* to do something. ("Congress shall make no law respecting an establishment of religion..." says the First Amendment. —And, through the 14th Amendment, most of these restrictions apply to state and local governments, too, not just the federal.) Others *imply* a duty *not* to do something. ("This Constitution, and the Laws of the United States which shall be made in Pursuance thereof...shall be the supreme Law of the Land." This clause from Article VI means that all lower levels of government have a duty not to encroach on the Constitution or federal law.) Virtually *all* federal appellate cases involve the question of whether or not some governmental entity has exceeded its powers (i.e., violated its duty to restrain itself) in some manner. The complainant has to allege that there has been harm because of an alleged breach of that duty, and that the breach has caused the harm.

(Note: I am using the language of "complainant" and "respondent" rather than "plaintiff" and "defendant." This way the discussion covers cases on appeal, not just at the trial level. Often the complainant on appeal was the defendant at trial. This is especially obvious in the case of criminal appeals.)

In property, the cases involve whether property rights have been violated by someone else or maybe by some governmental entity. (There is a duty to respect the property rights of others. Violation of those rights is the breach.)

All of these involve *definitions*. Given the facts of a particular case, the questions involved are 1) whether or not what the complainant says happened falls within the definition of "harm," 2) whether or not what allegedly happened to the complainant falls within the definition of "proximate cause," such that "the buck stops here" (i.e., in the respondent's lap), 3) whether or not the respondent's situation *vis-à-vis* the complainant falls within the definition of a "duty" the respondent owed to the complainant to make sure that the complainant did not suffer the alleged harm, and 4) whether or not what the respondent allegedly did or did not do fits the definition of a "breach" of that alleged duty.

It's a matter of testing the evidence to see if what you have fits each element of the definition of "duck." "*Does* it look like a duck?" One side says "yes," the other says "no." "*Does* it walk like a duck?" Same thing. Et cetera.

Sometimes, a court will say that even though a complainant claims to have suffered harm, there actually is no harm that the law recognizes as "**actionable**." (For example, hurt feelings.) Sometimes, a court acknowledges the harm, but says the respondent is not the "proximate cause" of that harm. Sometimes the court says the respondent had no duty to the complainant, even if the complainant suffered harm and the respondent's behavior caused that harm. (For example, a deranged person takes hostages at gunpoint, and the sniper on a police "SWAT" team kills that person just as he or she is about to shoot one of the hostages. The dead person's children, who were present at the scene, and saw it all, sue the police department because they're despondent over having seen the killing.) And sometimes the court says the respondent did not breach the duty the respondent admittedly had toward the complainant. (Example: a movie contains scenes so horrifying, and sickening, that the ads for it say, "Warning: This movie might cause you to have a heart attack. This is not 'hype.' We mean it." A 25-year-old, whose heart is in excellent condition, watches the movie in the theater—and, during one of the most shocking scenes, has a heart attack and dies.)

Within each area of the law, there are many "recognized causes of action" under the case law. (In criminal law, most criminal causes of action, i.e., crimes, are "recognized" by statutory law.) Each of those causes of action has its *own* set of elements. In Contract Law, for example, the very definition of "contract" consists of elements. In torts, the tort of "false imprisonment" consists of elements. And in criminal law, "kidnapping" consists of elements. These are all matters of *definition,* and of determining whether or not a particular document, act, or item of property *fits* a given definition. ("Is it a duck?")

> In order to BE "Black Letter Law,"
> EACH element is NECESSARY,
> though NO element, by itself, is SUFFICIENT.
> They come as a SET, for any given "cause of action."

The complainant has to prove ALL the elements of his or her cause of action in order to win. The respondent need negate only ONE element of the complainant's cause of action in order to win.

Then, however, there are the independent defenses against causes of action, called "**affirmative defenses**." In torts, for negligence, there's one called "contributory negligence" or maybe "comparative negligence" (depending on the jurisdiction). Then the shoe is on the other foot, and it's the *respondent* who has to prove *all* the elements. Assuming the complainant's case meets its own burden of proof, then all the complainant has to do is knock out only one of the elements of the respondent's affirmative defense in order to win. In Contracts, the affirmative defenses include "fraud," "coercion," "impossibility of performance," and more. In criminal law, the affirmative defenses include "self-defense," "defense of others," and "defense of property." In Civ Pro, it can take the form of a challenge "for want of jurisdiction," or others. (In fact, in "contributory negligence" jurisdictions, the complainant in Tort has a counter-affirmative-defense, in the form of the "Last Clear Chance" doctrine.)

What all these affirmative defenses have in common is that they are, in effect, a "Plea of Confession & Avoidance." The respondent (perhaps) does not challenge the proof of the elements of the complainant's (or State's) case. Instead, the respondent says, "Even if all that's true, I still win, because..." He or she is saying that the complainant's case is irrelevant—and in effecting is arguing "SO WHAT?"

As you can guess, virtually all of what's called Black Letter Law was originally "case law," i.e., **the common law**; not statutory. However, much of Black Letter Law is sometimes "**codified**" as statutes. A prime example is the old "law merchant"—the law of contracts and industry customs among merchants. It used to be private law, which was then absorbed into the case law (the common law). Today, most of it has been absorbed into the Uniform Commercial Code: statutes. (Family law provides several other examples: the Uniform Child Custody Jurisdiction & Enforcement Act, the Uniform Interstate Enforcement of Protective Orders Act, the Uniform Interstate Family Support Act, the Uniform Parentage Act, and the Uniform Premarital Agreement Act. And other areas of the law have their own Uniform Acts.)

So, Black Letter Law, I believe, can be thought of as the set of legal definitions—whether in case law or statutory form, and usually called "elements"—of basic principles of law.

You have to memorize these, and __understand__ them.

As Josephson put it:

> **Suppose, for example, that a student did *not* learn the meaning of terminology critical to an exam item or *did not remember all the elements of a particular rule.* If the missing information is so integral to an exam item that the student cannot demonstrate an otherwise well-developed understanding of the concepts involved in the question, the ability of the item to measure or any other level of competence is precluded...**
>
> [Boldface and italics added.]

In other words, if you can't "speak the language of the law," and in a way that shows you know what you're talking about (the concepts the words refer to and what they mean), your professor will "tune out" when grading your answers.

But this isn't just a matter of memorizing, say, a series of formulas, such as the ones you learned in junior high school for calculating the circumference or area of a circle. There's far more to it than that. You do, however, have to memorize the elements of Black Letter Law.

Policy "versus" Black Letter Law

"Policy" is a catch-all term that refers to thinking about the social and economic consequences of a decision. *All* courts (should) look beyond the the immediate dispute, to the effect the court's decision will have on future litigants in somewhat similar situations. But "policy" looks at the effect on society in general. (Yet, this is a false dichotomy, because the effect the court's decision will have on future litigants in somewhat similar circumstances also, obviously, is an effect on "society." But you can see what the distinction is getting at.)

There are those who say, "Only lower-ranked schools test Black Letter Law. But I'm at a *good* school, which emphasizes 'Policy,' so I have no need to learn Black Letter Law." This is perhaps the ultimate example of snobbery and one-upmanship among those who've been fortunate enough to get into a high-ranked school. Supposedly, there are some low-ranked law schools that *only* teach specific legal rules and statutes that will be covered on the bar exam of the various states in which each of those schools is located. These schools, it is said, use a "memorize and regurgitate" approach to the Law.

I doubt that even one such law school exists. (It strains credulity to think that a law school would be "teaching to the bar exam" even in *first*-year, when the "barzam" is still three years hence. The specific statutes and rules would change during the three years.) But even if it did, the very statement betrays the speaker's own abysmal ignorance of the nature of both Black Letter Law *and* "policy discussions."

Black Letter Law *IS* policy. Pick *any* rule of Black Letter Law, no matter what area of law it's from, and you'll quickly discover it *embodies* policy. And the counter-rule, if any, embodies a countervailing *policy*. The elements of the Black Letter Law concern our common-sense notions of justice—and thus are necessary to an understanding of "public policy" issues in the law.

It's nearly impossible, in the law, to discuss policy without *some* reference to Black Letter Law. The Law advances by adapting old legal policy to a new situation, by treating the new situation as though it were just yet another variation on an old theme.

For example, "space law" and "cyberlaw" are new areas of the law. But the legislative bodies and courts that try to work out the new rules of thumb for these things are not starting from scratch. Instead, every organization that wants the new rules to favor its own interest hires some hotshot lawyers. Those lawyers "argue by analogy" that certain *existing* law can easily be adapted to this new area. The interests of the various organizations often clash, of course. So, different lawyers look to different existing law, and say *that* law fits the new situation better than the existing law the other side wants to use as a model.

In situations like that, it should be obvious that the outcome depends on the *policy* that each set of existing law is based on. Those who are fashioning the new rules will decide which of the conflicting policy options (embodied in different Black Letter Law) makes better sense to them on balance. They then decide which existing law to use by analogy. (You have surely noticed that I stopped using the term "Black Letter Law" and instead began referring to "existing law." That's because the rulemakers will be looking at old case law and old statutes. But the case law and the statutes nearly always embody Black Letter Law. And if they don't, then there's a good chance the rulemakers will still bring in Black Letter Law, directly.)

Granted, there are times when a professor who's being cute will toss out something to which Black Letter Law seems not to apply. (One example: "Who owns the Moon?") But even there, you would argue on the basis of Black Letter Law, and try to analogize from old situations. (The same issue exists regarding "ownership" of the ocean floor in international waters.)

Even at the schools that serve as havens for the most other-worldly "policy wonks," a *pure* policy question" would be worth, at most, ¼ of your final exam in a course. Your professors may well spend 90% of class time, all semester long, discussing "policy," without reference to "Black Letter Law." But it is virtually certain that their final exams will *test* your knowledge of *specific* Black Letter Law, one way or the other…not your ability to B.S. about "policy" the way you did in class.

The only people who say otherwise are those who have yet to take even one exam in law school. They simply do not know whereof they speak. Those who turn their noses up at Black Letter Law are in for a most unpleasant surprise when they see their final exams and are expected to provide answers. Just ask Michael Josephson (author of that 1984 report to AALS, quoted earlier)—or the two professors quoted in Chapter 8.

And out in the real world, Black Letter Law is the *bedrock* of virtually everything you will do for your entire career. Wouldn't it be nice to learn it *before* you get your license?

Chapter 24, "Lookin' Toward the 'Barzam'," speaks of the value of having a good working knowledge of Black Letter Law, in terms of your *creativity* as a lawyer (and as a law student, for that matter). It says: *"[Y]ou'll gradually build up a general awareness, a sense of additional relevant points of law in any given situation.* And so, when you're working on a problem…, there will be things that come to mind that you might not have otherwise thought of. 'Seems to me I remember —somewhere in the back of my mind, something about…' *Your gut feel will alert you* to the possibility of something 'out there' that you might be able to use." *That's true on exams, too.*

New law is nearly always conceived by practitioners, not jurists. (Jurists turn it into "the law," and further develop it, but they usually get the ideas for their Opinions from the practitioners' briefs.) The more you know, and the better you know what you know, the better you'll be able to come up with a new argument that will impress whoever's sitting in judgment on your presentation. This is true in law school as well as in the real world. Law school is the time to lay the foundation for getting a reputation for deep insights and creativity in the law— which is based on a thorough understanding *of* the law…Black Letter Law.

Black Letter Law v. "Bright-Line Rules"

It's important to distinguish between "Black Letter Law" and "Bright-Line Rules." I think the snobs, discussed above, have confused the two. Maybe *that's* their problem (other than the fact that they don't want to roll up their sleeves and dig into the study of the law, instead of just bullshitting all the time). A bright-line rule is a specific, nitty-gritty legal rule that's absolutely clear. (Hence the term "bright line.") *Black's* defines "bright-line rule" as "A judicial rule of decision that tends to resolve issues, esp. ambiguities, simply and straightforwardly, sometimes sacrificing equity for *certainty*." (Emphasis added.)

Example: "to be valid, a will must be signed in the presence of two sane, sober, adult witnesses who are not named as beneficiaries under the will." Yes, that too is policy, and I said that Black Letter Law *is* policy. But while it's true that all Black Letter Law is also "policy," that does not mean that all "policy" is automatically Black Letter Law. "Policy" can take other forms—such as Bright-Line Rules. However, normally, once a Bright-Line Rule gets codified in statutory form, I believe it is no longer referred to as a Bright-Line Rule. Instead, it's just referred to as the statutory law on the subject. (And I believe the "two witnesses" rule is actually only in statutory form, so it should no longer be referred to as a "Bright-Line" Rule. A better example of a Bright-Line Rule would be "controlling" case law that says, "A child under the age of five is incapable, as a matter of law, of the 'mens rea'—i.e., the state of mind—required for a criminal act.")

Sure, in connection with a particular bit of Black Letter Law, a given Bright-Line Rule might be the test for whether or not a given element of that Black Letter Law has been fulfilled. So, in the example above, maybe an element of that Black Letter Law regarding wills says "disinterested" witnesses have to be present at the signing of a will; the Bright-Line Rule tells how many and exactly what kind.

Granted, there are times when it's hard to tell the difference between the two. But in general, keep this in mind: Black Letter Law usually involves a set of elements. A Bright-Line Rule stands alone. *More important, Black Letter Law elements tend to be general, with lots of "wiggle room." Bright-Line Rules tend to be specific, with "no escape."*

"Legal Maxims" & "Doctrines"

In between the Black Letter Law and the Bright-Line Rules are legal maxims. They're generally vague statements of a general policy, so they're not "Bright-Line" Rules. But they don't have "elements" to them, so they're not Black Letter Law, either. They're usually aphorisms.

Examples: "He who would seek equity must 'do' equity" (i.e., practice what you preach—judge not, lest ye be judged, in other words). "De minimis non curat lex." ("The law does not concern itself with trifles.") "Volenti non fit injuria" ("There is no injury to one who consents"—but this is actually just the Latin version of the affirmative defense of "consent" in the Black Letter Law in torts.)

Others are known (confusingly) as "doctrines," and thus sound like Black Letter Law. One example is the "Clean hands doctrine," which is really just another way of saying "He who would seek equity must 'do' equity." Another is "contra proferentem" (sometimes the second word is misspelled as "preferentum"); this is the "ambiguity doctrine." (When construing the meaning of a document, any ambiguity should be resolved in a way that goes against the person who wrote the document and who thus put the ambiguity in there in the first place.)

The Law School Learning Pyramid—
Level 2

After "Knowledge," the next level up in Josephson's "Law School Learning Pyramid" is "Understanding." Here's what he said about it:

> Understanding is the first *nonrote* step beyond "knowledge."
> It describes the mental capacity to <u>use</u> information as well as to store it...
>
> **A law student who understands a concept, argument, or principle should be able to restate or paraphrase it in his or her own words...**
>
> **A fundamental aspect of understanding is the ability to apply stored information to new situations...[applying—]**

(a) a known principle of *law* to given facts to determine whether the principle controls...

(b) a known statement of *policy* to a new situation to determine if the rule or principle generated by that policy should apply...

(c) a known holding of a case to a hypothetical case...

A fairly high level of understanding is manifested by a student's ability to *compare* two or more principles, cases, arguments, etc., and determine the extent to which they are similar or dissimilar...

A student...should be able to make rationally based *predictions* on the outcomes of certain arguments and evolution of the law.

This entails the capacity to *extrapolate,* to identify implications and consequences out of but extend beyond known information.

[The goal is to] develop the capacity to <u>read carefully,</u> to <u>read critically,</u> and to <u>think about what was read</u>...

The danger is that if the student [does not] "step back" and look at the overall picture, he/she may fall into a pattern of compulsive studying of *detail,* never making a serious effort to understand how to reconcile competing policies and inconsistent rules.

[Underlining in the original.
Italics and boldface supplied.]

As for that last part: beginning law students are often quite annoyed to see that there is no such thing as "the law," in the sense of having a set of rules where each situation has one and only one rule that's automatically applied to determine the outcome. Yet, this really should come as no surprise. Consider the following pairs of "countervailing wisdom": 1) "Two heads are better than one" v. "Too many cooks spoil the brew"; 2) "Look before you leap" v. "He who hesitates is lost"; 3) "The early bird catches the worm" v. "Haste makes waste";

4) "If it's worth doing at all, it's worth doing well" v. "Don't sweat the small stuff"; 5) "Eat, drink and be merry, for tomorrow we die" v. "Save your pennies for a 'rainy day'"; and 6) "All's fair in love and war" v. "Do unto others…"

In everyday life, we're constantly "reconciling" these "competing policies and inconsistent rules" in light of the facts of each new situation where they're relevant. (My personal favorite is from the famous wit of Dorothy Parker, a writer. As she and an acquaintance were about to go through a doorway, the acquaintance gestured for her to go ahead and then displayed a juvenile cleverness by saying, "Age before beauty." Parker went ahead. But as she did so, she shot back, "Pearls before swine!")

Getting a Head Start

As already discussed, your professors will do nothing to help you attain either Knowledge or Understanding, the first two levels of Josephson's "law school learning pyramid." So you're going to have to take the old fashioned do-it-yourself approach. However, once you're in law school, your professors will bury you under a mountain of make-work. —Or, to change the metaphor, they will put you on a treadmill, and you will have almost no chance to step off it.

So, you're going to have to get a head start.

There are some materials out there that can help you enormously. I call them "primers."* As the term implies, they take you through the basics, one step at a time. They are priceless.

The first is by John Delaney. It's called *Learning Legal Reasoning*. It is brilliant, but without being flashy. It's one of the very best books I've ever seen on the law. Delaney shows how the Case Method *ought* to be used, and how case briefing can be an invaluable source of mastery of the law—once you've learned the basics. *Learning Legal Reasoning* takes you to the mountaintop, so you can see the Promised Land. And it starts by giving you an orientation to various legal things, including some jargon.

However, seeing the Promised Land from atop a mountain is not the same thing as getting there.

For that, the primers to get are nearly all in Aspen Publishing's "Examples & Explanations" series. In each book, there's a section of "Examples" after each section. These "examples" are really *questions*.

---

* And by the way, *this* primer is pronounced as though it were spelled "primmer." (Pronouncing the "i" long refers to *paint*.)

Then, a few pages later, you get the answers. You're probably thinking, "big deal." However, as you will see in law school, you will get almost *nothing* that helps you understand the material you're studying. Quite the contrary. Best of all, the Aspen primers present fairly simple questions, appropriate to your stage of legal study—i.e., total beginner. You're told who has a problem, and what the problem is. It's up to you to figure out the answer. Then you check your answer against the correct one.

These books are worth their weight in gold.

Two of them are by the same author, Joseph W; Glannon: *The Law of Torts,* and *Civil Procedure. Contracts* is by Brian A. Blum. *Constitutional Law: National Power and Federalism,* is by two authors: Christopher N. May and Allan Ides. (As Chapter 1 said, Con Law is normally divided into two parts. The usual first year course, which lasts one semester, covers what's in the subtitle of the May and Ides book. The subsequent course, which is also one semester, is called Con Law II. It covers the Bill of Rights and then skips to the Reconstruction Amendments. Sometimes, both parts of Con Law are presented as one year-long course. But the course is still divided as described. There is another primer from Aspen on Con Law II, by the same authors. But this time the order of their names is reversed. This second book is *Constitutional Law: Individual Rights.* However, you almost certainly will not need it in first year—and, as mentioned in Chapter 1, you might not be taking Con Law, period.)

Aspen also does E&E books on Property Law and Criminal Law. But for these, other publishers have good books too. For property, I still recommend Aspen's. For crim, I don't—but as of this writing, the other has not been published yet.

The Aspen primer on property is just called *Property.* It's by Barlow Burke and Joseph A. Snoe. Its rival is from West Publishing, and is called *The Law of Property: An Introductory Survey, 5th ed..* Its authors are Ralph E. Boyer, Herbert Hovenkamp, and Sheldon F. Kurtz. As with the Aspen primer, it presents questions and then provides the answers. And for some topics, it covers them better than the Aspen primer does (but vice versa, too). The main reason why I recommend the Aspen primer over West's is because West's is in hardcover. (All the E&E primers are in paperback.) That means it's heavier, and it's priced higher.

Aspen's primer on Crim Law is called just *Criminal Law.* It's by Richard G. Singer and John Q. LaFond. (As Chapter 1 said, Crim Law is divided into substantive and procedural. Most first-year Crim Law courses focus on the substantive. That's what this Aspen book is for. They have another one on Crim Pro.) But I recommend someone else's book instead of the E&E volume. That someone else is John Delaney, author of the aforementioned *Learning Legal Reasoning*. Before Delaney became a law professor (at NYU, now, semi-retired, teaching one course at CUNY), he was a criminal defense attorney for many years. His book on substantive Crim Law is *Criminal Law Applied: Arguments, Exams, and Answers*. I have seen it in manuscript, and it is excellent. It's scheduled for publication in the fall of 2003.

There's one other area for which you need primers. The Blum book on Contracts for Aspen is excellent. (It is so excellent, in fact, that I often turn to it as a practicing lawyer, just to make sure I haven't overlooked something basic.) Blum's book concentrates on the Common Law of Contracts, though. Another major area is the Uniform Commercial Code. And you will need to read some additional primers to be fully "up to speed" on that in your contracts class. The American Bar Association publishes both of them, as part of its series, *The ABCs of the UCC*. (The UCC is divided into many "articles." In your first-year contracts course, you will be dealing with the first two articles. The second one is the biggie. It's on "sale of goods.") The two books to get are *The ABCs of the UCC—Article 1: General Provisions,* by Fred H. Miller and Kimberly J. Cilke, and *The ABCs of the UCC—Article 2: Sales,* by Henry D. Gabriel and Linda J. Rusch.

Chapter 16 discusses the cost of these materials, and where to get them. And the addendum to that chapter presents several timetables for reading these materials, based on how much lead time you have before you start law school (one year, eight months, six weeks, and zero).

The CALI Lessons Library

To further test yourself in the nitty-gritty of specific subjects, there's a wonderful product called the "CALI Library of Lessons," from the Center for Computer Assisted Learning Instruction, Inc. (a non-profit corporation). The Library contains 270 interactive lessons on 28 subjects. and often includes information on the history and policy of each item of Black Letter Law. I highly recommend it.

Many law schools have the Library available to students. You can access it free with your school's password. However, if you'd do better to get the Library on CD *before* law school. Work each subject after you've finished a primer in that subject. (There's also a book, from West you might need to get to be able to use the program most effectively.) The Center's website is http://lessons.cali.org/catalog.html.

See Chapter 16 for price and order information.

The Common Law...and Common Sense

Many laypeople believe law is all about "magic words." They think the practice of law involves encyclopedic knowledge of various specific phrases, which are then invoked like a Catholic priest (in the old days) reciting a stream of Latin that no one could understand, except (maybe) the priest. And, in fact, for much of the history of the law, that's the way it *was*. Under the old "choses of action," for example, a lawsuit had to be brought under the heading of a specific type of "action." And the "pleading" that was filed had to use exactly the right words for that type of action. The words were all legaldegook, of course. If a lawyer used *any* wrong "magic words" (such as for a different "chose" of action), the case was tossed out (and perhaps could not be refiled).

All of that nonsense is long gone—or nearly all of it. But sometimes, even today, there are specific "magic words" that have to be used...and if they are not, you lose. Yet, even here, there is a difference. Under the old way, it didn't matter if you described the substance of your case correctly, but used the wrong magic words. You had to use the *right* "magic" words, period. Today, even if you use "magic words" that apply to something else, there's a good chance the court will instead treat your case as being what's "laid out" in the substance of your pleading.

Today, when a case is tossed out because the wrong words are used, it's only because they *destroy* the case. Example: there's a settlement agreement that resolves some of the claims in a lawsuit. But the agreement, as written, uses standard phrases that mean the *entire* lawsuit has been settled. The plaintiffs had intended to proceed with the rest of their case after settling only some of the issues. But because the document they signed had phrases that meant they'd settled *all* issues, the rest of their case suddenly (and permanently), goes "poof!" (Typically, though, such things happen only because of a lawyer's negligence, i.e., legal malpractice. The lawyer did not *have* to use the phrases in question in order to present a document for the court's signature that resolved only the selected issues. The lawyer just got careless...and used the standard all-encompassing phrases without thinking about what they mean.)

—And that brings up the next area where "magic words" linger: legal writing. Many lawyers still use archaic legalese in all their writings because it's been tested in court and has held up under judicial scrutiny. But many times, the legalese is utter gibberish. The lawyers think they're playing it "safe" by contining to use it, without knowing what it actually means, but *thinking* it means certain things. Most of the time, they're right. But sometimes, as we've just seen, they're (fatally) wrong.

There has been a movement underway in the law for quite some time to abolish legalese and write in plain English. And it's been successful, for the most part. But some lawyers still use the archaic legalese because 1) they want to mystify their clients, and to put their clients "in awe of the law" (and by extension, in awe of those lawyers)—which actually was a major purpose of legalese in the old "choses of action" days; or 2) they're lazy, and merely re-use "boilerplate" legalese from old documents instead of creating new "model" documents; or 3) they're incompetent, and are not capable of setting down words on paper that clearly express what needs to be expressed.

Yet, even where a writing is in plain English, there are times when legal "terms of art" are best. Usually, this is in situations where a legal term takes the place of dozens of words in lay language. (And when writing for a court, the court prefers brevity.) Just the same, the occasions that call for legal terms of art are infrequent.

Perhaps one reason why snobs disdain learning Black Letter Law is because they feel that memorizing the elements of various aspects of Black Letter Law is to return to the days of legaldegook. They are wrong. The terms of Black Letter Law are a way to *speed* the *analysis* of a fact situation, not to get it bogged down in gibberish. And, more important, most Black Letter Law is in plain English, even though it does use legal terms of art. As mentioned before, the concepts in Black Letter Law are a crystallization of policy.

If you trace the history of the development of any area of Black Letter Law, you will see that it simultaneously gets clarified as to what it covers and doesn't cover. And it gets refined so as to effect justice in the widest possible array of situations that come under that area of Black Letter Law. In other words, despite occasional appearances to the contrary, the Law has always been concerned with justice...and with common sense. Granted, people can differ on what "justice" means in any given situation. And they can even differ as to what "makes sense." But over the long haul, there's a trend toward greater justice, and greater common sense.

I have seen various news items, and even entire books, that claim to expose contemporary "legal lunacies." Generally, these are humorous disclosures, meant to entertain. But sometimes their purpose is to show that "the law is 'a ass.'" (The "a" rather than "an" is not a typo.) When the published *exposé* is a statement from a statute or a court opinion, I've often checked the original. Nearly all of the time, one of two things is true. Either the publication misquoted the item, or it took it out of context and the context indicated a very good reason why the seemingly idiotic statement was made.

The phrase "the law is a ass" is from Chapter 51 of Dickens's *Oliver Twist*. Here it is, in context:

> "It was all Mrs. Bumble. She *would* do it," urged Mr. Bumble, first looking round to ascertain that his partner had left the room. "That is no excuse," replied Mr. Brownlow [the lawyer]. "You were present on the occasion of the destruction of these trinkets, and indeed are the more guilty of the two, in the eye of the law; for the law supposes that your wife acts under your direction."
>
> "If the law supposes that," said Mr. Bumble, squeezing his hat emphatically in both hands, "the law is a ass—a idiot. If that's the eye of the law, the law is a bachelor; and the worst I wish the law is, that his eye may be opened by experience —by experience."

Mr. Bumble was right; the law was wrong. *Oliver Twist* was written in 1838, and set in the London of 1837. It took nearly a century-and-a-half, but the eye of the law did open in this matter. The law no longer supposes that a wife is under her husband's direction.*

So why am I being so picky about this? Because, as you read and think about the law, it should "make sense" to you as a matter of common sense and justice. If it doesn't, the chances are good that you have missed something. (Of course, there *are* statutes, and case "holdings," that are idiotic. They're the exceptions. And from time to time, there are successful efforts to "make time stand still," or even to "turn back the clock.") More important, when you are thinking about trends in the law, or thinking about how a given case "ought to" come out, your guiding principles should be common sense, and justice.

(One of the keys to success in the law is meticulous, critical reading. Chapter 1 said, "[T]he *weakest* argument you can make to a court is to merely say, The law ought to be changed.' That's tantamount to merely making the child's plaint, 'It's not fair!'" Perhaps you now are thinking

---

* The most famous statement by America's most famous jurist—Oliver Wendell Holmes, Jr.—is "The life of the law has not been logic; it has been experience." (This is the opening line of his most famous work, *The Common Law*, consisting of the text of a series of his lectures on contract law.) Holmes was an avid reader of literature, especially English literature. I wonder if that line in Dickens about "experience" inspired Holmes's own.

I've just contradicted myself. However, the key word in that quotation is "argument." A good argument should consist of far more than your personal opinion or sense of justice. And if your sense of what's right is well-founded, you'll be able to back it up with meaningful authority. The point of the comments in this section on "Common Law and Common Sense" is that if you feel "something's not right with this picture" when you read a case or a statute, go with your "gut feel." Then come up with some good *arguments* as to why you're right...or else dig into it further and find out why you're wrong.)

As one student who was in the first semester of law school expressed it in an e-mail to me:

> I've noticed that the law itself is very easy.
> The concepts are baby talk, at least the first year
> courses. But the legal profession makes it look
> lofty and complex by giving each concept a
> fancy name and using high-powered language.
> What one needs to do to understand the law is
> only to put it in his or her own simple words
> and to cut through all the big talk.

That student is right. We'll return to this matter of putting into your own words, in order to understand it, in Chapter 4. (However, you nearly always will still have to *use* the fancy names and high-powered language in your exam answers.)

Ultimately (as Chapter 1 said), Black Letter Law is just a set of *"rules of thumb,"* to help guide society. Those rules of thumb can change. They are not a set of Platonic Ideas, hovering in another dimension, that are eternally valid, unchanging, perfect. They're just some concepts judges have worked out over time to create a set of general rules that can help resolve people's disputes in a way that makes sense and is fair. If a certain rule stops working that way, the rule gets changed, or else a whole new category of "exceptions" is created under that rule.

So, at the risk of being my usual overbearing self, please always remember two "legal" concepts above all others as you study the Law: common sense, and justice. Keeping those in mind can help you find your (and your future clients') way through the law's thicket.

Chapter 3 - Learning How to "Think Like a Lawyer"

> *The hardest thing of all for law students is learning how to "think like a lawyer."*

"Thinking like a lawyer" is actually quite simple. Yet, it's quite hard to master because it's completely new to you. It seems contrary to virtually all your previous experience, both personal and academic. However, it's also hard because—as the excerpts from the Josephson Report (in Chapter 2) made clear—law professors don't teach you how to do it. Nor do they even demonstrate it in class as part of the Case/Socratic Method. What you'll get instead is some vague statement such as, "You will learn how to 'think like a lawyer' here." And that's it. Nothing more...although you're led to believe that what occurs in class is some-how the essence of learning how to think like a lawyer.

Case Briefing as Rabbit Trail

What occurs in class is a process of sending students chasing down a rabbit trail. As Chapter 1 said, legal "education" uses the Case Method. As mentioned in Chapter 1, casebook opinions have been edited down. Students read several for each class, and should be prepared to discuss them. For this, the student is expected to "brief" each case.

The typical case brief, for a law school class, is a one-page summary, with the following:

1) what I would call "file" information—the "style" of the case (i.e., "X v. Y"), the court from which the opinion came, and (sometimes) the year of the opinion, along with the citation/s to the case reporter/s;

2) the *history* of the case (a.k.a. *procedure*)—the outcome in each of the lower court/s;

3) the *facts* of the case—as reported by the majority opinion, which may have slanted them* to make its decision look more justifiable;

4) the main *issue/s* to be decided (a.k.a. *question/s*);

---

* Or even falsified them. It happens, even with the Highest Court in the Land— as you will discover. These are appellate cases. The higher court/s are supposed to take the facts as "found" at the trial court level—by the jury, in a jury trial, or by the judge in a "bench trial." But sometimes a higher court gets
(Continued on next page)

5) the *holding*—i.e., the one-sentence "rule/s of law" the case announced,

6) the *judgment*—who the court decided for, with its effect on the lower court ruling/s; and

7) the *rationale*—the "why" of the decision (a.k.a *ratio decidendi*).

Sometimes there might also be *dicta*—more correctly known as *obiter dicta* (Latin: loosely, "other talk"), and sometimes called *"dictum"* (the singular form of "dicta"). This is where the opinion says something in passing that's not directly relevant to the holding of the case, but which might have significance all by itself. (Sometimes, it turns out to be the most important part of that case—as with the dicta that allowed professional baseball's exemption from the Anti-Trust Laws.)

Reading and analyzing cases is one of the most important things a lawyer (or court) does. Yet, it is not a real-world version of the Case Method of law school. It's worlds apart from the case-briefing for law school classes. And it's a tool you will have to learn how to use completely on your own. (More on that, later.) The way *professors* use the Case Method is counter-productive...by design. It's part of the effort Josephson described, to mislead students. Thus, only those who intuitively sense (or otherwise learn) what they need to know and how to find a way to learn it will do well on their exams. Even more unfortunately, *all* the books I have seen on "how to succeed in law school" emphasize that case briefing is the *sine qua non* of success in law school. And they tell you the *professors'* way, not the way that makes it an effective learning tool for you.

Judicial opinions are written for the benefit of attorneys and other courts. For that reason, they typically zero in on the narrow issue at hand—the facts and point/s of law on which the case turns. Attorneys and other courts already know all the relevant basic legal doctrines. There's no need for the opinion to go into any of that. The court implicitly assumes its readers have such knowledge. If you think of it in terms of Gestalt psychology, everything else is the (back)ground for the "figure" that stands out—the point/s explicitly discussed in the opinion. This approach makes complete sense for attorneys and other courts. It's highly efficient and concise. However, the casebook editors do nothing to provide students with the necessary background information to

selective, or creative. (This is a major reason the majority opinion and the minority opinion/s sometimes seem to be about entirely different cases, because the "statement of facts" by the two sides within the court are miles apart.)

help them put each case in context. Instead, the Case Method takes the inductive approach, i.e., students are supposed to gradually understand the individual trees well enough (even though some of those trees are deadwood) to eventually understand the nature of the entire forest.

The professors say "This is the way it has to be." But they are ignorant of the history of law school pedagogy. For one thing, Langdell's casebook (which, as Chapter 1 mentioned, was on Contracts, and published in 1871) was not the first casebook. More important, he included a *primer* on Contracts at the back of his book. (I suspect, but have not confirmed, that previous casebooks did likewise.) For decades afterwards, all casebooks included primers on the subject in question. In other words, the casebook itself contained a straightforward section on Black Letter Law, similar to the (much longer) stand-alone primers from Aspen, Delaney, etc., discussed in Chapter 2.

However, over the years, more law school graduates quickly went directly from being law school students to being law school professors. And, lacking meaningful experience "in the trenches," this new breed of professors apparently decided that casebooks should, at least in part, confuse the ignorant, instead of helping students to learn the law. And so, the "primer" section disappeared. The Great Game began: the talent search for those who are supposedly naturally gifted.

Then it got worse. Most of today's casebooks include a few cases that everyone agrees were *wrongly* decided. Or cases that are the law in only a *minority* of jurisdictions, not the "majority rule." Or cases on obscure, trivial points of law that have nothing to do with helping students get "the big picture." Quite often, these are the cases with which the casebooks start. The profs stay mum about these cases' shortcomings. Students—naively trusting that *these* cases represent "the law"—try desperately to master the points of law contained in them. Thus they're learning that which the law is *not*. This is all part of the "madness in the method" of law school pedagogy. It gives highest priority to identifying the few who are supposedly natural-born geniuses of the law. One of the marks of their supposed genius is that they intuitively sense a sham. This sham was and is perpetrated at the expense of the many who need to learn how to become competent attorneys even if they do not have a lot of "natural talent or 'vision.'"

It is extremely unlikely that you will ever be asked to recite a case brief as part of your answer on an exam. It is also extremely unlikely that, on an exam, you would be given the text of a case and told to "brief" it. Such things are unheard of. In fact, most professors who call on students to recite a case briefing in class will stop doing so after the first few weeks of the course. They give the impression to students that, at that point, students have mastered this "essential" skill, so there's no need to belabor it. Actually, though, there was no need to do it in the first place. Even when the professor continues to call for recitation of case briefing in class, nearly all the students stop doing a full-blown brief. Most rely on the case briefs in a Black Letter Law commercial outline (discussed in the next chapter). Others do "book briefing"—making notes in the margin of the casebook at the appropriate points in the text: "Procedure," "Holding," etc.

Case briefing, *as used by the professoriat,* is a *trivial* exercise…a trap for the unwary.

Analysis & Argument: Laypeople's v. Lawyers'

Many who go to law school do so because they like to argue. The essence of "thinking like a lawyer" is argument. But a lawyer, within his or her own mind, considers *both* sides of a dispute.

Some people take offense at this. They believe it means a lawyer doesn't care which side wins. And, in fact, often that's true: the lawyer argues only for the side that hired that lawyer, and would've been just as willing to earn his or her fee from representing the other side.

But this moral disapproval misses the deeper point. Being able to argue both sides of a dispute is based on being able to *see* both sides. And the lawyer (or law student) who is, at the outset, emotionally involved in one side of a dispute will fail to *anticipate* the arguments the other side might present. A lawyer wants to spot the other side's potential arguments ahead of time. If those arguments are too strong, the lawyer will not take the case, because it's a loser. Yet, even if the case is a good one, the lawyer still wants to think of the other side's arguments. That way, the lawyer can prepare to meet those arguments if and when the other side makes them. It's important to *dispassionately* and *objectively* evaluate a case. The lawyer then has a better chance of thinking of everything—and of being prepared for "anything." Counter-intuitive as it may sound, in the best analysis, a lawyer can state the other side's case in a way that at first appears to be just as convincing as that lawyer's own client's side of the case.

Out in the real world, *after* conducting a lawyerlike analysis (and taking the case), a lawyer who's handling a dispute will then change to the "advocacy mode" to get what the client wants. This advocacy might occur in negotiation, mediation, or litigation. And in the advocacy mode, emotion and moral suasion can be important and effective.

But one of the biggest mistakes law students make is to take sides, based on an emotional or political preference, from the very *start*. This is based on their experience. Usually, the disputes they've had in life have arisen suddenly. Or even when the person prepared an argument ahead of time (such as with a merchant), he or she didn't think through the other side of the argument. Such people, in effect, blind themselves to possible arguments the other side might use. And those points (or the response to them) then arise spontaneously rather than as the result of careful forethought. Out in the real world, that *can* "kill" you. On an exam, it *will*. —And it's a trap some law profs set on exams.

Ruggero Aldisert is a senior judge on the Third Circuit of the U.S. Court of Appeals. In his book, *Logic for Lawyers*, he says:

> Experienced judges have seen many eager lawyers, young and old, crusading with maximum passion and boundless energy, strident believers in their clients' causes, hopelessly shot down because their propositions were totally bereft of support in law or logic. To passionately feel or believe is one thing; to prevail in court is another. Those who put passion in place of reason seldom survive in the courtroom.

—Nor do they do well in law school.

Those who want to become attorneys because they like to argue almost invariably have only been involved in disputes where they took one side and never reversed roles. These might have been arguments in class, or with their parents, siblings, fellow students, or maybe lovers' quarrels. What all these have in common is that the person's *ego* or *heart* was involved. When "thinking like a lawyer," you have to put your ego and heart aside, at least to start. (Well, alright, as a trial attorney, I admit that ego is probably the prime moving force once the lawsuit has been filed. And sometimes one's heart is the deciding factor in taking the case.) *In your first-year classes in law school, you are NOT in the "advocacy mode."*

However, normally, being able "to see both sides" means that the person is open-minded and is reserving judgment, and not seeing the situation "in black and white." There are times (such as during a mediation or negotiation) when that's good. But in general—and particularly in litigation, after the attorney has switched to the "advocacy mode"—the purpose of being able to see both sides is to do a better job of *presenting* the dispute in polarized (black-and-white) terms…in *your* favor. (It also helps you convince your client that there really are *two* sides to the story—something that clients typically do not believe at first.)

There are those, however, who've participated in debate in high school or college, and have argued both sides of a question. Part of their job was to anticipate the arguments the other side might use, and to think of a good response to each one. That will stand them in good stead in law school. Yet, it really won't carry them all that far. That's because law school involves far more "conflict points" within each question, and far more sub-arguments, than high school or college debate. Further, in high school or college debate, you're told at the outset what the dispute is about—and it's always just one, narrow, issue. On most law school exams, *it's up to YOU to figure out what the conflicts ARE, including the POTENTIAL ones.*

"The Law School Learning Pyramid"
Levels 3 & 4

Chapter 2 introduced the Josephson Report's "Law School Learning Pyramid," whose foundational levels are "Knowledge" and then "Understanding" (of that knowledge).

The next level up "Issue Spotting." Above that is "Problem-Solving."

Issue-spotting and Problem-solving are the nuts and bolts of the day-to-day practice of law, for most attorneys. They're also the key to success during your days of reckoning in law school exams. As such, they are the major component of "thinking like a lawyer."

Issue-Spotting

Your grade in each course usually depends only on your performance on the one exam at the end of that course. That exam will nearly always be an essay exam. What it calls for is a good "lawyerlike analysis." And it should come as no surprise that a good lawyerlike analysis is based on "thinking like a lawyer."

Most law school essay exams are "issue-spotters." Usually, you're given a "fact pattern" as part of a problem. There's usually a command at the end of the problem. But the instruction is quite vague—often something like "Discuss all parties and issues." You then have to cut the problem up into little pieces, and to deal succinctly with each piece.

This issue-spotting has two parts. The first requires, as mentioned earlier, figuring out what the potential conflicts are in terms of *parties* and the *causes of action*. Chapters 6 and 7 will discuss that. From there, the second part is a lawyerlike analysis of the fact pattern. You go into the nitty-gritty of the claims or defenses for each cause of action, in light of the facts at hand. This is subdivided into two parts:

1. You have to elaborate on each side's potential claims against the other. And you have to present and discuss each side's defenses against the other's claims. This often takes the form of a dialectic: Smith says "A." Jones responds to "A" with "B," and presents argument "C" against Smith. Smith responds to "B" with "D," and to "C" with "E." Jones answers "D" with "F," and "E" with "G." And so on. This is sometimes called "The Dialectic of the Law."

2. You have to *weigh* each argument, in light of the counter-argument—and, especially, the *facts*. Figure out which arguments *will* fly, *won't*, or *might*. And it's a sure bet the "fact pattern" in the exam problem has items in each of these three categories. (And by the way, that's the reality you'll face in the practice of law, too.)

This second sub-part of "issue-spotting" is particularly concerned with those points where the argument is strong on *both* sides—i.e., the *key point/s at issue* within the claims and defenses. Out in the real world, *that* is where the parties will be fighting it out in court (or perhaps negotiating or mediating a solution). In other words, it's *not enough* to "spot" the "issue" as to who will be the parties to a dispute, and what their overall dispute/s will be about.

> The *key* "issues" you're trying to spot are the *issues-within-the-issues*. In other words, where will the major battle/s be fought in this war? (Your law profs will never tell you to do this, however. That's part of their "game.")
>
> On an "issue-spotter," the battlegrounds will nearly always involve only one *element* of a given cause of action. And that one element will be the battleground because of some fact that can be argued *both* ways, or because there are equally important facts on *both* sides with regard to that element.

This is why basic mastery of Black Letter Law is so important.

As the "Josephson Report" put it:

> **[T]he student must have sufficient knowledge and comprehension to *understand the significance of facts in relation to the substantive law.* Depending on the question, diagnosis can require a very sophisticated level of understanding.**
> [Boldface and italics added.]

Here are some rather *un*sophisticated examples...

"Ks" (Contracts)*

Different authorities use different words to define what a contract is. Section 1 of the authoritative *Restatement (Second) of Contracts* defines "a contract" this way: "a promise or a set of promises for the breach of which the law gives a remedy, or the performance of which the law in some way recognizes as a duty."

Note: according to the *Restatement*, it's redundant to speak of a "valid" or "enforceable" contract, and is incorrect to speak of an "invalid" or "unenforceable" contract. Something either is or is not a contract, period.

In his Aspen E&E primer on Contracts, Brian Blum provides a definition worded differently from that in the *Restatement*. And the various commercial outlines each have their own way of putting it. In law school, you use the definition your professor favors. The prof might not expressly say which definition he or she prefers. But it should be apparent from the cases assigned, or from class discussion. (In the real world, you use the definition the highest court in your jurisdiction has adopted.)

So, the words that follow are just one example, but they'll do for the purposes of this illustration.

---

* In sports, "K" is a baseball term, meaning a strikeout. But in law, "K" stands for "contract." The course, Contracts, is abbreviated "Ks." Although at first glance it appears that the abbreviation for Contracts should be "Con," "Con" is the designated abbreviation for "Constitutional," as in "Con Law." (Besides, since Contracts is in the plural, it would have to be "Cons"...and that just won't do. So, Ks it is.)

To be a contract, an agreement must satisfy the following elements:
1. Parties have legal capacity to contract
    A. Of legal age
    B. No insanity
    C. Not under the debilitating influence of drugs or alcohol at the time of making the contract.
2. Genuine agreement
    A. Based on a bargain
        1. Offer made
        2. Offer accepted
    B. Legal Detriment
    C. Involves one or more promises to perform
3. A lawful purpose for the agreement and of the means of achieving it.

This definition is more detailed than normal. But that's so you could see at a glance just how much is involved at the *outset* when "thinking like a lawyer" with regard to something that might or might not be a (valid) contract. (That checklist could be expanded even further.)

So, let's say you're taking a final exam in contracts. Here's the "fact pattern" of the first problem—

Jack and Jill are American citizens, and reside in Cambridge. Jill (aged 17) is a prostitute and Jack (aged 24) has been a third-year student at Harvard Law School. Jack wants to avail himself of Jill's services. But being a law student, he of course would never do anything illegal. So Jack has been trying to persuade Jill to have an "affair" with him, in which he will take her to expensive restaurants and on expensive vacations, and buy her expensive presents, rather than paying her money directly. She refuses. Then, on the evening of July 4, he is fortifying himself in a bar, as part of his preparation for the bar exam. He has been drinking heavily. Jill enters and he asks her to join him. He buys her several alcoholic beverages, which she consumes. She then tells him she will be 18 in a couple of months. She is moving to the U.K., where prostitution is legal, and will stay there a year. She tells him that if he's ever in London, he should "come up and 'see' me sometime," and gives him information on how to contact her there. Jack, now a recent law school graduate, writes up what he calls an "agreement." In it, he promises to contact Jill in London within the next year. She will let him have exclusive access to her, 24/7, for a week. During that time she will render services that are spelled out in the agreement. In return, he will pay a flat (but hefty) fee—half up-front, half at the end. Just above the signature line, it says "This instrument executed in Boston, Massachusetts, July 4, 2002." Jack and Jill sign it.

Jill takes it with her. In November, after learning that he failed the bar exam, Jack decides to console himself by going to London, where prostitution is indeed legal. He contacts Jill, who is indeed now 18, and pays her the up-front half of the fee. She honors her end of their agreement. But at week's end, Jack refuses to pay the other half of the fee. When Jill returns to Boston some months later, she sues Jack for breach of contract. Jack does not deny the existence of the written agreement, and admits making the down-payment on it. Nor does he deny that Jill fully performed under the covers—er, under the terms of that agreement. But he says the agreement is not a contract, so he does not have to pay the balance allegedly owed.

Then comes "the call of the question"—"Is there a contract?"

This is a simple example…though not as simple as it might seem.

Using the list of elements above, it's easy to see that the parties were not insane at the time they made their agreement, that an offer was made, and that it was accepted. No argument on these points. (Yet, in your answer, you would not just leave these out. Instead, you'd note the existence of the element in question, and then *explain, quickly,* why the element was fulfilled and thus there can be no issue about it. That way, when you get to the *real* "bone of contention," your prof will know you didn't just stumble onto it, or pick it by happenstance.)

The "legal detriment" part is also easy. "**Legal detriment**" exists when someone promises to do something that he or she is not legally obligated to do, or promises not to do something that he or she is legally free to do. If there is no legal detriment, the promise is "**illusory**," and there is no contract. (So, for example, there would be no legal detriment if a kid, who just turned 16 and got a driver's license, agreed to obey the traffic laws in return for use of the family car.) Jack and Jill both have legal detriment. (In an exam answer, you would *not* just make such a "**conclusory**" statement, though. You would *explain why*.)

At first glance, it appears Jack might have an "incapacity" argument. They had both been drinking heavily when they made their agreement. The incapacity-by-intoxication argument is used by a party to try to set aside all or part of a contract. Typically, the person seeking to avoid the contract says, "I don't remember signing anything," or "I know I signed something, but I don't know what it was or what it said," and then usually adds something like "I was so drunk I couldn't even see clearly." (And, in fact, the signature is usually not at all like the person's normal signature.) Here, though, Jack's condition at the time of the agreement is irrelevant.

This is because there are two other concepts of contract law that now come into play. The first is the **"benefit of the bargain."** —As a general rule, he or she who avails himself or herself of the benefit/s of a contract cannot then seek to avoid his or her obligation/s under that contract. Granted, though, if Jill had honored the agreement while Jack was still intoxicated, he might have a good argument.

But the facts of this case evoke a second concept of contract law: **"ratification."** Jack (presumably) sobered up between the time he made the agreement with Jill in July, and the time he went to London in November. And he did make the down-payment under the terms of their agreement, *four months after* the agreement was made. So, even if he lacked capacity when the two made the agreement, he "ratified" that previous agreement upon regaining his "capacity" for something other than large quantities of alcohol. —Actually, he did only a **"constructive"** ratification, but that'll do.

(In legal discourse, one does not use the words "explicit" or "explicitly." Instead, lawyers and courts speak, respectively, of "express" and "expressly." This is in contrast to "implied" or "impliedly." It's one of the lingering ways in which lawyers deliberately talk differently from laypeople, in order to show they're lawyers. At any rate: for some reason unknown to me, in contract law the dichotomy of "express" vs. "implied" is used only in connection with the existence of a contract itself. When it comes to talking about an "implied" ratification of a contract, lawyers and courts say "constructive" instead. Here, Jack's actions were an implied ratification of what may or may not have been a contract. It would have been an "express" ratification if he'd said or written, "I acknowledge this as a contract" when he was in London. The word "constructive" also comes up in connection with the "consent" doctrine in torts, and with regard to "constructive trusts." —And as long as I'm on this digression: the word **"construction,"** as used in the law, does not mean what it does in laypeople's discourse. Instead, it means "interpretation," or "meaning." But, as mentioned, "constructive" is not the adjectival form of "construction." As with so many things in the law, go figure.)

Back on track: those facts, along with the fact that he did avail himself of the benefits of the bargain, mean he's still on the hook.

He might try a second "incapacity" argument: that Jill was underage at the time the agreement was made. However, the underage-incapacity argument is used by the *minor* to avoid *his or her* contractual obligations. (And, in fact, the underage-incapacity rule is so strong that it usually trumps the "benefit of the bargain" rule.) So, only Jill can raise this argument, not Jack. And even if Jack could raise it, the ratification counter-argument would still apply, because Jill did not perform under the terms of the agreement until after she turned 18. (Page 17 in Chapter 1 gave the example of Bob Dylan, the rock-and-roll singer, as to how the underage-incapacity + ratification arguments normally work.)

So, it's all going to come down to what law applies: that of Massachusetts, or England. The agreement was *made* ("**executed**") in Massachusetts, but was to be *performed* in England (and *was* fully performed there, by Jill—and partially, by Jack). Element 3 (in my list) said "A lawful purpose for the agreement..." Under Massachusetts law, the contract is illegal, by statute. Under English law, however, it's legal. Therefore, this case "turns" on the "**choice of law.**" (A problem involving "choice of law" would never be part of a first-year contracts course. —And these days, neither would one that involves prostitution. But I thought you might enjoy the example anyway.)

Torts

Two buddies are on a fishing/camping trip. They're out in the middle of nowhere, with no one else around for miles and miles. They've been doing a lot more drinking than fishing. It's night. They're sitting around the campfire, and are quite drunk. The fire is dying, and they're out of wood. So one of the guys decides to chop some more wood. Because he's so drunk, he ends up whacking himself on the leg, causing a compound fracture and a severed artery. The injured guy is a doctor. He instructs his buddy how to apply a tourniquet to stanch the bleeding. But the doctor needs medical care, fast. He says that, at the very least, without prompt treatment, his lower leg will have to be amputated because of the lack of blood circulation. They don't have a cell phone. So they can't call EMS. The doc's going into shock. They'd come out here in his SUV. His buddy puts him into it and heads for town, "flooring it." Two blocks from the hospital, he loses control of the vehicle and crashes into a telephone pole. This causes further injuries to the doctor...who dies before the ambulance arrives. His family sues the doc's buddy.

In the typical first-year analysis of duty-breach-harm-cause, there clearly is harm. How about "proximate cause"? And what about alleged duty? And alleged breach of it?

Under normal circumstances, someone who's driving drunk and gets involved in an accident is negligent, period. But this situation is complicated by the fact that the doctor needed immediate medical attention and there was no way to get it unless the (other) drunk got behind the wheel. This is where the "reasonable person" standard comes into play. In these circumstances, what would a reasonable person think was the right, or wrong, thing to do?

Social policy comes into play here, too. Society wants to encourage people to come to the aid of others in an emergency. Say there are two possible rescuers, who are otherwise equal, but one is drunk and the other is sober. Obviously it would be better for the sober person to make the rescue attempt. But in this case, the *only* other person who was around when the doctor got hurt was his drunk buddy.

On a law school exam, you'd want to raise another point as part of your lawyerlike analysis. As a matter of law, no person has any obligation to come to the aid of any other person in an emergency. (There are exceptions of course. There are always exceptions in the law. One is the obligation of a parent to come to the aid of his or her minor child.) The uninjured guy was free to let his doctor buddy die out there in the boondocks. He could even have refused to put the tourniquet on.

However, once a person *starts* to come to the aid of someone else in an emergency, then the "reasonable person" standard applies to that person's actions. (And so, for example, the person cannot start the rescue effort, then abruptly change his or her mind and stop. Exception to the exception: where, given the circumstances, there's good reason for stopping, such as too much danger to the would-be rescuer.)

It might well be that this case would "turn" on how fast the driver was going when he lost control of the car. After all, he was just two blocks away from the hospital. He could have slowed down. Or maybe he could have found a pay phone *en route* and called for an ambulance. But maybe the trip from the campsite had been a long one, and the doctor had already passed out, and the driver was afraid his buddy was at death's door. —And remember: the guy *was DRUNK*. Is there such a thing as "the reasonable *drunk*" standard?

These are issues lawyers and judges think about. So should you, starting with the subject matter in each of your courses in law school.

Crim

A man sees a car parked in a "No Parking" area in front of the entrance to a drug store. The vehicle's door is unlocked, the key is in the ignition…and the motor's running. The car is old, and in bad shape. Smoke is pouring from the exhaust. But the man has just been released from prison (where he served a term for carjacking), and wants a set of wheels. So he jumps in and drives off. But he was spotted as he jumped in the car, and the cops are in pursuit. Then he hears a baby crying. The infant is in a "car seat" on the floor in the back. Right after that, the auto's power steering goes out. He loses control of the vehicle and slams into a telephone pole. He is not hurt, but the baby in the carseat is thrown out the back door and killed. The man's charged with felony murder.

Felony murder is the killing of a person while committing a felony. A bank robber, say, has to anticipate that people would be present in the bank and someone might end up getting killed. Here, though, the baby's presence in the car was happenstance. Yet, obviously, anyone who steals a car has to anticipate the cops might give chase, and thus the stolen car will be moving at high speed. *Someone* could get killed, such as a pedestrian in the wrong place at the wrong time.

Is this a felony murder? It depends, in part, on whether the jurisdiction in question allows "felony murder" to be charged in connection with *any* felony, or *only* in connection with dangerous felonies such as robbery, burglary, arson, kidnapping, or aggravated rape (involving use of a weapon). There might not be any statute on the books about it in this jurisdiction—but there might be case law. Say there is case law only, and it allows a charge of felony murder in connection with auto theft and flight. But then the question is whether the case law allows it because auto theft, in itself, is regarded as a dangerous crime (such as carjacking)—or whether a car theft (even if not inherently dangerous) *becomes* a dangerous felony when coupled with the high-speed chase.

The felony here is Grand Theft Auto. Or is it? Believe it or not, this case might "turn" on the value of the car. It's an old clunker, right? To be Grand Theft, the value of the car has to be sufficiently high to cross the threshold from misdemeanor into felony territory. —Then again, because of this very situation, some states have laws that say auto theft is a felony, period.

Back to the "flight"—if the car theft is a felony, do the rules about "res gestae" under the common law apply? Or does this jurisdiction use the modern statutory approach, which talks of "immediate flight," and considers whether the killing occurred "within the duration of the felony"?

Perhaps the underlying felony could be "kidnapping." "Kidnapping" does not require holding someone for ransom. But it does require a specific "mens rea" (state of mind), which in this case is "intent" to kidnap. And in the facts here, would that state of mind exist as soon as the driver became aware of the baby's presence in the car?

In the alternative, there's a possible charge for "criminal negligence" or "reckless manslaughter" in connection with the baby's death. Then, how does the failure of the power-steering figure in?

And so on.

Are we having *fun* yet? (If you are, that's a *very* good sign that you're cut out for a life in the law.)

Tools for Fools

Now you see why "case briefing" is a rabbit trail that leads you far afield from what you should be doing as you study the law.

A court's Opinion always *tells* you who the parties to the dispute are, and *tells* you what the issue is. On the type of law school exam that's given 90% of the time, you get neither of these. It's up to you to figure them out on your own.

A court's Opinion is narrowly focused. It deals with only a handful of issues, and often only with one issue. But the lawyerlike analysis of the fact patterns above were all multi-faceted: the more issues raised, the better.

A court's Opinion *closes* each issue. A lawyerlike analysis *opens up* each issue to further discussion. The (majority) Opinion in each case ' in the casebook is written to make it appear that the way the court ruled is the *only* way it could have ruled. But in a lawyerlike analysis, the goal is to see how far each part of the case will go in *both* directions.

A court's Opinion is *retro*-spective. Its tone is one of *certainty*. Issue-"spotting" on a law school exam is *pro*-spective. Its goal is not certainty, but *possibilities* and *probabilities*.

Here's another passage from the Josephson Report:

> Most law school test items tend to require a much broader view of the subject area than the day by day classroom experience would imply
>
> ...**This fact always seems to catch some students by surprise, as they discover** *a critical variance between the skills they were expected to demonstrate throughout the semester and those tested on the exam.*
>
> *The law teacher interested in maximizing student performance* and minimizing the *game* aspects of the testing process, **would do well to inform students that they should study for an exam differently than** *they prepare for an individual class* and that <u>perspective</u> and <u>over-view</u> are critical qualities for successful exam performance.
>
> [Underlining in the original, italics and boldface added.]

Josephson knew quite well that this "variance" catches nearly *all* students by surprise. He was being discreet, in deference to his fellow law professors. He also knew, but did not say, that very, very few law teachers are "interested in maximizing student performance and minimizing the *game* aspects of the exam process." *The biggest part of the game, of course, is figuring out what the game is...in time to learn the rules and play to win.* For that reason, there are virtually no professors who play fair with students and "tell it like it is" on how to prepare for an exam. The *real* test got underway *long before* the official one (the exam). (See Chapter 8.)

Case briefing, as it's used in law school, is a tool for fools. It's part of the professoriat's effort to fool the students, to lead them astray. Those students who know better ("instinctively" or otherwise) will keep their mouths shut about it. Sure, they brief the cases for class and can recite them on command. But they're aware it's just a sideshow. The real action of learning the law lies elsewhere. What goes on in class is just something to *fill the time* until finals.

I've received e-mails from students who say, "Okay. I won't even *read* the cases." I am *not* saying that you should not *read* the cases. After all, at the very least, the prof will probably be using them as the starting point for the Socratic Method in class. But the more important reason, by far, is that they provide the basic "fact pattern" you can use to create your own hypotheticals, as discussed in the next chapter.

The Fatal Default

As you've seen, learning Black Letter Law is the foundation of what Josephson called the Law School Learning Pyramid. It's important that you memorize the various causes of action, and the elements of each, along with the various defenses against causes of action and the elements of each, and that you understand it all.

But that is not enough. And this is the second area where law students really screw up.

Virtually all of your previous schooling was based on the "memorize-and-regurgitate" mode. As examples: "State ten major causes of the American War of Independence" and "Why did Prohibition fail?" Even analytical answers are based on the memorize-and-regurgitate mode: "Discuss the reasons for and against America's entry into the League of Nations." "Explain the concept of the 'Social Contract.'"

True, in mathematics and the sciences, you are given problems to solve. But there was always "a" right answer, very specific. Even on exams where the professor said "show your work," the prof wanted only to see if you knew the right formulas to use. The formulas were unvarying, for each type of problem. And you did not have to worry about some kind of "competing" or "countervailing" formula when working on a specific type of problem. You certainly did not have to reconcile various formulas, or analyze the problem in light of a "majority" formula and a "minority" formula, or "public policy," etc.

And, above all, as mentioned in connection with high school or college debate, in your previous schooling you were always *told* what the problem is, instead of being given a fact pattern and then being told to "discuss all parties and issues." (The only college major I know of that's—sometimes—similar to law is philosophy. One economics major has assured me that Econ is too, but I disagree.)

Yet, sadly, because most law students do not know what to do to do well, they default to doing what enabled them to do well in their previous schooling: memorize-and-regurgitate. They rarely even do a great job of memorizing all the elements of the Black Letter Law in each area, so they can recite those elements word-for-word in their exam answers. But even if they can do that, they let it go at that. They simply don't realizing that that's just the *starting point* of a good "lawyer-like analysis." (Even former debaters, who *start* with both sides, end up taking only one side, and try to crush the other in their answer.)

The watchwords here are "choose" and "use." You have to be able to *choose* the *right* Black Letter Law—both the "pros" and the "cons"—for the facts at hand. And then you have to be able to *use* them correctly. As John Delaney says, "The right path is a large part of the right answer." Rote memorization won't get you very far. It's *necessary*, but not *sufficient*. If you rely solely on the "memorize and regurgitate" approach, then—on the exam—you will end up "choking"...on your own vomit.

This chapter, and the one before it, showed you the right path—and the rabbit trail. In the next four chapters (and the addendum to Chapter 16), you'll learn the rest of the steps you'll need to take along that path to get where you want to go.

Chapter 4 - Pulling it All Together
—and Making it Your Own

As infants, we crawled, and later were able to stand on our own two feet. After becoming able to stand upright, we began to walk. After being able to walk, we began to run, skip, and jump. From there, we started to play "individual" sports such as tennis or racketball. And those who wanted to be winners first competed informally before entering tournaments.

In the "Josephson Pyramid," "knowledge" is the equivalent of crawling; "understanding," the equivalent of standing on your own two feet. "Issue-spotting" is the walking; and "problem-solving" is the running, skipping, and jumping. This chapter shows you how to pull everything together, and how to advance to the two highest levels of the "law school learning pyramid": "judgment" and "synthesis." Then in the next three chapters—in the language of the previous extended metaphor— you will learn how to play the game well...and how to be a winner.

Hang in There

Here are some items posted to my 2001 column on the internet:

Atticus—

I think I need a "pep talk" or some reassurance.

I am working through Glannon's Torts and I have never felt so stupid in all my life! I enjoy the book. I find it entertaining and challenging. But I am frustrated that I am not "delving" with my answers enough. I understand the concepts as I read them, but when I start to apply what I have learned to the questions, I flub up. Of course, I do not do this on all of them. On the ones that I do screw up, I understand (for the most part) why I got them wrong AFTER I have read the answer-explanation. But I am concerned that I am not "thinking outside the box" enough, and I worry that I will not be able to apply this new info to other hypos.

Is this normal? Or am I just freaking out over nothing? I feel frustrated much in the way I did when I studied all my LSAT analytical sections.

Okay...just wanted to make sure I am not completely far behind. Ai-yi-yi!!!!!!!! Thanks for listening. [Ellipsis in the original.]

[Here is the first part of my answer...]

At this point, as long as you understand *why* your answer was wrong, you're doing fine.

[I then told this first person to read the following exchange.]

Atticus—

I have been reading Glannon's primer on torts. I find myself confused when I work with the hypos. The problem is that I don't get enough feedback. The explanations that follow the examples often start with "It depends..." Although I know that the rules of law are flexible, having so many "depends" really confuses a beginner like me. So what should I do about that?

[My response...]

As you said, you are a beginner. In the analogy I have used in this column before, not only are you not yet a legal eagle, you are still "in the egg." That is not meant to insult you. Nor should you feel any sense of inadequacy or embarrassment about your situation. To invoke the old saying, "Rome wasn't built in a day." And the ability to do a lawyerlike analysis does not arise just from reading an Aspen primer and working its examples and explanations.

You will need to work with the Q&As in the book until you understand *why* "it depends." Yes, that does take time. But it's time well spent. This is where people so readily *mis*understand what Black Letter Law is all about—especially the snobs who turn their noses up at it and go directly to so-called "policy" questions. To repeat what I've said elsewhere, Black Letter Law is just the crystalization of policy. Part of what the answer depends on is the court's choice of the policy it wants to further. (This is where Delaney's *Learning Legal Reasoning* is particularly instructive.)

But you need to then go a step further. Change the facts, and see if that might change the applicable policy, and see if that changes the key element/s of Black Letter Law on which the case turns. You do that, and you will be developing an understanding of the nuances of the law, and of how the law and the facts work together in the same way that one hand washes the other. And you will be able to do an excellent lawyerlike analysis of a fact pattern.

Another misunderstanding of Black Letter Law is that people think that the process is routine, leading to just "the" answer. Nonsense. For almost any given case that's worth taking to trial, there really are two sides to the question (and often more). Each side musters its own "theory of the case," based on the strongest legal argument to make in light of the facts. In a problem on a law school exam, there is often no one right answer. What counts is your awareness of the issue/s and your analysis of the argument/s each side can advance, in light of the facts and the law that might be applicable to those facts.

So, "the" answer will *always* "depend"—not just in law school, but out in the real world. Therein lies good lawyering. But making the transition from the layperson's black-and-white assessment, with its one "right answer," to the lawyer's immersion in the shades of gray, is what a legal education is all about...or rather, should be.

I know from previous correspondence with you that you have mastered a difficult foreign language: English. Think about how frustrated you were at first, learning the bizarre variations in pronunciation that results from the exact same letters or syllables in English, but depending on what word they were in. Think of how you began with simple sentences, then worked up to more complicated ones. And think of how you eventually mastered the nuances of words, phrases, intonations, and so forth. I'm sure it was terribly discouraging at first. But you eventually mastered English—quite well. It will be the same way for you in mastering the law...if you keep at it with the same diligence you showed in mastering English. And you will eventually have the same sense of triumph in an arduous task. And that's when the *fun* of *playing* in the Law's domain begins.

As a now-deceased leader of your country of origin once said, "The journey of a thousand li begins with the first step." You have a long way to go. But keep at it, and you'll get there. (The only difference is that, in the Law—as in the mastery of English, even for native speakers—the journey is never-ending...and you will eventually come to *love* that.)

***

Three weeks later I received an e-mail from the person who'd sent me that first e-mail (above)...

Atticus—

I completed one of the reasoning exercises in Chapter 23 in the new edition of Glannon's Torts primer. I am very proud of myself with the response, and must gloat for you...

It's a small accomplishment, but stretches a long way in the confidence factor. I worked on an exercise (#4) and not only did I nail the answer, but it is what Glannon called a "subtle one" that "if a student even saw the issue I'd be impressed. I'd be bowled over if she offered a reasoned judgment about how it should be resolved."

Well...I not only saw it, I made it my primary answer and completely reasoned it out!

Ironically, I felt the whole time like I was giving a wrong answer, but I am feeling so much better about how all of this stuff is synthesizing.

I know I have far to go, but I appreciate the direction.

[Here's part of my response—]

As a general rule, if you feel you are giving the wrong answer, then you probably are. However, this does not apply when you are first starting out, as this student was. It takes awhile to get comfortable with a completely new activity, especially one where—at first—you feel as though you don't really know what you're doing.

* * *

The Nuts & Bolts:
Commercial (Black Letter Law) Outlines

Sorry to say, the primers won't be enough. You will also need to get a commercial outline for each course. The primers provide the conceptual overview, "the big picture." That way, you get some idea of how the pieces fit together: the logic of the overall subject. And what's also important, the primers take you through a rudimentary "lawyerlike analysis" of fact patterns.

Commercial outlines then provide the nuts & bolts of Black Letter Law: the elements of each cause of action and the defenses against each cause of action. They also discuss the cases in the casebooks. Some commercial outlines *only* discuss cases. They're sort of like the old Monarch Notes® or CliffsNotes™ that way: "briefs-in-a-can." Most, though, present both Black Letter Law and case briefs. (Some vendors do two sets of outlines: one is Black Letter Law, the other is just the canned briefs.) Some commercial outlines are geared to one, or perhaps two, casebooks. (They'll say so on the cover.) Commercial outlines nearly always are in an 8½" x 11" format.

Almost any law prof who is asked—and many who aren't—will tell you not to buy a commercial outline. (Josephson alluded to this—see page 44—when referring to profs who "disdain secondary sourses.") But the profs are not in your corner. Commercial outlines are absolute necessities. However, although they're absolute necessities, they're not sufficient.

Making It PERSONAL

One of the few times law professors are honest with students is when they tell them to do their own outlines instead of relying on the commercial ones. But, as usual, they don't explain why. Students get the impression that an outline is something that they're supposed to create in the final weeks of the course, to prepare for exams. You are indeed supposed to create it to prepare for exams. But you should be using it almost from *Day One*. Your outline synthesizes everything you've learned, from all sources—including the commercial outline.

HOW TO PROCEED

Your prof likely will provide a syllabus. It might have headings, telling what the topic is for each class. Then again, it might not. The syllabus will list pages in the casebook that you have to read before each class. Most of the assignment for each class will consist of cases. If the syllabus doesn't list topics, check the table of contents in the casebook; it might have headings, and you can see what heading each assignment is under.

If there are no headings, whether in the syllabus or in the casebook's table of contents, look in your commercial outline on the subject, especially if it's one that includes "canned briefs." (As mentioned earlier, some commercial outlines are "casebook specific," geared to one or more casebooks—and thus to that book's cases, obviously.) Sometimes a case is mentioned by name in a primer, too, and you find out from that what topic the case is used to illustrate.

Once you know what the topic of the case is, you can do either of two things: go to a primer or to a commercial outline. If you've prepped, and read the relevant section of a primer, you might want to quickly go over the topic again, in the primer, to refresh your understanding. But if you already feel comfortable with the topic at a conceptual level, you might want to go straight to the commercial outline. (Or, start with the commercial outline and then go to the primer. Your choice.) In Contracts, if the case is under the UCC (Uniform Commercial Code), consult the *ABCs of the UCC* book, discussed on page 60 in Chapter 2.

You then want to see what the elements are of the Black Letter Law on that cause of action, and the defenses against a cause of action. That's the first thing that goes into your outline.

But this is just the *starting point* of your outline.

PUT IT INTO YOUR *OWN* WORDS

The crucial part of mastering the material is putting it in your *own* words. It's when you try to do this that you'll realize what you don't understand. (As Confucius said, "Great Man is aware of what he knows—and of what he doesn't know.") If all you're doing is copying phrases from a commercial outline, or trying to memorize phrases someone else prepared for a personal outline, you'll never realize what it is you don't know. If all you can do is repeat things from memory, you won't do well on finals. But when you have to express it in your *own* words, and *apply* it, you'll become keenly aware of the gaps in your knowledge. Then you try to fill in those gaps.

Students have e-mailed me and said, "I got someone else's personal outline who'd taken this course from the prof last year. It's very good. So why should I make my own?" —Because there is no way someone else needed to understand exactly the same things as you, in exactly the same way as you need to in order to *truly* understand them. People often approach the same subject from different angles. Granted, in law school, one person's lawyerlike analysis should be pretty close to another's. But that's really just the *end* result. The way *you* "store" information, and *your* method of proceeding, might be quite different from someone else's, in *getting* to that end result.

For example, it is now well established that some people are visually-oriented. they like to draw diagrams, flow charts, and so on. Others want it all in words. True, it's easily possible that two people would both be visual, or verbal. But they won't visualize or verbalize in the same way.

Other students have written and said, "I got someone else's outline, but then started my own anyway. However, mine ended up looking exactly like that other one. I felt as though I were reinventing the wheel. So, I've stopped making my own personal outline."

Such people are kidding themselves. To repeat: there is no way your outline would end up looking just like someone else's, if you're doing your job right. When it bears an uncanny resemblance to some-one else's, the chances are pretty good the person who's writing the new outline isn't *thinking*—at least, not beyond the bare-bones. A good outline has muscle. And it takes regular exercise to build up muscle.

What someone else did might actually be better than what you do. But that's not the point. By making your own outline, you're making the subject your own. There's nothing wrong with comparing outlines after you've finished a section on some topic. But you should not look at someone else's outline until you've finished that part of your own. You'll just be subconsciously *copying* theirs.

(In years two and three you can rely on an off-the-shelf outline from someone else. Not in first-year, though.)

As an example of putting something into your own words, here's how I explained to myself the distinctions among an intentional tort, simple negligence, and gross negligence:

> Gross negligence occupies a middle ground between simple negligence and intent. The risk is so great, and so obvious, that "any damned fool would know" that it's just "an accident waiting to happen."
>
> Compare: "passive aggression." Normally, aggression is active. That's what an intentional tort is. Simple negligence is passive. Rather than being an act done on purpose, it truly "just happens." But in gross negligence, the tortfeasor has created a situation where you could say that someone gets hurt "accidentally on purpose."
>
> An intentional tort is a conscious "act of *co*-mission." *Simple* negligence is a thoughtless "act of *o*-mission." *Gross* negligence could almost be called "*willful* thoughtlessness."
>
> Usually, not always, with an intentional tort, the act is directed against a specific known victim (but see "transferred intent"). Virtually *always* with simple negligence, the situation itself is one that's "out of sight, out of mind" as to the tortfeasor: thus obviously the tortfeasor has no thought as to possible victims, even though such potential victims were foreseeable. With gross negligence, the risk has been "staring the (potential) tortfeasor in the face." Yet, his or her callousness regarding the safety of potential victims is so great that it's almost as though he or she *expects* someone to get hurt, but does not know who that person might be —and does not care as to either the victim's identity or the harm the victim suffers.

BUT USE THE "MAGIC WORDS" WHEN IT COUNTS

As mentioned, you put everything into your own words to make sure that you understand it. However, in your answers to exam problems, you want to use the wording your professor prefers (or seems to prefer), especially on the elements of Black Letter Law.

There are many different ways to express the elements of various parts of Black Letter Law. Page 72 in Chapter 3 gave the definition of a "contract" in the *Restatement (Second) of Contracts,* and then page 73 gave my own "checklist" of elements as an alternative.

It's quite possible your prof will have a preference. Yet, because profs play hide-the-ball, he or she will likely not tell you what wording to use. But pay attention in class. If the prof repeatedly uses the same wording on something, go with that. Perhaps the prof will instead spend a lot of time in class on a particular case. If the case has wording of the Black Letter Law (unlikely—it's an edited case, remember), use that. Or, if the prof pays a lot of attention to the *Restatement, use* the *Restatement's* wording.

The same is true regarding Bright-Line Rules and "Doctrines," discussed on pages 55-56 in Chapter 2.

You will want to *use the wording the prof seems to prefer. You should memorize that wording for the exam.*

However, don't get all worked up about this. You will have shown that you'd mastered the material by doing a good lawyerlike analysis in your answers on your exam. So, your prof will overlook the fact that you didn't "say it his or her way" with regard to the picky wording. (The prof might not have had one in the first place—and likely would have kept it a secret even if he or she did have one.)

And if you can't determine whether your prof does have a preference, don't worry about it. Use the wording in the *Restatement (*if applicable); or, at the very least, in a commercial outline. But, as mentioned, putting the Black Letter Law into your outline is only your *starting* point.

Digression: Dirty Professor Tricks

As you've seen, I urge you to read the primers before you even start law school. (To repeat: the addendum to Chapter 16 presents a timetable for prepping.) But even if you *have* prepared, that does not mean you'll have smooth sailing...

Atticus—

We've been in law school for 4 days and I'm thinking what the????

In Torts we've spent 4 days on one case and we have done this because the prof thinks it's a good starting point to let us know that both sides in a lawsuit can make a good argument.

I've picked up the Gilbert's Commerical Outlines and in the front it lists pages from various textbooks that correlate with sections in the outline. Well, the pages that this case are on in the casebook are not even listed in this index by Gilbert's!

So I'm thinking the case is virtually useless. I mean it does talk about negligence and strict liability in some ways but we aren't concentrating at all on those topics.

In Contracts we are actually beginning with DAMAGES awarded for breach of contract rather than starting with what is a contract. This is terribly backwards and even the 2Ls and 3Ls complain about the way my school teaches contracts. It just seems silly. Pages we are reading aren't listed at the beginning of Gilbert's.

It's sort of the same way with Civ Pro and Crim Law.

Anyhow, is this normal?

I know that PLS essentially says that the profs aren't going to teach us anything but I feel like I'm just treading water, going through the motions, until we start to cover something that remotely covers the black letter law.

I guess what I'm trying to say is that I have no idea where the classes are going right now. All they keep telling us to do is read these cases but when we go over them it's like we really aren't learning any fundamental rules, which doesn't lend itself to my outlining hopes.

Anyhow, what gives? Is this normal and should I just start strictly doing the E&E, Commerical Outlines, and the Restatements? When I do those 3 things I feel like I accomplish things, but when I'm mired in reading/briefing cases and spending time in class, I feel like I'm not learning a thing.

You aren't *supposed* to learn anything in class—nor from the cases themselves. From the professor's point of view, classes are, for the most part, just something to fill the time until exams. The prof is intentionally having the class just "go through the motions." It's "sink or swim." Yet, this "madness in the method" is *intended* to keep students *struggling*, merely treading water instead of learning how to swim. They figure it's up to *you* to learn how to swim, on your own (*without* any help from the cases).

With few exceptions,
you use the cases *only* as "topic signposts"
—to the *Black Letter Law* you need to learn...
and you *don't* try to learn the relevant Black Letter Law
directly from the cases *themselves.*

WHAT TO DO ABOUT THE "RANDOM" PROF

If you've prepped, you know what the logical order of the course should be. But that doesn't mean your prof will follow it. He or she might skip around from topic to topic within the subject, mixing everything up so there's no coherent order (as that e-mail just indicated).

My contracts prof, like the one this student had, started with a case on damages, from the back of the casebook. But the case came under the UCC, not the common law. Neither the casebook editor, nor the (edited) case itself, and certainly not the professor, let us in on that crucial bit of information. From the UCC case, he then jumped almost to the front of the casebook, for a case on "the battle of the forms." Everything throughout the semester was helter-skelter.

In these first few weeks, though, if your prof jumbles everything, don't worry about how all the pieces fit together...yet. Just put your outline's topics in chronological order—i.e., the order in which the prof assigned cases that dealt with those topics.

As you get more adept at doing a lawyerlike analysis (from playing with hypos), reorganize your outline to fit the logical order of the primers and the commercial outlines—as the *prof* should have done. There will be some gaps, of course (because of your prof's incoherent approach). But because you know where those gaps are, you'll still be able to see how everything fits together. Later, fill in those gaps.

DEALING WITH A PROFESSOR'S "OVERSIGHTS"

There are some profs, though, who *never* cover certain topics that *ought* to be covered. Maybe it's because the prof is just thoughtless. Or maybe it's part of the professoriat's standard operating procedure of keeping students in the dark. Regardless, if you don't understand the topic the prof *omitted,* it might be difficult for you to do a good a *thoroughgoing* "lawyerlike analysis" of the fact patterns in your exam problems. It's even possible that the prof will *tacitly* hold you *responsible* for the pretermitted topic. If a prof does omit a topic that he or she ought to have covered, you'd better fill in that hole in your outline.)

General rule: if the *primer* covered it, *you* should cover it, even if your prof didn't.

"MYSTERY CASES"

The primers usually don't mention cases by name. And the commercial outlines, even the ones that are entirely "canned briefs," don't cover *all* the cases in a casebook. Thus (as that last e-mail quoted indicates), the prof might assign a case that's not in a commercial outline.

(However, there are so many commercial outlines now, you ought to be able to find *one* that covers the case. But if you've already bought your commercial outlines, you don't need to buy yet another one. Instead, just go to the bookstore and look at the other outline there and see what topic that case covers; it will only take a couple of minutes. The commercial outline you already own has all the elements, etc., in that area of Black Letter Law. —And because "case briefing" is such a trivial exercise, you do not need to buy the commercial outline that has that case in it just so you can copy out the brief from that outline. It simply isn't worth it. Brief it on your own.)

But maybe the case is not mentioned in your primer or in *any* commercial outline. It might even be a case your prof edited and photocopied and then handed out. And you're drawing a complete blank as to what it's about. There's still at least one more way to skin this particular cat: either look the case up in the hardbound reporter in the law library, or else look it up on-line (the latter via Westlaw or Lexis). The casebook will give you the legal citation. Use that to find the case. (See Chapter 16 for a primer on legal research, to learn about "cites.") If it's a hand-out case, it might not have a citation, however. (See below on what to do then.)

It's almost *certain* that when you find the original version of the case, it'll have "headnotes" (informally known as "squibs"). These list all the points of law in that case—i.e., what the case is about.

However, if even after reading the headnotes, you still don't understand what topic/s the case covers, all is not lost. The headnotes use West's "key number" system. Every possible topic in the Law has been assigned a "key number" by West. And as part of each headnote, you'll see the key number for that headnote. It will be fairly easy for you to get a list of all the key numbers and what they refer to—and what *larger* topic each of them is a part of. (First-year only concerns the larger topics, not the minutiae, of Black Letter Law. You do not need to determine what the finely detailed topic is that the case covers. You just need the general topic—e.g., "impossibility of performance," in Contracts.)

But there's a tricky part to this when you're having to look up the headnotes. As you'll recall, the text of a case in a casebook has been edited. Sometimes this is because the case covers *several* points of law, in several different topics, and the casebook editor wanted only the material on the *one* topic. (The same thing is true with a photocopied hand-out.) So, when you look up the original text and see the headnotes, pay attention only to those that cover the *portions* of the full text that are reproduced in the *edited* version of the text that's in your casebook (or hand-out). Otherwise, you'll be chasing down many topics that are a complete waste of your time.

Sometimes the casebook editor or prof goes a step further, and leaves off the citation. So, you can't find the case and check the squibs...or so you might think.

If you have access to Westlaw or Lexis, though, you can do a "case-name" search, on-line, to get the citation (and, perhaps, the entire case, complete with squibs). But even if the case is not listed on-line (such as an old English case), you can still probably find it in the library by checking the "digests." (The legal research primer covers digests.) If it *is* an old *English* case, you'll probably be able to see it's an English case just from the wording, the title used when referring to the court or the judge, etc. So then you have to check *English* digests. (Of course, the prof will probably have tipped off the reference librarians, to keep them from helping students trying to find that specific case. So you either have to ask a general question such as "How do I find English cases when I don't have a cite?" or else you'll have to find a second- or third-year student who's willing to help you out.)

Note: I am *not* saying you should *always* look up the squibs. In fact, you should do that *only* when you have *no other* way of finding out what a case concerns. Time is at a premium in law school, and checking for headnotes (even on-line) takes time you can't spare.

THE "BAD LAW" CASE

Another favorite dirty trick was first mentioned in Chapter 3: assigning cases that are "bad law," (Either they were poorly-decided cases from the very start, or they've long since been overturned for other reasons.) But this is easy to deal with. A commercial outline should tell you that the case is "bad law," and why.

Specific Things to Cover

Chapter 2 recommended John Delaney's book, *Learning Legal Reasoning*. He has another book out, *How to Do Your Best on Law School Exams*. It's wonderful. And all of its Chapter IV is devoted to outlining your courses. It tells you just about everything you need to know. But here are some of the highlights:

Fact-Specific Examples. Create your *own* fact patterns to illustrate the rules from Black Letter Law. Do not just copy out the examples in a commercial outline. Rules have to be applied to specific fact situations, and their meaning has to be related to specific facts.

Policy. You've already seen the importance of understanding the policy behind any given bit of Black Letter Law. Just note that any given bit of Black Letter Law can serve *more* than one policy or purpose. As Delaney says, unless you understand each rule as a servant of policy purpose/s, it'll be hard for you to apply that rule.

Know the Limits. The policy behind a given rule might not apply to certain fact situations. So it's important to understand the purpose of the policy, and to understand situations where the Black Letter Law would not be applied. Make up examples where the rule does not apply. And have counter-examples ready where a conflicting rule applies or that illustrate an exception to the rule.

But this doesn't just concern the fine points of a particular rule. Sometimes, students forget that a particular rule only applies within one major area of law and not others. For example, "assumption of the risk" as an affirmative defense in tort can be invoked only in a *negligence* case, not in a suit for an intentional tort. In contrast, the rule on "infliction of mental distress" generally applies only to *intentional* infliction, not negligent. (In some jurisdictions, the latter does not even exist.)

Make Sure You've Mastered It. Don't just state the Black Letter Law and come up with a few examples, counter-examples, etc. Make sure you understand how that law works in practice. Don't "blow off" something you don't understand, just because you figure "Oh, it probably won't be on the exam." One of the most important laws of all is Murphy's Law: "If something *can* go wrong, it *will*." Besides, there is life beyond law school. And the rule you "blew off" in school may come back to haunt you—on the "barzam," or when you're out in the real world, or even in a later course in law school. So, take the time and stick with it until you've mastered it.

However—

Be Aware of Unsettled & Unclear Areas of the Law. There are some areas of the law that have yet to "gel" into Black Letter Law. Sometimes it's because there's a battle raging as to what the law should be. Other times, it's because there have been so few cases in some area of the law, and the cases within that area are disparate as to the fact patterns, so it's hard to say what "the law" really is.

Don't knock yourself out trying to make sense of it. But do be aware of the nature of the problem, and of the various holdings—especially when they point in different directions.

Conflicts. Profs love to pose problems where two or more rules of law might apply. Sometimes this is just a rule and counter-rule situation. But sometimes it's because there's a conflict in the law, as between the old law and the new, or between the majority rule and the minority rule in the common law, or between the common law and the statutory law (such as the Model Penal Code), or between the Black Letter Law in the case law common law and a *Restatement's* declaration of Black Letter Law. And sometimes it's a conflict between public policies.

In those situations, it might be that only one rule actually applies. (For example, a sale of goods comes under the UCC...but there are exceptions.) If the outcome would be different under a different rule (even if that other rule does not apply), it's worth your while to know that other rule and how it would affect the outcome. It's also worth your while to know why the other rule does *not* apply—and to be able to *quickly* explain that in an exam answer. (Extra points for you.)

Another area of conflicts involves ideology. For example, the Law & Economics "school" appears to define "justice" as economic efficiency, subordinating Law to the Market. The outcome of a case might be different under that heuristic.

"Bad Law." You do not need to spend much time on this. But it's helpful to understand why that case was or is bad. This is not for the purpose of discussing the case, but rather for deepening your understanding of the current Black Letter Law.

Trends & Novelties. Professors get bored teaching the same old stuff year after year. As with everyone else, they're attracted to the new and different. And so, what often interests a prof are (1) trends in the law, (2) new wrinkles in the law or new areas within old subjects, or (3) areas where the applecart of the law has recently been upset. *He or she might have an exam question on one of these.*

Chapter 24 advises you to get a subscription to the *National Law Journal,* as part of your long-range planning for post-graduate employment. *NLJ* regularly runs "think pieces" on legal trends and novelties.

"PSYCHING OUT" the PROF

Wording. No need to say more about trying to discover if the prof has any express or implied preferences as to the wording of elements of Black Letter Law, etc.

Topics. If your prof spends a great deal of time in class on a particular case, or a particular line of cases, or a particular area within the subject, the chances are good that he or she will return to it as part of an exam problem. Enough said.

"Themes." As Delaney explains, a theme is "an overarching perspective for formulating and analyzing the issues and doctrine. Professors are constantly relating the specifics in the cases to their favorite themes. It's important for students to understand the connection and what is going on." Another way of putting this is to ask, "How does the prof *'frame* the issues'?"

Different profs have different themes, of course. In my own first-year courses, there was a prof who was a flaming reactionary, and another one who was a flaming "politically correct" liberal. Every class with either was an hour-long harangue. The profs did discuss the cases, though. (You might not be even that "lucky." Instead, you might get a prof who assigns cases and then never mentions them, or even the points of law they concern, in class.)

As you will see in Chapter 6, you do not need to "give the professor what he or she wants" in terms of a particular political "spin." But you should certainly be aware of "where the prof is coming from."

If you have time, look especially for the prof's own writings on the subject of the course. It's unlikely any exist, because profs don't make their reputations, usually, on first-year subjects, but on some very fine point of the advanced courses. Sometimes, though, the prof who's teaching a subject will have done an article on a finer point within that subject. And the prof might have raised a point that you, in turn, might be able to raise in your exam answer, as though you'd thought of it all by yourself.

THE FINER POINTS

If you have time and think it's important, you can read articles in legal encyclopedias or academic law journals. Or you can consult a treatise or hornbook. (A hornbook can be useful for getting a quick historical survey of the subject. This can enhance your perspective, especially when considering the trend in a particular area of the law.)

The Killer Material

Chapter 2 recommended several primers for the Big Six courses. But four topics are killers, and three are in just one course: Property.

The first is **Estates & Future Interests.** Loosely, it concerns transferring possession of and title to real estate, espcially upon the death of the original owner. E&FI is a survival of medieval. You will either love it or hate it. Most, by far, hate it.

The various schedules for prepping for law school, presented in the addendum to Chapter 16, all allocate some time for E&FI. But even so, if your Prop prof decides to cover it, chances are you'll need more than what's in the primer on Property.

West has a good book out that will help orient you to the subject: *Introduction to the Law of Real Property: An Historical Background of the Common Law of Real Property and Its Modern Applications.* It's a slim volume and written in a surprisingly lively style. It's a classic. The original author was Cornelius Moynihan. His name is still on it, and most of what's in it is his work. However, for the 3d edition (2002), West brought in Sheldon F. Kurtz to be co-author. (Kurtz is one of three co-authors of West's general primer on property, discussed in Chapter 2.) Moynihan/Kurtz discuss the reasons how and why E&FI got to be the way it is. And for the new edition, Kurtz added questions and answers similar to the "Examples & Explanations" portions of the Aspen primers. After reading his book and working the problems in each section, the subject will *make sense* to you.

But if your Prop prof is serious about E&FI, you'll need even more than Moynihan/Kurtz. Fortunately, there are four other books that are magnificent. They have many practice questions in them, with answers. And those questions and answers can save your...uh, grade.

The first is by Robert Laurence and Pamela B. Minzer ("L&M"). It's published by Matthew Bender/Lexis Publishing. Its title is *A Student's Guide to Estates and Future Interests, 2nd ed..*

The second is by John Makdisi, and is published by Aspen. It's *Estates in Land and Future Interests: Problems and Answers, 3rd ed..*

A third book is from West. Its authors are Peter T. Wendel and Charles I. Nelson. Its title is *A Possessory Estates and Future Interests Primer.*

The fourth book is the one that's most popular. It's *Estates in Land and Future Insterests: A Step-by-Step Guide,* by Linda Holdeman Edwards, and is published by Aspen (but not as part of the E&E series).

As mentioned, all four have sample problems, with answers. You should answer these *in writing,* then see how well you did.

There's one other part of E&FI that's especially tricky. It shows up even outside real property: the notorious **"Rule Against Perpetuities,"** the "RAP." (Students add a "C" to the front of it, which stands for "Confounded.") I shall not discuss it, because it would get me too upset. Suffice it to say, it's hard; *real* hard.

Fortunately, though, Matthew Bender/Lexis Publishing has a book on it in their Student Guide Series. It's called, amazingly, *A Student's Guide to the Rule Against Perpetuities*. Its author is Frederic S. Schwartz. It too has questions, with answers.

Several students have e-mailed me to ask, "Why is this area of the law so important?" Here's why: as Chapter 23 discusses, nearly every state, as part of its "barzam," administers the Multistate Bar Examination (MBE). It has six subjects in it. One of those is Property. And Estates & Future Interests is an important part of the Property section. If you do not get a solid understanding of E&FI now, the chances of mastering it during your bar "review" course after graduation are about zero. So you will lose several points on your barzam score. Further, the state-specific portion of the barzam, in nearly all states, tests wills and trusts. E&FI— and *especially* the (C)RAP—are an important part of wills and trusts. Again, if you don't get a solid understanding of the (C)RAP now, there is no way you will be able to master it during your bar "review." And who knows? You might even end up writing wills for clients some day, and working in "estate planning." But you won't last long (or will soon get sued for legal malpractice) if you don't understand E&FI and the (C)RAP.

I do recommend that you get the Moynihan/Kurtz book and read it before you go to law school. However, you would do well to also get and study at least one of the four E&FI books, and the Schwartz book on the (C)RAP before you take a course in wills or trusts, and certainly before you take the barzam.

The second killer material in Property is **"real covenants and equitable servitudes."** Again, I won't go into what they are. (But see the exam problem and suggested answer in Chapter 7, which includes a section on this topic). As with E&FI, Real Covenants & Equitable Servitudes *will* be on the Property portion of the MBE, and you will not likely master it during your quickie bar "review" course. Further, if you end up handling real estate matters as a practicing attorney, you will certainly need to understand these topics.

The same is true of the final killer material in Property: **easements**— although easements are much less difficult than real covenants & equitable servitudes, let alone E&FI and the (C)RAP.

Matthew Bender/Lexis publishing's Student Guide Series has a book that covers easements, real covenants, and equitable servitudes. It's by Stephen A. Siegel. (I believe this is the same Siegel who has written many other student aids, for other publishers.) Its title is *A Student's Guide to Easements, Real Covenants and Equitable Servitudes*. As with all the books in the Student Guide Series, it has questions, with answers.

The fourth and final killer material in first-year is **Civ Pro,** almost in its entirety. The Glannon primer in the Aspen E&E series is excellent. But if your prof likes to get into the nitty-gritty of individual rules of federal civil procedure, you'll need more than Glannon's.

The book to get is one for practicing attorneys. (I use it regularly, in federal court.) It's *O'Connor's Federal Rules - Civil Trials, by* Michol O'Connor. It contains an excellent discussion, rule by rule, of the FRCPs (Federal Rules of Civil Procedure). It also cites to many cases on each rule, and discusses them. (There's a new edition each year. But unlike the trivially new editions of casebooks, this one could almost be updated every six months and it would still be a good buy.) If *your* Civ Pro prof starts to use a *rule-by-rule* approach to the subject, instead of the usual "leading cases" approach (with cases that date from *before* the FRCPs were adopted), you'd better get *O'Connor's...fast.*

O'Connor's publisher told me when the first edition of *O'Connor's Federal Rules* was published, the faculty at Baylor Law School (in Texas) got so upset at how clear it made everything that they *ordered* the school bookstore *not* to stock it, and not to take any orders from students for it. (The students, of course, just bought their copies elsewhere. Eventually, the faculty rescinded the ban.)

To learn what these books cost, and how to get them, see Chapter 16.

To learn what these books cost, and how to get them, see Chapter 16.

* * *

Some students have e-mailed to say that they found some other books that helped them clear up some fine points in various basic subjects. The books they recommended do not include Q&A material. But if you've read the primers, and want more to read, here they are:

Marvin A. Chirelstein, *Concepts and Case Analysis in the Law of Contracts,* 4th *ed.,* published by Foundation Press. From its title, it sounds like a casebook. But it isn't. It's a good book, in paperback.

Vincent R. Johnson, *Mastering Torts, 2nd ed.,* from Carolina Academic Press.

David A. Dittfurth, *The Concepts and Methods of Federal Civil Procedure,* also from Carolina Academic Press. Much of the material in the first few chapters strikes me as rather "Mickey Mouse." But when Dittfurth finally gets rolling, he gets good.

And Matthew Bender/Lexis Publishing has a "Legal Text Series" with volumes on several first-year subjects in it. Each book starts with the word *"Understanding..."*

Just to make sure there is no misunderstanding here: I am *not urging* you to go out and buy all these, not even the books on the "killer material," the way I urge you to get the books recommended in Chapter 2. Rather, I'm listing them because you might want to turn to them for further understanding after you've read a primer on the subject in question, while working on your personal outline. That's all.

"Hy-po, Hy-po, It's Off to Law We Go"

The "fact patterns" of the cases you're assigned to read in law school are real, not fiction. But, as Chapter 1 stated, each case your prof assigns will likely then be used as the starting point for a series of "hypotheticals," the "what if"/"suppose" questions.

Example: Chapter 3 noted it's common sense that, if someone is in danger, and two people—one drunk, one sober—are nearby, it's preferable to have the sober person (not the drunk) try to come to the rescue. But it also mentioned that (as a general rule) no one is legally obligated to try to come to the rescue of another. What if the sober person refuses to help, but the drunk "goes for it"? And what if the sober person is sure the drunk is heading to his doom? And what if the sober person then *restrains* the drunk? And what if the person in dire straits then dies, and that person's family then sues the sober person for having restrained the drunk? Or, suppose the sober person stands by while the drunk proceeds—and the drunk is indeed then killed during the attempted rescue, and the dead drunk's (pun intended) family then sues the sober person for *not* restraining him...and the person in dire straits had gotten out of danger on his or her own. What result? (You should already know the answer to this one.)

There are two kinds of hypotheticals: static and dynamic. The distinction is not important, though. The static hypo is where the "fact pattern" you get is not changed. That's what your prof will give you on your final exam problems called "issue-spotters." A "dynamic" hypo is where the fact pattern gets changed again and again. That is likely what your prof will give you in class. (It's also what you'll sometimes get on the Multistate Bar Examination, as a series of questions.)

It works like a kaleidoscope, sort of. The bits and pieces in a kaleidoscope are the same. But give the device a twist, and a whole new pattern forms. With a dynamic hypo, you're not only giving it a twist, you're changing one or more of the bits and pieces in view. The new pattern that forms might be a new *legal* pattern, in the sense that it brings into play *different* Black Letter Law (pro, con). Then again, it might not. Either conclusion has to be the result of a *lawyerlike* analysis. The fact patterns given in Chapter 3 (the examples regarding contracts, torts, and criminal law) were all static hypos. Chapter 1 presented a static hypo about Nasty Nephew. Next, it presented more facts without changing any of the original ones, so the new situation was still just another static hypo. Then some of the facts were changed, and thus it became a dynamic hypo. In the Aspen primers, most of the "Examples" problems are static hypos. Sometimes, though, a later static example is based on an earlier one, with the facts changed. So the two examples together are a dynamic hypothetical.

Static hypos are okay as a starting point when trying to master Black Letter Law and to do a lawyerlike analysis. But to get really good at "thinking like a lawyer," you should be working with *dynamic* hypos ASAP.

(Chapter 5 provides an extended example of how to take the fact pattern of a case as the starting point for creating your own hypotheticals and then playing with them. It then "spins out" even more hypos that are in the same topic as the original fact pattern, but which are independent of it.)

The Restatements

The *Restatements* are a good intermediate step between the Aspen primers' Examples & Explanations and creating your own hypos where you have no way to check your analysis.

Chapter 1 mentioned how, in the 1920s, the Committee on the Establishment of a Permanent Organization for the Improvement of the Law had criticized the "lack of agreement among members of the profession on the fundamental principles of the common law." The Committee achieved its goal (at least, with respect to establishing a permanent organization), and—in 1923—the American Law Institute was born. It's a *very* prestigious outfit.

The ALI is the source of the various *Restatements of the Law*. These are produced in keeping with its mission of "improvement of the law." Each *Restatement* is a multi-volume work. It's the product of some of the best legal minds in America, who spend *years* on it. (Law school faculty members who've served as *Restatement* "Reporters"—i.e., coordinators, with only one per *Restatement*—have *enormous* prestige.) They get a thorough critique of each draft, from hundreds of law professors, judges, and practitioners. It's been said that the *Restatements* have authority second only to U.S. Supreme Court opinions. That's an exaggeration, but not by all that much.

As their name implies, they restate legal principles (i.e., Black Letter Law) in an updated form. The first set of *Restatements* was done between 1923 and the end of WWII. A second one followed, starting in 1952. It's referred to as the *Restatement (Second) of*...whatever.

For Torts, Contracts, and Property (and others), the Second series is the current one. References to these works are abbreviated as "R2T," "R2P," and "R2K," respectively. The first series of volumes on Restitution, from several decades ago, has never been updated. The *Restatement of the Law on Lawyering,* on the other hand, is in its first series because it's new, a product of the 1980s and '90s. In 1987, ALI started on the *Restatement (Third)* project. In Property, the volume on mortgages is out, and the one on servient estates. But for other subjects in Property, the *Restatement (Second)* is still current.

Each *Restatement* proceeds by means of numbered sections. These are usually short (about a paragraph). As noted earlier, page 72 in Chapter 3 presented section 1 of the R2K, in full. Typically, below each section (or series of sections), the *Restatement* then provides one or more "illustrations," showing how that section or series of sections would apply to a given fact pattern. These "illustrations" are actually hypotheticals. Some are static. But other times, there's a series of illustrations, with the facts changed somewhat from one to the next—i.e., a dynamic hypo. And, as with the examples in the Aspen primers, they provide answers, at each step of the way.

Here's one from the R2T's §47, "Conduct Intended to Invade Other Interests But Causing Emotional Distress"—

> 2. A, who is annoyed by the barking of B's pet dog, shoots at the dog, intending to kill it. He misses the dog. B suffers severe emotional distress. A is not liable to B.

With the Aspen examples, you don't get the answer or the analysis until a few pages after the questions. But then you get the explanation as part of the answer—the "why" at the same time as the "what." With the *Restatement* illustrations, as you've just seen, you immediately get the "what." It's up to *you* to figure out the "why."

You might be wondering, "So how does this *help* me?" Here's how: between each "section" of the *Restatement* and the "illustration" (hypo), there's an official commentary on that section. The "Comment" presentation is short, usually just a few paragraphs. It explains the policy behind the section, why it's worded the way it's worded, and how this section is different from other sections on the same subject. These Comments are a *wonderful* way to further your understanding. What's more, there's a series of "Reporter's Notes." These "notes" provide a more detailed discussion. (So, the "Reporter" on a *Restatement* is actually far more than just a coordinator. That's the real reason why the role is so coveted among the professoriat—especially because the chance to become a Reporter comes along only about once in every other generation.)

Several students have said, "Okay, I play with hypos. But how do I know if my analysis is correct?"

The *Restatement* illustrations give you an immediate "reality check," by stating the correct conclusion. Obviously, if your conclusion disagrees with that in the "illustration," your analysis must be wrong, too. (This would not, by the way, necessarily be so regarding an answer to a problem on an exam. But the *Restatement* illustrations are narrowly drawn, and are simple.) So, knowing you were wrong the first time around, read (again) the Comment, or the relevant section in an Aspen E&E primer. Then try to figure out how you "missed the boat."

But even if your conclusion agrees with theirs, that is not enough. On an exam (and in the real world), it is not enough just to state your conclusion. (In legal jargon, as Chapter 3 noted, it's called "making a conclusory statement.") You must *explain* it—and, as an *advocate,* your analysis is actually more important than the conclusion. The "means" is almost more important than the "end." And on an exam, the why is (generally) more important than the what.

So, with the *Restatements,* you have an ideal opportunity to take the next step up from the Aspen primers. And you should definitely take advantage of that opportunity, for it is priceless. And after you've worked with the illustrations enough, you'll have the confidence to create your own hypos and deal with them, even when you can't check your conclusion and analysis against an authoritative source.

You should get a set of *Restatements* for Torts and Contracts, in addition to the Aspen primers and Delaney's books. (But you don't need the entire set of Torts. More on that in Chapter 16.) Unlike your casebooks, or even your commercial outlines—but *like* nearly everything *PLS* recommends—you'll be glad you have these *Restatements* when you're out in practice.

Because each illustration has the conclusion in the same paragraph as the fact pattern, you can't help but see it as soon as you reach the end of the hypo. So, make a photocopy of the illustrations. Then mark out the conclusion to each illustration. Set your photocopies aside before you start to work the illustrations as hypos. Then look only at your photocopied text, with the answers covered up. Next, just as with the Aspen E&E procedure, try to figure out the answers on your own. (As with the Aspen books, it's best to write your answer out, instead of formulating a "quickie" answer in your head. Also as with the Aspen primers, your answer should include your analysis, not just your conclusion.) After that, look at the book itself, and see the answer.

These books are useful for more than just playing with hypos. As mentioned above, the *Restatements* are highly respected by courts. It behooves you to become familiar with them, regardless of your area/s of interest. Yet, even so, the *Restatements* are not "controlling authority" —unless the high court in a particular jurisdiction says so. Further, although the ALI claims that the *Restatements* present a consensus as to what the common law is, sometimes part of a *Restatement* actually presents only the *minority* view. So, you cannot necessarily take a *Restatement* as Gospel.

In law school, you can score on an exam by knowing where the *Restatement* represents only the minority view, or where it conflicts with statutory law (as in Contracts, where it sometimes conflicts with the Uniform Commercial Code). Professors just *love* to pose fact patterns where the outcome will be quite different under different rules— common law, statutory law, or the *Restatement.*

A few students have e-mailed me to say their Torts or Contracts prof told them not to worry about the *Restatement* in that subject, because "The *Restatement* is not the law." That advice is in the same category as "don't use study aids." It's a trap for the trusting. Although it's literally true, it's extremely misleading. The *Restatements* aren't statutory law or case law in themselves, but—as mentioned—they *state* what the *Black Letter Law IS*...usually. Further, they're so highly respected that even when the *Restatement's* position is a minority position, it often eventually *becomes* the majority position. (The ALI presents these minority positions without acknowledging them as minority positions, knowing that by merely stating them, the ALI can perhaps promote a trend away from the majority positions. —Sneaky, but effective.)

The ALI publishes three different versions of the *Restatements.* The first is the hardbound set, complete with all the bells and whistles. It's what courts and many lawyers have. It lists many court decisions that have used a section of a *Restatement* as authority. You do not need that edition. It is far too expensive for law students.

The second version of the *Restatements* is called the "concise" edition. This is in paperback, and is primarily for lawyers. You do NOT want that edition, either. The "concise" edition has *cut out* many of the illustrations. After all, most lawyers don't need them. *You do.*

So, you want to get the STUDENT editions. They're in paperback. Chapter 16 tells where to get them, and gives their product I.D. numbers.

Not All Facts are Created Equal

In all hypos (and in the real world), you have to distinguish relevant from irrelevant facts. Having identified the relevant facts, though, you need to distinguish the insignificant from the "**material**" facts. "Material" is legal jargon for "important." That's why the cops talk about a "material witness." (I swear, I think I'd been out of law school for two years before I understood that. I'd thought "material" referred only to a *physical* item—as in "material goods"—vs. something intangible, rather than to something that was important whether it was tangible or not.)

All material facts are relevant. But not all relevant facts are material. They're the facts that the case "turns" on. And some material facts are so important they're "**outcome-determinative**," a.k.a. "**dispositive**."

Let's say there's an apparatus of critical importance at a factory. A green light is on when all's well. When something's wrong, the green light turns to red, as a warning. Color-blind people can't see the colors red and green (if I remember right), so they're not allowed to monitor that apparatus. But a person is working there who's kept his color-blindness a secret. His best friend is his supervisor, and knows the secret. But the color-blind guy is going to be laid off unless he has the job that includes monitoring that apparatus. So his supervisor buddy "covers" for him, and monitors the apparatus himself. But one day the supervisor is out sick, and a substitute supervisor is brought in from another department. Unbeknownst to that substitute, she has just become color-blind herself (like, as she arrived for work). She asks the subordinate for the "reading" of the light. The subordinate (honestly) says that he can't get near the apparatus to take the reading right away. The substitute supervisor takes a look and, not being familiar with the shade of green the apparatus uses, honestly thinks it's "green." But because she's now color-blind too, she doesn't see that it's red. The warning light is not heeded. While the subordinate is still away from it, there's an explosion. The whole truth comes out later.

In a suit for negligence, what are the relevant and irrelevant facts here? The material and immaterial? The outcome-determinative? Does it make a difference that the subordinate was color-blind? That his supervisor-buddy had been "covering" for him? That the sub-super was newly color-blind?

Maybe the most important fact, though, is one not disclosed in the fact pattern: whether or not the company had a policy of making sure whoever monitored that critical apparatus was tested for color-blindness, before being assigned to duties that included monitoring the light. Or another: maybe the *manufacturer* should have included a *flashing* of the light when there was something wrong, or a warning *sound*. (With this, you have a new potential defendant—one with "deep pockets." Noting the potential liability of the manufacturer can make a big difference to your success, both as a law student and as a practicing attorney...the latter especially with regard to the deep pockets. —In fact, to a plaintiff's trial lawyer, "deep pockets" is the most important "element" to look for!)

When playing with hypos, or an exam's fact-pattern, sometimes you have to go beyond the facts as given. But when you do, you need to make it clear you're doing one or both of two things: (1) drawing *reasonable inferences* from the facts *as given,* or (2) making *reasonable speculations* as to what the other (as yet unknown) facts *might* be.

Out in the real world, you'd have to follow up, regardless of which of these you're doing, because you don't want to just make inferences or speculate. You find out the rest of the facts, to clear the matter up. On an in-class hypo, or on a law school exam, you don't have that option. So you have to let your prof know what you're doing. (But you never write something that *contradicts* the facts as given.)

What causes the facts to go into the various categories is their *legal* implications. And this is where law students typically have another problem. It won't do to change trivial facts that have no effect on the legal analysis. In classes where the profs allow students themselves to change the facts in class, all too often the students only change immaterial or irrelevant facts. And the same thing often happens when students create dynamic hypos on their own.

In the Contracts fact pattern on pages 72-73 in Chapter 3, a meaningless change would be, "What if Jack didn't keep his promise to go to London within a year, but went later, and Jill was still there, and everything else was as in the original fact pattern?" (The answer: Jill would be said to have **"waived"** the "condition" that Jack keep his promise to visit Jill within a year, that's all.) On the Torts hypo, a meaningless change would be "What if it wasn't the doctor's SUV, or even the other guy's, but was a vehicle the doctor had rented—and, under the terms of the rental agreement, only the doc could drive it?" (That would be a separate issue, under contract law, and irrelevant to a problem in a torts course.) A meaningless change under the Crim hypo would be, "What if the guy had already done a carjacking since his release from prison, and there was a warrant out for his arrest?" (No effect.)

Meaningful changes would be these:

Contracts—"What if Jill were a prostitute (as before), but she and Jack were lovers, and he did not want her to go to England for a year, and their agreement was that she would take a week off to be with Jack when he visited her in London, and she would stop work there and move back to Boston within a year of her departure, and he would then reimburse her for her return air fare, and she kept her end of the deal but then he didn't keep his?" (Jack loses.)

Torts—"What if the doctor had brought his cell phone with him, but they were out of range, and they agreed that the doc would keep trying to call 911 until they were within range and the call went through, but the drunk buddy kept driving even after the call went through and an ambulance had been dispatched to meet them, and instead of running into a telephone pole near the hospital, he'd run into one out in the boondocks?" (Drunk buddy probably loses, although if the doc had passed out in the SUV, after the call went through, there might have been good cause to keep driving.)

Crim—"Suppose the person who'd left the car in front of the store had *stolen* that car, had *kidnapped* the baby in the carseat on the floor in the back, and went into the store to *rob* it—and the guy who drove off in the car did so because he'd seen the other guy put the mask on and then go into the store with a gun in his hand, and wanted to foil the getaway (because he'd been in prison with the robber and hated him), but he'd had no intention of stealing the car, and he'd heard the baby crying (as before)—and was heading for a day care center so he could leave the baby on its doorstep, but the power steering went out and the accident happened." (Assuming his story was believed—which it would not be, in the real world—the criminal charge might get "knocked down" to a misdemeanor "unauthorized use of a motor vehicle," and the baby's death might get reduced to a "vehicular homicide" charge.)

As Justice Ruggero Aldisert of the Third U.S. Circuit Court of Appeals likes to say, "We must separate that which is important from that which is merely interesting."

Circles: Virtuous or Vicious

As you can see, this ends up being a "chicken-and-egg" situation (or maybe a Catch-22, especially when you're first starting). If you don't have knowledge or understanding of the Black Letter Law, you won't be able to separate the relevant facts from the irrelevant, the material from the immaterial, and to discern the truly "outcome-determinative" facts. But if you aren't able to grasp the *legal* possibilities inherent in the facts, you won't be aware of the potentially appropriate Black Letter Law (pro, con). Whether it's a *virtuous* circle (an upward spiral) or a *vicious* one (and possibly a "death spiral") is up to you.

It's like an ecosystem: everything affects everything else. An intellectual ecosystem. (As Chapter 2 said, however, you'll probably do best learning the elements of the Black Letter Law, and the policy it embodies, first. Be sure to use *fact examples*.)

This is why practicing with hypotheticals is so important. The more time you spend playing with hypos, the more you will begin to "internalize" the Black Letter Law. You will no longer need to consult reference material and run through a "checklist" of the law. You will find that you have begun to memorize it. But you've memorized it in such a way that it's starting to become "second nature" to you. You'll reach a point where you almost automatically know the differences among facts that are irrelevant, relevant, material, immaterial, and dispositive.

To return to the analogy used earlier: it's sort of like learning a foreign language. Students spend a long time on vocabulary and syntax. You practice conversations with "pattern sentences." You translate readings. But in the early stages, what happens is you're still "thinking in English." So, you have to always stop and figure out, "how do I say this in _____?" Or, if you see something in the foreign language, you go, "Now, what does this mean in English?" Yet, those who stick with a foreign language, and get good at it, eventually reach a point where they can *think* in the foreign language. The translation step is no longer necessary.

The only way to "get there" is to keep at it.

> Playing with hypos
> helps you make a good outline.
> Making a good outline
> helps you analyze the hypos.
> One hand washes the other.

That's the key reason to play with hypotheticals: to test your knowledge in action. As mentioned, the next chapter presents an exhaustive example of how to use a case as a starting point for hypos, and a discussion of those hypos. The discussion there later spins further away from the case, using new fact patterns that required dealing with the same subject in a different way. That's what you should do.

Reworking Your Outlines

Each week, you *rework* your personal outline for each course. You'll be learning new material, learning more things about old material, etc. Just as a *hypothetical* has to be dynamic to be the best for you, so does the process of making your personal *outline*.

When you first learn something—anything—you have to commit many details to memory before mastering it. Remember when you first learned to drive? There was so much to keep in mind. Yet, within a very short time, driving became second nature to you.

If you now had to teach someone else to drive, how would you do it? —It would take you a good while to think it through, right? You could even try to write a manual. But you wouldn't need to write a manual for *yourself*. You already *know* how to drive—so well, in fact, that you don't even have to think about it. You just *do* it.

—And that's the key. You must *use* the law *regularly*: playing with hypos, reworking your outline. The more you work with it, the faster it'll become second nature. Then you won't need a *big* outline. You'll know most of it so well that it would take more time than it's worth to read it through.

Again, think of writing and then reading a "How to Drive a Car" manual for *yourself,* versus just getting in the vehicle and taking off in it. If you were about to drive someone *else's* car, the only mental notes you might want for yourself would be those concerning that car's idiosyncrasies. Perhaps you have to shift gears yourself—and it's a five- instead of a four-speed. Maybe the brakes tend to grab, or you have to push really hard on the horn, or the engine tends to stall, etc. Obviously, such mental notes would be minimal. That's the goal of your outline.

And this is why you should start your personal outlines from *Day One*. As you begin each new topic for a course, you'll have a lot of notes—from the Aspen primers and commercial outlines, especially. Because you want to make sure you get everything right the first time, you'll spell it all out. You'll thoroughly cover each point. So, each section will be a long one. Then you'll search out other sources of information and insights. You'll have new thoughts and examples to insert into your outline, especially after you've tested your knowledge with hypotheticals. (You'll have a folder for each course, containing your outline and other written materials. Even if you use a computer and have your outline on disk, you should still make—and study—a hard copy of the revised version for every subject, each week.) As you integrate those things into your outline, the relevant section will get bigger still. Your understanding will gradually deepen and broaden.

But then a funny thing will happen: you'll notice, each week as you rework your outline, that you don't need to cover everything so thoroughly as before: some of it has started to become second nature. So you condense it. Even though you're adding new text to the *old* parts of your outline, those parts will start *shrinking*. Meanwhile, the *newest* topics in your outline will be *growing*.

Your outline in each subject will be like a conquering army. At first, there's a huge commitment, because the struggle is still underway. Enormous resources are concentrated in one place. But assuming the army wins the battle, it then moves on. The front constantly changes. Only a garrison is left behind to occupy each conquered territory and to mop up any lingering resistance. But even in a pacified area, the occupying force remains on the alert. It conducts exercises and practices its skills. That's what you should be doing too, as your study group works new hypos on old subjects—and concocts hypos that cut across several areas within each course. (For those who dislike a military analogy, I invite you to create your own.)

In the alternative: picture your outline as a wedge. As you do a new draft of each outline every week, the older material gets narrowed down some more. Of course, there will be bulges here and there— more difficult material, new finds to integrate into old material. But the overall shape should be a lot like a golf tee.

Now you see why you should do your *own* outline, throughout the semester, instead of relying on someone else's end-of-semester, finished outline. The *process* of making it is more important than the *product*.

Note: reworking your outline each week is vastly different from rewriting (or typing up) your class notes each day. You have more important things to do than counter-productive make-work such as typing up your class notes. That's a waste of time. Don't kid yourself as to what you're doing, and what you're accomplishing. You should be taking few notes in class, anyway. (See Chapter 11.) But something that's worthwhile in your class notes should be worked into that course's outline at the end of the week. (Examples: you realize your prof has a preference as to the specific wording of the elements of a piece of Black Letter Law; or that the prof has a "theme.") Then you *throw the class notes away.* By the end of the semester, you want to have a minimum of written material to review for the final. In part, this is because by then most of what you need to know should be solidly lodged in your mind. You won't even have to look over the original text of *Restatement* material or law review articles, etc., that are in your course folder. Their key points should already be in your outline...and, especially, in your *head.*

Likewise, depending on how much time you have, do not look up the cases listed in the casebook footnotes. True, you could then "parse" those cases, *à la* Delaney's *Learning Legal Reasoning.* (See Part V.) But at least initially, you need to get the basics down pat. If you really want to read the note cases, you can come back to them later.

However, if there are *questions* at the end of an assigned case, it could well be worth your while to spend some time answering them.

Your "SUMMARY" Outline

Your personal outline for each course, discussed above, is actually your *Master* Outline. (I call it this in part because it helps you master the material.) But as exams approach, you want to create a new personal outline for each course. This one, however, is not just another draft of your old Master. (And you do *not* stop working on your Master Outline.) This one is radically different. In fact, it's only two pages, at most, for each course—because it's almost just a checklist. This is your Summary Outline.

Most law school exams are "closed book." (You can't consult any "outside materials" during the exam.) More important, when you're in the exam, the adrenaline (and caffeine, nicotine, or perhaps other substances) will be pumping through your body. No matter how well-prepared you are, there will be at least a little bit of tension. It's easy to "blank out." Regardless, it takes *time* to look things up in a Master Outline during an "open book" exam...and "time is of the essence."

So, if it's "closed book," in the last few weeks of the semester, you should memorize your Summary Outline for that course and *drill, drill, drill, on being able to reproduce that Summary Outline word-for-word in a VERY short time.*

Then, before the exam, find out how soon you're allowed to start writing. See if you're permitted to make notes to yourself on scratch paper before the exams are handed out. If you are, then use some scratch paper to quickly reproduce your Summary Outline in its entirety. The process of setting this down on paper should take only a few minutes. At the very latest, you ought to be allowed to start writing while the exams are being handed out. (Better yet, just go ahead and do it after you've been told to put all your other materials away and have only the scratch paper the proctor will likely have then made available.) *You want to have your Summary Outline written out on scratch paper even before you get the exam.*

—Of course, if it's "open book," you just bring your Summary Outline with you. (You should bring your Master Outline too. But, to save time, all you should consult is your Summary Outline, unless it's really important to you to look some *crucial* fine point in your Master Outline.)

Then, after you've outlined (on other scratch paper) your *answer* to a problem, you take a few moments to look over your Summary Outline, to see if there's anything you missed and should include in the answer you're about to set down for the professor's eyes.

That's another reason for reworking the Master Outlines: as the name implies, the Summary Outlines are just a further, *drastic* reduction of material that should already be quite familiar to you. Granted, your Summary Outline should include the elements of each legal basis of entitlement. But everything else should instantly trigger almost everything else in the corresponding section of the Master Outline.

Note: Aspen, Sum & Substance, and Harcourt Brace all publish very short sets of materials comparable to the Summary Outline. Please do not rely on these. If you want to, get one just to compare it with your own outline, if you must. But your personal creation should cover far more than these commercial products, in the same number of pages or less—because your Summary Outline is *your* creation, and is merely a "shorthand" reminder of things you've already completely internalized.

Most important of all, *your personal outline is specific to what your prof is holding you responsible for.*

Two Pitfalls in Outlining

FIXATION ON THE CASES

Many students believe that knowing the *cases* inside and out is the key to learning the Black Letter Law. And so, their outlines are organized around the cases, rather than around the Black Letter Law.

Granted, in Constitutional Law (and sometimes in Civ Pro), that tends to be the right way to go. However, for all your other subjects, the cases are not important—with the exception of certain "landmark" cases. (It will be made obvious to you, one way or another, if a case is a landmark.)

Do not, *do not*, DO NOT fill up your outline with information on the assigned cases. That would be a mere repetition of the methods you used in your previous schooling. And it's really just a slightly-disguised version of memorize-and-regurgitate. You should—at most—have a merely *parenthetical* mention of a case in the same section that discusses the Black Letter Law the case itself first alerted you to. (Again, though, Con Law is always the exception, and Civ Pro often is too.)

Sure, you feel like you're accomplishing something when you fill page after page of your outline with what's really nothing more than case briefs. But this is almost as pointless as typing up your class notes and saving them. You are playing a game with yourself...a *losing* game.

PLAYING *THE* GAME v. PLAYING *A* GAME

Many students only give lip service to getting away from the memorize-and-regurgitate mode. They do manage to stop relying on the idea that all they have to do is memorize the elements of the various causes of action and defenses in Black Letter Law. But then, almost in compensation, they often *obsess* about their outlines. And, unfortunately, my recommendation that you "drill, drill, drill" on *memorizing* your SUMMARY Outline seems to encourage their obsession.

However, getting all worked up about what's in (or is not in) your outline is just a variation on the memorize-and-regurgitate mode.

Consider this analogy: imagine someone who knows all the rules of baseball, the history of the game, famous players and their great accomplishments, and so forth...but who has never *played* baseball.

You have to step up to the plate, yourself. Take a swing at hypos "pitched" to you, even if you create them completely on your own (as with the verbal equivalent of a pitching machine). Practice playing the various positions and fielding the hypos others have hit.

Refusing to PLAY the game is a fall-back position that a lot of snobs use, by the way. They think that they're only going to be *umpires* (i.e., high court judges...or maybe law professors). It never occurs to them that in order to fairly evaluate a pitch or a play, it is crucial that even the umpire have had some *experience* playing the game...even if, in law school, only by playing with hypos. At best, they only play a little bit of "catch" and then let it go at that.

In "pop psychology," there's a phrase called "playing a game." It's a situation where someone pretends to be doing one thing in good faith but is actually doing something quite different. If you emphasize working on your outline instead of working with hypos, you are "playing a game" with yourself. You need to be playing *the* game instead: the game of hypotheticals.

—It's like what they say about management consultants (especially the ones who just got an MBA from a big-name school): he or she knows the *Kama Sutra* by heart...but has never had a lover of his or her own.

An outline is just a verbal inventory of your mental tools. If you haven't worked with those tools and "gotten the hang" of them, you'll be a lousy craftsman when it comes time to even *choose* the *right* tools, let alone to *use* them, for real. (And here, for "real" means on a law school exam. It's even more crucial out in the real world, though.)

Some profs even *encourage* an over-emphasis on outlines. They do so to pretend to be on your side, by making a grand show of offering to critique your outline during office hours. But they're mum as to what's *most* important.

PLAYING WITH HYPOS is the key to success. You should consult your personal outline as you do this. But after awhile (especially regarding the topics that are no longer new to you), you should have internalized what's on your outline and should no longer need to look up anything in it as you work a hypothetical.

Outlining can even become a "crutch"...a crutch that will *make* you a "cripple."

So DON'T "Jump the Gun" on Outlines

If you decide to prep, it will be all you can do just to stay on schedule (no matter which timetable you choose from the addendum to Chapter 16). It's more important for you to read and to work the problems in the Aspen primers than it is to start outlining even before you start law school. But, if you really have *lots* of time to spare before law school, it won't hurt for you to go ahead.

Believe it or not, though, even I think it's possible to do *too* much preparation. Outlining before you even start law school seems like overkill. Give the primers priority, and spend any spare time on the *Restatements'* "illustrations."

Study Groups/Partners

Most incoming law students think the purpose of a study group is to create outlines. Typically, they do it one of two ways. Each person does the outline for an entire course, or each person does various sections of more than one course. Either way, everyone then shares his or her product with everyone else.

No. No. No. As should be obvious from the preceding discussion, you have to do it all by yourself. While it's a good idea to compare outlines-in-progress, your study group should *never* split up the work. If the other members of your group want to do so, fight it. If you're outvoted, do your own outline for every course, anyway, in addition to your assigned part. (Better yet, find a new study group or partner, because the members of your present group are going about things the wrong way.) This is too important a matter to screw up because of ill-considered demands from others.

The main purpose of a study group is to play with hypos. You will do a better job of testing your knowledge and understanding, and your issue-spotting and problem-solving skills, when there's someone to play the role of Devil's Advocate for you.

Others will see things that you completely missed, and vice-versa. That's important. Perhaps their insights came from reading something you didn't—a law journal article, a leading case, part of a treatise, etc. Come exam time *you* will need to be able to think of *everything*, *quickly*, all by yourself. Even if you're a natural-born genius at the first four levels of the Josephson Pyramid, the input from others will enhance your judgment and skill at synthesis, discussed above.

One thing your study group *should* do collectively is to work old exams. (See Chapter 6.)

Your study partner/s should already at least have a feel for the elements of the causes of action you'll be discussing. Better one good partner than three mediocre ones. You don't want to have to spend much time going over the basics. And even though it's a great ego-trip, you don't want to constantly play tutor to the others.

On the other hand, there are those who think that they won't get anything out of a study group unless the other members are "bright" (as the people who think this way assume themselves to be). As a public service TV commercial puts it (in a different context), "You can learn a lot from a dummy." Even basic questions, that *seem* "dumb," can lead you to new insights and to new questions that are profound. So, the "dumb" questions might not be so dumb after all...for your purposes.

You and your study partner/s should take seriously what you're doing. You cannot afford to waste much time. So, no ludicrous hypotheticals or analysis in a bid for laughs. Keep the jokes, small-talk, and gossip to a minimum. *You* have better things to do with your time, even if they don't. Last, do not conduct your group study sessions over a pitcher of beer. Better for you to get a reputation as a hard-ass who aced the finals, than to be known as a Good-Time Charlie who finished as an also-ran. —Unless, of course, you go to law school only because you can't think of anything better to do, and you really don't care. (Then too, you might have a ten-million-dollar trust fund you're living off of—in which case, your future is set, regardless. Congratulations.)

Another advantage of a study group/study partner is in seeking out new external sources of insights. For any given course, there are cutting-edge cases. These include "big" cases that might be of interest only to those in the Law, including some that might not even have been decided yet. (That's another reason to read the *National Law Journal*.) These cases sometimes give profs ideas for exam problems. There are also law review articles, legal encyclopedia sections, treatises, and so forth—such as writings by your professor relevant to your course, as already discussed. Once you've reached a certain point, you'll be ready to go on scouting forays, legal research missions. (And you'll know whether or not you've reached that point.) They'll certainly help you to deepen and broaden your understanding, and might come in handy on a final. For your purposes, most of this is just potential icing on the cake you're trying to bake. However, sometimes you find something that enables you to *decorate* the cake—to the surprised delight of your professor. (But remember: you still have to *bake* the cake, first. If you haven't, spreading all the icing in the world will do you no good. So, do not give these scouting forays high priority. If you have time for them, fine. Otherwise, let them go.)

Your group can divide up the work of finding useful materials and photocopying them—with a copy for each member. Each member of the group then takes these materials and does with them what he or she will. However, you don't memorize cases, authors, excerpts, etc. And you certainly won't cite any of these on your finals. (As mentoined, except in Con Law, and maybe Civ Pro, you don't cite specific cases.)

How often to get together? That's up to you and your partner/s. —Once a week, at *least,* for at least an hour on each course. (As you will see in Chapter 5, playing with hypos is time-consuming.)

How do you select study partners? See Chapter 11.

There are those who want to be loners. However, it's very difficult to create your own hypos and then play with them on your own.

(Surely you'll agree that playing with someone else is usually better than playing with yourself.) It's almost like playing a guessing game with yourself—which is inherently impossible, because you already know the answer. Of course, with a hypo, it might be that you just *think* you know the answer. But, as mentioned regarding study groups, someone else might catch something you missed.

But there are those who have such a competitive attitude that they do not want to work with someone else and thus perhaps give that other person an edge on exams. That is a ridiculous attitude. For one thing, study groups exist only in first-year, generally. You still have two years to go. Those you work with might do better in first-year than they otherwise would have, because you worked together. But then again, so might you. Regardless, all of you will still have two years to go.

Your first-year courses are just *introductions* to each subject. And *no one* is a know-it-all, for real—not even professors or lawyers who've specialized in a given subject for years.

Reaching the Summit of
The Josephson Pyramid

The second-highest level of Josephson's "law school learning pyramid" is "Judgment." It has three aspects:

> As a student develops judgment skills, he/she learns to go beyond the narrow doctrinal and factual confines of a legal problem and perceive relevant *non-legal factors* which bear upon the problem-solving process.
>
> For example, <u>practical implications</u> involving issues of time, cost and the reasonableness of certain risks would be considered by a good lawyer. Purely academic solutions that are unrealistic or naive are not proposed by one with mature judgment skills.
>
> In the same vein, refined judgment entails an ability to perceive <u>tactical considerations</u> which may affect the wisdom of a particular course of action.
>
> Finally, judgment suggests an ability to perceive <u>ethical issues</u> and a sensitivity to the <u>human relations</u> implications of various options.
>
> [Underlining in the original, italics supplied.]

As Josephson then notes, "Some students (and lawyers) are terrific issue-spotters but poor decision-makers."

He also notes that "judgment skills are difficult to...test." And fortunately for you (though sadly for your fellow students), most of your fellow students will be so deficient at knowledge, understanding, issue-spotting, and problem-solving, that you don't need to worry about your judgment skills as a law student. (But out in the real world, it can make or break your reputation as a legal *counselor*.) Yet, calling attention to "non-legal factors"—especially the practical implications—can make you look savvy even to a professor.

I do believe, though, that the "practical implications" angle could be important to you in weighing arguments on hypos and exams.

The highest point of the Josephson Pyramid is "Synthesis." It's where you pull everything together, organize it, and set priorities.

> It requires application of all of the previous skills to permit a building of original theories, frameworks, systems. The skill will be manifested by an ability to rationalize previously irreconcilable positions, reorganize, categorize, classify, and otherwise "pull together" information, policies, and concepts....
>
> Many law school examinations are pitched at the synthesis level as they require the student to draft definitive judicial opinions, *new statutes,* or propose alternatives to an existing structure of system.   [Italics added.]

Josephson then says that term papers, rather than essay exams, are the better way to test a student's ability to synthesize. But, of course, term papers take a long time to read. In a first-year class of maybe 100 or more students, no way. Yet, even on an exam, he says, "We can, however, evaluate whether [ability to synthesize] exists as most of us 'know it when we see it.'"

If you have prepped for law school, and you follow the advice in this chapter, you will acquire the skill of "synthesis" as you go along. It is not something you will need to consciously strive for. Perhaps you will not even be aware that you have it. But your professor will be—as will your future employers when they see how you handle legal questions during a summer clerkship.

Even though the Josephson Pyramid has its somewhat artificial distinctions among "knowledge," "understanding," "issue-spotting," "problem-solving," "judgment," and "synthesis," these things occur together almost simultaneously once you get good. But you have to be good at everything. If you're not good at the knowledge, or the understanding, of Black Letter Law, and the policy it embodies, you won't be good at issue-spotting or problem-solving. But the act of spotting "issues" (and conflict-pairings) and solving problems will broaden and deepen your knowledge and understanding—your judgment and synthesis skills. "Knowledge-in-*action*" is what a good lawyerlike analysis is all about.

Teaching Old Dogs (and Puppies) New Tricks

Two psychologists, Amos Tversky and Daniel Kahneman, did a piece for *Science* magazine in 1974, called "Judgment Under Uncertainty: Heuristics and Biases." In it, they said that when people do not understand a proposition, they tend to regard it as inherently riskier than a proposition they do understand—even if the proposition they *don't* understand is actually *less* risky, objectively speaking.

To repeat: law school is unlike any academic experience you've ever had before. And the "proposition" of "The *PLS* Approach" is *completely* new to you. I know it's asking too much of you to accept it at this point, and it's perhaps even asking too much to expect you to understand it—in the sense of the "*why*" of it. So your natural inclination will be to *reject* it in favor of what worked so well for you in your previous schooling. *Don't do that.*

You'll be especially inclined, when you're under the stress of law school itself, to automatically revert to your old ways. If you succumb to that temptation, it will likely be a subconscious decision on your part. That's yet another reason to prep before law school. The better you've prepared before law school, the less stress you'll feel once you're in law school, and the less tempted your subconsious will be to take over in a knee-jerk reaction in which you revert to the M.O. of your previous schooling.

At least, before you make up your mind whether or not to.prepare, please read Chapters 8 ("The Walrus & the Carpenter"), 9 ("Professor Jekyll & Mr./Ms. Hide-the-Ball"), 14 ("Points of Error"), and 15 ("Winners & Losers, Whiners & Doers").

Chapter 5 - Playing with Hypos:
Munneke See, Munneke Do

One of the criticisms of *PLS* concerned statements in the first edition regarding a few unpleasant incidents (presented again in this edition) where professors were the instigators, at my law school. The critics declared that *PLS* was making the hasty generalization that *all* law school profs were ogres. Yet, as the original edition said (and this new one repeats), the incidents in question were surely isolated, and rare. They were reported just to let students know that such things *can* happen. So, students should not be shocked if and when they happen to witness, or to be the target of, such things.

The negative reaction was similar to denouncing someone for pointing out that, if you move to or visit New York City, there's a chance you'll be mugged, or your dwelling or car will be broken into and robbed, or your possessions might be snatched from you on the street or in the subway. Of the ten million or so people who live in New York, and of the many tens of millions who visit there each year, only a relative handful are crime victims. But that hardly means it's a "scare tactic" to say something about becoming a crime victim in New York City or of witnessing a crime there. After all, some people *are* crime victims there. I see nothing wrong with addressing crime in a book about New York City, or in offering advice to readers not to let it be an experience (if and when it happens) that gives rise to lasting trauma. (Especially these days, one can become a crime victim even in small town America. So I am not trying to stigmatize New York—where crime is *down*.)

Some of those who criticized *PLS* reported that nothing bad had happened to *them* similar to the incidents in *PLS*. To which, I said, "Good for you." It's as though someone who visits the Big Apple as a tourist comes home after *not* getting mugged there and then says the person who mentioned crime there was an "alarmist." (For the record: I lived in NYC for three years, for school and work. Not once—to my knowledge—did I even come close to being a crime victim. Nor did I ever witness a crime. I *love* New York. But I would advise people against going there in a spirit of absolute trust in the innate goodness of all the residents of Gotham. Even Philadelphia fails to live up to its name as the City of Brotherly Love.)

Several students have e-mailed me accounts of deplorable actions by law professors that happened in classes at their law schools. Unfortunately, each insisted on anonymity as to the name of the professor in question, and even as to the name of the law school. I suspect this is mostly because they do not want to besmirch the name of *their* law school. Law students—like lawyers—are averse to any disclosure that would perhaps diminish, even if only indirectly, their own prestige. But even if they'd been willing to permit full disclosure, there would still be the problem of confirming their reports.

But one incident, particularly appalling, occurred that has been fully verified...

Gary Munneke (pronounced MUH-neh-kee) is apparently in his early 50s. So far as I can determine from the information his publisher has provided, Munneke has never practiced law. Even though he is on the faculty of a law school just outside New York City, he is not a member of the New York bar. It appears that his entire career has been spent in legal academia, starting with an assistant deanship. Yet, from the information provided by one of his publishers, his C.V. is devoid of substantive scholarship. Instead, his writings are for prospective law students. He is the author, for example, of the introduction to *Barron's Guide to Law Schools*. He is also the author of *How to Succeed in Law School*. Munneke is a tenured professor at Pace University's law school, where he apparently mostly teaches torts.

He devotes pages 36-43 of the third edition (2001) of *How to Succeed in Law School* to the case of *Garratt v. Dailey*. It's a standard case in first-year Torts. It concerns the intentional tort of "battery." Unlike most cases in the casebooks, this one defines its subject. "A definition (not all-inclusive but sufficient for our purpose) of battery is the intentional infliction of harmful bodily contact upon another."

July 18, 2001, was the 50th anniversary of the events in question. The agreed-on facts of the case are these: Ruth Garratt, an adult, lived in a dwelling that had a backyard. One day, she was in her backyard with her sister, Naomi Garratt, who was also an adult. A child, Brian Dailey, was with Naomi Garratt at the time. Brian was five years and nine months of age.

Ruth Garratt did not serve as a witness at the trial. Her sister, Naomi, did. Naomi testified that, as Ruth was about to sit down on a wood and canvas lawn chair, young Brian pulled the chair out from under her. Ruth Garratt fell to the ground and are injured.

Brian testified that he had previously moved the chair from where it had been, and had then sat in it himself. However, he had then somehow realized that Ruth Garratt was about to sit down at the spot where the chair had been before—apparently without looking to see if the chair was still there. The alert boy, according to his testimony, then jumped up from the chair that he'd moved and had been sitting in. Thinking only of the welfare of Ruth Garratt, he'd tried to put the chair back to where it had been, in time for her to encounter solid support, not empty space. Alas, in his eagerness to rescue the foolish grown-up from discomfort and embarrassment, the child had failed to sound the alarm. But he was adamant that the chair had not been near Ruth Garratt. So he could not possibly have pulled it out from under her as she was about to sit on it. And he certainly had not thought to play any kind of prank. Rather, his quick-thinking action was a desperate attempt to save her from her own obvious negligence. A little prince, he.

The trial court rejected the testimony from the adult. It instead accepted as its "findings of fact" the testimony of the preschooler. The judge then ruled that the little cherub did not have the requisite *mens rea* for an intentional tort. So he dismissed Ruth Garratt's suit for battery, in which she sought $11,000 in damages she claimed to have sustained from the fall. That's $11,000 in early 1950s money. (Trial court judges pull stuff like this from time to time. They know most litigants will not appeal, usually because they can't afford to. We are supposed to have a system of justice under law, not capricious individuals. But sometimes that is a precatory piety.)

Garratt did appeal. The Supreme Court of the State of Washington saw through the sham—by both the child and the trial court. It could have reversed and rendered, which would have ended the case. Instead, it chose to remand to the trial court. Its opinion included some thoughts to "guide" the judge the next time around in the matter.

Interestingly, it said the child's age was virtually irrelevant. What the case "turned" on was the application of selected sections of the *Restatement of Torts*. (This was before the *Restatement, Second* existed.) Here the Court was playing judicial footsie.

As mentioned earlier in this book, an appellate court has to accept the facts as found by that lower court. (The exception is when there's overwhelming evidence that the facts were otherwise as found by the trial court.) Therefore, Brian Dailey's farfetched, self-serving declarations were "the facts." So the Court exercised some jurisprudential creativity to, in effect, stand those facts on their head.

Because battery is an intentional tort, it requires a certain state of mind (the "mens rea")—in this case, "intent." Having no choice but to accept that the well-intentioned lad had no thought whatsoever of playing a prank on his elder, the Court nonetheless noted that one of the trial court's findings had been that the lad had *intended* to move the chair. After all, he *had moved* the chair, deliberately, before sitting down in it himself. (The Court, wisely, did not spell out this part of its reasoning.) The Court then announced that the intent to move the chair, even absent an intent to cause Ruth Garratt's mishap, *"might"* be sufficient intent, as a matter of law, to sustain a cause of action for battery—*if* young Dailey had known or strongly suspected that Ruth Garratt would later try to sit down and that she would make her attempt without even looking to see if the chair was still there. Such reasoning was preposterous, of course. It amounted to a requirement that the child be nearly clairvoyant (which, of course, is virtually what he had claimed). But it was no more preposterous than the lower court's findings of "fact."

The trial judge got the message. (Part of the message was contained in the Court's holding that the boy's age was irrelevant. Thus the highest state court made it quite clear to the trial judge, near the bottom of the state's judicial totem pole, that—by reading between the lines—he would discern the Court was leaving him no "wiggle room" for more judicial shenanigans.) On remand, the trial judge reconsidered the matter...and *voilá!* He vacated his original judgment, ruled that Ruth Garratt had indeed established her claim after all, and awarded her full damages.

As a digression here: this is the sort of judicial reasoning that John Delaney discusses in *Learning Legal Reasoning.* When a court wants a case to come out a certain way, then, by God, the court will do whatever it has to do to *make* that case come out that way, despite giving lip service to controlling authority. The trial court's bizarre findings of fact, and the resulting denial of justice at the trial level, and the higher court's amazingly creative interpretation of the *Restatement of Torts* to ensure justice in the end, are excellent examples of how things work sometimes in the flesh-and-blood world of the law.

Perhaps the *Garratt* trial court judge had taken a bribe, or had a "special relationship" with the Daileys' attorney, or with the Dailey family, or he just loved the little brat, or hated Ruth Garratt or her lawyer. Or maybe he was just drunk at the time. Who knows? But that judge no doubt rubbed elbows with the Washington Supreme Court justices on various occasions, and—for whatever reasons—the justices did not handle the case the way they should have (i.e., reverse and render). But if the Court had done what it should have done, that would have severely embarrassed the trial court judge. So it ensured the same result by distorting the relevant sections of the *Restatement* almost beyond recognition. (Based on the high court's acceptance of the findings of fact, a legally *correct* application of the law would have *affirmed* the trial court.) Instead, the Supreme Court of Washington subtly directed the outcome, thus ensuring that justice would be done after all, but in a way that "saved face" for the trial judge. (The judiciary, like the legal profession, tends to look out for its own.) It happens all the time, out in the real world.

But this case is no way to teach Tort law.

As a second digression: this "deeper meaning" to the case shows why it's good to prepare before you even start law school. (The Aspen E&E primer on Torts covers the *Garratt* case...but only in the simplistic way in which it's taught in law schools.) Your fellow students will be desperately trying to make sense of *Garratt*. By having already grasped the "official" version of cases, you're able to delve into their deeper meaning...and you will have the time to do so because of your preparation. Nearly *all* cases, especially U.S. Supreme Court cases, have that "deeper meaning." There is far more to them than meets the eye. The best lawyers—and certainly the best lawyers among those who appear before the U.S. Supreme Court—understand that often what the case *appears* to be about is not really what it's about. Like an iceberg, 9/10ths of it is hidden beneath the surface. And this "deeper meaning" is frequently present even at the trial court level.

One reason law schools want students to come in totally unprepared is that they do not want students to start nosing around for this "deeper meaning." If students did that, three things would happen: (1) it would cause students to realize that the Law is not a set of "Platonic Ideas," that law is not a "science," and that the Majesty of the Law is analogous to "The Emperor's New Clothes"; (2) they would start asking questions far more sophisticated than they do now—questions that might stump the prof and make him or her look, shall we say, less than all-knowing*; and (3) they would realize that cases such as *Garratt*, because they are utterly preposterous, are the *worst* possible cases to illustrate elementary concepts in the law (in this case, "intent" in battery).

But the law schools continue to rely on *Garratt* and other off-the-wall cases, to supposedly "help" students "understand" the elementary concepts of the law. They do this, I believe, because they are trying to make things as difficult as possible for beginning law students. *Garratt v. Dailey* is an aberration in the law, not a valid leading case. But the professoriat figures that the "natural-born geniuses in the law" (such as themselves) will somehow figure it all out on their own and see through the Alice-in-Wonderland nature of the case and derive a legitimate Black Letter Law principle from it.

So, your Torts prof will use *Garratt*, as Professor Munneke states on page 42 of *How to Succeed in Law School, 3rd ed.*, for this purpose: "In the end, the student takes away an understanding of intent that is different from the concept of the term she brought with her to law

---

* And to maintain the illusion of being all-knowing, the prof would have to devote much more time to mastering the material, and to preparing for class.

school." His assertion about the case is as enigmatic as the Washington Supreme Court's rationale. Yet, he says it with the written equivalent of a straight face. However, "in the end," the student is left with no useful understanding of intent at all, thanks to the legalistic legerdemain of *Garratt*. And that, perhaps, is the end sought.

This is not to suggest that you should, if called on in class, give the analysis of the case as presented here. (Nor does Munneke do so in his discussion of the case in *How to Succeed in Law School*.) Quite the contrary. But I hope you want to become a good lawyer, not just a good law student. And to do that, you have to grasp that Black Letter Law, and even "policy," are still not the acme of legal reasoning. Out in the real world, your awareness of the *real* reality can mean the difference between winning and losing. (As Les McCann and Eddie Harris put it in a classic on their jazz release, *Swiss Movement,* "Try to 'make it real,' compared to *what?*") It helps to be able to spot a judicial sham. It also helps to be able to perpetrate one, when it is a counter-sham—as was the case in *Garratt*. But this is not just for future trial or appellate attorneys, either. Even "transactions lawyers," who write documents and never set foot in a courtroom, can benefit from this...in case something they've written shows up later as a contentious item in litigation.

The Real World Enters the Ivory Tower of the Law

So what does this case have to do with Professor Gary A. Munneke, sufficient to warrant the use of his name in the subtitle of this chapter?

As mentioned, Munneke teaches Torts, at Pace University's law school. In the first week of classes in August 2000 he assigned *Garratt v. Dailey*.

A student named Denise DiFede was in his course. Apparently Munneke had announced that if students were not prepared to discuss a case in class, they could advise him of that fact by e-mail. Ms. DiFede sent him an e-mail notice regarding *Garratt,* which was due to be discussed in the next class. Perhaps his students had been led to believe that they could expect mercy in return for their honesty.

Instead, he did what he no doubt would maintain was a re-creation of the facts of the case, as a "teaching tool." Ms. DiFede was in class, and Munneke told her to come to the front of the room, where a chair faced the students. Then he told her to sit in the chair. The professor was aware his student—not having read the case—did not know what was about to happen. As she began to sit, he pulled the chair away, and she fell to the floor.

She was wearing a dress. It flew up, exposing her to everyone in the class as she lay dazed. Ms. DiFede was 30 at the time, and is said to be quite attractive. After class, some of the male students made comments about her exposure that were, shall we say, insensitive. Further, she had recently had back surgery. Her fall apparently undid some of the improvements her back surgery had effected.

Denise DiFede never returned to her Torts class, or to any other. She dropped out of law school. Then she sued Munneke, in tort. Her suit included claims for intentional infliction of emotional distress and battery. Under the doctrine of *respondeat superior,* she also sued his employer, Pace University. (The contemporary media account is at http://www.nypost.com/news/regionalnews/33424.htm.)

By the way, this "Munneke trick" illustrates another legal concept: "You take the plaintiff as you find him." This is often coupled with mention of "the plaintiff with the eggshell skull." It works like this: say two people get in an argument, and one makes a shallow cut across the other's forearm with a metal fingernail file. But unbeknownst to the "slasher," the person cut is a hemophiliac, who bleeds to death before being able to get medical care. The decedent's estate sues (for the causes of action called "survival" and "wrongful death"). The defendant cannot argue that he or she did not know the victim was a hemophiliac. Too bad. The victim's hemophilia falls under the category of "the plaintiff with the eggshell skull." It was *foreseeable, as a matter of law,* that the victim *might* have been a hemophiliac. And as to the condition of Ms. DiFede's back: you take the plaintiff as you find her.

Pace University took no action against Munneke. He continued to teach all his classes, including torts—not just the next day, but ever since. When I last spoke with Ms. DiFede about this case, she said that Pace had refused to refund her tuition and fees. Instead, the university denied any wrongdoing by either Professor Munneke or itself, even before she filed suit. (She has since had more back surgey as a result.)

This incident is a bizarre illustration of how out-of-touch with the real world professors are. (I spoke with Ms. DiFede's lawyer, who said there was no evidence that Munneke had been drunk or on drugs at the time of the incident.) But Munneke, who'd apparently spent his entire career within the ivory tower, was so far gone that one might question whether he is *non compos mentis.*

There he was, "teaching" a case involving battery, where the court had found that *a child less than six years old* had the requisite intentional state of mind—even in conjunction with the *minimal* facts as found in that case—to make the child liable in tort. Yet Munneke, an adult and a *law school professor,* teaching *torts,* for Godsake, then commits a battery by deliberately imitating the (real) fact pattern of the case. In doing so, he showed far more obvious intent, even *planning,* than the darling Brian Dailey had.

What the Hell was he thinking? Does he believe that cases in a casebook exist in some twilight zone? Does he think that they do *not* illustrate basic principles of *Law* from the real world? Does he think that law school *professors* somehow exist *outside* (or *above*) the operation of the Law?

I am quite sure that Munneke is one-of-a-kind. (Well, I certainly *hope* he is.) But his practice of "Munneke see, Munneke do" illustrates the potential for professorial transgressions far more flagrant than the examples I had used in the first edition of *PLS.*

Thank God he wasn't teaching Criminal Law. He might have gotten it into his head to illustrate sexual assault.

The Munneke Case as Hypo

The preceding is an edited version of a piece I posted to a column I had on the internet in 2001. My comments generated a response from someone who was going to start law school that fall. He identified himself as "Mr. M." He'd been reading Glannon's primer (in the Aspen E&E series) on Torts, and wanted to kick the matter around.

The following exchange shows how to analyze a case and then turn a fact pattern into a hypothetical.

Atticus—

I enjoyed your item regarding the "irresponsible tort law professor," although I'm a little skeptical about some of the claims you imply the plaintiff would put forward.

For one, you suggested that the incident caused her to drop out of law school. I'm not so sure about whether she can prove the necessary proximate cause, though. I'd need more info on the facts. It would depend, for instance, on whether she dropped out immediately or at the end of the semester. (If the latter, defense counsel could argue that the proximate cause wasn't the humiliation of the event but the common stresses of the first-year experience.)

You could also argue that professors don't have a duty of care to ensure that their students wish to remain in law school. This is a much weaker argument, though.

Also, I'm a little skeptical about the claim for emotional damages stemming from the humiliation of the "blown-up skirt." Looking back on the Glannon text, I couldn't find any examples that included secondary emotional damages, like embarrassment. Most centered on direct emotional damages from the incident, such as fear, surprise, pain, suffering, or else the direct emotional damages from witnessing a close relative get injured (depending on the rule used, of course). My hunch is that the embarrassment claim, since it isn't tied directly to the action of the tortfeasor, but rather to the secondary actions of others, would be a tough one to make.

For instance, throw a counter-example such as this: say I am in a car accident in my own neighborhood, and am not at fault. If we assume that the above embarrassment claim holds, then I could likewise claim damages for embarrassment because I had to stand there and deal with the accident as my neighbors gathered or drove by and stared at me.

As Glannon writes, what we need here is a "certain toughening of the emotional hide" and not an action in tort. However, the emotional distress, if tied to the event itself (i.e., the shock and pain of the event, the fear of falling, etc.) probably would have more of a chance. But despite my reservations, I do think that the battery claim is (literally!) textbook.

I guess this is good practice.

Mr. M

Mr. M—

It *is* good practice. Nothing wrong with trying to pick the case apart.

Whether or not the incident caused her to drop out of law school is irrelevant. No part of her claim-as-made, as I presented it, was based on the fact that she had dropped out. However, were I her attorney, I would definitely go for causation in connection with her dropping out of law school. For one thing, she did drop out of law school immediately. So defense counsel could hardly contest causation —unless Ms. DiFede had already told others, even before the incident, that she was going to drop out imminently. As part of the damages sought, I'd go for a refund (with interest) of the money she'd paid for tuition, fees, etc. And the delay in getting her law degree would be a basis for further damages, because it would keep her from getting income she would otherwise receive as an attorney.

I would not advance the argument that professors have a duty to ensure that their students wish to remain in law school. But it was good of you to think of that one, and to then say why it was not a good one. That's what you should do, especially on a final exam. It's a minor issue, so you raise it, then dispose of it quickly and move on to more important things. Your score goes up another point.

I would, however, advance the argument that the professors have a duty not to torment students in a manner that includes battery. Yet, obviously, that argument gets subsumed under the duty not to commit battery. Yet, then again, there are cases that have held that certain providers of services (innkeepers, railroads) have a special relationship with their patrons, and therefore owe them a higher duty. I don't know of a case offhand that applies that to schools, especially to schools where *adults* are enrolled, but again, it's an issue worth raising on an exam—and disposing of quickly. It would also score some rhetorical points with a jury, especially given that the plaintiff is an attractive young female and the tortfeasor is a middle-aged male.

As for your criticism of the emotional damages argument—well, as a practical matter (vs. a law school exercise), that is where the major damages would come from. I do not know how badly her back was hurt by what happened. For the sake of discussion, let's assume her back was not hurt at all. Then, the damage award can only come from the punitives, or for actuals for emotional distress a.k.a mental anguish. And I'd want to play those up big-time. (I would also want to have a female judge, and an all-female jury. The defense would, of course, want to have a female attorney representing its side.)

And I flat-out disagree with you about the claim for emotional damages. Any jury, trial judge, or appellate court would likely agree that what Munneke did fits the definition of intentional infliction of emotional distress. He clearly intended to humiliate her. He probably did not even think that her dress might fly up, but he is held responsible for the consequences of his action. It is not the dress flying up that provides the foundation for the claim, and I did not mean to give that impression. That's just the icing on the cake.

The test of intentional infliction of emotional distress is usually phrased as "shocks the conscience" or "goes beyond the conduct allowed in a civilized society" or "outrageous" behavior. Those are pretty broad, and extreme. Pinochet, Milosevic, and Bin Laden clearly fit it—at least, with respect to the conduct part. But it was intended to cover more acts than theirs, and developed before any of these guys "did their thing." Whether or not what Munneke did shocks the conscience, etc., is a fact question. That's why I'd want an all-female jury.

But I do not think your argument about tying the *legal* basis of the "embarrassment angle" to the action of "others" would fly. That would be to arbitrarily say that the emotional distress can be measured only by the subjective distress of the victim, without taking into account the objective situation. In fact, in a typical emotional distress claim, it is vastly preferable to look at the objective situation. Otherwise, you're left with a claimant seeking big bucks who starts sobbing and says, "Oh, I was so humiliated," and who could well be playing a courtroom version of *Who Wants to be a Millionaire?* (A social policy argument.)

For example, let's say the plaintiff's professor was a female, and the only witnesses to the event were other females. Ms. DiFede would have a difficult time arguing objectively that she had suffered all *that* much embarrassment. But because the prof was male, and presumably many members of the class who observed the victim's disarray were male, the objective reality—and her resulting emotional damage—was much greater.

This isn't a tough argument to make at all. The viewing by others naturally becomes the focal point of the claim. As for the analogy you proffered, where a person was in an auto accident and suffered embarrassment when neighbors happened by, there you have not only a difference of *degree,* you have a difference of *kind.*

The most obvious difference is that the other guy presumably did not intentionally cause the accident, so you have a negligence case rather than one for battery. That changes the picture considerably. Claims for emotional distress as a result of the tortfeasor's negligence are much harder to make than for an intentional tort. (In some states, they're not allowed, as a matter of law.) But even if, somehow, the "accident" was not an accident, and someone deliberately ran into the plaintiff—road rage?—then the degree of embarrassment would not rise to the level of passing the giggle test. Rather, the "toughening of the emotional hide" counter-argument would readily dispose of it.

Let's play with this a bit more, though. Did you ever see the movie *M.A.S.H?* (The movie, not the TV show.) It's dated. There was a scene in it where the men all wanted to see "Hot Lips" nude, to determine if she were a natural blonde. So they arranged to have the shower walls pulled away while she was in the stall, thus leaving her completely exposed...as they checked her out. No act of battery there. But I would argue the woman would still have had a cause of action for intentional infliction of emotional distress. And it would be a stronger claim than Ms. DiFede has based on the fact that her dress flew up in front of the whole torts class. (That is not to say, however, that Ms. DiFede's claim is not a strong one. The "Hot Lips" case is the *extreme* example.)

AF

Atticus—

We can make the argument that the plaintiff, through her actions, <u>consented</u> to an offensive touching.

First, she agreed to come up to the front of the class for a demonstration of the case.

Second, she actually sat when asked to at the front of the class. Using the "reasonable person" standard, she should have thought that "something was up." After all, the professor's behavior was strange, given that she was not familiar with the case and why he was doing what he was doing.

But plaintiff's counsel might reply that she did not know the facts of the case presented, and she did not know what was coming— as shown by her e-mail. Yet, I find it hard to believe that she would just proceed sheep-like into that strange situation (strange to her, in her—supposed—ignorance of it). What she did makes no sense. Wouldn't she at least ask why the professor was doing this?

Well, the only reason I think she did not ask why was because she already knew. I would try very hard to show that the plaintiff (through discussions with classmates, preliminary comments by the prof, etc.) was given a rudimentary understanding of the facts of the case—enough of an understanding that she knew the case involved a chair being pulled out from under someone. If we can establish that key fact, the argument is <u>much</u> stronger.

The plaintiff might not have given <u>express</u> consent. But given her agreement to proceed to the front of the class for a demonstration of the case, and given the fact that she did then attempt to sit in the chair, and <u>if</u> she knew enough of the facts of the case, then we can claim that her gestures and conduct reasonably manifested consent to the offensive touching. This wasn't a battery. It was just a misunderstanding...

Also, plaintiff's attorney claims that the professor acted in retaliation for the plaintiff's lack of preparation, which he knew about because of her e-mail. I would claim that this just <u>assumes</u>, but does not prove, that the professor actually <u>read</u> the student's e-mail before class. So the defendant was just honestly doing what he thought would be a good demonstration for the class, and that plaintiff was "playing along." The fact that the person he picked had not read the case was just an unfortunate event.

Okay, at least I put up a fight on the battery claim. I don't think my arguments are strong enough to win on the merits, but I do think they're strong enough to keep the plaintiff from getting summary judgment in her favor.

Now, onto the direct infliction of emotional distress, where the big bucks lie. Glannon dodges the question of direct infliction. "It is difficult to summarize the state of the law on direct infliction claims, other than to say that it is exquisitely unclear." Thus, my previous argument on the direct infliction claim was based on no law at all. But now I shall discuss it in light of the applicable standard, "shocking to the conscience/civilization."

But first, I want to play with your comments on causation for damages in the plaintiff's dropping out. Well, even if we conceded that the plaintiff dropped out immediately, can we claim that "but for" the defendant's action the plaintiff would not have dropped out? Yes, we can argue that but for his action she would not have dropped out then, when she did. But we already have evidence (her e-mail) that she was falling behind in her studies. Defense counsel should try very hard to put forward as much evidence as possible to show a pattern of such unpreparedness. Sure, we might not find enough to have us overcome the preponderance of the evidence before us. But we might as well try, we at least have a starting point. I think it would be irresponsible for defense counsel not to contest the causation claim on this one.

On to the intentional direct infliction claim. Again, I would put forth the claims I put forth above to make this whole thing look like a misunderstanding and not this dastardly deed by an off-whack professor that "shocks the conscience of civilized society." There is much that a law professor will do that will upset his or her students: calling on them, for instance. This professor was just trying to conduct his class and edify the students. That certainly shouldn't shock anyone's conscience. Had plaintiff simply read her case, the good professor would have simply had a nice little role-play at the front of class (which he perhaps was expecting), and not the misunderstanding and disaster that occurred.

Failing that, I would try to convince the jury that the distress was mild, and would call for very little damages. But as I don't know the standards for determining emotional distress damage amounts, I'm not even going to bother going there. But basically, I would try very hard to make the defendant not seem like the jerk plaintiff's attorney would paint him as. I would instead try to paint him as a very hard-working (and even innovative!) law professor who was victimized by horrible bad luck and his lazy student's unpreparedness when he was trying to bring the case to life and teach something. If we can convince the jury of this we can at least avoid high punitives and maybe a judgment against us altogether.

And surely you don't think defense counsel will let you get away with an all-female jury?

Mr. M

Mr. M—

You and I are considering two things at once: how to handle this on a law school final exam, and how to handle it as a real-world lawsuit. Nothing wrong with that. I do need to make it clear, though, that our talk of how high the damages should be, and who should be on the jury, is relevant only to the real-world lawsuit. They would not be appropriate topics for a final exam answer. So I shall discuss the real-world parts first, to get them out of the way.

You are quite right in saying that defense counsel's efforts would be directed foremost to getting a decision against the plaintiff, or that (in the alternative) defense counsel would be trying to minimize the damage award. This is why the moral and emotional factors often weigh so heavily in a trial.

This is one reason law school professors use appellate cases, not trial cases. The professoriat finds no value in discussing emotions— or morality. That is one reason why those who want to become trial lawyers are so bad at it when they first get out of law school: a key ingredient to success in trial advocacy has been denied them by those who were supposed to be teaching them how to become successful even as trial lawyers. More important, though, the battle regarding emotions and morality is what determines what the findings of fact *are*. Juries—and *judges*—at a subconscious level, are leaning toward one side or the other early on. They then "rationally" evaluate the evidence to determine what the "facts" are. Not surprisingly, they usually find that the facts are in agreement with their emotional predisposition. Even the outcome of appellate cases, as the Washington Supreme Court's handling of the *Garratt* case shows, are determined on an emotional or moral basis first. Then the court emphasizes the facts that support its predisposition...or, as in *Garratt*, finds a way to get around the facts as "found" at the trial court level. There is nothing necessarily wrong with that. What's wrong is that the law schools pretend it doesn't exist...especially among judges.

You are quite right that the chances of getting an all-female jury would be about zero. I'd be willing to take a couple of "SNAGs" ("Sensitive New Age Guys"—Alan Alda and Phil Donahue types). And, assuming that the jury verdict does not have to be unanimous, I might deliberately seek to have an unreconstructed MCP ("Male Chauvinist Pig") on the jury, just to be my unwitting Devil's Advocate and alienate everyone else and drive them up the walls. Then they'd quickly unite against him and come in with not only a favorable verdict, but a much larger damage award against *Munneke* just as a way to vent their collective spleen against the MCP in their midst. (By the way, I don't know to what extent, in New York, a case on these causes of action is *allowed* to be presented to a jury. Despite the merger of "law" and "equity" in virtually all states, some retain the distinction insofar as they do not allow jury trials on the latter.)

Okay, now on to the case as hypo:

The "Consent" Affirmative Defense

Good of you to think of it. You would pick up points on an exam just for raising that. I don't think it flies, though. So, you would want to dispose of it quickly in your answer.

Analogy: a man and woman are on a date together, and in a restaurant. They've been dating awhile, and she knows he likes to play practical jokes of a juvenile nature. The host shows them to a table for two. The man says to the woman, "Why don't you sit down here?" She moves toward the seat. The man pulls it out for her, and nicely says, "Sit down." Yet, he has *never* done anything chivalrous before, such as opening and holding open a door for her...or pulling out a chair for her. And whenever he's thinking of playing one of his little jokes on someone, he has a funny smile on his face. He has that smile now. When she starts to sit down, he pulls the chair out from under her.

He could not argue "consent" by saying she ought to have expected "something was up." For all she knew, he was going to present her with a phony engagement ring, and then ask her to marry him, but all as a joke. Consent can't be nebulous. Although the person who's subsequently harmed need not have consented to each and every foreseeable harm, the person does have to at least understand that he or she is at risk for *physical harm,* of a type that a reasonable person would say was foreseeable in those circumstances.

Let's change the facts of the real-world situation, though. Say it was common knowledge at Pace Law School that jolly ole Munneke, every year, would sometimes find a student in class who had not prepared *Garratt*. And every year, he would have a chair set up at the front of the class, facing the students. And every year, he would tell an unprepared student to come down to the front of the class and to sit in the chair. And every year, Munneke would then pull the chair away as this student sat down. Now, assume Munneke was *notorious* for this. "Everyone" knew about it. Even those who had not read the case had heard that he picks on someone and pulls a chair out from under that person in front of the whole class. And not one person on whom Munneke had pulled this trick had ever complained.

If all this were true, and Ms. DiFede knew about it, how would that affect your "consent" argument?

One more slight change: if all this were true, but for some reason Ms. DiFede were the only person in her Torts class who did *not* know about it, how would that affect your "consent" argument?

Another change: Ms. DiFede did not know about it, but Munneke —based on his awareness of his own notoriety regarding this "Munneke trick"—thought she did know about it. How would that change your "consent" defense, if at all?

And yet another change: Ms. DiFede did not know about Munneke's reputation, and he neither knew nor cared whether she knew about it. But everyone else in the class did know about his peculiar pedagogical practice. So, when Munneke called on her to "come on down," everyone else in the class started making premonitory sounds, such as groaning, or saying "UH oh," or "Wo-oh," or "Here it comes." And assume Ms. DiFede heard all these sounds. What then of your "consent" defense?

Still another: Munneke had been doing something like this for years, and everyone knew about it. However, on all the previous occasions, he had given the student the following instructions: "When I tell you to sit down, I want you to start to sit down. But then stop without actually coming into contact with the chair. Okay, now, sit down." The student would start to sit down, and Munneke would pull the chair away. And then he would say, "Okay, now reach around with your hand and feel the chair." The student would reach around with his or her hand, and—no chair. Then Munneke would ask, "Now, if you had not stopped the process of sitting down, what would be the legal situation of what the result would surely have been?" And from there, the discussion of battery would begin, and the student would be sent back to his or her seat among the other students. But this time, with Ms. DiFede, Munneke forgets to say the part about starting and then stopping. Instead, he just tells her to sit down, and then pulls the chair away. Ms. DiFede had heard about Munneke's in-class demonstration, and knew that it involved pulling the chair away. But she also knew that it did not involve causing a student to fall to the floor. So she was expecting something, but something other than what happened. How does this affect your "consent" argument?

(By the way, counsel, you tried to "slip me a weenie" in your oft-repeated statement that Ms. DiFede had voluntarily come to the front of the class to participate "in a demonstration of the case." There is no evidence of that. She did come to the front of the class. But it was not necessarily voluntarily. And she did not come forward with the knowledge that she was going to be a participant in the demonstration that ensued. Yet, your words suggested that. Clever advocacy! You might even be able to get away with it in the courtroom, if opposing counsel is not alert.

—Full disclosure time: I've been slipping you a rhetorical weenie of my own. Notice that, nearly every time I refer to the plaintiff, I call her "Ms. DiFede," not "the plaintiff," or "Denise." I am emphasizing she is a flesh-and-blood person, and giving her some dignity by using the "Ms." But every time I refer to her professor, it's just as "Munneke" —which ties in with the phrase I'd use from time to time in a trial: "Munneke see, Munneke do." Or course, neither your ploy nor mine would be appropriate on a law exam.)

It was I who added the argument that Munneke was retaliating against Ms. DiFede. Her lawsuit, as filed, does not mention the e-mail to Munneke before class. Nor does it allege that his action was an act of retaliation. It was *very* good of you to raise the issue of whether or not Munneke had *read* her e-mail before class. And perhaps that is why Ms. DiFede's pleading does not even mention it. Munneke would almost surely deny that he had read it. So, sir, you caught me on that one. Well done. Whether in a courtroom or in your answer to a final, that perspicuity will stand you in good stead. (By the way, I checked with Ms. DiFede after you caught my oversight. Before class, Munneke *responded,* by e-mail, to her e-mail.)

So, just for fun, let's keep the reprisal allegation in as part of the hypothetical. What if Munneke had a reputation for being "brutal" toward students who came to class unprepared, despite the fact they'd let him know before class that they're unprepared? In fact, what if he was known to be *especially* brutal on those who'd had the nerve to tell him *before class* that they were unprepared, instead of those who were unprepared and were "caught" after trusting to luck that they'd not be called on? What if Ms. DiFede knew of this, but had come to class unprepared anyway, after foolishly trusting Munneke and sending him that e-mail? And what if her knowledge of his reputation took the form of stories that were wild exaggerations, stories of his doing things far worse than pulling a chair out from underneath a student in order to illustrate a battery case?

At this point, I congratulate you for not invoking "assumption of the risk" as an affirmative defense. And I assume you did not do so because you know quite well that A/R is an affirmative defense only to torts of *negligence*, not to torts involving an allegation of intent. Yet, I'm also sure you speculated that "consent" and "assumption of the risk" are ultimately the same thing. (In days gone by, a woman's shirt was called a "blouse." A "shirt" was something only a man wore. A man wore "trousers," a woman wore "slacks." Granted, to reinforce the spurious distinction, there were some artificial differences: a man's trousers had the zipper in the front, a woman's slacks had the zipper in the back; a man's shirt had the buttons on the right and the buttonholes on the left, and the woman's blouse had them the other way around. The difference between A/R and "consent" is sort of like that.) It's almost what the law calls "a distinction without a difference." But the artificial separation still remains—and there are plenty more like that in the law. So it's good of you not to get them mixed up, because even though the distinction is just a matter of using a different word for the same concept, using the wrong word can hurt you on an exam. And on the exam, you would mention A/R, but then dispose of it in the same sentence by saying, "but A/R is an affirmative defense only to negligence; hence irrelevant here, as battery is an intentional tort." More quick and easy points for you.

Emotional Distress

As for Ms. DiFede's dropping out, you are setting a *mighty* high standard if you're saying she was "already falling behind" just because she hadn't prepared *Garratt* for that day's Torts class. After all, the facts as given indicated that this incident occurred in the first week of class. (It was August 21, 2000, to be exact.) One of the things you have to be careful about on a final exam is arguing based on facts that are not contained in the fact pattern. All we know for sure is that she had not prepared this one case for this one class. However, you are free to raise the *possibility* that she was already falling behind in her studies —as you did. (Then again, a counter-argument would be that *all* first-year students quickly fall behind in their studies, because the law schools plan it that way. Further, it is quite common for students in the first few days of classes to feel hopelessly lost, and to at least half-seriously consider dropping out.)

But let's add that to the hypo, too, and take it as a given. Say the incident happened a month later: at the end of September. And say Ms. DiFede had indeed established a record of not being prepared for *any* of her classes. What then, Mr. M?

What I'm about to say is a cheap shot, but what the hell: your argument about how the incident was a "misunderstanding" reminds me of how, to this day, Japan still refers to its systematic atrocities of World War II—including the infamous Rape of Nanjing—as "unpleasantness." (Okay, that's over the top. But give me time enough before trial, and I'd come up with a toned-down example to use on the jury.)

Where is the "misunderstanding" here? Did Munneke not understand what he was about to do? Did he not understand that Ms. DiFede would fall to floor? Did he intend that she magically somehow *not* fall to the floor? Did he think she would catch herself and end up doing a deep kneebend? Using the "reasonable person" standard, and the precedent of *Garratt* itself regarding intent, you're going to have a big problem arguing "misunderstanding" with a straight face. (The most likely interpretation is that he was aware of all these things, yet assumed she would neither be physically harmed nor offended by her fall—which presumably was exactly the same self-serving assumption Brian Dailey, *a five-year old*, had made. Ah, the irony.)

<u>The Dress</u>

Such facts as are known are stacked pretty heavily against Munneke. So let me change a fact regarding the emotional distress claim and see how that affects the argument you can make. Ms. DiFede's pleading (the lawsuit filed) does not mention the dress flying up. It did in fact occur, however. So I brought that in as a key part of the claim for emotional distress.

Mr. M, what if the plaintiff were in the habit of wearing no underwear? I am not trying to be salacious here. Seriously, what would this change in the facts do to her claim about extreme embarrassment?

AF

[Note: in this next, final installment of the exchange between Mr. M and me, I responded to each point he made, as he made it, rather than reproducing his entire letter and then posting my entire response, as separate wholes. His comments are in italics. Mine are not.]

Atticus—

It's been a pleasure sparring with you over our unhappy tortfeasor professor, quite an interesting game.

Yes, it has been a pleasure. And that's what law school *should* be. It's part of "The Joy of Lex." You and I are demonstrating that one can find almost an entire legal universe in a grain of sand. Although I do not advocate it, it's not all that much of an exaggeration to say that nearly all of the first year of law school could be based on just this one case, and on almost *any* case (insofar as one could raise arguments from other areas, by analogy. They cannot be used as analogies, however, unless you *understand* them. And that's why it's so important to know Black Letter Law backwards and forwards as you head into finals. If you can go to the heart of disputes, and use a lawyerlike analysis to succinctly deal with them, you'll ace your exams. However, on a final, you do *not* bring in analogous law from other courses. Save that for when you're arguing to a court, not a law prof.) The better you know Black Letter Law and the policies behind it, the more speedily you can deal with exam problems...and the more ground you can cover, i.e., issues you can spot and discuss well. That's what your professors are looking for in your answers. And that's what, out in the real world, you will be doing as a lawyer: thinking of *all* the possibilities, and then quickly seeing which ones *will* fly, *won't*, and *might*...and thus are worthy of further investigation.)

I am glad you noticed some of the tongue-in-cheek character of a few of my previous claims. Yes, for many of them I would have trouble keeping a straight face. But I was trying to do the best and still remain somewhat faithful to the facts-as-given. Now, though, since you've started throwing a few hypotheticals around, I'll join you. And I shall remove the guise of defense counsel and see what I can do, as objectively as I can, with the metaphorical clay of the new hypotheticals.

Your best has been pretty good so far.

First, a Grain Assault

Omagawd. You're a punslinger. So you're heading to law school at the University of Punsylvania?

There is a cause of action that plaintiff's counsel did not raise, namely, assault. Assault is an intentional action by the defendant that puts plaintiff in the reasonable fear of an imminent battery. Do we have that here? Well, we could argue that plaintiff was taken by surprise, did __not__ see the battery coming, and so __no__ assault occurred. However, there may be an assault action here if we are creative enough, given the unusual fact pattern.

Think about this: there is a small interval between Time (A), when the plaintiff expected she would come into contact with the chair, and Time (B), when she instead came into contact with the floor. During the window of time between (A) and (B), the plaintiff came to realize what was up (i.e., not her), and was put in fear of the (extremely) imminent battery that was (no pun intended) to befall her. [Note from AF—Oh sure, no pun intended!] *to rephrase, to match my rule statement above: the professor's intentional action of pulling away the chair created a situation, prior to and directly preceding the plaintiff's harmful contact with the floor, that put her in reasonable fear of an imminent battery.*

Mr. M, very good of you to raise the possibility. Even just seeing it might get you a couple of points on an exam. Also, very good of you to consistently say *"reasonable"* fear. The use of that one word would be worth another point on a final. But you wouldn't want to spend much time with this at all, because it will not be a hotly contested issue; the argument on one side is too weak.

The distinction between assault and battery (which distinction exists only on the civil side, not the criminal) is that an assault is apprehension of an imminent battery that might in fact *not* occur. Further, assault is claimed only when the battery *does not* occur. If the battery does occur, the assault claim gets merged into the battery claim. —But that's only true out in the real world. On a law school exam, it's a good issue to raise, for the sake of scoring some quick points.

The reason why the argument is weak is that the battery was *already underway.* Ms. DiFede's apprehension was of what *actually was to occur* rather than what she merely feared *might* occur. True, technically, the battery had not yet occurred, because there was no touching until she hit the floor. Perhaps, then, it is technically incorrect to say the battery was already underway.

But here's an analogy. It's worthless from the real-world point of view but might make the point valid nonetheless: a guy on an 18th-century sailing ship has been made to "walk the plank." He's out on the plank. There's clearly an assault because he is in reasonable apprehension of an imminent battery (actually, of his imminent death by drowning or as shark food). But at that point, those in control could still change their minds and let him walk back aboard ship. Once they have begun to tip the plank, though, he will lose his balance, and having nothing to grab onto, he will fall off into the sea. Somewhere in there is the point of no return. It is a battery in progress, even though the offensive contact has not yet occurred. At least, that is what I would argue.

Let us say, however, that the chair Munneke used was high—something like a barstool. But Ms. DiFede is standing on a platform. Thus, to sit down, she must still lower herself to the chair rather than somehow raise herself up to the seat as would normally be required with something like a barstool. And let's say Munneke had an assistant standing by with a second chair, a chair noticeably lower than the first. So, Munneke tells Ms. DiFede to sit down on the tall chair, which is right behind her (but on the floor, not the platform). As she begins to do so, he yanks that tall chair away. But then the assistant swiftly puts the lower chair (which has a big beanbag cushion to it) underneath the falling Ms. DiFede, gently catching her and ending what would otherwise be described as a fall. (And let's further assume she was wearing jeans that day, so nothing could be exposed.)

The plaintiff would probably have a hard time making out a good case in battery. But your scenario regarding a cause of action for *assault* just might work there, especially if (1) Munneke made sure she saw—after it was too late for her to stop her downward movement off the platform—that he'd pulled the chair away, and (2) the assistant with the lower chair had not entered the room until Ms. DiFede was facing the class, so she was unaware of the second chair. And for good measure, throw in (3) Munneke was aware that Ms. DiFede had fallen from a highchair when she was an infant, and had to be hospitalized, and the experience had given her a lasting fear of falling to the floor when a chair is involved in any way.

Okay, now on to your hypos.

Playing with the Consent Defense, or, Battery Not Included

Mr. M, are you *sure* you want to become a lawyer? You are obviously a man of considerable wit and talent. It might be wasted on a career in the law. Then again, in the right sort of case, it would be most welcome in an appellate opinion...or, for that matter, in a law review article (in case you have an interest in a law professorship). I hope you don't lose this gift of yours in your progress through the law's thicket. I suspect you're also a poet...who writes in iambic *pun*tameter.

(1) Every year, defendant pulls a chair out from under an unprepared student, and is notorious for it. Plaintiff knew about this.

Here I think we have a good case for a consent defense. This is an even stronger version of the fact pattern I put up last time. We know that the plaintiff knows what the defendant is doing. And here plaintiff's actions, essentially playing along, show a manifestation of consent.

You're right. The key factor is that the plaintiff *knew* what she was in for.

(2) Same facts as (1), but plaintiff does not know.

Here I don't think the consent defense holds. Showing that the plaintiff has some prior relationship to, and knowledge of, the strange custom is important in helping us to determine her state of mind. Sure, I (as defense counsel) in the previous round derided her for not wondering what was up in this strange demonstration. But how many of us have been in similar situations, say at a magician's show, where we go up to the front of an audience and the performer points to a chair and tells us to "Have a seat"? Thus, I don't think that she can infer from plaintiff's actions, knowing her ignorance, that she was expecting anything more than just "having a seat." Therefore, her actions and what we know about her state of mind do not show a reasonable manifestation of consent.

I agree, Mr. M.

(3) Same facts as (2), but defendant is aware that his practices are notorious, and he (erroneously) believes plaintiff is aware of his notoriety.

This one is easy. The consent doctrine rests entirely on the mental state of the plaintiff. Whether or not defendant believes such consent exists is not sufficient for the consent defense. Plaintiff must show consent or a manifestation of consent. So, if my analysis in (2) is correct, then the same analysis holds here. The defendant's mistaken belief is irrelevant.

Again, very good points. And again, I agree...but this time with a caveat: to say "manifestation of consent" adds nothing to the word "consent." The former is not a term of legal art. On an exam, you'd need to break it down into "express" consent, which is undeniable, and "implied" consent, which gets into the "reasonable person" standard with regard to the *defendant's* state of mind. So, with implied consent, the defendant's belief, although mistaken, *is* relevant...and might be reasonable, thus leading to no liability.

(4) Same facts as (2), but with a noisy class making warning sounds.

This is a gray area between (1) and (2). It is enough to make this situation a very unusual one for the plaintiff. It isn't quite the innocence of "have a seat." But neither does it give any hint that plaintiff should be expecting what eventually happens. The class might just be unusually rowdy and expecting the professor to chew out the student for being unprepared. I don't think we can stretch these incoherent warnings into plaintiff figuring out that a chair will be pulled out from under her. There is no reason to see her actions as manifesting consent. Thus, I would analyze this one as (2), above.

Yup. Normally, only the plaintiff has the "burden of proof." (In a case like this, my guess is that in New York State the burden would use the "preponderance of the evidence" standard.) All the *defendant* has to do is raise sufficient doubt as to whether there is a preponderance of the evidence on *any* element of the plaintiff's case. (In the same way, in a criminal case, all the defendant has to do is raise sufficient doubt as to whether there is proof *"beyond a reasonable doubt"*—the *highest* burden of proof—as to even just *one* element of the State's case.) However, an "affirmative defense," which is what "consent" is, sort of puts the defendant in the shoes of the plaintiff. The defendant has to meet the same standard of proof as the plaintiff. (Note: in a criminal case, though, the defendant with an affirmative defense does *not* have to meet the same standard as the State, i.e., "beyond a reasonable doubt.") So, assuming Ms. DiFede met the burden of proof for battery, she would win, even if Munneke raised the affirmative defense of "consent"—*unless* he could meet *his* burden of proof on that defense. In the facts given above, he could not.

(5a) Defendant has been doing this for years. He usually gives instructions and a warning. He does, as usual, this time.

First, we should deal with the simple case implied by your hypothetical. Let's assume he *does* give the warning this time, but things go wrong somewhere and plaintiff sits anyways and is injured. Is this a battery? Well, as we know, battery is an intentional action by the defendant that causes a harmful or offensive touching to the plaintiff. I would say this does not meet the standard. Why not? Because it fails in the intent requirement. Defendant has given a warning to plaintiff to what he is doing. He clearly does not want her to come to harm. Thus, he does not intend for a harmful touching to occur.

I agree, sir.

Okay, so it is not a battery. Is it negligence? Negligence involves a breach of a reasonable duty of care by defendant that causes damages to the plaintiff. Given that definition, I don't think we have negligence, either. By giving his warning, I think we can argue that defendant acted with reasonable care in advising plaintiff of the situation and what was going on. Thus, there was no breach. And without a breach, we can have no negligence.

D'accord.

(5b) Same facts as (5a), but defendant failed to give instructions this time. Plaintiff had heard about defendant's behavior, but did not know it involved falling to the floor. She was expecting something other than what happened.

Is this battery? I don't think so. Here again, I think the intent element cannot be sufficiently proven. Defendant has been doing this for a long time. On all previous occasions, he had made sure he informed his students what he was up to. Thus, we have no reason to think he had the intent to do anything different this time. He just might have forgotten, or perhaps he felt it was unnecessary given his reputation.

I'm with you. Plaintiff's counsel, however, might want to argue the retaliation angle, especially if previous practice involved choosing a student at random and this was the first time Munneke had called out someone he *knew* to be unprepared. But it's a weak argument for the plaintiff.

So is it negligence? A stronger case, and I tend to think so. When creating a risky demonstration like this, defendant has a duty to make sure the student knows what is going on and won't get injured. Think of our buddy, Mr./Ms. Reasonable Person. Wouldn't that person say to defendant, "You better be careful and let her know to halt her sitting action or she might very well take you literally, sit down, and come crashing to the floor"? Thus, defendant's negligence was evident in his breach of a reasonable duty of care in making sure that his students were well informed about the nature and risks of this demonstration. This breach caused the plaintiff to fall and be injured.

Hey, you're no fun anymore, Mr. M. You're getting everything right, and exactly so, nothing missing. How can I inflate my ego at your expense, by pointing out your errors, when you are making *no* errors? (And now you see another reason professors don't want students to prepare for law school by studying primers, etc.)

Okay, but do we have any affirmative defenses available to us? (Even if we assume it is battery). Well, defendant has clearly breached a custom, and a prior relationship existed with plaintiff. However, the end result of that custom was unexpected to her. Thus, she consented to the action, but was ignorant of the final result. So, the question lies in what is the scope of her consent? Plaintiff sat, knowing the nature of the custom defendant had created, but not necessarily knowing the exact result of it. If I remember correctly, the rule is that once plaintiff has consented to the touching, then she cannot complain of any consequences that were not reasonably foreseeable, so long as the defendant's action is substantially similar to what she was expecting. So, the question is, "Was what happened here substantially similar to what she had heard about before?" I think it was—the only difference being ignorance of the final consequence, which is insufficient to rebut the affirmative defense.

I take back what I said about your perfection! "Unexpected" does *not* equal "unforeseeable."

Try this analogy (taken from real life, by the way): actors are presenting a play. In one scene, someone gets stabbed. Throughout rehearsals, the attacker had used a "stage knife"—the kind where the "blade" retracts when it makes contact with something, thus giving the illusion that the knife is being plunged into someone's body. The "victim" had consented to this, and had good reason to expect that nothing unusual would happen in performance before an audience. But in fact, somehow, a *real* knife was in the "props box" before one performance.

When the stabbing occurred, it was for real. "Unexpected" does not equal "unforeseeable."

But change the facts: say that the trick knife was the one in the props box, and that's the one that was used. However, for an inexplicable reason, the "blade" did *not* retract during the performance. As before, the stabbing was for real. Let's further assume that the knife had been checked out before the performance, and was in good working order; the blade retracted. Now *that* is a situation where the unexpected and the unforeseeable were one and the same. But "unforeseeable" is the legal term of art, so "unexpected" should not be used...especially not in an answer on an exam.

Too many hypos.   Too little time.

Uh, Mr. M, I believe the original of that was "So many women, so little time." However, if you prefer your formulation, I can safely say you are already well into thinking like a good law student.

And by the way, on a final exam, that is exactly the problem: too many potential issues to do a thorough discussion of them *all*. One of the key ingredients of examsmanship is the ability to spot the *key* issues, and to then devote the bulk of your time to *them*. And the key issues usually are so because there is a hotly-contested fact capable of interpretation in a way that favors one side, but also in a way that favors the other side, or there is a countervailing fact, and it's an issue the case might "turn" on.

But I can't let you go off without some hypos of my own. I want to play with different kinds of affirmative defenses a little more.

And you now see why profs make sure students get to ask few questions in class—or, at least, that the students don't get useful answers. At least I am in cyberspace and have plenty of time to consult reference materials and think these things through before putting words to electronic paper. Okay, gimme your best shot...

<u>*Affirmative Defenses Hypos*</u>

(A) *Defendant calls plaintiff to the front, intending <u>only</u> to grill her in front of everyone about the case. He knows she didn't read it. He offers her a seat in a chair up front. However, someone (not the defendant) had been eating their lunch in the classroom earlier and had used a very sharp knife to peel an apple. That person had accidently left the knife on the chair, cutting edge upward. Defendant sees this at the last minute. Fearing for plaintiff's safety, and with no time to shout a warning, he pulls the chair away as she is lowering herself onto it, causing her to fall.*

Not bad! Not bad at all. Hmm. No cause of action for battery, because there was no intent to cause a harmful contact. This is similar to a situation where someone pushes another out of the way of a car when the car's brake has slipped and the unattended vehicle is rolling silently down a hill and is about to strike someone in its path. But the person who gets pushed out of the way then falls and breaks a bone or two, and sues...the *rescuer*. I'm going to be lazy and not look up the exact legal doctrine, but it might be something like "The Good Samaritan defense" (which is what it's called in medical malpractice law).

But there is a case here for negligence. If the prof planned to have the student sit on the chair, the prof should have checked the chair out first—even to the extent of making sure it would not collapse. He should have noticed the knife. But then again, so should the plaintiff, so there's a contributory/comparative negligence argument here, too. Not looking good for the plaintiff, Mr. M.

(B-1) *Defendant has a rickety old wooden chair that was used extensively by James Madison at the Constitutional Convention. (Humor me, folks. I'm making this up here.) Defendant owns that chair and keeps it at the front of a classroom that only he gets to use. The chair has great sentimental value to the defendant as well as financial value. (He's a member of the Federalist Society.) The chair is <u>extremely</u> fragile, and it is known to be unable to support even a light load. Plaintiff is a fairly large person. Defendant calls plaintiff to the front of the room, again intending only to grill her. He offers her a seat. He expects plaintiff to sit in a sturdy metal chair that is also at the front of the room. Instead, plaintiff begins to sit on the Madison chair. Defendant, seeing the imminent destruction of his prized possession, pulls it away, causing plaintiff to fall.*

By the way, there is one, and only one, chair still extant that's known to have been used at the Constitutional Convention. It was none other than George Washington's. So you are on solid ground as to your starting fact. As to causes of action...

Battery. Defendant did not intend to cause the offensive contact with the floor when the plaintiff fell. But he also obviously intended the action (pulling the chair away) that led to the offensive contact with the floor. The fact that defendant was motivated by a desire to save an important historical artifact can be used to try to mitigate damages; but it is not in the same category as the exposed knifeblade, legally, and thus is irrelevant to the defense against the cause of action itself. Even so, plaintiff has a weak battery there (hey, I can pun too), because she ignored the obvious chair in favor of the Madison chair. (Presumably, too, she *knew* it was the Madison chair, or at least could see that it was quite fragile. Or so the argument would go.)

Negligence. Defendant did not indicate which chair the plaintiff should sit in, so was careless. This is particularly telling given the immense value of the chair. Arguably, he should not have had it in the classroom in the first place, because he clearly could not expect to be in the room *any and every* time someone else was present. When he pulled the chair away, he was likely not thinking about what might happen to plaintiff. He was thinking about what would happen to the chair if he did not pull it away. Thus, he arguably showed a "reckless disregard" for plaintiff's well-being, which perhaps gets us into "gross negligence" territory (especially given earlier facts noted in this paragraph).

By the way, there was a real-world situation similar to this, though it did not become a lawsuit, because there were no damages. A woman who collected antique chairs had invited friends over. One of the friends was quite heavy. The hostess did not say which of the antique chairs were delicate and which were not. There was one chair that looked sturdy, but was actually fragile. Sure enough, the heavy friend began to sit on that chair. And the hostess did indeed pull it away from her. But as the hostess pulled it away, she cried out "Wait!" Then, very embarrassed at her own failure to anticipate just this situation, she explained to her friend that the chair was too delicate for "anyone" to sit on. (Everyone present noted this polite fiction, and to spare the heavy person's feelings, no one sat in that chair while she was present.)

(B-2) Same facts as (B-1), but defendant pulls the chair away after seeing that there is no time to warn or stop the plaintiff from sitting.

There must be a typo here, as I see no difference between this and the facts of (B-1). So let's add that the defendant calls out a warning before pulling the chair away.

Technically, it seems the same analysis holds up as to both battery and negligence. However, the belated warning knocks out the "reckless disregard" in negligence, so the gross negligence claim is gone and we're left with simple negligence...and no punitive damages.

It might seem that it would be unfair to hold the defendant liable under either cause of action. But here's where the social policy kicks in. Let's assume the plaintiff has been injured as a result of the fall. And let's assume there are medical bills to pay, lost wages, etc. Who should bear the burden? The completely innocent plaintiff? Or the defendant—who set it all in motion? Keep the social policy in mind, and it's easier to see why defendant "has to" be liable. (That's the unspoken basis for the Washington Supreme Court's holding in *Garratt*.)

(B-3) Same facts as (B-1), but the chair has a big sign on it saying "FRAGILE. DO NOT SIT HERE!" Does this make a difference? Is this fact relevant?

Indeed it does and is. It also complicates things.

We're still working with the fact that the chair is a valuable artifact. Assuming plaintiff could read, and assuming plaintiff clearly would have demolished the chair by sitting on it, I believe the battery case would fail. This involves some hair-splitting, though. Defendant would argue that he did not have the intent to move the chair in such a way as to cause an offensive contact for plaintiff. (We're back to the possibility of a deep kneebend, for example.) Of course, that's what defendant would have argued above—and would have lost on. Here, though, defendant would have argued "defense of property." Plaintiff clearly intended to take an action that a reasonable person would know would destroy the chair. Arguably, plaintiff knew the chair was a valuable artifact. But even if plaintiff did not, plaintiff knew the result of his or her action of sitting on a fragile chair (again, under the reasonable person standard). A property owner is permitted to take reasonable measures, in light of the circumstances, to defend his or her property. Pulling the chair out from under plaintiff—especially if defendant had called out first—would meet the test of defense of property, particularly given that this is a valuable artifact.

If, on the other hand, it were a completely ordinary (albeit fragile) chair, then defendant had no right to pull it out from under plaintiff and risk harm to plaintiff. The defendant could have instead let the plaintiff ignore the warning and sit down, even if the chair collapsed and the would-be sitter were injured. (And the chair owner could then have sued that person for damages, for the destruction of the chair.)

The "consent" doctrine comes in on the intentional tort (battery) side—and the "assumption of risk" doctrine comes in on the negligence side. (Both of them as defenses by the chair's owner, of course.)

The only way I can think a cause for negligence could possibly come in here is if the plaintiff is (a) blind, (b) illiterate, or (c) not literate in English, and in either (b) or (c) the sign did not appear to be a warning. There might be other bases for negligence, but those will do for now. In any of these situations, assuming—under the reasonable person standard—that it was foreseeable that such a person would attempt to sit in the chair, then the defendant could be held liable in negligence for unreasonably failing to anticipate the presence of such a person, or to take further measures when he or she knew such a person was present.

Two can play the hypotheticals game!

And as *PLS* said, it's more fun to play with someone else than it is to play with yourself. Playing with hypos is almost the *only* valid reason for having a Study Group. And the group should be kept small.

You and I have spent *hours* playing with hypos—first from the Munneke case itself, and then from spinning off into new fact patterns. That's what doing a good job of playing with hypos is all about. Of course, you cannot afford to spend hours in law school on hypos generated by *each* case that's assigned for class. But that's another good reason to get a head start on law school...as you are doing. "The more you know, the more you see"—not just when playing with hypos, but on the final exam...which is what playing with hypos prepares you for. Regardless of whether or not someone has a head start before law school, once you're in law school, you will have to allocate your time for hypos across all the cases you're assigned.

It's like a musician practicing several hours for each minute he or she will be performing before an audience. And practice makes perfect, or close enough to it. Granted, too, we changed the facts around a *lot*. On a final exam, it would be 99.9% certain that there would be only one set of facts, with no change-ups. (This is not true on the Multistate Bar Exam, by the way.) And on the final exam, you would have maybe 90 minutes, at most, for each problem, to sort out what was important from what was not, both as to facts, arguments, and counter-arguments, and to organize your thoughts and present them in a crisp, coherent manner, in a descending order of importance, while trying to at least *mention* everything that can get you more points merely for noticing it. That *definitely* takes practice. So don't forget your Delaney's examsmanship book, and especially the LEEWS "Ugly But Effective" (UBE) system. [See Chapter 6.]

Just remember, though, to eventually spend a fair amount of time writing out answers to old final exams under *timed* conditions.

✳✳✳

Munneke and Pace filed separate answers to Ms. DiFede's suit. Both answers consist almost entirely of denials and demurrers. However, both defendants have raised the same "affirmative defense." And even though they're represented by different law firms, both firms are apparently using the same "form book" for the wording of their pleadings. Munneke's answer says, "[I]f Plaintiff sustained injuries as alleged in the Complaint, said injuries would have been brought about and caused in whole or in part by Plaintiff's own negligent and/or culpable conduct." Pace's answer says: "[I]f the plaintiff sustained injuries as alleged in the Complaint, said injuries would have been brought about and caused in whole or in part by the plaintiff's own negligent and or culpable conduct."

Update (May, 2003) - The Munneke case has not settled. Nor has it been set for trial. Check the *PLS* website for further developments.

✳✳✳

In practical, day-to-day terms while you are in law school, this chapter is the most important in this book. It shows:

• The callous disregard law schools feel for law students. True, Munneke is the extreme. But the fact that Pace University's school of law apparently did nothing whatsoever to discipline him speaks volumes.

• The value of getting a head start by preparing for law school with the primers, LEEWS (see next chapter), and Delaney's books. "Mr. M" was not yet in law school when he proffered his comments, and was only using Glannon's torts primer, not even a commercial Black Letter Law outline. Yet, by the end of the dialogue, he was already capable of doing a far better "lawyerlike analysis" than all but a handful of law school students who've spent an entire semester in Torts.

• The value of playing with hypos. Did you notice how Mr. M's analysis became tauter, more sophisticated, and simultaneously more wide-ranging as the dialogue continued?

• The importance of reading carefully, and not "reading into the case" things that are *not* there—such as my assumption that Munneke had seen Ms. DiFede's e-mail. (Because this was a real-world situation, not an exam, I was able to check it out. But had it been just an exam, the assumption would have hurt my score.) However, it is okay to *speculate* about reasonable possibilities, as long as you state you are speculating and you don't go too far afield.

• The value of learning how to *weigh* the arguments on each side, in light of the *facts presented*—and to thereby spot the *key* issues in the fact pattern on a final exam, on which you should then spend the bulk of your time, even as you raise (and summarily dispose of) minor issues that get you quickie points—which can add up to a big difference in your place on the grade-curve.

I never heard from "Mr. M" again after our exchange during the summer of 2001. (At least, I never heard from anyone who acknowledged being Mr. M.) So, I do not know if he ever went to law school (or for that matter, if he is still alive). And if he did go to law school, I do not know how well he did on his finals. But I think it's safe to say that, if he followed through on the magnificent head start he showed here, he did very well indeed.

You can too.

Mini-Addendum

On October 15, 2002, Professor David J. Garrow of the Emory University School of Law was suspended for six months, for committing an assault and battery against a member of the administrative staff. (Garrow does not have a J.D., but a Ph.D. He teaches a course for first-year students on legal methods, and an upper-level course on civil rights.)

Gloria Mann is Emory's operations director, responsible for the university's physical plant and operations, maintenance, construction, renovation, security, telecommunications, parking, room reservations, and special-event planning. According to her, Garrow and she got into an altercation in late September, 2002 outside her office. When she attempted to walk away from him, he followed her into her office, grabbed her wrist, pushed her backwards, and began shouting at her. Two other Emory employees then intervened, and Garrow departed. Mann's account, and that of the witnesses, was sufficiently compelling that Garrow was arrested and criminally charged by police.

Emory automatically begins in-house proceedings to investigate such matters. William J. Carney is the Emory law prof who chaired the three-member-panel inquiry. According to him, Garrow was asked to attend a proceeding in early October on the matter, but repeatedly indicated he wouldn't. Therefore, in effect, he allowed a default judgment to be taken against him, leading to his six-month suspension.

Mann filed for a temporary restraining order to keep Garow away from her. (I do not know if the order was granted—or if it was, if it was then turned into a temporary or permanent injunction.) As of this writing (November, 2002), Garrow is considering filing suit against Emory, and Mann is considering filing suit against Garrow for battery, defamation, and intentional infliction of emotional distress.

Does Pace University, unlike Emory, not have administrative procedures for dealing with alleged attacks by faculty? Or did Emory invoke its procedures only because criminal charges were filed against one of its faculty? Or perhaps Emory took the matter seriously only because it involved an alleged attack against a university administrator rather than against a "mere" student? Beats me.

Regardless of the reasons, the contrast between the two law schools' handling of the matters in question is indeed stark. To this day, Pace's Munneke is in good standing, as though nothing ever happened. At Pace University's school of law, and no doubt at many others, the rights and dignity of students are unworthy of serious consideration.

Ironic that should be the case at a *law* school, don't you think? —And perhaps also disturbing that *law* students so meekly accept it.

Chapter 6 - Taking Exams: Lawyerlike Analysis When Your Future's on the (Written) Line

Have you ever watched figure-skating competitions? In the Olympics, for example, those who go for the gold have been practicing for several hours a day for years. In the final round, they only get one shot—of just a few minutes. The winners are not necessarily the best figure-skaters in the world. *But they're the best in the world at figure-skating when they're under intense pressure.*

That's the way it is with final exams. It isn't enough to know what you know, and to be able to "think like a lawyer." You have to be able to *prove* it, on paper, to the prof, *fast*. The stress you endured in the time-pressured LSAT is nothing compared to the stress you will experience on law school finals, which consist of a battery of exams spread over two weeks, at most. (But the stress of the bar exam is even worse: all day, every day, for as much as four days straight.)

It isn't fair...but that's the way it is, and you have to grin and bear it. This chapter and the next one are on how to "strut your stuff" when it counts most. "Examsmanship"* is the name of the game.

Roll Over, IRAC

For half a century now, law students have been told to follow "IRAC": (1) spot the **I**ssue and state it, (2) state the **R**ule of Law that applies, (3) **A**pply the Rule to resolve the Issue in light of the facts, and (4) state your **C**onclusion.

(It's interesting that, for generations, law profs have told students it's not important to know the "rules" and to be able to apply them, and have told students not to consult any study aids—but then have turned around and told them to use the Issue-**Rule**-Application-Conclusion method of examsmanship.)

However, IRAC is designed for just one type of exam problem, the "issue-spotter." Although probably at least 90% of all law school exams are of this type, there are others. Further, the words the acronym represents give a misleading impression. They imply there's only one rule for any given issue, whereas there could be (and usually are) opposing rules, each championed by one side that seeks to have *its* rule be the

---

* I know, I know: in these days of gender-neutral language, it should be "examspersonship." But I just can't bring myself to write that.

"controlling" one. (Granted, though, one's understanding of "IRAC" could be expanded to include the statement of a contrary rule, and an analysis of the issue based on each rule, and then a conclusion based on the student's evaluation of the pro and con arguments in light of the facts.) Last, often—as we saw regarding hypos—there's a "chicken-and-egg" situation: sometimes the rule itself is what gives rise to issues, rather than the other way around.

This is not to say that IRAC is bad. In fact, it's good. (It's certainly better than having nothing at all.) But it just isn't good enough. (By way of analogy: long ago, quinine was the only treatment for malaria, and quinine certainly was helpful. Today, though, it's pointless to stick with quinine when modern pharmaceuticals are available.)

The biggest failing of IRAC is it ignores the fact that law professors love to play hide-the-ball *even on exams*. (That's why this type of exam is called an issue-*spotter*.) A favorite trick is when the prof does not even tell you *who* the parties to the dispute/s are, let alone *what* the dispute/s are. So, you have to play detective even as to that. (Thus, this type of exam problem isn't just an *issue*-spotter.)

There's a better way to go about it, even as to the "issue-spotter" type of exam problem, and certainly as to the other types of problems. So, issues...

Types of Issues

Chapter 3 noted that the third level of the "law school learning pyramid" is "issue-spotting." The Josephson Report discusses several types of issues. These fall into two main groups: real issues, and non-issues.

You might think that a non-issue is, by definition, not an issue. But you have to keep in mind we're talking about law school exams here. It's important for you to show you've spotted things that perhaps *appear* to be issues, but *aren't*, as well as to show that you recognized the *real* issues. You won't get as much credit for each of the former as the latter. But you will definitely get credit. And if you fail to state the non-issues and to *explain why they are non-issues*, you miss potential points. Profs love to throw in a lot of things designed to send students off on wild goose chases in their exam answers. It makes it so much easier to grade the answers quickly. First, though, the real issues...

Josephson describes these as "legitimate points of controversy." He says they're what "two well-informed creative lawyers would fight about."

Law teachers expect good students to perceive more than the obvious arguments and interpretations; we expect them to discover or develop contentions which, though not "dead bang" winners, create a legitimate chance for success. There are two criteria for the point-of-controversy issue: first, there must be a decent chance of winning the point; and second, the point has to be worth winning, that is, it has to be significant enough to affect the outcome. It is sufficient if there is a <u>plausible basis for the argument</u>, and a significant possibility of success.

[Underlining in the original. Boldface added.]

He goes on to say that "real issues" are either (1) legal, or (2) factual.

A legal issue can arise in several ways. Sometimes there are different rules that could be applied. (For example, the traditional rule v. the modern rule, majority rule v. minority rule, standard rule v. an emerging trend, statutory law v. case law v. the *Restatement.*) Sometimes there is no clear rule "on point," at all. This could be the result of something that's truly "new under the sun." (Space law or cyberlaw, to use the examples of Chapter 2; or surrogate motherhood.) Sometimes there's a rule that's "on point," but it's subject to different interpretations, and those different interpretations will produce different outcomes.

Josephson continues:

More *subtle* issues exist when the point of controversy is less obvious as where a particular view of the law is clearly dominant and the only chance of success is to *persuade the court to limit, reverse, or distinguish the law* based on an analogy to another case, the law in another jurisdiction, or a commentator's view...

The *"C"* student will be expected to perceive the *obvious* legal issues, while the "A" and "B" students will be expected to perceive those issues as well as difficult or subtle issues not so readily apparent.

[Italics and boldface added.]

So even if you catch *everything* that *has to* be caught, you're still just showing average competence (i.e., you're *mediocre*). It's only when you catch the "extras" that you're good. Remember doing things for "extra credit" on tests before law school? Well, now, unless you *get* the "extra" credit, you don't get much credit at all. You're just an "also-ran."

As to real issues that are "factual" in nature, Josephson says they concern facts "critical to the invocation of a legal rule." (This brings us back to the chicken-and-egg question.) And as with legal issues, you're only *mediocre* if all you do is hit the obvious factual issues.

> One *obvious* form of factual issue occurs where the applicable legal standard contains terms that inherently demand factual analysis. Thus, factual issues arise in almost any problem-solving questions of "materiality," "reasonableness," "probable cause," "relevance," "good faith," "necessity," and the like. Another easily recognized factual issue arises from any question where the facts seem to be well balanced—some support the potential plaintiff and some support the potential defendant. In both cases, the *average* student can be expected to "discuss the facts."
>
> **More *subtle* factual issues can be found by a critical examination of facts in relation to each specific legal requirement: (e.g., was the defendant really predisposed to commit the crime?; was the plaintiff actually injured by defendant's libel?; was the buyer's purported acceptance sufficiently unequivocal?)**
> [Italics and boldface added.]

In other words, as Chapter 2 put it: *Does* it look like a duck? Walk like a *duck? Quack* like a duck?

He continues*:

---

* I quote Josephson at length because, as mentioned in Chapter 2, his 1984 report was prepared for the Teaching Methods Section of the Association of American Law Schools, and is entitled *Learning & Evaluation in Law School*. That means two things: (1) it was an official document, prepared for use "within the temple," and not for law students' use, and (2) much of its analysis, and many of its conclusions, are identical with what the first edition of *PLS* said. So you're no longer being asked to just take "Atticus Falcon's" word for it. (I apologize for any and all repetition, but I believe it serves a useful purpose.)

The best issue spotters tend to adopt an ardent advocate's outlook as they comb the problems for weaknesses, and opportunities to argue for the reversal of a controlling rule or for its expansion or contraction. If there is one skill that seems to unequivocally demonstrate a student's ability to "think like a lawyer," it is the skill of critical analysis which produces this form of issue-spotting.

This also applies to identifying *non*-issues (which Josephson also calls "negative" or "near-miss issues"). Blunter terms for these are "false issues," "bogus issues," "red herrings,"...and "traps for the unwary."

A second and more troublesome form of issue is **the "near miss" issue which occurs when the law teacher, unwilling to assume that a student knows the law and has applied it properly, wants to see the student discuss possible points of controversy even if it is clear that there is no legitimate basis for dispute.** For example, a test item...might well pose a fact pattern where every element...[of a cause of action] is present except one...[A] well-informed student should theoretically conclude that [it] is a non-issue; reasonable lawyers would not fight over this point...**Nevertheless, the savvy law student knows he/she should discuss the issue...and state why there is none in this case.**
A failure to raise the issue could be a costly examsmanship error because most law teachers expect students to discuss "near miss" issues (that is why they put all those...facts in the question).
Unfortunately, most students do not realize the need to discuss negative issues of this type and it is certainly not intuitively obvious that one should discuss an inapplicable rule. *An exam will be much fairer and more valid if the teacher explicitly informs his/her students how near miss issues should be handled.*
[Italics and boldface added.]

But professors are not interested in making their exams fair *or* valid. They're interested in making them easy and quick to grade. They assume the cream will rise to the top. If the cream has to pass through a number of filters on the way up, so much the better: the quality of what does rise to the top is thus even further assured, they believe.

Chapter One of the Josephson Report is "Basic Principles of Testing and Grading/The Pursuit of Valid, Reliable, Fair Exams." This is not the place to discuss the contents of that chapter. Suffice it to say that its overall conclusion is that law school essay exams, especially "issue-spotters," are a *very* poor way to test students' ability to do a lawyerlike analysis.

One reason the Josephson Report had no impact on the law school professoriat, and so quickly disappeared, is that Josephson's conclusions implicitly called into question the basis on which law school professors lay claim to their purported "natural talent or 'vision.'"

Four years after his report was published, Josephson left the ivory tower. Given his deep concern with fairness, it should come as no surprise that he founded the Josephson Institute of Ethics. (It's named for his parents, Joseph and Edna Josephson.) I have no doubt those few members of the professoriat who were even aware of his efforts to get them to clean up their act heaved a sigh of relief at his departure from their ranks.

In a future work, I hope to provide a detailed discussion of his analysis, and of what needs to be done by way of reform. But for now, it's still "business as usual" in the ivory tower. —And *you* have a far more pressing need: how to make the best of a *very* bad situation.

Somehow, you have to avoid falling victim to the pervasive (and perverse) "hide-the-ball" pedagogical malpractice of law schools, and to instead *take* the ball and *run* with it...and *score*. To help you do that is the (short-run) purpose of *Planet Law School*.

Josephson uses the term "transaction" for anything in a fact pattern that has potential legal significance. He describes the typical "issue-spotter" as a "multi-transactional problem." "Transactions" include the following: (1) "every separate event or occurrence which has legal significance"—this includes each motion in Civ Pro, each harm suffered in Torts, and every agreement in Contracts; (2) "every separate party whose rights or responsibilities must be discussed"; and (3) "in areas such as Real Property...each listed item of property which must be discussed is the functional equivalent of a transactional issue."

Some questions read like Russian novels where a parade of separate parties do strange and aberrant things to each other. In such cases, the first issue-spotting task is to recognize and label each transaction of legal significance so that they will be addressed in the discussion.

However, Josephson was writing for his fellow law professors, not for law students. His own task was to identify the problems regarding "learning and evaluation in law school" (which is the official title of his Report). Therefore, while he identified the problem, he did not address how those who are law *students* can try to deal with it.

He did say this, though:

Issue-spotting requires a *systematic* examination of:

(1) each potentially important transaction (transactional issues);

(2) each potentially applicable legal theory as it relates to each transaction (legal theory issue);

(3) each legal proposition or rule as it relates to each legal theory (legal proposition issue); and

(4) the factual and legal sufficiency of each element of an applicable legal proposition (element issue).

Beyond the intellectual power required to decide which of the *potential* issues are *real* issues, the simple discipline of *systematic analysis is essential to well developed issue-spotting skills.*
[Emphasis added.]

He also comments that "Issue-spotting [the third level of the pyramid] relates to finding and defining problems, problem-solving [the fourth level] deals with the discussion and resolution of those problems."

So, it's not enough just to *spot* issues, just as it is not enough merely to memorize and regurgitate Black Letter Law.

The Fruitcake

Many trial lawyers like to tell juries that the case is like a "picture puzzle," and they're going to assemble the pieces of the puzzle to give the jury the complete picture. Law school "multi-transactional" problems are like a *jigsaw* puzzle. But with a jigsaw puzzle, you *get* all the pieces, in the box. And the box has a picture on it of what the puzzle should look like when all the pieces are put together. In a law school exam, you don't get that picture. You don't get all the pieces. And *some* of the pieces you do get are from a *different* puzzle, and don't belong in the box at all.

What Josephson calls a "multi-transactional problem" is also like a fruitcake. A fruitcake is dense. It has bits of lots of things in it: currants, citron, nutmeats, dates, slivered almonds, candied orange peels, chopped figs, and candied cherries. It's quite "rich."

A "fruitcake" law school exam problem is also "rich"—in issues and parties. But many of its bits and pieces are hidden...and there are often little bits of poison in there too.

There is a systematic way to deal with it, though.

Step 1

Look for any and all people or organizations in the "fact pattern" who have a "gripe" about something that happened (or didn't happen).* On rare occasions, the prof will tell you who all the potential parties are. More often, the prof keeps some of them hidden. (For that reason, in Chapter 4's hypothetical involving the color-blind employees and the explosion, the fact pattern I provided deliberately did not even mention the manufacturer.)

As part of Step 1, figure out what each aggrieved party's gripe is all about—*in layperson's terms*. Do not immediately jump into a legal analysis. At this point, you just want to get a quick survey of what the conflicts are, and who's involved.

The end result of Step 1 will be "conflict pairings." You will have a list of aggrieved parties, with corresponding gripes against one or more corresponding defendants. In this first step, some of the defendants might have counter-grievances.

---

* If the complainant is *very* upset, I suppose you'd have to call these...yes, "gripes of wrath." (Sorry—couldn't resist.)

Step 2

Convert these complaints from layperson's terms to legal terms. (You do not do this as part of Step 1 because some gripes in layperson's terms can be converted into *more* than one complaint in the law. If you immediately jump to the legal terms, you might be satisfied with the first one you spot, when there are others, more subtle, awaiting discovery.)

Each complaint, when put into legal terms, becomes a "legal basis of entitlement." You invoke the relevant cause of action.

Step 3

Figure out "the other side of the story" for each legal basis of entitlement. What are the possible defenses to each claim or counter-claim? You put those in legal language.

Step 4

Quickly run through your Summary Outline, to see if it piques your memory as to something you missed—whether as to a possible claim, a possible defense to that claim, a possible counter-claim, or a possible defense to the counter-claim.

Step 5

Break each claim and each defense into its *elements*. Look for *facts* that establish or contradict the existence of each element of each claim or defense. This is where you have to be good at distinguishing the relevant facts from the irrelevant, and relevant facts that are "material" from those that aren't.

Step 6

Evaluate, *element-by-element,* the claims, defenses, counter-claims, and counter-defenses for each "conflict pairing." This will reveal what the potential *issues* are—and are not.

If there's something that (in Josephson's words) "informed creative lawyers would fight about," that's an issue. If your analysis indicates that one side almost certainly wins or loses on an element because of the facts in light of the law, you quickly note why. But your main concern will be those elemnts in a claim or counter-claim where it's "iffy." It might be that, of the four meta-elements required to prevail in a cause of action, or the elements required to prevail on an affirmative defense, one or more sub-elements in each are "dispositve" of that meta-element. ("Dispositive" means it disposes of the issue, i.e., it resolves it.) Say the the facts clearly favor the plaintiff on most of them, but they favor the defendant on another. And those facts favorable to the defendant might be strong enough to knock out that one element of the plaintiff's entire cause of action (in which case the defendant wins). Or, the defendant might have an "affirmative defense" that the plaintiff cannot surmount, in which case the plaintiff's own element-by-element mustering of the facts on his or her cause of action becomes almost meaningless.

Step 7

Divide the conflicts into major issues, minor issues, non-issues, and near-miss issues.

The non-issues exist where the situation is so one-sided that it's a slam-dunk for one side or the other, either on an element or an entire cause of action. You will not want to spend much time on those. Here, there will likely be obvious "outcome-determinative facts," and you want to note them in your answer.

The minor issues are, as the name implies, of minor importance. So you won't want to spend much time on them, either. Save them for last. If you don't have time to cover some of them, no big loss.

The bulk of your answer-time will be spent on the major issues. But you also will want the prof to know that you did not fall into the trap of the near-miss issues; you did not go chasing rabbits.

How do you distinguish among all these? That's what you should have been spending your entire semester on.

Wentworth Miller's LEEWS

The foregoing discussion (Steps 1-7) is a revised and condensed version of the "Legal Essay Exam Writing System"—"LEEWS." Its creator is Wentworth Miller.* (Miller originated the terms "conflict-pairings" and "legal basis of entitlement," used above.)

LEEWS takes the old IRAC approach and vastly improves on it. LEEWS is a Godsend...and Wentworth Miller is its Prophet, bringing the tablets down from the mountaintop.

---

* *Wentworth* Miller is not to be confused with Robert Miller, author of the how-to-succeed-in-law-school book, *Law School Confidential*. (Nor is Wentworth Miller to be confused with his son by the same name, who's now becoming established as a movie actor, as in *The Human Stain*, with Nicole Kidman and Anthony Hopkins.)

(He calls his system "putting the problem through The Blender." But a blender turns different substances into a uniform whole. Seems to me that what LEEWS does is more like putting a fruitcake into a centrifuge. But no matter.)

To return to the analogy at the outset of this chapter: it isn't enough to be the best figure-skater in the world. You have to be the best under pressure. And Wentworth Miller is a great coach.

As he explains it: "The purpose of LEEWS is to simplify what seems a complex process, to make addressing any hypothetical (the fact pattern exercises that together make up the law school exam predictable) —a series of units (corresponding to 'issues'), each getting roughly a paragraph of analysis."

In Miller's view, you shouldn't think about "exams" at all, at least not in terms of "how to handle them." Law exams are composed of hypotheticals, made up of fact patterns. Professors call these fact patterns "questions." Miller points out that this is a misnomer, characteristic of the sloppy thinking of law professors (his words, and I agree), who typically are untrained and inexperienced in the more nit-picking process *real* lawyers use when analyzing a problem.

The hypos contain the "issues." He teaches you to identify *all* the issues (including perhaps some the prof missed when putting together his or her own "checklist" of "issues spotted" to use when grading).

Miller notes (and again, I agree) that profs don't like the idea that all essay exams can be approached in this way. They denigrate LEEWS by saying, "Different professors want different things. No one can know what *I* want in an answer." But that is just professorial vanity. There is a standard methodology to legal problem-solving. Thus (as you'll see in Chapter 8), all profs want the same thing, whether or not they inform their students of that fact. —And if they *don't* want a "lawyerlike analysis," why are they *law* professors?

Miller presents his program on-site around the country, as does his associate, JoAnne Page. In 2000, I (again) sat in on the full session each one presented. These two are magnificent teachers. Their styles differ, but each is amazingly good. The program runs on a tight schedule: roughly six hours, one day, with short breaks and a short lunchtime. But Miller and Page are each so good that the time passes quickly.

It is truly disgraceful that a LEEWS-type program is not part-and-parcel of every law school's pedagogy. It is even more disgraceful that many law school professors tell students "Don't take LEEWS." (At some law schools, at the plenary session for new students, one of the *deans* will tell students not to take LEEWS.) These people are *serious* about making law school as difficult as possible for you.

Miller also has a set of audio tapes from the program. Whether you attend the on-site program or listen to it on the tapes, you get an excellent manual on examsmanship. I recommend that you get the program on tape, and listen to it after you've read at least some of the primers (see Chapter 16) and before you start law school. LEEWS costs, at most, about $100. It is the single best deal you will ever find in law school. (Chapter 16 tells how to get it.)

"Ugly But Effective"

This book has talked about how hard it is to change your way of thinking, to effectively "think like a lawyer." But even once you've accomplished that, you still have to be able to "strut your stuff" for the prof, to *prove* you have it. Unfortunately, this is where a lot of students who are really *good* at "thinking like a lawyer" fall down on the ice.

For one thing, they somehow get it into their heads that what they're writing is a judicial opinion. So they go for the elevated, erudite style. Forget that! On a final exam, you want quick and dirty, not slow and elegant. You're dancing the jitterbug here, not a minuet. You don't get points for style, only for substance. As with a video "combat" game, you want to hit as many targets as you can, as fast as you can, to rack up points before time runs out. Save the loftiness for when you're ensconced on a high court.

For another, even when students avoid sounding like a judge, they sound like freshman English students. They have "topic sentences," or at least little introductory phrases. Forget that too. Time is of the essence here! You want to hit the deck running...and Miller shows you how.

He's developed what he calls the "Ugly But Effective" (UBE) writing method. This is *not* what you use on the exam itself. But it *is* what you use to *train yourself* at writing out a swift, concise, legal analysis of a fact pattern. Just as you need to use a systematic, one-step-at-a-time approach to analyzing a fruitcake exam problem, so you need to use a systematic, one-step-at-a-time approach to articulating your analysis for the prof. That's what the UBE can do for you.

Miller advises students to practice the UBE for at least 20 minutes at a time, at least two or three days a week. But, based on e-mails I've received, it has become clear that students do not take his advice.

They want to stick with their old ways, the comfortable ways—the ways that served them so well in the past, but which can sabotage their chances for success on law school exams. They think that just taking the LEEWS course, and reading the manual, will be enough. It isn't. As Aristotle said: "Sow a thought, reap a deed. Sow a deed, reap a habit.

Sow a habit, reap a character. Sow a character, reap a destiny." I don't think Aristotle was quite right about that regarding a life itself, but it certainly applies to your destiny in law school.

NOTE: There are profs who limit the length of your answer. (One restricted his Contracts students to 31 lines...and did not announce he would do that until *the day before the exam.*) If you've been practicing the UBE method regularly, you can take limitations in stride. That means you will not have to spend precious time trying to edit your answer down to the prescribed maximum length.

The SUPER-Fruitcake

In his Report to fellow law school professors, Josephson noted this:

> **A major source of content unreliability is that many exams are written in haste [by the professors] and are, therefore, carelessly constructed. This is particularly true in the case of essay questions.**   [Boldface added.]

That makes sense. The professors don't bother to teach you anything. Nor have they even bothered to "articulate learning objectives," in Josephson's phrase. So why should they bother to carefully construct the exam problems? They already know there will be winners and losers, because of the forced curve. And they do not care who those winners and losers are. The former, if they're winners across-the-board in all their first-year exams, will be dubbed natural-born geniuses of the law, worthy of consideration as future law school professors. As for the rest, who cares—outside a small circle of friends (and family) of the "losers"?

Wentworth Miller has shared with me some lovely examples students have sent him of what I call "Super Fruitcake" exam problems. The first three are from unknown sources. On a Torts exam: "What are your thoughts on no-fault insurance?" That's it. From a Con Law exam: "The Equal Protection Clause...What do you have to say about it?" (Ellipsis in the original.) The third is my favorite. This, on a Property exam: "Who owns the Moon?" Cute. Really cute. The fourth is from a professor at Duke whose name I (unfortunately) do not have: "The words, 'if not, then...' in the context of the Rule Against Perpetuities...What do you have to say about that?" (Ellipses in the original.) *This was the ONLY question on a two-hour final exam in Property.*

These professors were clearly contemptuous of their students, and displayed it in a less subtle manner than law faculty normally do.

Miller's solution is simple. If an exam problem provides you with no structure whatsoever, then you *structure* it. You pose your own series of hypotheticals, each of which invokes some relevant aspects of Black Letter Law. Then you engage in your own dialectics, just as if the question itself had posed the hypotheticals you just created.

The prof who asked the "Moon" question was not seriously looking for you to answer the question of ownership of the Moon. He or she wanted you to show you know the relevant Black Letter Law and how to conduct a lawyerlike analysis—same as on a "normal" fruitcake problem. It's just that this particular prof was particularly lazy. He or she is in effect calling on you to create your *own* exam problem. And that's exactly what you do. The same is true of most open-ended exam questions such as the examples given.

(I am not going to provide detailed answers. In part, that's because there are dozens more questions like that. These are just the few that have come to my attention. Also, in part, I have learned many students read the discussion of LEEWS in the first edition of *PLS*, then foolishly decided they did not need to take LEEWS itself. I am not about to do anything that would encourage that short-sightedness this time around.)

*　*　*

Full disclosure: Miller and I have a friendly disagreement. He sincerely believes that "All you need is LEEWS." (Reminds me of the old Beatles tune, "All You Need is Love.") On occasion, when asked about the primers *PLS* recommends, he has told students they do not need to read any of them. Neither he nor JoAnne Page mentions primers during their on-site program, nor does he mention primers on the LEEWS tapes. He maintains that if you read the primers, you will reinforce your pre-existing academic approach to the law, i.e., memorize-and-regurgitate. He emphasizes that the process of conducting a lawyerlike analysis is paramount, and students should do nothing that distracts from it.

He does say that it's important to get commercial outlines to find the Black Letter Law and the policy behind it. But it seems to me the best way to learn that is through reading the primers and working the problems in them—and in working the "illustrations" in the *Restatements*, before proceeding to commercial outlines and then the old fruitcake exams.

You've already seen that I agree with him that students tend to stick to what they're comfortable with—the approach they used in their previous schooling. And I agree with him that doing so is a formula for disaster. But it is not enough to have what he calls the "toolbox." Tools are fine. But as with any "shop" class or apprentice tradesman ("tradesperson"?), you have to gradually build up your skills by starting with simpler tasks. I believe you will be able to put LEEWS to work for you better and faster if you've read at least parts of the primers first.

(I strongly suspect that Miller values *PLS* at all only because it so strongly recommends LEEWS. But even though the respect is not equal in both directions, I still say LEEWS is a Godsend.)

But even if he's right that all you need in *law school* is LEEWS, once you're out in the real world you'll discover how much substantive law you need to have already learned before you got your license—and how difficult it is to make up for lost time. At the very least, the primers and *Restatements* will deepen and broaden your understanding. That can come in *mighty* handy.

Dipping Your Exam in "Delaney's CIRI(P)"

LEEWS is necessary, but it's not sufficient. It's the best approach to "fruitcake" exam problems. But again, Miller and I have a friendly disagreement. Even for policy discussions, he says, "All you need is LEEWS." And it's true that many questions, such as the super-fruitcakes, *appear* to be "policy" questions but actually are just *disguised issue-spotters.* And it's true that about 90% of all exams are either fruitcakes or "super-fruitcakes." But that leaves the other 10%, particularly those that are "pure policy," or that call for drafting a proposed statute.

Chapter 4 introduced John Delaney's second book, *How to Do Your Best on Law School Exams,* and touted its excellent chapter on outlining. But, obviously, the book is about examsmanship. I highly recommend it.

Delaney has his own improved version of the old IRAC approach. He calls it "CIRI(P)." The acronym stands for **C**onclusion - **I**ssue - **R**ule - **I**nterweaving of Facts and Rule - **P**olicy.

You've heard the slang expression, "This guy is 'toast'"? —It refers to someone who's about to get "scorched" or "burned." And you know what "French toast" is. (Just in case: it's bread dipped in egg batter, then toasted in a skillet and covered with syrup.) You want to make (French) "toast" of the prof's problems. And you do that by performing a red-hot lawyerlike analysis. And one of the best ways is to dip it in Delaney's CIRI(P).

As his book explains, there are variations, depending on what type of problem your prof gives you. Two variations are of particular interest here. The first involves "elastic standards." Other than Bright-Line Rules, virtually *all* standards in the Law are elastic. But what Delaney's referring to here are terms that are almost open-ended, such as "nuisance" in tort. And in a second variation, he discusses how to handle your answer when the problem involves a rule that clearly has to be overturned.

When working old exams or hypotheticals (and *only* then), he also has what he calls the "HATRI" method. It's an elaboration of the unifying concepts of the law (duty - breach - harm - cause) discussed in Chapter 2. This second acronym stands for **H**arm - **A**cts & Parties - **T**opics - **R**ules - **I**ssues. (The "Topics" part refers to legal areas implicated by the fact-pattern. The "Rules" part refers to the specific Black Letter Law or statutory law.) It is excellent.

I do have one friendly disagreement with Delaney, too, though. As his CIRI(P) formula indicates, he says to put your conclusion at the beginning of your exam answer, versus at the end as under the old IRAC. (Out in the real world, when you write a legal memo, you will indeed put the conclusion at the beginning.) But in your answer to an exam problem, the conclusion is always less important than the analysis. And the best conclusion usually includes some "waffling" as to who should win—and that seems a rather wishy-washy way to start. (Of course, even if you do put your conclusion at the outset, you do not actually write it in until you've done the analysis. That way, you can make sure your conclusion reflects your analysis—including some "wiggle room"—rather than being something that contradicts the analysis you've written.)

The LEEWS manual and Delaney's examsmanship book both include sample exams and model answers. Delaney's has a unique feature: in addition to the "model" answer, he also provides a "poor" answer and a "so-so" answer to each problem. This is wonderful. Students who only see "model" answers often assume (naturally) that they can come up with something similar. But in fact, most students either write poor answers or mediocre ones. (See next chapter.) So, when you write out your answer to Delaney's sample problem, you can then check your own answer not only against the good answer, but against the other two. That will give you a good feel for how far you have to go yet to get good.

LEEWS & Delaney as Complements

Students err in thinking they'll do fine if they just master either LEEWS *or* the CIRI(P) without the other system. However, this is *not* a matter of "Six of one, half a dozen of the other." But neither is it a matter of "apples and oranges." Although perhaps Wentworth Miller and John Delaney see their respective examsmanship methods as rivals, they're complementary. Their similarities are more numerous, and important, than their differences.

It's like the difference between a ballpoint pen and a felt-tip pen. A ballpoint pen is great for writing when you're making carbon copies or writing on non-carbon-reproducing forms. Ballpoint pen ink won't smear easily, and won't wash out. A felt-tip pen, on the other hand (*in* the other hand?) can write at almost any angle, on almost any surface, and usually leaves a thicker track so it's better for underlining. Most of the time, though, either one will do fine.

Or, consider the difference between America's *Wall Street Journal* and Britain's *Financial Times*. Both are business newspapers. The *WSJ* (usually) covers American business and finance better than the *FT* does. The *FT* (usually) covers foreign business and international business better than the *WSJ* does. But the bulk of their content consists of overlapping coverage.

Likewise, LEEWS and the CIRI(P) are both tools. You choose the tool appropriate for the job. For most exams, either one will do the job quite well. But for certain problems, LEEWS might be better; for others, CIRI(P). You need to know how to use both. And gradually, you'll see when one or the other is clearly more appropriate.

Getting to Maybe:
On Balance, the Verdict is "No"

GTM was published after the first edition of *PLS*. When it came out, I posted a short, favorable review of it to Amazon.com. I did so largely for three reasons. First, I was delighted to see a couple of current law professors (Michael Fischl and Jeremy Paul) who are trying to *help* students. Second, the authors' criticisms of IRAC are right-on.* Third, I really enjoyed their—very brief—discussion of the *joy* to be found in "playing" with a problem.

---

* Wentworth Miller had been criticizing IRAC for 20+ years. But students apparently assumed he was doing so only to boost attendance at his on-site program. Yet, oddly, everyone took Charles Whitebread's 1989 book, *Success*

(Continued on next page—)

But now I must back off somewhat. After years of further reflection, prompted largely by e-mail conversations with law students, I see I was too hasty.

GTM spends nearly 130 pages on various types of "forks" to look for. Its classification system is quite elaborate: forks of law, forks of facts, twin forks, concurrent forks, proliferating forks, hidden forks. But what these all amount to is a method for issue-*spotting*. When it comes to conducting a lawyerlike *analysis*, the authors really only say "just add reasons" (and they use that exact phrase).

Well, gee. That doesn't help you much.

I went through the book again before writing this section, and read all the passages I'd marked. It does have some good stuff. But it just isn't nearly good enough. For example, the authors hardly mention hypotheticals. It appears they discuss thinking up your *own* hypos only once. And even then, it's in passing, when they advise you to anticipate what problems the prof will pose on your exam. But as you've seen, creating your *own* hypos and working them is a *crucial* step in learning Black Letter Law and how to conduct a lawyerlike analysis.

There's virtually nothing in the entire book about the *vital* importance of "interweaving" facts and law in your answer—something that both Wentworth Miller and John Delaney stress.

Nor does *GTM* even mention the importance of spotting the *"near-miss"* issues, and quickly disposing of them.

And more important still, they do not even mention the significance of *time*. There's no discussion of setting priorities, and of developing a method of providing a swift, concise answer. (The model answers they provide to their sample exam problems at the end of the book were apparently written in a leisurely manner, and would take up far too much time to write out on a real exam.)

But what perhaps bothers me most of all are the problems they pose as their "sample exam questions." The problems are simple, on the level of the examples in the Aspen primers. They *tell* you who the parties are (and there are always only two), and what the issue is (usually just one). On a real exam, especially a fruitcake exam, you usually have to figure everything out on your own. (Again, see next chapter.)

---

in Law School: Exam Taking Techniques—which advocates IRAC—at face value. However, Whitebread, unlike Miller, is a "member of the guild, i.e., a law professor. Thus, there's reason to believe he was practicing less than "full disclosure" of what success in law school *really* involves. (Delaney is one of the few exceptions.)

So, ultimately, I am sorry to say, *Getting to Maybe* is not anywhere near as good as I'd thought in my initial burst of enthusiasm for it. Its main virtue is in the title itself. Unless your prof says otherwise, you are indeed going for a "maybe," an "it depends," rather than a narrow-minded, one-sided analysis of "yes" or "no." (Part of your analysis, of course, is to show how it *could* be "yes," and how it *could* be "no." And perhaps you will end by saying it's "most likely" one or the other...unless your prof has expressly told you to reach a *firm* conclusion.)

Actually, though, I'm now embarrassed to say that, at bottom, *GTM* is misleading. Its style is great. Its substance is lacking. If you have the time and the money, you might get and read it sometime after you've started law school. But you should give it your lowest priority as an aid to examsmanship. In fact, spending time on its overly elaborate system of merely finding forks will very easily get *you* "forked" on your exams.

However, to end on a positive note: Fischl and Paul make one point that is *vital*. They speak of an "information dump," where students try to write down *everything* they know on the subject. It's as though the student were saying, "See! I know *this,* and *that,* and this *other* thing, and *this* thing over here!" Gee, how nice. But the essence of Thinking Like a Lawyer is separating the *relevant* from the *irrelevant*. If you are able to *choose* and *use* the *relevant* stuff, the prof will assume you *also* knew the *irrelevant* stuff. But if all you do is dump everything from your head onto the page, it will be clear that you did *not* know what was important, and what was not. What Fischl and Paul call the "information dump" is another way of describing the "memorize-and-regurgitate" mode, and carried to an extreme. Their warning against it is dead right-on. Ignore it at your peril.

Working Old Exams

As discussed in previous chapters, you should start with the Examples & Explanations in the Aspen primers, and then move to the "illustrations" in the *Restatements*. But you should start working old exams *very* early in the semester. Yes, I know, you're thinking, "But I need to know the material first!" The best way to get to know the material is by *testing yourself* on it—first with the E&E material, then with the "illustrations," then with your hypos...and "finally" with the old finals. ASAP.

There is no reason on earth why you should work each old exam only once. In fact, it will be a tremendous boost to your self-confidence if you work an old exam early in the semester, and then come back to it months later and see how much better you do the second time around. (If you've prepped before law school, even the first run-through should please you at least somewhat.)

To get good at both CIRI(P) and LEEWS, use both of them when working old exams. When slicing through a fruitcake for the first time, try LEEWS first. Then switch to Delaney's CIRI(P)—and especially his HATRI.

Begin with the old exams from your own prof who's teaching the course you're taking, if they're available. If there are model answers, consult the model answer on only *one* of them. Save the other model answers for later, when you work those other old exams a second time. "Counter-intuitive" as it may sound, you're actually better off working old exams from your prof that *don't* have model answers—although at some point it's important to see what your prof regards as a "model" answer, just to pick up some idea of that prof's idiosyncrasies as to what he or she wants students to deal with exam problems.

Move on to old exams from *other* professors who've taught that course, including old exams that you can find on-line, posted on various law schools' websites. (In his E&E book on torts, Glannon has a practice exam in the back, with a model answer.)

Also, a product line called "Study Partner" has two series of exam questions, with answers. The first series is called "Issue Spotting." It's in three volumes, available separately. Volume I is on torts, contracts, and substantive crim law. Volume II is on civ pro, prop, and evidence. Volume III covers Con law, crim pro, and corporations. Corresponding to each volume in the "issue-spotting" series is a volume in Study Partner's "Exam Writing" series. (Chapter 16 tells what these cost and where to get them.)

And at some point, early on, work the exams in Delaney's examsmanship book. See if your answer is in the "poor," "so-so," or "good" category. (If you get his new book on substantive crim law, it also has exam problems with a "good," "so-so," and "poor" answer for each.)

As Chapter 4 mentioned, the main purpose of a study group or study partner is to practice creating and working hypotheticals. After awhile, though, you should work old exams, collectively. This is *not* a time to play one-upmanship games. You are there to *spot everything,* and to *cover* everything. This includes quickly separating the relevant facts from the irrelevant, the material from the immaterial, and identifying the outcome-determinative facts. It includes spotting all the conflict pairings, all the major issues, all the minor issues, and all the red herrings, and then setting priorities for your answer. Each session, or each exam, one person acts as secretary, writing everything down.

As mentioned above, time is of the essence on a real exam. After you've worked old exams as a group, collectively, you should get together as a group and work a selected old exam individually, under *timed* conditions. Then compare your answers when time runs out. Different people will cover different things in different ways. As a group, you discuss all the possibilities: why each person chose to cover what he or she did, and why it was covered in the way it was covered. —But again, this is not a matter of playing self-aggrandizing one-upmanship games. Be *considerate* of others' need to save "face."

You do not need to then compose a collective answer. What's important is the comparison and contrast of answers. Each of you then draws his or her own conclusions as to what's important, and why. (To minimize the gamesmanship aspect, you should do this only with old exams that do *not* have model answers, if possible. That means you should save some exams without model answers for later in the semester.)

As the time for exams approaches, everyone in your study group should do one more thing: work an old exam under real-world conditions. This means you go to the law school, preferably on a weekend, and go to a classroom similar to the one in which exams are administered. One person hands everyone a copy of the (same) exam. (No peeking ahead of time, not even by the person handing them out.) You then start work. When time runs out, stop. Just by working that exam in a classroom, with others there, you will come closer to what it will be like on the real thing. The more you can familiarize yourself with the "exam experience," the less likely you are to feel stressed on the real thing.

Note: if your exam will be closed-book, part of what you do as finals approach is practice writing out your Summary Outline before the exam is handed out in your practice sessions.

Obviously, you should have been practicing the LEEWS "UBE" system —even though, as mentioned, Miller says you do *not* use it for writing out the answer you will be turning in to the prof.

The "Rainbow" Method

I am not necessarily recommending the following, but offer it for your consideration...

The book *Law School Confidential* speaks of the importance of briefing cases the law school way. As you've already seen, I think that's silly. And *LSC* then goes a step further, and tells you to use several pens, of different colors, to mark up your casebook. One color is for the holding, one for the facts, and so forth. I think that's *really* silly. (JoAnne Page, of LEEWS, dismisses it as what she calls "The Rainbow Method." And I certainly don't think it will help you get any pot of gold.)

However, the "Rainbow Method" just might be a good idea for working *old exams:* one color for the parties, one for issues, one for what Delaney (in his examsmanship book) calls "red-hot facts," and so forth. If your study group works old exams while everyone's together, but works the exams individually, the "Rainbow Method" can help everyone to instantly compare and contrast their initial "take" on the contents of the exam itself. (This works, though, only if everyone has agreed which color to use for what). Just a thought.

"Connect the Dots"

Remember how, when you were a small child, you'd be presented with a page of dots, and each dot would have a number by it? You had to start at the dot by #1 and then draw a line to the dot by #2, and so on. Eventually, the lines connecting the dots formed a complete figure.

On law school exams, you have to be sure to connect *all* the dots. Don't leave something out just because it's "so obvious I don't even need to mention it." Not so. (That, by the way, is one of the biggest mistakes *I* made on law school exams.) Your professors have spent an entire semester keeping you as ignorant as possible. And they assume that you *are* ignorant—ignorant and myopic. They know that, in the panic that surrounds law school finals, there's a good chance that, in the dark, even with a flashlight you couldn't even find the nose on your face. And most of the time, they're right (metaphorically speaking).

The official motto of *The New York Times* is "All the news that's fit to print." But the *un*official motto (and the paper's real attitude) is: "If it isn't in *The New York Times*, it didn't happen." Your profs have a similar attitude toward your exam answers. If something isn't in your answer, they assume you completely missed it. You have to "spell it out" for them—but you can spell it out in *shorthand* when it concerns something that seems "so obvious I don't even need to mention it."

The Rush to "Policy" Discussions

Far too many students ignore a Black Letter Law lawyerlike analysis in favor of BS-ing about policy. Their profs, who spent most of class time BS-ing about policy, encourage this. (The profs then grade down those who ignore Black Letter Law, of course. See Chapter 8.)

But in your answer to your exam problems (and out in the real world), if you go straight to a policy discussion, others will wonder, "Doesn't this person know the *law?*" If you want to discuss policy (especially if your prof said you should), fine. But *start* with the nuts-and-bolts Black Letter Law lawyerlike analysis.

Policy is especially relevant as a *tie-breaker.* If both sides are equally strong, look to the policy behind the Black Letter Law—or look to policy that might *change* the Black Letter Law, to reach your conclusion. (Yes, it helps to throw in something about policy, as in the policy behind the Black Letter Law. But emphasize it only if it strengthens the argument. Otherwise, give it low priority, with the exceptions as noted. See Part V for a real-world case analysis that properly invokes policy.)

When the Prof Gives You a Break

The theoretical material on deception refers to something called a "second-order lie." One party tells the *truth—knowing* the other will think it's a *lie.* I don't know if law profs do this. But students often have a *misplaced* suspicion (versus an appropriate one) of their profs' fact patterns on exams. Then they insist on "proving a given."

If, for example, your prof *tells* you in the fact pattern that there's a contract, do not waste your time discussing the elements of a contract. Take it as a given, and move on to whatever the prof has in mind. (And it's a sure thing, if the prof does give you a freebie, the prof wants you to spend your time on something else...which just might be hidden from you.)

Special Situation: "What does This MEAN?"

Sometimes, you have to apply a criminal statute or regulatory statute. But it might have many possible interpretations. The outcome of the case will depend on which interpretation is chosen.

This situation comes up in the case law, especially when the courts are trying to deal with a statute or High Court ruling that seems to change the law. Knowing how to spot all the possible interpretations, and how to argue for and against each, is a good skill to have.

Some profs like to spend a lot of time on this in class. But it's very hard to create a problem that would test this on an exam. The fact pattern would pretty much have to lay it all out for you as to what the various interpretations *are*. Profs like to hide the ball, even on exams.

So, keep this general rule in mind: if the prof laid it out for you in class, chances are it won't be tested.

The "Politically Correct" Prof

You *will* have at least one prof in first-year who makes it a point to constantly subject you to his or her ideology, be it liberal or conservative, militant feminist or "Law & Economics." The prof figures you're a captive audience, so why not try to make converts? —Or at least introduce you to his or her way of seeing the world. (See Chapter 26.)

Many students believe that, on a final exam, they should—wherever possible—provide an answer that parrots the prof's harangues. They fear that if they say something that is obviously not "politically correct" in the prof's eyes, the prof will give that student a lower grade.

I ran that by John Delaney, who's been a law school prof for decades now. Here's his response (reprinted with his permission):

> 1. There are ideologues of the right and left who could be offended by "incorrect" analysis. But they should be easy to identify: they do not like "deviationist" reactions to their party line in class. If they're intolerant in class, they'll be intolerant on exams.
>
> 2. But many can be charmed by an *opposing* analysis, *if*
>
> a) it presents a decently organized analytical argument, even contrary to the professor's own;
>
> b) it demonstrates an awareness of the arguments in the relevant assigned materials;
>
> c) it demonstrates *knowledge* of and an appraisal of the professor's arguments, and is not simply a conclusory rejection of them;
>
> d) it avoids what I call "political campaign talk" with all of the usual logical and analytical weaknesses: non sequiturs, extreme overstatement, mostly emotion, demonizing and personalizing opposing views, etc.

Many professors like to be surprised by a *thoughtful, well-argued* dissent...especially since so many exam answers are just dreck.

Multiple Choice Exams

Multiple-choice is fine for quizzes, but there's no excuse for any law school *exam* to have a multiple-choice component.

As Gregory S. Munro (a law prof at the University of Montana) put it in his book, *Outcome Assessments for Law Schools*—

> It is a problem when a law professor gives students an end-of-semester multiple-choice final exam on which they are not allowed to write any comments or assumptions and which will be graded by a scat-tron device. The students have no way of stating the premises which may make their answer right or of identifying ambiguity or problems in the question.

The ABA's "Interpretation 303-1" to Accreditation Standard 303 says "Scholastic achievement of students shall be evaluated by written examinations of suitable length and complexity, [or by] papers or other documents..." "Written" means "essay" or at least short-answer.

But the professoriat is getting lazier by the year. It's so much easier just to turn over "bubble-in" answer sheets to a computer to grade. So, there's been a gradual increase in MC exams. The ABA blithely looks the other way. (Perhaps printed multiple-choice *questions* can also be called a "written" exam even though the *answers* are not. But if so, taking advantage of the ambiguity in the word "written" is shameful.)

And so, for example, on the first day of class in the fall of 2003, Sheldon Halpern of Ohio State U's law school announced that the only exam in his Defamation Law course would be an *entirely* multiple-choice final. (See page 316—the second addendum to Chapter 10—for a further discussion of this episode.) But *the* laziest prof I've heard of is Gerald Torres, at the University of Texas. In the fall of 2001, the final exam for his first-year Property class included 38 multiple-choice questions. He took all but a handful of them, *word-for-word*, from a set of *commercial practice materials* for multiple-choice tests on property.*

---

* The use of the "canned" mulitple-choice questions showed Torres's contempt for his students, as well as his laziness. But he also *[Continued on next page.]*

(See page 304 for a further discussion of multiple-choice exams, including a defense of them.)

Emanuel's, the commercial outline vendor, has a new series of books out called *Crunch Time*. Each book is on just one subject. In addition to fruitcake problems with model answers, each book has short-essay problems with answers...and multiple choice questions with answers. If you know (or suspect) that your prof will have at least *some* multiple-choice questions on the final, you might want to get the *Crunch Time* for your subject. (In fact, you might want to get it anyway, for its fruitcake and short-answer problems and answers.)

The LEEWS *manual* also covers multiple-choice.

Special Situation:
The Absolutely Worst Professor Possible

A student e-mailed me in the spring of 2002 that a prof had given a multiple-choice final (of the prof's own creation, unlike that of Torres) consisting of questions such as (1) "Which justice [on the U.S. Supreme Court] made the following statement in the case of blah-blah-blah?" (2) "In what case did Justice So-and-so make the following statement?"

Even more than the Torres final in property at the Universtiy of Texas School of Law, this showed utter contempt for the purpose of a legal education.

(The student insisted I not disclose the name of his law school or the subject in which that exam was given. He would not even tell me the prof's name. However, I assume this prof will keep giving the same type of exam. Regardless, the student has promised me that if no one else reveals the prof's name before this student graduates, he will.)

I hope that if there is a Hell, that when this prof is despatched to it (as he surely would be), he spends an eternity answering idiotically

---

gave a short take-home problem as part of the same exam. (It's unclear how much each part counted toward the overall grade, as it appears Torres did not disclose that. But neither part was apparently less than 40%.) The essay portion went something like this: "Humans have finally made contact with extra-terrestrials. The aliens, however, do not know of American property law. Please explain to them the central characteristics of American property law. Maximum four pages, double spaced, one-inch margins." That has almost nothing to do with a "lawyerlike analysis," and is more appropriate for a college-level course on "Introduction to American Law." So much for teaching students, and evaluating their ability, to "think like a lawyer." To me, the assignment showed Torres has even more contempt for the very idea of legal education as a *professional school* program than he does for his students.

picky multiple-choice questions such as the ones he forced his students to endure on that exam. And as I am fully confident that (if there is a Hell) I am going that way also, I shall be sure to look him up and inflict my own personal retribution upon this miserable excuse of a legal "educator."

Special Situation:
The Second-Worst Professor

There are professors who play even dirtier than normal, and say things like, "On the final exam, if you see a situation like this, be sure to cite the holding of blah-blah-blah [some specific case]." These are the same profs who told you all semester long that there was no need to memorize rules. But what is a holding in a case, if not a form of rule?

These professors are disingenuous. They are sending you chasing down another rabbit trail. Exams test your ability to apply Black Letter Law in a lawyerlike analysis to a fact pattern. Memorizing case holdings is obviously just a form of memorize-and-regurgitate. You do not need to do that. You do not need to know the history of the cases as they came up through the courts, or what the positions of each party in each case were. And you certainly do not need to memorize the case citations. (The citation gives the volume and page number of the "reporter" in which the case is found.) These professors are testing the limits of your gullibility. Do not fall for this.

—That said, however: yes, for Con Law and Civ Pro, especially, there are "landmark" cases that you ought to know by name and holding. There aren't many of them. In the other "Big Six" courses of first-year, you might memorize the name and holding of a "landmark" case or two, also. But, unless the model answers on file to your prof's old exams show that you need to know the case names and holdings, you don't.

To Type or Not to Type?

Type. (Surely it's unnecessary to explain why.)

Haste Makes Waste

When you get into the exam room for the real thing, and the exams are handed out, this is sure to happen: within three minutes, at least one or two people will start writing/typing their answer. This "spooks" a lot of people. They figure, "Wow. This problem is so easy that So-and-so saw the answer right away. *I* must really be *dense*."

This is another example of the survival of the mentality from earlier schooling. Previously, a student either would or would not know the material, period. If you knew it, you could start answering immediately, and could quickly finish the exam. However, as both LEEWS and Delaney say, you need to spend some time *planning your answer.* (More on this in the next chapter.)

Further, in your previous schooling, if you knew the material "cold," you could easily finish answering the question/s before time expired, and turn your answer/s in early. However, in law school, that is insane. A big part of what the exam is about is that there's *never* enough time to cover *everything.* Part of the "test" is to see how well you set priorities, covering what *must* be covered—plus as many minor issues (or non-issues) as possible, but then letting the rest go.

To be charitable: the person who starts writing/typing his or her answer immediately is probably trying to relieve his or her stress by doing *something* instead of just sitting there in a stupor. Less charitably (and in the alternative), that person is like the "gunner" in class: a blowhard who is so insecure that he or she has to compensate for it by trying to intimidate others in his or her quest for reassurance.*

The same alternative explanations are quite likely as to the student who makes a big show of packing up early, turning in his or her answer/s and leaving the exam room ahead of time.

(At my law school, a prof who'd been hired from another school was teaching at my school for the first time. He put no old exams of his on file. But one student declared that she had obtained all his old exams from his former school. But she refused to share them. The prof knew of this, but said nothing. *After* we'd taken his final, however, he passed the word that he'd *never* put old exams on file *anywhere.* So the prof had tacitly colluded with the cutthroat student's effort to increase everyone else's anxiety.)

Intellectual Inversion

Atticus—

I'm a 1L at [one of the "Trinity"]. My prof spent the first five hours of class sessions talking about different interpretations of statutes and case law. He NEVER gave HIS opinion of the law.

So when I outline, I end up writing down all sorts of theories. I wonder how I can incorporate these theories into exam answers.

---

* Yes, I know: if I'm so set on playing amateur shrink, I ought to follow in the footsteps of Benjamin Sells, author of *The Soul of the Law,* and give up the practice of law to become a psychotherapist.

I love the LEEWS approach. It's so systematic...However, when I have a premise for a fact pattern, there might be competing interpretations or fact patterns, or branches as suggested by GTM. Am I supposed to get into these competing theories or rationales?

For instance, there is a relevant statute regarding a fact. Supposedly, I spot an issue. There might be many applications of the rule; a key term in the rule has different interpretations. The legislative intent can also be argued. And reference can be made to the relevant cases. Because the professor never gave HIS interpretation of that particular statute, I have no choice but to analyze all the competing arguments.

As you can see, this approach poses a few problems. First of all, my outline—containing tons of cases, rationales, and policy discussions—will be too long for both reviews. Second, the LEEWS approach does not work well any more because of having a streamlined outline that gets to the point, I have endless policy discussion that runs forever.

I remember that you said some professors just love to talk about policy in class but give typical exams with just hypos. If that's the case, are the lectures of these professors important at all? I really don't feel I've learned any Black Letter Law in these discussions. I talked with some 2Ls who had this prof last year. They said he talked about policy the whole semester, then just gave a BLL exam at the end.

But he told us he wants to see competing applications and interpretations of law on his final, and Black Letter Law does not interest him.

I am not quite sure of the mentality here. Quite a few people in my section say they think policy and philosophical discussion is what this law school is all about. They say Black Letter Law can be learned in just a few months. I am thinking maybe I'm a little tunnel-visioned.

What's your take? Is it now time for me to take the "Getting to Maybe" approach for this class—i.e., to concentrate mostly on class notes and try to learn policy?

On the one hand, the student says: *"I talked with some 2Ls who had this prof last year. They said he talked about policy the whole semester, then just gave a BLL exam at the end."* Yet, the student also wrote, *"But [the prof] told us he wants to see competing applications and interpretations of law on his final, and Black Letter Law does not interest him."*

It was staring this student in the face that this prof is a typical professorial hypocrite: saying one thing, doing the other. (This student, of course, did not have the benefit of *PLS2*, with its excerpts from Josephson's report to the AALS or of Chapter 8's discussion of the two pieces by law profs about the routine "bait and switch" practice.)

This chapter has discussed why a "What does it *mean?*" problem on an exam is quite unlikely. But even if the prof were to test policy, you've already seen how to deal with it. To get more specific, though: if you have to work with "competing applications of a rule, different interpretations of a statute, legislative intent, or the meaning of a key term," well, *that is part of the STANDARD LEEWS approach.*

It makes no sense that this student says that "the LEEWS approach does not work well" for this. As near as I can figure, this student is "hung up" on the fact that there appear to be no "conflict pairings" here. But there *are* conflict pairings. Instead of *parties,* they're conflicts of what Wentworth Miller calls "premises," i.e., "legal bases of entitlement." The "different interpretations of a statute, legislative intent, or the meaning of a key term" are *all* what Miller calls "premises."

The prof supposedly intends to *drop* the need to spot conflict pairings of parties. So the problem the prof allegedly will pose lets the student go straight to the interweaving of facts and rules. That's still a straight LEEWS-Delaney analysis.

This student is perpetuating the *false dichotomy* between "Black Letter Law" and "policy." I'll say it again: Black Letter Law IS policy. It's just "old, well settled" policy that has gelled into a list of specific elements. It's nonsense to think of Black Letter Law *versus* policy. Typically, as discussed previously, for any given fact pattern, there will be two *conflicting* rules of Black Letter Law. Each rule will incorporate a "policy." A good lawyerlike analysis takes into account those competing policies, and then argues both sides as to which policy (i.e., which rule of Black Letter Law) should take precedence *in light of the facts presented.* (On a law school exam answer, unless the prof specifically tells you to, you do *not* take the role of advocate and argue that one rule or the other should prevail. Instead, you interweave the facts and the law—*à la* Delaney—and state that one side or the other is *likely* to prevail.)

That is why it is utterly specious of this student's fellow 1Ls to say that "Black Letter Law can be learned in just a few months." For one thing, you only *have* a "few months" between the first day of class and the final exam. For another, it is not really a matter of "learning" Black Letter Law. Sure, the *basics,* the first-year Black Letter Law—*the BABY STUFF*—can be learned in a matter of *hours.* But acquiring a *sophisticated* understanding of Black Letter Law is a *lifetime* project...in large part because *there will always be new fact patterns that give rise to new "wrinkles."* The know-it-alls who have yet to handle even one real-world case (which includes most of the faculty, by the way) are as foolishly arrogant as they are naive.

It also troubles me that this student said "Because the prof never gave *his* interpretation of that particular statute, *I have no choice but to analyze all the competing arguments.*"

Ironically, this professor is doing students a *favor* by *not* disclosing his own interpretation of the statute.

Out in the real world, you will need to consider and evaluate *all* the possibilities—including situations where the dispute largely "turns" on what interpretation of the statute the *court* will adopt. No *judge* should ever give you an "advisory opinion" and tell you what he or she thinks is the "correct" interpretation of a statute *before* hearing both sides of the case in *light of the facts* (even if only during a preliminary hearing). Why expect a *prof* to? —As though some prof (any more than some judge) had the law's equivalent of "Papal Infallibility."

Despite taking LEEWS, this student has yet to disabuse himself of the notion that there is *one* "right" answer. The essence of a good lawyerlike analysis is to come up with *lots* of *possible* answers, and to weigh them *in light of the facts*. This is not a graduate school of engineering, where every technical problem has one (and usually *only* one) "right answer."

But this student *also* wanted to simultaneously go to the *opposite* extreme (from the one "right" answer), via *GTM's* "forks." Apparently, he wanted to eschew the detailed outline and just wait and see what fact pattern the prof would throw at him on the final...and then start spotting "forks."

No point in repeating the comments about *GTM*. But the allure *GTM* has for this student reinforces why I'd changed my mind about the book's value. When "crunch time" comes, this student will spend far too much time looking for "forks" instead of knifing through the exam and spoon-feeding the prof a good lawyerlike analysis *à la* LEEWS. He will run out of time, and his analysis will be hurried and poor.

Another reason why he will likely run out of time is that, apparently, he is only going to prepare a Master Outline, and not also a Summary Outline. (See Chapter 4.) It appears he intends to consult it when cramming for finals, and perhaps even during the exam itself (if the exam is open-book). He thinks of outlining as the creation of a finished *product,* rather than as the *process* of constantly reworking his outline-in-progress. The journey *is* the destination. You "internalize" your outline by creating new examples and counter-examples of Black Letter Law in action. But this student, *without realizing it,* is sticking to the memorize-and-regurgitate mode.

However, by the time his exams begin he should no longer *need* a Master Outline at all. So, whether or not it's "streamlined" is irrelevant. (Granted, though, it should not be overly long.) In fact, the only purpose of the *Summary* Outline will be as a checklist to make sure he's not overlooked something before he starts writing out his answer for the prof.

It would make no difference if this prof decided to "change his ways" and stop giving Black Letter Law exams. For a pure policy exam (versus a disguised fruitcake), the student would have a simple task. He need only run through each of the applicable policies, rationales, etc., that bear on the facts the prof provides, to see how well each applies to those facts. Straight LEEWS or CIRI(P). He'd need *to discuss them ALL*. But it could be done with a simple flow-chart analysis. It would be hit-and-run: hit each point quickly, then move on (as with a Black Letter Law exam).

Bottom line: yes, he has to pay attention to policy. And yes, he has to put down all the possibilities in his outline. But assuming this prof (and other profs like him, who play the "bait-and-switch" discussed in Chapter 8) remains true to form, *top* priority should go to Black Letter Law. The prof's old exams proved that he *talks* policy but *tests* Black Letter. That's typical. After all, it's the *bedrock* of *everything* you'll *ever* do as a lawyer.* Ignore it now at your future peril, both as a law student and as a lawyer. And this is true even for graduates of "The Trinity." (See the testimonial essays at the end of Chapter 15 from students at Boalt, HLS, and NYU.)

---

* And, of course, as a judge. Several years ago, I was in a state district court where a jury trial was in progress. The jury was recessed so the attorneys could argue a point of law to the court. One lawyer said that the doctrine of "force majeure" controlled. Hizzoner's head snapped up. The judge then said *"Force majeure?* What's *that?"* (I am not making this up. There is a transcript.)

Even educated *laypeople* know what "force majeure," a legal term of art, means. But not this judge.

Three things made his ignorance particularly appalling. First, he'd been on the bench for more than six years. Second, President Bush, *père,* had nominated this guy to be a *federal* district court judge. Had the nomination been approved (which, thank God, it was not), this ignoramus would have had *lifetime tenure.* Third—and what made it personally embarrassing to me, indirectly—was that this goofus had attended the same law school *I* went to... one of the "best" in the country.

Chapter 7 - Slicing through a Fruitcake

The pedagogy of law school brings to mind a famous slip of the tongue by Richard J. Daley, Sr., for decades the notorious Mayor of Chicago. (The current mayor is Richard *M.* Daley, one of his sons.) The Vietnam War was at its peak in 1968, and the Democratic National Convention was being held in the Windy City. Large numbers of Chicago's Finest went berserk and repeatedly attacked peace demonstrators who'd gathered at some distance from the convention site. Upon receiving reports that his "thin blue line" had rioted, Hizzoner stated, "The policeman is not there to *create* disorder. The policeman is there to *preserve* disorder." (Obviously, he'd meant to say "prevent" rather than "preserve.") Every time I think of law school professors, I remember that statement of Richard Daley's. The professor deliberately both *creates* disorder *and* seeks to preserve it. It's *your* job to bring *order* to it—especially to the mess presented to you as the essay questions of your law school finals. (And by the way, it's similar to the practice of law.)

Here's part of an e-mail I received in mid-autumn 2001 from a student in his first semester of law school:

Atticus—

My property professor is a real wacko. I was working on one of his exams from last year, and I have to say that it's the weirdest thing I've seen in my entire life. I wrote out an answer. But there is no model answer on file, so I went to discuss it with the prof.

He basically said my answer was off and that I needed to do more work. His words were: "You need to spot the issue. State the rule. Apply it. Then talk about policy."

Now, I'm really worried about the final. I'm not even sure what the issues are on this old one. Apparently, what I think are issues are not issues, and I miss what the prof thinks is relevant. I have no idea what I'm supposed to be spotting.

I talked to some 2Ls who had this prof and they said that people cried during the final last year.

What do I do?

I'd received e-mails reporting that a prof had caused someone to cry in class. Also, there were those who reported that a student, upon seeing his or her grade on a final, would burst into tears...and they were not tears of joy. But this was the first report of a prof who caused students to cry during an exam. It brought to mind the words from Omar Khayyam's *Rubaiyat* (as translated by Edward J. Fitzgerald):

> The Moving Finger writes; and having writ,
> Moves on: nor all your Piety nor Wit
> Shall lure it back to cancel half a Line,
> Nor all your Tears wash out a Word of it.

It was no surprise, though, that the prof made only cryptic remarks to a conscientious student seeking help. From the prof's point of view, there really was nothing that could be said, because he—as with vitually the entire professoriat—believes "Either you have it, or you don't."

Curious, I asked the student to e-mail me a copy of that old exam. It turned out to be one problem from an exam.

The Exam Problem

Suzy Creamcheese, M.D., is the founder and owner of the Mothers of Invention Clinic. She established the clinic to implant fertilized eggs in women who (if the implant were successful) would then become pregnant with that egg. (The clinic's name is from the saying, "Necessity is the mother of invention.") Most of her patients are women in a marriage or other "committed relationship." Dr. Creamcheese surgically extracts eggs from them. The women's husbands/"significant others" provide sperm. Dr. Creamcheese then unites the eggs with the sperm, in vitro, and surgically reimplants one of the (now fertilized) eggs in the woman. Sometimes the procedure must be repeated several times before it "takes" and pregnancy occurs.

From the beginning, however, Dr. Creamcheese would also acquire eggs and sperm by purchasing them from donors. This was because some of her patients were women whose eggs were incapable of fertilization, or else the woman in question had a serious genetic defect and did not want to pass that defect along to her child. For these women to become pregnant, Dr. Creamcheese would use eggs from one or more other women who had sold them to her to be fertilized and implanted in her patients. And it sometimes happened that a woman's partner also was infertile or had a serious genetic defect and did not want to pass that defect along to his child. So, at the couple's request, Dr. Creamcheese would use the sperm of another man to fertilize the eggs to be implanted in the woman. Starting within the past two or three years, though, more of her implant patients have been single women alone, who do not have a committed partner and who want to become pregnant by a sperm donor.

Sperm and as-yet-unfertilized eggs, along with fertilized eggs, were all kept in cold storage. The cost of storage was not billed separately, but was built in to the fees Dr. Creamcheese charged her patients, as an overhead expense. If a woman wanted her own eggs implanted in her, it was necessary to have more of her eggs available in case the initial implant failed. Also, even when an implant was successful and a pregnancy occurred and was carried to term, sometimes a woman would indicate that she might want to have one or more additional children some day, so her eggs (usually already fertilized by her husband or partner) would be held in storage for further possible use. (Typically, Dr. Creamcheese would extract around two dozen eggs, nearly all of which would be found to be worth implanting. But for any given pregnancy, it had never taken more than half-a-dozen reimplants before pregnancy occurred or the woman in question gave up.)

Donors who were paid for eggs and sperm are carefully screened to make sure they are genetically and medically "sound." Although the names of donors are not disclosed to patients, the patients can get a complete profile, including a genetic profile, of the person who provided the egg or sperm in question. The donors have to sign a release of all claims to the donated matter. For women who had their own eggs extracted for reimplanting in themselves after fertilization, Dr. Creamcheese would keep their eggs in storage until and unless the woman signed a "release for destruction" of those eggs. (Yet, from the very beginning, some of her patients were married or in a "committed relationship" but were unsure of how long the marriage or relationship would last. They would privately instruct Dr. Creamcheese to keep at least some of the extracted eggs separate and unfertilized. That way, if the woman remarried or entered a new relationship later and wanted to have a child by her new love, it would not be necessary to surgically extract more eggs. Dr. Creamcheese would store these unfertilized eggs, identified and clearly separated from those unfertilized eggs that the clinic had purchased, until such time as she received a release for the eggs' destruction, from the woman the eggs had come from.)

The Mothers of Invention Clinic is by appointment only. Appointments are booked only in the afternoons, and only on three days of the week: Thursdays, Fridays, and Saturdays. During those times, Dr. Creamcheese receives those who wish to sell eggs or sperm to the clinic, extracts eggs from women or accepts semen from the men, conducts in vitro fertilization of eggs, and implants fertilized eggs in patients. On a typical day there is only one surgical procedure, whether extraction or implant (on an out-patient basis), and generally no more than five or six people visit the clinic.

The clinic is on the first floor of a two-story structure. It is a house. Dr. Creamcheese purchased it years ago from the Zappa family and immediately converted it. The foyer of what had been the Zappa residence became the reception area/waiting room. What had been the dining room is now used for private consultations with potential (or current) patients or donors. The master bedroom was converted into the outpatient surgical theater, where eggs are extracted or implanted. The master bath, off the old master bedroom, is still used as a bathroom, but the tub and bidet have been removed. It is also used as the room where sperm is "extracted." Patients' files and the bookkeeping records are in what had been the family room, which is also on the first floor, and that room also serves as Dr. Creamcheese's office. The kitchen was turned into a laboratory where eggs are united in vitro with sperm. The cold-storage units are also there, along with small medical equipment such as the microscope and autoclave.

Dr. Creamcheese lives, alone, on the second floor of the house. She converted the recreation room (which had a "wet bar" in it) to a new kitchen. One of what had been bedrooms is now her personal study and library. Another former bedroom is now a "gallery," in which she keeps her valuable collection of Barbie® and Ken® dolls, and various paraphernalia related to them. The other former bedroom is still used as a bedroom: hers.

The building is in Young Pumpkin Estates. It is a subdivision, created out of what had been all of Uncle Bernie's Farm. After the developer, Moon Unit, had purchased it, company officials persuaded the authorities to change the zoning of the farmland to "single family residential." The tract was designed to consist of single-family residences (i.e., houses). Deeds conveyed by Moon Unit to the original homebuyers contained covenants specifying the property was for a single-family residence. The Zappas' deed did not contain the covenant.

One couple who came to Dr. Creamcheese were Jimmy Carlyle Black and his wife, Valarie. They provided sperm and eggs, respectively, at the Clinic, and Dr. Creamcheese had immediately fertilized all of Valarie's eggs with Jimmy's sperm. In the same week that Jimmy and Valarie were there, a woman named Aybea Sea had some of her own eggs extracted, to be united with sperm the Clinic had purchased and whose donor Dr. Creamcheese had carefully screened (as always), and whom Aybea Sea had chosen to be the source of the sperm. Immediately after extracting Aybea Sea's eggs, Dr. Creamcheese united them with the designated sperm. The first implant for both Valarie and Aybea Sea was scheduled for two months later.

Frank Dweezle is a self-proclaimed "post-modern entrepreneur," who had already made his fortune twice over. His first was from establishing KRUD-FM, a "radio station." But instead of broadcasting, KRUD engaged only in "streaming" into the internet. Its format of "grunge" and "hip-hop" music, and "bathroom humor" proved hugely popular on a global basis. Its worldwide audience was estimated at more than 50 million, most of whom were fluent in English. KRUD is said to have a market value of $340 million. Dweezle's second fortune was made from a company called Home Stretch. Dweezle had somehow obtained an ongoing supply of Viagra®, in huge quantities. He then took orders through the Home Stretch website, for prices far lower than pharmacies charged. To evade U.S. laws, the Viagra® was shipped from outside the USA to customers within the USA, from several points that were constantly changing. Dweezle still owns that company. Home Stretch has an estimated value of two billion dollars.

Having become quite wealthy, Dweezle wanted to benefit humanity even more than he already had—and make another fortune in the process. He sought to establish a website from which women could acquire fertilized eggs for implanting in themselves. He contacted Dr. Creamcheese, who agreed to provide fertilized eggs that had been "released for destruction." In addition to receiving money from Dweezle for each sale, the Mothers of Invention Clinic would receive free advertising on KRUD, and promotional material would be included on the new venture's website.

Dweezle then launched "Motherly Love" as his new company in cyberspace. The price he charged for fertilized eggs was triple what he paid Dr. Creamcheese. Those who bought them got a Certificate of Authenticity with the product. But before Motherly Love would ship the product to a customer, it had to have a signed release (via digital signature) saying, "I as sole purchaser/we as joint purchasers of fertilized human eggs agree to hold Motherly Love harmless for any problems encountered in the implantation or carrying to term of the fertilized human eggs purchased from the Motherly Love website." Despite the very high price charged, business was brisk. Dweezle was on his way to making a third fortune. Dr. Creamcheese had already expanded the hours of her clinic, to five afternoons a week, to accommodate more donors and to receive more eggs from women who wanted them implanted. Yet, Dweezle was already heavily back-logged with orders. So, at Dweezle's urging, Dr. Creamcheese agreed to start supplying more fertilized eggs from among "extra" fertilized eggs that she believed she would not need to use for implants.

Shortly thereafter, the Clinic called Valarie and Aybea Sea to inform them that, "due to circumstances beyond our control," a defective cold-storage unit had warmed up and the eggs, fertilized eggs, and sperm in it were all effectively destroyed. What had actually happened to their fertilized eggs is that Dr. Creamcheese had sold them to Frank Dweezle's Motherly Love. Dr. Creamcheese offered to extract more eggs at no charge, and to carry on as before. Valarie agreed at once, but said she could not come in for a few weeks. Aybea Sea said "I'll think about it."

Two of Dweezle's earliest customers were a lesbian singing duo, "Wowie" and "Zowie." Their "art" was characterized by what *The New York Times*, in its usual restrained manner, referred to as "intimate cavorting on stage." The two women (both 18) had hair that was, in various places, deep green, turquoise, white, and purple, arranged as spikes in places. They took pride in disclosing that "everything on our bodies that *can* be pierced *has* been pierced," and they wore various rings, etc., at the site of each piercing. In this age of "hype," they existed for pure shock value...and were making millions of dollars at it. They were hated not only by "mainstream" people, but also by lesbians who detested the image of lesbianism "Wowie Zowie" (their name as a duo) were creating in the popular mind.

To raise their "shock schlock" to a higher level, Wowie and Zowie, during an interview on MTV, announced that Wowie was pregnant, with an egg extracted from an (unknown) other woman and fertilized by an unknown male whose profile the two women had approved together. Further, after Wowie gave birth, Zowie would then become pregnant, the same way. They announced they'd bought the eggs from Frank Dweezle's website, Motherly Love, and the second fertilized egg was currently in storage at the Mothers of Invention Clinic. Dweezle, subsequently interviewed by an MTV "veejay," declared (perhaps truthfully) that most of his customers were lesbian couples, especially those in states where, by statute, gay and lesbian couples were barred from adopting children. The audio from the Wowie Zowie's MTV announcement, and of the MTV veejay's interview with Dweezle, were replayed together many times on KRUD.

Of course, as intended, these revelations generated huge publicity. Dr. Creamcheese accommodated more people by further expanding the hours of the Clinic. But the publicity also caused a lot of people to Freak Out. Jerry Drawlwell and Pat Faubusson, televangelists, called for "action." Even "Burnt Weenie Sandwich," the "alternative newsletter of cyberspace," declared that this was just too much. The Speaker of the U.S. House of Representatives, Gingrich Newton, promised "something will be done—immediately." And it was. A bill was quickly rushed through both houses of Congress, and signed by President Mesquite the same day. It made it illegal to sell, "directly or indirectly, fertilized human eggs." The statute was a felony, punishable by fine. Congress and the President also directed that "all artificial insemination, surgical extraction or implantation of human eggs, or in vitro fertilization of human eggs" be done only in "an accredited hospital."

Very shortly thereafter, Frank Dweezle filed suit on behalf of Motherly Love, in state court, alleging that the new regulation was a taking of his firm's property rights. Almost immediately after that, people who had provided eggs or sperm to the Mothers of Invention Clinic joined the suit. This group formed a class, and included Jimmy Carlyle Black and Valarie, and Aybea Sea. (At this point, no more eggs have been extracted from either Valarie or Aybea Sea.) They claimed their property rights had been violated by the unauthorized sales. And within a few days after that, Dr. Creamcheese, and a group of people who had purchased fertilized eggs from Motherly Love (and thus, indirectly, from the Mothers of Invention Clinic), joined the suit as another class. They included "Wowie Zowie," who of course greatly boosted the notoriety of the pending litigation. This new class also claimed that its members' property, in effect, had been taken, and further claimed that the federal statute interfered with their Constitutional right to procreate.

Then, within just a few more days, the Young Pumpkin Estates Homeowners Association joined the suit, to challenge Dr. Creamcheese's Mothers of Invention Clinic in Young Pumpkin Estates.

Shortly thereafter, the government filed a motion for summary judgment claiming there was no taking because there were no identifiable property rights affected and that the statute was constitutional.

Today is your first day as the new judicial clerk for the Honorable Igors Boogie, presiding judge of the state district court where all these pleadings are on file. The judge has just said to you, "Kid, I want you to write me a memo. In it, I want you to examine all the property rights of the relevant parties. And examine the quagmire of the regulatory takings doctrine, while you're at it."

DISCUSS.

Allotted time: 75 minutes.

[Note from AF: the recommendation of 75 minutes includes the time it takes to read the problem itself.]

After reading this problem, I sent an e-mail to the student, which said in part:

"Your prof might well be wacko, but I don't see it from his old exam problem. Rather, he is quite clever—and a bit devious...in other words, a typical law school professor."

I then asked the student to send me his proposed answer—the one he'd shown his professor.

Student's Proposed Answer

<u>Jimmy Carlyle Black & Valarie, and Aybea Sea (JVA) v.
Creamcheese (C)</u>:

Who acquires property rights in the egg?

[Commentary from AF—This is the wrong way to start. It might at
first appear to be the logical starting point, but as we shall see, it is not.
The prof set a trap. The student has already stepped into it.]

JVA will argue that property rights were acquired
in the egg by virtue of the fact that this is their
personal property, and C acquired a bailment. A bailment requires: 1) acceptance and delivery, 2) actual
physical control. The first element is established
when JVA leave the egg at C's clinic, and C took the
egg from them, promising to hold it. C then exercised
physical control as the egg was in her possession.

[The student is already in trouble. He'd started off by asking "Who
acquires property rights in the egg?" But the Black Letter Law regarding
bailments was irrelevant to that question. Bailments is an entirely separate area of Property Law. Then he does not state the two elements of
a bailment completely and accurately...and he omits the third element.]

JVA will argue that this is a mutual bailment
because JVA would receive the benefit of fertility
and C would receive money. As this is a mutual bailment, C had to exercise a reasonable standard of care.
JVA will argue that a reasonable person would carefully guard DNA rather than sell it over to the
highest bidder.

[He's digging his academic grave even deeper now. "Mutual bailment"
is indeed relevant to the standard of care...but only in an action for
negligence. He hasn't mentioned negligence. So, at the very least, this
discussion of the standard of care is premature. But as we shall eventually
see, there is *no* negligence here. So this discussion is entirely irrelevant...And
he's already cutting loose from the facts, with his reference to "the highest
bidder." The "fact pattern" said nothing about an auction.]

C may assert that JVA lost their property rights due to abandonment which requires 1) relinquishing possession, 2) an intent to give it up to the first person who finds it. The second element, however, is not established because JVA will point out that they planned to come back to C's clinic for a fertility treatment. Moreover, no release form was ever signed.

[It appears the student has come back to bailments. And in fact this matter should be discussed under bailments...in which case the approach should be entirely different. Abandonment is relevant, but not with regard to JVA. And he has misstated its second element.]

As a matter of policy, the court will have to consider whether property rights should be acquired in eggs. On the one hand, the court in *Moore* stated that property rights should not be acquired in spleens because society needs to promote socially useful research and reduce litigation. In this case, society needs to promote procreation. JVA may point out that a rule which allows anyone to utilize eggs left at fertility clinics may actually hurt procreation. As in JVA's case, they may go to a fertility clinic for the purpose of procreation and have their intent frustrated by not being able to utilize the eggs for a treatment. On the other hand, perhaps this should not be dealt with under a property schema at all because eggs have the potential for human life, and the court has never held that we can acquire title in human beings.

[Here the student is desperately looking for a way to discuss "policy," as per the prof's suggestion. He is on to something here. But his third and fourth sentences leave me baffled. And I believe it's a mistake to try to "punt" this out of Prop Law (into Con Law). Further, the student wrote "a rule which allows anyone to utilize eggs left at fertility clinics may actually hurt procreation." He surely meant to write "a rule which does *not* allow..." Carelessness costs.]

<u>Dweezle/Creamcheese (DC) v. Government</u>

Did the statute amount to a taking when it did not allow DC to sell eggs?

[I'd said in my initial response to seeing the prof's exam that the prof was a bit devious. I believe that part of the prof's deviousness concerns the matter of "takings." (More on that later.) The student here has fallen for it.]

There is only a taking if DC acquired title to the eggs. DC may assert that title was received via prior possession. The prior possessor always prevails over everyone except the true owner, and since the govt is not the true owner, it doesn't acquire title. The govt may counter that JVA have better title than DC. However, DC will point out that based on the doctrine of relativity of title, the govt can only recover on the strength of its own title, not on the weaknesses of DC's title. DC may also argue that they acquired title to the eggs via abandonment.

Certain eggs were given up with permission, and certainly these donors had the requisite intent for the sperm/egg donations to go to the first person who found them.

A taking of property occurs if: 1) the statute deprives the property of all economic viability, 2) the statute was arbitrary, or 3) the statute frustrated investment backed expectations. Respecting the first element, DC will argue that the eggs have no economic value since they can no longer be bought or sold on the market. The second and third elements are probably not satisfied as the statute applied to all eggs, and the government made no explicit promises that eggs could be used for economic purposes.

Assuming there was a taking, DC will argue that just compensation is based upon the 200 percent markup that Dweezle used. The govt will argue that this amounts to extortion, and the value should be what C received from Dweezle.

[Assuming I am correct that the "takings" issue is a *false* issue, this student has just wasted a lot of time on arguing the *merits* of the issue, when he should have been *quickly* explaining why it is a *false* issue. Further, "extortion" is a *crime*. No law student should ever use a legal term as a figure of speech to enhance his or her rhetoric in an exam answer. —In fact, no law student should be rhetorical in an exam answer. Remember: *you are not in "advocacy mode" during an exam.*]

Wowie & Zowie, and Others (WZ) v. Govt

WZ only have a claim for taking if they acquired property rights in the eggs. WZ may acquire title if DC originally acquired title and passed title to WZ. WZ may have other venues for recovery.

[The student is still chasing down the "takings" rabbit trail, and is still conflating the "takings" issue with an issue as to who has property rights in the fertilized eggs.]

By common law, a bona fide purchaser recovers if the owner entrusted the property to a merchant who sold it to a bona fide purchaser. JVA entrusted the eggs to C. C sold it to Dweezle who sold it to WZ.

[And now he swings back to bailments, which is what this paragraph concerns...although the student erred by not expressly referring to bailments, instead of "the common law." In general, he is "on to something" here. But he is presenting this in the wrong place, and in the wrong way. Further, he has failed to indicate from *whom* the bona fide purchasers can recover, and *what* they might be able to recover— unimplanted fertilized eggs, damages (i.e., money), or both. But he is speaking of the *wrong* parties' rights, here.]

Are WZ bona fide purchasers? The govt will say no because WZ had a duty to investigate who owned the eggs when they bought them from the website. After all, these are sensitive pieces of DNA which could potentially be stolen. The website failed to mention where the eggs came from. WZ will assert that the website seemed genuine to them, so a unilateral duty should not be imposed on the purchaser.

[The "genuineness" of the website (whatever *that* means) is irrelevant. And he misstates the law regarding BFPs (Bona Fide Purchasers). In fact, there IS a unilateral duty, in hindsight, when one seeks to claim the status of BFP. The purchasers should have investigated the provenance of the fertilized eggs, and should have scrupulously confirmed that Dweezle had a right to sell them.]

WZ may also recover on the basis of UCC which states that any entrustment to the merchant gives the merchant the right to transfer the rights of the transferor to a bona fide purchaser in the ordinary course of business. WZ will point out that when Dweezle sold the eggs to them, it was via a website and was within the "course of business;" Dweezle was a merchant in the business of selling eggs.

[This is a Property exam, not a Contracts exam, so a discussion of the UCC (the Uniform Commercial Code) should at most be a digression here, not an argument. Besides, a *bailment* is an "entrustment"—and the merchant/bailee has *no* "right" to transfer "the rights of the transferor" (which is not a term of legal art) "in the ordinary course of business", (which *is* a term of legal art.)]

As a matter of policy, it may make more sense to deal with this problem under constitutional law, rather than property rights. WZ may have a basis of recovery due to the fact that the government is interfering with their procreation rights. Property law may obscure the idea that we are dealing with "goods" that have the potential for human life.

[Here again the student is trying to work in policy. But because this is a Property Law course, what the prof had in mind was policy regarding *property* law. The student, in desperation, has veered off into pure Con Law...specifically, the "penumbra of the Constitution"—and the term is certainly apt here! He vaguely senses what the argument should be. But (like "Wrong-Way Fenway") he's not going in the right direction.]

Creamcheese v. Government

C may assert that there was a taking based on the fact that she can no longer practice her profession on her property due to the new statute. A taking requires: 1) deprivation of economic viability, or 2) arbitrariness, 3) or frustration of investment backed expectations.

[The student has again headed in the wrong direction. The prof may well have included a section in the course on "job rights" as property rights. But that is usually covered only in upper-level courses, specifically courses on employment law. I doubt the prof got into that during this semester. But if he did, then that changes the picture somewhat...but not much.]

Respecting the first element, C will assert that the house loses all economic viability since she is no longer able to practice her profession within it. The govt will counter that the house may still be bought and sold and used for residential purposes, which is what it was originally intended for. The statute was not arbitrary as it applied to everyone, and the govt gave no explicit guarantees so investment backed expectations were not frustrated. The govt may also assert as a matter of policy that we should allow the statute to stand because it protects the health of people. We don't want medical procedures being performed in someone's kitchen.

[Now we've suddenly gone from the right to earn a living to "takings" regarding the house. The student has conflated the two. As he points out, to be a "taking" regarding the house, the government has to have done something to make the house valueless *as a house*. But his paragraph conflates the Real Estate issue with a "livelihood" issue. And as we shall eventually see, the entire "takings" issue is a red herring.]

Neighbors (N) v. Creamcheese (C)

N may try to recover on the basis of real covenant or equitable servitude doctrine which requires, *inter alia*, that the covenant be in writing. As this element is not satisfied, N can't recover on this basis.

[Wrong. If a covenant is an equitable servitude, it does not have to be in writing. Only a real covenant requires a writing.]

N may be able to recover based on an implied reciprocal negative servitudes which requires: 1) common grantor, 2) inserts restrictions into many deeds, 3) to fulfill a general scheme, 4) and C has some sort of notice. We don't know from these facts whether a common grantor inserted the restrictions into the neighborhood deeds, but there seems to be a general scheme to create a single family neighborhood. C may also be on inquiry notice as he could see that this was a neighborhood and not a commercial area.

[This is not a correct statement of the elements, because, in part, it conflates the elements of a real covenant with the elements of an equitable servitude. The student has tossed out the term "implied reciprocal negative servitude" in an obvious attempt to dazzle the prof with his alleged knowledge of legal jargon. The same is true of his use of the Latin, "inter alia" ("among other things"). —Wentworth Miller *recommends* the use of Latin terms. He and I have another friendly disagreement on this. I think Latin terms add little, and can *hurt* you: if your analysis is poor, such terms look like a desperate attempt to "suck up" as appears to be the case here.) But then the student uses the appallingly unprofessional phrase "some sort of notice"! The guy has not only dug himself into a very deep hole; he is now pulling in the dirt on top of himself.]

Did C breach the servitude? C will say that the upstairs was still used as a residence, and only the downstairs area was used for fertility purposes. N will point out that the bathroom was being used for sperm treatments, the kitchen stored eggs, and that another bathroom was being used for in-vitro fertilization. A single family home is typically not used for these purposes.

[Again, the student is on to something here. But he has not addressed the issue adequately.]

    If C breached it, she may have a defense
    based on prescription which requires: 1) continuous,
    2) adverse, 3) notorious, 4) open use of the property
    in violation of the servitude. The use was probably
    continuous as she used the property as a clinic for
    years; Adversity depends on the test employed by the
    jurisdiction which could either be: 1) intentional,
    2) good faith, or 3) objective. C was probably unaware
    of the covenant, and so she would likely meet the
    good faith and objective tests, but not the inten-
    tional test. The notorious and open requirements
    would be problematic because no one could really see
    the in-vitro fertilization process going on in her
    house. C may argue that the neighborhood could see
    patients going to her house, but N will say that N
    had no idea that the patients were going there to
    donate sperm and eggs.

[At this point, the burial is complete. The student refers to a "prescription." It appears he was thinking of an "easement by prescription." But easements have nothing to do with this problem. His discussion then concerns the elements of *adverse possession,* not *easements*—and even then, his statement of the elements of adverse possession is incorrect. Last, adverse possession is a way of *acquiring title* to property. But Dr. Creamcheese *already owns* the house.]

General Commentary

As Wentworth Miller says, "you want to show your prof 'a lawyer coming off the page.'" And as John Delaney says, there are *lots* of ways to go about doing a "lawyerlike analysis"—*but not on an exam.*

I've heard of profs who brag that they never take more than five minutes to grade a student's exam answers, on average. I used to be outraged about it. Now I understand it. Within 10 seconds of starting to read this student's answer, I knew it was not good. Virtually all law schools have a forced curve, with a set number of each letter grade allowed. My hunch is that a prof takes all the student's answers, and does a first run-through to sort them into three piles. Those three piles are the same as Delaney's three categories of answers: good, so-so, and lousy. Were I a law prof, this student's paper would immediately go into the "lousy" stack. But if the "so-so" stack was too small, I would end up having to move some of those from the "lousy" stack into the higher category, merely because of the forced curve. I'll bet the typical prof then spends a fair amount of time with each answer that looked "good" during the first quickie run-through; less time with each answer in the "so-so" group; and almost no further time at all with those in the "lousy" pile. After all, if a student is "out of the running" for a grade of 90 or better, it makes no difference if the student gets a 66 or a 71 (assuming that anything below 66 is an F).

I believe the grade for the student's proposed answer, even on the curve, would be no better than a D+. If it received a grade on an objective scale, that grade would be an F.

I do not see this as a reflection on the student's ability, but the professor's opacity. This "teacher" could have taught his students the relevant Black Letter Law, and how to play with hypos, and how to do a lawyerlike analysis. At the very least, he could have *alerted* them to the importance of those things, as the Josephson Report urged. But as Chapter 2 discussed (quoting the Josephson Report), this professor was (typically) playing hide-the-ball. Hence the vague instructions to "Spot the issue. State the rule. Apply it. Then talk about policy." —All of which (with the exception of the advice regarding policy) was just IRAC.

I have no doubt that well over half the students in this property law class were at *least* as lost as this one was. And that's the way the prof wanted it and intended to keep it. And when his students did not do well, he no doubt engaged in "Blaming the Victim." (It used to be the standard response to rape victims, for example. "What happened is your own fault. Somehow, you brought it on yourself.") That's still the accepted response to law school students who are certifiably incompetent when they graduate. (The short-term memorization for the bar exam definitely does not provide the knowledge graduates need to practice law.)

This professor should have been ashamed of himself. Instead, I am sure he was quite pleased with himself. (See the reviews of the "how to succeed in law school" writings of two members of the professoriat, in Chapter 8.)

LEEWS and Delaney, Applied

This is the type of exam Josephson called a "multi-transactional problem"—and chastised as being "far too reliant on the relatively minor skill of isolating transactional issues." It's what I call a "fruitcake."

Both Wentworth Miller *and* John Delaney say to take about one minute, when you first get the exam, to do a "preliminary overview." Read the overall instructions at the start of the exam, which apply to the *entire* exam. Next, quickly flip through the pages of the exam, just to see how long it is. But do not read the various problems in it.

Then, go to the "call of the question" at the end of the first problem. In other words, find out what the prof wants from you. Then quickly see how long the problem is, and glance through it—but *without reading it*. The exam here is dense with facts. That's all you need to know at this point.

Because this is a "fruitcake" problem, use LEEWS.

One of the traps the prof set was that he said to examine the property rights of the "relevant parties." He did not say the *named* parties (which includes the classes). This is an "issue"-spotter, and that includes spotting *parties* not specifically named in the fact pattern.

The prof named several parties, and referred to two "classes" of litigants, too. The student naively thought those were the *only* parties. And the student had only five issues—the ones the prof handed him on a platter. As a general rule, if a prof says, for example, that a contract exists, you do not question that. You take it from there. And if a prof says something like "Discuss the claims and liabilities A and B have toward each other," that's what you go with. But when a prof says something like "examine the property rights of the relevant parties," watch out...especially when the prof names specific parties and issues but then does not tell you to limit your discussion to those parties and those issues. There's more than meets the eye, here.

The next step in LEEWS is to read the fact pattern, carefully. As I read through it, I circled the names of the parties, and also circled the word "class" when the facts near the end talked about the litigation. I also marked the issues that the prof "telegraphed" to students. I made a marginal note ("Issue?") when what Delaney calls "the lightbulb of issue-spotting" was triggered by something in the fact pattern. And I underlined what appeared to be "material" facts. The ones that appeared to be what Delaney calls "hot facts," I underlined with a *thick* line. (As Chapter 6 said, you could use the "rainbow" technique, with different-colored felt markers to indicate parties, issues, material facts, etc.)

As I'd read through the fact pattern, I'd seen that the student missed a key angle that would have led to additional conflict-pairings and discussion of more potential causes of action: There's a distinction between those who *sold* sperm and eggs to Dr. Creamcheese, and those who provided sperm and eggs to her for their *own* use. The fact pattern used the word "donors" for both, but that was another trap. "Donors," in *law*, is a term of art. It comes under the law of Gifts. *Some* of the people who supplied eggs and sperm were sellers. But apparently most were not. Most were what's called "bailors." Because this is a property exam, it was obvious that the prof had embedded an issue of bailments in the fact pattern, and cleverly hidden it. The student spotted "bailments." But bailments is irrelevant to the *sellers*.

This, in turn, raised what Josephson calls a "near miss" or "negative" issue, and I call a "bogus" or "false" issue. In other words, it's a "red herring." This one concerns those sellers. As Chapter 6 said, you don't ignore such non-issues simply because they are spurious. Quite the contrary. Your prof might be testing your ability to spot *them*, too—and your ability to explain *why* they are non-issues (which is really no different from explaining why other things *are* issues). And I'd bet my next paycheck that this prof was doing exactly that.

Another non-issue concerned the information that those who provided eggs and sperm of their own, for reimplanting, did not pay a separate fee to the clinic for the storage of those items. Payment is irrelevant to whether or not a bailment exists. But the prof knew quite well some students would go chasing after that as a material fact that supposedly raised a real issue.

One issue that *might* be a "near-miss" concerns whether or not Dr. Creamcheese had the right to sell fertilized eggs after the original owners signed a "release for destruction." This is part of the discussion of bailments.

As I'd read through the fact pattern, a "red flag" went up on another *bogus* issue. I believe the prof was also devious in a manner that "cut *both* ways." He tossed out what appears to be a "red herring"…or, depending on how you look at it, a "freebie," a giveaway. This was a trap for those who did not catch it, causing students to go chasing down a rabbit trail. Hence the red flag. But for those who did catch it, it SAVED them an enormous amount of thought, effort, and *time*.

Here it is: the professor specifically asked for a discussion of "the quagmire of the *regulatory* takings doctrine." But the bulk of the federal statute in question was a *criminal* statute (a "felony"—which means it's criminal, and in this case punishable by a fine). It's another "near miss"/ "negative" issue.

Yet, the "call of the question" also specifically said that the answer was to be thought of as a memo, of sorts, for the presiding judge in this case. The judge would want to address the "takings" issue. A student's answer should let the prof know the student spotted the trap/freebie—and then quickly dispose of it, while paying attention to the supposedly important part: the *regulatory* aspect of the statute (which, even so truncated, is a bogus concern, because it is not a "colorable" claim).

It seemed to me that there were two overall issues. One concerned bailments, and the other, the covenants. There's an "abandonment" sub-issue under bailments—which the student caught, but then fumbled away. And there were three negative issues, related to the overall issues. These were: 1) the claims of the egg and sperm "donors" who'd *sold* those items to Dr. Creamcheese, 2) the "hospitals only" aspect of the federal legislation—which was *different* from the ban on the sale of fertilized eggs, and 3) the constitutionality-summary judgment issue. All of these were traps, along with the "takings" non-issue.

It took me almost 14 minutes to read through the fact pattern carefully and to mark it up. Because I'd used less than a minute for the "preliminary overview," I now had 60 minutes left of the professor's suggested allotted time of 75 minutes.

Both Delaney and LEEWS advise dividing up the rest of your time into "planning your answer" and then writing it. Miller says you should use a fourth to (at most) a third of the allotted time for "planning your answer." This includes making a *very* abbreviated "answer outline" of conflict pairings and issues. Delaney gives similar advice. (This "answer outline" is for your use only, and is *never* to be prepared in such a way that you can hand it in to your prof if you run out of time. As Miller points out, if you have in mind that you will be turning that "outline" in, you will spend far too much time on it. Time is of the essence here, and you need to use it for better things.)

In planning your answer, you should quickly review the "Summary Outline," discussed in Chapter 4. (As mentioned there, you should have written it out on "scratch paper" even before the exam was handed out...if that was allowed.) You do this to see if you missed anything as to possible issues. (I confess that I didn't have a Summary Outline to work from, because I tossed my law school outlines when I got out of law school. —Truth be told, I gleefully burned them, along with my casebooks, in a "good riddance" ceremony. And I'd never made any *Summary* Outlines in the first place, because I didn't know any better.)

LEEWS recommends that you divide what Josephson calls a "multi-transactional" problem into its major parts. I put the above items into three groups: 1) bailments, 2) the covenants, and 3) the "takings" non-issue. As mentioned, it would be important to let the prof know that I'd spotted the red herrings *as* red herrings, and to explain why they were so. But that should not take long. So I allowed three minutes for planning the answer to these, and only five minutes to writing. That left 52 minutes for the other two. As for the bailments part, I knew bailments well. (I sing "Won't You Come Home, Bill Bail*ee*" in the shower.) But the bailments aspect was still a bit tricky because of the conflict pairings and issues I'd spotted and the abandonment issue. So I allocated eight minutes for planning the answer, and 20 minutes for writing it. As for the real covenants...well, the covenants issue looked pretty simple to me, especially because there were two non-issues associated with it that could be disposed of quickly. However, real covenants is a difficult area of property law, and it is not my strong point (to put it mildly). So I set aside a bit more time to think that one through than I otherwise might. Therefore, I allocated nine minutes for "planning" and 15 minutes for writing. But that left no time for checking my work...which can prove fatal.

In the suggested answer that follows, I did not exactly do it the way LEEWS says to. Partly, that's because I wanted to "flag" each issue. This would let the prof see at a glance that I'd spotted the hidden issue/s about bailments, and would make a good first impression. Nor did I do it exactly the way Delaney recommends. He says to put the conclusion at the beginning of the answer. As Chapter 6 said, I strongly disagree with that. So I used the LEEWS approach and put the conclusion at the end of each section.

A Suggested Answer

1. THE BAILMENTS ISSUE

First, we must distinguish between those who provided eggs and sperm to Dr. Creamcheese as BAILMENTS, and those who provided them as "goods" SOLD to her.

1-A. There was a BAILMENT as to SOME "Donors"

The elements of a bailment are: 1) Physical delivery (usually) of the item by the bailor to the bailee for a particular purpose, 2) bailee's intent to exercise physical control over the item, and actual exercise of such control, and 3) an express or implied understanding that the goods will be returned.

Couples or individuals who sought in vitro fertilization for *their* benefit delivered the respective items to Dr. Creamcheese with the expectation that they would receive a fertilized egg that would be implanted—i.e., a return of the "goods." There was physical delivery, and Dr. Creamcheese, as bailee, had intent to exercise physical control and did exercise physical control. (A bailment can arise without payment for it. So the fact that the cost of storing the fertilized eggs was "built into the fees" the clinic charged is irrelevant.)

Couples or women who received an implant of a fertilized egg could also authorize destruction of the fertilized eggs that came from *them*. Thus, the issue is whether this is really a bailment, because there was not necessarily an expectation of a return of ALL the goods—i.e., fertilized eggs that were not implanted. However, arguably the test of a bailment has been met to a sufficient degree to call this a bailment.

Jimmy Carlyle Black & Valarie, plus Aybea Sea, as well as some members of the class of persons whose names are unknown at this point (and who meet the test described above) are bailors, not sellers.

1-B. BAILORS v. Dr. Creamcheese

The transfer from Dr. Creamcheese to Dweezle, of the bailors' fertilized eggs, was wrongful, outside the scope of the bailment agreement. It was knowing, and deliberate, and part of a commercial transaction between Dr. Creamcheese and Dweezle. The intentional nature of Dr. Creamcheese's act is amply demonstrated by her deceit, when she told Jimmy Carlyle Black & Valarie, and Aybea Sea, that their fertilized eggs still in storage had been accidentally destroyed, when in fact they had been sold to Dweezle. The facts suggest that she also deceived others. Dr. Creamcheese is liable to the bailors who had not signed a "release for destruction" (Jimmy Carlyle Black & Valarie, and Aybea Sea, etc.), and—per 1-D—perhaps to *all* the bailors for the intentional tort of conversion.

There is no need to discuss the levels of negligence required for a bailee to be held liable in tort based on who gains the primary benefit from the bailment, because here there was no negligence, just an intentional act.

1-C. EGG & SPERM "Donor"-SELLERS
Third parties who acted as isolated individuals provided eggs or sperm to Dr. Creamcheese as a sale of goods to her. The releases signed by the donors of the sperm and egg donors make it clear that these were not bailments, and that the providers relinquished all interest in the items provided.

There is a contracts issue of "fraud in the inducement." It is possible these sellers would not have sold had they known the eggs and sperm were not going to be implanted by Dr. Creamcheese but might instead be resold by her to others who would resell them yet again. However, this does not come under the law of property, but of contracts.

These third-party sellers, because they are not bailors, have no cause of action sounding in property law against Dr. Creamcheese, Dweezle, nor against end-users who purchased fertilized eggs from Dweezle.

1-D. The "ABANDONMENT" DEFENSE
The facts suggest that Dr. Creamcheese did sell to Dweezle some fertilized eggs for which she had a "release to destroy" from the providers. (This assumes the fertilized eggs came from the woman in whom they were to be implanted. See 1-C, above, when the case is otherwise.)

Abandonment is 1) a physical abandoning of personal property, combined with 2) the intent to abandon it.

Dr. Creamcheese might argue that the "release" for destruction is different from an ORDER for destruction. The release was a tacit abandonment of the fertilized eggs, and she therefore had the right to their ownership (and to sell them to Dweezle).

Normally, however, "abandonment" is used in relation to one who *finds* the abandoned property. Dr. Creamcheese did not "find" the fertilized eggs.

She might argue that this is like the abandonment that occurs when a patient's diseased or damaged organ is removed and then used for medical research. *That* abandonment is tantamount to a *gift*—to medical science. But the "released" eggs were not to be used for medical research. And the very fact that Dr. Creamcheese apparently never disclosed, to any of her patients, that she might *sell* some of their fertilized eggs to Dweezle is a tacit admission on her part that she knew the women involved would quite likely forbid it (or else would have demanded their "cut"!).

Further, the bailors would argue that Dr. Creamcheese had in effect been appointed as the *agent* of the original providers, for the purpose of *destroying* the eggs, and had no discretion to do otherwise. (A property owner—usually—has the right to destroy his or her own property, and can authorize a third party to destroy it without the owner's regaining possession before the destruction.) But, given what this "property" involved, Dr. Creamcheese was not given *discretion* to destroy the fertilized eggs (and certainly not to sell them).

The claims against Dr. Creamcheese by those who had "released for destruction" the fertilized eggs that they'd originally intended to be reimplanted in *them*, will "turn" on whether the court construes a "release" for destruction as an "order" for destruction. It is likely to do so, given the nature of the "property" involved. Dr. Creamcheese already had a conflict of interest re her patients' fertilized eggs. To interpret the "release" as anything other than an *order* would be to reinforce that conflict of interest.

Social policy is crucial here. A *fertilized egg* is not in the same category as a removed organ. If implanted and carried to term, it will be a human being who walks the face of the earth. Thus, a couple whose own sperm and egg have been united in vitro have now placed their own potential children in Dr. Creamcheese's hands.

Thus, Dr. Creamcheese's "abandonment" defense will almost certainly fail.

1-E. BAILORS v. Dweezle
1) Damages for Wrongful Purchase

Ordinarily, a bailee cannot defeat the rights of the bailor by transferring to a bona fide purchaser (BFP). However, if the bailee is a DEALER in goods of that kind, even if the transfer is wrongful, the bailor cannot recover from the BFP. The issue is whether Dr. Creamcheese was a dealer in goods of that kind. The facts state that for years, she had accepted eggs and sperm (whether from those seeking implants or from those selling eggs and sperm) for use only to provide fertilized egg implants to HER women patients. Although the facts do not say exactly how short-lived her practice was of selling them to Dweezle, it apparently had not been going on long. Further, the facts strongly suggest that there was no established "industry" of the buying and selling of fertilized eggs on the open market or in exclusive, on-going supplier-purchaser commercial relationships. Therefore, the idea of a "dealer" in these goods was a novelty. Dweezle was clearly aware of that, because the very idea of selling fertilized eggs on the open market was apparently HIS brainchild, and thus HE CREATED this "infant industry" (pun intended).

So Dweezle is not a BFP, because Dr. Creamcheese is not one of many "dealers" in "goods of this kind" for purposes of Dweezle's avoiding liability.

He is also not a BFP because, given the (shocking) novelty of selling fertilized eggs on the open market, then, under the "reasonable person" standard, he was "on notice" that he should have investigated the provenance of the fertilized eggs rather than buying them "no questions asked." The "bona fide" part of "bona fide purchaser" literally means "good faith." Dweezle did not purchase in good faith with regard to the provenance of the "goods."

He would argue that he trusted Dr. Creamcheese to be selling him only those fertilized eggs that she allegedly had authorization to destroy. However, his request for "extra eggs" arguably indicated his desire to obtain more "product," regardless of the circumstances.

Given that the frozen eggs were actually conceived members of the human species, that is all the more reason for one who desires to sell fertilized eggs to inquire into their provenance—and with the utmost scrupulousness. Dweezle did not do this. His way of doing business as to his source for Viagra suggests a lack of conscientiousness.

Unless the abandonment argument prevails against *some* bailors, *all* those who provided items as bailments to Dr. Creamcheese—the unnamed class members, Jimmy Carlyle Black & Valarie, and Aybea Sea—will prevail against Dweezle.

2) Constructive Bailment

Equitably, because Dweezle was not a BFP, he could be held to have entered into a "constructive bailment," acting as a subsidiary bailee for Dr. Creamcheese on behalf of the bailors, and holding the fertilized eggs "in trust." An injunctive action to replevin the unsold inventory, and an action in trover seeking damages against him for conversion (regarding fertilized eggs that have been implanted), would then prevail for Jimmy Carlyle Black & Valarie, and Aybea Sea, etc.

1-F. BAILORS v. WOWIE & ZOWIE and other END-USER PURCHASERS ("Users")

Dweezle was not intentionally a bailee with regard to the fertilized eggs. He was a merchant who had purchased the fertilized eggs from Dr. Creamcheese, for resale. To repeat: given the (shocking) novelty of selling fertilized eggs on the open market, other Users were, under the "reasonable person" standard, "on notice" that they should have investigated the provenance of the fertilized eggs rather than buying them "no questions asked." The Certificate of Authenticity apparently means nothing more than that the goods sold are fertilized human eggs capable of gestating to term. Arguably, then, the Users are not BFPs, and thus are liable to the bailors (except those, if any, against whom the "abandonment" argument succeeds). If the bailors can access the records of Dr. Creamcheese and Dweezle, they could trace the path of their eggs and sperm to the ultimate end-users of fertilized eggs, and sue them as individuals. Then they could either recover damages in an action for trover (if implanting had already occurred—such as with Wowie) or secure an injunction under re-plevin (for the return of unimplanted fertilized eggs—as with Zowie). But, per 1-C, the egg and sperm *sellers* have NO cause of action.

Further, if Dweezle is held to have a "constructive bailment" and to be holding the fertilized eggs "in trust," then he is a sub-bailee to Dr. Creamcheese. This breaks the Users' potential argument to claim the status of what might be called "holders in due course," and makes it easier to undermine their claim to BFP status.

2. NEIGHBORS v. Dr. Creamcheese
2-A.   RUNNING COVENANTS

The case involves a negative covenant a.k.a restriction. It would be either a "covenant running with the land" (in law) or an "equitable servitude" (in equity). The two are lumped together by some commentators as "running covenants" or "servitudes," and the trend in the courts is to treat them as the same. But there is still a difference in many juris-dictions.

They have two elements in common: 1) The provi-sion in question must "touch and concern the land." ALL courts have held that a restriction to "single family residences" touches and concerns the land, so that element is satisfied here. 2) There is an "intent to bind" successors in interest.

This is probably not a covenant running with the land (at law). To be so, courts generally require a Declaration of Covenant/s in the deed, as proof of "intent to bind." The Zappas' deed did not have one. However, some courts have held that a subdivision plat filed by the developer can satisfy the recording requirement of a covenant running with the land (at law), in part because of the rules for proof of "intent to bind successors." Young Pumpkin Estates is a development, and presumably there was a plat filed. So there is a fact question as to exactly what writing is on the plat Moon Unit filed.

Moreover, the third element of a covenant running with the land at law involves "privity," both "horizontal" (as between the original owners) and "vertical" (as between the original covenanter and a subsequent owner who acquired ALL of the original owner's interest). Dr. Creamcheese did not buy her house from the developer (Moon Unit), but from the Zappas—who might or might not have bought from Moon Unit. So, she does not have horizontal privity such as would make this a covenant running with the land (at law).

The argument of the privities can be thorny, and could make the plaintiffs vulnerable here. It would be easier to analyze this as an equitable servitude—in part because it appears that the neighbors are seeking only injunctive relief, not monetary damages. (Monetary damages are usually not available in a suit in equity.)

The third element of an equitable servitude, in contrast, is notice—either actual, "constructive," or "inquiry." It appears Dr. Creamcheese did not have actual notice, because the Zappas' deed omitted the covenant. However, she probably had constructive notice because she was in a development formally designated as Young Pumpkin Estates, and probably was aware that the Homeowners Association existed (because she was likely paying dues to it and receiving a newsletter) before it sued her. A stronger argument under "constructive notice" was the existence of the zoning law restricting the area to single family dwellings. Even if she was not aware of the law, her ignorance is no defense. The same thing is true regarding the Moon Unit's plat on file in the recording office, if the court accepts that as proof. Dr. Creamcheese also had "inquiry" notice, which falls under the "reasonable person" standard. In part, this is again because she lived in a development that had its own official name:

Young Pumpkin Estates, and she could easily see that it was "part of a common scheme," and that all the buildings in it (apparently) were houses and were used only as single family units, not as apartment houses or businesses. There were "implied reciprocal restrictions," even if she was not aware of that legal term of art. A reasonable person would say that Dr. Creamcheese's alleged ignorance of the restriction was willful and self-serving, and thus no defense.

2-B. Dr. Creamcheese's possible defenses

The first is "laches." Under laches, she could argue that she had been using her house as a place of business for some time, and her neighbors knew of and had acquiesced in that use, and are suing now only because of the publicity. However, the laches defense is good only against a FIRST complaint. Once the complaint has been made, laches is not available as a defense against complaints regarding subsequent violations of the restriction. So laches is no defense against an injunction seeking to bar further use of her house as a clinic.

Dr. Creamcheese's second possible defense is "relative hardship." But this only applies in situations where a building owner is on the MARGIN of an area with restrictions and is on the border with ANOTHER area that has no such restrictions. Thus, it is argued, the building on the edge is not clearly a part of the restricted area and thus is not openly and notoriously in violation of the area's restrictions. There are no facts to support that here. A further argument against this is that Creamcheese is a medical doctor with a practice that is apparently lucrative. She can easily afford to establish her clinic in a building outside Young Pumpkin Estates. She could continue to live in her house and thus the house would not lose its value to her as a result of having to move her clinic out.

Her final potential defense is the best: this cause of action could well "turn" on whether or not the restriction specifically says that the houses can ONLY be used for single family residences and for NO OTHER PURPOSE, or whether the restriction is worded to suggest that the only RESIDENTIAL purpose of the houses is as single family residences.

Dr. Creamcheese's clinic is discreet. The facts suggest that there is no signage in front, nor a parking lot on her property. The volume of visitors to her clinic is apparently quite low. (All of this, of course, helps account for the previous lack of protests from the neighbors.)

By analogy, an investments advisor with a select, short list of clients ought to be allowed to work "from home" if his or her work involves only occasional face-to-face meetings with those clients. Likewise, a book editor who only occasionally meets with writers whose works he or she is editing. (But then again, such persons do not convert an entire floor—*half*—of a two-story dwelling into what can only be used for business purposes, as Dr. Creamcheese did here.) If the case law says that a restriction such as the one here MUST say EXPRESSLY that a single-family dwelling house can only be used for RESIDENTIAL purposes, then this "loophole" might allow Dr. Creamcheese to prevail. However, the neighbors would argue that visitor traffic has increased, and is likely to increase further still.

It is highly likely that the neighbors will prevail, in light of all the facts here.

3. THE "TAKINGS" ISSUE

The "takings" claim is not colorable, especially with respect to the fertilized eggs. "Takings" is a form of inverse condemnation, brought by a property owner, rather than the usual condemnation proceeding, which is brought by the government. It concerns only REAL ESTATE, not PERSONAL property. Further, the statute banning the sale of fertilized eggs is CRIMINAL in nature (a "felony"), and is outside the scope of a takings case. The law regarding regulatory takings is not implicated here.

It is not necessary to rule on the constitutionality of the statute, as legislation should be interpreted to avoid raising constitutional issues whenever possible, and there is no need to do so here, as no constitutional issues are implicated in the first place, with respect to PROPERTY law.

The criminal nature of the prohibition is similar to the law that made it illegal to possess or distribute cocaine. At the time, one of the key ingredients of Coca-Cola was a form of cocaine. (Hence, the name "Coca"-Cola, as cocaine is from the coca plant.) There was no "taking" of Coca-Cola's property, as a matter of law. Nor is there here, given the criminal nature of most of this statute.

Even if this were a purely regulatory, civil statute, this rule is permissible. The banning of the sale of fertilized eggs is arguably similar to a ban on the sale of clothing and bedding for very young children that is not fire-retardant, as a health and safety measure—which regulation destroyed the value of many firms' inventories. But the government is not required to compensate property-owners each and every time government action diminishes (or even destroys) the value of their property—even realty, let alone chattel. The regulation here effected a "legitimate state interest," and would be invalid only if it were "palpably without a legitimate foundation." The burden is on the challenger to the regulation. Here, the challengers would not likely succeed.

4. "HOSPITALS ONLY"

It is unclear whether the "hospitals only" law is part of the criminal statute discussed in #3 above.

Regardless, the law regarding "takings" is irrelevant to the requirement that all "fertility work" be done in an accredited hospital, because "takings" law only applies to real property, not to the right to earn one's living in a particular setting. There are no facts here to suggest that the regulation severely diminishes or destroys the value of Dr. Creamcheese's house as a HOUSE, which would be the only basis for a claim under the law of "takings."

Final Commentary
on
This Exam Problem

This is the first time I've answered an exam problem since I was in law school. So, I'd not been practicing the LEEWS "Ugly But Effective" writing method. You should—regularly. (Just remember, it's a method of organizing your thoughts while *preparing* for an exam, and *not* a method of writing out your answer on the real thing.) As you can probably tell, I took longer than the time I'd allotted myself for writing out the answer. But then again, this was a *practice* answer. As such, it was a *learning tool*. Were I still in law school, and had I been practicing the UBE method, it would have been possible, I think, to write more concisely and to cover the same ground within the 40 minutes I allocated. Also, because this answer is appearing in a book, I tried to make it at least somewhat "polished." In an answer to a real "live" exam, you would never do that, because it would take too much time. Substance is far more important than style. "Quick and dirty" and *thorough* beats slow and elegant and *incomplete* any day. —**And had I been answering this exam as a law student, I definitely would have set aside time to check my work and correct careless errors, ambiguities, etc.**

What I have provided here is a generic answer. On a real exam, this answer would be customized for the prof. Throughout the semester, I perhaps would have checked any published writings of the prof in the area of property, to see if there's anything that would alert me to what might be on the exam, or to what the prof's preferred line of thinking is on something. And, of course, I would have tried to pick up on any clues the prof provided in class, whether the clues were intentional or not.

I of course was not sitting in on the student's classes. I do not even know what casebook the professor had assigned. It's possible that I am wrong in some of my comments on the student's proposed answer. Or, perhaps the prof treats "takings" as somehow applying to personal property. (Or, for that matter, maybe my understanding of the law is wrong, and it *does* apply to personal property, though I think otherwise.) It's also possible that he regards a criminal law as being a regulatory law, or, again, that my understanding of the law is wrong and a regulatory law can be a criminal law. (Normally, a regulatory statute carries a fine with it, so it appears to be somehow criminal in nature. It is not, though. It is possible to have a fine even under a strict liability regulatory statute—no "mens rea" required, and mens rea is one of the required elements of a criminal act.)

What the prof wants trumps LEEWS, Delaney, the primers...anything. If the prof who gave this exam wanted elements stated in a certain way, then that's the way you state them, rather than using the wording in a commercial outline. Likewise, if the prof apparently wants a particular way of doing a "lawyerlike analysis."

There are even some professors who say "I don't want to see any Black Letter Law in your answer." They are being highly disingenuous. What they invariably mean is they don't want to see legal jargon or a presentation of the elements (all together) of a cause of action or defense.

So, say the prof here had said "No Black Letter Law." Then, for example, under 1-A in the bailments discussion, you'd *leave out* this: "The elements of a bailment are: 1) Physical delivery (usually) of the item by the bailor to the bailee for a particular purpose, 2) bailee's intent to exercise physical control over the item, and actual exercise of such control, and 3) an express or implied understanding that the goods will be returned."

Instead, you'd go into a discussion of each element, without *calling* it an element. For example, "People who did not *sell* their eggs to Dr. Creamcheese provided sperm and unfertilized eggs to her to be combined into fertilized eggs and to then be reimplanted in the women who provided those eggs. Dr. Creamcheese had physical control over these items, and both intended to have that control and did exercise that control in the process of creating fertilized eggs." *Et cetera*. In other words, you go straight to the step of what Delaney calls the "interweaving of facts" with the relevant law...but without using legal jargon, in this case. Check the prof's old exams with model answers, though. See if the instructions say "No Black Letter Law," and then see if the *model answer* does indeed avoid legal jargon, elements, etc. There's no point in being "played for a sucker" on this one.

You might have noticed that I skimped on privity, under 2-A. If it had become obvious (during class discussion or based on the amount of reading the prof assigned on the topic) that "privity" was important to this prof, I would have learned it better and then discussed it more in my answer, instead of skipping over it so lightly.

Throughout the answer, I "led with the facts." Issues arise from facts. Facts determine the outcome of issues, because the facts—with lawyers trying to "spin" them to bring them under one set of legal principles or another—determine what legal principles apply. As mentioned, this is what Delaney calls the "interweaving" process. It is very important.

Also, I brought in some stuff from the "real world," such as the part about the cocaine in Coca-Cola, or the analogy about investment advisors or editors working "from home." This is okay, as long as you use it only for the purposes of *illustration* or *analogy*...which I did. But those "outside facts" ought to be known to the prof too, to enhance the credibility of the illustration or analogy. They're what Josephson referred to in his discussion of "arguing by analogy."

Notice also that I hedged wherever I thought I could get away with it. That's why you see words like "usually," "generally," "the facts suggest," "apparently," "presumably," "probably," and "arguably." I hoped this provided some "wiggle room" when I was making some reasonable inferences. These would perhaps get me the benefit of any doubts in the prof's mind, regarding possible exceptions or counter-arguments. It also saved time, though, by not having to spell things out with regard to the point in question, when the point was not a major one.

I did not use legal terms such as *"infra,"* *"supra,"* or *"arguendo,"* despite the advice of LEEWS to do so, because that can be seen as a "gimmick"—one that can backfire on you. But I did use appropriate legal terms wherever possible, such as saying something was "no defense" rather than "no excuse," or using "chattel" instead of "personal property," or referring to a claim as "colorable."

Under 1-B, a short paragraph discussed how the level of care required is irrelevant because Dr. Creamcheese's tort was intentional rather than one of negligence. (A discussion involving torts would normally be out of place on a property exam. But the tort of conversion straddles torts and property, and belonged in the bailments discussion here.) This was included to impress the prof that I knew about it, and that I recognized it was irrelevant and why. That could be a way to pick up a quick and easy extra point or two on the score. Same thing regarding the quick discussion under 1-A of the irrelevance of the fact that the cost of storage was built in to the fees charged patients rather than billed separately.

Remember: *do not omit showing* that an element is proven or disproven by the facts at hand, just because it's *obvious*. That is one of the biggest mistakes on exams by first-year students. As Chapter 6 put it: "connect *all* the dots, to make the figure."

I do not have any commercial outlines. The discussion in my answer is based on reading the relevant sections in the Aspen E&E primer on property by Barlow Burke and Joseph A. Snoe, and in the West primer, *The Law of Property: An Introductory Survey,* 5th ed., by Ralph E. Boyer, Herbert Hovenkamp, and Sheldon F. Kurtz. And for the discussion of servitudes, I also used *A Student's Guide to Easements, Real Covenants and Equitable Servitudes,* by Stephen A. Siegel (part of the "Student Guide Series," from Matthew Bender). As you know from Chapters 2 amd 4, I highly recommend these primers.

You should know all this stuff cold. And, as mentioned in Chapter 4, you should have created a "Summary Outline" that you would reproduce on scratch paper before the exam is handed out (if that's allowed). An open-book exam would not really have been helpful here, because you would lose too much time looking up stuff.

I spent less than an hour trying to "get up to speed" on the relevant law, *in lieu* of having just spent most of a semester in a Prop course. So, my analysis might be "off" in places. If anyone sees more conflict pairings, issues, etc., or disagrees with my analysis (either of the student's answer or of what's in my own), please e-mail me. If there is sufficient interest, it will be posted to the website.

Note: Egg "Donors" v. Sellers

My proposed answer distinguished true egg "donors" from those who *sold* their eggs to Dr. Creamcheese. However, the December, 2002 *Atlantic Monthly* had an article, "Grade A: The Market for a Yale Woman's Eggs," by Jessica Cohen. It said the term "donor" is used even for those who sell eggs.

But I stand by the distinction. The legal position of *true* donors is different from that of "donors" who are really sellers. Noting the distinction, and discussing the different legal positions, gets you more points, despite the fact that the word "donors" is used in the market-place to describe both sources of eggs.

And this distinction touches on a crucial difference between essay exams and multiple-choice. Because this was an essay exam, my proposed answer could make the distinction by exploiting the hidden ambiguity of the term. Even if the prof was not looking for it, the prof would not be annoyed. (Quite the contrary, most likely.) But that distinction would not have been possible by just "bubbling in" one of several multiple-choice answers. A student would have no choice but to assume that "donors" applied to both groups of suppliers. That's another reason why, when going beyond the mere mastery of terms and definitions, essay exams are the only *appropriate* "test instrument" in law school.

Old Exam as Source of Hypos

Suppose Dr. Creamcheese extracted eggs from women, and those eggs would then be fertilized by sperm from the respective woman's husband or "significant other." But suppose Dr. Creamcheese fertilized only *some* of those extracted eggs with the sperm of the husband or significant other—and (unbeknownst to the couple) fertilized the rest with sperm from males who'd *sold* it to her. If Dr. Creamcheese then segregated the former from the latter, and never sold the former to Dweezle but did sell him the latter, how would this affect the analysis?

Likewise, what if Dr. Creamcheese used *some* of the sperm from the husbands/"significant others" to fertilize the "bailment" eggs, but used the *rest* of the sperm from the husbands/S.O.s to fertilize eggs *sold* to her? (Given that it's a lot easier to get sperm than eggs, this example seems really farfetched. But then again, the sperm source might have been an Olympic decathlon medalist who was also a rocket scientist. Many women might be willing to pay dearly to have such a guy get into their genes.)

And would the potential claims of the *women* who supplied eggs for implanting into their own bodies be different from the potential claims of their husbands/significant others, after the eggs had been fertilized and sold to Dweezle?

Another wrinkle: the fact pattern mentioned that some women who were married or in a committed relationship privately instructed Dr. Creamcheese to *not* fertilize *some* of their extracted eggs, in case the current marriage or relationship did not work out. If a woman later signed a "release for destruction" of those *un*fertilized eggs, how would that affect the analysis?

And one more: What if Dr. Creamcheese did not sell Dweezle any *fertilized* eggs, but only shipped him sperm and *unfertilized* eggs, and Dweezle then hired *others* to fertilize the eggs supplied with the sperm that was also supplied? And what if he only bought unfertilized *eggs* and then used his *own* sperm to fertilize them? (This last is not as "far out" as it sounds. There was a highly publicized case where a "fertility doctor" was treating "barren" married women via artificial insemination. He obtained sperm from their husbands. But that's not the sperm he inserted into the men's wives during the artificial insemination procedures. Instead, he used his own. Truth is stranger than law school exam fact patterns—even the fact pattern in this one.)

All these possibilities move farther and farther afield from property law, though (into torts, contracts, and—with the last—even into family law, i.e., paternity actions)...which is probably why the prof who wrote this exam problem did not "go there." But unlike "live" exams (where you should stick to what the course is about), hypos allow you to cut across the categories of the law...as is often the case in the real world. So, it's good practice in what might be called—especially given the nature of *this* exam problem—"cross-fertilization."

The Mystique, and the Tragedy

In his wonderful book, *On Writing: A Memoir of the Craft,* Stephen King says something about how you either have it (talent), or you don't. However, he doesn't let it go at that. Instead, he distinguishes among *incompetent, competent, good,* and *great* writers (if I remember right). And he says that if you don't have the basic minimal talent to even be competent, there's nothing to be done for you. But he says that if you have enough raw talent at least to achieve basic competence, you can go on from there and become a good writer, if you work at it. But if you do not have the enormous raw talent for greatness to start with, you will never be able to go from being good to being great, as a writer.

I believe the same thing applies to trial lawyers, for what that's worth. More important, I believe it applies to law students. Yet, it seems to me that anyone who's able to get into law school in the first place has enough raw ability to achieve at least basic competence. And most can go from being competent to being good.

However, the professoriat doesn't see it that way. They're looking only for greatness. That's all they value. And, of course, they fancy that they themselves had the raw talent for greatness all along.

One of the great tragedies of law school is that the professoriat would rather enhance the Mystique of the Law than try to *help* students become at least *competent* law students (and competent future attorneys). At least 75% of all first-year students fail to achieve competence, even though they're among the 99.9% who pass their courses. Most students don't ever get any good. They just get by.

Meanwhile, the professors—like the Medieval monks who fattened on the offerings of the peasants in the surrounding countryside and the largesse of wealthy benefactors who were worried about getting into heaven—have long betrayed their moral obligations to society in general, and to their students in particular. They are an unworthy elite.

Fear

Some of those who read this chapter in manuscript, and who are not yet in law school, said they were intimidated by my suggested answer in contrast to the student's proposed answer. They said they would have been proud if they could have even come up with something approaching the student's answer. One of the people who read this chapter was convinced, at first, that law school would be just too difficult.

I am not exaggerating when I tell you that my suggested answer was all just *"baby stuff."* I do not practice in Property Law, and have never had a case even remotely related to what's in this exam problem. Nearly all of my suggested answer came "off the top of my head," although I did then check the reference materials mentioned. What makes it seem to you, perhaps, to be such a great accomplishment, maybe even a dazzling display of analysis, is that this is all so completely new to you. But any *high school* student of fairly good intelligence could have come up with at least 90% of what I did, after reading the appropriate primers and practicing his or her examsmanship skills.

In his book, *How to Argue and Win Every Time*, Gerry Spence (perhaps the greatest trial lawyer in America) wrote:

> This fear that so disables us—how do we deal with it? I feel it squalling in my belly whenever I stand up in the courtroom to begin an argument. I feel it whenever I begin the cross-examination of an important expert witness who is armed with a much greater knowledge of the subject than I. Will I fail? Will I be seen as incompetent?

Then, a bit later, he says:

> **THE KEY: Fear is our ally. Fear confirms us. Fear is *energy* that is convertible to power —our power.**
> [Boldface in the original, italics added.]

Fear is a big part of what drove me as I worked on this manuscript: fear of not writing well; fear of leaving out something important you need to know; fear of leaving out any of the wonderful tips and insights that so many people have shared with me, or of leaving out my response to thought-provoking questions or criticisms that have come in since the original edition; fear of making a mistake in a name, a date, a quotation, a citation, a point of law, or even of misspelling or misusing a word; and above all, fear of failing to get through to you.

Spence is right: while fear is a source of determination to do everything possible to avoid failure, it is also a source of immense energy.

Put your fear to work for you—and, as Wentworth Miller likes to say, you might reach a point where you are *looking forward* to your exams...a great *opportunity*, to go for the gold and win it.

I hope you see the suggested answer as a challenge, not as something intimdating. And I can promise you that if you work "The *PLS* Approach" conscientiously, you'll be able to do an answer to this fruitcake problem that's *at least* as good as mine—while you're still in your first-year Property course.

Remember when you first learned to ride a bicycle? But once you'd "gotten the hang of it" you perhaps looked back on the learning process and wondered why it ever seemed so hard. The same thing is true in examsmanship.

The law school mystique is hype. *You have what it takes to do well.* It's just a matter of following through (but in the *right* way)—and of having a little bit of luck by (1) not having a class where *all* the students followed through the right way (and thus merely shifted the grading curve to the right), and (2) not having a *truly* "wacko" professor who has no interest in your ability to do a lawyerlike analysis and who instead gives you an exam that's *truly* "off the wall."

I responded to the student who'd sent me the exam problem and proposed answer, and provided my suggested answer. Fortunately, he'd contacted me with sufficient time left in the semester to "clean up his act"—not just in Property law, but in all his courses (because doing a good lawyerlike analysis cuts across the curriculum).

During the summer of 2002, I heard from him again, for the first time since the fall semester of 2001. He'd done quite well on all his exams, and had graded on to Law Review (and this at a well-respected school). He now intends to seek a judicial clerkship with a federal appellate judge.

I'd like to end this chapter by saying "Good luck!" —But it really shouldn't be a matter of luck. Not for you. This Part I has now pointed you in the right direction. It's up to you to make the journey...on your own.

You *can* do it.

Part II:

The View from the Ivory Tower

Chapter 8 - The Walrus & the Carpenter

Normally, I do not comment on specific published advice that I disagree with on "How to succeed in law school." However, readers of my column that was on the internet in 2001 called my attention to two items, and asked me to comment on them. The first appears to be a piece original to the internet. The second is an article from a law review, and the article was also posted to the 'net.

The following is a revised version of the review I posted to my column in two parts, on July 3 and 5, 2001, regarding the first item.

"Understanding Law School"
by Prof. Kenneth W. Graham, Jr.
http://www.casenotes.com/uls.html

Graham is identified as a full professor at UCLA's law school. Reportedly, he is quite popular with the students.

He starts out right-on, by stressing the difference between "learning the rules" and "acquiring skills."

But he soon veers into la-la land. He suggests that you ask yourself "How should I define success?" (in law school). He indicates that there really is no such thing as a one-size-fits-all definition of "success." What's important is to "define it in terms of things you can control rather than those that are in the laps of the gods..." For some, "success" could mean "studying 10 hours on Saturday."

This appears to be part of the "self esteem" movement that has swept the country at lower levels of academe. It used to be that "the power of positive thinking" could be used to help people achieve their goals. But evidently that was not good enough, because too many people did not succeed. (*Reality* might have something to do with that.) Now the "Feel Good about Yourself" school of thought urges us to pretend we have *already* achieved a worthwhile goal, even if other people are not impressed by the achievement of that "goal." No one should ever have to feel inadequate in any area where he or she wants to feel *adequate*. So a way has to be found to "put a good face on it" when the aspirant is obviously less than successful.

Thus, presumably, if your first-year grades don't turn out so well, by all means smile and look the interviewer from the law firm right in the eye and say, with sincerity, "My first year in law school was very successful. I studied 10 hours every Saturday." Hey, who knows? Maybe he or she will buy it. (Ten ours a day is too much, by the way.)

As for acquiring skills, Graham recommends that you "keep time sheets." Honest. "Go through your daily time sheets at the end of each week and 'bill' each professor for the time you spent studying for each class and 'bill' yourself for the rest." Graham says this habit will keep you from spending too much time on a subject just because you enjoy it more than the others, when you need to spend more time on the others. However, I have a feeling that anyone who's gotten good enough grades to get into law school does not need to do timesheets to know if he or she needs to spend more time on certain subjects.

Hey, again, who knows? That "skill" might *really* help you on your final exams. And maybe your interviewer from the law firm will offer you a job on the spot because you already have so much experience in filling out timesheets. (However, timesheets at law firms, of course, are used for the purpose of billing clients. Thus, they bring money into the firm. Further, new associates' value to the firm is determined in large part by their timesheets. So they put money into the *associates'* pockets, too. In other words, the time lawyers spend doing timesheets is well worth it. But given the time crunch on law students, is it really worthwhile to do timesheets in law school?)

Graham's next tip is "Know the Enemy." He is referring to your professors. He says it is very important to understand each prof's politics and especially his or her values. And to do that, he suggests you "read or skim any books or articles the professor has written."

But as Graham well knows, what's on at least 90% of all law professors' final exams is Black Letter Law, not the prof's politics or values. Yes, it is a good idea to read or skim books or articles the professor has written. But the reason for that is to spot the professor's pet topics within the subject matter of the course. Yes, it also helps to know the prof's politics or values. But if you've prepped for law school, you will easily be able to pick up on your prof's concerns and biases, even the subtle ones, in class. That's because you'll already know the subject fairly well, and can concentrate on listening for the nuances, including the prof's idiosyncrasies. Granted, a law review article might present something the professor has not disclosed in class, such as a line of thought you can raise in an answer on your exam. However, most students have not gotten the head start of "The *PLS* Approach." They cannot afford to spend much time on this outside reading, trying to "psych out" their profs. But even those who do will find that sucking up by being "politically correct" on your finals will not get you the grade you want, if you've not done the *basics:* a good lawyerlike analysis based on Black Letter Law. Icing is not cake.

As for study aids, Graham largely dismisses them. "Their nostrums range from flashcards to computer programs, from songs you can sing in the shower to weekend seminars in flea-bag hotels." He says most are proffered by "well-meaning quacks or fast-buck artists."

Yet, Graham says he has not "tried" *any* of them. Of course, as a law professor, he no longer needs to try them. But the effect of his dismissal is that, as far as his readers can tell, the Aspen primers, the CALI "Library of Lessons," Delaney's books, and LEEWS are no better than all the rest. (*PLS*, however—as you've seen—contains *highly recommended* items, after I evaluated nearly every study aid I could find.) Graham is more subtle than to come right out and say "Don't use study aids," but the effect of his words is the same...and is insidious.

Ironically, Graham's commentary appears on the website of Casenotes, a publisher of commercial outlines for law students. And Graham himself is the author of an outline for Casenotes. Seems to me the phrase, "Watch what I do, not what I say" is relevant here. Or does he regard commercial outlines as being something *other* than study aids? In fact, Graham puts "commercial outlines" under a separate subhead, much later in his paper. There, he says they serve two purposes: (1) to provide a ready-made outline for students who "don't have time" to make their own personal outlines, and (2) to provide what he calls a "second opinion" on each topic in the course, so the student who has made a personal outline can check his or her understanding. I agree with the second point. But it seems both purposes mean the commercial outline is a study aid.

Letting the Cat out of the Bag

Under the subheading "Preparing for Law School Exams," Graham writes: "A sage once observed that legal education resembles the method used to induce schizophrenia in laboratory mice; namely, you train them to run the maze in one way, then abruptly change the goal. *All semester, law students are told that rules are not important and are rewarded for making oral arguments, then on final examinations, they are expected to memorize a bunch of rules and make good written arguments.*" (Emphasis added.)

Mind you, he is not apologizing for that. In fact, he cheerily states it as a given. **His words are just about the clearest possible admission one could ask for, regarding the hypocrisy, and even the duplicity, of law school professors.** And it comes straight from the horse's...uh...mouth. Yet, even here, Graham's interest in the truth is open to question.

How are students "rewarded" for making oral arguments in class? Surely Graham knows that the term "oral argument" normally refers to the oral argument that occurs in appellate advocacy. Surely he also knows that the "oral arguments" he refers to as occurring in class have nothing to do with the oral arguments of appellate advocacy. His choice of that term appears to be equivocation, giving the impression that class discussion involves acquiring a skill that will be useful in appellate advocacy.

And does Graham seriously maintain that students' grades really have any component for "class participation"—and that students can improve their final grade by showing skill in class discussion?) See the addendum to Chapter 9.) And on what basis would students be showing their "skill," anyway? Graham has just admitted that the "rules" (i.e. Black Letter Law and the policies behind it) are ignored throughout the semester. These "oral arguments" sound more like the sort of "bull sessions" that typically occur at lower levels of academe.

It's disturbing that a law professor would speak of Black Letter Law (although he does not use that term) only as "a bunch of rules" to "memorize." It's worth noting, too, that he says that this memorization is to occur *"on"* final exams. Not "in time for," but "on," the meaning of which suggests *"during."* That is impossible, of course.

What goes on, and what Graham has just admitted occurs, is called "bait and switch," out in the real world. Ordinary merchants get sued for this, under laws against consumer fraud. But to the merchants in the "unreal" world of the ivory tower of the law, it's standard operating procedure, year in and year out. They have no fear of being called to account for it, because all law school students accept it as a "given." Those who do well (and eventually rise to positions of power within the profession) love it, of course. Those who did not do well keep quiet for fear of being humiliated (and the law school professors make sure their students know the sting of being humiliated, so the students will never again want to be humiliated in front of their peers).

And then Graham ducks out. His very next sentence says, "Why we test you on what is testable on a written examination rather than on your mastery of all the skills you are taught in class is too important to be discussed here."

Oh?

"Too *important*"?

To *whom?*

...and *why?*

Writing is just *words,* on paper. So, the skill of a lawyerlike analysis on a written exam should have the same content as the spoken words uttered during the "oral argument" that allegedly occurs in class. But Graham has already made clear that the latter bear no resemblance to what has to be written out on finals. So what are all these "skills you are taught in class"? He does not say.

His very *next* sentence is, "But this practice creates a tension between learning what you need to be a good lawyer and learning skills that are only useful on examinations." Does he believe that what makes for good lawyering is the sort of discussion that occurs in a law school classroom?

Out in the real world, cases usually "turn" on whatever aspects of Black Letter Law can be made to apply to facts. No matter what the facts are, there will be Black Letter Law on *both* sides of the dispute. If law *students* are going to reason about something, then they should be using the tools of legal reasoning. And the most important tools of legal reasoning comprise Black Letter Law. In other words, *the lawyer-like analysis called for on a law school essay exam is fundamentally the same as the lawyerlike analysis called for in the practice of law. There is NO "tension" between them.*

Yet, as Graham has stated, in law school the professors regard Black Letter Law as irrelevant in connection with "teaching" students anything during class time...anything that can help them to become better lawyers out in the real world.

By dismissing Black Letter Law as "a bunch of rules" (without ever referring to it as Black Letter Law), Graham insinuates that what he's talking about is really just a relatively arbitrary collection of regulations similar to the IRS Code, a state Probate Code or Family Code, etc. Such codes can be easily changed, and frequently are. By using the phrase "a bunch of rules," Graham implies that Black Letter Law is utterly superficial and transitory, hence *unworthy* of notice. Yet, as he knows well, the great bulk of Black Letter Law has been stable for generations. *That's why it's called Black Letter Law.* Even so, as quoted above, he has admitted that the only reason final exams even concern Black Letter Law at *all* is because *that's* "what's testable on a written examination."

Ironically, one set of statutes is part of the syllabus in probably every first-year Contracts course in the country: the Uniform Commercial Code. Its name implies that it's the same throughout the country. But it is not. All 50 states have enacted the UCC, but many have made their own changes to it. But the UCC itself is largely just a codification of the old "law merchant" of the Common Law—i.e., it's Black Letter Law, now in statutory form. If Graham is serious about ignoring Black Letter Law because it smacks of being "a bunch of rules," how does he explain the inclusion of the UCC in the first-year law school curriculum?

So, what might be the reason/s for the pedagogical "bait and switch" that's "too important to be discussed here"? I believe they're twofold. First, law professors themselves are not necessarily all that competent in the subjects they "teach." They fear being held accountable, in effect, in each day of class for knowing *well* the very things they would suddenly hold students accountable for on final exams. By telling students not to prepare for law school, telling students not to use study aids, then endlessly playing "hide-the-ball," the professoriat ensures that students remain ignorant all semester long. And the professoriat's own relative ignorance is thus never exposed. Second, law professors pretend that successful law students are just naturally gifted.

Recall that Graham had said, regarding success, that it's important to "define it in terms of things you can control rather than those that are in the laps of the gods..." That is why he urged students to adopt a definition of success other than getting high grades. But the implication is that success in law school is one of those things that's "in the laps of the gods." In other words, Graham is tacitly saying that "either you have it, or you don't, and if you don't, well, that's not my problem."

During WWII, when the Allies had gained a foothold in France after D-Day, they pressed the attack. From time to time, they'd encounter signs at crossroads, such as "Malmédy, 42 km," with an arrow pointing in a given direction. Malmédy might indeed have been 42 km away in that direction. Or it might not. What often happened was that persons unknown had turned a sign, so that it pointed in a different direction. Or they'd moved it to a different crossroad, or even changed the names of the towns or the distances shown on those signs. The purpose, of course, was to confuse the Allied troops and stall their advance.

Even though Graham refers to law profs (of which he is one) as your "enemy," we all know that he is only using that as a figure of speech, and joking. These people really are "on your side." They really do want to help you...right? What could possibly be more sincere than pointing you in the right direction by writing an article called "Understanding Law School"?

* * *

The following is a revised version of the review I posted to my column on July 3, 2001.

"When Fear Knocks: The Myths and Realities of Law School" by Prof. Peter F. Lake
Stetson Law Review, Vol. 29, No. 4 (Spring, 2000)
http://www.law.stetson.edu/lawrev/lake.pdf
Legal *"cite"* - 29 STETSON L. REV. 1015 (2000)

Lake is identified as a full professor at Stetson U. College of Law.

He discusses what he calls 18 "myths," two "half-truths," one "little lie," and one "myth + half-truth" about law school. I shall comment on only a few of them.

Just as Graham advocates coming up with a definition of "success" that leaves you feeling good about yourself, so Lake says, "[I]t seems to me that what we believe substantially creates our kind of reality, and some realities are better than others." Yes, and what's generally *called* "reality" tends to be more "real" as "a" reality than the "reality" Lake's readers might believe after reading his article.

He says it's important, when you arrive at law school (or, presumably, before—via the internet), *not* to get information about the school, professors, etc., from second- and third-year students. They really don't know what they're talking about. And to some extent, I agree. But as with Graham, Lake soon veers into la-la land. "[T]he finest source of wisdom about the law school experience can be found in the professors and instructors, and also in members of the legal community who have practiced for many years."

Ah, but wait. Maybe you shouldn't trust the practicing lawyers. "However, one caveat is important. Law school has changed considerably in a relatively short period of time and promises to change even more considerably in the years to come."

What law schools, especially well-respected ones, have undergone any change beyond the merely cosmetic in more than a *century?* (As for future changes, well, don't hold your breath.)

But Lake continues: "So, you may find that although you can get some wisdom from people who have experienced law school in the past, to some extent the realities of modern law school are being created as you are going through law school. This may put a greater burden on students to assimilate the realities while they are in the process of learning in the educational programs, because realities are shifting so fast."

I burst out laughing when I read that—and cannot help but wonder if Lake was at least smiling as he wrote it. A *glacier* shifts faster than almost any major law school he can name.

Lake set up a straw man here, and then knocked him down. It would have been suspect of Lake to say "the finest source of wisdom about the law school experience can be found in the professors and instructors," and let it go at that. So he first says that lawyers who graduated "many years" ago can also be a source of wisdom about law *school. Why?* Why recommend lawyers who've practiced for many years, instead of lawyers who *recently* graduated from that school? After all, he just said that law school "has changed considerably in a relatively short period of time." So, wouldn't a *recent* graduate be more likely to be qualified to comment on the quality of the legal "education" he or she got at a given school, with all its "fast-shifting realities"?—And especially regarding the quality of specific profs still on the faculty.

The "bottom line" of his caveat is this: the *only* ones you can trust, in this fast paced world of changing law schools are...*surprise!* —"your law school professors and instructors." *They're* the only ones who are truly on top of the rapidly shifting pedagogy, and thus can help you stay on the cutting edge of this reality.

Of Truths and Half-Truths

I do agree with one point he makes. Far too many students think that Black Letter Law, for example, is just a set of rules they have to memorize and regurgitate. The law professors encourage that belief— but only for the purpose of tacitly denigrating Black Letter Law...until final exams, that is.

To excuse his own pretermission of Black Letter Law, Lake notes that the Florida legislature (Stetson is in Florida) had recently rewritten the state's tort statutes. That process was part of a nationwide movement by business interests to "reform" tort law, to make it more difficult for people to sue businesses, or to at least minimize the "damages" plaintiffs get if they win. Lake complains that the statutory changes are an example of why there's no point in teaching Black Letter Law.

But here he engages in verbal sleight of hand. For one, as with Graham, he would apparently have his readers believe that Black Letter Law consists of arbitrary and transitory regulations. Yet, as a law professor, surely he knows that Black Letter Law is the body of general principles of law that have "gelled" over generations. True, sometimes Black Letter Law gets codified, turned into statutes, as with the UCC. But what happened in Florida (and elsewhere) was just a political coup. It did not change the nature of the Black Letter Law with regard to torts, as to general legal principles. Nor would any changes to Florida's version of the UCC cause any changes in the way the text of the "model" UCC is taught at Stetson. Last, although Stetson is not a "national" school, I seriously doubt that Lake, or any other Torts professor there, uses a casebook that is Florida-specific, and which gives priority to statutory law over the common law.

His own half-truths do not stop there, however. "Students often complain that the professors are attempting to 'hide the ball' or are 'unclear' or 'theoretical' or whatever. Naturally, if you come to law school assuming you are simply a vessel into which black-letter knowledge will be poured, then this type of education would be a cruel hoax."

Yes, students do come to law school assuming they are simply vessels into which knowledge will be poured. That's what all their previous schooling has been like. Just because the one extreme is bad (which it is), that hardly justifies pretending there is *no middle ground*...and then going to the opposite *extreme*.

Students are right to complain when their professors *withhold* virtually *all* knowledge from them. Granted, it is not a hoax to force students to eschew the role of passive vessels, in favor of one that forces them to become "pro-active" (to use a fashionable term). But it is indeed a *cruel* hoax to play hide-the-ball (or, as Graham indicated, to pull a bait and switch). An *inter*active approach, that is *meaningful*, is what the students seek...and need. Lake has pulled a very clever verbal sleight of hand with his specious dichotomy.

More interesting, from a logical point of view, is his all-or-none approach to Black Letter Law. Presumably, the purpose of learning how to reason is to learn how to reason *about* something. Logically, what law students should reason about is the law—and figuring out how the law applies to a given fact pattern. Therefore, starting with the ABCs (Black Letter Law) would seem to be a good idea. But Lake will have none of that. Instead, he argues that, because there are so many legal rules, it is better not to even try to teach students any of them. (Imagine a physics professor saying, "I'm not here to teach you physics. I'm here to teach you how to 'think like a physicist.' As for the laws of physics and so forth...well, there are so many of them that it's better not even to try to teach any of them to you.")

Yet, several pages later in the article, Lake says:

> [T]he simple fact of the matter is that most top exams become top exams not by particularly brilliant insights and new ideas, but rather by the careful and somewhat tedious process of *laying out accurate rule statements,* identifying central and obvious issues, analyzing the facts in the question, and drawing reasonable conclusions...[W]hat typically distinguishes students on exams is not flashy or particularly brilliant insight, but again, covering *the basics.*
> [Boldface and italics added.]

This is exactly what Michael Josephson said in his Report.

Yet, with respect to *Lake,* here we again have the "bait and switch" that Graham (using different words) spoke of in connection with schizophrenia. This is exactly what Josephson had criticized in his Report. But Lake, like Graham, is talking out of both sides of his mouth...in the same piece of writing.

As Lake has just indicated, what he calls "the basics" are the basis of success on law school exams. (They're the basis of success out in the real world, too.) Then what is the problem with trying to *help* ensure that law students can do these things? Why play hide-the-ball, and tell them not to consult any study aids? Why is it that the teaching of Black Letter Law, and of how to do a good lawyerlike analysis, is somehow beneath the professoriat's dignity? Why is *teaching* beneath these "teachers'" dignity?

According to Lake, "Students must be able, in a sense, to teach themselves as they go through their career. If the legal education process is successful then, in effect, you become your own self-contained professorial unit." And you have to start that *self*-education process in law school.

Here yet again he is engaging in verbal sleight of hand. He says, "if the legal education process is successful..." But the purpose of a good education in *any* subject is to help the student to *continue* the education on his or her own, for life. Normally, however, a "good education" provides students with a *foundation,* of knowledge and skills, for that future *self*-education. It is not based on keeping the students in the dark.

Paradoxically, Lake implies that the universal need for law graduates to *continue* to teach themselves somehow implies that the law school is doing students a *favor* by *NOT giving them a foundation of knowledge and skills.*

No·wonder Graham had mentioned schizophrenia. On the one hand, students are subjected to hide-the-ball throughout the semester, and told not to consult study aids. Yet, on the other, this is somehow part of a legal "education" process that will make them aware they damned well *better* find some study aids once they're *out* of law school. Although students are each expected to be a "self-contained professorial unit" *in* law school, the only tool they're supposed to use is their own brain. And, *as has been seen, EVEN THE PROFESSORS say that what goes on in the classroom has nothing to do with the lawyerly skills that the final exams test.*

So once again, we're back to "either you have it, or you don't; and if you don't, that's not my problem." *No* other graduate school—let alone a *professional* school—operates this way.

Question: If students are supposed to be their own "self-contained professorial units," *why do they have to pay as much as $30,000 a year in tuition* to support the law professors who teach them nothing of value? Why not have the law profs just *write the exams* and *grade* them? It doesn't take a full professor to keep the lamp of knowledge extinguished. *Teaching assistants* (second- and third-year law students) could do that just as well—and would be happy to, just for free tuition. This would perhaps greatly reduce the cost of a law school "education."

The Answer, My Friend
is (You're) Twisting in the Wind

Lake then says, with no awareness of the enormity of his statement, "After all, in no time at all, you will be sitting in an office and someone will be asking you questions. These may be *life and death* questions, and there will not be a law professor or an authority figure there to handle that issue for you." (Emphasis added.)

That is exactly *my* point. Yet, in law school itself, your own "teachers" will play Sphinx with you, rather than "handling the issue for you." So, if you don't learn "the basics" on your own *in* law school, how will you be in a position to start from scratch *after* you graduate? Well, that's not Lake's—or the law schools'—problem.

And what *about* that client who might be asking you "life and death questions" as to the survival of his or her livelihood, or family, or any number of other things that can mean the difference between a happy future and devastation? **The fact that Lake would casually refer to "*life and death* questions," and then not explore his *own* responsibility to help future lawyers be able to provide *good* answers to those questions, reveals his own callousness and utter amorality.**

Commenting on the relationship between law school and the practice of law, he then says this about the former. "No doubt that during this process you will feel at times as though you have been abandoned; however, this is an important part of the growth process of becoming a lawyer."

Do you know what a "snipe hunt" is? Were you ever taken on one as a kid, deep into the woods, maybe during summer camp? Do you feel that the abandonment of the snipe-hunter (the victim of the juvenile "bait and switch") was an important part of a "growth process"?

Lake continues: "Today, many law firms and legal operations expect young lawyers to enter the profession more or less fully equipped to shoulder the responsibility of day-to-day decision-making." Pray tell, how can law school graduates accept responsibility for day-to-day decision-making when they never even received a grounding in the *basics* while they were in law school?

A few sentences later, Lake goes even further with his argument that the law schools' abandonment of their students actually does them a favor: "So the next time it is 1:30 a.m. and you have not finished the assignment, and *you are still not sure exactly what it is you are supposed to learn*, and you are cursing your professor, you might stop for a minute and say, 'Thank you sir, may I have another?'" (Emphasis added.)

(For those unfamiliar with the phrase—"Thank you sir, may I have another?"—it's from the elite English boarding schools. A student who was being *punished* would be told to bend over and drop his pants. The teacher—and back then the teachers and students were always male—would give the student several *very* hard whacks on the bum with a large wooden paddle. After each whack, the student was required to say, "Thank you, Sir. May I have another?" It was a sadistic practice...in a—*proudly*—sado-masochistic environment.)

You might take a moment to think about what Lake said there...and what it means.

On the subject of *grading* exams, he says this: "You [i.e., a prof] want to find an exam that can clearly and concisely work its way through the basic issues, *stating the rules clearly*, analyzing the facts, and drawing reasonable conclusions." (Emphasis added.) A good lawyerlike analysis...which the professor has been ignoring, even *belittling*, all semester long.

One of the basics that Lake himself might want to spend more time on is correct spelling. Throughout his article, he spells "impostor" as "imposter." It's particularly disturbing that none of the students who serve as second-year slave labor on the Stetson Law Review, nor the articles editor, even ran a spell-check to catch the repeated error.*

Lake himself is doubly-Harvard-educated (A.B., J.D.). I suppose nothing can be done to stop him from hiding the ball, ostensibly for his students' own good. But maybe he should at least start keeping a dictionary in plain sight, for *his* own good.

Speaking of himself and his fellow law professors, with regard to students, he writes: **"We give them *more work than a human being can realistically accomplish* in a period of time... We also *set people at each other* in ways that foster competition. We put in motion the wheels that *fracture* people."** (Boldface, italics, and ellipsis added.)

—And he's proud of it...because it's all for the *students'* own good, of course.

Ah, "the finest source of wisdom about the law school experience." You can trust me: I'm your *professor*.

...Even if you end up drowning in this lake of *lies*.

* * *

As Shakespeare's Hamlet said, "One may smile, and smile, and be a villain."

---

* Granted, §3.404 of the UCC, when referring to what would otherwise be called "counterfeit" goods, instead uses the term "impostor"—but in a handful of states, it is spelled "imposter." However, Lake was educated in Massachusetts, and has been making his living in Florida. Those states' version of the UCC both spell the word "-or," not "-er."

I first read his article as a print-out from the internet. Suspecting that the text had been re-typed for cyberspace, I checked the bound copies of the Stetson Law Review. These errors are in the original. However, at one point in the cyberspace text, it refers to the "IRAC" examsmanship as "IRAQ." That error is not in the original.

The Walrus and the Carpenter
by
"Lewis Carroll" (Rev. Chas. Lutwidge Dodgson)

The sun was shining on the sea,
Shining with all his might;
He did his very best to make
The billows smooth and bright—
And this was odd, because it was
The middle of the night.

The moon was shining sulkily,
Because she thought the sun
Had got no business to be there
After the day was done—
"It's very rude of him," she said
"To come and spoil the fun!"

The sea was wet as wet could be,
The sands were dry as dry.
You could not see a cloud because
No cloud was in the sky:
No birds were flying overhead—
There were no birds to fly.

The Walrus and the Carpenter
Were walking close at hand;
They wept like anything to see
Such quantities of sand:
"If this were only cleared away,"
They said, "It would be grand!"

"If seven maids with seven mops
Swept it for half a year,
Do you suppose," the Walrus said,
"That they could get it clear?"
"I doubt it," said the Carpenter,
And shed a bitter tear.

"O Oysters, come and walk with us!"   [Law school classes begin.]
The Walrus did beseech.
"A pleasant walk, a pleasant talk,
Along the briny beach:
We cannot do with more than four,
To give a hand to each."

The eldest Oyster looked at him,   [Having prepped via
But never a word he said: "The *PLS* Approach"]
The eldest Oyster winked his eye,
And shook his heavy head—
Meaning to say he did not choose
To leave the oyster-bed.

But four young Oysters hurried up,
All eager for the treat:
Their coats were brushed, their faces washed,
Their shoes were clean and neat—
And this was odd, because, you know,
They hadn't any feet.

Four other Oysters followed them,
And yet another four;
And thick and fast they came at last,
And more, and more, and more—
All hopping through the frothy waves,
And scrambling to the shore.   ["I've wanted to be a
                                      lawyer since I was twelve!"]

The Walrus and the Carpenter
Walked on a mile or so,
And then they rested on a rock
Conveniently low:
And all the little Oysters stood
And waited in a row.

"The time has come," the Walrus said,
"To talk of many things:
Of shoes— and ships— and sealing-wax—
Of cabbages— and kings—
And why the sea *is* boiling hot—
And *whether* pigs have *wings*."

[The Case/Socratic Method]

[A hypothetical]
["Policy" discussions.
(Emphasis added.)]

"But wait a bit," the Oysters cried,
"Before we have our chat;
For some of us are out of breath,
And all of us are fat!"
"No hurry!" said the Carpenter.
They thanked him much for that.

[The kinder, gentler
professoriat.]

"A loaf of bread," the Walrus said,
"Is what we chiefly need:
Pepper and vinegar besides
Are very good indeed—
Now if you're ready, Oysters dear,
We can begin to feed."

[Ah, exams.]

"But not on us!" the Oysters cried,
Turning a little blue.
"After such kindness, that would be
A dismal thing to do!"
"The night is fine," the Walrus said.
"Do you admire the view?

"It was so kind of you to come!
And you are very nice!"
The Carpenter said nothing, but
"Cut us another slice:
I wish you were not quite so deaf—
I've had to ask you twice!"

"It seems a shame," the Walrus said,
"To play them such a trick
After we've brought them out so far,
And made them trot so quick!"   [The "bait and switch."]
The Carpenter said nothing but
"The butter's spread too thick!"

"I weep for you," the Walrus said:
"I deeply sympathize."   ["Either you have it, or
With sobs and tears he sorted out   you don't. Too bad."]
Those of the largest size
Holding his pocket-handkerchief
Before his streaming eyes.

"O Oysters," said the Carpenter
"You've had a pleasant run!
Shall we be trotting home again?"
But answer came there none—
And this was scarcely odd, because
They'd eaten every one.   [On a forced curve,
                                        though, 10% or so are spared.]

ATTICUS FALCON, ESQ.

Chapter 9 - Professor Jekyll
& Mr./Ms. Hide-the-Ball*

To separate the myths of law school from the realities, you must look at the situation from the faculty's perspective.

Pursuing the Path of Least Resistance

Most college and grad school profs have a Ph.D. That sometimes takes three years of courses, just like law school. But the other future professors already studied their subject extensively in their undergraduate days, as required preparation. Future law profs, in contrast, have no prior exposure to the subject, and then do their three years only on the *basic* law degree—formerly known (as Chapter 1 mentioned) as "*Bachelor* of Law."

Also, in many graduate schools, Ph.D. candidates must take general competency exams in addition to their individual class exams or papers. Sometimes, there's a set when they complete their master's level work, and then a second set before they're certified to get the Ph.D. But future law school profs, because they only get the J.D., only have to take the normal exams all law students take. (Granted, though, there's also the bar exam...although many law profs have never taken it.)

Further, aspiring professors outside the law must then do another one to three years of "doctoral research" and write a doctoral dissertation, to prove themselves worthy scholars. And then, after a student has passed all the exams in grad school, his or her "dissertation director" can reject the student's Ph.D. thesis—and even if the director approves it, the dissertation *committee* can then reject it. We're talking about a *completed* doctoral thesis here...after perhaps as much as six years of graduate work (including the research). Would-be law profs face no such potential dead-end.

Thus, not only is it much easier to become a law professor than a prof at any other type of school, the situation is comparable to a college professor having only a college degree. (And it might not be too much of an exaggeration to say it's comparable to a 6th-grade teacher

---

* Doug Knox, who as of this writing is a second-year student at the University of Florida's law school, used this phrase in an e-mail to me. With his permission, I now give him the credit he's due—with gratitude.

having only a 6th-grade education.) Even business school professors, who teach MBA candidates, are required to have a doctorate in business. But unless one of your profs has an advanced degree in the law (which is extremely unlikely), each year you complete in law school you acquire 1/3 as much formal legal education as your professors.

Of Apples & Oranges
...and the Color of Money

A law school professor teaches all of two courses per semester. It's 6-8 hours a week, max. (And I do mean max, because each "hour" of class is actually just 50-55 minutes.)

A typical law school full professorship means a base salary of between $100,000 and $150,000 a year...for 34 weeks' employment. (The typical college or grad school prof makes considerably less. This has been the source of much internal complaining at universities that have law schools.) At six hours a week, and making $100,000 per academic year, that's over 490 bucks an hour. If it's eight hours a week, and still "just" $100,000, the rate drops to a mere $367 an hour. But at eight hours a week and $150,000, it jumps to $551 an hour. And at six hours a week for $150,000, it soars to $735. Nice. Very nice.

The profs at the top schools have seen their top graduates get annual starting salaries of as much as $200,000 (including, sometimes, a "signing bonus"). So they say they have to "keep pace." Thus, for several years straight now, law schools—whether public or private—have had annual tuition increases of 10% or more. *Your* money pays for the faculty's feather-bedding. (Actually, though, at a law school that's affiliated with a university, the parent institution rakes off between a tenth and 40% of each student's tuition and fees. The skimmed funds then subsidize other programs and schools, especially in the sciences. Medicine, in particular, is a chronic money-loser.)

The professoriat looks only at the bottom line, the dollars. They ignore the fact that in the first few years of practice, their hotshot former students making the big bucks have to work not just 50 weeks a year, but 52, not 34. (New associates at big firms are told they can take a vacation. But only the foolish dare use more than a few days of it.) And the new associates are expected to work at least 60 hours a week, and often more than 80; not 6-8. At 60 hours a week, that's $64/hour. At 80 hours a week, $48. Besides, *very* few law firms pay $200,000 a year to new associates. The usual peak starting salary (as of now) is more like $150,000 (including the standard bonuses). But the firms still want those hours. At 60 a week, that's $48; but at 80, only $36.

It's a grind. Hence the term "law factory." But in a *real* factory, the blue-collar workers have a choice about working overtime. And they get paid time-and-a-half for it, and sometimes double-time. In the white-collar "law factory," there is no overtime pay—and *no choice* about what would otherwise be called "overtime." Many a new associate has had to work on Thanksgiving Day, Christmas Day, even New Year's Eve. In contrast, try to find a law prof at your school who's available more than two or three hours a week outside of class (despite his or her posted "office hours"), let alone who's available on any of these holidays (or the day before a holiday—or almost *any* day before 10 a.m. or after 3 p.m.).

The key concept at the law factories is "billable hours."* The rule of thumb is that for every three hours worked, two should be "billed out" to one or more clients. It is not unusual for new associates to be expected to bill at least 2,500 hours a year. To do that requires working an average of 72 hours a week, all 52 weeks of the year. (And at some law firms, the expectation now is *3,000* hours.) If you fall short, you're "eased out."

Although the new associates are getting paid at the "wholesale" rate of (at most) $36-$64 an hour, their time is billed out "at retail," i.e., $250-$300 an hour. So, in return for their $150,000-$200,000 salary, each new associate brings in between $625,000 and $900,000 to the firm.

What do *law profs* bring in to the law *school,* in return for the $367-$735 an hour they're making? More important, what do law *students* get as "enhanced value" in return for the now-routine tuition hikes of 10% a year they're *paying?*

A prof's office is rent-free. Secretarial services are free, too: the school pays the secretary's salary. The phone, lights, copier, etc., are also free. Granted, for attorneys at the law factories (versus sole practitioners, who comprise two-thirds of all attorneys in the private sector), the overhead does not come out of their own pockets. However, no lawyer makes as much money with such little overhead or effort—and such a low performance standard. Most *judges* do have such a low overhead. But no judge gets by with working so little. Yes, there are faculty meetings, schmoozing with the powers-that-be, etc., all of which is virtually mandatory. But it's not exactly a stressful way to make a living.

Unlike lawyers, most law profs (as with professors at colleges and grad schools) are "tenure-track." And most do have tenure. (An "assistant"

---

* If there were an organization just for major law firms, its national headquarters would of course be in...Billings, Montana. (I've often thought the American Bar Association should move its headquarters there.)

prof is a tenure-track prof who does not yet have tenure. When he or she gets tenure, there's an automatic change in title, to "associate" professor. Adjunct professors, instructors, lecturers, and most "legal clinic" faculty are not tenure-track. Their contracts are reviewed periodically, and thus they have no job security.) Tenure means virtual immunity from dismissal. Tenured faculty can do almost anything, as long as they do not (a) shoot up heroin or snort cocaine—in class; (b) throw daggers at or fire guns at their students; (c) engage in *coercive* sexual relations with their students; or (d) otherwise indicate that they're a menace to society. Barring that, they can't be fired. (Chapter 5 discussed this in connection with a professor at Pace University's law school.) So a tenured law prof's base salary is *guaranteed,* no matter what. No lawyer has such a deal.

The Name of the Game

The law profs also ignore the fact that, unlike their hotshot grads' income, the professoriat's six-figure base salary, as the term implies, is just the beginning.

For the typical college or grad school prof, salary is maybe 90% of his or her annual income. Sure, some have investment income, maybe even a trust fund. They can also teach summer school, and pick up some extra money. And there are those who get royalties from published writings. But for most college and grad school professors, what they know has virtually no demand outside the ivory tower. (Economics and business profs are—sometimes—the exception.) For the law school professoriat, it's different.

In America, we proudly say we have "a government of laws, not men." But the laws have to be written, and administered, and interpreted by men and women. We do indeed have a government of laws: we are heavily regulated by statutes, treaties, administrative regulations, ordinances, and case law. Lawyers handle all of that.

This means there's a demand for legal experts. They serve as consultants when legislation or rules are being drafted and when arguments are being prepared for court. They're hired to advise corporations on the meaning of new statutes and rules—and sometimes of old ones. The cachet of "law professor" is *enormously* valuable in this market.

It doesn't take a genius to figure out the result. It's a matter of incentives. But just in case you're resisting the analysis, here it is:

You have a job where all you have to do is show up in a specified location at specified times, a total of 6-8 hours a week. (And you can cancel a class—or even a week's worth of classes—and make them up later.) Outside class, your time is almost entirely your own.

Now, what are you going to spend the rest of your time on?

A. Preparing diligently for class—reading law review articles on the first-year subject/s you teach; discussing your intended approach with others; thinking of new examples to use, new questions to ask, etc.

B. Further developing a good reputation in some esoteric or fast-growing area of the law, so that *you* can become the hired consultant, the hired expert witness, etc.—and make bunches more money from these outside activities…without jeopardizing the income you get from supposedly teaching your students.

If you picked "A," you are not cut out to deal with the real world of the Law—or the real world of *anything*. "B" is the path to profit and glory. And that's (supposedly) what life's all about.

Hypothetical Example

You're a law professor, tenured. In recent years, there's been a dramatic growth in "identity theft." Criminals, using stolen information, have devastated many people's credit record and financial position by impersonating those people in cyberspace. And, of course, there have been lawsuits. Many lawsuits.

You have no experience as a trial lawyer, but you want to get a piece of the action. And you know that a lot of trials (and all appeals) turn on interpretations of the law rather than interpretations of facts—and interpretations of the law are argued to judges, on paper, not to a jury. And right now, "identity theft" is a new area of the law where "the ball's up in the air." *You* want to be one of those who can grab it and run with it…and score some big bucks. (After all, the consultant/expert witness gets paid, no matter which side wins the case.) So let's say you want to become a consultant in the area of identity theft.

You take on a research assistant or two, selected from your students. You don't have to pay them. They're in it as willing slaves, trying to bask in what they hope is—or will be—your reflected glory as the "leading expert" on the subject. (The *school* might be paying them, though, under a work-study program. Even then, it's minimum-wage.)

You decide to submit a law review article for publication. Your students do all the research, and maybe even all the writing. The article gets published, preferably in a prestigious law journal. (You mention your student helpers in the acknowledgments, with a quickie expression of gratitude. But the by-line on the article is yours alone.) You then start to work on another article—a variation on the theme. You might get some op-ed pieces into the *New York Times, Washington Post, Wall Street Journal,* or a newspaper chain via syndication. These could lead to an interview on ABC's *Nightline,* an appearance on PBS's *Frontline,* and so forth. Maybe you even do a casebook on the subject.

These things get you noticed by the lawyers who'll handle the I.D. theft cases...and by the prestigious schools that want to have "the" leading expert in this area on *their* faculty. If you're lucky, you'll be invited to testify before a state legislative or Congressional committee that's drafting legislation, or get hired as a consultant by a government agency that's drafting regulations.

Meanwhile, you teach a second- or third-year class in the subject. (Or maybe you just do a seminar—easier, because you don't need to use notes. And seminars involve far fewer students, so there are fewer potential demands on your time during office hours.) The law school thus *pays* you to maintain a credential (the teaching of the course) that you'll use as part of your "drawing card" for getting considerable income—income you don't have to share with the law school.

Getting There

According to an item in *The American Lawyer* magazine several years ago, Laurence Tribe—the prominent Harvard Law professor—was then billing his time for outside work at $1,200 an hour. (That's one thousand, two hundred. I hate to think what his hourly rate is now.) The magazine estimated his annual income then was 3-4 million dollars. Tribe, of course, is at the very capstone of the American law school pyramid; no doubt, faculty at lower schools make less from their "moonlighting." And were he to devote *all* his time to private practice, he might make even more. (For all I know, he's a good teacher, and devotes a great deal of time outside class to his students and to class preparation. Regardless, you see how the system works.)

One of my law school courses was in the law of defamation (libel and slander). The professor was a recognized expert in the subject. Numerous publishers and broadcasters had him on retainer. Yet, he bluntly told us in class, several times, that "this area of the law is so complicated, and so confusing, that it's really impossible to teach it." And so, he didn't. But that hadn't stopped him from repeatedly offering the course, to enhance his credentials. Granted, he assigned cases, and we discussed them in class. But he told us it was "impossible" to provide even a simple definition of basic concepts such as slander *per se* and libel *per quod.* Yet—as we could see from the discussion of defamation in our commercial outlines from first-year torts—even a *sophisticated* discussion on these topics was readily available.

After graduation, I naturally saw former classmates from time to time. Once in awhile, one of them would have a case—or know of a case—that involved defamation. Without exception, if the case was important, his or her first reaction was to recommend good old Professor X as a consultant. A major purpose of Professor X's class was to drum up future business for himself. His hourly rate was staggering (though not nearly as high as Tribe's), as was his retainer.

In addition to their base salary and consulting work, law school professors sometimes receive tens of thousands of dollars in "research grants" that are channeled through the school by outside sources. So, when a law professor points out that his or her job involves all that time spent on research, it's true—but not the whole truth. In fact, it's quite misleading. Only a handful of law school profs in America do research in the subjects that comprise the *first-year* curriculum—the foundation of future attorneys' skills. Their research seldom concerns what's supposed to be their primary responsibility: educating future lawyers.

Many people work a full-time day job and then "moonlight" part-time. However, for most law school professors, the "full-time" *day* job is the moonlighting. Unfortunately, law school profs are not required to disclose how much time they spend each week on "outside" work. And they are not required to report (except to the IRS) how much money they make from it. Based on my own observations, and those of fellow former students, it's reasonable to assert that an ambitious law school professor easily spends as much as four times as many hours on outside-income-producing activities as he or she does in class—and makes perhaps four times as much money from it.

In sum, the faculty salary is just the *starting* point: one of a number of potential income streams that are tributaries to a law prof's financial well-being. Or, to look at it differently, the law school professorship is just the hub of a wheel with many potentially lucrative spokes. The more prestigious the law school, the more valuable the credential. (For prestige value, even a mere assistant professor at a big-name school beats a top attorney at most law firms, despite the fact that a top lawyer in that area knows vastly more—especially as to how things work in the *real* world of the law.)

But without that faculty position, the prof would be just another lawyer (if, that is, he or she has even taken and passed the bar exam).

The law school professoriat (which sees itself as "natural-born geniuses of the law") has found an answer to the question, "If you're so smart, how come you're not rich?" With the sole exception of clinical law profs (discussed in Chapter 19), they are definitely getting there.

Failing to Spot THE Issue

To further enhance its students' job prospects, Harvard Law sets its forced curve in such a way that over *half* of the graduating class each year is *cum laude* or better. Last time I checked, however, there had been only three people in the school's history who'd graduated *summa cum laude*. One of them is Charles Nesson, who became (and still is) an HLS professor. (He became well known for devoting the first 15 minutes of class to having his students do calisthenics in the room.)

A Civil Action, by Jonathan Harr, concerns a federal class-action toxic tort suit. Nesson served as a consultant to plaintiffs' counsel, Jan Schlichtmann. According to Harr, one of the first things Nesson did was to urge that Schlichtmann seek a *billion* dollars in damages from the defendant multinational corporation. The law firm's staff promptly started referring to Nesson as "Billion-Dollar Charlie." The movie, like the book, made Schlichtmann out to be a greedy plaintiff's attorney—which he was. But in the movie, Nesson's involvement was not even mentioned, let alone his advice. Harr's book did not state how much Nesson's retainer for consulting was, or whether or not he was to get a piece of the action on a contingency fee basis. (If the latter, perhaps that explains his advice.)

Around the time the case was progressing, Court TV hired Nesson to serve as host and moderator for a series of programs on trial advocacy. (Ah, more outside income.) Clips from real trials were shown, and then Nesson and guests would discuss the performance of each lawyer in each clip. One of his guests was none other than...Jan Schlichtmann. ("You scratch my back, I'll scratch yours.")

Chapter 2 of *this* book discussed four concepts that cut across nearly everything in the law: duty - breach - harm - cause. One would think that Schlichtmann, as an experienced personal injury lawyer, would have been mindful of those four basic necessities. And one would certainly think that Nesson, as a summa cum laude HLS grad/prof, would have caught what the lawyer missed. Yet, the lawsuit was thrown out on *summary judgment* because the plaintiffs had failed to provide even minimal evidence to establish cause-in-fact. (The movie made the judge appear, shall we say, less than impartial—and perhaps even less than mentally balanced. The book makes it clear that the judge did indeed have some unpleasant quirks. But that's true of most judges...and most human beings.)

However, any decent first-year law student, taking a "fruitcake" exam based on this real-world situation, would have checked if there was a potential issue on the element of causation. Apparently, though, neither Schlichtmann nor "Billion-Dollar Charlie" even *thought of* the need to establish the existence of cause-in-fact...until the defendant filed the motion for summary judgment. (Summary judgment is almost never granted, because, normally, the **"prima facie"**—Latin: loosely, "plausible face value" case—is sound enough to withstand such a challenge, even though that case might eventually lose at trial.)

That illustrates the greed and the grossly inflated self-image of law school professors. It is also a sad illustration of the consequences of the isolation of the ivory tower from the real world of the law.*

Research v. Teaching

Here's the real kicker: the *law school's* reputation is based on how many nationally (or internationally) recognized experts it has on its faculty. (So, they would argue, the "outside activities" are actually integral.) It's a symbiotic relationship between the law school and the law profs, from the point of view of making money for both.

In this, it works like the reputation of universities' science departments, which depend on the number of Nobel prize-winners they have. But there's a difference: the typical Nobel-winner actually *teaches*—and teaches only a handful of students at a time, whom he or she *rigorously* trains. Sometimes these students are so well trained that they eventually win Nobel prizes in their own right. Such is not the case with law school professors. First, law school profs often have large classes. Second, unlike science, the realm of untapped potential *meaningful* research in the law is relatively small.

The "publish or perish" rule determines a faculty member's career. (This is the same as with college and grad school faculty.) An assistant professor must get two articles published in reputable academic journals to prove that he or she is a real scholar, and thus worthy of tenure. Typically, to be promoted from associate to full prof requires more published articles in reputable journals. After that, the professor can coast for life...and many do. Or, he or she can keep cranking out articles of "high quality" in hope of getting an offer to join the faculty of a more prestigious school.

However, the professor who is writing knows that those who will be evaluating his or her work are not interested in the same old stuff. Being human, they're attracted to the new, the different. Originality is paramount. But first-year courses concern Black Letter Law ("old,

---

* Nesson is now positioning himself as the country's leading expert on "law and cyberspace."

fundamental, well settled"). Unless the writer can find a way to try to completely upset the applecart in some area of Black Letter Law (which is extremely unlikely), he or she does better to look elsewhere for subject material. That's another reason faculty who teach first-year are often far less conversant with the subject matter than you would expect.

The law school concurs in the faculty's desire to give first-year courses bottom priority. (And because law school casebook publishers provide a free teacher's manual, the professor need only consult that for any new developments in the subject.) The *AALS Directory of Law Teachers* lists all full-time tenure-track faculty in America's law schools, and what they teach. But it never lists the *first-year* courses they teach. Those are irrelevant. All that counts is the upper-level courses, the areas of the profs' "expertise."

Almost no law school professors bother to try to become good *teachers*. After all, why should they? Their pay is not based on how well they teach. It's based on how important they are as legal scholars. (The major law schools are constantly trying to steal superstars from one another. Occasionally, one succeeds. It's quite a coup.)

Maybe you're in (or went to) an undergraduate school big enough to employ "teaching assistants" (TAs). In the largest, most prestigious universities, often teaching "assistants" do *all* the teaching. The professor's name is listed as the person conducting the course, but the professor is nowhere to be found. Teaching the freshman undergraduates is the last thing that 99.9% of the college professoriat wants to do. Their interest is in the advanced classes, preferably seminars with seniors or graduate students—who serve as their (unpaid) research assistants.

Law school also has TAs. However, they teach only the two courses thought to be beneath the dignity of professors: legal research and legal writing. In all your other courses, throughout your three years of law school, you will be taught by a genuine professor. So, at least on paper, there's a big difference. Sounds good.

But wait: the problem with the first-year courses is that, nine times out of ten, the law school professor feels the same way as the college professor who teaches freshman English (if, indeed, your freshman English course had a real professor presiding in the classroom): he or she really does not want to be there. And it shows. Often, the professor takes it out on the students. Especially in first-year.

(Students have e-mailed me that a professor at the University of Texas law school, Alan S. Rau, is particularly abusive in his first-year Contracts class. Students respond with scathing evaluations at the end of the course. One wrote—paraphrasing a line from a movie—"We are all dumber having heard you speak...May God have mercy on your soul." Rau apparently *revels* in the criticism: he posts the scathing evaluations on the outside of his door. Rau, of course, has tenure.)

For most law profs, the classroom experience is a necessary "evil," a chore to be endured much as they endured performing household chores when they were kids. For most members of the professoriat, students are a nuisance. Law school professors want to spend their time feathering their own nests—which is understandable. Students aren't even fledglings yet, let alone legal eagles; your professors do not want to attend to the needs of insistent hatchlings, all of whom have gaping, chirping beaks and wildly flapping wings. Would *you?**

Richard D. Kahlenberg is a 1989 graduate of Harvard's law school. In 1992, his book, *Broken Contract: A Memoir of Harvard Law School*, was published. At one point in it, he discusses a bull session with other students. All were unhappy.

> The main complaint was that we students were ignored. "Sometimes I feel as though the law school grinds on and the students are just extras," one student said. "As if the real purpose of the university was to allow professors to do their thing, and that the students were just here to make it seem like a university."

Yup, that's it—not by accident, but by *design*. It's true of America's universities in general, but particularly true of America's law schools.

Excursus into Intellectual History

The tradition of scholarship in the West is now almost 900 years old. The "Dark Ages" of Europe occurred in a political sense because of the Fall of Rome in 410. However, arguably, the Dark Ages began in an intellectual sense even earlier. For with the triumph of Christianity, zealous Christians began destroying all evidence of "pagan" religion—including the magnificent libraries. In general, the only writings of the ancient Greeks and Romans that survived were in the Levant.

---

* At some law schools, there's a library just for the faculty. It's off-limits to students. Officially, this is so the professors will never have to worry about being able to find a book they're looking for. However, law profs are generally pretty bad about returning books they've removed from the library—and sometimes even about "signing them out." The real reason for the faculty law library is so that professors won't encounter students. Students, by definition, are pesky.

The 7th century saw the advent of Islam in that region, and soon the rise of the Caliphate. Moslem leaders valued the pre-Christian writings. (This was understandable in part on the principle of "The enemy of my enemy is my friend." Islam expanded its territory at the expense of the Christian—Byzantine—Empire, which it obliterated in a campaign that lasted a thousand years. The Christians, before the Moslems, had obliterated the "pagans.")

In the 9th century, the Arabs established what could be called the world's first university, the House of Wisdom, in Baghdad. Its purpose was largely to study the pre-Christian materials. Gradually, copies of those writings became available in the West, through the Arabs and Moors (often with Jews acting as the conduit). Christianity by that point was the universal (and official state) religion. "Pagan" intellectual discourse was no longer seen as "offensive to God." Further, the Christians knew they lagged the Moslems in the life of the mind.

So, in the 11th century, *Europe's* first university was founded: the University of Bologna in Italy. Other countries, wanting to keep up, quickly founded their own universities. The curriculum was based entirely on the newly circulating ancient writings. The subjects were the Trivium (grammar, rhetoric, and logic—this last called "dialectic") and the Quadrivium (basic mathematics, geometry, astronomy, and music).

But, interestingly, the most important subject (to both the Church and the secular rulers) was neither in the Trivium nor the Quadrivium. It was Law—in particular, the study of the Justinian Code, based on ancient Roman law—and the development of canon law. (Most of the Popes in those centuries were Doctors of Canon—i.e., Church—Law.)

"Scholarship" quite rightly involved the study of the ancient writings in order to understand them, to work out their implications, and to analyze conflicting beliefs of various writers. Thus, research was truly "re-search," in the sense of searching through the ancients' writings again and again, looking for things others had missed and trying to challenge the conventional analysis on some point or other. This bore spectacular fruit for the West. The 12th-century Renaissance (and Saint Thomas Aquinas's *Summa Theologica*) resulted from these studies. "Re-search" became the only approved method of demonstrating one's scholarship.

However, surely after nine centuries it's time to end this *exclusive* method of determining "scholarship." Today, scholars are notorious for "knowing more and more about less and less"—and for not being able to teach it to anyone. Like the mandarinate that eventually led to China's demise in the 19th century, it's a "diminishing returns" situation. Scholars have lost sight of their original purpose (and the reason for tax-subsidized universities): to gain greater understanding and then to share it with others for the benefit of all society. Instead, the professoriat sees itself as similar to medieval monks, cut off from the rest of society *by choice*, yet entitled to deference and material tribute from society merely because, with their superior knowledge, they're privileged characters. It has nearly become a matter of all take and no give. (Herman Hesse tellingly gave the title "Magister Ludi"—"Master of the Game"—with the alternative title of "The Glass Bead Game"—to his subtle, yet devastating, novel on the surrealism of academe.)

Tainted Research and Fraudulent Objectivity

Law professors sometimes *cultivate* the image of fuddy-duddy, otherworldly academic "monks." This helps them maintain a group identity distinct from that of the "hard-headed" *practitioners* of law. So, when the supposedly non-intellectual lawyers who are out in the real world criticize the supposedly intellectual law school professors for their alleged impracticality, the latter often just smile timidly. They just can't help being the way they are. But the "otherworldliness" is often a facade for a very real *this*-worldliness.

In recent years, the federal government has cut its funding for scientific research. Universities have turned to corporations. The corporations have often been happy to oblige—but often on condition that they get complete control over what information is released about the research. Often, the reported results are slanted to create the impression the sponsoring corporation desired when it commissioned the "research."

Many of the research grants that go to law professors come from corporations or organizations that have a legal axe to grind. So they ask the prof to look into it for them. The prof does the research, and then has a law review article published reflecting that research. And "He who pays the piper calls the tune."

Several published articles on the same subject make the prof an "expert." This expertise means not only can the prof be hired for consulting work, but the prof can be hired as an *expert witness* on a point of law. Even if the prof is not hired, his or her articles can influence the thinking of others. But the connection between the funding and the article is not disclosed. (See the Coda for an example.) And no law school that I know of *requires* its professors to disclose this conflict of interest.

Aloof in the Ivory Tower

Nowhere are the consequences of this process more disastrous than law school, and the "education" of future lawyers. To return to Chapter 2's analogy of medical school: what if medical schools valued their faculty only on the basis of the faculty members' ability to write "impressive" articles? What if the faculty actively sought to keep future doctors "in the dark" about medicine, the way law school faculty members—as attested by the Josephson Report, and illustrated by Graham and Lake—do law students? Medical school faculty members are expected to be good doctors. Law school faculty members often do not even have a license to practice law.

The path to a tenure-track teaching job with a reputable law school is great grades in law school, followed by a judicial clerkship—preferably with a U.S. Supreme Court justice, or at least with a federal appellate judge.

Notice what's missing? Proven ability to teach. The performance standard is "drudgeship"—the ability to grind away for grades in law school, and ability to grind away as slave labor for a federal judge. (It's the same criterion big law firms have when hiring new associates, by the way.) Drudgeship is hardly conducive to creativity and spontaneity, which good teaching often involves. At least a future Ph.D. starts out as a T.A. (for what little that's usually worth). Future law profs don't start out as TAs. Instead, they Make Law Review. (See Chapter 18.)

In 1994, two law school professors, John Mixon and Gordon Otto, did a law review article called "Continuous Quality Improvement, Law, and Legal Education."* Regarding the idea of even *asking* if a law school gives good value for what it charges, they said:

> The merest suggestion brings howls of complaint that students do not know what is good for them, that customer feedback (particularly in teaching evaluations) is suspect, that the participating bar has nothing to say, and that law school faculties best serve their customers by producing law review articles.

* 45 EMORY L.J. 393, at 436-37

As two other law professors, Jay M. Feinman and Marc Feldman, noted in a 1985 law review article:*

> At most law schools, the purposes and methods of teaching are regarded as unfruitful, if not unfit, topics for conversation.

Nothing has changed since Feinman and Feldman wrote in 1985, just as nothing has changed since Mixon and Otto wrote in 1994.

Notice what else is missing in a law professor's background?—Experience in the *practice* of law. (And I am not referring to "getting your ticket punched" by a one- or two-year stint in a law factory. There, new associates usually don't even come face-to-face with a client, let alone assuming responsibility for a case.) In fact, at the very top schools, those who have more than a year or two as attorneys in the real world are regarded as "tainted," and are unwelcome as tenure-track junior faculty. Exceptions are few.

Both of these patterns were established by Christopher Langdell of HLS. He'd had little success as an attorney in private practice. He had less success as a teacher of law. Determined, however, to impose his vision on legal education, he sought to fill the Harvard Law faculty with professors who were entirely of his own making. His chief protégé, James Barr Ames, went straight from being an HLS student to being a member of its faculty, and later succeeded Langdell as Dean. One thing the two had in common was utter contempt for lawyers and judges—i.e., those who chose to make their living in the real world.

It might have made sense, initially, for Langdell to employ only faculty created in his own image, but untainted by experience with other pedagogical methodologies or the vagaries of law-in-the-real-world. Surely, though, now that more than a century has passed, it is time to reexamine the mold from which law profs are made, for it is truly moldy—a toxic mold.

---

* *Pedagogy and Politics,* 73 GEO. L.J. 875

It isn't from Ignorance

Educators have long known that the best way for students to learn is through feedback mechanisms in the learning process itself. Final exams, of course, are a feedback mechanism. But by then it's too late to correct one's errors. That's why students have homework assignments, "exercise questions," and quizzes beforehand. These are reality checks, to use a buzzword (which itself is a buzzword, come to think of it).

Yet, you get none of this in law school. Two reasons why. First, profs don't want to do any more work than they absolutely have to in return for their $100,000-$150,000 a year base salary. For example, the detailed critique of a student's proposed answer to just one "fruit-cake" exam problem in Chapter 7 took me quite some time to complete. Granted, I could have covered everything in a face-to-face meeting with the student in a fraction of the time. However, first-year classes usually are large. Even a half-hour meeting per student, just to go over a practice exam, would require perhaps as much as 50-70 hours, total...hours that do not put another dime into the prof's pocket.

Also, as Chapter 7 discussed, because there are so few *good* exam answers, the profs can grade *all* the answers quickly. But if the students' answers were typically much better than they are now, grading would take far more time.

Further, many students who haven't "gotten it" by the end of first-year still haven't gotten it by the end of second-year, or even third. So their exam answers in *later* years don't take much time to grade either. Thus, the prof who tries to help his or her students do a good lawyer-like analysis in first-year is making much more work for himself or herself down the road, too. It just doesn't pay.

In his report to the AALS, Michael Josephson said,

> If a student, for any reason, fails to recognize or discuss any transaction of significance, he/she will miss the opportunity to resolve the problems arising therefrom and his/her exam score will suffer severely...This so substantially [overweights] the value of spotting a transactional issue that *it can render the exam invalid.* Failing to discuss a significant transaction in a multi-transactional question is like failing to discuss a whole question in a multi-question exam.
>
> [Emphasis added.]

But that's the *whole idea*. It's the *prof* who gets to decide on the exam's validity.

By making everything "hang" on your ability to spot the conflict-pairing or the issue (or non-issue) in the first place (what Josephson collectively calls the "transactions"), professors can dispose of a student's entire answer to an exam problem in a matter of seconds.

It's sort of like missing your exit on a highway, or the correct turn on a lesser road, when participating in a "car rally." There's a route you're supposed to follow, which includes taking several exits and turns. If you miss one, and realize your mistake, you can always go back. But you've lost a great deal of time. And if you don't realize you should have taken that exit or turn in the first place, you might not reach your destination at all.

Of course, the profs are supposedly there to help you learn the law. So, shouldn't they be giving you some feedback along the way? Then you would have a measure of your own progress (become aware of your weak spots and so forth), instead of having only the one exam as a performance measure.

That brings us to the second reason why the profs don't care whether or not you learn anything: they do not see it as their job to teach you at *all*. (The Josephson Report, quoted in Chapter 2, addressed this point, as did the articles by Graham and Lake, which Chapter 8 discussed.) They figure that if you're any good, you'll learn it on your own. And if you can't learn it on your own, there's no hope for you: you just don't have what it takes. So there's no point in helping you in the first place. In other words, as to their possible efforts on your behalf, if it's not worth doing at all, it certainly isn't worth doing well. This plays both ends against the middle...with the students in the middle.

Many law school professors don't even return graded exams to students. Or, if they do, there are almost *no* comments on the graded exams other than the occasional general remark. This is not just to enable the profs to be lazy. It also *hides their pedagogical incompetence from scrutiny—and accountability.* Even if all the professors were to really *teach,* and then returned students' graded finals, there is virtually no way two students could compare their exams to see why each of them got the score he or she did—because there are no comments to help them understand their results.

Nor is there any way a student who got a low score can challenge the result by saying, "Hey! Wait a minute, professor! You showed us how to do a lawyerlike analysis. Take another look at *my* analysis here and you'll see that it's exactly what you wanted. So, how about changing my grade to something better?" —Such a challenge is impossible because *the profs have deliberately kept students in the dark throughout the entire first-year course.*

For the same reason, if a prof turns in an *erroneously* low grade for a student, that student cannot determine that it was obviously a mistake.

Smoke & Mirrors

Given that the teaching in law school is so bad, and that hide-the-ball is at the heart of it, nearly all students fail to master even the foundational levels of the Josephson Pyramid. If students' abilities were tested on an objective performance scale, most of them would fail the course. But that would reflect badly on the professor's teaching ability, wouldn't it? So, the obvious solution is twofold:

(1) put the grading on a curve, so that even if *no one* in the course learned much of anything, it *appears* that *some* students "got it," and others didn't, so it's all (allegedly) a matter of the students' ability to learn (or lack thereof), not the professor's ability to teach (or lack thereof); and

(2) because the prof—or someone working for the prof—does the grading, the prof can guarantee that there *will* be grades that seem to indicate that some students really *did* "get it," even if they didn't.

With a curve, the "best and brightest" might actually be just the least incompetent of the incompetent. (But don't tell *them* that.)

The law profs do not merely grade on the curve, though. They use a "forced" curve, also known as a "normalized" curve. With a regular bell curve, it's possible that 15% of the class deserves an A+, A, or A-. But typically, with a forced curve, only five percent can get those grades. So the competition for the top scores is keen.

The law schools say they have to do this to ensure "uniformity" and "fairness" in grading. On the surface, that makes sense. After all, profs vary. Some are easy, some hard. But a forced curve creates only a meaningless uniformity. The Josephson Report discussed several experiments in which different graders reviewed the copies of the same set of students' answers on exams. The grades they gave varied widely for *each* student. Thus, there was no objective fairness, because of the subjectivity factor. The resulting uniformity of grading on a forced curve is real enough, but it does not reflect a uniformity of *standards*. And so it does not uniformly reflect the students' actual abilities.

But to the professoriat, that does not matter. They really don't care who wins and loses. All that counts is that there *be* winners and losers.

I am not advocating that law schools convert to objective, multiple-choice tests. That is not the problem. The problem is that the law schools fancy that their role is to separate the alleged wheat from the alleged chaff. *That* is deplorable.

It reminds me a lot of NASA's attitude toward the astronaut corps. Until recent years, astronauts had to be former military pilots. They came from a very "macho" culture. Astronauts were those who had "the right stuff." There was a mystique about them. Then, just a few years ago, the Russians, desperate for hard currency, announced that they would allow "space tourists" in return for the payment of millions of dollars. NASA strongly opposed this. It said that space was too dangerous for ordinary civilians without all the special training. The U.S. government nearly begged the Russians not to go through with it. The Russians ignored them. So far, two wealthy men have taken them up on the offer. Neither, to my knowledge, was a former military pilot, and the "training" each received was rudimentary. Both men completed their missions without mishap.

Is this to say that just anyone can put on a space suit and blast off and all will be well? Of course not. Those guys were there as tourists, not crew members, let alone as shuttle pilots. But their trips all but destroyed the mystique of astronauts. (And now NASA has joined in, by allowing a rock star, among others, to ride the shuttle into space.)

Of course, the first-year of law school is not a "tourist deal." Quite the contrary. But it is unworthy of the mystique that surrounds it. It's fatuous of the law schools to assume that at the level of first-year, they have to awe students by totally confusing them. Instead, as anyone in *any* walk of life knows, the better you are at what you do, the more you appreciate the really *great* ones, and the better you understand *why* they're great...even if you know that you can never rise to their level.

If a student does poorly on exams, then as long as that student passes, he or she will be able to "sit for the bar" upon graduation from law school. And if that student then passes the bar exam, he or she will be assuming responsibility for clients' legal problems. But if, objectively speaking, that student was incompetent every step of the way in law school, that student-as-newly-licensed-attorney is a walking case of legal malpractice. By playing hide-the-ball, the law schools *guarantee* this effect on most graduates.

Instead of pitting students against one another on a forced curve (or any curve at all), the law schools should establish a standard of competence. That standard should be set *high*. And it should be particularly rigorous in first-year.

I believe that all first-year law students should have to score at least 90% on their exams, on an objective scale. And they can do it... *if the professors stop playing hide-the-ball and start TEACHING.*

Law students are smart, highly motivated, and hard-working. They couldn't have gotten into law school were they otherwise. And they are desperate to understand the law, and to ascend what Michael Josephson called the six levels of the Law School Learning Pyramid. But the professoriat does everything it can to keep them from mastering even the foundational level.

I've heard or read where someone described lawyers as being merely "mechanics with words." That's not so. However, in the first year of law school, it's *close* to the truth. Mastering the Black Letter Law, and learning how to do a good lawyerlike analysis, at the *basic* level that first-year requires, is indeed close to merely "slotting the right things into the right places."

Nearly *all* incoming law students have "the right stuff." And the law schools should ensure that *all* first-year students have mastered at least the first four levels of the Josephson Pyramid. But that means better teaching. It also means an end to pitting students against one another on a forced curve in first-year. *Second*-year grades, based on papers or even forced-curve finals, can be used to separate those who allegedly are the potential great ones from those who are "merely" competent.

But at least those who *are* "merely" competent *will* be *competent*. That would make all the difference in the world to the quality of the legal profession, and to the quality of legal service that's provided to ordinary clients (versus the big-bucks clients the "best" students end up serving in the law factories).

And it would make law school a much more civil place, and thus perhaps help make the legal profession less uncivil in these days of "Rambo tactics."

One reason law schools emphasized first-year grades so heavily was that, until the 2002-2003 academic year, the federal courts made their decisions about hiring judicial clerks two years before students graduated. Students thus were chosen in the fall of second-year, to begin a judicial clerkship roughly 18 months later. And the only grades the judges had to go on were the grades from first-year.

That has now changed. Federal judges now are often choosing their judicial clerks only from those who have completed two years of law school. One wonders why it was ever otherwise.

What this means is that students can now use their performance in *second*-year courses as proof of their ability. So there's no need for the law schools to emphasize first-year as a way of separating the "masses" from "those who are destined for bigger and better things."

The Ivory Tower & The Barzam

Law schools report the percentage of their graduates who pass their state's bar exam on the first try. They make a big deal of it, to boost their ranking in *U.S. News & World Report*. But have you ever wondered why there's no data available as to the average *score* a school's students got on the bar exam—let alone various parts of it? (The data exists. It's just not released.) Given the fact (as Chapter 23 explains), that a *passing* score on the bar exam is exactly that (i.e., the lowest possible score you can get and still not flunk), and given that the passing score is often around *55 or 60*, wouldn't you like to know if a given law school's graduates had an average score that was closer to one end of the scale than the other? Wouldn't *that* tell you more about the quality of the "legal education" you're paying to get from that school than *any* other bit of information possibly could?

I think so. And maybe you do too. But the law schools do not want the state bar examiners (who track that information) to give that information out.

Breaking Free from the Toxic Mold

There are some law professors who not only have a conscience, but have the desire to try to change the system. One is Gerald Hess. In 1991, he founded the Institute for Law School Teaching, at Gonzaga* University (in Spokane, Washington). Its mission statement says:

> The Institute for Law School Teaching recognizes the obligations law schools owe to their students and to society to provide a learning environment to help students achieve the highest academic standards and to prepare students to assume their responsibilities as effective, moral attorneys.

This statement is revolutionary—in part because it's sincere. Law schools and the professoriat generally feel no such obligation, either to their students or to society. They are utterly uninterested in helping students achieve, academically. They certainly do not care about

---

* The first "a" in "Gonzaga" is long. Aloysius Gonzaga was a 16th-century Jesuit college student who was canonized. He was Italian, not Spanish.

preparing students to become effective, moral attorneys. And as Chapter 25 will discuss, they actively discourage students from being moral.

The group's statement continues: "The Institute is committed to improving the quality of teaching and learning in legal education."

ILST sponsors a conference every summer, for two or three days, with presentations on law school teaching. Participants can teach a mock law school class, and have their performance critiqued by pedagogical experts. If they wish, their presentation is videotaped. Then they can review the tape and try to eliminate some of their counterproductive techniques and quirks as pointed out during the critique. The exercise is perfunctory, at best. But it's a start.

Only about 50 law profs attend the conference each year. Yet, it law *schools* cared about making sure that their "teachers" could teach, they would require—and pay for—new hires to go through a training program on effective law school teaching. (Yes, AALS also offers a semi-annual program for new law profs. But see the addendum to the next chapter.)

In 1999, ILST published *Techniques for Teaching Law,* by Gerald Hess and Steve Friedland. In it, they noted that "Research shows that frequent evaluation improves student performance on the final exam." In any place but law school, that's been common faculty knowledge for decades. Hess and Friedland also discuss effective pedagogical methods such as "Classroom Assessment" and "Small Group Instructional Diagnosis." No point in discussing those here, but they would be a huge step in the right direction for law school pedagogy.

That book is the first ever written just for teaching law—and so far, is the *only* one. Yet, in the three years since it was published, it has sold a grand total of only 500+ copies...in a country where there are nearly 10,000 full-time professors, deans, and other administrators at law schools. (The total excludes law librarians.) *That* speaks volumes.

In 2000, the Institute published Gregory S. Munro's *Outcome Assessments for Law Schools,* quoted in Chapter 6 and in this one. As of this writing, Munro's book has been out for 30 months...and has sold a total of about 270 copies. That too speaks volumes.

In it, he gingerly speculated, "[T]eachers may cling to ineffective teaching and testing patterns simply because they are most convenient, least time consuming, and easiest."

—And those teaching and testing methods also support the professoriat's self-image as "natural-born geniuses of the law." (I doubt even Munro would take exception to that.)

Gonzaga is not a big-name school. And the members of the ILST's advisory committee do not come from big-name schools. As of this writing, they're at Vermont Law School, Arizona State University College of Law, Mercer University School of Law, Seattle University School of Law, Brooklyn Law School, and Queen's University Faculty of Law (Canada). Not one professor from a high-ranked school has gotten involved in the effort. Granted, it's better to have sincere people involved from low-ranked schools than to have people from high-ranked schools who only give "lip service" to the need for good teaching. But the fact that professors from big-name schools eschew the Institute speaks volumes about the attitude of the "powers that be" at the high-ranked schools. If professors thought it was a "career-enhancing" move to get involved with the Institute, they would. They don't.

The law school profs who are involved, however, are caught between a rock and a hard place. They know how bad the pedagogical malpractice of law schools is. Yet, they dare not strongly criticize it (the way *PLS* does). Nor do they even gently criticize law schools the way Michael Josephson did in his report to the Association of American Law Schools in 1984. And in fact, they've been too circumspect. The annual conference—and occasional articles in *The Journal of Legal Education* (which is not a prestigious academic journal)—are the extent of the Institute's efforts to date. They do have "Seven Principles for Good Practice in Legal Education" on their website (http://law.gonzaga.edu/ilst/ilst.htm). They reinforce the principles with "inventories," which consist of checklists for what law school teachers should be doing and encouraging their students to do. Most of the "inventories" seem to me to be "Mickey Mouse," as are ILST's three videos. But again, it's a start.

The only law school I know of that, across-the-board, *insists* that all its teachers actually be able to *teach* is Massachusetts School of Law. It's an independent school, not affiliated with a university. At MSL, when a prof is new to teaching, some of his or her classes are video-taped and then the prof sits in on a criticism session similar to that at the ILST's summer conference. And staff auditors continue to sit in on professors' classes from time to time, to make sure the profs are continuing to do a good job of teaching. (The American Bar Association has class visits as part of its accreditation and reaccreditation process. But those visits are a joke. This chapter gives an example, later.)

Of course, MSL might merely be making a virtue of necessity. It's not and will likely never be a big-name school. Since it can't compete with the high-ranked schools in "scholarship," it competes by producing "effective" (and perhaps even moral) lawyers. Regardless of the reason for MSL's approach, it appears to be unique. And that is tragic.

The "Kinder and Gentler" Professoriat

I regularly get e-mails from students saying "You're all wrong about professors. At *my* school, they're really nice. They *care* about us." One guy wrote that "I have a prof who's the greatest. He and I play racquetball together almost once every week." Another wrote, "One of my profs divided the class into groups. Each week, a different group goes to his house for a free dinner."

Gee, how nice. Pray tell, how does that help you learn the law and do a lawyerlike analysis?

As early as 1959, in his book, *The House of Intellect,* Jacques Barzun said, "A teacher is liked because he is a 'good guy.'...A faculty of good guys would make the ideal college, one of friendly and informal equals, warm as a family." Today, of course, it's probably even better to be a "cool dude" than it is to be a "good guy" (or gal). This seems to be a peculiarly American desideratum, this desire for "warm and fuzzy feelings." The students who want this have failed to realize that they're no longer in college...or should I say perhaps, no longer in nursery school? Time to grow up.

This reminds me of British colonial administrators in the heyday of their Empire. Quite often, above all, they just wanted to be liked. Or at least that's what they wanted the natives to think. But especially as the British colonies neared independence after WWII, it behooved these administrators to do what they could to prepare the locals for it. Instead, they did what they could to ensure that British industries would be able to continue to exploit the locals even after independence. And I think that's why, in so many countries that gained their independence after WWII (not just from Britain, either), the countries are a mess.

There are those who blame the locals, and say it's all a matter of culture, and there never was any hope for those countries anyway. But until the rise of the "Tigers" of Asia (Japan, Hong Kong, South Korea, Singapore, Thailand, Taiwan-Republic of China, and now Malaysia and the People's Republic of China), experts were saying that *those* places would never amount to anything economically because of their culture. It's always "blame the victim."

Now that the word is getting around about the Aspen primers, there are a few profs who put a primer on the "recommended" list, and even a few who require students to buy one. Yet, these professors still require students to do the same massive amount of make-work reading as before. Apparently this allows these profs to keep their consciences clear. But they know perfectly well their students do not have time to read the primers, from scratch, in addition to the assigned material.

Law profs may have gone from one extreme to the other, from the Kingsfield Syndrome (discussed in Chapter 11) to "Nice-Nice." But their underlying attitude is the same: "Either you have it, or you don't, so there's nothing I can do for you. And if you *don't* have it...well, that's not *my* problem."

An Illustration

One of my first-year professors was zealous in proving that he was our friend, that he really cared about us, about teaching, about the Law, etc. He even threw a big "get acquainted" party for us at his house early in the first semester. Many of us loved him, because—unlike the other professors—he was clearly on *our* side in the struggle to master the Law.

However, for some strange reason, try as he might, he could never make the Law clear to us. The more questions we asked, the more confused we became on hearing his answers. He was generous with his time outside of class. He'd recommend materials for "further reading." However, these were always abstruse, sometimes downright opaque. We just thought that's the way the Law is. Gee, it was hard. We felt very humble, even humiliated, in the face of this body of learning—and the professor's seeming familiarity with it all. If only we could penetrate the mysteries, join the ranks of the initiates. Someday. But when? It seemed as though we'd never find the key to unlock the door to the Hall of Understanding.

Because we were convinced that the professor was trying so hard to help us, we didn't want to let him down. We were sure he felt badly because we just weren't getting it—although he didn't let it show. And so, most of us probably put more time in on that course than any other...to no avail. We felt so much sympathy for him, because we were obviously so stupid and unworthy of his sincere exertions in our behalf. We all voted for him as Teacher of the Year. (He won.)

This was the Contracts prof I spoke of in Chapter 4, who used a helter-skelter approach. He habitually led people on, then let them down—or let them tear themselves apart, as in his first-year class. This was his routine practice; many unsuspecting students fell for it, and suffered for it. (His "seduce and abandon" method continued in the advanced courses.)

The worst enemy is the one you think is your good friend—until he or she stabs you in the back. This holds true in the practice of law, also, but I was surprised to have found it in law school...or rather, in a law school professor, especially such a seemingly likable one.

I later learned that—after doing very well at a top law school—he'd spent one year working for a federal appellate judge. Then he'd spent one year as an entry-level associate at a *very* prestigious law firm. But he'd never handled a contracts case. He probably couldn't have made things clear to us even if he'd wanted to; he really didn't know what he was talking about, period. (He taught a 3rd-year course in contract-drafting, even though he'd never written one in his life.) That is not uncommon among law school professors. As long as they know more than their students, it's easy to fake expertise.

The Blum primer on contracts in the Aspen E&E series was not published until years after I got out of law school. It was only upon reading it that I understood contract law, sorry to say.

"Con" Doesn't Stand Just for "Constitutional"

Imagine a situation where you want to learn how to invest money in publicly traded stocks. So you hire an advisor to teach you. The advisor charges several hundred dollars an hour. He tells you fascinating stories of his adventures in investing. And along the way, he uses terms such as "ex-dividend," "limit order," "puts and calls," "convertible debenture," "preferred common," "short sale," and "IPO."" But he never explains what those terms mean, and won't tell you what they mean. You're able to figure out some of them on your own, though. And this advisor/instructor is such a nice guy. You can't help but like him.

But after giving him thousands of dollars, you realize you still don't know how to invest your money well. In fact, you really don't know much about securities at all. And then he says, "Ah, well, you see, my job isn't really to teach you about securities. My job is just to teach you to think about securities. You have to take a 'review' course (which costs a couple thousand dollars) to actually learn how to invest in securities. But unless you'd paid for my advice, you wouldn't be eligible to sign up for that course. So, you definitely got your money's worth from me." And he's right: his "schooling" is what made you eligible for the "review" course, and you would not have been able to take it otherwise. Further, once you've taken that "review" course, you might get yourself into a situation where you'll have opportunities not only to invest, but to make some serious money.

However, did you get your money's worth? Did you *really* need him? What if you could have gotten into the "review" course without paying that advisor first, and you could have studied securities and investing on your own? As long as there were a final test that *everyone* had to take, what difference would it make how you learned the material for the test, such as on your own or from a hired advisor?

Perhaps you've been in love with someone who was not in love with you, yet who was very good at stringing you along. Any time there was an argument, it was because *you* "misunderstood" something—and it was always *you* who would end up apologizing. Somehow, when things weren't right, it was all *your* fault.

In the term "con artist," "con" stands for "confidence." It refers to gaining the intended victim's confidence, i.e., trust. Hence the expression, "Don't try to 'con' me."

Only the rarest of con artists is *not* "friendly." But at least when the con artist finally strikes, he or she usually disappears, *fast*, after running the "con," for the victim has discovered the truth.

The very *best* confidence artists, though, "keep the 'con' on."

A Suggested Compromise

In *Outcome Assessments for Law Schools*, Munro says:

> An essay exam at semester's end will test a student's knowledge in a summative fashion and provide almost no feedback to the student. On the other hand, suppose a teacher presents students with incremental problems of increasing complexity at the start of each chapter of a law textbook and requires students to analyze and solve the problems by seeking out and applying the law to the facts of the problem. When completed, the teacher reviews the answers and gives the students feedback. This is a type of formative learning experience that provides significant experience to the student.

Well, duh. I am not trying to make fun of Munro. Rather, the point here is that the situation in law school is so bad that a sincere, conscientious writer such as Munro has to use such circumlocution instead of saying, "Hey, guys! Isn't about time we start doing what we're getting *paid* to do—i.e., *teach?*" What Munro described is not some speculative venture, but the *minimal requirements* of teaching. Yet, it's obvious that he realizes it will be *news* to his fellows in the law professoriat

Chapter 16 of this edition of *PLS* has a do-it-yourself program of independent study of the law. The "examples and explanations" in the Aspen primers, the "illustrations" in the *Restatements,* the CALI

"Library of Lessons," along with the practice exams, accomplish what Munro recommended. And although you might not be interested in really learning the law, surely you're at least interested in doing well on your exams. As you saw in Chapter 8, your law professors are not sincerely interested in helping you learn anything—although, admittedly, some of them do a very good job of "keeping the 'con' on."

Given that the law school professoriat doesn't want to do any *teaching*, and detailed review of a practice exam such as discussed in Chapter 7 would involve a lot of work, what follows is a suggested compromise...

Professors could start handing out Exercises early in the semester. For example, upon the completion of each topic in the course, the prof could hand out some problems similar to those in the "Examples" sections of each chapter of the Aspen primers. Students could work out their answers over the next few days. The prof would then hand out model answers, similar to the "Explanations" sections of the Aspen primers. (The questions and answers could instead—or also—be posted to a website, or distributed via listserve, of course.)

If the prof were determined to give a "fruitcake" exam at the end of the course, he or she could hand out a practice problem early in the semester, after covering several different topics within the course. But instead of seeking a complete answer, the prof could just say, "identify all the possible conflict pairings, and all the possible causes of action." A few days later, the prof could hand out the answers.

The third step would be for the prof to hand out a "fruitcake" problem that *told you* what all the "conflict pairings" and the possible causes of action were. Your job would then be to analyze those causes of action, and the defenses to them (including the affirmative defenses), and to weigh the arguments on both sides. This would include, of course, spotting each *non*-issue, and explaining *why* it was a non-issue. As before, a model answer would then be handed out later.

The fourth and final step is the only one that profs do even partly now: providing a "fruitcake" problem (usually several, in old exams "on reserve" in the library), and require the sort of answer that would be needed on the real thing: conflict pairings, causes of action, spotting the element/s on each cause of action where there would be an issue, and a thorough discussion. However, this fourth step would include something new: handing out an explanation of *why* various alternatives to the model analysis were *in*correct (as Delaney does in his books).

Thus, the professor's additional work would be minimal, as he or she would not have to grade any of these assignments. (And doing the assignments would be voluntary.) I doubt more than a very few profs would be motivated to do this, however, given their "natural-born genius of the law" mentality...and their natural indolence.

For those rare profs who were more inclined to earn their pay as *teachers,* they could arbitrarily divide the class into practice-exam groups, and tell each group to submit a collective answer to the problem. (Many students would already be in study groups. The prof would then only have to assign to practice-exam groups those who had not joined a study group.) But this time, instead of merely providing a model answer, the prof could meet with each group, as a group, and go over its answer in detail. During the meeting, the prof would give *meaningful* answers to students' questions (unlike the nebulous comments of the prof quoted by the student in Chapter 7). Instead of going over as many as 100 exams (or even more), the prof could set the size of the groups working on the exams so that he or she would not have to deal with more than, say, a couple dozen proposed answers.

The title of this chapter is taken from an 1886 novel by Robert Louis Stevenson, *Strange Case of Dr. Jekyll and Mr. Hyde.** Dr. Jekyll was a scientist and a good guy. But he developed a liquid substance that he then drank. The formula turned him into a murderous fiend, who became known as "Mr. Hyde." It was only much, much later that it was discovered that Dr. Jekyll and Mr. Hyde were one and the same.

As your friendly Professor Jekyll gives you warm and fuzzy feelings, just remember his or her exam awaits you. But of course, if you don't do well, it's all *your* fault. You just didn't have what it takes.

Decades ago, a shrink named Eric Berne published a book called *Games People Play.* One of the games was called something like "Let's you and him fight." As part of this game, the person who pitted the antagonists against one another remains "above it all" and a "friend" to both sides. —This is a favorite tactic of executives regarding subordinates, by the way. (FDR, in particular, did it all the time.) When you and your fellow students deteriorate into a "dog-eat-dog" attitude as finals approach, give thought to the kindly dogcatcher.

And when you see that exam, and realize how little your "caring" prof clued you in as to how to learn the law and how to do a good lawyerlike analysis, maybe you will realize, at that fateful moment, that your Professor Jekyll was Mr./Ms. Hide-the-Ball all along.

For those who insist that their profs are "great" because the profs are so friendly and "accessible," here are three suggestions.

---

* That is not a typo. The title is not *THE Strange Case...,* just *Strange Case....*

1. Ask them to implement the proposals above.

2. If you really think your prof is "on your side," ask him or her why your law school uses a forced curve in first-year, pitting all the students against each other for the top slots, instead of ensuring that *all* first-year students attain a (high) minimal level of competence in Black Letter Law and doing a lawyerlike analysis.

3. See how closely your profs resemble Graham and Lake, before you declare them good.

Just for fun, tell the "good" prof you're interested in becoming a law school professor yourself, and you've heard of the Institute for Law School Teaching. Then ask, "Can you tell me something about it?" Or ask if the prof knows of the Hess & Friedland book, *Techniques for Teaching Law,* or Munro's *Outcome Assessments for Law Schools.* Quite likely, the prof will claim to know about these, but will say something like "However, I really can't say much, off the top of my head.")

The "new and improved" law school professoriat, that's "kinder and gentler," brings to mind an old children's poem:

The Spider and the Fly
by Mary Howitt (1799-1888)

"Will you walk into my parlour?" said the Spider to the Fly,
"'Tis the prettiest little parlour that ever you did spy;
The way into my parlour is up a winding stair,
And I've a many curious things to shew when you are there."
"Oh no, no," said the little Fly, "to ask me is in vain,
For who goes up your winding stair can ne'er come down again."

"I'm sure you must be weary, dear, with soaring up so high;
Will you rest upon my little bed?" said the Spider to the Fly.
"There are pretty curtains drawn around; the sheets are fine and thin,
And if you like to rest awhile, I'll snugly tuck you in!"
"Oh no, no," said the little Fly, "for I've often heard it said,
They never, never wake again, who sleep upon your bed!"

Said the cunning Spider to the Fly, "Dear friend what can I do,
To prove the warm affection I've always felt for you?
I have within my pantry, good store of all that's nice;
I'm sure you're very welcome—will you please to take a slice?"
"Oh no, no," said the little Fly, "kind Sir, that cannot be,
I've heard what's in your pantry, and I do not wish to see!"

"Sweet creature!" said the Spider, "you're witty and you're wise,
How handsome are your gauzy wings, how brilliant are your eyes!
I've a little looking-glass upon my parlour shelf,
If you'll step in one moment, dear, you shall behold yourself."
"I thank you, gentle sir," she said, "for what you're pleased to say,
And bidding you good morning now, I'll call another day."

The Spider turned him round about, and went into his den,
For well he knew the silly Fly would soon come back again:
So he wove a subtle web, in a little corner sly,
And set his table ready, to dine upon the Fly.
Then he came out to his door again, and merrily did sing,
"Come hither, hither, pretty Fly, with the pearl and silver wing;
Your robes are green and purple—there's a crest upon your head;
Your eyes are like the diamond bright, but mine are dull as lead!"

Alas, alas! how very soon this silly little Fly,
Hearing his wily, flattering words, came slowly flitting by;
With buzzing wings she hung aloft, then near and nearer drew;
Thinking only of her brilliant eyes, and green and purplish hue—
Thinking only of her crested head—poor foolish thing!
At last, Up jumped the cunning Spider, and fiercely held her fast.
He dragged her up his winding stair, into his dismal den.
Within his little parlor—but she ne'er came out again!

And now dear little children, who may this story read,
To idle, silly flattering words, I pray you ne'er give heed:
Unto an evil counsellor, close heart and ear and eye,
And take a lesson from this tale, of the Spider and the Fly.

* * *

Snicker all you will at this old, corny poetry, and call its inclusion in this book "over the top." But you (perhaps) shall see.

"Better Learning, Better Lawyers: Building Toward a Better Future"

The first edition of *PLS* was criticisized for its unrelenting condemnation of the law school professoriat (as no doubt this edition will also be). They will say that most professors are good, and that most professors "care." Here's another offer of "proof of facts" for them...

The subheading above was the title of a program to be held August 8–10, 2002 in Austin, Texas. It had two "tracks." One was for legal educators, and was called "Humanizing Legal Education." Its co-sponsors included four Texas law schools. The two-day program included presentations on the following topics:

> "Law Student Distress - The Scholarly Literature"
> "Law Student Distress - The Students' View"
> "Possible Causes of Phenomenon" Part I -
>   *Methods of Instruction"* (emphasis added)
> "Possible Causes of Phenomenon, Part II -
>   *Methods of Evaluation"* (emphasis added)
> "Possible Causes of Phenomenon, Part III -
>   *Tacit Negative Values"* (emphasis added)
> "Legal Education in the 21st Century:
>   Radical Design for a Changing Profession"
> "The First Year: The Legal Research & Writing Course"
> "Lawyering Skills Courses"
> "The Large Traditional Course"
> "Humanizing the Practice of Law"
> "Where Do We Go from Here in the Academy?"

The first five presentations were scheduled for 1 hour, 15 minutes each. "Legal Education in the 21st Century" was to be 30 minutes, the presentation on "The Legal Research & Writing" course was to be 45 minutes. The presentation on "Lawyering Skills Courses" was to last 50 minutes, "The Large Traditional Course" was set for 55 minutes. "Humanizing the Practice of Law" and "Where Do We Go from Here in the Academy?" were each scheduled for one hour.

Twenty-four law school professors and one non-law prof, representing 20 schools, were to present papers and serve on panel discussions.

The "legal education track" within the two-day program was geared to the nearly 10,000 full-time law professors and administrators. (This total does not include law librarians or adjunct law school faculty, the latter of whom, alone, number in untold additional thousands.)

Timely notice of the program went out to the dean of every law school in the country. Other co-sponsors of the program were entities within the American Bar Association, the Texas State Bar, and a private dispute resolution center; these sent out their own announcements.

The program was cancelled...due to *lack of interest*. Only *eight* professors wanted to learn about such topics as "law student distress," "legal education in the 21st century," and "humanizing the practice of law."

The person in charge of handling the reservations was an employee of the Texas State Bar. She said that she'd been at her job for years, but could not remember *ever* having to cancel a program because of insufficient sign-ups.

She said that law schools have limited budgets for sending professors to programs, and perhaps there was a scheduling conflict with a more important program (that she was not aware of). Or maybe the professoriat had already attended enough programs of a similar nature (even though the program in Austin was, to her—and my—knowledge, the first of its kind).

Yet, even among the hundreds of law professors at the nine law schools in *Texas,* and even with *four* of those schools (the public ones) serving as co-sponsors, there was insufficient interest despite the program's convenient location in the center of the state.

Other than a signed declaration from the members of America's law school professoriat, admitting that "*PLS* is *right* in what it says about us," I cannot think of better evidence of the faculty's true attitude...except, perhaps, the articles (and others like them) quoted in Chapter 8.

It's especially discouraging that, of the two dozen law school professors who were scheduled to present papers or serve on panels during the program, not one was from a high-ranking school. And although I was unable to obtain a list of registrants, to see what law schools they represented, I seriously doubt that any of the eight professors who signed up to be in the audience was from a big-name school.

Because *PLS* is indeed critical of the law school professoriat, here is a list of those who were scheduled to be on the program faculty:

Benjamin, Andrew G.H. - Affiliate Prof. of Law and Clinical Professor
of Medicine, University of Washington
Collett, Teresa - Prof., South Texas College of Law
Curcio, Andi - Prof., Georgia State University College of Law
Daicoff, Susan - Prof., Florida Coastal School of Law
DiPippa, John M.A. - Prof., University of Arkansas at Little Rock,
William H. Bowen School of Law
Floyd, Daisy Hurst - Prof., Texas Tech University Law School
Floyd, Tim - Hadley Edgar Professor of Law, Texas Tech U. Law School
Glessner-Fines, Barbara - Prof., Univ. of Mo. at Kansas City School of Law
Hessler, Kathy - Prof., Case Western Reserve University Law School
Iijima, Ann - Prof., William Mitchell College of Law
Kerr, Irwin - Prof., The George Washington University School of Law
Krieger, Larry - Director, Clinical Externship Program, and Prof.,
Florida State University College of Law
Lustbader, Paula - Director, Academic Resource Center, and Prof.,
Seatlle University School of Law
Morin, Laurie - Prof., University of the District of Columbia,
David A. Clarke School of Law
Organ, Jerome Michael - Prof., University of Saint Thomas
[Minneapolis] School of Law
Post, Deborah Waire, Professor, Touro College, Jacob D. Fuchsberg
Law Center
Rapoport, Nancy, Dean, University of Houston Law Center
Schuwerk, Robert P., Prof., University of Houston Law Center*
Sheehy, Richard (J.D., Ph.D.) - Assist. Prof., Counselor Education,
Drake University
Silechia, Luria Ann - Prof., The Catholic Univ. of America School of Law
Silver, Marjorie A. - Prof., Touro College, Jacob D. Fuchsberg Law Center
Suni, Ellen Yankiver - Prof., Univ. of Mo. at Kansas City School of Law
Teeter, Jr., John W. - Prof., St. Mary's University School of Law
Wexler, David - John D. Lyons Professor of Law, Prof. of Psychology,
University of Arizona, James E. Rogers College of Law
Winick, Bruce - Prof., University of Miami School of Law

These, along with those who are affiliated with the Institute for Law
School Teaching, are among the very few who probably really *do*
care—about something other than their own prestige and paychecks...
who really do care about legal *education.*

* Schuwerk was also the Director of the ill-fated program.

Cui Bono? *

Roughly half a century ago, the man who was in charge of General Motors, "Engine Charlie" Wilson (not to be confused with "Billion-Dollar Charlie" of HLS), made a statement that went something like this: "What's good for GM is good for the country." The attitude of the law schools is "What's good for the professoriat is good for the students and, in turn, good for the legal profession and, in turn, good for the country."

There are those who've criticized *PLS* because, they say, it alleges a "conspiracy" among law school professors and deans, etc. Apparently they put those who believe in a possible conspiracy in the same category as those who believe they've been abducted by intergalactic aliens and taken aboard "flying saucers."

The term "conspiracy" became a basis for personal attack as a result of the controversy surrounding the assassination of President Kennedy in 1963. Interestingly, JFK's successor as President, Lyndon Johnson, said—after he'd left the White House—that *he* had always believed JFK died at the hands of a conspiracy. And the 1979 Report of the House Select Commission on Assassinations said there *was* a conspiracy.

The word "conspiracy" is just a pejorative for a cooperative effort involving a relatively small number of people. When President Eisenhower, in his farewell address in 1961, announced the existence of a "military-industrial complex," was he a "conspiracy theorist"? Or how about the efforts of Enron, Exxon, and other energy companies to gain control of George W's energy policy in 2001? This involved a series of secret meetings with top government officials, including the Vice President of the United States. And their behind-the-scenes efforts were successful. Was that a "conspiracy"?

Regardless, *PLS* is in good company, for in 1995 the U.S. Department of Justice filed a civil antitrust suit against the American Bar Association in connection with law school accreditation. "Beginning at least as early as 1973 and continuing until the date of this Complaint, the ABA and its conspirators have engaged in a continuing conspiracy in unreasonable restraint of interstate trade and commerce in violation of Section 1 of the Sherman Act," the feds said. In its Competitive Impact Statement filed as part of the suit, the Department of Justice stated that "[R]ather than setting minimum standards for law school quality, and thus providing valuable information to consumers, the legitimate process of accreditation, the ABA at times acted as a guild that protected the interests of professional law school personnel."

---

* Latin: "For whose good?"

The suit alleged 11 points of "anticompetitive standards and practices" by the ABA.

Point 1 was the domination of the ABA's accreditation process by law school faculty and deans who have a vested interest in continuing the anti-competitive practices their predecessors at the ABA had put in place.

If you took American history in high school, you surely remember that when the original federal agencies were set up to regulate industries that were "ripping off" the public, it did not take long before those various agencies were soon "captured" by representatives of the industries they were supposed to regulate. Well, the same thing exists, even now, with regard to America's law schools. The federal government deferred to the ABA as a quasi-official regulatory agency. And the major law schools soon saw to it that they dominated the ABA's accreditation committee. Would it surprise you to learn that *90% of the committee's members were full-time law school professors or deans?*

Point 2 concerned what can be called a Faculty Perpetual Salary Increase Motion Machine.

The racket worked this way: a statistical "median" in a set of data is the middle figure in the data. It is not an "average" (more properly known as a "mean"). Rather, the median is the number that splits the data points in half; half the other numbers are above that figure, and half below it. So if half the full-time full professors of law in the country were making over $125,000 a year in base salary, and half under, then $125,000 would be the median salary.

The ABA told law schools below the salary median that they should pay "closer to the median." But when a school paid more, that pushed the median up. And, of course, every time a school *above* the median raised its faculty's salaries, that *pulled* the median up. Thus, the pushing and pulling worked in tandem, in a never-ending process—a perpetual motion machine to boost the salaries of full-time law school profs.

As Anne K. Bingaman, then in charge of the antitrust division, told the press, "The ABA's accreditation process required that universities raise salaries to artificially-inflated levels, and meet other costly accreditation requirements that had little to do with the quality of legal education they provided."

Point 3. "The ABA has required that an accredited law school must be organized as a non-profit institution. The ABA has never accredited a proprietary law school", according to the federal complaint.

Point 4 dealt with the ABA's continuing discrimination against schools not ABA-accredited. It had a rule *forbidding* ABA-accredited schools from accepting transfer credits from students who'd come from non-

ABA schools. It also forbade schools from allowing their own students to get credit for courses taken at non-ABA schools. And those who'd obtained their basic law degree from a *non*-ABA school could *not* get an *advanced* law degree (such as the LL.M.) from an ABA school.

So, students enrolled at ABA-schools were effectively barred from taking courses during the summer at non-ABA schools, because they could not count those credits toward graduation from their home school. Likewise, a student who'd completed first-year at a non-ABA school could not transfer to an ABA law school, but would have to apply (and if accepted) start over as a first-year student. (And given the inherent advantage someone would have who'd already completed a year of law school, it's extremely unlikely that any ABA law school *ever* admitted a student who'd already been through first-year elsewhere.)

Point 5 noted that the ABA required a student-faculty ratio of no higher than 20:1 for accreditation. However, only *full-time tenure track* professors counted as "faculty." There was no provision for counting *adjunct* faculty, or law school *administrators* who also taught a course from time to time, or *emeritus* faculty who continued to teach after official retirement. Even *full*-time faculty were not figured into the student-faculty ratio if those faculty (1) were also teaching in another school at the same university, or (2) in some instances, were *visiting* professors (teaching at this school for a year before returning to their home schools), or (3) were clinical education profs, lecturers, or instructors—unless they were tenure-track (which is almost never the case for teachers in these categories).

The refusal to give even "partial credit" to adjuncts, administrators, and non-tenure-track teachers had a particularly debilitating impact on schools that primarily offer *evening* programs. (Most of the proprietary schools are "night schools.")

Point 6 concerned teaching loads. The start of this chapter of *PLS* noted that profs teach 6-8 hours a week, max. That's because of an *ABA rule*. (And, of course, because law profs dominated, and still dominate, the accreditation process, "the ABA rule" requiring light workloads for law profs was really just a rule enacted by the professors themselves.) If a prof taught two sections of the same course in any given semester, that prof was allowed to carry as much as ten hours of class a week. Otherwise, eight was the limit.

Point 7 dealt with the ABA rule that law schools give each prof at least a year off on a regular basis. The rule did not require that it be a *paid* leave of absence. But as the suit noted, "in practice, the ABA has required" it. So, a school that wanted to hold down students' tuition by not paying for sabbaticals would jeopardize getting or keeping accreditation from the ABA. And that was the whole idea, from the point of view of the law profs who controlled accreditation.

Point 8 was on bar "review" courses. (We'll return to this in Chapter 24.)

Point 9 challenged the vagueness and misuse of the ABA's requirement that a law school have an "adequate physical plant," a.k.a. "adequate facilities."

Point 10 complained of the vaguess and misuse of the ABA's requirement that a law school have "adequate resources" to "sustain a sound legal education program." This is a euphemism for "money."

Point 11 concerned the "Operation of the Law School Accreditation Process." This related to the secret, arbitrary (even capricious), vague, and inconsistent practices of the ABA in granting or withholding its approval.

(When I was in law school, one day the professor teaching a course announced that two reps from the ABA would be showing up the next day. He warned us students to "be good" in class. Only one rep came, however...and fell asleep within ten minutes. A few days later, the prof disclosed—outside of class—that he and another prof had taken the two ABA reps out to dinner and then a night on the town. They'd made sure both guests were well lubricated the night before the class. Chuckling, he then said that the rep who'd failed to show for class had been "indisposed" after the night out—and the one who did show had not realized that he'd slept through the class. However, the one who sat in on the class had assured the prof that the class was great and that he and the other rep would give a glowing reaccreditation report to the ABA. So much for quality control...and impartiality.)

Running into the Wahl Commission

As mentioned, the Department of Justice filed suit against the ABA in 1995. However, it began its antitrust investigation in 1994—perhaps in response to the private antitrust suit filed in 1993 against the ABA by the Massachusetts School of Law. The DOJ action was resolved by settlement agreement. (MSL, in contrast, lost its suit.)

On Point 1, the ABA agreed that no more than half the members of the Accreditation Committee or the Council that oversees it would be "law school deans or faculty."

On Point 2, the ABA promised to neither solicit nor gather data on faculty salaries, nor to use faculty salaries as a criterion for accreditation.

For Point 3, it agreed not to use a school's non-profit or for-profit nature as a criterion.

Addressing Point 4, it promised not to bar graduates of non-ABA schools from eligibility for advanced law degrees from ABA schools. And it said it would allow students to transfer credits from non-ABA schools (but only up to one-third the total credits required for the basic law degree at the ABA school).

So, the consent decree resolved only four of the 11 points.

As for the rest, it noted that the ABA had set up an in-house review panel on accreditation policies and practices. (This was only after the Massachusetts School of Law had filed its suit against the ABA and the Department of Justice had begun its investigation of the ABA.) The court referred to this as "The Special Commission to Review the Substance and Process of the ABA's Accreditation of American Law Schools." The consent decree required the Commission to complete its review and file its report with the judge. The panel was to address the seven points of complaint not covered in the agreed judgment.

The panel was informally known as the "Wahl Commission" (after its chairperson, Justice Rosalie E. Wahl of Minnesota's Supreme Court). What turned out to be the Commission's initial report is dated August 3, 1995. Its Supplementary Report is dated October 31, 1995.

Of the Commissiion's 15 members, six were law school deans at the time, and one was a former law school dean then serving as president of a university. Justice Wahl had been a law professor from the time she got her law degree until her appointment to the Minnesota Supreme Court. I do not know how many, if any, of the remaining 47% of the members were, as with Justice Wahl herself, *also* long-time former law school faculty or deans (or former non-legal academicians).

As to Point 5 of the federal suit, on student-faculty ratios and the definition of "faculty," the Commission stated (page 7, Supplementary Report) that "the contribution of individuals who do not come within the definition of 'full-time faculty'" should be considered if the school's student-faculty ratio is *above* 20:1. Thus, it appears that the three groups of teachers listed on page 283 in this chapter *still* would *not* be counted—except to bring the ratio *below 30:1* (which is the limit for ABA accreditation)...but only after the ratio has exceeded 20:1.

Point 6 concerned teaching loads. The Wahl Commission recommended scrapping the "quantitative approach." Insted, it endorsed a rule whereby "qualitative factors" could be considered, such as the time the prof spent "preparing for class," or in "office hours" to be available to students, time the prof spent on "research," or in faculty meetings, etc. It appears that this "qualitative approach" is intended to justify a claim by faculty members that their *real* "workload" is already vastly higher than 8-10 hours a week.

Point 7 was on faculty leaves of absence. The Commission said (Initial Report, page 27; Supplementary Report, page 5) that the ABA had never *required* that sabbaticals be with *pay*. So, there was no need to change the ABA's rule requiring law schools to give full-time faculty leaves-of-absence on a regular basis. But what the antitrust suit had said, recall, was "In *practice* [emphasis added], the ABA has required that law schools provide their faculty with paid leaves." Thus, the ABA's special commission intentionally ignored the heart of the federal complaint on Point 7. "Problem? *What* problem? No problem *here*."

Point 8 was on in-house bar prep courses at the law schools. (See Chapter 24.)

Point 9 concerned the requirement of an "adequate physical plant" a.k.a. "adequate facilities." (In practice, this has most often meant "having a big library.") As with Point 7, the Commission said it was all a misunderstanding. The ABA's accreditation people were *not* "excessive" about this. Rather, the Commission's two reports implied, when the ABA criticized a law school about its physical plant or facilities, it was because the administration and faculty at that law school had raised the point *themselves*—and wanted to use the ABA's criticism as leverage to get more money out of the alumni to address a serious problem. Thus, the ABA was merely following the lead of the people who had to deal with the problem day in and day out. No need to change *that* rule.

Point 10 dealt with "adequate resources" for law schools. According to the Commission (Initial Report, page 13), what the feds had been upset about was that the ABA had supposedly been "extreme or unreasonable about enforcing the Standards on allocation of resources." It then said, "The Commission is unable to comment on whatever information may be in the possession of the Department of Justice that gave rise to this implication." Never mind that the DOJ had collected "over 200 boxes" of material from the ABA. Apparently the Wahl Commission had no idea what the Department of Justice had discovered during its year-long investigation before it filed suit.

The Commission interpreted Point 10 to refer *only* to "the allocation of resources between the law school and its parent university" (Supplementary Report, page 12, referring to Initial Report, page 32-33). This is a discreet way of referring to the funds a university skims off its law school (and thus from the law school's students).

Many (perhaps all) law schools affiliated with universities have written agreements stating how much of law students' tuition and fees the law school must pay to the parent university. Sometimes these payments are inflated charges for security or maintenance or other "university services." (It operates in a manner similar to the "transfer pricing" multinational corporations use to avoid taxes.) But usually the payments are just blanket transfers of funds—as mentioned, a *surcharge* on *law* students by the parent university.

"Ensuring that adequate resources are available" is a polite way of saying "the parent university shouldn't kill the goose that lays the golden eggs." (Interestingly, the Commission defended the ABA by saying that it "had received no complaints" about this from any law school dean or any president of a law school's parent university. Small wonder. Given the power the university exerts over the law school, the silence of the law school deans is not surprising. And given the wealth the university extracts from law school students, did the Commission actually think it possible that a university president would "complain" that his or her university was entitled to skim off even *more?*)

Point 11 concerned the operation of the accreditation process. In response, the Wahl Commission focused at great length on the nitty-gritty of the "site visitation" teams, whose members "inspect" law schools for accreditation or re-accreditation. They did not address the ABA's continuing ability to exercise arbitrary (even capricious), vague, and inconsistent practices in granting or withholding its approval.

The Sham...and the Shame

The proposed consent decree was held in abeyance for a year, to allow public comment on it, and on the Wahl Commission Report concerning Points 5-11. On June 25, 1996, the consent decree was rendered as the court's final judgment. *United States v. American Bar Association,* 934 F. Supp. 435 (D.D.C. 1996).

Several things are disturbing about the federal suit and the consent decree.

First, the proposed agreed judgment was filed with the court on the *same day* as the lawsuit itself: June 27, 1995. So, there were no formal "discovery" procedures (depositions, interrogatories, etc.) that might have become public records. Nor, for the same reason, were there any formal court proceedings (such as hearings) that were open to the public while suit was pending.

Second (and related to the first), whatever the Department of Justice found during its investigation is now "under seal." (This is standard operating procedure when a federal civil antitrust case is resolved simultaneously with the filing of a formal lawsuit.) Now there's no way to see the evidence—including "over 200 boxes of documents submitted by the ABA," according to the federal government's response to public comments about a proposed modification of the consent decree. This means that any subsequent private suit would incur very high discovery costs, because the plaintiff/s would be starting from scratch.

Third (and related to the previous two), it's obvious that the Department of Justice and the ABA had been *negotiating a deal* behind closed doors throughout the "investigation." Granted, though, that sometimes happens in federal civil antitrust cases. But because all the feds' evidence is now under seal, it's impossible to know whether the agreement they reached reflected the merits of the feds' case.

Fourth, the consent decree was responsive only to Points 1-4 of the DOJ's suit. The Wahl Commission had whitewashed the ABA regarding the seven remaininng points. It had denied a problem existed on Points 7-11, and all but openly stated that the feds' case had no merit on these. As to Points 5 and 6, it recommended only cosmetic changes. *Yet neither the Department of Justice nor the Court objected to this.*

This is especially troublesome because of the ABA's response to Point 7, the faculty sabbaticals. The DOJ had noted *in its suit* that the ABA had no express rule requiring *paid* leaves of absense, but that it was the ABA's *sub rosa* rule. The Wahl Commission ignored this concern—and thus indirectly told DOJ to get lost. So there was all the more reason for the feds (*and the presiding judge*) to question whether the Wahl Commission was acting in good faith on *any* of the seven points it was supposed to address. Yet, not a word was raised in protest.

(Granted, with a proposed settlement agreement, a judge is not to delve into the details. If the parties are satisfied, the court is supposed to merely ensure that the proposed judgment, as written, meets certain minimum standards. However, a proposed settlement in a civil antitrust suit is a different matter. Especially when the federal government is the plaintiff, the public interest is strongly implicated. And it's the responsibility of the court to scrutinize the proposed settlement to ensure that it serves the public interest. The court apparently did not do that in *this* case—for had it done so, it would have realized the Wahl Commission's whitewash, and the empty gesture of the consent decree.)

Seven Years After

Point 1, recall, concerned the law schools' dominance of the accreditation process.

For the 2002–03 year, the "accreditation committee" (officially, the "Section Committee on ABA Standards for Appraisal of Law Schools") has 19 members. The chairman is a law school professor. The vice-chairman is a law school dean. Eight other members are law profs, and three others are law deans. So, *nearly three-fourths* of the committee are still law school academics.

But the Council of the ABA Section of Legal Education and Admissions to the Bar is the locus of the far greater power.

Under Standard 801, the Council determines, by *itself,* all the "policies," "standards," "rules," and "interpretations" that govern it. True, it's required to inform the ABA's House of Delegates of any changes. The House of Delegates, at its regular meeting, "shall at that meeting either agree with the Council's decision or refer the decision back to the Council for further consideration." Note, there is no option for *overruling* the Council's decision. Standard 801 then also says: "If the House refers a Council decision back to the Council twice, then *the decision of the Council following the second referral will be final and will not be subject to further review by the House.*" (Emphasis added.)

Also under Standard 801, "The Council shall have the authority to grant or deny a law school's application for provisional or full approval or to withdraw provisional or full approval from a law school."

So who's on this Council? As of April 2003 its chairman is Thomas Sullivan, dean of the University of Minnesota's law school. (Coincidentally, he'd been a member of the Wahl Commission.)

Sixteen other people are listed as "members." Seven are current full-time law school academics (including two deans).

So, at first glance, the ABA has complied with the consent decree's 50% limitation on law school academics' membership. However, two other members are former law school academics (one prof, one dean). Thus, of the 16 ordinary members of the Council, 57% are likely committed to seeing things from the perspective of the legal professoriat. The ABA thus is technically within the letter of the consent decree, but has violated its spirit.

Further, one of the "public" members is another dean, but just not at a law school. And there's a "law student member"—who is unlikely to buck the system. So nearly 70% of the Council's members can arguably be classed as adherents of the guild, even without considering the influence of the law school dean who is the Council's chairman.

(You can confirm all this at the ABA's website, which is http://www.abanet.org/legaled.html. Look under "sections.")

Although the ABA is barred from denying accreditation because of "inadequate" faculty salaries (Point 2) or a school's proprietary nature (Point 3), it still has a free hand to deny accreditation supposedly for other reasons that have nothing to do with these. More on this, below.

Under Point 4, ABA schools cannot bar students' transfer credits merely because those credits are from non-ABA schools. But of course there's still nothing to stop a school from turning down a *student* from a non-ABA school—a student who went to a non-ABA school for first-year and wants to transfer to the ABA school, or who completed the basic law degree at a non-ABA school and now wants to enroll at an ABA school for an advanced degree. There is no "compliance mechanism" in place to ensure that the boycott has not continued in a new way.

As mentioned, under Point 6, the Commission endorsed an *expansion* of the ABA's discretionary powers in connection with denying accreditation or re-accreditation based on teacher workloads.

Point 9, "adequate facilities," is what provides the biggest opportunity of all for the ABA to exercise arbitrary power. There are no objective standards as to what "adequate facilities" means, so "inadequate" facilities becomes the catch-all for continuing discrimination by the ABA. And there's no way to question the soundness of their decision.

(When *you* get to law school, you might find it interesting to keep track of how many library books you use during your three years. And you might want to ponder what legitimate purpose all the other books serve relative to *your* legal "education"—and what you're actually paying for.)

Point 11, which the Wahl Commission (and eventually the DOJ and the court) also "blew off," concerned the very nature of the accrediting process itself.

Gary Palm is a law professor who served on the ABA's accreditation committee for six years. Then he served on the Council that makes final decisions on recommendations from the committee about accreditation. In 2000, after ending his time on the council, Palm sent the U.S. Department of Justice a letter. In it, he said that law schools with powerful friends receive less scrutiny in the accreditation process than others do. He also said, "There is no system in place to ensure consistency." Is it a coincidence that new schools that get approval have typically hired former members of the accreditation committee to advise them on how to go about it?

The ABA still only rarely releases a report filed by those involved in the accreditation process, and the release is entirely a matter of *its* discretion. The law school involved *cannot* release the reports about itself. The deliberations of the accreditation committee and the Council are all in secret, even now. Just as with the professors themselves within their own law schools, there is no scrutiny of what they do, and they have no accountability. The vagueness of the standards for accreditation, combined with the secrecy of the accreditation process, lends itself easily to unfair discrimination. But what's at stake, for thousands of law students as well as dozens of law schools, is staggering.

If an *official* governmental regulatory agency did business this way, there would be a nationwide outcry. But as it is, the only prominent person I know of who's protested this ABA Star Chamber is Thomas Sowell, of The Hoover Institution at Stanford University.

A.B.A. Über Alles

The antitrust suit did not address the ABA's continuing campaign to become the *sole* accrediting agency for *all* law schools.

As of this writing, California, Alabama, Tennessee, Mississippi, and Massachusetts are the only states left that require their law schools to have accreditation only from the state. ABA approval is optional.

But states that *require* their law schools to be ABA-accredited also have (at the ABA's urging) a rule that says anyone who graduated from a law school in another state can take this state's bar exam only if the law school the student graduated from in the other state is ABA-accredited. (In some states, however, the graduate is allowed to take the state's bar exam...after being licensed elsewhere for *several years*.) To provide graduates of the non-ABA states' law schools with the freedom to accept job offers and practice law in other states, this rule in the ABA states puts enormous pressure on the non-ABA states to fall in line.

Before the antitrust consent decree, Georgia did not require its law schools to have ABA accreditation. But when the ABA stepped up its campaign to convert the hold-out states, Georgia soon caved in. All the law schools there then had to scramble to put themselves under the ABA's thumb. One of those schools was the John Marshall School of Law, in Atlanta (not to be confused with the John Marshall School of Law in Chicago). It was a freestanding, proprietary law school. And guess what happend to its application for ABA accreditation?

The U.S. Higher Education Act, and the Department of Education's regulations interpreting it, require that an accrediting body be "separate and independent" from an affiliated trade group. As discussed earlier (page 289), the ABA's House of Delegates have no power over the practices and decisions of the Committee on Accreditation or the Council. The Committee and the Council are a law unto themselves.

However, it was proposed to the Department that authority to accredit law schools should no longer reside in either the Committee or the Council. Instead, law schools would be accredited *only* by state or regional authorities. The Department *vetoed* that proposal, saying it would be "impractical." Thus, again thanks to the Department of Education, power remains concetrated in the secretive ABA.

Supposedly the ABA cannot take into account that a law school is freestanding (i.e., not affiliated with a university). But there's more than one way to skin a cat. The ABA has been especially harsh with freestanding law schools, particularly those that are "for-profit."

Robert J. D'Agostina fought a long, losing battle against the ABA to get accreditation for Atlanta's freestanding John Marshall School of Law. According to him, at one point the ABA told him to spend another *million* dollars on the school's *library*. They didn't tell him *how* to spend it, just to *spend* it. —And, of course, the expenditure meant the school had to charge students more tuition.

That was the point. Most prospective attorneys would prefer to attend a decently ranked law school. So the ABA helps ensure that the only decently ranked law schools are those that are affiliated with a university. (The process continues when profs and deans affiliated with universities are asked to "evaluate" law schools for *U.S. News & World Report's* annual rankings. The vast majority of law profs and deans are at university-affiliated law schools. Not surprisingly, virtually all the freestanding law schools are ranked in the fourth tier. *USN&WR* also accepts at face value the ABA's propaganda that the sheer number of books in a law school's library has a qualitative effect on that school's "educational program.")

High costs needlessly imposed on law students enable parent universities to continue to skim high dollar amounts. Freestanding law schools are not subject to this rake-off. Thus, they have the option of charging *lower* tuition and fees—unless, **to gain or keep ABA accreditation, the ABA forces them to spend so much on "adequate facilities" that the freestanding schools *have to* charge tuition and fees in line with those of the university-affiliated law schools.**

This is the *real* meaning, in practice, of "adequate resources" for the law school: are the students being charged enough to ensure their tuitions and fees are in-line with *university-affiliated* law schools?

Many students would attend a lower ranked law school if its cost were far below that of attending a university-affiliated school. And that is what, for example, the Massachusetts School of Law is. The ABA still refuses to accredit it, even though MSL is not-for-profit. Originally, it charged only $8,000 a year in tuition. In an effort to placate the ABA, it spent so much money that it has now (as of this writing) raised tuition to $12,000 a year.

But MSL would quite likely gain ABA accreditation within a matter of months if it raised its tuition to $20,000 a year—because then MSL would no longer be a *low-cost* alternative to the university-affiliated law schools in the greater Boston area. (*All* the law schools in the Bay State are *private*. Thus, they have no competition from any public law school, with the "low" in-state tuition rates of most public law schools.)

If students have to pay at least $20,000 a year in tuition regardless of where they go to law school, then obviously the only ones who will apply to a freestanding, lower-ranked law school are those who can't get in anywhere else. But with low tuition, even many people with high GPAs from prestigious colleges, and high LSAT scores, would seek out the freestanding law schools.

So, arguably, the major reason the U.S. Department of Education continues to recognize the ABA as the *only* national accrediting agency for law schools, and the reason why the university academics who dominate the accrediting process will continue to conspire *against lower* legal education costs, is that the federal government itself is part of a "conspiracy" to subsidize America's *universities*. (In the same way, federally guaranteed students loans are also a massive subsidy to universites...and to the banks that make those loans. Yes, the loans benefit the students. But the subsidizing also drives up their costs. So what they gain on the one hand they nearly lose on the other.)

As long as "Uncle Sugar" and the ABA cooperate to continue this inflationary spiral, there will be no serious efforts to end the pedagogical malpractice of law schools or to legitimize low-cost innovations in legal (or any other) education. The ABA's recent—successful—effort to virtually "gut" on-line legal education (which was rightly perceived as a low-cost alternative to traditional residential programs) is a prime example.

In its suit, the federal government said it wanted a permanent injunction barring the ABA from its conspiratorial practices.

But in the consent decree, the feds agreed that it would only last for *ten* years. **Thus, as of June, 2006, the ABA will be completely free to *resume* its conspiratorial practices with regard to faculty salaries and the boycotting of proprietary schools and non-ABA schools.** Care to guess what will happen to law school tuition rates, and the effect on the renewal of accreditation for freestanding law schools?

Perhaps another purpose of the consent degree was to *forestall* other private antitrust suits, and thus to buy time for the ABA to complete the acquisition of an *absolute* monopoly over all U.S. legal education—at which point, its anti-competitive practices would be moot. (If *every* state requires its law schools to be ABA-accredited, the ABA's total monopoly would be the result of all 50 states' freely choosing to act, individually, rather than as part of a conspiracy. Right?)

Plus Ça Change...

As Alphonse Karr, a 19th-century French novelist, said in *The Wasps,* "The more things 'change,' the more they stay the same."

Why is American legal education so bad? And why is it the same throughout the land? Old saying: "If it ain't broke, don't fix it." For the nearly 10,000 full-time faculty, deans, and other administrators at America's ABA-accredited law schools (and their parent universities), the American system of legal education *works,* quite well indeed.

Talbot D'Alemberte is a former dean (1984-89) of Florida State University's College of Law. In 1991-92, he was president the ABA. He also served as a member of the Wahl Commission.

Of the pedagogy of law school, he said, "People who conduct this kind of educational program are not trying to educate." Then, as Munro had, he shifted to a more delicate way of putting things:

> But it's also possible to conclude that we run
> legal education in a way that is least burdensome
> to professors, and most advantageous to the uni-
> versity systems ...[O]ne way of looking at this
> whole thing is to ask who benefits from such a
> system...In whose interest are we running legal
> education?*

---

* Talbot D'Alemberte, *Law School in the Nineties: Talbot D'Alemberte on Legal Education,* ABA Journal, September 1990, page 52.

Addendum to Chapter 9 -:
The AALS Workshops for New Law Teachers

The Workshop for Those Teaching the Big Six Courses

Every summer, the Association of American Law Schools (AALS) holds a two-day "workshop" for new law teachers. It's open only to those who've been hired to start teaching at law schools the coming fall, or who have already been teaching for just a year or two.

I'd called AALS and explained I was a lawyer-writer, but not a present or soon-to-be law prof, and that I was working on a book on legal education and wanted to sit in on the workshop. Initially, they said that would be fine, though I'd have to pay the highest rate on the fee schedule to attend. But later, AALS informed me that I would not be allowed to observe the proceedings after all.

So, I registered anyway—giving a fake name and claiming to be a new law prof at a school I've never even set foot in. (I gave AALS the school's street address and phone and fax numbers as my own, and made up an e-mail address based on the school's.) It cost a total of $2,000 to attend (registration fee, air fare, lodging, meals, cab fares, etc.) But it was worth it.

The program's first day was on techniques of teaching the law; the second, on finding topics for the law review articles that would get the writer tenure. About 150 new assistant professors of law attended the program.

I spoke privately with several of the speakers after their presentations, and with several of those in attendance. I shall not disclose the name or law school affiliation of anyone whose statement/s are repeated here, not even statements made as part of a speaker's formal presentation to everyone. Whether their statements were public or private, the people who made them assumed that those statements were "off the record" with respect to those outside the guild. I do not want to discourage the openness and truthfulness of speakers or attendees of future programs. Hence the lack of identifying information as to the source of specific remarks.

Several speakers emphasized how fortunate a law prof's life is. One noted that a law professor only works 24 weeks a year, and has the other 28 to himself or herself. (In the main body of this chapter, I spoke of 34 weeks' annual employment. I had neglected to consider vacation time during and between semesters.) A participant with whom

I spoke privately said, "In my first year, my salary will be more than double that of older friends of mine who got a Ph.D. and have already been teaching for years now—and they have four times the teaching load I'll have." Another attendee with whom I spoke privately pointed out that those who get a Ph.D. and hope to get hired as professors have to prove their worth as "scholars" (in the form of their doctoral thesis) before they even get job *interviews.* And they have to pay as much as $30,000 a year in tuition while trying to prove their worth. New law profs, in contrast, *already have* the job. *Then* they are, in effect, *paid* to try to prove their worth as scholars, because they're expected to produce the two law review articles required for tenure only *after* they've gotten the job (joined the faculty).

One of the speakers said that if a prof does a seminar for second- or third-year students, it's a good idea to get the students to write their papers on topics of interest to the professor—so the prof can use the students' ideas and research as source material for future law review articles that the prof can do. Another speaker said that, after getting tenure, producing casebooks can be lucrative. And yet another spoke of how media appearances can lead to consulting work.

Participants were told: "Never change a student's grade, except in the case of an arithmetical error." A student's exam grade should not be changed because "the grade you gave that one student's answers was in the context of all the students' answers you'd seen. To take that one student's exam out of context and to re-evaluate it would be unfair to the other students." Interesting. The only way to review one student's answers would be if the prof would then also review all the other students' answers, to re-establish the "context." And that was the only reason a prof should give to a student who asks that prof to take another look at that student's exam with a view to possibly upping the grade.

But there were two other reasons, apparently not to be disclosed to students. The first was that the recorder's office at the law school gets annoyed when a prof wants to change a student's grade. It means more work for the recorder's office. So, especially among new (untenured) profs, it's best not to annoy one of the law school's fiefdoms. The second additional reason for not changing a student's grade is that it could "violate the forced curve." If the school's forced curve dictates that only, say, three students can get an A-, and changing this student's grade now means that four students get an A-, then the prof will get in trouble for that. And the only solution would be to change another student's grade too—a student who got one of the A- grades from before.

Implicitly, this reasoning also applies to changing a student's grade for any other cause, *such as "class participation."* (As Chapter 11 will note, adding points for class participation is B.S. This AALS workshop provided the proof as to why.)

As was to be expected, nearly everyone in the audience was young—and idealistic. And all the speakers, even those with decades of teaching experience, were idealistic. The teaching techniques recommended on Day One were wonderful. (Gerald Hess, of the Institute for Law School Teaching—discussed in the main body of this chapter—was one of the presenters.) However, nearly all the speakers advised the attendees that in their first year or two of teaching, it will be all they can do to just "get settled in" as teachers, and to start working on the law review articles that will get them tenure. The teaching techniques presented were far more worthwhile than the Socratic Method (although one presentation was on how to go about using the Socratic Method the *right* way). But all of them "require a lot of work." Further, the consensus among the speakers was that it's better to play it safe in the early years of teaching law. Until the new prof gets tenure, it can be risky to be "too different." Better to do things pretty much the way they've always been done until the new prof "gets established" (i.e., gets *tenure*).

But the speakers who talked privately with me all admitted that by the time a new prof gets tenure, doing things the old way has become a *habit*. And, of course, once a prof has tenure, there is no incentive to *change* his or her ways. One speaker, in formal remarks to all participants, noted that once a faculty member has tenure, he or she will be asked to serve on various committees, and will have little time for further scholarship. (This assumes, of course, that once the prof has tenure that he or she will even be interested in further scholarship.) Given that the teaching techniques presented during the first day of the program "require a lot of work," and given that the old ways of doing things will have become a habit by the time the new prof gets tenure, and given that once the prof has tenure he or she will have little time or incentive for the work needed for a change in pedagogy, the reasonable conclusion is that AALS knows that nothing will change, despite its lip-service. (The cover of the materials at the workshop had the slogan, "The improvement of the legal profession through legal education.")

In fact, just as law students themselves are subjected to a "bait-and-switch" (discussed in the main body of this chapter), *so are these new law profs.*

If just a significant minority of the legal professoriat were as conscientious and dedicated as the attendees at this workshop appeared to be, legal education would be at least one order of magnitude better than it is now. But, inspiring as the presentations by the experienced law profs were, they are the exception to the rule. They, and AALS, know quite well that "the system" will grind these new professors down, despite the idealism and high hopes. Eventually, all but a handful of these new law professors will be just like those who've preceded them in the ivory tower of the law. (One speaker played the key lines from "folk-rock" singer Bob Dylan's recording of his most famous song, "The Times They Are A-Changin'." But the speaker obviously had no awareness of the irony: The song came out in 1964, nearly two generations ago. And nothing of substance had changed at the law schools since. True, there are now more female students, and more female faculty—and more faculty "of color" or openly "gay." But to the student who gets shot down, it makes no difference the gender or color or sexual preference of the person who fired the bullet.)

Despite all the attention paid at the workshop to trying to *teach* law students, not one speaker mentioned the heartbreak that all but the top 20% of the class will feel after their grades come in from the fall semester's courses. As will be discussed in Chapter 25, law school *breaks students' spirits*. It is *meant* to. All the wonderful teaching techniques, even if perfectly executed by all profs (old as well as new) would not change the fact that *after only one semester* in law school, the vast majority of students' dreams have been permanently shattered...because of the forced curve. Even if all the students in class, objectively speaking, scored higher than 90% on the final, 80% of the students will still be excluded from the job opportunities that will thenceforth remain open only to the top 20%.

In May 1998 the *Harvard Law Review* published a Note by a student there, Sharon Dolovich. Its title was "Making Docile Lawyers: An Essay on the Pacification of Law Students." (Its title, all by itself, is significant.)

In it, she discusses the impact of the forced curve.

> After the grades come out, many people experience a profound loss of self-esteem and confidence, as well as a significant shift in their self-perception—but no one talks about it. For these people, the information about their grades becomes a discreditable stigma, one that they do their best to hide. This process takes its toll...

As she noted, "For the majority of students, this means a considerable lowering of their expectations, an adjustment that can't help but be psychologically painful."

Two of the speakers at the AALS workshop privately told me, "Yes, we really need to do something about that." But all they had in mind was helping new law profs do some hand-holding for students who'd not done well. They did not question the "need" for the forced curve.

Further, only three of the speakers were from big-name schools. (One was from UCLA, another from USC, and the third—a last-minute substitute—was from Yale.) Nearly all of the attendees were from relatively low-ranked schools. (The exceptions were Northwestern, with three participants; and UNC, Illinois, and Indiana-Bloomington, with one apiece.) The data imply that the very top law schools are not interested in providing even a rudimentary "introduction to the teaching of law" to their new faculty. And because the very top law schools are the role model for all others as to pedagogy, the message is clear: skill at teaching is not important. No doubt this explains the dismal sales figures for Gerald Hess and Steven Friedland's book, *Techniques for Teaching Law,* and for Gregory Munro's *Outcome Assessments for Law Schools* (discussed in the main body of this chapter), despite the fact that America now has over 10,000 full-time law school faculty (not counting librarians listed as faculty).

Granted, at least one speaker knew of a new law teacher who was eventually denied tenure because that teacher's student evaluations were so negative. And the speaker also knew of a professor who was asked to become a visiting professor at another school (and thus was going to be looked over as a possible recruit to that law school's faculty), but was not given a job offer after the year as a visiting prof because the student evaluations were negative. I am skeptical. The speaker was not from a big-name school, and I doubt that a big-name school would have cared about student evaluations, even if the two schools the speaker had in mind did care.

One attendee with whom I spoke privately told me that she had already been teaching for two years. We discussed casebooks. When I complained that they were intentionally confusing and that students needed a straightforward presentation of Black Letter Law before getting into the fine nuances of case law, she told me two things that still cause me to shake my head in wonder:

1. "There is no such thing as Black Letter Law." I am not kidding. She told me that the "elements" of each item of Black Letter Law—such as battery, or a contract—varied so much from state to state that there was no uniformity, and hence no point in trying to teach them. When I tried to make her realize she was mistaken, the woman almost literally sneered at me. "*You* must be a *skills* teacher," she said. ("Skills" teachers teach students how to practice law, in the same way that med school profs teach students how to practice medicine. But in law school, the "real" profs are contemptuous of the teaching of "skills.")

2. When I asked her what was the purpose of a casebook, she replied, "To launch students into discussions of various public policy topics." God help her students. And God help the future clients of her students. I have encountered much hypocrisy among the law school professoriat. But this was the first time I had encountered a professor who was truly deluded.

***

Because most of the attendees were joining the faculties of relatively low-ranked schools, there was no one-upmanship…for a few hours. But when we broke into small groups for discussion, one woman in the group I sat in on made sure everyone knew that she had attended Yale Law School. It took less than three minutes for another woman in the group to let everyone know that *she* had attended *Harvard*.

At the luncheon on the third day, I sat next to a guy who'd graduated from Stanford Law School. On the other side of him sat a woman who'd attended Washington University's law school (which is in Saint Louis, not Washington State or D.C.).

The Stanford grad sniffed, "I didn't even know Washington University *had* a law school." Then, to make sure the woman got the point, he added: "I don't even know anyone who went to Wash U's law school." The Stanford guy had been raised in the Midwest. He knew enough about Washington University to know that it's informally referred to as "Wash U." But he claimed not to be aware of the existence of its law school.

***

The Workshop for Those Teaching Legal Writing

The third day of the AALS program was a separate "workshop" for teachers of legal writing.

In contrast to the 150 who'd attended the workshop for teachers of the Big Six courses, only about half as many were at this second workshop. There was little overlap as to the participants. Another difference was that very few of those in the first workshop had already been law teachers, and even they for only a year or two. But it appeared that most of those at the second workshop had been teaching legal writing for years, even decades. A third difference was that most of the legal writing professors, as mere "skills" teachers, were not tenure-track. Some were adjuncts (part-timers).

As Chapter 1 mentioned, at most law schools, legal writing is only a first-year course. Few schools have additional legal writing courses, such as contract- or statute-drafting, in second- or third-year. So, few participants in the second workshop had expectations of ever teaching upper-level courses.

The main thing they had in common with those at the first workshop was their idealism. But their most marked feature of all was their resignation to Fate. They accepted that their law schools committed scant resources to what's inherently a labor-intensive activity. The TAs (teaching assistants) merely graded homework assignments. It was up to the teachers of legal writing to edit or critique all their students' writing, all by themselves. A "regular" prof merely posts office hours. Legal writing profs, to do their jobs, have to meet with each student— sometimes for an hour or more. (One of the participants, who would be teaching for the first time, said she would have a class of 60 students. Another, who'd been teaching for years, said there were habitually more than a hundred students in his legal writing class.) Their workload is staggering; their pay far below that of the tenure-track teachers of the Big Six courses.

A perhaps even more disturbing aspect of the resignation to Fate was their acceptance of the fact that many students who enter law school cannot write: they have not mastered basic grammar, syntax, punctuation, or even spelling (despite "spell-check" software). These students do not understand the purpose of paragraphing (other than to break up a text block into chunks). And these students do not know how to think things through and write their thoughts out in a coherent, well reasoned manner free from irrelevancies and internal contradictions.

(Interestingly, there were two other categories of "problem students": (1) those who had been "creative writers" and could not or would not convert to the demands of legal writing, and (2) those who had been expository writers and could not or would not convert to the demands of legal writing. Both groups apparently insist "I already know how to write.")

As Chapter 1 noted, the Big Six courses are on the forced curve. But at most law schools, legal writing courses are either "pass-fail" or "credit-no credit." Given that the courses are not graded, participants reported that students gave their writing assignments bottom priority. Several teachers spoke of students who were supposed to hand in an outline, then a rough draft, an intermediate draft, and a final draft—but who only handed in a *partial outline* as their "final draft." They spoke of students who failed to show for the student-teacher conference at which the student's work was to be discussed.

But if the teacher had failed these students (or reported "no credit"), the law school powers-that-be would take that as a cry for help from the teacher—a cry for help in the form of more resources. The powers-that-be do not want to hear any such cries for help. And while the school was likely to have committed resources to an "academic support" program for marginal students to help them to merely obtain *passing* grades in the Big Six courses, the law school was not willing to set up a remedial writing program.

The legal writing profs thus had no choice but to make the best of a very, very bad situation.

So, what the presenters advocated was little more than "hand-holding" for those students who were willing to put forth *any* effort, however minuscule. And the thrust of this hand-holding was an attempt to build up students' self-esteem, *however misplaced*, as writers of legal documents such as memos. The speakers repeatedly said that "too many" corrections and "discouraging" words would cause many students to give up altogether.

All these factors combined mean that most students of legal writing get the equivalent of a "social promotion." ("Social promotion" is where a poor student in, say, 9th grade, gets held back a year, but then gets promoted to 10th grade the year after, even though there has been no improvement, because otherwise the student will no longer be among his or her age peers.)

As Chapter 1 said, essay questions on law school exams are a form of legal writing. They require students to *quickly* draft a concise, taut, and thorough "memo." So, instead of letting students "drag their feet" in the legal writing course, wouldn't it make more sense to *push* students, so that the students would then have a *chance* to write well under pressure? Students, though, do not see the connection—and their legal writing instructors do not tell them, nor do any of the "real" law profs. (It's even possible that they're not even aware of the connection.) By letting students "slide by," the legal writing teachers unwittingly contribute to their students' poor performance on finals.

Perhaps those teachers have resigned themselves to the extreme likelihood that students who need remedial instruction in writing will never place in the top 20% of the class. Yet, many of those at the AALS program were at schools where the *only* graduates who will find jobs are those in the top 20%.

And surely those teachers also know that two-thirds of all attorneys in private practice are sole practitioners. (Often this is because, not having found employment upon graduation, they had no choice but to hang out their own shingle.) But sole practitioners, by definition, have no one outside their "firm" to critique their work and compel them to draft legal documents of *decent* quality. New sole practitioners *can* eventually learn substantive law, and procedural law and skills, on their own. But someone who graduates from law school without ever having learned to write well will almost *never* make up for this deficiency during his or her career in the law. (The same is true of those who go to work for all but the biggest law firms.)

This is a major reason the overwhelming majority of legal documents—from memos, motions, and briefs, to wills, contracts, and even letters to clients—are so appallingly poor in quality. And this in turn means that these future lawyers' future clients will suffer terribly at the hands of opposing counsel more competent at legal writing, even if the opposing counsels' cases are the far weaker, objectively speaking.

The big law firms, of course, *weed out* their new associates who got top grades but who never learned to write reasonably well (which happens). Rarely, the big law firms will make sure their new associates *learn* to write well, instead of just firing those who cannot.

Thus, the law schools' unwillingness to ensure that their graduates do write well ensures that the grads who become solos or small-firm lawyers are at a serious disadvantage when going up against lawyers at the big firms. (More on this in Chapter 25.)

NOTE: Even those students who got top grades might be asked to provide writing samples as part of the interviewing process. —**And** *all* **judges interviewing potential** *judicial clerks* (see Chapter 22) **will insist on writing samples.** Those with mediocre writing ability will probably not get hired, no matter how stellar their grades. Although many big firms do not request writing samples, they will (as mentioned) cut from the payroll any new associate who appears to be hopelessly inept at legal writing.

The bottom line on legal writing is this: in the long run, it's cruel to be kind to marginal students. And it is pedagogical malpractice for the law schools (with the approval of the AALS) to slight legal writing programs (despite an annual one-day "workshop" for teachers of legal writing).

One person who read page 179's discussion of multiple-choice exams, and how the ABA's Standard for Accreditation 303 "disfavors" them, said that one reason why MC final exams are proliferating in law school is that *law students these days cannot write a lawyerlike analysis.*

But out in the real world, there are no multiple-choice exams.

You will be expected to write. Granted, you can use "form books" as your models (discussed in Chapter 17). And maybe you'll be at a firm where *paralegals* (out of sight of the clients) do all the work of lawyers (without the clients' knowledge, of course), and the lawyers just meet with the clients and make the court appearances. But paraglegals should not be entrusted with the work of lawyers any more than a bookkeeper should be entrusted with the CPA's work of preparing an income tax return.

If you can't WRITE, it doesn't make any difference that you can still READ. You have no business being in law school...and any law school that accepts such students or lets them get a degree ought not to be allowed to remain in business.

—**And that includes any law school that allows is faculty to use multiple-choice final exams (as contrasted with multilple-choice quizes or tests before the final that measure only the students' ability to memorize and regurgitate).**

* * *

Although AALS no doubt is annoyed that I attended their workshops under false pretenses, using a fake name and giving a false affiliation with a law school, if they have any brains (which, I fear, is doubtful), they will realize that I am trying to do them a favor here.

Chapter 10 - A Trial Memo

As Chapter 9 briefly discussed, educators have long been aware of effective educational methods. Yet, the law school pedagogy completely ignores these methods. Chapter 8 presented reviews of two articles by law professors who openly, even proudly, described what can be called the "bait and switch" nature of legal education. There are many more documents of a similar nature, by law school professors.

Several chapters, starting with Chapter 2, discussed the Josephson Report, commissioned by the Association of American Law Schools. As has been mentioned elsewhere in this book, there are many more documents of a similar nature, commissioned by various foundations, the ABA, and others.

Yet, nothing has changed, in over a century.

So maybe it's time to sue the bastards.

—A class-action suit, most likely in federal court, against America's law schools, the Association of American Law Schools, and the American Bar Association. A court would not likely countenance high monetary damages from these defendants, so the primary remedy sought would probably be injunctive relief: a court order that law schools adopt sound pedagogical practices, as to first-year courses. However, it could get a jury trial only if presented as an action at law rather than equity, I think.

In the proposed suit, the first cause of action would "sound" in antitrust. This is not so fatuous. As Chapter 9 mentioned, the federal government itself sued the ABA in 1995, in a civil antitrust action, in connection with its accreditation policies and practices.

The second cause of action would be for the intentional tort of consumer fraud. And there might a third, for breach of fiduciary duty.

Another possibility would be to invoke the Racketeering Influenced and Corrupt Organizations Act, a federal statute. This too would not be fatuous. The RICO statute, as it's called, was originally a weapon against organized crime. But now it's used against non-criminal wrongdoing also, in civil suits. (The federal courts "disfavor" civil RICO, though.)

The fifth cause of action would "sound" in contract.

In American law, it's possible to allege causes of action "in the alternative." So, "in the alternative" to the intentional tort/s in the second (and possible third and fourth) cause of action, there's negligence, specifically gross negligence.

Chapter 2 discussed "policy." The first part of what follows is an example of "public policy considerations."

It's Time for a Change

Hazel Glenn Beh (pronounced "bay"), of the University of Hawaii's law school, did a law review article concerning colleges that's also germane to law schools: *Student versus University: The University's Implied Obligation of Good Faith and Fair Dealing,* 50 MD. L. REV. 183 (2000).

On page 194, in footnote 52, she says:

> The government has turned over much of the oversight function to private accrediting agencies by requiring institutions receiving federal funds to be accredited by federally approved and recognized accrediting agencies. In essence, "the Secretary of Education accredits the accreditors." See Jeffrey C. Martin, *Recent Developments Concerning Accrediting Agencies in Post-Secondary Education,* LAW & CONTEMP. PROBS. 121, 125 (1994) (discussing the historical and the current relationship between the federal government, private accrediting agencies and higher education institutions).

On page 185, she'd noted that "Increasingly, higher education is viewed and *views itself as a business with education as its product.*" [Emphasis added—AF.] As authority, she cited *Andre v. Pace Univ.,* 618 N.Y.S.2d 975, 979 (City Ct. 1993), *rev'd.,* 665 N.Y.S.2d 777 (App.Dist. 1996). She also cited, in support, Richard A. Matasar, *A Commercialist Manifesto: Entrepreneurs, Academics, and Purity of Heart and Soul,* 68 FLA. L. REV. 781, 792-93 (1996).

> The federal government has long recognized the *consumer nature* of education and the need for congressional oversight. The Student-Right-to-Know provisions of the Higher Education Act [20 U.S.C. §1092 (1994 & Supp. 1998)] evidence congressional recognition that *higher education is both a product and a relationship that begs for external review.* (194) [Emphasis added.]

Beh also stated (224): "Ignoring the consumer nature of the relationship allows the institution too much discretion."

She reported (211-212) that "[M]any scholars and commentators have found numerous sound reasons to hold colleges liable for professional negligence claims…" Footnote 143 then provided authority for her statement, including the following: "Johnny C. Parker, *Educational Malpractice: A Tort is Born*, 39 CLEV. STATE L. REV. 301, 302 (1991), (asserting that 'educational malpractice is a viable theory and that traditional negligence analysis and public policy support the recognition of such cause of action'), Laurie S. Jamieson, Note, *Educational Malpractice: A Lesson in Professional Accountability*, 52 B.C. L. REV. 899, 964-65 (1991) (arguing for recognition of educational malpractice)."

As the title of her article indicates, however, her main focus was on contact law, specifically "good faith and fair dealing." (In your Contracts course, you'll deal with this in §1-201(19) of the Uniform Commercial Code—which applies to the sale of goods—and under the common law, as §205 of the *Restatement (Second) of Contracts*, which in turn uses the UCC's definition.) Beh comments (216):

> At the performance stage, good faith and fair dealing demands cooperation, observation of reasonable commercial standards and excludes behavior inconsistent with common standards of decency, fairness, and reasonableness, and with the parties' agreed-upon common purposes and expectations. [Citing cases.]

She also says (215-216, quoting case law), "Although good faith and fair dealing terms are usually left unexpressed by the parties, courts generally agree that these terms exist and are implied in every contract."

Then (218) comes a zinger:

> [W]ithout good faith and fair dealing to restrain [universities], *students are at the mercy of the school and societal interests are not served.*
> [Emphasis added.]

From "good faith and fair dealing," she moves to a discussion of "contracts of adhesion." Your Contracts course should cover this. For now, suffice it to say a contract of adhesion is one where the two sides have grossly unequal bargaining power, and the powerful side presents the contract to the weak side on a "take it or leave it" basis.

In this regard, Beh says (183), "[S]tudents are not invited to bargain with the institution over the terms and conditions of the educational contract—a contract that is largely implied or finds its terms scattered throughout various unreadable publications that contain fine print disclaimers of institutional liability." She cites Victoria J. Dodd, *The Non-Contractual Nature of the Student-University Contractual Relationship,* 33 U. KAN. L. REV. 701 714-18 (1985), "(discussing adhesion contracts and arguing that 'the student-university contractual relationship' is an example of an adhesion contract)."

Beh had noted (212), that "courts have roundly refused to recognize educational malpractice." But as she notes on the final page (224) of her article:

> Without a well-defined judicial role, the unchecked deference accorded to institutions *leaves students vulnerable and without adequate remedy when institutions of higher education place their own economic and commercial goals over their students' educational needs.*
>
> [Emphasis added.]

All I can say to that is: "Hallelujah!—and Amen."

Breaching the Walls of the High Citadel

The first breach of the heretofore impregnable jurisprudencial walls of the higher education Establishment occurred with a lawsuit filed in tort and contract by a medical student. Only the contract cause of action survived the pre-trial phase. But the plaintiff got that to a jury, which found in his favor. The trial court then ruled his only "damages" were his payments of tuition and fees, which the court ordered the school to refund to him. The higher court reversed as to the damages, and said the plaintiff could recover for *income lost as a result of not graduating from the school by the time he thought he would.*

The case is *Sharick v. Southeastern Univ. of the Health Sciences,* reported at 780 S.2d 136 (Fla. 3d DCA 2000).

The appeal had originally gone before a three-judge panel, as is the norm nearly everywhere. But the panel's decision alarmed (as it well should have) the University of Miami, the Independent Colleges and Universities of Florida, and the American Council on Education. They intervened, and asked for a rehearing of the case by *all* the judges who serve on that appellate court. (This is called "*en banc*," and being Norman French, is pronounced "ohn bahnc" in the French manner.) Ten judges (including the original panel of three) did hear oral argument on a *motion* for rehearing. (An 11th chose not to participate.) The *en banc* court then denied the motion, apparently by a 6-4 vote. (This meant the three-judge panel's decision stood.) There was then an effort to have the case heard by the Florida Supreme Court. But the high court refused, dismissing the appeal on jurisdictional grounds.

The *en banc* appellate court's decision was issued *"per curiam,"* which meant no one wrote an opinion in the name of the court to explain the decision. However, one judge, Juan Ramirez, Jr., wrote a "concurring" opinion. It's reported at 780 S.2d 142 (Fla. 3d DCA 2001). (There is also a dissenting opinion, joined by three other judges.)

As had Prof. Beh, Judge Ramirez first spoke of a "traditional deference to colleges and universities." In student-school disputes, the courts kept hands off, practicing "judicial abstention" in the same way they do regarding disputes within institutions of organized religion. As to schools, the hands-off policy was because the schools were said to be *"in loco parentis"* (Latin, loosely, "in the stead of the parents"—NOT "The parents are *loco*," despite what students thought). Courts are loath to interfere in the parent-child relationship. However, Ramirez noted *"This view is now disfavored because it no longer represents contemporary values."* (Emphasis added.) Virtually all students in higher education, these days, are legally adults. So, the student's relationship with the school, Ramirez continued, is at least somewhat contractual in nature.

That is at the heart of one aspect of the "policy" argument, for it implicates such matters as good faith and fair dealing, implied-in-fact contracts, contracts of adhesion—and also consumer law, especially consumer fraud.

In an op-ed piece in *The Chronicle of Higher Education* for November 8, 2002, Scott D. Makar (a former practitioner of and teacher of education law) said, "Imagine the worst-case scenario: a class-action suit seeking damages for the value of the entire student body's future earnings."

I'm imagining it, all right—for the entire student-body, *nationwide.*

Defenses and Responses

Based on the discussion in this book, the pleadings in the proposed suit are obvious as to duty, breach, harm, and proximate cause. So I'll proceed to three likely defenses.

The first possible defense is that "A court order to adopt certain pedagogical practices would not issue, as the matter is too subjective."

However, as mentioned, there has long been a consensus as to sound pedagogical practices. Expert testimony could easily establish that. As for implementation, the experience of the Massachusetts School of Law (discussed in Chapter 9) could serve as a model.

The second defense, taken at face value, seems much more serious — namely, that "It would be an interference with academic freedom."

However, the term "academic freedom" is *substantive* in nature. Requiring teachers to exhibit certain minimal *procedural* skills *as teachers* does not impinge on their intellectual freedom. After all, if a professor is to teach a first-year course in Property, then the professor has agreed that the subject to be taught is Property. The law of property, at the level of a first-year course, is well settled. If a prof "teaches" a second- or third-year course in a completely different subject (or even a seminar in property, but on, say, "philosophical alternatives" when "thinking about property"), then—in those subsequent courses— the prof would be free to return to pedagogical malpractice. But by then the students would have finished first-year, and presumably would have received a solid grounding in the basics of Black Letter Law and how to do a good "lawyerlike analysis." Thus, the deleterious effect of a recrudescence of the prof's proclivities would be minimal. Profs would be free to continue to develop expertise in subjects on which they intend to serve as paid consultants.

(Note: the pedagogical malpractice discussed in this book, and to be presented in such a lawsuit, is restricted to that of law school. As the reviews of the two articles discussed in Chapter 8 indicated, law school is unlike any other academic experience. No school of medicine, dentistry, engineering, architecture, or even business uses a pedagogy of "hide the ball" and "bait and switch." Law school is unique.)

No doubt the defendants would respond that it would nonetheless be an infringement on academic freedom to require that teachers be able to teach, because many good scholars are incompetent as teachers. They will say that "In *higher* education, schools are for *scholars* (the faculty), not just *students*." But the response to this is simple—what's called a "think tank."

"Think tanks" have been around for a long time. For example, The Brookings Institution, according to its brochure, "traces its beginnings to 1916 with the founding of the Institute for Government Research, the first private organization devoted to public policy issues at the national level. In 1922 and 1924, the Institute was joined by two supporting sister organizations, the Institute of Economics and the Robert Brookings Graduate School. In 1927, these three groups were consolidated into one institution, named in honor of Robert Somers Brookings...a St. Louis businessman..." Brookings is a freestanding entity. As its brochure also says, "In its research, The Brookings Institution functions as an independent analyst and critic, committed to publishing its findings for the information of the public. In its conferences and activities, it serves as a bridge between scholarship and public policy, bringing new knowledge to the attention of decisionmakers and affording scholars a better insight into public policy issues." Brookings has no students or classes.

There's also The Institute for Advanced Study, in Princeton, New Jersey. Because it's often referred to as "The Princeton Institute," there's a widespread belief that it's part of Princeton University. But it too is an independent entity, *located* in Princeton. As its brochure states, it's "an independent, private institution dedicated entirely to the encouragement, support and patronage of learning through fundamental research and definitive scholarship across a wide range of fields. It was founded in 1930...as a center where intellectual inquiry can be carried out in the most favorable circumstances." The Institute is organized almost entirely into what it calls "schools," all of which are either in mathematics or the natural sciences. Its brochure continues: "Each School has a small permanent Faculty, and some 180 fellowships are awarded annually to Visiting Members from other research institutions and universities throughout the world." (Albert Einstein was on its faculty from 1932 until his death in 1955.) According to the brochure, "The Institute has no formal curriculum, degree programs, schedule of courses, laboratories, or other experimental facilities."

But it's the final example that's most relevant here: The Hoover Institution on War, Revolution and Peace. According to its brochure, The Hoover Institution "is a public policy research center devoted to advanced study of politics, economics, and political economy—both domestic and foreign—as well as international affairs." It was founded in 1919 by Herbert Hoover, ten years before he became the thirty-first president of the United States. Like the "think tanks" above, it has resident scholars...who teach no classes. However, The Hoover Institution is on the campus of, and under the auspices of, Stanford University. (Hoover was a Stanford alumnus.)

Professors who can't teach don't belong in the classroom. Aspiring scholars who are incompetent as teachers would instead go into a Think Tank affiliated with the law school. Those people would have absolutely no teaching duties at all. But perhaps selected lawyers, judges, etc., could become Visiting Fellows for various lengths of time, to be exposed to the Great Thoughts of these Great Scholars. (Of course, unlike what happens now, the Think Tank ought to get a share of the income its scholars-in-residence made from their independent consulting. After all, the women in a brothel give a hefty cut to the House.) Law school students could serve as research assistants to these Great Legal Minds, and receive law school credit for it.

The faculty of the law *school* would consist only of capable *teachers*. (And the best teachers *are* often the best minds.)

Thus, a rich law school could have its cake and eat it too. Schools with less money to spend on big-name faculty (*or that wanted to hold students' tuition down*), would forgo an affiliated think tank. They would strive to make their reputation on the ability of their graduates to "hit the deck running" in the practice of law. (Of course, the rich schools could compete in this regard too.)

The third defense that comes to mind (against the proposed suit) is that "Everybody does it this way, so this has to be the right way." Thus, the "standard of care" to be observed is that set by "industry custom"— in this case, the legal education industry. However, a long line of cases has already demolished that possible defense.

The earliest involved personal injury suits by railroad employees who'd been injured on the job. (Chapter 1 discussed the legal doctrines employers used to defeat those suits. But even in the late 19th century, the courts carved out some exceptions to those defenses.)

In *Wabash R. Company v. McDaniels*, 107 U.S. 454, 461, 2 S.Ct. 932, 27 L. Ed. 605 (1882), the Supreme Court (Harlan, J.) said:

> And to say, as [a] matter of law, that a railroad corporation discharged its obligation to an employé—in respect of the fitness of co-employés whose negligence has caused him to be injured— by exercising, not that degree of care which ought to have been observed, but only such as like corporations are accustomed to observe, would go far toward *relieving them of all responsibility whatsoever for* negligence in the selection and retention of incompetent *servants*. [Emphasis added.]

Twenty years later, Justice Oliver Wendell Holmes, Jr., writing for the Court in *Texas & P. R. Co. v. Behymer*, 189 U.S. 468, 470, 23 S. Ct. 622, 47 L. Ed. 905 (1902), said (citing *Wabash*):

> What usually is done may be evidence of what ought to be done, but what ought to be done is fixed by a standard of reasonable prudence, whether it usually is complied with or not.

Behymer, though, was another railroad / personal injury / fellow employee case. The "leading" case on the subject of "industry custom" came 30 years later, from a U.S. Court of Appeals, *T. J. Hooper v. Northern Barge Corp.*, 60 F.2d 737 (2nd Cir., 1932).

T. J. Hooper was an admiralty case. The facts arose in 1928. Radio was then barely 15 years old. Ships had devices to transmit distress signals in Morse Code (as did the *Titanic* in 1912). That had become an industry-wide custom (after the *Titanic* went down). By 1928, radios existed that could send *voice* messages. Other radios existed that could only *receive* voice messages...such as weather reports (or the movements of icebergs, for that matter). But the radio manufacturers apparently had not yet created equipment that could both send and receive voice messages. Many shipowners merely continued with the old devices that could only send out messages, in Morse Code. That's what the owner of the tugboat *T.J. Hooper* did. When the boat left port, with barges in tow, the weather was satisfactory but later got a bit rough. Weather reports that went out on the radio said things would shortly get worse. But, of course, the *T.J. Hooper* did not hear those reports. It lost one of its barges at sea. The owner of the barge, and the owner of the cargo that was in the barge, both sued the owner of the tug...and won.

T. J. Hooper is in many first-year Torts casebooks. It's regarded as a "products liability" case. However, it's on point to the proposed lawsuit, for Learned Hand, writing for the court (and citing *Wabash* and *Behymer*), said (at 740):

> [A] whole *calling* may have unduly lagged in the adoption of new and available devices. It never may set its *own* tests, however persuasive be its usages.
>
> [Emphasis added.]

Sound teaching methods are analogous to the devices in question in the *T.J. Hooper* case, and law school teaching as a "calling" has severely lagged in the adoption of those methods. Further, the "tests" the law schools set for the adequacy of the industry's longstanding methods might be persuasive to the professoriat, but—to repeat the words of Justice Harlan in *Wabash*—the effect has been that of *"relieving them of all responsibility whatsoever for negligence in the selection and retention of incompetent servants."* Following what Justice Holmes said: that which *ought* to be done is *fixed by a standard of reasonable prudence,* even if is it is not complied with.

The Josephson Report, the Institute for Law School Teaching at Gonzaga University School of Law, and The Massachusetts School of Law have shown how to comply with a "standard of reasonable prudence" concerning teaching, without infringing upon academic freedom. The legal education Establishment cannot argue that the proposed remedy is not practical or feasible.

* * *

Plaintiffs, of course, must have "standing." I don't, as I've been out of law school too long; all possible statutes of limitations have run. But those currently in law school would have standing.

If anyone would like to share some thoughts on this (including further legal research, or "parsing the cases"), please let me know.*

---

* To repeat, the website address and my e-mail address are on the first page in this book, facing the inside front cover.

ATTICUS FALCON, ESQ.

First Addendum to Chapter 10 -
The Themis Institute

The Themis Institute (named for the Goddess of Justice of ancient Greece) is a non-profit corporation.

Its purposes are educational, charitable, and public interest litigation, to wit:

1. To conduct research on legal training or education, on the law, and on the legal profession, and to provide resources either tangible or intangible (e.g., books, a web site), and advice and instruction, to prospective law students, current law students, and recent law school graduates, to assist them in becoming good law students and good lawyers—in both senses of the word "good.".

2. To receive contributions for the charitable purpose of paying them over to degree-granting institution of higher learning and to other institutions or organizations that have tax-exempt status under §501(c)(3) of the Internal Revenue Code in furtherance of the corporation's desire to improve the quality and accountability of pre-law and law school training and education and pedagogy.

3. To receive contributions for the charitable purpose of paying them over to individuals (or their designated organization or institution of higher learning) as scholarships for pre-law and legal training or education.

4. To litigate in the public interest, in furtherance of the corporation's desire to improve the quality and accountability of pre-law and legal training or education programs and institutions, and to improve the quality and accountability of the legal profession and of professional legal organizations directly connected with legal training or education either as degree-granting institutions or otherwise.

(As of this writing, I am neither a member of the Board of Trustees, nor an officer, nor the incorporator, nor the registered agent of The Themis Institute...but I intend to be involved in its activities.)

The Themis Institute
3112 Windsor Road - Suite A-103
Austin, Texas 78703 - 2350

(No phone number or fax as of this writing.)

e-mail: themisinstitute@pdq.net

Second Addendum to Chapter 10 -
The Halpern Matter (and Student Self-Help)

Page 179 in Chapter 6 discussed why multiple-choice exams are a poor measure of students' ability—and that ABA Accreditation Standard 303 "disfavors" them. MC exams have some justification in, for example, the LSAT, because there hundreds of thousands of students must be graded. But page 179 also noted, in passing, that Prof. Sheldon Halpern of Ohio State U., on the first day of his Defamation Law class in the fall semester, 2003, announced that his students' grades would depend on their score on a final that would be entirely multiple-choice.

I contacted Prof. Halpern and invited him to comment on that, in light of Standard 303. I shall not quote our subsequent exchange of e-mails, as no doubt he would insist his statements are protected by copyright. Suffice it to say, however, he was displeased by my inquiry.

In the next session of the class, Halpern spent perhaps a quarter-hour denouncing *PLS* and its author. He declared that *"No one* is in a position to tell me what to do and to threaten me." Yet, all I'd done was ask him to explain the reasoning behind his action in light of ABA Accreditation Standard 303. Given that his course had only 15 students in it, grading essay exam answers himself did not seem too burden-some. But Halpern announced to the class that if "an overwhelming majority" *wanted* him to, he'd give an essay final instead...and it would be *six hours long*. You know the response to *that* gambit.

As you will see from the numerous e-mails to me that are repro-duced in Chapter 15, many, many professors are, shall we say, less than professional in their dealings with students. I deleted the profs' names reported to me in those e-mails. It is now too late to go back and insert them. (And I can add these comments about Halpern only because the printing of *PLS II* is far behind schedule, at the printers.)

If any of your profs behaves badly inside (or outside) class, or gives an MC exam or otherwise displays poor pedagogy, please let me know. I'll post the report on the website and ask for confirma-tion from others who were witnesses. *Negative publicity might help motivate the professoriat to start cleaning up its act and accord students the respect they deserve. (It might also help the best applicants decide where to seek admission to law school.)*

I'll keep your name out of it, **of course. If the prof discovers your identity and retaliates, I'll publicize that, too—and seek legal assistance on your behalf from The Themis Institute,** *pro bono.*

If you're unwilling to take even *minimal* **steps to protect your** *own* **dignity and rights, what use will you be to your future clients?**

Part III:

Tips...and (More) Traps for the Unwary

Chapter 11 - Classes: "DOs & DON'Ts"

First thing: do not even *think* about trying to hold a job during first-year. You simply cannot balance employment and full-time law school. Law school itself is full-time work. (I am told that in the movie *Love Story*, the hero held *three* jobs in first-year, and still placed third in his class... at Harvard Law School. Sure. —The novel on which the movie was based was written by someone who'd never spent a day of his life as a law school student, anywhere...Then again, the author was a Yalie. So perhaps that was his very sly way of knocking Harvard.)

Second-year employment is okay, but even then it should be something directly related to the law. (See Chapter 18 regarding internships and research assistantships.) If you believe you can handle full-time first-year and even *one* part-time job, you're headed for a fall in the fall.

Now, with that out of the way, the rest of this chapter concerns only classes...

$$* * *$$

As has already been emphasized, *things will not be explained to you in class.*

Your goal should be to know the jargon and to understand the concepts before you go to class. Ironically, if you don't, class will be almost a complete waste of time.

—Actually, class will be almost a complete waste of time anyway. As has also been emphasized, what happens there has almost nothing to do with what's on the exam. Therefore, *what happens in class has almost nothing to do with your grade.* You should be taking *very* few notes in class...because you've already mastered the material.

So why go to class at all? Well, in some schools it's mandatory; points are deducted from your final grade if you miss too many sessions. (This is becoming more common, as more students realize that class is almost a complete waste of time. If the rule exists at your school, you'll know.) Regardless, there is a very good reason to attend: it's another way to *test* your mastery of the material.

Nothing should happen in the classroom that leaves you feeling worried. The main reason you go is to pick up the occasional insight about Black Letter Law, here and there. If someone says something useful (which is unlikely), and it's something you hadn't thought of on your own, make a note of it. Then revise your personal-outline-in-progress in light of it. (Also, the prof might disclose—intentionally or not—what his or her favored approach is to a problem or what his or her preferred wording of an element of Black Letter Law is.) As Chapter 4 indicated, the key to doing well in law school is constant review of the material, updating it and *applying it to new hypotheticals.* You should be grateful any time someone gives you a hint as to a new way of looking at something, because it enables you to expand your repertory of analysis. Or, something said in class might pique your curiosity about a point of law, or cause you to think of new questions and hypos on your own. The more angles you can expose, the fewer are left hidden. That, in turn, means whatever you get on the exam is unlikely to take you by surprise.

(Speaking of being taken by surprise: assignments for your section's very first day of class in each course will be posted together, some-place. Find out where that place is, and then do all the assignments in time. —And by the way: most law schools now use the continuous-surface desktop rows arranged in concentric arcs. At most schools, each student is assigned a specific seat. But those who come to class unpre-pared sit in the back row, which is normally empty. The professor typically doesn't call on a student until confirming that the student is in the assigned seat. So the "back bench" is a sanctuary....However, some professors regularly violate this alleged sanctuary.)

Another good reason to go to class—the "final" one, though not the last one: your professors might explicitly state (or strongly hint at) what will be on their exams. This is particularly likely as your courses near their end. (But sometimes the professors don't keep their word.)

Your performance in class is irrelevant, as far as your grade is concerned—although some profs make a big show of promising to add a point or two to the final grade of students who do exceptionally well in class. As the addendum to Chapter 9 said, that's B.S. But it's harmless.

However, just because class doesn't count, that doesn't mean you can get cute, or be the class clown, or get sarcastic, or defiantly fold your arms and say "I don't know" when called on. Those things can get you marked for punishment, such as being repeatedly called on—and ridiculed. (Also, see "blind" grading, in Chapter 13.)

On the other hand, don't try to show off in class. If you follow the recommendations of Chapters 2-4, you'll know far more than the average law student. *Don't let it show.* Your fellow students will probably resent it if you do. Your professor will feel threatened by it and will make it a point to put you back in your place ASAP. And no matter how much you know about the law, the professor—perhaps—knows more...or at least, can do a better job of faking it. (This also applies to discussions of non-law topics on which you may well be a bona fide expert. The prof does not want to hear your "useful information.") You are not even there to engage in a true *dialogue* with the professor, let alone a *contest*. Trying to out-shine the prof is a no-win situation. You'd do better to leave law school altogether if you can't resist this one-upmanship urge, because it is suicidal.

True, the prof might appear to be impressed by your in-class brilliance, and not feel threatened by it. However, all that matters to the prof is how well you do on the exam. If you were brilliant in class, but then only so-so on the final, the prof will think something like, "Hmph! Must have been a 'flash-in-the-pan.' Too bad. For awhile there, I was impressed." Then the prof will think even *less* of you than otherwise.

Resisting the one-upmanship urge especially applies in your very first class on the very first day. Typically, the professor will ask each student to briefly introduce himself or herself. This is no time to brag. If one of your ancestors once sat on the U.S. Supreme Court, do not inform your fellow students of it. (The professor already knows: the admissions committee will have passed around any tidbits concerning various members of the entering class. Count on it.) If you won six Gold Medals at the most recent Olympics, keep a lid on it. (The professor already knows.) On the other hand, don't be timid, self-deprecating, and so forth. Also, avoid the *false* modesty routine; the smugness always shows through the facade. Don't be a comedian. If you're a direct descendant of Jesse James, John Dillinger, or Al Capone, don't make a joke about it—at least, not in class...unless it's criminal law. And above all, make no observations about how the legal profession is held in such low esteem by the public. Let the prof do that.

You don't get a second chance to make a first impression. From Day One, you want to come across as a mature, well-prepared, articulate professional. But don't overdo it, acting like a pompous ass. Save that for your clients and the media, after you get your license.

The key word here is "crispness." It's a buzzword, but "crispness" expresses that air of calm self-confidence that you want to have. (Herman Hesse, in *Magister Ludi*—Latin for "Master of the Game"—describing the hero: "Although humble, he was completely at ease." That's the way you want to be in class.) Of course, if that's not you, so be it. You have to be true to yourself—but at least try to be true to your *better* self.

* * *

Do not ask the professor a question in class, even if the professor invites it (rare). Join the after-class crowd at the lectern, or wait until office hours (if the prof has them). Better yet, take the matter up with your study group. In class, you want to keep a low profile. Do an adequate job when called on, but no more—even though you could. And don't play "teacher's pet" and raise your hand to answer a question someone else has struggled with. That's something to have outgrown by the end of grade school.

If you've been brilliant in class, and bomb on the final, your in-class brilliance will come back to haunt you. The word *will* get around to your fellow students, even if you try to keep it secret, that hot-shot you didn't do so well come crunch-time. (They'll know when they see you didn't Make Law Review.) *Save the in-class brilliance for years 2 and 3... if ever.*

(It might wound your *amor propre* to keep a low profile and have others assume you're dim-witted. But if and when you ace the exams, your true ability will be obvious. "Success erases all failures"—including a failure to "shine" in class.)

However, if you do choose to show off in class, you'll have *another* problem even before the the grades come in: your fellow students will call upon you outside of class to answer *their* questions. Answering others' questions is indeed a good way to test your own knowledge. And unlike the process of answering practice questions in a book, it's a real ego trip. But it gets old, fast. You'll soon find you can't handle all these people's demands on your time. If you then start turning them away, they'll not forgive you for it; nor will they forget it...*ever.* They'll make you the scapegoat for their poor performance. Playing know-it-all tutor is what economists call a "diminishing returns" situation. Much as it paiins me to say this: better to hide your enlightenment under a basket and let others continue to curse their own dimness instead of cursing *you.* (Exception: your study group—but they shouldn't have to ask anyway; they should already know.)

Here's another reason to go to class: to scout out your fellow students. True, after the self-introductions in your very first class, each student will be called on perhaps only once in the entire academic year, in each course. But you'll take all (or nearly all) your first-year courses with this same group of people. By attending class regularly, the odds are you'll hear many of them speak at least once in class during the first few weeks of law school. Also, as mentioned, during those self-introductions, you'll get to observe the pose everyone strikes during this opening tableau. That's important.

These first few days are when first impressions are made—and first impressions are hard to dislodge. (That's another reason for you to be prepared for class. I can still remember a few of those who gave particularly incompetent answers in first-year classes. And I *very* clearly remember the time I gave a totally wrong answer, in torts.)

There will be contact outside of class, yes. (But spare your fellow students the bragging—and any false modesty—even then.) However, what happens in-class has a special weight. Assuming you and your classmates don't scatter to the winds after graduation, your paths will cross. (Three-fourths of all attorneys practice within 200 miles of where they went to law school.) You'll have these people as allies, opponents, and consultants from case to case. You need to learn who's reliable, who's a quick thinker, who's lazy, who's foolhardy, who's timid, who's belligerent, etc. Class is a good place to start doing that, to see what their standard operating procedure is—and how they perform under pressure.

Above all, in the short run, you need to find worthy partner/s to study with, as you bounce hypotheticals back and forth—discussed in Chapter 5. True, the show-off might be brilliant. And maybe that person won't regard you as a worthy study partner unless you too have displayed brilliance in the classroom. However, hold off until you're in a 1:1 or small-group encounter *outside* class. Then the "genius" will be properly impressed. And if this star is *truly* brilliant, he or she will fully understand and appreciate your in-class discretion.

But if you still aren't accepted, don't worry about it. My experience with the genius show-offs is that they're a pain in the neck. In trial law, the key to success is "preparedness—plus fighting spirit." It's no different with law school finals. High intelligence and a brain that works fast are important. However, regardless of their mental endowment, *the study partners you want are the solid types, even the plodders, who stick with the material until they have it all down.* It doesn't take brilliance to do this. And it doesn't take brilliance to concoct hypotheticals. *It does take mastery of Black Letter Law and knowing how to Think Like a Lawyer.*

Although many lawyers—and nearly all law professors—like to pretend otherwise, the Life of the Law is not the Life of the Mind. (More on this in Chapter 27.) It certainly is neither rocket science nor brain surgery. The more you work at it, the better you'll get...as long as you work it the *right* way, and not how your profs tell you to. You might even discover that you've become "brilliant" yourself by the time the exam questions are handed out.

Very few of your section mates will have read *Planet Law School*. So, if you have a study group composed only of those who *have*, it will be a real powerhouse. Then, it will just be a question of which person in your group is #1, #2, etc., in each of your courses when the grades come in. You want to find those people. Even though they're your natural rivals, you want them on *your* side. You've heard of "synergy"? —"The whole is greater than the sum of its parts." This is especially so when everyone in your study group is first-rate. The rich get richer, etc; and the rich (usually) know when to stick together regarding their common interest. By forming a study group of "gifted" students, the members will gain more from each other, by working *together*, than they would by each joining various other study groups composed of those who haven't taken advantage of *Planet Law School*.

But you don't want to let on to *everyone* that you've prepped the *PLS* way. I say that not because you should be sly. Rather, it's because the panic will set in, on the first day of classes, among your fellow students. If they think you *might* know *anything* more than they do, they'll make a beeline for you, to get help. Then you have the same problem that was discussed above.

Here's a way to "lie low": before the very first meeting of your very first class, everyone will look at the posted chart to find their assigned seats. Post your own notice right next to it: "Section ____ PLS Study Group to Form." Then put your phone number or e-mail, no name. Those who've read *PLS* will know what you're talking about— and (presumably) will contact you. Then all you have to do is make sure that they've done more than just *read* this book. (The second addendum to Chapter 16 presents another possibility.)

If you get no response, here's an alternative: the ones who impressed you as being sharp during the opening tableau, but who then did not speak up in class (unless called upon), are the ones you want to check out: the strong, silent types.

But you have to put your study group together *early*.

What about the Weekend?

Even if you've prepared, there will be stress in law school. And so, you'll want to "blow off steam" sometimes. Fine. Just don't overdo it.

Many students apparently believe that law school is only a part-time activity, during business hours Monday through Friday. They then spend Friday and Saturday nights carousing...and all day Saturday and Sunday sleeping it off or sobering up. They wait until Sunday evening to begin preparing for the next week's (usually just the next day's) classes—and, of course, end up burning the midnight oil. That is not only irresponsible, obviously; it is also insane.

I strongly suspect such students are in law school only because they couldn't find anything to do that appealed to them after college, and thus wanted to "stall" for three more years before entering the real world. For many, their parents are picking up the tab. Because it's "OPM" ("Other People's Money"), they don't care about getting a good return on "their" investment (at least, on "their" *financial* investment). It apparently never occurs to them that someday they might actually be practicing law...and people will be paying them hard-earned money for sound legal advice. "Out of sight, out of mind." I hope that when they botch it, they get fired (at the very least) and get sued for legal malpractice, for they will be the sort of lawyer who gives lawyers a bad name.

Some might think that there are certain low-ranked law schools that are "party schools." And there probably are. However, as the book *Brush with the Law* showed, there are appallingly immature and irresponsible students even at HLS and Stanford. (And by the way, the fact that the book's authors even survived law school—thanks solely to their respective schools' forced curves, which benefit the *in*competent as well as penalizing the competent—is one of the best pieces of evidence of the pedagogical malpractice of Harvard's and Stanford's law schools.)

At most law schools, students have approximately 10-12 hours of class a week. But these are scheduled with a lot of "down time" between classes. It's hard to do anything other than reviewing for class. So, you can't make productive use of much of your time during business hours Monday through Friday. Thus, use *most* of each weekend to re-work your outlines, to review the primers and *Restatements,* and possibly to meet with your study group or partner. The weekend is also the time to work old exams (which, as mentioned, you should start doing *early* in the semester).

But "All Work and No Play"

It's easy to think this book wants to turn you into a real "drudge." However, as you'll discover, if you've prepared for law school with "The *PLS* Approach," you'll have far more free time than your fellow students.

For one thing, because you'll already have a basic understanding of the concepts and jargon, you won't be spending hours and hours trying desperately to get up to speed the way your fellow students will. And because you recognize that most assignments are make-work, you'll be able to devote *minimal* time to them—again, unlike your fellow students. Those who are working themselves to death will indeed be working hard, but not "working *smart.*" You, in contrast, will.

Sex

Don't burn the midnight oil. Get your own fire lit instead, if you wish (and *can*). It's the better way to work yourself into an 11th-hour frenzy. And the emotional and physical release will improve your academic performance. Seriously. —On the other hand, beware involvements that can lead to emotional upheavals.

The next chapter will discuss law school as portrayed in *The Paper Chase* and *One L.* In the former, the protagonist got laid fairly regularly. More power to him. The author of the *One L* memoir, in contrast, had the far more typical experience: even though he was married, he had no sex life; he had neither the time nor the energy. Yet, I have no doubt that had he used "The *PLS* Approach," he would have had more of both.

Chapter 13 will discuss, in part, the stress that law school places on "committed relationships"...and suggests a way to deal with it.

Other Stress-Relievers

You should get some vigorous physical exercise on a regular basis through sports, calisthenics, jogging, etc. (Believe it or not, law students—and lawyers—often have stooped shoulders, and back problems. This comes from lugging around all those law books. If you take Chapter 16's advice regarding casebooks, you can avoid those afflictions.) But just to be safe, your exercise program should include things that will keep your back in good shape.

You might also consider learning how to do something like Transcendental Meditation®...especially in the morning before classes, and in the hours before each exam.

Last, Chapter 30 will discuss, in part, the importance of "taking humor seriously," and treating yourself to regular doses of robust laughter.

As those who already do any or all of these things know, these will improve your *mental* vitality and resilience. Unlike getting drunk or high, or "boogeying all night," they'll *reinforce* your ability to "think like a lawyer."

...And they'll make your life a whole lot more enjoyable, and help you not only "survive" law school, but *thrive* in it.

Deflecting Intimidation

Much of your stress will occur when you're "cold-called on" in class. It's an intimidating experience. Profs know that, and deliberately do it. They say it "helps the students learn." Nonsense.

Here are a couple of e-mails I received in the fall of 2002:

Atticus—

I can only complain again how foolish is the way they are "educating" us. Supposedly, the Socratic Method and class discussion are beneficial to students because they learn to think like lawyers and learn from others students' questions. Fool of it!

First, when the professor questions a student in class, that student does not by definition learn to think because (a) he or she is scared to death and embarrassed; (b). probably doesn't know what the professor wants; (c) can't give the right answer because of massive lack of knowledge. Other students are mostly trying to read up the case before the prof. picks on them, or can't hear the "victim" because either the class is too big or the "victim" speaks quietly. And again, a regular 1L can't follow up on the professor's train of thought.

So, there is no intellectual enrichment, only satisfaction of the professor's desire to look smart.

And even if the professor is a devoted teacher like one I have, it still is a waste of time because of all these reasons.

Yesterday, the contracts professor called on a woman, and she just kept quiet because she didn't know what to say. If I were the professor, I would have turned to the next student the moment I realized she wasn't ready. Firstly, not to humiliate her, and secondly, since she wasn't ready, I would not have accomplished my teaching objectives.

The professor, however, kept her sweating in dead silence for at least 20 seconds, and even then didn't let her go and kept on asking her questions for a couple of minutes before picking on someone else.

Did someone learn from her answers? Not I.

Atticus—

I have a prof who, when she calls on a student for grilling, makes the student stand up. That adds to the student's stress, of course.

Today, she called on a woman. The woman did not do well. The prof then said, "If you can't understand the law, you shouldn't have come to law school." The student burst into tears.

The prof let her stand there, crying in front of all of us, while the prof stared at her coldly. That just made the crying worse.

If you look bad in class, try, try, try not to let it get to you. Sure, it's embarrassing, and you'll probably never forget it.

But always remember: *what happens in class does not count.*

If a prof makes a cutting remark about your "inept" performance, try this: raise your eyebrows, and assume an expression of utter nonchalance. Then, very calmly, even casually, say something like, "Even a good student can have a bad day" (or, if you want to give it a bit of an edge, say, "As I'm sure you remember from your own days as a law school student, even a good student can have a bad day"). Or just shrug your shoulders and say, "Beginner's mistake"—and look sincere. *(How you say it can be even more important than *what* you're saying.)*

Believe it or not, the prof will *probably* be secretly impressed that you are not intimidated. He or she will even wonder, because you (like the prof) do not take what happens in class seriously, that perhaps you have the makings of a natural-born genius of the law.

Do NOT "get into it" with a professor (such as the one mentioned in the second e-mail, who was a bitch). *But nicely yet firmly let the prof know you will not be intimidated by those bullying tactics.*

You have to keep your cool. For those of you who intend to practice trial law, this is especially important. (There are many judges who love to try to intimidate lawyers in their courts. And there are many negotiators who use intimidation as a technique. Perhaps you've already had a "stress interview" when you applied for a job, to test your cool. Stress interviews are idiotic, I think. But the insulting prof has no method to his or her madness, only the madness.)

Admittedly, though, if you hold your ground, even in a nice way, the prof may become even more obnoxious. He or she might say, "With that attitude, you'll never be a good lawyer!" —or something like that, including "You are obviously an idiot!" (which some professors do say to students in class). If that happens, you can again *casually* say, "Maybe I'll get lucky and do well on the exam."

The more unprofessional the prof becomes, the more professional and restrained *you* become. The effect, especially in the eyes of those who witness the exchange, is devastating.

But for Godsake, assuming you get the upper hand, do not press your advantage. (That is asking for serious trouble. It always helps to give you opponent an avenue by which to make a graceful exit and to save face.) If you've shown you know how to handle yourself in a tough situation, the prof will give you a wide berth.

(Please take a look at page 791 in Chapter 28, for a discussion of an ezcellent book by Dr. Suzette Haden Elgin: *The Gentle Art of Verbal Self-Defense.* It can be a life-saver, both in law school and after.)

Chapter 12 - Caught Up in the Madness:
The Paper Chase and *One L*

Anyone who's considering law school is often told to see one movie and to read one book, to "find out what it's really like." The movie is *The Paper Chase;* the book, *One L.* Both concern a student's first year at Harvard Law School.

The Paper Chase (1973) was based on a 1971 novel by John Jay Osborn, Jr., a 1970 HLS grad—who'd written his novel while a 2L. The novel is out of print, but the film is available on video. Timothy Bottoms had the lead, playing a character whose surname is Hart (get it?). John Houseman was the main supporting actor, in his classic role as Professor Charles W. Kingsfield.

One L was written by Scott Turow, the lawyer-novelist, and was published in 1977. Unlike Turow's subsequent works, this one is non-fiction. "One L" is shorthand for a first-year student at HLS, and as a 1L, Turow kept a diary, which was published after his 2L year. (He changed the names, descriptions, and backgrounds of the people involved, to protect the innocent...and the guilty). *One L* is still in print, a solid backlist title.

If you have not yet encountered these works, approach them with extreme caution. The problem is not that they give a false impression. Quite the contrary. What they present is the truth. But it should not be true for *you.* The reality depicted in those works should not become *your* reality. They're "What it really should *not* be like."

You've heard of the so-called "self-fulfilling prophecy"? Well, regarding lawyers-to-be, *The Paper Chase* and *One L* both set you up for a bad time. The reality they present is actually a bizarre "unreality." Together, they're the single biggest trap for the unwary with regard to law school. That's why this entire chapter is devoted to showing what's wrong with the model they present.*

---

* Certainly Turow was not deliberately setting a trap. He obviously didn't cherish his experience. I've not read the novel on which *The Paper Chase* is based, so can say nothing regarding that author's intentions. However, the movie takes a real "macho" attitude toward surviving the tortures and terrors of first-year...similar to the Marine Corps' explicit statement that "boot camp will make a *man* of you." (And even Turow fell into this, somewhat.)

The Kingsfield Syndrome

From a future law student's perspective, the key figure in *The Paper Chase* was Professor Charles W. Kingsfield, who teaches contracts. He is brilliant and aloof. He is also merciless in his pedagogy. But *The Paper Chase* would have us believe that this was the academic equivalent of what's now being called "tough love." Kingsfield's seeming antipathy toward his students supposedly masked a deep concern for their intellectual progress. "Hart" had quickly concluded that Kingsfield's disdain and ruthlessness were for the students' own good. The awe he felt toward Kingsfield from the very beginning had grown even stronger by film's end. Hart had supposedly gained a mature understanding of the true nature of the Great Scholar, and of the Law's Majesty. Hence his mystical utterance about "Having a true Socratic experience."

One L was published six years after *The Paper Chase* was, and four years after the Osborn novel had been made into a movie. Surely, as a teacher of creative writing at the time the novel came out, Turow had read Osborn's work at some point. And even more surely, he would have seen the film before going to Harvard Law. Yet, he mentions neither in *One L; The Paper Chase* is conspicuous by its absence. However, Turow's commentary on it screams from between the lines.

Turow also reported *his* experiences in a contracts course, with a Professor "Perini." I have not attempted to learn from the author of either book if the contracts professor was modeled on a specific HLS prof. However, I have spoken with several people at Harvard Law School, some of whom were employees there prior to the publication of either book. They reported much speculation as to who the "real" Kingsfield or Perini was, but no agreement. Therefore, I believe it is too much of a coincidence to be a coincidence that Turow's Perrini teaches the same subject as Osborn's Kingsfield.

(In the alternative, it's possible that both Osborn and Turow had their professor teaching Contracts because—as Chapter 1 noted—the first use of the Case/Socratic Method at Harvard Law School was by a Contracts professor, in 1870.)

As with "Hart," Turow began the academic year in awe of his contracts prof. However, unlike the movie's constantly increasing adulation, Turow's opinion moves in the opposite direction.

As with Kingsfield, Perini was a pompous asshole and a bully. (But Hart was usually oblivious to that.) However, in the movie, Kingsfield spoke with an upper-class British accent. This makes his academic brutality easier to overlook. (Americans have been conditioned to genuflect at the sound of an upper-class British accent.) To make Perini's obnox-iousness more apparent, Turow went to the other extreme, and has Perini speak with a distinctively Southern accent. (Americans have also been conditioned to believe that anyone who speaks with a strong Southern accent is either a fool, an ignoramus, a "con artist," a dissolute libertine, a bigot, a brutal sadist, or some combination thereof. Perini fit the brutal sadist stereotype.) To make him even more clearly objection-able, Turow goes out of his way to mention that Perini's law degree was from the University of Texas...and we all know how odious any-one from Texas is, right?

But the movie's image of Kingsfield in *The Paper Chase* naturally overwhelms *One L's* written image of Perini. In fact, it has led to what I call the Kingsfield Syndrome: many law school professors have—subconsciously or deliberately—imitated it. (This life-imitating-art is similar to the way the world's mobsters have quite consciously imitated the dress, choice of automobiles, and methods of speaking and acting portrayed by American gangster films.) Unfortunately, the many professors who imitate Kingsfield are able to copy only the aloofness and the harshness, not the brilliance. They mistake sarcasm and sadism for education. They self-indulgently abuse their authority in the name of pedagogy.

As with Hart, students are conditioned to respond with fawning adulation to this display of arrogance and cruelty. It is no exaggeration to compare this to the "battered wife syndrome." The victimized spouse decides to stay in the relationship because—however oddly by objective standards—she thinks, "If he didn't care so much about me, he wouldn't be so abusive."

(By the way, the episode in *The Paper Chase* when Kingsfield starts to throw Hart out of his class is based on a true incident at HLS. The real-life professor's name was Edward Henry Warren, who taught Corporations Law and Property Law at Harvard from 1904-43. He had a nickname: "The Bull."* In the movie, Hart gives a smart-alec response to an inquiry from Kingsfield. In the real-life incident, the student's response was merely inept. In the movie, Kingsfield summons Hart to the lectern, hands him a dime—the cost of a payphone call in 1973—and orders Hart to call his mother to tell her that he does not have the makings of a lawyer. In real life, "Bull" roared at the student, "You will never make a lawyer! You might just as well pack up your books now

---

* "Bull" Warren is not to be confused with *Earl* Warren, the former Governor of California who served as Chief Justice of the U.S. Supreme Court from 1953-69.

and leave the school!" The student, shocked, stood and gathered up his belongings. In both the film and real life, he then moved toward the exit—but then turned and faced the professor. In the movie, Hart loudly says, "You are a son-of-a-bitch, Kingsfield!" Thereupon, Kingsfield replies, "Mr. Hart, that is the most intelligent thing you have said today." The class bursts out laughing...thereby distracting us from the truth of Hart's statement. Then Kingsfield tells him, "You may take your seat." In real life, the student had declaimed to Professor Warren, "I accept your suggestion, Sir. But I do not propose to leave without giving myself the pleasure of telling you to go plumb straight to Hell." Immediately, the Bull replied: "Sit down, Sir. Sit down. Your response makes it clear that my judgment was too hasty." Don't know about you, but I prefer the true version.)

Mistakes in Common

Although *The Paper Chase* and *One L* finished with opposite views of their respective contracts professors, the students in both works made the same major mistakes. As with lemmings jumping off the cliff, they mindlessly followed what others were doing. Neither Osborn nor Turow understood (at the time) how students could avoid the trauma these authors described.

However, any future law student, turning to either of these works, would naturally and naively assume this is the way law school is, ineluctably. And so, like the fatalistic cavalry in Tennyson's "The Charge of the Light Brigade," they vigorously attack. ("Theirs not to reason why, / Theirs but to do and die.")

Don't you be that way. In law school, there is no safety in numbers (exception: your study group—which is a very *small* number). Don't follow the herd...because the herd is unwittingly headed for the slaughterhouse. Be a maverick. You're thinking about going to law school because you have a good brain. *Use it.*

Here's how the students of *The Paper Chase* and *One L* screwed up...

BURNING the MIDNIGHT OIL—and the 11th-HOUR PANIC

If you're burning the midnight oil, you're doing something seriously wrong. As the Opening Statement of *this* book put it,

> You're going to have to work hard, no matter what. But hard work by itself doesn't guarantee success—not in law school, and not in life. In fact, for those who think that way, hard work is sometimes counter-productive.
>
> It isn't enough to *work* hard. Nor is it enough to *be* smart. You have to *"work smart,"* too.

And there's more to it than that. As mentioned in Chapter 11, you need to take good care of your health and to build up reserves of energy. Each day—and especially as you begin your exams—you want to be fully rested, yet completely alert. Constantly burning the midnight oil, playing some kind of macho (or "macha") game to see how few hours' sleep you can get by on each night, is academically suicidal. I assume you do not have a death-wish. So don't work yourself to death.

You've heard the saying, "If it's worth doing at all, it's worth doing well"? Nonsense. In law school, there's too much to do—and much of it isn't worth doing at all...And if it's just barely worth doing in the first place, it certainly isn't worth doing well. To again quote the Opening Statement: "You have to acquire a sense for what's important, what's not. Set your priorities. This is especially so that all-important first year of law school. You can't know *everything*—but you *can* know what really *counts*..."

Neither Hart, nor Turow (nor anyone else) had the foggiest idea of what it took to do well on exams. True, *The Paper Chase* leaves the audience with the impression that Hart did well. But we never find out—for good reason: the odds were that he was destined for a Hart-breaking discovery, given the way he'd approached his courses. Turow, after *his* finals (and before the grades were issued) said he and his fellow students *still* didn't know whether or not they'd done well.

That's how it goes, for all students at all law schools. —And it tells you something about what's wrong with law school pedagogy: success is virtually haphazard, even among "the best and the brightest" who've worked so hard to master the material.

Long ago, Wall Street discovered that a randomly-selected stock portfolio, chosen simply by throwing darts at a list of securities, would perform about as well as one chosen by professional investors. However, because that didn't require managers or any of the other big-ticket costs, any investor would do better to buy a dartboard and dispense with hired advice. Naturally, that has never happened. Everyone, especially those who *succeed,* wants to *believe* in the system —and that they can beat it through more than sheer luck. I'll bet that if Harvard Law School had chosen *x* number of students at random, and had declared *them* to be at the top of the class (regardless of their performance on finals) their subsequent careers would have fared the same as those who won the finals lottery, as long as their secret didn't get out. Of course, no law school would dare conduct such a longitudinal comparison test, because then the myth would be shattered, the mystique would be gone. (However, with *Planet Law School,* it will not be a matter of chance for *you*—if you follow through.)

Both Hart and Turow crammed for finals. But there's a difference between cramming and intensive studying. It's more than semantic. Cramming is the hare's approach, and hare-brained. Intensive study, at less than the frantic level of cramming, is the tortoise approach. (A determined tortoise can cover a lot of ground.) It's more practical, determined, and thorough. Just before finals, Hart and a fellow student spent a few days together in a hideaway. They tried to quickly memorize all the material for each course, in one marathon session. That's cramming —and foolish.

There is absolutely no reason to spend the final days before an exam working yourself into a frenzy, burning yourself out at the very time you most need to be in top condition, both physically and mentally. And there is absolutely no excuse, now that you're reading *Planet Law School,* for running around like a chicken with your head cut off, the way students in *The Paper Chase* and *One L* did...which is the way it still is, even today.

(You might, perversely, be looking forward to such a traumatic experience—thinking that, years hence, you'll look back on it and laugh. If so, the joke will be on you. And it won't be funny, even then.)

Granted, Hart had been doing intensive study throughout the semester. So had Turow. But neither of them knew how to "work *smart.*" So they both just worked *hard*—very hard. Too hard. Yes, *too* hard. *Good* work is all that counts, and it's indicated by the *results.* In law school, there's no such thing as "An 'A' for effort."

MISTAKES re. CLASSES, STUDY GROUPS, and OUTLINES

In both *The Paper Chase* and *One L,* many students tried to play teacher's pet in class. They raised their hands, sure they had the right answer. They desperately wanted to outperform some unfortunate fellow student who had just failed to shine. As Turow discerned, students "tended to see classroom performance as an index of standing" —i.e., of how good they were. Further, in *The Paper Chase,* there were several scenes where students made cutting remarks in class about answers another student had just given. They pumped themselves up by putting others down. Professor Kingsfield encouraged this dog-eat-dog approach. That is sick. (Unfortunately, it's also the norm.) Yet, as Turow also noted, when the grades came out, often those who seemed smartest in class had been washed away, somehow.

(From your point of view, though, what's most important about class is that all of this is irrelevant. That's why all of Chapter 11 dealt with how to play the in-class game correctly.)

In both portrayals of law school, study groups formed early in the year. However, after the initial meeting, they did not begin work as a *group* until several weeks before the exams. *Big* mistake. As Chapter 4 showed, your study group should be working *together* on *hypotheticals,* starting with the first week of law school.

In *One L,* Turow said it was a problem that the members of his study group couldn't agree on how to approach each subject. That's because they didn't know what they needed to do. You do.

Neither work made the distinction between Master and Summary Outlines that *this* book makes. What their students did were Master Outlines. In *The Paper Chase* and *One L,* the study group members divided up the task. In the former, each person outlined only one course. Then they exchanged outlines just before finals—or were supposed to. In the latter, each worked on some material in every course, so the outline for each course was a collective work.

To repeat: you can't very well internalize someone else's outline, or someone else's part of a collective outline. All you can do is memorize it—and even that is unlikely, given the short time remaining before exams. As Chapter 4 explained, to internalize your own outline, you have to write the material in your *own* words and to *constantly re-work* it. Your outline should contain what's useful to *you.*

And as *The Paper Chase* and *One L* both showed, sometimes others either provided a very poor outline, or none at all. One of the best things about doing your own outlines is you don't have to worry about someone leaving you in the lurch during the final countdown to finals.

In both *One L* and *The Paper Chase,* the outlines were far too long, anyway. In the former, one "outline" was more than 400 pages; in the latter, there was an *800*-page outline. Even during an open-book exam, it would be impossible to make use of one of those monstrosities, even if on disk and indexed. If the students had been reworking their outlines, as discussed in Chapter 4, they could have pared each Master Outline down to 50 pages at the most.

The most important purpose of a study group is to practice hypotheticals and work old exams, not to split up the work of making outlines. Do the one, not the other.

CHEATING

Unlike Turow, Hart cheated. *The Paper Chase* finessed it, but he cheated. He committed a breaking-and-entering of the law school library in the wee hours. He sought, and got, the notes Professor Kingsfield had taken when *he'd* been a first-year law student in contracts (at Harvard). Hart wanted to make sure he'd completely "psyched out" Kingsfield, the better to anticipate what he, Hart, should say in answer to the final exam questions in contracts. What better answer to give than the professor's? Hart could easily have mined Kingsfield's own thoughts by consulting other sources. In fact, he did—Kingsfield's published articles, for example. But that clearly wasn't enough. He wanted to give himself that extra, *unethical* edge.

Thus, *The Paper Chase* gave the subtle, and false, impression that, as a result, Hart *did* have an extra edge. (Maybe that's why he wasn't worried about his grades at film's end—or, at least, his contracts grade.) But *success in law school is a very simple matter:* Black Letter Law; Thinking Like a Lawyer.

There's no magic to it, no Secret Writings such as the Red Set, hidden in a locked room the way they were in the movie. Yet, this is the message the film conveyed. But even if Kingsfield had freely given all his students copies of his first-year notes, the effect would have been minimal. (And his notes certainly didn't include the problems he'd be posing on finals he'd be giving to his own students in years to come.)

There is simply no need to even *try* to give yourself an extra edge by doing something unethical. (That includes pulling "dirty tricks" on fellow students...which tends to happen as finals approach.) —And if the penalty for getting caught is "death," doing something unethical borders on sheer lunacy. It simply isn't worth it, given that the additional benefit is trivial, at best, and probably nonexistent. It could even be counter-productive: you'd take it easy, counting on what you think will be an easy score, instead of preparing to meet the real challenge.

Another message from this episode in the movie was that it's okay to cheat if you're a "good guy." But what "bad guy" *doesn't* think of himself as a "good guy" who deserves a break...even if it involves break-and-enter?

Of Aptitude...and Lassitude

According to *One L,* Scott Turow's LSAT score was in the *99th* percentile. So, theoretically, Turow should have aced first-year. He didn't. The very lack of a correlation between his LSAT result and his initial HLS performance is a good indication that something is terribly wrong with the system. The correlation—or rather, the lack thereof—between LSAT scores and first-year law school grades is, no doubt, yet another well-kept secret that enables the academic emperor to claim he is fully dressed as he struts about the classroom. (Then again, I shudder at the thought of Professor Kingsfield buck naked.)

Actually, like the Emperor's New "Clothes," it's a "secret" that's out in the open. *Law Services Report* is a newsletter of the Law School Admissions Services—LSAS, the folks who do the LSAT. In its March, 1988 issue, there was an interesting statement from the then-director of services and programs for LSAS. She reported that there was a *very disappointing correlation* between LSAT scores and "early" law school performance. Because "early" performance (i.e., first-year) is the only one that really counts, her statement was fraught with enormity. —But never mind, it's still business-as-usual regarding the LSAT and its crucial importance as a basis for the law school admissions decision. (To the best of my knowledge, the LSAT people have not done an updated study, and would no doubt prefer that earlier study be forgotten.)

More and more, it appears the LSAT does not test aptitude for law *school.* However, perhaps it *does* accurately test it for *law*—or rather, for one's *potential* to Think Like a Lawyer. There's a difference between the one and the other.

And no doubt that is why it's just called the "Law School *Admissions* Test." And that's all it is: a device to enable law schools to quickly decide who gets in, based on a bare score (combined with the applicant's undergraduate gpa to create an "index score"). Admissions people are even lazier than the professoriat. (Admittedly, they're also far more heavily burdened, especially with the huge increrase in law school applications. Given the skimpy resources they have, they've almost no choice but to look almost *solely* at the index numbers.)

Students with natural athletic, musical, or artistic talent still need to be guided in the nature of the skill in question. They aren't expected to learn it on their own. Yet, law school *itself* is *sabotaging,* for its own selfish and cynical reasons, the very people entrusted to its charge.

Given Turow's intelligence and humanity, what he experienced was tragic. The same could be said of hundreds of thousands of others.

The fault lay not with the students, but with the deliberate pedagogical malpractice of law schools. Someday, perhaps decades from now, *One L* will have only historical interest, in the same way that we read about how, once upon a time, all surgery was done by *barbers*— without anesthetic.

So What?

Back to the *Chase*: Almost at the very start of the movie, Kingsfield gives a little speech. In it, he says something about how his questions probe the students' brains and reshape the students' cerebral mush into something that enables them to Think Like a Lawyer.

I beg to differ. True (unless you use "The *PLS* Approach"), you don't go into law school already knowing how to Think Like a Lawyer. But I've seen plenty of people who came *out* of law school *still* not knowing how to Think Like a Lawyer. What the Case/Socratic Method does is to turn your layperson's brain *into* cerebral mush. It's up to *you* to reshape that mental mess into a fine instrument capable of good legal analysis. Most law school students never get good at it. They just get by.

You might think it odd of me to go off on such a tangent about a movie. But I practice trial law. And trial lawyers know that a jury remembers only a small fraction of what it hears, and an even smaller fraction of what it reads in documents. However, a jury remembers a very large percentage of what it *sees*...especially if what it sees has been chosen for visual impact. (It probably results from "left-brain" v. "right-brain" processing, respectively.) Most of all, a jury remembers what it sees and *simultaneously* hears, especially if it's something dramatic. A movie, as a form of drama, is by definition dramatic. That's why Kingsfield will be remembered and revered, even though Perini is truer to real-life. Unfortunately, that's also why errors *The Paper Chase* students made will stay in your mind much better than the lessons of *Planet Law School.* You might even forget that the students' mistakes in that film *were* mistakes. (Another thing any trial lawyer can vouch for is that people's minds play tricks on them. Memories are amazingly faulty, and open to suggestion.)

You should not watch that movie.

Sorry to say, the only reason for you to see *The Paper Chase* (or to read *One L*) is to learn how *not* to go about being a first-year law student. Better to avoid these altogether. Turow, Hart, and their fellow 1Ls made almost every mistake possible. (So did I—and then some.) If you've already seen the movie or read the book, keep it in mind as a cautionary tale. And if you find yourself feeling or acting the way Turow, Hart, and their fellow students did, the tocsin should sound in your brain, for you are doing something terribly wrong. Use *PLS* to avoid such travail. One, two or three, law school shouldn't be 'ell for you.

Mini-Addendum #1: *Legally Blonde*

Between the first edition and this new one, the movie *Legally Blonde* was released. Perhaps, as with "Hart" in *The Paper Chase*, the protagonist's name includes a play on words: the heroine of *Legally Blonde* is one Elle (pronounced "L") Woods.

Unlike *The Paper Chase* and *One L,* it has almost nothing to do with law school. True, it's *set* in law school (Harvard, of course). However, it has little to with what the *real* world of its setting is like. And as with virtually all films (and TV shows) that include courtroom scenes, the trial was pure hokum. Ms. Woods would not have lasted two minutes in a real trial. (Besides, no first-*semester* student can take a course, or work on a project, that involves litigation.)

Unfortunately, though, the lecherous male prof *is* realistic. The woman prof, however—who evicts Elle from the very first class because Elle was not even aware of the assignment for that class— is later "redeemed." This happens when she exhorts Elle to remain in law school despite the sexual harassment. (Notice how that female prof didn't say a*nything* to Elle about maybe filing a *complaint* against the lecherer? The professor's tacit attitude in the movie is typical of that of real life: although Elle should not "bare it," she should merely grin and *bear* it. No "sisterhood" here. That's the way it goes.)

If you think this movie will help you "understand what law school is really like," you're wasting your time. —But then again, unlike *The Paper Chase* and *One L,* at least it doesn't pretend to depict what law school *is* like. *Legally Blonde* is almost pure fantasy*—though harmless...and (also unlike *The Paper Chase* and *One L)* is *charming.*

---

* Including the fantasy of beating the odds by getting a perfect score on the LSAT, and then not only being considered at all for admission to HLS, but getting in, long after the deadline for applications had passed.

Mini-Addendum #2: *The Bar Review Pitch*

Chapters 23 and 24 discuss, respectively, the bar exam and preparing for it. Commercial vendors provide "cram courses" after you graduate. However, at many schools, student "reps" (sales people) solicit first-year students in the very first weeks of law school. They urge students to sign up for a bar review course now, even though the students will not be taking it for another two-and-a-half years. They tell students that "the price will go up" each year. By signing up "now" (and paying a hefty deposit), you will "lock in a guaranteed price, and be protected against further price increases."

The price does go up each year. However, a deluxe cram course (which the student reps solicit for) covers both the Multistate Bar Exam and the state-specific bar exam. But *if you have the self-discipline to prep for law school itself,* you will also have the self-discipline to study the *Multistate* subjects on your own. (You'll see why, in Chapters 23 and 24, it's much less difficult than the student reps for the deluxe vendors would have you believe.) Then, the only bar review course you'll need after law school will be one that covers the state-specific subjects you'll have on the "barzam" in the state where you want to practice law. And you do not have to put down a deposit 30 months ahead of time.

By not following the herd, and not signing up for a "deluxe" cram course, you can easily save $1,500 or more.

I mention this now because you might choose not to read Chapters 23 and 24 until after you've finished first-year. But by then, you'll have already signed up for a full-scale bar review course (and paid the deposit). At that point, you'd still save money by dropping that deluxe cram course (thus forfeiting your deposit) and then paying only for a state-specific bar review. But most students don't go through the cost-benefit analysis. Instead, they stay with the deluxe, and end up paying a total of more than $2,000 for their bar review, simply because they did not want to forfeit their deposit. The "deluxe" cram companies know that. That's why they put the "hard-sell" on you when you're new to law school, to get you to sign up and put your money down.

That's yet another aspect of "getting caught up in the madness."

Even if you do not have time to read all of this book before starting law school, please—if you are pressured by some fellow student who's a sales person (and sometimes faculty members are also in on it) to sign up for a full-scale bar review course in your first semester of law school—read Chapters 23 and 24 before you make your decision.

Chapter 13 - Let the Student Beware

"Blind" Grading

Virtually every law school uses blind grading on written exams. It's similar to the SAT or LSAT that way. (Those, of course, are multiple-choice, and computer-graded. Most law school exams are essay, and graded by a human.) You're assigned a number. You write that number on each "bluebook" you use during the exam ("0103—43rd [book] of 43," etc.). The professor only sees the bluebooks with the code numbers. (At some schools now, students use computers—without memory—to type their answers, but are still assigned code numbers.) There's a receipt, of sorts. It's in two parts. The first part you turn in to the exam proctor. Your name and code number are on it. When the prof turns in the grades, the grade sheet shows the score each student got, but only by the student's code number, not name. So the registrar's office then refers to its own list, which has students' names *and* code numbers. Next, it enters the score each student got, onto that student's record. The grades are posted, with scores listed by code number, just as on the gradesheet. Each student has kept the other half of the exam code number receipt, and uses that to look up his or her own score on the posted gradesheet. (At some schools, however, the grades are posted by the students' I.D. numbers or Social Security numbers. And some schools provide the grades directly to the student, in person or by mail.)

Because the prof doesn't know whose answers he or she is grading, personal bias can't enter into the final score. True. However, *afterwards,* a *tenured* professor can find out the grade he or she gave to a particular student, by name—*before it's recorded.* The professor can then raise or lower that score before it's entered on the student's transcript. (He or she will then change the score in the student's answers, too, before returning them, of course—if, indeed, the graded answers are returned.) It happens. If asked, your law school will deny it, but it happens. Rarely; but it happens. (We'll get to another practice that belies the preaching—one that's far more common—in Chapter 18.)

The moral is: don't think you can thumb your nose at your prof just because you're sure you'll ace the final. True, a professor can't change your grade and flunk you if you did well. But a half-dozen points can make a *big* difference in your class standing—so even if you do ace the final, you still lose. (And please don't dream that just because the professor seems to like you so much, you don't have to worry about your final grade—as though your friendly professor will change it to something better if you don't do well. That happens only in the movies...and not in movies about law school. Although theoretically it can work in both directions, in practice it's usually just one way: down.)

You'd better get used to it right now, if you haven't already: some lawyers lie. (Gasp!) And nearly all law school professors are lawyers (at least, on paper). Don't let the pretense of the academic "above it all" attitude fool you. Behind the façade, these people can be just as petty and vindictive as you or I...and you're on *their* turf, playing by *their* rules.

The "Character & Fitness" Committee

Part of the P.R. the legal profession persists in spouting is that all future lawyers are screened to determine their "character" and "fitness" to see if they're "worthy" of entering this noble profession. When you start law school, if you intend to practice law in the state where your law school is located, you must file a "Statement of Intent to Study Law" with that state's supreme court, bar association, or other agency authorized to license attorneys. Then the Character and Fitness (C&F) Committee decides whether or not you're entitled, on moral grounds, to join the ranks of those engaged in the virtuous calling of the Law.

You will be scrutinized. But the bar is too cheap to conduct more than a perfunctory investigation on its own. Instead, it relies on *you* to tell it the truth and the whole truth, first on your Statement of Intent, and then on your Application for a law license. (In most states, you also have to provide your fingerprints, at your own expense.) If at any time the powers-that-be discover you lied, *you* will discover just how much power they have—and the clever tortures they can inflict effortlessly. So, if you were put on probation for a semester in college because you never returned 20 long-overdue library books, you'd better report it.

Once you *have* a law license, you can seduce clients, perjure yourself, bill for work never done, rip off the trust fund you set up to provide for a rich client's heirs, etc. Almost *anything* goes—as long as you don't *flaunt* your turpitude *and* you're well-connected with the powers-that-be in your state's regulatory agency. (I am not exaggerating—as you will see for yourself once you're admitted to the guild. And no, I have not engaged in unethical behavior myself...well, not *seriously* unethical behavior. But I know of several lawyers—and judges—who have engaged in *heinous* behavior, again and again, yet have never received anything more than a token slap on the wrist for it, despite strenuous efforts by their victims.) However, until you *get* that union card, you'd better at least *pretend* to be a sanctimonious pinhead.

The C&F committee is often more concerned with dishonesty *vis-à-vis* the C&F Committee than with the transgression itself. Let's say you have 90 unpaid parking tickets. That's bad. It means you're a scofflaw. But if you "come clean," and confess, then at least you've proven you're an honest scofflaw. Or maybe you can concoct a convincing story as to *why* you didn't pay those 90 tickets. (Sample: "I sold that car to my sister, but we never got around to having the registration changed regarding the license plates. *She's* the one who accumulated all those tickets. I even have correspondence to that effect, between the two of us and between the city and me." Good luck. You'll probably need a written confession from your sister, which you're unlikely to get.— Then again, maybe someday she'll want the free services of her lawyer sibling. Hmm...)

Here's the one that really gets to me most of all: if you go through any type of psychological therapy or counseling, you might be required to report it to the C&F people. *You might also have to sign a waiver giving them access to your file.* In the state where I went to law school, it was a Catch-22 situation: the strain of law school was enormous, but students were explicitly advised *not* to seek counseling...because it might jeopardize getting a law license in that state! We could go to a counselor, but anything we said about having doubts regarding the Law, or lawyers, could be used against us. It could also be used against us if we ever felt like committing suicide in law school (which feelings were not so rare, actually), or felt like murdering a professor (which feelings were *definitely* not so rare).

Even if a therapist-patient privilege exists in your state, you might be asked to waive that privilege. Refusal to do so will count heavily against you. We're not talking Constitutional Rights here. We're talking about the Character & Fitness Committee. As far as they're concerned, you have no rights. And the U.S. Supreme Court, for the most part, has backed them up.

The other thing that can jeopardize your future license is lack of gravity. I was not joking when I said you have to appear to be a sanctimonious pinhead. The C&F people have absolutely no sense of humor—and very little sense of humanity.

I am not making up the following: a student (at a law school that shall remain nameless) filled out the Statement of Intent to Study Law form. There was a question on it as to whether or not he would "uphold" the Constitution of the United States. It was (and still is) a ridiculous question to ask. So he gave a flippant answer: "Of course: I'm a 'constitutional' kind of guy." His state's Board of Bar Examiners decided, on the basis of that one answer, that the student in question was unfit to practice law. It refused to allow him to sit for the bar exam. He sued. *Years* later, his state's Supreme Court ruled in his favor. By then, of course, his prospects for a career with a reputable firm were gone, as was his bank account. (However, I don't know if he ever passed the bar exam: It was—and is—based on "blind" grading...and guess who, in that state, gets to grade 60% of it?)

Another example, also involving "loyalty" to "the Constitution": a black student was at another, anonymous, law school during a time when a number of "racial incidents" were going on around the country. One day in class, she said she was uncertain of her loyalty to the U.S. Constitution because it was the basic document of a system that was so oppressive to blacks. A fellow student (white) reported her to that state's C&F committee. The Committee conducted a full investigation. In my opinion, she was cleared only because she was black. There was a danger of adverse publicity—perhaps even "racial incidents"—if she was barred from the bar. (I have no quarrel with letting her off the hook because of her race, if indeed that's why she got off. My quarrel is with a regulatory agency that comes down hard on a student who makes such a thoughtful comment*—and then looks the other way while licensed attorneys routinely and deliberately subvert the Constitution, the rule of law, the "justice" system, and so forth.)

Never, never, *never* raise your voice to anyone who's on or connected with the C&F committee—whether on the phone or (metaphorically) in writing. They have even been known to make extensive notes of any conversations, whether on the phone or in person. These people have all the power. They know it. They often act it.**

Actually, the experience is good training for dealing with superiors in your law firm, or with judges: no matter what they say, no matter what they do, they're right. Remember that dictum from the Middle Ages? —"The King can do no wrong." Well, the Character & Fitness Committee can do no wrong—while you're under their authority. Nor can a judge—while you're in that judge's court. Nor can a superior at

---

* I disagree with her, but that's beside the point; at least she was thinking and refusing to take things at face value...and after all, that's part of what a good lawyer is supposed to do.

** I speak from (second-hand) experience, having counseled a law school graduate who ran afoul of my state's C&F committee because he'd run afoul of a department chairman at a grad school he'd attended. The professor had set out to ruin the student's life—and nearly succeeded.

your law firm—while you're an employee of that law firm. No matter what they do, you grin and bear it—although there are ways to politely and discreetly take issue with them. (Yes, I am exaggerating...though a lot less than you'd think—or I wish. Even so, there really *are* limits to how much you should shut your eyes to.) Above all, be humble and respectful, even to the point of humiliation. No matter how petty, ridiculous, or stupid these people seem (and, often, *are),* they have the power over your future.

Granted, for the vast majority of law school students and graduates, the process of getting vetted goes smoothly. It's a routine procedure. Don't be the exception who proves the rule.

Sexual Harassment

Chapter 12 already "touched" on this (as it were). There are rules against it, but it happens. Welcome to the real world of law school. Remember, the professors have tenure. True, (male) *college* profs these days can have their lives *ruined* by mere *accusations* later proved to be utter *fabrications* motivated by spite, caprice, or greed. But law profs are different. They're immune. (And if an assistant law professor, without tenure yet, is stupid enough to harass others about sex, that person doesn't have what it takes to play the faculty's games anyway.) The rules are largely for P.R. purposes—just as the "rules of ethics" that supposedly guide practicing attorneys are largely just for P.R. purposes. You file a complaint, see what happens to it...and see what happens to you.

(Chapter 5 had an extensive discussion of an appalling action by Professor Gary Munneke of Pace University's law school. Granted, that did not involve sexual harassment...although, given that Ms. DiFede was not only female, but an attractive female, I strongly suspect there was at least a subsconscious sexual component to Munneke's battery of her. Regardless, the law school at Pace not only never lifted a finger to come to her assistance in the days that followed, it has actively been contesting her claims for *years* now—despite the fact that the entire first-year torts class witnessed the battery.)

Sure, there are exceptions. If you're the editor-in-chief of your school's Law Review (the flagship publication, not some other academic journal), *and* you're the daughter of an attorney who's a prominent member of the state bar, you can get some action—maybe even something as drastic as a *private reprimand. (That'll* show'm.) Otherwise, you'll be subjected to a very stressful round of interrogations, meetings, hearings, etc. Just what you need when you're trying to get good grades in law school.

There is the retaliation factor, too. (See "blind" grading, and the "character and fitness" committee, above. —There's more than *one* way to screw a student.)

So what to do? I'm sorry, but I am going to dodge the question. I am not a trained counselor, have only handled one sexual harassment case (I represented a female plaintiff; the case settled), and am male. There are people far better qualified than I to give you advice. All I will say is it's better to head it off at the pass (as it were). If you can attend any presentations, or read any material, that helps you to protect yourself, I urge you to do so—*before* you go to law school (or even college, as the case may be). An ounce of prevention, etc. Planet Law School is like nothing you've experienced before. Don't let it turn into *Invasion of the Body-Snatchers.*

Here are two incidents I observed, personally, in law school. Obviously, since I was present (and not a participant) these weren't in 1:1 settings. In fact, all my section-mates were fellow witnesses.

The first was directed to the female students in general. My Torts prof—male—launched a discussion of "social utility" as a concept for imputing liability in tort. He steered the social utility concept into the realm of *criminal* acts, within the context of civil liability for same. He then picked rape as his example.

He said *civil* liability for rape should be based on a "balancing test." In the one scale was the social "disutility" as to the rape victim. However, this "disutility" was only potential, and might be minimal. "And she might *enjoy* it." (Yes, he said that.) On the other hand, the rapist obviously derived pleasure from committing the rape. So there was a "social *utility*" to weigh against any disutility. Theoretically, then, given a certain fact pattern, an act of rape could be a benefit to society. (I am not making this up. More than 100 people can confirm this. —And I graduated from law school in the *'90s*, not the '50s.)

The second example was directed to an individual. As one of its main cases, my first-year Civ Pro casebook discussed *Owen Equipment and Erection Company v. Kroger.** The civil procedure professor, male, thought it would be cute to embarrass a female student by asking her about it. He called on the most attractive woman in the class—one of the most beautiful women I have ever seen, in fact.

"Tell me about *Owen*," he said.

She started to brief the case. He interrupted her.

"I see this company's full name is 'Owen Equipment and Erection Company.' Which would you prefer: 'Equipment,' or 'Erection'?"

---

* 437 U.S. 365, 98 S.Ct. 2398, 57 L.Ed.2d 274 (1978)

She politely said either one would do. He wouldn't stop.

"I'm surprised. I would think *you'd* want *'Erection'*—although I suppose an erection is impossible without the equipment for it. Could you tell me why you might *prefer* 'Erection'?"

She did not become flustered, nor did she respond, other than to calmly say, "No, I can't." Good for her. Having failed to unnerve her, the prof let it go.

Granted, these incidents were minor forms of sexual harassment. But they *were* sexual harassment, in my book (and this *is* my book, after all). In neither of these instances did anyone voice a complaint in class (or afterwards, to my knowledge). Why? —Because we were all in our very first semester of law school, and living in fear and trembling...which is the way the professors liked it. I think it's more than coincidental that no similar incident occurred *after* first-year.

Racial Harassment.

I am not referring to racial harassment by fellow students, but to racial harassment by professors. Yes, that too happens, even today. It's rare, at least in its overt form, but it still happens. I never witnessed any such incidents while I was in law school. However, I heard of one. It involved yet another of my first-year professors, and quickly made the rounds of the entire school.

This particular professor was a (white) "flaming reactionary." He hated anything that he regarded as reverse discrimination, and had written extensively in opposition to it. My school had several students from minority groups in it. One of these students, a black, was in the professor's course. One day in class, the prof called on the guy, who gave an inept answer. The professor glared at him silently for awhile, then said, "You're the best argument I've ever seen against affirmative action."

Never mind that white students had often given inept answers. Never mind that even good students sometimes have bad days. All the prof cared about was that this student was black—and as far as the prof was concerned, the only way a black could get into this particular law school was as the result of reverse discrimination. In short, the professor was a racist.* His remark was as savage as it was uncalled for.

---

* This is not to say, by any means, that *all* whites who oppose affirmative action are racists. However, racists do use their opposition to affirmative action as a socially-acceptable stalking horse for their bigotry. (As a logical proposition: "All 'A' are 'B'" does not mean "All 'B' are 'A'.") (Continued on next page.)

Because I was not an eyewitness, I cannot swear it happened this way, or that it happened at all. But I had occasion, later, to discuss it with another faculty member, who confirmed it. He said the professor who'd made the remark was privately urged not to be so indiscreet again...and that was the end of the matter.

Once again, I shall duck the question of how to cope—in part because I'm a WASP. But once again, if you're a member of a minority group, I urge you to attend presentations and read relevant material before you even enroll in law school. (However, if the student hadn't been so stunned, he might have shot back: "And you're the best argument I've ever seen against tenure.")

According to reports from some black students, some profs have not called on blacks (or other minorities) when those students have raised their hands hoping to be called on. If it's a systematic exclusion, it's clearly discriminatory (by definition). And were I in those students' shoes, I would be offended too.

However, you shouldn't want to be called on in the first place. You shouldn't even be raising your hand. (See Chapter 11.)

But, students say it shows a lack of respect from the profs. True. But the profs don't respect the white students either, even though they might do a better job of masking their disdain for them.

You've heard the saying, "A black in a job has to be twice as good as a white in that same job just to be regarded as *equal*"? (Unfortunately, affirmative action has reinforced that.) My advice: *ace your exams.*

These days, top black grads are not only getting preference in *hiring* by firms and government agencies, the *firms* are paying them a *premium* over white grads. (Whether they then get *promoted* at the firms is another matter; but that's a topic for another time.)

Choose your battles carefully. If it's just a subjective matter of perception, consider letting it go. And even if it obviously is some mild racism, I'd say consider letting that go too—as long as it it isn't vicious, disgusting, etc. (Yeah, I know: "Easy for you to say, Whitey!")

But, by God, where it's something *major,* and you can not only prove it objectively, but you can nail someone dead to rights, go for it! Choose your battles carefully...so that when you do fight, you win a clear victory that "sends a message" to those who might otherwise want to exercise their racist tendencies.

This professor's own bigotry was ironic, as he was descended from late-19th-century immigrants whom WASPs had heavily discriminated against because of their religion and national origin. This group only won acceptance in "polite society" through the power of the ballot box, by voting as a block in big-city elections.

Difficulties for the Disabled

This section concerns only those in wheelchairs. I apologize for leaving out those with other physical disabilities. My only excuse is that, if you're deaf, etc., it's very easy to determine whether your prospective law school is considerate in this regard. Such is not the case regarding promises of wheelchair accessibility. (And as for other disabilities, I apologize for my ignorance as to your needs.)

If you're in a wheelchair, you already know that the symbol indicating "access for the disabled" is sometimes fraudulent. The "wheelchair ramp" turns out to be at a 35-degree angle, accessible only to a motor-driven chair with *very* high power; the interior doors (especially to the restrooms) aren't wide enough to accommodate passage of a wheelchair; or the sole elevator turns out to be the freight elevator by the loading dock—and you have to find a janitor with a key to make use of it.

At my law school (a wealthy one) accommodations were minimal. To the best of my knowledge, while I was there no one in a wheelchair was ever on the premises—perhaps for good reason: I could easily see attending classes would have been very difficult for such a person. Despite this, the school's promotional materials proclaimed that it was fully wheelchair-accessible.

If the buildings of your proposed law school are relatively new (built, say, within the last decade), they're probably truly barrier-free. Regardless, if a given law school accepts you, it might have a videotape it can send you, showing that it's wheelchair-accessible. But don't trust the self-serving proclamation in the promotional literature, and perhaps not even a videotape (which, of course, has been carefully edited). And don't even take the word of a disabled person on the *faculty or staff*. (Faculty and staff don't go all the places at the school the students do.) It might be worth the expense of a visit before you decide to enroll there. Check out the auditoriums, classrooms, elevators, cafeteria and snack bar, the lounges—everything. This includes living quarters and transportation arrangements. If you can't afford the visit (or even if you can) ask if there's a *student* there who's disabled, or a recent graduate who's disabled. Get that person's name and e-mail addrress or phone number. Insist on it, before you'll further consider enrolling at that school. Contact him or her (or, if you visit, meet that person face-to-face if you can). Of course, as was the case at my school, there might be no such person. You either make the visit, or you take your chances.

At a previous school I attended, the administration deliberately lured disabled students by promising to create a "barrier-free environment" in a special dormitory for them. In the years I was there (which was more than three years after the promises were made) nothing was done. (Years later, I checked again. There still was no barrier-free dorm. My hunch is the school was getting federal money for the project—and then diverting the funds.) The disabled students I spoke with were very bitter; rightfully so.

You don't need such an additional burden anywhere—but especially not in law school.

For several years, a law school in the Boston area (whose name I forget) built up a good reputation for itself for accommodating the disabled. This included help for students with dyslexia—such as providing assistants for taking notes in class and giving the dyslexic students extra time to take exams. Then the administration abruptly reversed its policy, without notice. It took a lawsuit against the school to get the problem resolved.

Perhaps there's no way "looking before you leap" could have helped. One day the administration was supportive, the next day the students were left in the lurch. But that sort of situation is surely rare.

Domestic Difficulties

Law school puts stress on marriages and other "committed relationships." Divorce is sometimes the result. As you saw from Lake's article reviewed in Chapter 8, law school deliberately pits student against student, in a very sick game. Unfortunately, that indoctrination often spills over into students' relationships with others.

Have your significant other read relevant portions of this book, to get an idea of what you will be or are going through. Better yet, have him or her spend a day attending classes with you—including time to listen in on conversations between you and other students, to see how law school is affecting others. Try to get your other half to realize what it is you're up against, and to bear with you.

However, do *not* turn this into a "game," whereby you use law school as an excuse to be insensitive, abrupt, critical, argumentative, demanding...and in general, a jerk.

You are *both* going to have *work* at it, very hard, to keep law school from ruining your relationship.

> An ounce (or more) of prevention is worth a pound of cure, no matter what the subject.
> (This applies when counseling your future clients, too.)

Addendum to Chapter 13: What the Dean Did

On November 27, 2002, John Dwyer—professor at and dean of the University of California at Berkeley's law school (Boalt Hall)—announced his resignation from both positions as of January 1, 2003.

Dwyer stated he was leaving because of "an allegation of sexual misconduct that violated the university's sexual harassment policy." He said the accusation was based on "a single encounter two years ago that was consensual, but there is no allegation that any form of sexual intercourse occurred." He also said, "I acknowledge that this reflected a serious error in judgment on my part and was inappropriate."

Laura Stevens, the attorney for the the unnamed complainant, disclosed alleged details of the incident. Dwyer was socializing with a group of law students at a cafe in Berkeley. He and five of them, including the woman in question (who was then in her second year at Boalt), later went to a bar in Oakland. (Question: this dean went *bar-hopping* with his *students*? That alone is…inadvisable.) When the group was calling it a night, everyone got separated at the bar. Dwyer offered the quite intoxicated woman a ride home, which she accepted. He asked if he could use the bathroom in her apartment, and she said "yes." While he was in the bathroom, she passed out on her bed. She later awoke to find her skirt and blouse had been pushed up and her pantyhose removed—and her dean had his head at his student's breasts and his fingers in her vagina.

According to attorney Stevens, the woman was treated at the university's health center. Later, she attended individual and group therapy sessions for victims of sexual assault.

She then made an anonymous call to the school's Title IX officer, who's responsible for university compliance with federal laws on sexual harassment. The attorney says the student was told that if she complained, the person ultimately responsible for following up would be… Dean Dwyer. In the corporate world, *alternative* channels are available when a sexual harassment complaint is to be made against the person who normally is ultimately responsible for handling such complaints. But at Boalt Hall, the Title IX officer told the student she was not aware of any other channels. For that reason, the student was concerned about both the handling of her potential complaint and about retaliation.

U. Cal. has a *90-day deadline* for filing sexual harassment complaints. Care to speculate as to the effect on students who fear publicity and possible retaliation?

Stevens says the student also consulted with three female members of the Boalt faculty. Two of the three did not yet have tenure. They were concerned about retaliation against themselves. The student had wanted to speak with another female professor, Linda Krieger, but Krieger also did not have tenure at the time. So the student waited until Krieger received tenure (in spring 2002) before approaching her. Attorney Stevens indicates Krieger was concerned that she (Krieger) might have a legal duty to report the alleged sexual assault regardless of the student's wish. But when Krieger spoke with the Title IX officer and the University's General Counsel, neither could answer that question. Krieger then urged the student to retain an attorney and file a complaint.

In his resignation statement, Dwyer belittled the event by noting it had occurred two years before. However, it's understandable that the woman had waited until she'd graduated from law school (in May, 2002) before filing her complaint. (At the graduation ceremony, she received her sheepskin from the fingers of...Dean Dwyer.)

The university says she visited the Title IX office in May, 2002, but did not file a complaint because she allegedly refused to identify Dwyer as the perpetrator. The university also says she received vigorous assurances there would be no retaliation against her. (However, because she'd graduated by then, the point was moot.) She filed her complaint—under the faculty Code of Conduct, which apparently has no deadline, rather than under the university's sexual harrassment rules—on October 16, 2002, after hiring attorney Stevens.

The San Francisco *Chronicle,* Boalt's faculty, and many students were very sympathetic to...the dean. Dwyer, 50, a bachelor, had been married and divorced twice. He'd met his second wife when she was a student at Boalt and he a professor there. The *Chronicle* quoted her as saying "He wouldn't assault somebody. He's really principled that way." Other articles in the newspaper emphasized that female students found Dwyer physically attractive and charming, and that it was well known that he flirted with them and they with him. (The subtle message, of course, was that the student's claim of "assault" was not made in good faith.)

Commentary from fellow denizens of the ivory tower emphasized Dwyer's brilliance as a student (in both law school—Boalt—and in grad school—Ph.D. in chemical physics at Cal. Tech.), along with his brilliance as a legal scholar and his accomplishments (especially in fund-raising and hiring of new faculty) during the two years he'd been Boalt's dean. The message was "Why should this great man and this great law school have to lose so much over something so minor?"

Well, that student did the dean (and Boalt Hall) a *favor,* by not having promptly filed a *criminal* complaint against Dwyer. It appears he chose to resign on his own. Good for him; the man has *some* sense of honor. Had it been up to the university, though, I've no doubt he would have received only a slap on the wrist.

Addendum to the Addendum (!)

In January, 2003, the *PLS* reader who'd alerted me to the Dwyer case alerted me to items on the matter by several "Internet columnists."

One stated that by resigning from Boalt Hall as both its dean and a faculty member, Dwyer was not necessarily engaging in a *mea culpa*. The columnist speculated Dwyer's departure "could also be motivated by, say, a fear of wrongful persecution by a school community that has a faction of **hysterical militant feminists**." (Boldface in the original.) And some commentators said the dean was the victim of a "get Dwyer" campaign by radical feminists and groups composed of people of color who'd opposed his hiring as dean in 2000.

Yet, in his letter of resignation, Dwyer had said "I acknowledge that this [incident] reflected a serious error in judgment on my part and was inappropriate." If that's not a *mea culpa,* pray tell, what is?

Further, the commentators overlook these facts: (1) the complaint against Dwyer was made privately, not publicly (on October 16, 2002); (2) a behind-closed-doors investigation was underway, unbeknownst to all but a handful of people; and (3) Dwyer resigned on his own (on November 27) while the investigation was proceeding. Had it cleared him of any wrongdoing, and had he (and the law school) then been *publicly* accused notwithstanding the investigation's findings, the commentators might have had a good point.

Further, *Dwyer* created the public issue himself. He could merely have said he was resigning "for personal reasons." Many government and corporate officials have done that. (Granted, though, the rumor mill would have buzzed with speculation as to the *real* reason, as always.) Instead, he subtly portrayed himself as the victim of a vindictive female law student. He insinuated she'd changed her mind after a willing sexual encounter and was accusing him of impropriety.

Had Dwyer *not* uttered his innuendos, and had the woman's lawyer, Stevens, *then* released the alleged details anyway, the commentators would have had a good point. But Dwyer brought it on himself by casting aspersions on the woman's character even while admitting his own wrongdoing.

Stevens perhaps overreacted by *immediately* releasing the alleged details. However, had I been in her situation, I would have "hit the roof" too, after seeing Dwyer's public statement. He'd set a subtle "smear campaign" in motion. That he had "tactfully not named his accuser" (in the words of one columnist) is irrelevant. It was just a matter of time before the woman's identity became known—and only Dwyer's insinuations would have been "out there."

And Dwyer's defenders did indeed follow his lead. One woman said that because the student was an adult (25 at the time), she had to accept some blame for what happened. After all, she'd been drinking heavily. So had Dwyer—and she ought to have known better than to let a drunk man into her apartment, even if he was the dean of her law school and old enough to be her father. And, of course, she passed out on the bed while he was in her bathroom, so what did she expect?

Granted, it was unwise of her to get drunk. However, that does not excuse Dwyer's (alleged) actions. He too was apparently drunk at the time. But an excessive intake of alcohol cannot *completely* dissolve a person's sense of right and wrong.

And what should the woman have done? The man had given her a ride home. He'd asked to come into her apartment to use her bathroom. Was she to have refused him because she feared he was using the "call of nature" as a pretext for a *different* "call of nature"? Or should she have said, "Sorry, Dean, I'm afraid I'm going to pass out as soon as I get inside, and well, frankly, I'm afraid you'll take advantage of me while I'm unconscious"?

One critic posted this: "If Dwyer's such a stud, doesn't it seem unlikely he'd be groping someone who's passed out, even if [Dwyer's] drunk?" That is especially surprising coming from a woman. (One of the standard defenses in rape cases is "The accused is so handsome and charming that he has no problem 'getting women.'")

Another said, "We can't know what *really* happened that night," and dismissed it as a mere "He said/She said" matter. And the woman's chief critic emphasized that nearly ten percent of all complaints of sexual assault filed with the police are later shown to be lies.

Interestingly, the columnist also mentioned that nearly ten percent of almost *all* types of crimes reported to the police are found to be lies. (In fact, the vast majority of crimes, including muggings, are just one person's word against another's. But that's hardly a reason to forbear investigation and prosecution.) And most important of all, Dwyer not only admitted he'd done *something* wrong of a sexual nature, he regarded it as serious enough to warrant his resignation both as dean and professor.

The woman's chief critic figured out who she was, *and disclosed her name on the internet.* He then began a character assassination attempt. He reported that, in law school, she'd been a member and leader of left-wing activist groups. Further, he stated that Linda Krieger—the professor who'd advised the woman to hire a lawyer and file a complaint—had been the woman's thesis advisor, and was an ardent feminist and former civil rights attorney. And after graduating, the student had not taken a job as a "public interest" lawyer, despite her attorney's press release to that effect. Instead, she'd gone to work for a left-wing political advocacy firm.

The columnists also argued that the two-year delay in filing the complaint was evidence of the alleged "get Dwyer" campaign. However, if she wanted to "get" him, wouldn't it have made more sense for her to have *immediately* filed—when Dwyer was new on the job, and before he'd had a chance to ingratiate himself with the Boalt Hall community and to consolidate his position as dean?

Stevens says the woman had gone to the campus health clinic the next day for what was apparently a medical exam to see if she'd been raped, and had enrolled in counseling for victims of sexual assault. Assuming that the clinic and the center maintain records, investigators could have checked out these alleged facts. (And perhaps they did, before Dwyer resigned.) If the student was concerned enough to promptly do those things, does it make sense she would have then kept silent for two years just to await an opportune moment to "get revenge"? (There's no evidence that anything was occurring at Boalt Hall to make Dwyer particularly vulnerable in October, 2002.) To suggest the student had been "lying low" because she had a sinister motive is...bizarre.

Yet, one woman critic noted, "Former Dean Dwyer now suffers the ultimate negative consequence for what he admits was inappropriate 'cocktail party' behavior—excommunication from not just his livelihood, but from a community that was his life."

"'Cocktail party' behavior"? (Yes, this happened in *Berkeley, California.* But even so...)

Moreover, excommunication is an act of expulsion. Dwyer was not expelled nor even asked to leave, by others. He departed on his own. If that was "his life," he's the one who chose to jeopardize it.

A male defender stated: "The University granted [the woman] unfettered power to anonymously destroy the academic career of a caring, committed, not just hard-working, but driven and dedicated servant of the Boalt Hall community and the legal profession. What a tragedy for Boalt to lose him."

The *woman* did not destroy Dwyer's academic career. All she did was file a complaint. (And it's quite likely Dwyer will be back in the ivory tower, somewhere, before long.) Nor did the woman act anonymously. Would the critic have preferred that all initial complaints be made as press releases? He makes Berkeley's confidentiality procedures sound like the *truly* anonymous denunciations by secret "informers" during the McCarthy Era.

Can there be any doubt what the rest of this woman's law school experience would have been like had she filed her complaint promptly— and its existence (and her identity) had "accidentally" become known even to just the faculty, let alone to her fellow students?

Remember, Denise DiFede? (Chapter 5 discussed her situation.) She filed *her* complaint (a lawsuit) promptly. Yet, despite having over a hundred witnesses to Professor Munneke's action, to this day, both he and Pace University's law school vigorously deny any wrongdoing on his part...and, in their pleadings filed with the court, have attempted to shift the blame to *her.*

Dwyer's defenders have also criticized the woman's lawyer, Laura Stevens. One critic said that Stevens is a "civil rights lawyer" who has previously represented clients suing corporations and universities (including U. Cal - Berkeley) for discrimination. He implied there was something wrong with that. He then quoted Stevens as saying corporations can often be persuaded to change their ways without a lawsuit, because they realize it's cheaper to switch than fight. The critic then said that this "switch or fight" threat was also wrong.

Forgive me for sounding like an attack-dog attorney, but I see nothing wrong with the "switch or fight" negotiating technique. And I have sometimes advised my own clients to reach a settlement agreement instead of fighting it out and possibly losing and then having to pay far more (including expenses and my fee).

The former dean's defenders also charge that there is a "political agenda" to the aftermath of his resignation. They say Professor Krieger is trying to expand her power base at Boalt Hall, and that she and attorney Stevens are working together. The two are now trying to force the law school to institute "sensitivity" training and a far more elaborate set of regulations regarding student-faculty sexual contact (and to hire more militant feminists and people of color).

There might well be something to that claim.

So what?

—That is an entirely *separate* matter, a "political" one.

Lawyers (and future lawyers) should not "work downwards" from their general political opinions to the facts of a specific dispute. Nor should they read into a case facts that either were not there to start with, or are irrelevant.

Dwyer did *something* wrong. He knew it, admitted it, and voluntarily paid a very high price for it, *whatever* it was he'd done. That's *all* we know for *sure.*

Wise judges write their opinions to apply as narrowly as possible. Wise lawyers (and future lawyers) try to stay as "close to the ground" as possible when working on a case, rather than soaring into clouds of ideology.

One reason why *PLS* denigrates those who want to think of law *only* in connection with "policy" is that the aftermath of Dwyer's resignation illustrates what happens: dogma causes them to lose sight of the facts, in the name of "policy."

Policy is important, as Chapter 10 ("A Trial Memo") showed. But the nonsense that passes for "policy" in the name of legal thinking is wrong in several ways. First, it becomes the "go-to" choice, a path of least resistance for those who are not *really* interested in "Thinking Like a Lawyer," but who instead are would-be "public intellectuals." In short, they would rather bullshit than roll up their sleeves and do some serious mental *work*.

Most courts, most lawyers, know that the real work in the law has little to do with "policy" arguments beyond the policies that have already gelled as Black Letter Law. Rather, they know that the real work in the law is to analyze specific (known or likely) *facts*, in light of specific *rules*, to reach specific *decisions* about specific disputes, defended by specific *reasons*.

It appears that all of Dwyer's defenders, quoted above, were either students at or graduates of Boalt Hall. And Boalt, as one of the "best" law schools in the country, is a bastion of "policy." If the woman's critics are typical (and I believe they are, not just of Boalt but of most law schools), Boalt Hall and its students should be concerned about something far more important than the Dwyer matter.*

---

* Having criticized Dwyer's defenders, who are anti-radical-feminist, I am sure some readers will jump to the conclusion that I am pro-radical-feminist. In that case, please read Chapter 26 before you make up your mind.

Part IV:

Dissent
&
Response

Chapter 14 - Points of "Error":
A "Banker's Dozen"

The old-fashioned neighborhood baker (who no longer exists) had a reputation for generosity. Hence, a "baker's dozen" was 13. Bankers, in contrast, have a well-deserved reputation for stinginess. So this chapter presents a *"banker's* dozen" (11) criticisms of *PLS* that have appeared in the five years since the original edition was published. (The page facing the inside back cover, though, presents one other—my personal favorite.)

In appellate litigation, the advocate looks at what happened at the trial court level. He or she then picks out various legal points (not factual ones, by the way) on which the advocate's client lost. The next step is to gauge the chances of success on appeal by challenging the judge's rulings on some of those points of law. The challenges are called "points of error." (Actually, these days, most courts call them "issues.")

PLS's critics raised their points of error in their appeal to a higher authority: prospective *PLS* readers, i.e., you. This chapter addresses their contentions. The decision who's right is yours to make.

1. *"Don't Worry, Be Happy (Play Now, Work Later)"*

The first argument against *PLS* is directed to those who've recently wrapped up one degree and will soon be starting law school. It usually goes something like this: "You've just finished years of schoolwork. Well, law school involves a lot *more* work. And once you've started there, you'll never be able to relax and enjoy yourself again for more than a couple of weeks at a time, for the rest of your life. If you don't get a lot of R&R now, you will quickly burn out in law school. So, use these final months of freedom to have lots of fun. Party hardy, hit the beach, bum around Europe, etc."

That argument has intuitive appeal. And, of course, it implies "The *PLS* Approach" is a grind, as though *PLS* says the process of studying (and practicing) law is and *should* be a matter of "all work, and no play."

But here's a question for such people. Professional sports are *very* big business in America. Yet, we speak of *"playing"* baseball or football. Despite the fact that we call it "playing a game," professional athletes with even several years' experience in the big leagues still show up for spring training (baseball) or summer camp (football). So the question is: Why? (Okay, it's in their contract. But *why?*)

These guys love the game. They want to be among the very best at it. They want to be winners. And so, they're willing to start preparing for the real thing months in advance. They know their preparation will pay off.

Further, professional athletes usually have already had several years' experience in the sport before joining the pros. In contrast, prospective law students have had zero first-hand experience of what they're in for. ("Playing lawyer" in mock trials in high school or college does not count.) Yet, the prospective law students who adopt this "Don't worry, be happy" argument do not even want to learn anything about the game before they start playing it for real—with their future on the line. Go figure.

Question: ever hear of the fable, "The Grasshopper & the Ant"?

There is no way to prepare for law school *other* than "The *PLS* Approach." The law schools themselves, for reasons I shall not go into here, deliberately wiped out all the old "pre-law" programs that were similar to the "pre-med" programs that still exist. Even the old pre-law programs were not good preparation in the way the pre-med programs were and are. But at least they were a good-faith attempt. No such good-faith attempt is available these days, period.

True, many law schools have a "recommended reading list" for those about to enter law school. And, in fact, that is another claim made as to why "The *PLS* Approach" is not valid. (See Point 3.)

But think it through: if there's no way to prepare for law school, the law schools themselves should not be posting their own recommended reading lists. And if there *is* a way to effectively prepare for law school, regardless of what that entails, then those who say not to prepare perhaps have an ulterior motive. (After all, it's one thing to say that "The *PLS* Approach" is not the right way, or not the best way, to prepare. It's quite another to say "Don't prepare," period.)

2. "PLS itself says there's a good chance each professor will leave out some stuff. So I should wait until I can see what each prof will cover, before I prepare."

It makes a mockery of the word "preparation" to say you'll start "preparing" for law school only after you're *in* it.

Most of law school is "make-work." But you won't be able to spot the make-work for what it is if you've not *already* prepared. You certainly won't have the courage to skip the make-work when nearly all your classmates are treating it as "the way to go." So what would happen is that you'd decide to do the make-work after all. You'd only look at the primers, etc., in your "spare time." But if you're doing the make-work, it's part of the law school's pedagogy that you *won't have* any spare time. You'll be just another stressed-out lemming, rushing toward the edge of the cliff. A major purpose of "The *PLS* Approach" is to help you spot and skip most of the make-work. That will save time (and help you greatly reduce the stress) once you're in law school.

Some law schools are so determined to make it as difficult as possible for students to do well that they don't even tell the students what *courses* they'll be taking until two or three days before the courses begin. This is especially common among law schools that have either gone from a semester system to a quarter system or have cut year-long courses down to one semester.

Ironically, some *PLS* adversaries have used that as the basis for further criticism of this book. They argue that if students find out that they won't be taking, say, Contracts until the spring, why should they read the Contracts primer the summer before? Surely—they continue— by springtime students will have forgotten everything they'd learned about Contracts from reading its primer before starting law school. So, it's better to wait until the vacation after first semester, and to read the primers for their second-semester courses then, they say.

However, after your first round of final exams, the last thing you're going to want to do during winter vacation is to study two or three more primers from *scratch*. (Besides, you simply wouldn't have enough time.) And especially if you will not be taking Property until the spring, and your course will cover Estates & Future Interests, or real covenants and equitable servitudes, the *very* last thing you'll want to do will be to master *those* topics over the holidays. Also, at some law schools fall exams are given *after* the winter holidays. Students use the winter vacation to cram. But if you thus spend your winter vacation, you certainly would not then be preparing for your spring courses.

Further, the primers themselves don't cover "everything." By definition, primers are not exhaustive. Each covers all the major, basic parts of its subject. So, the odds are good that your professors will cover everything that's in each primer. (Students have reported that some profs have used one or more questions from the "Examples" sections in an Aspen primer, almost word-for-word, as short-answer essay problems on final exams.) Also, a given prof might be inefficient, and not cover particular areas of the subject in class. The prof will have *assigned* material on everything he or she had *intended* to cover. But even though the semester ended before the inefficient prof got to the material at the end of the syllabus, he or she will still hold you responsible for it on the final. Thus, you're expected to magically find the time to do that extra reading between the final class and the exam. If you've completed an overview of the entire course, though, on your own, before the very *first* class, the chances are quite high that you'll be able to take that extra work in stride.

So what about if you read something months before you start law school, and then don't take a course in that subject until your second semester (or quarter)? Even though you might not consciously recall each aspect of the material, you will find that it comes back to you rather quickly. It will take you much less time to get up to speed. (Obviously, during the winter vacation, you should *re*-view the primers you read before the fall semester for courses that you will not be taking until spring.)

As this book has already said, law school is not like your previous schooling. But this is not just in terms of the difference in pedagogy. Another major difference is that law school prepares you for a *professional* career. Unlike, say, grad school in literature, much of what you cover in law school *will* come up again in the real world. Just because you don't need to know something in order to get ready for a particular prof's final in that subject, that does not mean you're "home free" forever.

In fact (as Chapters 23 and 24 will discuss), *five of the six* subjects on the Multistate Bar Exam are *first-year* subjects. (These are Con, Crim, Ks, Prop, and Torts. The sixth of the Big Six, Civ Pro, moves to the state-specific part of your "barzam." On the Multistate, it's replaced by Evidence.) So, even if your Property professor does not cover Estates & Future Interests, it is certain that the MBE will test it (again, see Chapter 23). If you get the first-year subjects under control before even starting law school, you will understand them better in first-year. Thus, you'll not only do better on your law school exams, you'll also find the Multistate "barzam" a whole lot less stressful (and easier to pass).

3. "I trust my law school
—or, at least, my professors—
to tell me everything I need to read and do
in order to do well."

Just for fun, here are some other beliefs of a similar nature:

1. "I trust that my high school teachers and the principal only made rules that were in the students' best interest. And I trust that the teachers and school officials always attempted to be completely thorough and fair when evaluating interpersonal situations and meting out rewards and punishments."

2. "I trust the local police officers' union when they say the crime rate has increased because there aren't enough officers on the force, and when they say there aren't enough officers on the force because patrol officers' pay is too low and their hours are too long and they don't get enough (paid) vacations."

3. "I trust that the appointed officials of government agencies (whether local, state, or federal), and all elected officials (whether local, state, or federal) tell the truth about issues that concern me as a citizen."

4. "I trust that the manufacturer of the shampoo I use is honestly telling me the best way to clean my hair when, on the container's label, it says, 'Lather - Rinse - Repeat,' and that the manufacturer has no desire to get me to use up my shampoo (and thus cause me to need to buy more of their product) twice as fast as necessary."

5. "I trust the auto mechanic who tells me that my car needs a new whatsit and a replacement thingamajig. I trust him when he estimates it'll take $2,800 in parts and labor. I trust him when he says it won't cost any *more* than that. And I trust him when he tells me my car will be ready in two days."

6. "I trust that major auditing firms, especially Arthur Andersen, sincerely try to present an accurate picture of their clients' financial situation, and that auditing firms are not influenced by any desire to make more money by doing their client's bidding and 'fudging' the numbers, ever. And I trust that 'Generally Accepted Accounting Principles' really do yield an accurate statement of any major corporation's financial situation."

Perhaps you still believe that law school professors, and law schools, are "above it all." Maybe you think they're somehow immune from the near-universal proclivity to feather one's own nest, whether with money or prestige, and to "get by" with as little work as possible. If you still trust your law professors and your law school after reading this book, all I can say is, good luck.

Most beginning law students find themselves in total darkness. They're desperate. It's natural that they would turn to their professors (or a law school administrator) for guidance. After all, we've been brought up to revere our teachers, and to look back on our previous educational experiences with indulgent memories, even if a given teacher's methods seemed harsh. Why should law school be any different? And so, when professors or school officials set out a bright light, which seems to dispel the darkness and enlighten their students, the students rejoice and fly toward it.

...But it's a *bug light*. When the grades come out, you'll hear a series of "Sssszzzt!" "Sssszzzt!" That's the sound of most students' hopes being incinerated in a flash of *real* enlightenment.

4. "The PLS Approach is overkill. It's just too much work."

I am giving the benefit of the doubt to those who make this point. They apparently think the work *PLS* advocates before law school will not reduce the amount of work required once you're in law school. Therefore, it's just "more of the same," and thus too much, they say. In the alternative, the argument assumes that without the *PLS* approach, law students will be told what material will be tested on their final exams, and how to prepare. The "extra" work *PLS* calls for can indeed provide something more, but the effort required is not worth it, they say.

Regardless of which alternative, the argument fails, for two reasons.

First, it assumes that the first year of law school involves clearly defined tasks, and students will be told what these tasks are and how to accomplish them. (This latter part, of course, is Point 3, above.) Second, it assumes that it takes a certain amount of time to accomplish these tasks, period.

It's as though law school were a farm...say, the traditional American farm with "40 acres and a mule." Each subject would then be a separate field. (Contracts and Property might each be the equivalent of nine of those 40 acres. Civ Pro and Torts might each be seven acres, and Crim Law and Con Law four acres apiece.) Each field has to be plowed and sowed with seed. The sprouted seeds have to be cared for and the crop eventually harvested (on your final exams).

But if the analogy is valid, what happens is that the law school tells you to find an old-fashioned hand-held plow and then hitch it up...to a mule. You're to follow behind the mule, on foot, up and down each field in those 40 acres, over and over, busting sod. Then you're supposed to walk through every field again, one row at a time, planting the seeds. And this process repeats with the weeding and eventually the harvesting. Even so, if there is insufficient rain (i.e., you don't have enough "natural talent or 'vision'"), your "crops" will fail anyway.

However, with modern equipment, a farmer can plow a large field *and* sow seeds in it within a vastly shorter time. Maintenance (such as weeding) is also much easier than in ages past. So is the harvesting. And, of at least equal importance, modern agriculture uses hybrid seeds that produce dramatically improved yields over those of ages past. It's one thing to go over the same ground more than once. It's quite another to go over it time and time again in the *least* fruitful manner.

Delaney's *Learning Legal Reasoning* and his new primer on Criminal Law, along with the Aspen primers and the ABA's series *The ABCs of the UCC,* are your hybrid seeds. With them, you can get a far greater yield on your final exams than you could get from the materials your professors insist you use exclusively. Wentworth Miller's LEEWS and Delaney's examsmanship book are your modern tractors, combines, and harvesters. You can accomplish what you need to in a fraction of the time it would have taken if you'd stuck to the old-fashioned approach...the approach your law school professors insist you use exclusively. And instead of relying on "rainfall," you set up your own "irrigation system."

In other words, you can have a far greater harvest with far less time and effort, because "The *PLS* Approach," conscientiously applied, enormously increases your productivity.

Your professors and the law schools are not interested in qualifying you for entry into a highly competitive agribusiness industry. They say "your bar review course will cover all that." Instead, they would have you pretend that you are members of 4H or FFA (if even that much). They do not even view crops as being grown for the purpose of feeding people desperately in need of legal sustenance. They view crops, instead, as an opportunity to find one or two specimens to be entered at the County Fair, to win a blue ribbon and be shown off to everyone. As long as they occasionally get that, they're happy. If you're the one who turns in that prize specimen on your finals, fine. If not, too bad for you and your need to put food on the table as a lawyer someday. Too bad also for your future clients.

Given that most people's exposure to farming consists only of looking through produce in the supermarket, here's a different analogy: China's Great Wall was built almost entirely by hand, with rudimentary tools. That was the only way to do it, back then. But if for some reason China decided to create a second Great Wall, today, surely it would use modern methods. Your law professors are expecting you to construct a great edifice...and to do it by primitive means. Yet, as Chapters 2 and 8 showed, and the response to Point 3, above, further argued, neither your law professors nor the law schools themselves will tell you anything worthwhile as to what your specific tasks are and how to accomplish them.

To briefly return to the response to Point 1: in the short run (especially during the summer, when your friends are having a good time), "The *PLS* Approach" does indeed seem to be a lot of unnecessary work. But once you're in law school, you'll see it's *law school itself* that involves a lot of unnecessary work. The law profs want students to spend *x* hours *trying* to learn something that you could have *already* learned, and made *sure* you learned...in a *fraction* of the time, by using the "The *PLS* Approach." So, yes, you do indeed spend a lot of time before law school on work when you could have been playing. But you will get to spend a lot more time on R&R *in* law school—while others are working their tails off or are running around like chickens with their heads cut off. (And remember Aesop's fable, "The Grasshopper and the Ant"?)

Most important of all, because you will have already mastered the basics, *you can spend proportionately far more of your time in law school on the finer points—the finer points that will get you more points on your final exams.* Instead of desperately trying to understand the "baby stuff" the way most of your fellow students are, you'll be looking up relevant law review articles in the subject each of your profs is teaching...articles written by your profs. And you'll be much more alert in class to the "subtext" of what each prof is saying. Thus, you'll have a better feel for their pet interests and theories, their biases and intellectual idiosyncrasies. You'll be *way* ahead of the game...*which is a big part of what this book is about.*

In short, if you're satisfied with the thought of merely being an "also-ran," go ahead—play the game by the law school's rules. But if you want the best possible chance of being a *winner*, it behooves you to try to beat them at their own (sick) game.

5. "Why go over the same thing more than once?"

Here critics attempt to turn *PLS's* own argument around and use it against *PLS*. After all, *PLS* stresses efficiency and productivity, and not "going up and down rows within a field time and time again." Because "The *PLS* Approach" covers what they'll be going over in law school, they see it as a pointless duplication of effort.

While their contention bears a superficial resemblance to Points 1, 2, and 4, above, there is a difference: cutting away the fat is not the same thing as failing to "dress" meat altogether. In the latter case, you miss out on nearly all the potential protein and other nourishment.

You and I haven't met. But if you're one of those who makes the "once is enough" argument, I know you. You're the person who announces smugly, "I've read Plato," or who casually says, "I studied Shakespeare in high school." And you're the person who would always read only the Monarch Notes® or CliffsNotes™, never the original text.* You're the one who thinks that because you spent a total of three hours in class BS-ing about some statements Socrates made, you thereby "know" Plato's "philosophy." Or maybe you saw Mel Gibson's movie version of *Hamlet*, or Kenneth Branagh's version of *Much Ado about Nothing*. So, you think you "know" Shakespearean drama. You're the sort of person who says, "Oh, I've been to the Louvre," as though that means something about your ability to appreciate the art there.

Perhaps this will come as a shock to you, or at least as a disappointment, but...as a general rule, something that's profound usually requires more than one exposure to make the most of it.

---

*   Don't misunderstand me here. I can't remember whether I used Monarch Notes® or CliffsNotes™, but I would not have even *passed* the second semester of 9th-grade English without whichever one of these it was I used. The teacher spent the entire semester on *A Midsummer Night's Dream*. It was way over my head. And her approach killed whatever potential interest I had in the Bard. Years later, though, I had the great good fortune to see that very play performed at Yale Rep. It was one of the high points of my cultural life, and turned me on to Shakespeare ever after. But I'd no choice about slogging my way through *MND* as a junior-high student, and would never have volunteered to study it, at that age—so the "minimalist" approach, via Monarch Notes® or CliffsNotes™ was fair. (Besides, Monarch Notes® and CliffsNotes™ are helpful even to the committed, conscientious student.) In contrast, going to law school is a matter of your own choice; no one *ordered* you to.

Arthur Rubenstein (1887-1982) was one of the greatest pianists of the 20th century. His repertory included the Fifth Sonata of Alexander Scriabin. Rubenstein had given the work its London premiere early in the century, and therefore believed he understood the work intimately. When he was around 70, he heard, for the first time, a Russian pianist who was not yet 45, Sviatoslav Richter. Richter's program included Scriabin's Fifth Sonata. In *My Many Years,* (the second volume of his autobiography), Rubenstein says this of his experience hearing Richter's interpretation of it: "Then came a revelation...and now I heard a brand-new piece, miraculously played."*

Those who say they don't ever want to go over anything more than once will not "get" that anecdote. Nor will they ever gain much insight from reading Plato, Shakespeare, or anything else more intellectually demanding than a novel by John Grisham or Tom Clancy.

For such people, it probably really is a waste of time to delve into the Law enough to begin to see its beauty, its possibilities for creative play of the mind, and so forth. But my response to their argument is not written for those people. Rather, it's for those who hear the "once is enough" argument, do not think it through, and thus uncritically accept it. But some of them are capable of better things in the Law. Some even have the potential to become giants of jurisprudence. So this response is meant as a wake-up call for them.

6. "Other 'How to succeed in law school' books don't say what PLS says, so I ignore PLS."

For those who think that way, here are some questions.

The first is: Do you know the story, "The Emperor's New Clothes"? (Do you *know* it, *all* of it, not just "Have you heard of it?" There's more to it than just its famous "punch line.")

Let's call the other questions "historical hypotheticals."

Say it's 1492. You're an official attached to the royal court of Ferdinand and Isabella of Spain. Some guy named Christopher Columbo, from Genoa, shows up and asks for money to pay for a sea voyage to India by heading *west*. But "everyone knows" the world is flat—and that anyone who sails into the horizon will sail right off the edge of the planet. What's your advice to Their Majesties?

---

* Too bad he didn't say "It caused a tremor in my soul—a 7.3 on the Richter Scale."

Say it's 1799. George Washington left the Presidency two years ago. Now he's come down with a serious throat infection. Medical science of the day says illness is caused by "bad blood." The solution is to start draining it off, by applying leeches to suck it out. This process continues until the patient recovers...or dies. (Back then, no one knew anything about white corpuscles and their role in fighting illness and disease.) You are one of the physicians who's been called in. If some other doctor shows up and starts telling you that draining off blood would be the *worst* possible thing to do, you'd label that doctor a "quack," wouldn't you? (And so you would have been one of those who, with the best of intentions, killed the Father of Our Country.)

Say it's 1925. You're an Army officer. You've been ordered to serve on the panel of judges in a court martial. The defendant is a brigadier general named Billy Mitchell. For years, he's been saying that battleships are obsolete protection for America's shore installations. According to him *air* power is the wave of the future. He insists that air power can sink battleships. Yet, "everyone knows" that airplanes are an important weapon only against civilian populations, in what later will be called The Third World. Even when the Navy puts Mitchell's theory to the test (and loses several old battleships in the process), the results are dismissed as a fluke. The only people who take Mitchell seriously about battleships' vulnerability to air power are some naval officers in Japan...but you don't know about that. Mitchell won't shut up. So, he's on trial for insubordination. Tell me, what is your likely verdict?

The "conventional wisdom" is called the conventional *wisdom* for a reason. But as circumstances change, what started as wisdom can become folly. And sometimes it was folly *all along*.

Those who dismiss *PLS* on the grounds that it is a minority of one commit either or both of two informal logical fallacies: *"argumentum ad verecundiam"* (in this Point of Error 6), and *"argumentum ad populum"* (in the next point of error). I see no point in doing a favor for those who dismiss *PLS*. So, rather than give the meaning of those terms, I shall just say they're defined in the logic books *this* book touts (in Chapter 17).

7. "Law school students, some of whom are in second- or third-year, and some of whom did well in first-year, have told me PLS is all wrong. So I'll take their word and ignore PLS."

There are those who've been in law school only a few weeks, and who thus have yet to take their first exam in law school, yet who present themselves as know-it-alls to would-be law students. This Point of Error 7 does not address that group.

So, what about someone who's finished first-year? The first question to ask is, "Did he or she *really* do well?" It's highly unlikely the student will let you see an official copy of his or her first-year transcript. So, the only way to know for sure is if the school in question allows students to Make Law Review only on grades, and the student who's talking to you is indeed on Law Review. (As discussed in Chapter 18, it's possible at most schools for students to Make Law Review via the "write-on," as well as through grades. So it's possible that a student who's on Law Review got there "through the back door," as it were. Think he or she will disclose that?) Of course, there will be students who will tell you something like "I graded on to Law Review, but decided it was too much work, so I turned it down." Or maybe it's this one: "I finished first-year in the top 11% of the class, but Law Review only takes the top 10%. Even so, I clearly did quite well." Again, maybe they're telling the truth, maybe not. And, of course, if they're at a school where it's impossible to grade on to Law Review, and where the school refuses to tell its students where they rank in the class, then you're out of luck.

You should take a student's claim of first-year excellence with a *block* of salt unless you can obtain clear proof. As you will discover, law school is rife with one-upmanship games. "Résumé-padding" is even more common there than it is in the real world.

For the sake of discussion, though, let's assume that the person who's telling you that *PLS* is wrong is someone who can prove that he or she did well in first-year. But that brings us to the second question: "Did he or she really 'blow off' *PLS*?"

With this, we get into the problem of "the myth of the natural-born legal genius." It just amazes me how many law professors and law review editors say, "Oh yeah, I took LEEWS. And I aced my finals. But LEEWS didn't have anything to do with it. I would have aced my finals anyway." There are others who will not even admit at first that they took LEEWS.

I've received several e-mails from people who say something like this: "I'm in law school at [one of the top three, or five, or ten, or 15] law schools in the country. I used 'The *PLS* Approach' to first-year—got the primers you recommended and studied them before law school, got LEEWS on tape and listened to the tapes and read the manual before law school, read Delaney's books, etc. And sure enough, I aced all my exams and graded on to Law Review. I am now in third-year, and am the Law Review's [whatever] Editor. I just wanted to let you know that I feel indebted to *PLS* and to LEEWS and John Delaney. Without them, I'm sure I wouldn't have made it. But I'm following in the footsteps of others who did well and who want everyone to think they're what you called 'natural-born geniuses of the law.' For that reason, sorry to say, I must insist that you hold all this—including my name—in strictest confidence. But I did want to share my success story with you, and to thank you, Atticus."

That attitude flabbergasts me. There's not much I can do about the situation (although the second addendum to Chapter 16 mentions one possibility).

Everyone's heard of the myth of humble origins, in politics. Few political candidates from wealthy families want it known that they were born into riches. Most pretend either not to have wealth, or else to have pulled themselves up by their own bootstraps. (In the late 19th century, of course, it was fashionable for Presidential aspirants to claim they'd been born in rural poverty, *à la* Lincoln.)

Much the same thing occurs, in *reverse,* with those who do well in law school. They don't attribute their success to hard work alone. In fact, many a hard-studying student claims not to be. Thus, he or she has it covered both ways: (1) if the student does well on finals, he or she appears to be a natural-born genius of the law; (2) if the student does not do well, the student can shrug his or her shoulders and say, (a) "Gee, guess I should have studied harder," or (b) "It's all random, a matter of luck." (I'll address that last possibility shortly.)

For the sake of discussion, though, let's assume that the person who's telling you *PLS* is wrong really is someone who aced first-year without using "The *PLS* Approach." Does that prove anything?

It *might* be the case that this person really *is* a "natural-born genius of the law." I doubt it, though. More likely, it merely illustrates the working of the curve, as discussed in Chapter 9. By definition, 10% of the students will be in the top 10% of the class—even if, were their ability to be measured *objectively,* they would not even be good enough to pass at all. Unfortunately, your mastery of the subject matter, and your ability to think like a lawyer, are really tested in a verifiable manner only once you're practicing law. Your ability that was good enough to get you an "A" from a prof, on the curve, might not be good enough to get you beyond Square One out in the real world. Only time will tell.

Another way of looking at this *does* involve luck—though not in the way the "random success" adherents would have you believe...

Winston Churchill was Britain's Prime Minister during most of WWII. He was educated at Sandhurst, Britain's public military academy. As a young officer (and later as a war correspondent), he was in combat. It is well documented that Churchill deliberately and constantly exposed himself to enemy fire during battles. Yet he never received so much as a flesh wound.

George S. Patton, Jr., was an American general during WWII. In a well-known episode from that war, his jeep was strafed by a German fighter. His driver and aide took cover at the side of the road. (The movie, *Patton,* changed the facts of this incident.) Patton, however, stood up, pulled out one of his famous pearl-handled revolvers, and began firing at the plane even as its bullets ripped up the jeep he was standing in.

Both men obviously survived their encounters and achieved greatness. Does this mean, then, that soldiers who hope to achieve greatness should never take cover, but should instead rashly expose themselves to enemy fire? Well, consider the possibility that there are umpteen men now six-feet-under who could have achieved the same greatness as Churchill or Patton, but who were cut down by enemy fire when they refused to duck—either because they were too proud or because they felt they had Divine Protection. In other words, just because *someone* rises to the top after doing things the wrong way, that does not mean the wrong way is thereby proved to be the right way.

(For those who have difficulty with those examples, try this one, which is a reverse example: Many people say that, in their moment of greatest need, they cried out to their god, and their god came through for them. They then go on to say this proves their god exists and that those who believe in that god and are worthy of that god, and who cry out at a time of great need, will be saved by their god from whatever it was. But you never hear from those who cried out to their god in similar situations and whose cries were *not* heeded. They went down the tubes. Besides, the fact that their cries were not heeded allegedly proves that those people were somehow unworthy of divine assistance.)

The Churchill and Patton examples (and the religious one) illustrate another informal logical fallacy. This one's called *"post hoc, ergo propter hoc"*—or, in English, "false cause."*

But there's another myth at work, besides the one about the natural-born genius of the law. This one says that "Success in law school is a matter of luck, and is entirely random." For obvious reasons, this claim usually comes from those who did *not* do well in law school.

However, if success in law school is entirely a matter of luck, consider the implications of that alleged fact:

1. Whether law school professors are *good* at teaching is *irrelevant.*

2. If the quality of law school teaching is irrelevant, why hold classes? Why not let students read books or learn from CDs on their own, from whatever sources they choose?

3. *Why require a law degree?* The law schools themselves freely admit that students "learn what they need to know to pass the bar exam" from taking a *commercial vendor's* bar "review" course *after graduating from law school.* (This despite the fact that, as mentioned, five of the six MBE subjects are *first-year* subjects.) So, if law school exams are of trivial relevance to getting a law license, why not allow people to take a bar exam regardless of whether or not they've attended law school? Then, probably the only people who would go to law school (and give up three years of their lives—and thus, three years of potential income, and maybe $125,000 out-of-pocket for a law degree) would be those who only wanted to go to a law school whose top graduates can get one of those jobs fresh out of law school that pay $200,000 a year.

Regardless of your response to these implications, here's something that's undeniable: there is such a thing as a "lawyerlike analysis." Chapters 3 and 6 discussed it. Chapter 3 explained why "learning how to think like a lawyer" is the hardest thing, *psychologically,* for law students to do. Those who say success in law school is entirely random, a matter of luck, are tacitly admitting they don't even know what a lawyerlike analysis *is.* Yet, as Chapter 3 said, learning how to "think like a lawyer" is simple. —But it takes a *lot* of effort to get good at it.

---

* The religious example, if I say no more, will upset the devout. So here's the rest of the analysis, which ought to set their minds at ease: the fact that the devout person's claim is based on faulty reasoning does not mean the devout person is *wrong.* It just means that the proof offered for his or her argument is not logical reasoning. There are many things in this world that are true, but which we cannot prove. And to the *really* devout person, this failure of proof is *good.* It means that his or her god will reward those who do sincerely believe in that god despite the fact that they cannot prove, logically or empirically, that this god even exists.

8. "PLS says, 'Don't buy the casebooks.' and thereby forfeits its credibility regarding ANYTHING about law school."

Chapter 16 in this new edition of *PLS* again states the argument as to why you are wasting your money if you purchase casebooks—and that you have a perfect right to waste your money if you wish. Yet, the sheer vehemence of those who dismiss all of *PLS* just because of this casebook matter is most curious. Such people protest too much, methinks.

For the sake of discussion, though, let's assume these critics are correct that there's something aberrant, to put it mildly, about advising future law students not to *buy* any casebooks in their first year of law school. But even if that's so, how does that destroy the credibility of all of *PLS*?

H.G. Wells was a great 20th-century writer. Yet, he hated the Catholic Church. (He once said he'd never be able to drive a car in France, because if he did he'd be tempted to run over a priest.) I don't know if his works are tinged with animosity toward Catholicism. But even if they are, does that mean he forfeited his credibility as a writer?

Speaking of the Catholic Church—Everyone knows about how Galileo was hauled before the Roman Inquisition, and forced to recant his announcements that his discoveries (using the newly-invented tele-scope) confirmed the Copernican view of the universe—which view contradicted the Church's theology. He later reversed himself, and again championed Copernicus...for which he was again hauled before the Roman Inquisition. The first time, in 1616, the Pope was Paul V. The second time, in 1633, it was Urban VIII. But Europe was then wracked by the Thirty Years' War. (The new Bourbon dynasty in France was challenging the old Hapsburg dynasty of Austria for continental domi-nance.) And all the while, the Ottoman Turks were taking advantage of the strife. They'd conquered the Balkans—and wanted the rest of Europe. The Papacy alone was able to put things into proper perspective... to no avail. And here was Galileo, naively announcing discoveries that threatened one of the intellectual pillars of Christendom from within (and thus, Christian morale) at the same time the Turks were threatening Christendom militarily from without. Are Paul V and Urban VIII discredited?

One more: Sir Richard Woolley was Britain's "Astronomer Royal" from 1956 to 1971. This meant he was the most prominent, prestigious astronomer in the whole British Empire. Yet, in the very year he became Astronomer Royal, he declared, "All this writing about space travel is utter bilge. To go to the *Moon* and back would cost as much as a major war." A year later, the Russians launched *Sputnik*. And two years before

Sir Richard's tenure as Astronomer Royal ended, an American walked on the Moon and returned safely to Planet Earth. But does the fact that Woolley was so wooly-minded about the practicality of exploring space mean that all his work as an astronomer was automatically discredited?

There are hundreds of additional examples possible here, but you get the idea.

Here's a true story: in the late 1920s, a visitor was observing military exercises involving units of the British Army. He happened to be present as an artillery battery fired some rounds. As the gun crews went about their business, there was another soldier standing at attention within a few feet of *each* fieldpiece. The observer asked why the extra men were there. After all, they were doing *nothing*. No one could explain it. They just said "That's the way it has to be." Curious, the visitor began searching through old artillery manuals. He discovered that the presence of the additional man standing at attention by each gun dated from the days before the internal combustion engine. The extra man was there to *hold the reins of the horses that had hauled that gun to the site*. His task was to keep the horses from fleeing when the artillery began firing. Never mind that horses no longer hauled fieldpieces. The superfluous soldiers had been kept on—a major waste of manpower—because no one had ever thought to re-evaluate the need for them in light of changed circumstances.

I hope you "get my drift."

What *I* don't get is why some people are so eager to clutch at straws—*any* straw—to discredit *PLS*. (However, the end of this chapter presents my hunch.) It's especially disappointing that these critics pounced on something that was intended to help students *save money* without thereby sacrificing anything that could help them do well in law school.

9. "I don't trust the word of anyone who hides behind a pen name."

The response to Point 6, above, mentioned a couple of informal fallacies in logic: *argumentum ad verecundiam,* and *argumentum ad populum*. The argument of point 9 relies on another informal fallacy. This one's known as *"argumentum ad hominem."* It's a form of personal attack. It's intended to dispose of an unwelcome message by disposing of the messenger. (Here's another example, but in reverse. It's from comedian W.C. Fields: "Anyone who hates dogs and children can't be *all* bad.") This one can be disposed of quickly.

To pick just four examples from American history—from the 18th, 19th, and 20th centuries:

People who are thinking about going to law school ought to at least have heard of *The Federalist Papers.* They're a series of pamphlets and articles published in 1787, after the Constitutional Convention had finished its work. Their purpose was to persuade people to support the effort to ratify the new Constitution. It had three authors: John Jay, Alexander Hamilton, and James Madison. Not one of them signed his real name to any of the publications. Instead, even though they wrote their various contributions separately, each always identified himself as "Publius." Jay became the first Chief Justice of the Supreme Court; Hamilton, the first Secretary of the Treasury; and Madison, the fourth President. (By the way, the leading anti-federalists also published under a collective assumed name, "Cato.")

When Abraham Lincoln was still a small-time politician in Springfield, Illinois, he wrote numerous articles for local newspapers that were critical of political opponents or policies. Quite often, these articles were either anonymous or under various pen names.

During the Cold War, America's policy toward the Soviet Union was called "containment." It was first publicly proposed in a 1947 article, "The Sources of Soviet Conduct," in *Foreign Affairs.* Its author was George F. Kennan, who'd been merely the *chargé d'affaires* at the U.S. embassy in Moscow. It was published under the *nom de plume* "X".

It would be one thing if *PLS* were a vehicle for a personal attack on one or more individuals based on alleged first-hand experience with them. (For example, claiming to have been a participant in an alleged orgy at the Clinton White house, or to have been a dealer from whom George W. allegedly bought crack cocaine.) In such a case, the use of a pseudonym would indeed be suspect, to put it mildly. But as the above examples show, expository writing is a different matter altogether.

10. "PLS is motivated by bitterness, and is therefore unworthy of serious consideration."

Another *argumentum ad hominem.* For the sake of discussion, though, let's say that *PLS* is indeed motivated by emotion—specifically, bitterness. So what?

In 1979, the five-year-old daughter of a woman named Cindi Lamb became a quadriplegic for life when the car she was riding in was struck in Maryland by another vehicle. The other driver, who was at fault, was intoxicated. He had a record of arrests for drunk driving. Lamb immediately launched a campaign to toughen Maryland's punishment for DWI (or DUI, if you prefer). In 1980, the 13-year-old daughter of a woman named Candy Lightner was killed in a car crash in California. The other driver, who was at fault, was intoxicated. He had a history of DWI arrests. Every time, he'd gotten off with just a "slap on the wrist"—including one just 48 hours before he killed Candy Lightner's child. Immediately, Lightner and other women launched a campaign to toughen California's punishment for DWI. That same year, Lamb and Lightner joined with others to found Mothers Against Drunk Drivers (MADD). It's now a big, influential organization, as I'm sure you know. Does its founders' motivation of bitterness mean they (and MADD) are unworthy of serious consideration?

Nearly all the feminists of the 20th century, and the suffragettes of the 19th and early 20th centuries, were motivated by deep bitterness at being second-class citizens in America solely because of their gender. Their bitterness helped them maintain the will to endure their decades-long struggles.

And do you think those involved in the struggle for civil rights for racial minorities—and before that, those involved in the struggle to end slavery—were unworthy of serious consideration because they were largely motivated by a sense of outrage?

Now let's go back to the very birth of the nation. The Founding Fathers were largely motivated by bitterness. They'd been denied the rights of Englishmen, especially in regard to being taxed without having any say-so in the matter. Firebrands such as Sam Adams, Patrick Henry, and—above all—Thomas Paine certainly made easy targets for an *ad hominem* attack based on their emotions. Those who dismiss *PLS* as motivated by "bitterness" would almost certainly have been firmly on the side of the Tories in the years before and after 1776.

It has become obvious that more and more *PLS* readers are not Americans. So here are some examples, from foreign histories:

Mohandas Gandhi, from India, had been educated in London to be a lawyer. He had then gone to South Africa, where he became a success. In 1893, when he was 23 years old, he bought a first-class train ticket. But upon taking his seat in a first-class compartment, he was told he would have to move to a lower-class car; first-class was for whites only. When he refused, he and his baggage were put off the train. The immense bitterness Gandhi felt at that instant caused him to begin his civil rights movement in South Africa—and later, to return to his native India to continue the struggle for equality by seeking India's independence from Britain. What, pray tell, was wrong about his being motivated, at least initially, by bitterness?

In March, 1917, the Mensheviks overthrew the Tsar of Russia. They were largely motivated by bitterness. Tsar Nicholas II—truly one of history's greatest incompetents—had kept Russia in WWI against the Germans. Yet, there was not enough food to feed even the people at home, let alone the army. Unfortunately, the new Menshevik government—a democracy—was overthrown barely six months later by a communist coup (the Bolsheviks). The communists were not motivated by bitterness, but by a pure lust for absolute power. Is that better than bitter?

You've probably heard the expression "Not for all the tea in China." Until the late 19th century, China was almost the only source of the world's tea. When the English took up tea in a huge way, they imported it from China. And they bought so much that the balance of payments in China's favor threatened to deplete Britain's treasury of its reserves (of silver, as in "the pound sterling"). The British wanted to sell goods to China to cover their previous bilateral deficit and to establish an on-going equality in the value of goods traded. But the Chinese weren't interested in buying much. So the British surreptitiously introduced opium into China. When the Chinese imperial government tried to keep the dope out, Britain formally declared war—not once, but twice, in the mid-1800s. (That's how China lost Hong Kong for 155 years.) Even their official name was The Opium Wars. This was about the same time the white nations forced China to adopt a so-called "open door" policy. But on the doors to the exclusive clubs for white foreigners in Shanghai (China's commercial capital), the signs read, "No dogs or Chinese allowed." (Chinese *servants* in the clubs were an exception, of course.) To this day, the Chinese government and people are quite bitter concerning roughly a century of being treated as nothing but "coolies" despite the fact that, off and on for thousands of years, China's civilization had been the highest in the world. Those who dislike bitterness are free to try to explain to the Chinese why the Chinese, because of their lingering resentment, should now have zero credibility regarding any country's foreign policy toward China.

The late Simon Wiesenthal was world-renowned for tracking down top Nazis who'd gone into hiding after WWII. Perhaps he was at least partly motivated by bitterness at what they'd done to the Jews of Europe. And when Adolf Eichmann was found, captured, and tried for his war crimes and crimes against humanity, was the whole effort somehow disqualified, morally, because the Jews who eventually executed him in Israel were largely motivated by bitterness? You tell me, pal.

There's something about human nature when it comes to making a serious commitment to a long-term struggle that might well prove hopeless. Most people do a cost-benefit analysis…and decide it isn't worth it. This is especially true when the people in question have nothing to gain from the cause's success. (For example, even if you completely agree with everything in this book, what's the likelihood you'd be motivated to try to change the pedagogical malpractice at your law school, even after—*especially* after—you've graduated?) In terms of *rationality,* it usually makes absolutely no sense at all to buck the system. (The Declaration of Independence, for example, expressly acknowledges this: "[A]ll experience hath shown that Mankind are more disposed to suffer, while evils are sufferable, than to right themselves by abolishing the forms to which they are accustomed.")

It generally takes an *irrational* impetus to get someone to say, "Damn the torpedoes! Full steam ahead!" and to then stay the course no matter what. Emotions are sometimes irrational.

Perhaps you believe only "positive" emotional motivations are acceptable. But many a would-be reformer who claims to be motivated by, for example, love, actually has an ulterior purpose. Perhaps you think it's possible to determine a person's "true" motives. But if you still insist that an emotional impetus be "positive," you've just condemned the entire Reformation. (Recall that it was set off by Martin Luther's *anger,* which caused him to nail his famous 95 Theses to the door of the Catholic church at Wittenberg in 1517.) So, if you're Christian, I hope you're not a Protestant (Note: "Protestant," as in "protest")—and especially not a Lutheran.

Is *Planet Law School* motivated by bitterness? *You're damned right it is.* If and when you ever *practice* law, and see what happens to the vast majority of clients, whose lawyers are as certifiably incompetent as they are greedy, then you may sit in judgment on my bitterness. But until then, please knock off the "holier than thou" routine, because you are either an ignoramus or a pious fraud.

11. *"Atticus Falcon admits he did NOT do well in law school, so he has no right to set himself up as an authority on law school."*

Good point—even though it's yet another *argumentum ad hominem.* However, for the sake of discussion...

The best book on military strategy in the history of the Western world is *On War.* It's by Carl von Clausewitz, and was published in 1832. Yet, Clausewitz never was a military commander. And as a junior officer, he'd been taken prisoner by the French in 1806 and was held for three years. He later became a staff officer and a military instructor. Although he was at the Battle of Waterloo, he was not there as a commander of troops.

So, Clausewitz was not qualified to write *On War.* Napoleon was. But Napoleon didn't. Clausewitz did. And his work has withstood the test of time. Although WWII made many of his theories obsolete, enough are still valid that his book is studied by military people around the world, even today.

The Art of Courtly Love was written by a man named Andreas Capellanus, around 1180. It's widely (and wrongly) regarded as the origin of Western notions of romantic love. However, "Andreas Capellanus" is Latinate for "Andrew the Chaplain." You see, the author of *The Art of Courtly Love* was a Roman Catholic priest—i.e., a celibate. While, granted, a lot of priests (and monks) broke their vows regarding sex (in *those* days, anyway), nothing's known about A.C. to indicate he was among the hypocrites. Therefore, objectively speaking, he was not qualified to write *The Art of Courtly Love.* But he did. And his work has withstood the test of time. It became one of the most influential books in the Western world for the next several centuries, at least among people of "refined tastes."

Now here's the most audacious analogy of all: after Jesus of Nazareth was executed, 11 of his Disciples were still alive and at large. (Judas Iscariot had killed himself, as you'll recall.) Christ's own brother, James, was still alive and well. So was Peter, whom Jesus had told would be "the rock on which I shall build my church."

So why is it that virtually the entire Christian scripture (nearly everything after the Book of Acts) consists of letters written by some guy named Saul, from *Syria*—a guy who'd never even *seen* Jesus before the entombment?

Well, Saul (saying his name was now Paul) gives what he (and Christianity) regard as valid justification. Perhaps that's because his readers realized that the message was more important than the messenger...and thus did not resort to ad hominem attacks against him.*

Before law school, I'd qualified for membership in MENSA, the national organization for people who are supposedly in the top two percent (or something like that) of the population in terms of intelligence. In college, I'd taken American Political Theory, Western Political Theory, Constitutional Law, Accounting, and a year of Business Law (that last one taught by an adjunct prof—a corporate general counsel)...and aced them all. Throughout high school and college, several attorneys had told me that I "think like a lawyer." Because I could not afford the (then-) $600 cost of an LSAT prep course, I took the LSAT "cold"...and still hit the 94th percentile.

Yet, when I went to law school, my supposed high intelligence and pre-law courses and natural "gift for the law" were of little avail. In fact, I ran into a brick wall, and suffered massive injuries. (*Head* injuries, as you can tell.)

Curious, I decided to investigate what had gone wrong, and why. My curiosity was heightened by my awareness that there were several students in my classes who, objectively speaking, were not all that bright, yet who did quite well in one course or another. That just did not make sense to me. Also, I'd learned in third-year that *every* editor on my school's Law Review had taken LEEWS. It was just too much of a coincidence to be a coincidence. From there, it was fairly easy to do a post-mortem and figure out the cause of my own demise (which was the same cause as that of hundreds of thousands of others).

The result of my experience and analysis (and five years of input from more than two thousand people) is the book you now hold in your hands. Yes, I screwed up—BIG TIME—in law school. It's your right to assume, therefore, that what this book has to say is worthless. Were I to do it over again, I would certainly follow "The *PLS* Approach." But, you only get to go around once, whether it's law school, or life itself. And the best I can do at this point (other than trying to be a good lawyer, in both senses of the word "good"), is to try to help others, who want to become good lawyers, to avoid the horrible mistakes I made in law school.

* * *

* And now some people will be upset because this supposedly likens *PLS* to the New Testament. Oy vey!

On Writing: A Memoir of the Craft, by Stephen King, talks about those who insist they want to become writers, but who really just don't want to put in the work. On page 143, he makes this point:

> I'm not asking you to come reverentially or unquestioningly, I'm not asking you to be politically correct or cast aside your sense of humor (please God you have one). This isn't a popularity contest, it's not the moral Olympics, and it's not church. But it's *writing,* damn it, not washing the car or putting on eyeliner. If you can take it seriously, we can do business. If you can't or won't, it's time for you to close the book and do something else.   [Emphasis in the original.]

Amen. And what he said about wannabe writers is true *a fortiori* for wannabe lawyers. After all, if you say you want to be a writer, yet "play a game with yourself" and don't do what you need to in order to become a competent writer, only two bad things can happen: either you won't ever get published, or you'll get published and your book will not sell. But even those who are not really serious about becoming lawyers can still get a law license, and can have paying clients. And God help those clients. In other words, unlike lousy writers, if you're a lousy attorney, you hurt others far worse than you hurt yourself.

Then again, maybe that does not bother you in the slightest.

I believe that all 11 "Points of Error" discussed above are motivated primarily by laziness.*

At first, admittedly, that claim seems absurd. After all, law students typically spend long hours studying. So how could they be accused of laziness?

—Because the people who make the arguments discussed above are *intellectually* lazy. They would rather have the emotional comfort of being part of the herd than do any serious thinking on their own. With their intellectual laziness, they're already destined to be mediocre lawyers (perhaps judges), no matter how well they happen to do in law school.

---

* And yes, this is an *argumentum ad hominem.*

Point 8, above, mentioned that those who criticize *PLS* seem to be clutching at straws in their efforts to dismiss it. It's as though their attitude is "Don't try to confuse me with the facts! My mind's made up!"

On Writing is appropriate here, too. When discussing the laziness of some who claim they want to become writers, King says (page 107): "No one can be as intellectually slothful as a really smart person; give smart people half a chance and they will ship their oars and drift..." (Ellipsis in the original.)

Usually, law students and would-be law students are smart people. The "points of error" discussed above are all good examples of how these people can be ingenious at putting their "smarts" to work in behalf of their intellectual indolence.

As an attorney, I'm always game for a good argument, as sport. The purpose of the adversary system—whether as competition in business, or in "the marketplace of ideas," or in a courtroom—is to keep everyone involved on their toes. But it helps to have a worthy opponent, who at least knows whereof he or she speaks, to make the contest fun.

One of the things that is particularly galling about the *PLS* critics is that they present little or no evidence to back up their claims. In the language of the law, their statements tend to be merely "conclusory." Even if they are in law school, and their own experience has been different from that described in *PLS*, they generalize from their own experience. I doubt that any of them have read any books about legal education or the legal profession. And I am certain they've not been in touch with literally thousands of other law students.

I attend at least three conferences a year on legal education. At these, I hear presentations and then discuss legal education and the legal profession with current law school faculty and administrators. And I'm regularly in touch, via e-mail, with some of these people. I read several law review articles and books each month, just on legal education.* So, while I cannot claim exhaustive knowledge of the subject, I am definitely not "shooting from hip," as I believe these critics are.

—Then again, as one wag said, "He too serves a purpose who only stands and *jeers.*"

> *If I tell the truth, they rush to beat me,*
> *If I lie, they trust me.*
> Kabir
> (15th century Sufi poet and philosopher in India)

---

* These conferences and materials cost me over $4,000 a year, out-of-pocket.

Here's an e-mail I received in late January, 2003, from a first-year student who'd not yet received his grades from the fall semester:

Atticus—

I still believe that it's worth it to train with "The PLS Approach."

Even if my grades are not higher than those of other students who came in "blind," still, I will have gotten the same grades as everyone else with only maybe 30% as much effort as theirs. I didn't kill myself during all that time.

Besides, I probably have a better understanding of Black Letter Law.

If, on the other hand, I make the law review, then the PLS approach benefit is even more obvious.

Also, I know for sure that in case I did poorly, I would have done even worse had I followed the regular path.

And to top it off, people who did poorly with the PLS approach probably screw it up somewhere along the way. Some people simply [are] not mature [as evidenced by] their wondering whether it would have been better for them simply to start LS "blind."

Knowledge can't harm here, no way. It's childish to think otherwise.

So, whatever my grades are, I won't complain.

Chapter 15 - Winners & Losers, Whiners & Doers

Excerpts from a "thread" on a message board...

Posting from "anon 25"—
I have the time before the fall, and was wondering if there is anything you would recommend doing beforehand.

Posting from "DaBears"—
Relax! Don't worry about preparing for law school. Those who try to learn their classes before law school starts sometimes miss out on the learning process in class because they're too obsessed with learning and memorizing all the rules. Also, people who start early sometimes burn out, or so I'm told.

Posting from "Toboggan"—
Besides, it's not like they don't teach law in law school.

Posting from "Army jag"—
As a 2L, I agree. You will have PLENTY of law soon enough. I read a few books before because I was excited about law school (One L and A Civil Action)...Relax, have fun. You've got the next 3-4 years of law study ahead of you. They teach you what you need to know.

Posting from "KimChee"—
Get in shape, stabilize your life, if you've been meaning to stop smoking, do so...and just generally get yourself physically and emotionally ready. If you need to get mentally ready, read some law thrillers, Grisham or Sherlock Holmes or something. Otherwise, just chill.

Posting from "A Fortiori"—
I agree with the general theme of those who have already posted. Don't waste your time learning the law; you'll have plenty of time to do that come fall.

Posting from "Menexenus"—
Planet Law School *was a complete waste of time, full of falsehoods and stupid advice...*

* * *

Now here's a series of items from a student at Boalt Hall (one of the top law schools in the country). Her statements appeared on a members-only message board. She always posted under her full name, which I have deleted. My comments (not posted to the board) follow.

Her initial posting was on August 12, 2000, before the fall semester began. Referring to the various books for those starting law school, she said, in part:

> *I found contradictions among the many books and in some cases an author will write in a very authoritative way something that can only be their opinion because another author will state the opposite point just as adamantly.*

She gave no examples of different authors saying opposite things. However, it's rather odd that someone about to enter law school apparently had a problem with the fact that various authors allegedly disagree on things. Further, most authors do just give "their opinion," rather than providing a survey of the opinions of others. And, of course, if all books for prospective law students were saying the same thing, they wouldn't all be on the market, would they?

Yet, ironically, all the other books *I've* seen for prospective law students do say esentially the same things. These are what I call the "Law School Lite" books. And they're what caused me to write *this* book. Regardless, this student said she'd decided to "do her own thing"—without saying what it would be—once law school started.

As she explained in that same posting:

> *If I had not been in school last year or had been in a less demanding semester, I would probably be more serious about prepping but I know that I have needed the R&R.*

In other words, the last semester of her previous schooling had been so demanding that she just had to take off the *entire summer* before law school to recuperate. (God help her if she ever becomes a lawyer in a big-firm "law factory," and is expected to work 60-80 hours a week for her first three or four years straight.)

The other excuse she gave for not preparing was:

> *I just have to believe that my school has this covered and knows what they are doing by giving us a less-demanding orientation.*

(Boalt, as with all law schools, does not tell students what they need to know before classes begin. Hence the "less-demanding orientation.")

Then on August 25, 2000, came this:

Right now, I feel totally scattered, confused and fairly DUMB. None of my friends can believe I'm having a nervous breakdown after only 3 days of classes (my classmates understand completely though).

This is typical. It is also what the law schools *intend.*

The August 25, 2000 posting included these passages:

Office hours with a professor? I have NO idea what to even ask a professor at this point. What do I say other than "I have no idea what is going on three quarters of the time."...Whenever a professor asks a student a question in class, I think "I'm glad he didn't ask me that. I have NO idea."...They warned us the very first day that in the next few weeks we will question (big time) our decision to go to law school and their decision to let us in. The admissions dean warned us we will feel like NOW the world will know how stupid we really are and they will realize they made a BIG mistake by letting us in. I feel so completely inept. Does this get any better? I am wondering if I will remember all of this for my exams or even from class to class. Tired and confused. [Ellipses in the original.]

As you see, the school *planned* for *all* its students feel this way.

A month later (September 27, 2000), she posted this:

I'm a 1L...and had lunch with my..."mentor" and she said a lot of stuff a la PLS about not sweating the small stuff but prepping for exams (outlining early and often). However, I'm not at that stage yet...I feel like I do all the reading and prepping and I go to class and become totally lost almost immediately. Everything is Sanskrit. As I read through my casebooks, I try to really work through the cases and figure out what in the world they have to do with black letter law of the class (or vice versa) and I feel that I would like to relax from that position *if I could* but right now I feel too paranoid to do so. I hope this gets better...either this feeling of being perpetually lost...or this feeling that I must digest every single word..............somehow I want to be vested in all this AND understand and I want it NOW!!!! Argghhh. It's so frustrating!! [Long ellipsis in the original.]

Recall that, in her initial posting, she'd said she'd looked at books, apparently including *PLS*, for prospective law students. Now here was her student mentor giving her advice similar to that in *PLS*...and the student "blew it off," just as she'd blown it off while awaiting the start of law school. —And yet, she continues to "vent" about how things aren't going well for her.

Then comes her posting of December 16, 2000:

I'm in the middle of finals...I think I posted the first month of school that I never felt so dumb. Didn't think I would ever get it. Had no idea what was going on. Well, I caught on...

—Or so she thought.

February 9, 2001:

I did everything "right" last semester and wasn't thrilled with my grades...

No, she did everything *wrong* her first semester. So her disappointing grades are no surprise. But here's the full passage, including the rest of that sentence:

I give myself more free time this year [i.e., second semester] because I definitely burnt out last year long before finals. I'm trying to see the big picture and not get lost in the details as I did last semester. I did everything right last semester and wasn't thrilled with my grades so I am trying to focus on things that will help with exams (the big picture, black letter law, exam writing, analysis) and not get bogged down in the day to day experience of briefing cases.

Well, she got it half-right as to what she needed to do. She certainly needed to stop getting bogged down "in the day to day experience of briefing cases." No wonder she burned out. (This is not to say she should not have been briefing cases at all. But she gave *top* priority to briefing, when it should have been at the *bottom*.) Had she "prepped," she could have paced herself in law school, instead of burning out, because she would have avoided most of the crushing make-work of first-year. Notice that she says nothing about having taken LEEWS or making use of Delaney's examsmanship book.

She continues:

I used to be overly prepared...I knew so much that sometimes I couldn't tell what the prof was asking (all kinds of info swimming into my head). [Ellipsis in the original.]

Let's see now—She knew *so* much that she *couldn't tell what the prof was asking?* In other words, she's suggesting that her prof "dumbed things down" by simplifying them. *She,* the "overly prepared" student, didn't have enough to go on from the prof to able to figure out just what over-simplification the prof had in mind. The woman flattered herself rather than face up to her shortcomings as a student. She was not "overly" prepared. In fact, she was not prepared at all, because she had spent her entire first semester "preparing" the wrong way. As this book has already said, "It is not enough to work hard. You have to work *smart.*" To put it charitably, she did not "work smart." She paid the price.

Her student mentor had tried to clue her in ("a la PLS") during that lunch the two of them had. But as the student had said, she was "not ready," at that time, to take her mentor's advice. Apparently, despite her poor first-semester grades, she *still* was not ready...

Now I tend to skim things, pick out the issue, note the holding and why and figure out how the facts apply to the law and vice versa and let the nitty gritty go. If it works, great. If not, we'll try a third approach in the fall.

In other words, she was *still* relying on case briefing. No LEEWS, no primers, no Delaney, no nothing other than the casebook. (She does not even mention commercial outlines, let alone doing her own personal outlines.)

At that point, I stopped monitoring the board she was posting to. But I think it a safe bet that her new approach was also destined for failure.

Now you see why judges, major law firms, and government agencies that hire graduating law students prefer to interview only those with top grades. At least then they (probably) don't have to worry that their prospective hires are "flakes," such as the student who was quoted above.

(And now you also see how it is that most profs have a default attitude of a secret contempt for their students.)

That same message board had another member who posted frequently. She did not discuss study methods or *PLS.* Yet, her posting of January 9, 2001 is as sad as it is instructive:

> *I got all my grades today...[W]ith the exception of legal writing, where I got an A—and that's only worth one credit—I got mostly B's and C's (and I won't even talk about Civ Pro where I'm at least happy to report that I passed...) The thing that really gets me is that I got the C's in the classes I studied for the most!*
>
> *So, my question is, to anyone who got mostly B's and A's— How did you do it? I know, it's important to study and I did every night but I had a hard time just keeping up with the amount of reading to have any time to digest it (and just to figure out what's going on). So how?...*
>
> *I did mostly everything MY PROFESSORS said to do and that DIDN'T get the grades I wanted. IS IT JUST A MATTER OF SMARTS? If not, how should I study? (IS PLS RIGHT?)*   [Capitalization added.]

Yes, *PLS* **is** right. There are none so blind as those who will not see. The two people quoted above simply shut their eyes to what's in *PLS.* The first student trusted her law school to tell her how to adequately orient herself. The second trusted her professors to tell her what to do. And so, both were left wondering, in the words of the second student, "Is it just a matter of smarts?" Well, that's what the professors (and the successful students) want you to think. But given that the content of the first year of law school is at the level of "baby stuff," it's likely that *every* student in virtually *all* law schools could score in the 90th percentile or higher on their finals. (This is an *objective* score, not on the curve.) After all, law students are *smart.* But to get students to the point where the entire class would know the material well, the profs would have to drop their hide-the-ball approach...and do a *lot* more work. That won't happen.

More important, if they laid it all out clearly for the students, the way the primers, Delaney's books, and LEEWS do, students would realize that it *is* all just "baby stuff" in first year...and they would quickly become too sophisticated for their professors. They would demand a *genuine* legal *education*—something that simultaneously prepared them to assume professional responsibilities *and* had intellectual merit, instead of something *high school* students could easily master...if it were taught in a straightforward manner.

* * *

The following items are e-mails sent to me privately, or comments sent in when I had a column on an internet website in 2001.

Atticus—

I have noticed something that is especially strange, at least to me.

In my Crim Law class, our teacher lectures quite a bit, interspersed with asking us for voluntary input. Our casebook has a lot of readings between the cases, with scholarly, historical, and philosophical writings of relevance. He told the class that he feels that these writings are more important than the cases. In class, we simply use the cases to extract the relevant rules of law.

We don't spend a lot of time on the cases per se. We simply talk about what the case "turns" on, what the reasoning is, why it creates problems, etc. Then we continue on to the readings, discussing the same issue the case brings up, but with a variety of authors' perspectives.

While I find the professor to be very dry in his method, I think that it is very clear where we are going, and what he thinks is important.

However, many, many students in my class have talked about how they think he doesn't know what he's doing, because he "doesn't teach the class like a REAL law school class." They are upset that we don't spend more time on the cases, whereas I feel that we just skip the irrelevant stuff that the other professors fill up the day with. I just can't understand why they would rather use the "real law school class" method, where most of the same students are CONFUSED, never extracting the most important elements from a case.

[AF—My response...]

I'm with you.

People who deal with horses a lot will supposedly tell you that if a horse is in a barn, and the barn catches fire, it is *very* difficult to lead the horse to safety. It wants to stay in the barn...so much so that it constantly attempts to turn back, and will even try to re-enter the barn when it first gets out.

This prof is teaching a course that has *genuine* intellectual content, versus the BS-ing in the name of "policy" that goes on in most courses that eschew Black Letter Law...let alone what goes on in most courses that eschew policy in favor of a straight Case Method. Yet, he is also starting with the basics—as he should. (If students can't even read and write, they'll never be able to appreciate Shakespeare.)

I hope he has tenure, though. No doubt "the powers that be" at your law school are annoyed by his forthright and intellectually *worthwhile* approach.

But your fellow students have been successfully conditioned by the traumatic experiences of the first few weeks of law school, in their other courses. (Many people in countries that were formerly said to be "behind the Iron Curtain" vote for the communist ticket, because they prefer the predictable somnolent mediocrity of communism to the excitement of capitalism and freedom.)

Atticus—

I read PLS last March and started up right away on the primers, LEEWS, and some other materials. I have been very surprised at how accurate your predictions of law school were. I have actually had profs tell the class they don't have time to teach us black letter law, we are graduate students and should be able to figure that [out] on our own. So these profs then spend all class going into policy (but all their exams on file have only black letter law questions). A lot of my classmates are already lost in some classes (Contracts & Con Law seem to cause the most problems) and if not for my preparation I don't know if I would be having it so easy. Also, from legal writing: "There are twelve of you and only one A." There is a forced downward curve of 2.7 to 3.0 in all classes. I think it's going to make some students become very competitive. I've already heard stories that past exams disappear out of the library come November.

[AF—It won't make them competitive, in the sense of becoming competition, because they do not have a chance of being "contenders." But as you noted, it will likely make them "play dirty" with their fellow students. (I have a file of reports of "dirty tricks"—things cutthroat students have done to hurt other students' chances of doing well.)]

* * *

Here are some particularly disturbing items...

During 2001 (and perhaps even now, under another name), a person using the identification "Bonehead" regularly posted to message boards, and was critical of prepping for law school. For example, on May 18, 2001, he posted this to the Princeton Review board:

Take it easy. There is no way to prepare for law school. It is like nothing you have ever done before. Unless you are taking a class by Glannon, don't waste your time on his primer.

Later that month, I made some comments of my own (on the column I had on the 'net at the time) about those who denigrate prepping, and I mentioned "Bonehead's" posting. Shortly thereafter, this e-mail came in directly to me:

Atticus—

I frequently belittle the importance of your book on the Review website because I am kind of a bastard. You have to know that we currently have very different goals. I want to have as little competition in law school as possible, and you want to help people make the most of their legal education and become good lawyers. Yours is a laudable goal, but until you can assure me that no one in my Top Ten school (with a reputation for cutthroat competition) is reading your book, I am going to publicly disavow all knowledge of its utility.

Bonehead

Did this come from the *real* "Bonehead"? I have no way of knowing. (Then again, those who are severely critical of *PLS* will say that I have made all this up anyway.) But as I noted in a subsequent column, Bonehead is not just "kind of a bastard," but a bastard, period. It would be bad enough if he made comments only to fellow first-year students at his own school. Yet, supposedly because he doesn't want to take *any* chances, he was reaching out to a *national* audience. His self-defense that maybe someone who reads the Princeton Review board might end up as one of *his* classmates, is ridiculous. Like Iago in Shakespeare's *Othello,* the guy just likes to manipulate innocent people into destroying their future.

On January 19, 2002, someone who used the identification "blboy" posted the following item to the Princeton Review board, in response to a question as to whether students should prepare for law school:

I'm a 2L—here's the truth—they teach you everything you need to know from scratch. Read a few books if you are excited about starting law school, but preparing before you get there doesn't work. By the way, a few months into semester one, you will have had your fill of dense case books, so relax for now, work hard when it actually counts.

To be blunt, "blboy," like "Bonehead," is a liar.

More disturbing is that, on June 24, 2002, "blboy" was back on the Princeton Review board in response to a question similar to that of five months earlier:

> *I'm a 31 do nothing, relax, they teach you need to know from scratch.**

The consistency between claiming to be a second-year student in January and claiming to be a third-year student in June strongly suggests that "blboy" *is* a law student who indeed was a second- and third-year student, respectively, at the time of those postings.

However, "blboy" knows better...and is again lying. Why, I do not know.

Most law students who've finished second-year go to work as "summer associates" at law firms before returning to law school for third year. June 24, 2002 was a Monday. It was not a holiday. The posting came at 4:20 p.m. EST. Yet, "blboy" was reading the Princeton Review board during normal business hours, and then posted his message at 4:20. (Even with the time difference, 4:20 p.m. EST is during normal business hours even in Alaska and Hawaii.)

Seems to me either he had not been able to get a summer job in the law at all, or else his attitude toward doing work he was to be paid for was just as casual as his alleged attitude toward law school itself.

"Blboy" is either a fool, a fraud, or both. He has the makings neither of a good law student nor a good lawyer. I strongly suspect he is one of those who was attracted to the law because he regards a law license as, literally, a license to lie, cheat, and steal.

* * *

More e-mails...

Atticus—

After only three days of classes, I can tell that the prep is going to be very useful. Example: In Con Law today (our first meeting) the prof introduced himself, tooted his own horn for a bit ("I graduated number one from my law school, Harvard"), etc...not too self-promoting!

[Continued—]

---

* Punctuation, missing words, and upper-case/lower-case spelling in the original.

Then he went on at length about how he thought the Socratic Method was useful, and told us he would use it...At that point, he asked a question about the Constitution, and why the courts sometimes refuse to look at some issues that might, at first glance, seem very important. (He was getting at "political questions.") SILENCE in the classroom. No hands go up.

Now, I remembered very well your comments in PLS about the non-incentive to participate...lay low if you can, after all, the final is what counts, etc. But the silence was, as the saying goes, deafening.

The answer I had for him was the answer he eventually "pried" out of me using the Socratic Method. But, he wouldn't let me spit it out! I tried to answer, got about ½ way through the answer, and he jumped in with a question. So, I answered that, and tried to get back to the original question. But he cut me off and asked another question. So I answered that, and tried to get back to the original question, etc., for about 5 rounds, before he finally let me answer the original question, though he kept "hiding the pea under a different shell" a few times.

Anyway, what was amazing to me was that about 30 seconds into the so-called grilling, I was clearly remembering this discussion from the Con Law E&E volume. The questions he asked me were following the logic of what I had read a few weeks back. It was almost as if we were having the dialogue right out of the E&E book.

Atticus—

Well, I've finished my first two weeks at the University of Michigan. Exciting stuff.

When I got here, I thought the professors were quite nice. I still do. But they have said and done things to make me believe you have them accurately pegged.

First, my torts professor one day started to wax eloquent about tests and finals. He said two things about this: 1) whether you do well on tests comes down to talent. Some people have the talent and other people don't. 2) Ultimately, it doesn't matter how much talent you have for the tests; you can still succeed as an attorney.

[Note from AF—#2 sounds like the lover who breaks up with you and then says, "But we can still be 'friends.'"]

[Continued—]

Second, even though the professors speak of so many moral issues, etc., what the tests come down to is black letter law. The torts professor gave us a mock exam today so we could see what they were like under pressure. I was nervous about following LEEWS (well not really...the test doesn't count) because the prof had been talking so much about policy, etc. When we got the test, it was your standard hypo. He had been emphasizing the need to make arguments, so I did that. With that being said, it was straight LEEWS.

Atticus—

I just wanted to let you know that today marked the first day of orientation at the [name of school deleted]. An associate dean informed us that 1) No matter how hard we studied most of us would make a 2.7, because it's a forced curve, 2) We don't need study aids, and 3) Our lives are basically going to go down the drain for the next three years.

Some people are already being neurotic and competitive (although they are acting low key).

Atticus—

I have to say, you are right on about law professors. I can't imagine what I would be doing or thinking right now if I never read PLS. It is only Day 2 and people tonight have already been freaking out. (Nobody seems to know what they are supposed to be learning from these arcane cases.)

Atticus—

I have been accepted to study law at the University of Montana. I spoke with the dean of admissions at the UM law school this morning. I asked her for curriculum and book lists...She assured me that I was worrying needlessly! She urged me to simply relax, enjoy the summer and come to law school ready to work. Obviously, I'm not so inclined.

Atticus—

Thanks for writing PLS. Without it, I'd never have started prepping this summer and discovered how much of a struggle it is. I think if I'd found out how lousy my answers were only after school had started, I might be crying myself to sleep at night.

[AF—Most students don't find out how lousy their answers are until they see their grades. "The Moving Finger writes..."]

Another series from a message board...

Posting from "I love it"—

If you show up [at the start of law school] well-rested and waiting for the profs to teach you what will earn you A's then you really will have trouble sleeping. OR you can teach yourself the first-year subjects before the first day of class. Do yourself a favor and invest now before all your extra time is used up by the profs.

Posting from "anon o me"—

The above post is pure PLS-inspired bullshit. You don't need to spend your summer prepping to see the red herrings the profs throw out. You need to go to class, do the reading, and read (at least) the headnotes for the squibbed cases. Get in a study group of people who also go to class, do the reading, and discuss law rather than football or the hottie in class. That's all there is to it.

Posting from "SU2L"—

Read what you want to read because you won't get to read for fun for the next year (3 of my 5 profs even assigned massive reading over winter break). Spend time with your family/friends—another thing you won't get to do too often during school.

Look through cookbooks (websites, magazines, whatever) for recipes of food that you can cook batches of 10 meals, that freezes well, that doesn't turn moldy for a week in the fridge, takes only 2 or 3 minutes and cooks in five minutes.

Make sure you and everyone in your (resident) family has enough underwear, socks, pants, etc., to last 1 week, better yet, 2 weeks without doing laundry...

Posting from an "anon"—

I am taking a different stance to this from most other posters. I have already started preparing by reading and outlining...

I am set on making law review and/or a prestigious journal in law school (top 15), and I see no better way to improve my odds than to start studying now...

I see this as a perfect opportunity to enter law school ahead of the pack...I really enjoy reading and studying the material anyway.

Posting from "SU2L" (again), in response to "anon"—

[R]egardless that nearly all the current/former law students tell you no prep is necessary, you refuse to believe it. That's your choice. The pathetic part is you actually believe what you're doing will make a difference. I've met plenty of people like you; butt their heads against brick walls that others tried to help them avoid. Then they wonder why their head hurts. Why do you think former 1Ls post the advice they do? I can only assume you think we're trying to throw you off the winning plan...You've deluded yourself into believing you know what prep will make a difference...Get used to being pitied. With your attitude, you're going to experience a lot more of it. The vast majority of 1Ls know the black letter cold by finals.

[Note from AF—I did some checking on SU2L, who claimed to be a "former 1l." When she posted, she was still *in* first-year, as a *part*-time student (at Seattle University). She'd received only *one* grade at the time...from her legal writing course.]

Posting from "New 2L" in response to SU2L's second posting—

I agree. He has NO fucking clue what he is talking about... He doesn't even know what the HELL will be taking place four months from now. There is no way on earth to prepare for it... This yo-yo is going to ruin his summer and in October he'll be crying. So be it. Too bad for him.

* * *

Back to the e-mails...

Atticus—

My first exam is about two weeks away. My classmates are falling apart. Most of them are STARTING their outlines THIS WEEKEND and will do AN old exam THE NIGHT BEFORE the final.

One person was crying after class the other day. I really want to help everyone and tell them that the world is not about to end. Unfortunately, I would feel the same way if I just sat around the whole semester and then tried to cram everything in during the last two weeks.

The madness is truly intensifying, to heights I never would have thought possible.

I want to thank you for your book. I know that I prepared in the best way possible and worked as hard as I could. I'll just have to wait and see what happens.

[AF—What then happened is that this student got a 3.89 GPA in first-semester. As of this writing (April, 2002), she is now finishing the second semester of her first year. If she continues at this rate, perhaps there will be a testimonial from her in the *next* edition of *PLS*. (See addendum to this chapter.)]

Atticus—

I just wanted to let you know that you were absolutely right about prepping before law school.

I bought PLS last spring and out of fear alone I bought the primers. I was a bit dubious about the necessity for law school prep because of virtually all of the law students who post to the Princeton Review board and Greedy Law Students board. They all seemed to be so sure that prepping would not be beneficial and it would even be counter-productive. But I was scared to death about law school so I went through the primers and Delaney's book on legal reasoning.

I should have prepped more but I was working full-time. Truth be told, I was a bit lazy. I did not spend enough time on the primers. Sometimes I cut corners on the examples at the end of the chapters. I suppose I was looking for excuses to waste time last summer so I justified it by listening to law students' advice. They all said that law school was so unique that there was no way to prepare beforehand. And while I didn't completely believe them, I gave some credence to their advice. —Or perhaps just used it as an excuse to spend time with friends this summer instead of going through the primers in a more focused manner.

Getting back to my original point...

Your advice to prep before law school was right on target. I've just finished my first week of law school, so take my opinion with a grain of salt.

First, as to the argument that you can't prep because you don't know what the professor will concentrate on during the semester, the syllabus that I got in each class roughly followed the topics in the primer. It looked like there perhaps were topics that I studied in the primers that will not be covered in class, but that does not bother me. And it looks like most professors have a pet subject that wasn't covered in detail in the primer, but again that doesn't bother me because that's a small part of the class.

[Continued—]

You were right about what the classes would be like. The professors said they didn't recommend buying commercial outlines. They all claimed the best way to understand the law was to read and discuss the cases. After a week of going through cases, I am firmly convinced that they are wrong. How are we supposed to learn the rules from the cases if we spend the whole hour listening to the professor talk about his/her favorite constitutional issue?

Also, some of the professors have given some good hypos after we discuss a case. But if I had not already known the law before the class, I don't think that the hypos would have made any sense to me.

[Note from AF—Nor are they meant to, except to those who are "natural-born geniuses of the law." For everyone else (i.e., 90% of the class)...that's not the prof's problem.]

You were also right trying to caution against showing off in class. Every professor made a comment about how they can grade for class participation. And after they said that, about half the class would raise their hands for every question he/she asked. I did the math and realized that the class participation points are pretty meaningless to my overall grade.

[AF—Those profs were treating the students like trained seals...and the students were happy to oblige. But points for class participation is another "myth" that law profs propagate.]

It's really hard for me to resist the urge to show off. It's very important to me that everyone recognize that I'm smart, and it bothers me that the "smart" people here have already decided that I'm not one of them because I don't talk in class. I tried for a little to think of "bright" comments to make that would impress the professor and my fellow students. And I realized that I stopped listening to what the professor was saying and began concentrating only on what I would say. So now, I won't play that game.

There's a required class for first-year students called "Legal Process." We've discussed four Supreme Court cases so far, dealing with the same topic. From these cases, we are supposed to be learning legal reasoning. Thankfully (because of your advice), I'd read Delaney's book. From talking with other students, I can already tell that most of them are very confused and have been misled about the purpose of the class. Delaney's book was excellent, because it cut through all the BS about political opinions, etc., and focused on real legal reasoning. I've already glanced at an old exam and know the prof doesn't ask any questions about Justice So-and-so or about any of the prof's pet constitutional issues. It's an issue-spotter.

Also, the advice in Delaney's book, about briefing cases, was much more helpful than what we were taught in the "briefing workshop" last week.

The instructors only mentioned outlining in passing, as though it's something we're not supposed to start until later in the semester. (We'll have a "workshop" on outlining—in about a month!)

Thanks to your advice, I'm not freaking out like many of my classmates. I know that I've got lots of work to do, though.

Atticus—

You'll love this one. I asked one of my professors about policy questions on the exam since he's devoting a fair amount of class time to "policy" discussions. He told me that the general guideline I ought to use is to discuss as much policy as a lawyer in court would. There are points of policy which have to be raised and points which don't.

I asked him how was I supposed to know what a lawyer in court would say? I am not a lawyer and haven't been in a courtroom even a day in my life.

He smiled and said that it was a good question, but they, professors, test—among other things—that magic ability of some select students to feel what a lawyer would say in court. Some do, and "some" (most," he meant) don't. I thought it was pretty amusing.

The Civ Pro professor discussed Long Arm jurisdiction only. He didn't mention the California-type jurisdiction which is discussed by Glannon at a decent length. So I played dumb, and asked him after class why didn't we talk about it. I told him I loved Civil Procedure and had looked through some books, and they discussed the California-type jurisdiction. He said he'd never heard about it and wasn't sure he knew what I was talking about. I'd understand if he skipped it because he held it to be marginal, but I'd expect him to be familiar with the concept.

Atticus—

Thought you might get a kick out of what happened today. Civ Pro had been wearing me down with its rules and details. (I am even outlining the primer because of the fine details.)

I was kind of fed up, so I decided to look at an exam to test if any of it was sinking in. I printed out a Civ Pro exam from the Harvard Law School website (Prof. Shapiro, January, 2000). It was a problem on the pros and cons of a motion to dismiss, involving long-arm statutes and an auto accident in one state after the car had been worked on in another state.

To my surprise, I began asking questions like, "Where did the brake job take place?" "Where did the transaction occur?" For jurisdiction purposes, does this meet the Washington v. Intl. Shoe *test?*"

At the end of it all, I was confident that I could—at a minimum—pass the exam. **Given that I have not even darkened the door of a law school, that's not bad.** [Boldface added—AF.]

However, I realized that what I needed now was an organized system for going through all of the issues and for practicing the writing out of answers in a lawyerlike fashion. I used the LEEWS method. The LEEWS manual breaks it all down, step-by-step: one, two, etc. On the exam you were to put it all together and DANCE. I found out that I really like dancing. Even a Civ Pro exam became a very fun intellectual exercise.

But don't worry. I don't think I know it all. My approach is just like I use to cross even ONE-way streets in Moscow: look BOTH ways, repeatedly; move speedily…and expect some madman to come out of nowhere and attempt to run me down at any moment.

To those who say just kick back and relax before law school, I say, "Bullshit." There is no way that showing up for law school bare-assed and optimistic can compare going in with eyes wide open and with a working knowledge of the issues.

Atticus—

My professor for contracts is the typical sort of prof you described in PLS. He is the most confusing man I have ever seen in my life… He tries to make easy concepts quite difficult. I must admit that contracts is more difficult than torts and criminal law, because we are not familiar with the jargon. All my classmates are lost and already hate law school. (This is only our first week.)

Even I felt confused in class sometimes and I tried to rigorously prepare the PLS way. However, my contracts primer has clarified a lot of my confusion. Usually, once I play with the hypos in the *primer, I start to see how things come together. It is extremely time-consuming, and I feel so slow at understanding things. But, usually, after many hours of playing with hypos and changing around the facts of my case, I finally come to an understanding of things.*

I feel bad for my classmates who do not understand what is going on right now because I am sure it is going to get even more difficult quite fast.

The prof also told us that under no circumstances should we use commercial products. He qualified this statement, however, by saying we should run out and by a hornbook or a treatise on contracts...HA...HA!

Just thought I'd let you know. I'm sure you understand the fun that we are all dealing with. Really, thank you for your book. I would be completely lost without your advice.

Atticus—

I am involved in a pro bono/habeas "death row" case [as a law student]. I went over the 86-page habeas petition and there was nothing that did not make sense or that I did not understand. From claimed errors in the voir dire to diminished capacity, it all made sense. Even the crim pro items were clear. (I'd read about them months before, in the Aspen primer.)

A funny thing happened when I was preparing for my crim law test last semester. While going through BarBri practice tests, I noticed I was scoring about 98% correct on the crim pro questions, and I could not for the life of me explain how I knew all that stuff. That made NO sense, because my crim law course last semester had only been on the substantive crim law, not procedural.

It was only after I started the pro bono case and I flipped through the Aspen crim pro primer that I realized I had read the book months before—and obviously had remembered the material.

Atticus—

My contracts professor (Ken Hegland), made us buy his book, Introduction to the Study and Practice of Law *(a Nutshell book), and reading it is the entire first week's assignment. He also told us how complicated law was, and then proved it, by having us read a case with the holding edited out, and then (as a group) trying to figure out what the ruling would/should be. We all agreed we didn't know.*

[AF—Hegland's book is good as to the "practice of law" part, but not the "how to study" part. Too bad he didn't assign Blum's primer on contracts in the Aspen E&E series, instead, and spend a week on *that*. It would seem to be a better use of class time…and students' money.]

Atticus—

My property professor told us not to ask her questions if we are confused. She said we should go to the library and figure it out ourselves. She also said we should not use commercial study aids and that we should not begin our outlines until late in the semester.

Atticus—

Seems to me no one (I may be hedging) used PLS. In each of my classes, the students are writing down the most trivial things, scrambling to get what "she" said, etc. I on the other hand am making a few notes here and there, listening to the reason why the law is the way it is and thinking of hypos.

***

From the message board of the Yahoo group, Planet Law School (http//groups.yahoo.com/group/planetlawschool)…

Exhibit "A"—

I don't think many of my fellow students have prepared. All I can say is I am very glad I found PLS and trusted my instincts that AF was telling the real truth. I would be totally caught up in the madness by now (yes, after only 4 days) instead of just feeling a little unnerved.

I also really appreciate having this discussion board as a "compass" b/c it helps to know others are experiencing the same feelings, speeches, styles of profs. I think it's amazing that law schools can be so very much alike all over the country.

Exhibit "B"—

During the first week of classes, the law school was the asylum of the nicest people on earth. People just wouldn't stop smiling to each other and be nice and warm.

[But now]…I feel like I'm back in high school even though I've been out of high school for awhile…People are split into factions. I wonder how can they do that so fast. I have a feeling that the sense of competitiveness will soon break through…

[Continued—]

I spoke to several people in my class asking them what they thought about our classes, i.e. the Socratic Method. All except one said they believed the professors had a plan they would follow to lead us to understanding of the material. All believe that professors work hard to teach us, so it's up to us to work hard to understand. One said he began to smell the rat but still wanted to remain an optimist.

Meanwhile, one professor is so bad, he refuses to answer questions even when asked in class. His answer is simple:

"THINK ABOUT IT YOURSELF, 'CAUSE I WON'T MAKE THIS COURSE EASIER THAN WHAT IT'S GOTTA BE." These are his exact words.

I haven't met even one person who has more or less clear understanding of what that professor "taught" us in two weeks.

I'm the only one, because I went through Aspen books and commercial outlines. I also have not met a single PLSer, even though I'm bad at meeting new friends. But from the people's behavior it seems they are all already screwed up. So, I guess, they didn't read...PLS.

Exhibit "C"—

Well at my law school, the professors are staight up dragons.

My CRIM LAW prof apparently graduated #1 from Stanford and then clerked under Rehnquist so he came in and class began QUICKLY!

This was the first day mind you. Luckily for me, I didn't get called on, but he tore up a couple of people because they hadn't read the cases carefully.

Our Torts class is a lot like that as well except the professor just embarasses us a lot more by essentially saying we are pretty error-prone.

My Crim Law prof actually did call on me the 2nd day about some obscure case in the notes of the actual case we were supposed to have read and luckily I had actually briefed that case out of curiosity so my time went fairly smoothly although I did get hammered a couple of times.

Civ Pro and Contracts aren't as bad but are pretty much the same.

Mr. Falcon is ABSOLUTELY RIGHT about class...It's nuts. At first I thought that maybe it wouldn't be as bad as Atticus said, but he's right on the money.

Exhibit "D"—

I'm learning contracts from Genghis Khan, or at least I get the impression that my professor looks to Genghis Khan as a role model in pedagogy. I'm not joking here. Some examples:

You cannot look at him. If you look at him, he yells, "What do you think, Mr. So-and-so, is this a visual experience here? Do you need to see me? Or do you think it's a cerebral experience? Do you think you need to see me, or might it be better to take notes during class? Some people have a problem here, let me tell you. Some people have a real problem. They're looking at me and not taking notes."

[AF—If you have the nerve for it, and if he asks *you* "Is this a visual experience here?", you could immediately shoot back, "Actually, it's a *religious* experience." And if the prof is so foolish as to ask, "Why is that?", you respond, "Witnessing an incarnation of the divine, of course: the Word made flesh."

If the prof insists you keep your head down and appear to be taking notes, I do not think you need to comply. If the prof orders you to, you can respond with, "I'm willing to accept responsibility for how I absorb what's said in class. Call it a *student's* right of academic freedom." If the professor throws a fit, just say, "Perhaps we should inquire of the dean in this matter—or the Institute for Law School Teaching." The prof, of course, will not have heard of ILST. You might get to then explain to him or her what it is.]

I think he enjoys the terror he instills in everyone. He also insists on people having the case book and briefs. It's insane. He has people read from their briefs. He also loves asking questions like, "How many reasons were in the court's opinion? Which one was the strongest? Where is it?" Actually, the "where is it?" is constant. He always wants to know what page and paragraph something is. He asks questions about footnotes. If someone hasn't looked up a word in Black's Law Dictionary (and he will ask folks, he'll even ask where they got the definition). He asked one student to give him the definition of "restitution" and when this student (a 42-year-old man, international businessman) didn't have an exact definition (as in, from Black's Law Dictionary) but just tried to wing it, he called the man "unprepared" and "unprofessional."

He gave out a sample of the ideal student notes for his class. Question and answer, verbatim of one of his classes. It worked out to about 8 pages. We should just type down everything he says and everything the students answer for every class. This, he tells us, will not only help us in reviewing for his exam, but also for the bar exam. Alright, I'm a novice, but forgive me if I'm a tad skeptical.

My CivPro professor gives an exam that is primarily multiple choice. On top of that, he is—hands down—the winner of the hardest exam-maker for 1st year students. In previous years, students supposedly left his exam wanting to drop out of law school. One 2L told me she cried afterwards. Of course, everything is graded on a curve, so it really doesn't matter if everyone does poorly or great, since a curve is a curve is a curve. He does put 1 hypo on his final, but 75% of the exam is multiple choice.

Much of the beginning of ConLaw was going over cases like Marbury *that seem to espouse nothing more than general principles.*

Now that we're doing Commerce Clause, and Substantive Due Process, there are specific tests and elements that can be applied, but our professor spends class time just cutting down the arguments of sides, majority and dissent, in the opinions.

I am making sure I do the readings, but focusing on E&E, and the C[ommercial] O[utline]s to get the black letter law needed to apply to hypos. I'm answering the questions in the E&E books (I did some of the books 2 years ago, so I find I'm rusty) and in the COs to make sure I get the basic stuff down. I feel like I'm going to want to start practicing hypos soon.

After reading PLS, I knew exactly what I was getting into, so to speak, so I can't say nobody told what it would be like. I don't know what I would have done if I hadn't read PLS. (Once again, Atticus, thank you!)

Exhbit "E"—

In our contracts class we started with DAMAGES from breach of contract!!!!!! Even then we've only covered expectancy damages in the first two weeks.

In my tort classes we are "supposedly" covering negligence (again, why aren't we starting with, "what is a tort?") and we've barely covered that!

In our civ pro class we are not even close to learning how to file a complaint because we are too busy trying to figure out what justice is ?????

We don't have con law first because we have crim law, but it is a little better.

Exhibit "F"—

We started in Contracts by learning that there can be no punitive damages. Then we went on to study reliance damages, then on to consideration, studying old cases where they only required detriment to P _or_ benefit to D. Then on to mutuality, which as I take it from [Aspen's] E&E [primer], is no longer good law. I'm guessing we are "tracing the development in the field of contract law...which is interesting to me, but confusing as hell to everyone else.

Exhibit "G"—

Everyone complains of being so lost in Ks. Thanks to E&E, I don't feel lost. (To me it would make more sense to start with offer-acceptance in Ks like the E&E does.) One of the cases we studied last wk, Webb v McGowin, turns on "moral obligation" which, after spending 30 min. discussing, the prof said the case was decided incorrectly and is not an example of the law. Someone objected to having to learn it. Needless to say, that was met with an icy stare!

People in the class are still complaining about that, a week later, and are so outraged like they think it was a total anomaly or something. Thanks to PLS, I'm not surprised.

Exhibit "H"—

Today in my TORTS class the professor says, "We [law professors] are not here to teach you the Black Letter Law. We are here to re-create the way that your mind thinks."

Today in my CRIMINAL LAW class the professor says, "You people better understand that I'm not going to teach you the rules or Black Letter Law of Criminal Law! You reciting the rules is not what's going to be on the exam! The exam is going to be a fact situation and you are going to have to analyze it!"

Today in CONTRACTS class, when asked about supplements, my professor says, "Any supplement that doesn't have a case index in the beginning of the book is a bunch of crap! Look at your casebook! It's got a case index in the beginning! If you need material to supplement what you are reading in the cases, go to other casebooks or the reporters themselves." He also went ahead to talk about how he didn't like the Restatements!

Then we had a required seminar for 1Ls!!! We had 2 law professors (both Civil Procedure profs for 1Ls) who told us that it was the job of the law school to teach us how to think like lawyers. We need to get away from this notion that we need to learn the rules of the law or the Black Letter Law, and should instead really try to pull what is going on out of the casebooks. We need to study the casebooks extensively and try to pull together what all the cases are saying as a whole.

Anyhow, as you can see, my day was eventful, but in sort of a negative way, but just like everything else I've experienced in law school, I look over at the seat next to me and there is Atticus Falcon with PLS in hand saying, "I told you so."

Exhibit "I"—

Does anyone else have Teaching Assistants? I have one for each of my classes except Legal Writing & Research, and all of them hold review sessions. I was skeptical about how helpful this would be, but decided to attend one session and evaluate.

I went to the Torts review session and was pleasantly surprised. The TA focused on blackletter law only, and the exam. Yes, this early, she talked about how to write the exam. She said next wk we would look at some hypos and write exam answers for them. People were asking her about cases, what we would need to know, etc. and she told them, "Forget about cases. You don't need to remember anything about cases. You need to know the rule of law cold." She even talked about writing the outline for yourself at the beginning of the exam as Atticus has suggested.

This prof has no old exams on file, and all his exams are "closed book"

Out of my class of 50-some people, there were only 7 of us there.

Exhibit "J"—

I think some of my classmates are clueless as to what they really should be learning. A student who sits next to me in Torts was making elaborate flash cards for cases—with the name of the case at the top, the facts, issue, rule, blah-blah-blah, and she was memorizing them. She thought that's what the final would be!

Exhibit "K"—

I am so grateful for PLS, this board, and AF. This first semester of law school has been an academic experience like no other, even with a grad degree.

Last night we had a review session with a prof. All semester this prof has referred to case names, had us compare cases, everything is case, case, case, so much so that nearly everyone in the class was certain he would want case names on the final. [Continued—]

I distinctly remember one point early in the semester, a student asked him if we would need to know case names for the final. He said something to the effect of, "No, not necessarily, but it could help if you did, blah blah blah." (Of course, to the average over-achieving law student that means "learn those case names to get those extra points.") Thanks to PLS I never fell for it. (Okay, I did check it out with a 2L buddy who had this prof last year also. But isn't that the PLS way too?)

Anyway, <u>at this review session yesterday this same prof says under no circumstances should we write a case name on the final.</u> [Underlining added—AF.] *He only wants to see Black Letter Law. He said it would be best not to reference cases in any way as some of them were exceptions to BLL and you could really screw up using them.*

The woman sitting next to me had a stack of hand-written case briefs three inches thick that she had been studying. She looked physically ill. She honestly thought the review session would be a review of cases.

Where else, but law school, could this happen? —At the 11th hour, the prof basically says that all the stuff we read and learned and talked about in class all semester is not what you need to know. You need to know something else.

[AF—And I'll bet he didn't tell the class *what* it was "you *do* need to know," instead of just suddenly telling what they *didn't* need to know. (As you see, the subtitle of this new edition of *PLS* is *not* hyperbole.)

However, it could have been even worse (and for most students, it is): most profs who lead students on during the semester *never* tell them the truth. Maybe this prof was able to keep his conscience clear by finally (as it were) levelling with the class, albeit at the 11th hour (actually, only at 11:59 p.m.).]

Exhibit "L"—

I empathize with the plight you are all going through. I'm a 2L at a top tier school and graded onto law review using the PLS method. It will work if you put in the time and energy.

It takes a lot of time, but 2L is not really much better (except you know what you're doing and can do it a little bit faster).

Keep grinding away and good luck. Post here if you have any qs, but it sounds like you are all doing the right thing.

[Continued—]

PS—I noticed that many of you are briefing. I briefed according to the LEEWS method. **Yes, I did get called on and often looked stupid, but it doesn't matter now. People in my class actually thought I was a stupid dolt. They changed their tunes when they saw I graded onto law review.**   [Boldface added—AF.]

* * *

Another series of comments posted to a message board—

1. *"If it weren't for the curve, you'd all fail," says a professor about our upcoming law exam.*

2. *Tell him, "If it weren't for the sleep, I'd never show up."*

3. *Tell him he's lucky he has a teaching job because he obviously couldn't handle real employment.*

4. *Ask him why his teaching is so poor that none of his students can score above an F.*

5. *I bet that if it wasn't for the curve, only two to five out of the 120 students in my contracts class at UVA would pass...I bet most raw scores are below 60%. Thank God we'll all get a B+ in the end. It's just all my fault...I'm too stupid.*

6. *Just ask your prof about that famous saying, "Those who can't DO, teach."*

* * *

More e-mails...

Atticus—
   I'm really starting to believe that the administration at my law school is inherently evil. An assembly was held the other day on study skills. The Dean told everyone NOT to use LEEWS. I feel really bad for everyone around me. They are all going nuts and there is no need for it.

Atticus—

There are a scant few who know what they are doing around here...the few who have read PLS (I found them by discreetly hinting that I'd read a book about law school called "PLS," and of course those who'd read it said, "Atticus Falcon?")...and I am happy to say I am one of them.

Everything that comes up has been forewarned by your book. My torts professor, [name deleted], is pretending he is Professor Kingsfield from The Paper Chase.

Atticus—

In my contracts course, 30% of the grade is based on a paper. When we did the first draft, we were not allowed to go to the prof or the TAs for help. The prof said the reason why we could not go to the TAs was because the TAs had not read the cases for the project.

The professor lied! In my meeting with a TA a couple of days before the paper was due, she said the TAs are the ones who FOUND the cases and then wrote the assignment for the class! The professor had very little involvement.

This professor spent 55 minutes of class talking about the minority rule, then the last five minutes on the majority rule. Naturally, we got confused, and thought the minority rule was the majority rule. So then she accused us of not listening in class.

Atticus—

I'm starting week 2 here at [name of school deleted], and in my section of 95 students not one person responded to my posting about forming a PLS study group. I guess that can be viewed as good or bad: good because it means there are no other students who've prepared as I have; bad because I don't have anyone to study with who's up to my speed. I must say, though, that I'm enjoying the "deer caught in the headlights" look so many in my section always seem to have on their faces.

Atticus—

PLS is working for me. For example, we are covering homicide in criminal law. The professor decided to skip over the whole "mens rea" deal, which made it somewhat hard to figure out the definitions in the Model Penal Code. So I went back and read that part of the primer. Then I used the hypo in the casebook, and used the LEEWS approach. It WORKED. After many hours of toil, I finally understand.

Atticus—

The administration at my law school was saying last week, at the Admitted Students' Day, that we should just take it easy over the summer and there was no need to prepare. I asked a professor who teaches Property what he thought of Moynihan's book as a preparation for Property class. He encouraged me just to enjoy my summer and not get caught up with reading material.

[AF—Moynihan's book (now "Moynihan/Kurtz") is one of the background primers, recommended in Chapter 4, for Estates & Future Interests.]

Atticus—

Just had an experience that is bizarre. [Name deleted]—an author of one of the Aspen E&E primers—is a professor at one of the schools I have applied to. I attended a reception for prospective students, and he was one of the faculty people there. I told him I was reading his primer. Then, just for fun, I asked him if he knew of any other books that might help me prepare for law school. He appeared to think it over a moment, then said, "No." !!!!!!

[AF—This is like the law prof who writes a commercial outline, then tells his or her own students not to buy commercial outlines. The hypocrisy of those people never ceases to amaze me. Dangle a few bucks in front of them, and they'd sell their soul…if they have one, that is.

But this prof is actually worse. The guy *has* to know that *his* primer is just *one* in the Aspen E&E series. And surely he has a copy. So he knows the back cover lists the *other* books in the series. Unlike the prof who writes a commercial outline and then advises his or her students not to buy commercial outlines, this prof was outright lying.

But at least he wrote a good primer.]

Atticus—

Re. your comments about the cooperative nature of the law school experience. You mentioned that the cooperative feel of a class starts to evaporate, and quite quickly. Well, you were right on the money. Just around the edges, I have noticed it starting to erode. As people are called on in class and begin to stumble, I watch people grinning and enjoying their fellows' pathetic plight. Someone in class the other day was "cold-called" on, and she made an ass of herself, clearly hadn't read the material, and hadn't even bothered to listen to the conversation in class. It was painful. Yet, after class, many people were chuckling about it. I don't know how much of their laughter was of the "Gee, I'm glad it wasn't me" kind, and how much was of the "Oh well, screw her, she got what she deserved" kind.

Many of your other insights are starting to occur as well. Example: I have been in what I would call an informal study group with two other guys. We have an hour break between classes almost every day. The two other guys and I have been using that time to prep for the next class: reviewing cases, extending the issues via hypotheticals, parsing out phrases and rules, etc. (I know it sounds like I'm blowing my own horn, doesn't it? I guess I am. But I'm working hard. Why not toot for awhile?)

Anyway, we have been doing this since Day One. We made the terrible mistake of getting together today to talk about the material in a crowded area where there were others from our classes hanging out. It didn't take more than 3-4 minutes before we were interrupted with, "Hey, you sound like you get it. Can you explain this to me?" Or, "Wow, I'm just now starting to read for class. Can you give me a heads-up?" (This, about 30 minutes before the class the reading was for.)

As you noted in PLS, it puts a person in a lose-lose situation. Answer questions and there goes our study time before class. Don't answer questions, and voilá, you are the class asshole.

Atticus—

Your comments about competition brought back memories of my time in grad school.

Anyone who doesn't look for a competitive edge is, in my view, an idiot. Everyone is trying hard to do his or her best. And ofttimes, it is a "zero-sum" game: your gain is someone else's loss. In grad school, funding, teaching privileges, TA assignments, etc., all rested on your performance in relation to others.

This, as you note, doesn't mean you have to be a cutthroat asshole. The few who took that approach were quickly shunned, and usually revealed to be largely incompetent.

The single best student there (and someone with whom I work now, as it turns out) was very quiet about his work. And, not surprisingly, he was respected by other students and the faculty.

[AF—In law school, the benefits are similar.]

Atticus—

I have never been "put off" by your method, as it is systematic in its approach. Before going to law school, I was in business for myself and followed a four-year journey towards profitability, and later worked for other companies/businesses. I learned early on of the value of training and continuing education, and the value of following a system. Even in sales training, it wasn't just a matter of how to successfully close the sale, but how to carry the right attitude, too, and how to practice the right behavior, to go hand-in-hand with the technique of making the sale.

Without going into detail, I have seen from the experience of executing this system, for long stretches of time in my life, that it works. Maintaining the inner energy level to work the system, and having the confidence to go at it even if you are alone, has been one of the ways I have gotten through my young adult years.

Bear in mind, though, that I "floundered around" through most of my 20s, so I feel like I am making up for lost time. I wish I had known this attitude and behavior (discipline) when I was 23 instead of 33. But as the saying goes, the journey is the prize.

Success in law school (or anything else in life, for that matter) follows the same method: possessing the right attitude and knowing how to adjust it/tune it to maintain perspective, practicing healthy behaviors and remaining balanced, and hitting the books for learning how to learn the tools of the trade.

Atticus—

I'm currently working as a legal assistant for a large law firm and will begin law school this fall. Many of the attorneys I've talked to here say that your advice is right on the money (especially the part about the classes that "don't count now"). And many of my friends who are currently attending and doing well (i.e. made Law Review) said that your advice will put me "head and shoulders above the competition" in law school.

Atticus—

I read your book (repeatedly), took LEEWS, read Getting to Maybe, *actively read all the* E&E *books, got the Bryan Garner books, etc., but I simply choked on all the in-class exams. I entirely blame myself for my grades, as although I did read your book and the* E&E *books, I did not keep up with my outlining, did not do all the questions in the* E&E *books, and came up short in several other areas.*[Cont'd—]

I am not criticizing your book or your recommendations at all; on the contrary, I recognize that if I had followed them to the letter, I would have likely done better (particularly if I could be less nervous on the in-class exams).

[AF—Sadly, if he *had* followed through better, he *would* have been less nervous during his exams.]

* * *

From a posting (#143) to the aforementioned Yahoo group, Planet Law School...

My guess is that Atticus really layed out the terrain in Planet Law School *by saying that the [Aspen] E&E [primers] are the best things out there to go by if you are going to law school. However, he didn't say that everyone would take advantage of these materials either. I played pro baseball for a year and really got to see the inner workings of some organizations. There are all these new methods of evaluating talent out there, and every organization seems to think they have the upper-hand on each of these methods, but in all honesty, every organization knows the same things. It just all depends on who takes advantage of these methods and who uses them in the best way to evaluate the best talent. This is the way good organizations in baseball are built, i.e. the Athletics, Giants, and Padres.*

I"m guessing it's the same way in law school. At first, I was thinking when I read Planet Law School *that I had a guide that was going to lead me to the Promised Land because nobody else had it. I was a little naive, but somewhat right in that I had a guide that was going to lead me to the Promised Land. But it wasn't going to be because nobody else had the resources. It's because I'm going to be the only person who takes advantage of the materials in the best way they can be taken advantage of.*

I'm guessing this is what Atticus Falcon was getting at. It's one thing to know about the materials. It's another thing to have the materials. It's yet another thing to use the materials. And it's yet another thing to use the materials in the best way possible. I think this is the crux. Atticus gives us the play-by-play on what to do to be successful, but he can't put in all the hard work that we'll need to put in order for the PLS method to work for us.

[AF—Yup. He hit the nail right on the head...or, because he's a former baseball player, perhaps I should say he just "homered."]

Atticus—

At the beginning of last summer I read your book and purchased what you recommended: LEEWS (attended the lecture and bought the tapes, but basically never practiced LEEWS), and the Aspen E&Es for all my classes (but lightly read them). Regarding commercial outlines, I never really opened them, until the last week before finals.

I never really practiced what you preached, but merely said oh the system will save me.

In first-year, I then got these grades: Crim C, Ks C-, Torts B-, Civ Pro D, Prop C-, writing course C, and Con Law C-. (Grading is on a B curve, 20% As, 50% Bs and the rest C/Ds, but rarely is a D given.)

I have a 1.9 and I am on probation this Fall semester. Unless my average gpa reaches above 2.0, I will be kicked out..

Basically, last year I felt unmotivated to try, and this time around I really feel a sense and a motivation to start getting things done. I really want to read the E&Es now and don't want to procrastinate like last year.

* * *

Wentworth Miller, of LEEWS, forwarded this e-mail to me:

Ever wonder about those people who say they are giving more than 100%? Here's a little math that might prove helpful.

If "A B C D E F G H I J K L M N O P Q R S
      T U V W X Y Z" is represented as

1 2 3 4 5 6 7 8 9 10 11 12 13 14 15 16 17 18 19
     20 21 22 23 24 25 26.

Then: HARD WORK (8+1+18+4+23+15+18+11) = 98%
  and KNOWLEDGE (11+14+15+23+12+5+4+7+5) = 96%
  And BULLSHIT (2+21+12+12+19+8+9+20) = 103%...
which, of course, is literally impossible (and the bullshit artist always fails to deliver).
  Further, ASS KISSING (1+19+19+11+9+19+19+9+14+7) = 118%.

* * *

From a posting to a message board, in response to someone who'd put up an item about using "The *PLS* Approach" to preparing for law school:

I find it amusing that you honestly believe that all of this prepara-tion is somehow going to throttle you past the rest of us. Certainly you might have a better initial grasp of some of the concepts. But what really matters in the end is just how much "gray matter" you have and how you use it to your advantage. I remember there used to be guys in college who would spend the summer preparing for advanced mathematical courses, and I would just survey the material in the summer before. These same guys seemed to know the stuff in the early weeks, but before long the truly talented in the group (yours truly included) blasted past them. Their surface knowledge of the material could not make up for an innate lack of ability.

Frankly, I think it's great that you are preparing and that you feel very good about it. But it would behoove you to not get your hopes up too high, because no matter how much time you put into it, the cream always rises to the top. Reading will help you become knowledgeable, but it won't improve your innate intelligence.

[AF—My comments...]

Now, that's interesting. It is, of course, the myth that law schools—especially the professoriat—have been propagandizing for decades now. And they honestly believe it. This anonymous poster has obvi-ously bought into it hook, line, and sinker...or perhaps is waging a "disinformation campaign," *à la* "Bonehead." And who knows? Perhaps he or she truly is a "natural-born genius of the law." If so, then this student might well ace all of his or her finals, perhaps without even having conducted a "survey [of] the material the summer before." But I would raise three objections to this attitude.

The first is that law school is not college. I cannot imagine why anyone *without* a "high degree of innate intelligence" would sign up for a course in *advanced mathematics*. Regardless, the material in the first year of law school is, objectively speaking, in no way comparable to advanced math. It's more like simple arithmentic, and plain geometry. It's only the Case/Socratic Method (and especially "hide-the-ball") that makes it *seem* hard.

But for the sake of discussion, I'll assume the poster was sincere.

Even so, my second objection is that in any respectable law school virtually *all* the students were at the top of their college classes, including students at the most rigorous schools in the country. Trusting to their own innate intelligence, and their success in previous schooling, they assume they have what it takes to excel in law school. Too late, they learn that law school is different. *Quite* different. And success in first-year is not primarily a matter of intelligence or intellect.

As discussed earlier: in college, your textbooks and professors try to "lay it all out for you." So it makes sense that—after being handed everything on a silver platter, as to information and resources—"innate intelligence" *is* what makes the difference...that, and hard work. But in law school, you're thrown into the water—during a *typhoon*—and told it's "sink or swim." Then you'll be handed an anchor, and told it's a life jacket. And you're told not to try to swim toward a life buoy—because it only *looks* like a life buoy; actually, what you're seeing, they say, is a shark's fin, and you'd be swimming to your doom.

My third objection is this: giving that writer the benefit of the doubt (and assuming he *is* brilliant), how sad that he wastes his brilliance by his arrogant indolence. What insights might he have achieved were he willing to *work* at *learning* the law rather than merely "surveying the material" in time for the exam?

Here are two of my favorite quotations...

The first is from the foreword to a fine novel by Anton Myrer, *Once an Eagle*. The foreword is by John W. Vessey, Jr. (U.S. Army, Retired), who was Chairman of the Joint Chiefs of Staff from 1982-85. The novel is largely about what goes into the making of a good army officer. Vessey mentioned the Army War College, and said its purpose is "to move future leaders from cocksure ignorance to wise uncertainty."

The smug twit quoted above typifies the all-too-common "cocksure ignorance" of far too many law students...and lawyers. Sadly, legal "education" never even *tries* to reach the top two levels of the "Josephson Pyramid"—but if it did, perhaps students like this one might develop some *judgment*, the essence of which is "wise uncertainty." They might also develop some humility.

—Which brings me to another of my favorite quotations. This one's from the late Cal Tech physicist (and Nobel prize-winner), Richard Feynman. "I was born not knowing and have had only a little time to change that here and there."

Those who prepare for law school are (perhaps) already exhibiting the humility (despite his brilliance) of Richard Feynman, and the wise uncertainty extolled by Gen. Vessey. These are ultimately among the marks of a good lawyer, too—"good" in *both* senses of the word "good."

Addendum to Chapter 15 —
Testimonial Essays

The PLS Approach and How it Worked for Me
or
"How I Lost 20 Pounds and Got Great Abs
in Just 15 Minutes a Day on the PLS Diet"

Because I wanted a career in L.A., I had originally applied to UCLA and U. Cal - Berkeley (Boalt Hall), with no luck. The University of Florida had accepted me, but—because I was desperate to leave the state of Florida—UF did not seem particularly attractive to me. The deadline to accept admission there was June 1ˢᵗ. I opted to accept on June 2ⁿᵈ. Luckily, they let me do it. I also realized quickly that transferring to UCLA was a possibility.

In any case, I knew transferring required me to do fairly well first year. And, I thought perhaps it would be good to get some idea what this whole "law school" thing was about. So, I did what I always do when encountering a new area: I searched for a book on the subject.

I distinctly remember paging through the various books on the shelves at the store. Most of them were pretty generic. *PLS* kind of jumped out at me. I picked it up and glanced through it. It promised it was different than the other books; it had information they didn't—but I needed to know. Well, I had no basis for evaluating these promises. But I have always lived by a simple principle: if it's different, it's probably better. A rebuttable presumption, but one that had served me well in the past. This decision would prove no different.

A quick read of the first few chapters of *PLS* convinced me that Law School would be an entirely unique experience. I felt way ahead of the game just having the information from the book in my hands—I felt like I was starting to really understand what I was getting into; the fear of God entered my heart. The book was scary, but persuasive. The chapter on professors had an especially profound effect on me—that sure sounded like a sweet job to me. Still: law school sounded like quite a scam. Could it really be as bad as Atticus painted it?

Either way, his preparation advice seemed both obvious and intuitive. What could possibly be lost by spending the time and money to prepare for law school? If it was really as tough as Atticus painted it, *any* edge would be welcome, especially if I wanted to transfer. And, given how important first year grades are, preparation seemed like an obvious choice. Sure, it would cost money (it turned out to be quite a lot), and sure it would take time, but how could having read the entire year's curriculum ahead of time NOT give me an important advantage?

I only had three months. This wasn't going to be too easy.

I immediately ordered the primers and the tapes. Commercial outlines were available at the same bookstore where I had bought *PLS*. I began by reading the Torts Primer. I have to say that this was a great place to begin; the subject matter was basic enough so that it could serve as a good introduction to the rest of the books. I then moved on to Contracts, which was significantly more difficult for me. I then read Criminal Law. About this time, I found out that my school was on a semester system with only three of the 6 subjects assigned per semester. Luckily for me, my first semester consisted of exactly these three subjects. This was good, because time was running short (and I doubt I could have remembered second semester stuff anyway). I crashed hard on these three courses—listening to the tapes and reading the commercial outlines. The week before school I read the Delaney books and listened to the LEEWS tapes (which I found *quite* useful).

I was one of the nervous few to place a notice for a *PLS* study group on the bulletin board at my school. No one ever responded. This was good news, I thought; I may have been the only one at my school.

And, because of *PLS* I really did start my outlines early. I was outlining by the end of the first month (once we really had enough material). This move really helped me a lot. I was way ahead of the pack—most of whom didn't even consider starting outlining until it was too late. I don't want to pretend I kept this practice up in future semesters, but it certainly made the first one a lot smoother.

I didn't find law professors to be nearly as scary as Atticus made them out to be. Of my four professors, only one was less than helpful. Of the others, one actually *assigned* Glannon's on Torts (which shocked me). She was, of course, quite young. My contracts professor was the closest thing I ever saw to Kingsfield, but he was fair and obviously cared about his students. At the end of the semester he took time to assure all of us that grades were not nearly as important as we thought and that we would all be ok. My legal writing instructor was terrific; she became a friend, and we are still in touch to this day.

My first semester was good, but not outstanding. It required a tremendous second semester to lift me into transfer territory. I knew that to get into UCLA I would need to get into the top 10% of my class. Halfway through the year I realized that Berkeley would also be an attractive option. To assure myself entry there I would need to get into at least the top 5%. At the end of my first semester I was in the top

15%. I needed a near-perfect effort second semester to do so. In the end, dedication and motivation paid off. I finished the year 4th in my [first-year] class out of 195 students, just about the top 2%. I graded on to the Florida Law Review. However, I never joined the journal. I was accepted as a transfer applicant at NYU, the University of Chicago, and Boalt. I chose the last option. Early in my first semester at Berkeley, I wrote on to their law review. This year I served on the editorial board.

I doubt I would have been as successful without having read *PLS* and, more importantly, taken its advice. Law school is really about teaching students a particular way of thinking—a method they call "thinking like a lawyer." Because it requires an entirely new system of thinking, this method takes a lot of hard work and many hours to grasp and master. However, once you get it, it's like riding a bicycle—you know exactly what you have to do to succeed. Everyone eventually understands the system. Some get it quickly (the "top 10%") and others pick it up second semester, or second year, or even in practice.

The biggest edge *PLS* gave me was a head-start. Reading the primers and doing LEEWS got me a significant first look into both the substantive material and the method of thought. That way things "clicked" faster than they normally may have, allowing me to enter the top ranks along with several people who, for whatever reason, in each year, are natu-rally inclined to pick up the system the quickest. I also got a head-start in beating out the psychological terror that law school can be. I knew the system I was getting myself into and could brace myself.

As I've said, I found the primers and the prep work to be extremely useful. I found the Aspen series to be absolutely necessary. I still use it to this day—in many cases in *place* of casebooks. In fact, I've often selected a course based on whether an Aspen Primer is available for that course. They're that good. Most of my friends who did very well think so too—even the ones who didn't use *PLS*.

One fantastic part of *PLS* was the mostly good advice the book gave on *which* commercial products to use. You are deluding yourself if you think you will never use books outside of your casebooks in law school. It's absolutely necessary because the casebooks simply aren't the best way to teach the law.

Everyone in my first year class quickly got on the commercial materials bandwagon—but no one had any guidance on what good and bad products were. Entire 100-person sections stared aimlessly at "Legal Lines" attempting to "cliff note" cases. None of them understood that part of the point of the case experience was to integrate the reasoning—and that doing so required you to read the cases and brief them yourself. I tried my best to subtly hint at how good the Aspen series really was; but I had no credibility.

The materials recommended in *PLS* certainly are expensive—and it definitely will mean extra work for you. But guess what: it will be worth it. The costs involved represent an insignificant initial investment when you consider the increased likelihood of your success in the law and throughout your career from doing well first year. Think about how much money and time you're already investing in law school. If an extra thousand dollars[*] and some more hours mean that you can get a lot more out of it—learn a lot more—and be more successful in your ultimate career, I think you'd be remiss not to do it.

Nevertheless, as I have written, I still worked extremely hard. There are no short-cuts to success in law school. But working really hard alone won't get you there. Working *smart* will. And that's what *PLS* and these materials helped me to do. And that's one big reason that I'm about to graduate from Boalt Hall, the #7 Law School in the Country.

Robert Brayer, J.D. (2002)
U. Cal. - Berkeley (Boalt Hall)

---

* Note from AF: Actually, as you'll see in Chapter 16, it's now just a little over $500, total, for the "must-get" items..

The State of the Planet
or
Coup d'Etat: A Practical Handbook

Writing on law schools these days runs the gamut from the seminal (*One L*) to the degenerate (*Brush with the Law*). *Planet Law School* is in a league of its own. Part memoir, part jeremiad, part how-to manual, its chief advantage might be its humility. [In the first edition,] Part I of the book [was] entitled "Landing in a Strange, Little World." The author explains professor-student dynamics in a chapter entitled "Professors: What's in it for *You* v. What's in it for *Them*." [*Note from AF*—That material is now mostly in Chapter 9, but not only there.] By putting together one of the best resource guides on law school, the author equips the prospective law student with a wealth of strategies (from the tactical to the technical) to confront her law school experience.

I was given a copy of *PLS* by a friend, and have found it to be the single best available guide to the sundry study aids and supplementary materials that stock the typical law school bookstore's bloated shelves. The author has provided list after annotated list of what he considers to be the best and most helpful resources out there, and in so doing saved me a considerable amount of time and money.

PLS also provides the law student with a playbook of successful law school strategies. The author's systematic approach to preparing for class, handling class, and preparing outside of class served me well during my first year of law school, arguably the most important of a law student's formal education. *PLS* focuses on that vital first year, and while the particulars of a legal education differ from school to school, the 1L curriculum is nearly identical no matter the school you attend.

PLS equipped me so that I was able to survive in the classroom while still being able to pursue opportunities here at Harvard Law that are very important to me: I'm the President of the Harvard Law School Federalist Society, Deputy-Editor-in-Chief of the *Harvard Journal of Law and Public Policy*, will be working this summer [2002] with two of the world's top firms, and will be clerking upon graduation for a judge on the D.C. Circuit. I feel very blessed, and part of that blessing was finding *Planet Law School* at just the right time.

Brian J. Hooper
Class of '03
Harvard Law School

Not a Magic Wand

I've heard it said that the only way to get rich from a "get-rich-quick" book is to write one. It seems that there is no correlative for law school how-to manuals. Not only is it my understanding that Mr. Falcon has yet to strike it rich on *Planet Law School's* thunder, but as a reader I have personally benefited a great deal from the content of this guide-book. I do not know Atticus Falcon personally. In fact, he still refuses to reveal to me his earthly identity. Nevertheless, as a service to the community, I wish to communicate my unqualified endorsement of the *PLS* strategy, and to share my experiences with the Way of the Falcon.

As of this writing, I am a second-year law student at New York University School of Law. My experience with *PLS* began early in the summer before I began law school at NYU. I was looking for something to read. Out of college 2 years, I was a little rusty—as a reader, that is. Sure, I could do it. I was a college graduate, after all. But I knew that law school would involve a quantity and class of reading thereto-fore unfamiliar to me. I wanted to get primed, and I had a sense that I wanted to read about law so it wouldn't be wholly unfamiliar to me when I began. But I struggled for material. I read novels about lawyers, second-class law school how-to guides, and even some works of legal nonfiction. It was good to get back into the habit of reading again, but looking back, I can't see as any of that was particularly helpful. And then I discovered *PLS* on Amazon.com.

I flew through the first edition of *PLS,* cover to cover, in a matter of days. During that time my erratic and ineffective drive to prepare for law school was transformed into a systematic campaign, with a clear roadmap and, most importantly, a list of required reading.

It was June by this time. As you've likely noticed by now, AF prescribes an expansive list of recommended materials. At such a late date, there was virtually no chance I could read them all. But I could read some. At a local law school's bookstore, I purchased Glannon on Civil Procedure from Aspen's Examples and Explanations series. I chose to begin with Civ Pro because I thought it would be the most foreign of the first year subjects from the outset. Glannon's Civil Procedure primer is a masterpiece. I can't imagine how difficult it must be for first year students to navigate Civ Pro based on a string of cases alone. Glannon is easy to read, surprisingly enjoyable for a book about an area of law devoid of substantive subject matter, and an excellent piece of groundwork upon which to build your understanding of what you will be given once law school begins

Short on time, I didn't get all the way through the Civ Pro primer on the first pass. I devoted a couple of weeks to it, but saved time to take a look at Glannon on Torts, and Blum on Contracts—also from the E&E series—during the course of the summer.

Finally, as the last few weeks of summer wound down, I read Delaney's *Learning Legal Reasoning* and did his briefing exercises. AF loves this book. I liked it. It's short enough, and worth looking at. Delaney teaches you how to look at a case. What are the most important parts? What should I be looking for? What should I be writing down? I never had a problem reading the cases, and I think Delaney deserves at least some of the credit for that. I will say this: the less you know about what goes on in a law school class and what is expected of you in law school assignments, the more helpful *Learning Legal Reasoning* will be.

Day 1 came up pretty quickly. My first class was Civil Procedure. I had read about 300 pages of Glannon's book, so I thought I would be in pretty good shape to understand my first assignments. But, wouldn't you know it, I was completely unfamiliar with the very first topic my professor chose to send at us—Judicial Standing Doctrine. (I have since learned that this is an area of law more commonly associated with classes in Constitutional Law or advanced Federal Courts.)

But there's an important lesson in this: virtually every law professor varies even basic courses in ways that cannot be predicted by the student, by Atticus Falcon, or by any primer's author. As far as I'm concerned, that's the most important reason to have the traditional parts of a law school course figured out as early as possible. Hit the ground running and you can avoid the cascading confusion crashing down around your less well-prepared classmates.

Eventually, nearly everything Glannon treats in his primer was covered in my Civ Pro class. The same was true in Torts and Contracts. Everything these books had covered came up in class. Of course, I didn't remember everything I had read over the summer as it came up. That's impossible. But as topics I had covered came up in class and in the reading, instead of being frozen in fear by new and unknown subject matter, I found much of it was familiar. When we'd be assigned cases and other students may have been wondering what to derive from each case, since I had an overview of the subject matter, it was much easier to see the main point of each case as it came up. Think about it: how much easier is it to understand something the second time you see it than it was the *first* time? There's really no room for disagreement on this point.

My professors all liked to add a little extra to the mix—your professors will have grand theories, schools of thought, modes of analysis and intellectual currents they will wish to impress upon you. There's no way to prime for that. But if you're ever going to understand it, you'd better know the basics—the Black Letter Law. Especially at "high ranking" law schools, professors love to neglect Black Letter Law to talk about their scholarly interests in a given subject matter. My Torts professor was fascinated by insurance and algebraic formulas for calculating ideal tort deterrents. My Contracts professor added a feminist critique of our casebook to the required reading. In Property, we discussed theories of judicial decision-making as thoroughly as we covered what it means to "own" something. It was generally very interesting stuff. These were smart, smart people and they made my classmates and me more thoughtful students of the law. But I can see that it may have been very easy for a student to underestimate the importance of knowing the nuts and bolts of our subjects.

Regardless of how uninterested your professor seems in Black Letter Law, it will be assumed that you have mastered it when you sit down on test day. If you have not mastered it, simply stated, you will make serious mistakes. Even for professors whose approach seems highly theoretical, it is important to be able to communicate to them in your exam that you know What the Law Is.

LEEWS provides a good system for getting this stuff down in your blue book. During your first set of law school exams in December, it is going to be easy to panic. LEEWS will give you a clear and organized way to structure an answer to a traditional issue-spotter question. The lessons of LEEWS can also be applied to other types of question you may encounter. I took the day-long course in early November with a buddy of mine from my section. We swore each other to secrecy, because it's quite a nerdy thing to be doing with your Saturday. But I think it was helpful. Again, the less you know about what to expect coming in, the more helpful LEEWS is likely to be. It's not going to turn you into a master of examsmanship overnight, but it's an important set of basic tools for exam-writing. Some people have an instinctive knack for effectively organizing the answer to a sick and twisted exam question. Many people do not. Ignore the basic tools at your peril.

I have had terrific results from my law school efforts thus far. I graded onto Law Review. Last summer [2001], I split my time between a competitive fellowship at NYU and a high-paying gig at a major, national law firm. This summer, I'm working at one of the most well-respected firms in the country. When I graduate, I am set to clerk for a judge on the U.S. Court of Appeals for the Second Circuit. In short, I have seen results.

Can Atticus Falcon and *Planet Law School* claim full credit for these accomplishments? Absolutely not. Law School is hard work, no matter what you do to prepare—and AF won't do it for you. If you are to succeed, you need to devote massive amounts of time. One NYU professor is fond of saying that if you're serious about law school, you need to give over a year of your life as a 1L to mastering the art of being a law student—and do nothing else during that year. He's right. This comes naturally to almost nobody.

PLS is not a magic wand. It is not a book of tricks, and there are no shortcuts. But the approach is sound, and it works. When you arrive on Planet Law School, you are not there for a vacation, you are there to make war and conquer. The enemy is formidable, foreign, and has vast resources aimed at making you weak. Some react by showing disrespect to classmates, by flying into a frenzied panic, or by giving up altogether. If you're serious about conquest of Planet Law School, you can never fall into any of these traps. Victory takes confidence, energy, relentless attack, and a battle plan. Forgive me my long and jingoistic metaphor, but *PLS* is an intelligent plan of attack. Stay on plan, stay focused, get up early in the morning and by December of your first year, you will see all the forces aligned against you are in complete collapse.

Many thanks, AF. You know what you're talking about.

Robert Schwartz
Class of '03
New York University School of Law

[AF—As of this writing, Robert has completed two years at NYU. He has given me permission to disclose that he has yet to receive a grade lower than A-. Further, he's one of the top ten students in the Class of 2003. (That's top ten *students*, not top ten percent.)

Quite possibly, Robert was a natural-born genius of the law, all along. But if so, he showed his genius, in part, by not taking any chances. He used "The *PLS* Approach." (Thomas Edison's most famous saying is, "Genius is *one* percent *in*spiration…and 99% *per*spiration."

Gen. Vesey and Dr. Feynman (quoted at the end of the main body of this chapter) would be proud of lawyers-to-be such as Robert Schwartz…and Brian Hooper and Robert Brayer.]

Chapter 16 - Of Dollars—and Common Sense

It just might be that you don't care about getting a starting salary of close to $200,000 a year (including the standard bonuses). Or even if you're not interested in a big-bucks job after law school, perhaps you're also not interested in getting a big merit scholarship. In either case, maybe you aren't concerned about doing well in law school. —But if you took out loans to pay for it, your pre-graduate indifference to the "green" might turn into post-graduate "blues" with astonishing speed when you have to start "servicing" your debt.

Yet, whether you're in an organization (law firm, government agency, or NGO/non-profit) that's large or small, whether you're on salary or living off contingency fees, you'd better have learned how to do a good lawyerlike analysis in law school anyway. Otherwise, the other side will "kill" you. Don't know about you, but I *hate* to lose, even when I took the case at no charge. (And if you screw up often enough on the job, you'll soon be *out* of a job.)

I'll bet half the people in law school didn't really want to go there. They went because they couldn't find anything else to do that satisfied them. Law school just was the "least bad" option. Typically, they got a college degree in a major with no marketable value. Then they didn't want to accept the consequences of that choice. And they bought into the myth of the J.D. as the "all-purpose" degree. So there they are, in law school, basically just "marking time." And after they graduate, they'll continue just to "mark time" in whatever jobs they have.

These people will not be competition to you (whether as law students or lawyers)...except for the very few, the very fortunate, who really are "natural-born geniuses of the law."

I also guess that about a third of those who are in law school are there because they think Law is a glamorous career. They've watched various lawyer TV shows and movies, and decided, "Hey! That's for *me!*" What they want is what they fancy will be an "exciting lifestyle." They were often too snobbish to consider business school (which is the only other place you can go to after college with absolutely no preparation for it)—and wanted to be able to say, "*I am an attorney.*" And when they get into law school, and discover how much work it is, they too eventually just mark time. They too (with the exception as noted above) will be no competition to you.

The remaining sixteen percent or so are divided into several groups, but I am not going to take up your time to discuss them here. Even though I've mocked those who say, "I wanted to be a lawyer since I was 12 years old," the fact is, I did too. That's called having a "fire in the belly." This is not to say people should go to law school only if they see it as a calling. But your competition will mostly come from those who take it seriously—i.e., fewer than 20% of your classmates, even at the top schools. **It's easy to beat a 2.7-3.2 forced curve, if you know what you're doing. But even if you know what you're doing, it isn't so easy to get into one of the top slots.** And, truth be told, the more people who read *PLS*—and *follow through* on it—the stiffer the competition at the top will become. (At a *professional* school, the curve itself is an abomination. But that's a battle for another day.)

The "do-it-yourself" items recommended in Chapters 2, 4, and 6 can get you where you need to be. But it really is up to you. All the substantive materials listed below will be of value to you as reference materials even when you are a practicing attorney. As for the reasoning and examsmanship materials, they will help you develop *skills* that will be of value to you as a practicing attorney.

Investing in Your Success

"MUST GET" MATERIALS for FIRST-YEAR

Delaney Books*:* JohnDelaneyPub.com   (No orders by phone.)
  Learning Legal Reasoning $29 (including shipping)
  How to Do Your Best on Law School Exams $32 (including shipping)
  (If ordered together, the two books are $55.35 including shipping)

American Bar Association Books - $30 each   abanet.org   (800) 285-2221
  Miller & Cilke, *The ABCs of the UCC — Article 1: General Provisions* (product #5070306*)*
  Gabriel & Rusch, *The ABCs of the UCC — Article 2: Sales* (product #5070312)

Aspen Books $35 each   aspenpub.com   (800) 234-1660
  Blum, *Contracts, 2nd ed.*
  Glannon, *The Law of Torts, 2nd ed.*
  Glannon, *Civil Procedure, 4th ed.*
  May & Ides, *Constitutional Law: National Powers & Federalism, 2nd ed.*
    (Note: at some schools, Con Law is not required.)

The CALI "Library of Lessons" http://lessons.cali.org/catalog.html
  $20 - Many law chools make it available for free, once you're in.
  But I *urge* you to get it *before*, to get a head start. It's worth the $20.

Choices in Property and Criminal Law

Property:
Burke & Snoe, *Property* $35 (Aspen E&E primer) (My preference)
or
Boyer, Hovenkamp, & Kurtz, *The Law of Property: An Introductory Survey,* 5th ed. $43 (West Publishing) westgroup.com (800) 328-9352

Crim:
Delaney, *Criminal Law Applied: Arguments, Exams, and Answers.* $26 (My preference)(Forthcoming, fall 2003),
     or
Singer & La Fond, *Criminal Law* $35 (Aspen E&E primer)

LEEWS (Legal Essay Exam Writing System) leews.com (800) 765-8246
Tapes or Live Program, & Manual - $100 (max.)
(Group discounts available, which can reduce the price to $80.)
Note: for an extra $50, you can get the tapes *and* do the live program. The live program is only during the academic year. I recommend getting the tapes during the summer and listening to them (and reading the manual). Then, if there's a live program nearby soon after you start law school, it would be good for you to attend, as a refresher.

STRONGLY RECOMMENDED for FIRST-YEAR

American Law Institute Books (ALI/ABA) ali.org (800) 253-6397
Restatement (Second) of Contracts - ***STUDENT*** *Edition* $46.
These are sold as a set of 3 "pamphlets" product #5152

Restatement (Second) of Torts - ***STUDENT*** *Edition* $69.50
There are 4 "pamphlets." The product numbers are a bit odd.
"Pamphlets" 1 & 2 are a set, with product #5207.
"Pamphlet" 3 has product #5208, and the fourth is product #5415.
The price listed is for all four, together.

Legal Research
I am not *recommending* that before you start law school you get a primer for legal research. You need to put your time in on these other materials. However, several students have asked for a recommendation. I don't have any favorites. Everything I've seen has been good. Any bookstore for law students will have a variety of titles on this. All are in paperback, and are priced around $25.

RECOMMENDED - SUPPLEMENTAL EXAMSMANSHIP MATERIALS

I am not saying you should necessarily get *all* the following. But you should seriously consider getting at least some of them. Your choice.

Finals Law School Exam Series   discovery-press.com
  (800) 200-7110 (outside L.A. only - inside L.A. check local listing)
  Separate book for each subject, @ $28.

Study Partner - Exam Series bsmsphd.com   (800) 743-7394
  lawbooks@adelphia.net
  "Exam-writing Secrets" - on the webpage, tips to download, free.
  The "issues" books are $15 each; the "exams" books, $19 each.
  Exam Writing I - Torts, Contracts, & Crim Law (Substantive)
  Issue-Spotting I - same
  Exam Writing II - Civ Pro, Prop, & Evidence
  Issue-Spotting II - same
  Exam Writing III - Con Law, Crim Pro, & Corporations
  Issue-Spotting III - same

(Emanuel's) "Crunch Time" Books - By subject, @ $18.
  Essay questions, short-answer questions, and multiple-choice questions, with answers.

* * *

Even if you take Con Law in first-year (and thus have to get that book), and even if you get all these materials at the *list* price (and do not take advantage of multiple-item purchase discounts), and even if you choose only the *higher*-priced alternative presented as to prop law and crim law, your total cost is $459 for the "Must Get" materials, and another $115.50 for the *Restatements,* for a grand total of $574.50 (excluding the supplemental examsmanship materials).

If you're graduating from college, perhaps you could get these items as a graduation present. Sure, they're not as exciting as a new car or a trip to Europe. But in the long run, they'll help you get the wherewithal to pay for *many* new cars and *many* trips to Europe, if you wish. (Besides, a car will cost you several thousand dollars a year for insurance, gas, and routine maintenance. These books would be a graduation present that would eventually put money into your pocket instead of taking money out of it.)

You are about to go off in a significant new direction in your life. Sort of like getting married. And when a couple gets married, the bride "registers her pattern" so people who want to give china or crystal can get together and divvy up who will buy what. (I've never been through this process, but am told that's how it works.) Perhaps you could work something similar regarding these books, as you head toward law school. So, photocopy these pages and give them to whoever's asking you what you want for a graduation present.

FOR the "KILLER MATERIALS"

Except for the Moynihan/Kurtz, you can wait and see if you need them:

Prop - Estates & Future Interests

Moynihan/Kurtz, *Introduction to the Law of Real Property: An Historical Background of the Law of Real Property and Its Modern Applications, 3rd ed.* $34 (West) westgroup.com (800) 328-9352

Edwards, Linda Holdeman, *Estates in Land and Future Interests: A Step-by-Step Guide.* $30 (Aspen) - See information above if you wish to order directly from Aspen.

Laurence & Minzer ("L&M"), *A Student's Guide to Estates in Land and Future Interests, 2ⁿᵈ ed.* $24 (Matthew Bender/Lexis Publishing) bookstore.lexis.com (800) 223-1940

Makdisi, *Estates in Land and Future Interests: Problems & Answers, 3ʳᵈ ed.* $30 (Aspen)

Nelson & Wendel, *A Possessory Estates and Future Interests Primer,* $22. (West) - See Moynihan/Kurtz book, above, for direct order info.

Schwartz, *A Student's Guide to the Rule Against Perpetuities* $24 (Mathew Bender/Lexis Publishing) - See L&M book, above, for direct order information.

Prop - Other

Siegel, *A Student's Guide to Easements, Real Covenants, and Equitable Servitudes, 2ⁿᵈ ed.* $24 (Matthew Bender/Lexis Publishing)

Civ Pro

O'Connor, *O'Connor's Federal Rules - Civil Trials* (updated edition each year) STUDENT DISCOUNT PRICE: $31 (including shipping). Jones-McClure Publishing) jonesmcclure.com (800) 626-6667

OTHER SUPPLEMENTAL MATERIALS

Get any of these only if you really want to dig further into a subject—

Chirelstein, *Concepts and Case Analysis in the Law of Contracts, 4th ed.* $25 Foundation Press (West)   fdpress.com

Johnson, *Mastering Torts, 2nd ed.* $25   Carolina Academic Press cap-press.com   (919) 489-7486

Dittfurth, *The Concepts and Methods of Federal Civil Procedure* $20 Carolina Academic Press

Various authors, Legal Text Series: *Understanding [various subjects]* Matthew Bender/Lexis Publishing   (See above for contact info.)

* * *

As mentioned, Chapter 17 will discuss books on legal research; and also legal reasoning and legal writing. The addendum to Chapter 19 will discuss Resources for Future Litigators.

But if you get them now and try to read them now, you'll be biting off more than you can chew. As it is—and as you will see from the addendum to this chapter—you have plenty enough to do.

Some General Websites for Books

amazon.com	barnsterbooks.com	eBay.com
barnesandnoble.com	bestwebbuys.com	half.com
	discoverypress.com	lawswap.com

Problems with Ordering

In the past five years, many people have reported problems ordering some of these materials.

There have been those who even posted nasty reviews of *PLS* to Amazon.com, saying that the books *PLS* recommends are not available. Apparently some general vendors *still* list some of these books as "out-of-print." But the people who complained to Amazon obviously did not attempt to contact the publishers, even though *PLS* provided information on how to do so.

There have even been problems with Aspen. Until quite recently, their own website did not list any of the volumes in its E&E series. That has been corrected...sort of. As of this writing, you have to look under each area of the law to find the primer. They are not listed together on their own page, the way Matthew Bender/Lexis Publishing lists its *Student Guide* series on one page. (And as of this writing, the new primer on property is not listed at all.) Even so, be sure you have the authors' names and the exact titles when you enter the website. Look for the words "Examples and Explanations" as the subtitle.

ALI/ABA, the only source for the *Restatements,* also is a problem sometimes. They might split your order up into separate shipments, weeks apart. You might get two or three volumes from one *Restatement,* and one volume from the other, in the first shipment. Then the rest follow in a second, or even third, shipment. Always check the packing slip to make sure they know they still owe you some books, if you haven't received everything the first time around.

I have not heard of any problems when students have ordered from any of the other publishers. But if you have no luck with their websites, try calling their toll-free numbers.

And, of course, you can probably get these books from any of the general book vendors listed above...although some still don't give the correct information regarding Delaney's.

If you're having difficulty ordering books, please check more than one source. If you do not receive books you've ordered, and the vendor is proving unhelpful, you can e-mail me about it, if you wish. I'll do what I can to try to get them to clean up their act. If necessary, I would publicize the problem in my new column on the Net. (When people had repeated problems getting Aspen to ship their orders in 2001, even after the new editions were available, exposure in the column got prompt action.)

You Can Lead a Horse to Water

Based on e-mails I've received and message board postings I've seen, the people who don't make use of the independent study materials *PLS* recommends fall into five groups.

The first is composed of those who don't like *PLS* itself. They sometimes say, "*PLS* is just a book that tells you to buy lots of other books." I leave it to you to decide the accuracy of that observation, especially regarding this new edition. But, having supposedly gotten "burned" on *PLS,* they're not about to spend money on anything it recommends.

The second consists of those who like *PLS*, and could afford to buy the recommended items, but think it a waste of time even more so than money. I might be making a hasty generalization here that is entirely inappropriate, but there seems to be a pattern along gender lines within this group. A disproportionately large number of e-mails from women say, "I'm relieved just to have gotten into law school. I know I could *never* be a top student. I'll be happy just to get the law degree, pass the bar exam, and get a job as a lawyer." Such little self-confidence, after doing what it takes to get into law school in the first place, astounds me.

A disproportionately large number of e-mails from men say (expressly or tacitly), "I do not need to prep. I might consult one of the primers if I run into a point of law I don't understand. But I expect that to be rare. And I will cross that bridge if and when I get to it." Ah! A natural-born genius of the law!

In short, it really does appear that at least some women are too intimidated to try to learn to read a map, while at least some men are too "macho" to ask for directions.

The third group is composed of those who object to the total cost of these items. "I can't afford these," they insist.

Oh, really?

Years ago, a study was published about departmental budget committees at corporations. At each company, half a dozen low-level managers from various departments routinely met to allocate their budget. The people who monitored the process reported that the committees usually spent hours wrangling over little things, such as what paper cups to buy for coffee—an item that cost several hundred dollars, at most. But they'd typically spent less than 30 minutes allocating several hundred thousand dollars for "big ticket" items such as training programs.

The observers concluded that what happens is this: people spend the most time on what they're familiar with. And that means things within the realm of their personal experience. Everyone on all those committees had, in their personal lives, allocated several thousand dollars—but not hundreds of thousands. And so they lingered over the small stuff..(But as then-Senate Minority Leader, Everett Dirksen, Republican of Illinois, once remarked: "A billion here, a billion there— pretty soon you're talking about real money.")

The future law students mentioned above think absolutely nothing of forking over $20,000 or more a *year*, for tuition—plus another $10,000 or more for food and lodging, and hundreds of dollars for casebooks...and giving up potential income by becoming full-time law students. Yet, they begrudged a few hundred dollars for do-it-yourself materials that could literally prove worth *millions* of dollars to them.*

Part of the problem is an "easy come, easy go" attitude with respect to financial aid. Many students take out large federally guaranteed student loans. Often, the check gets mailed directly to the student's school. The student then shows up and endorses the check over to the school. The student sees the check for all of about 10 seconds. In the student's mind, it's not *his* or *her* money. The money never really went into their pockets, so—in their own minds—the money never really came *out* of their own pockets. It all happened so fast, "now-you-see-it, now-you-don't," and was so smoothly done. After that, they don't think of the day of reckoning, when they have to pay those loans back (with interest). Nor do they think of whether or not they really get their money's worth from the law school that just tapped them for a bundle (and will tap them again, and again).

But in the meantime, "The *PLS* Approach" urges them to take money from their own pockets (several hundred dollars of it, in fact) long before the financial aid check comes in. And they have a real problem with that. The LEEWS course costs, at most, around a hundred bucks. With the group-discount option, students can bring the price of LEEWS down to as little as eighty bucks. Yet, few students go to the trouble of rounding up a group. They'd rather moan and groan about having to pay "so much" for a course that, by itself, could be worth a fortune to them, as a return on their investment. But that's all out-of-sight, out-of-mind to them. All they can see, and think of, is what's right in front of their faces: a hundred dollars, about to go from their pocket into Miller's. (Miller has raised his prices by only five dollars in something like the last decade. His program is a "steal" for what he charges. He really isn't in it to get rich. The guy just loves to teach...and loves to thumb his nose at the legal education Establishment.)

There's an expression, "Penny wise, pound foolish." (The "pound" is as in British currency, the pound sterling.) People who balk at paying for the resources listed in *PLS* are often both pound and "*penny*" foolish.

These same people will almost certainly panic after they've been

---

* By the way, this same pattern of sticking with the familiar is, as Chapters 2 and 3 mentioned, a big reason for students' poor performance in law school. What they're familiar with is the old "memorize-and-regurgitate" mode of scholarship. At some very deep level, they would rather stick to what they're comfortable with than venture into the new realm of "thinking like a lawyer." Then they pay the price, and say, "Gee, I guess I must not be so smart after all." They're right—though not for the reasons they think.

in law school awhile—probably about the time they realize final exams are fast approaching. Then they'll grab anything and everything they can get their hands on, and will spend far more than is recommended here. The law school "study aids" industry knows this. That's why so many study "aids" are worthless.*

And that's also why I've constantly tried to evaluate everything I can get *my* hands on, and to recommend to you only the ones I think are truly worthwhile (and cost-effective). But even those who, late in the semester, end up buying only what *PLS* recommends will find that they are doing too little, too late. They won't have time to make effective use of what they've bought...in part because these students will be too frazzled (the "deer caught in the headlights" syndrome).

This brings us to the fourth group, the largest by far: those who bought the primers, or got the LEEWS program on tape...but then never followed through.

Some e-mails to me have said, "I took the LEEWS course, but didn't do well. So, LEEWS is pure hype." I then question those students as to what they actually did. Typically, those who respond say something like this: "I bought the tapes, and listened to about half of them." Sometimes they say they even listened to all of them. Regardless, it turns out that they never read the LEEWS manual. Or else it's this:

---

*   A funny thing happened while the manuscript for the first edition of *PLS* was in progress: the firm that was going to publish it got a call from a high corporate executive at a *major* publishing firm. He'd heard that *Planet Law School* was in the works, and wanted to buy the title. Not the manuscript, just the title. He thought that the title, all by itself, would sell a lot of copies of the book. (He was probably right about that.)

During the conversation with the head of The Fine Print Press, Ltd. (my publisher), the man said his firm's name was so well-respected, and its market penetration was so high, that they could "move" several thousand copies of *anything* for law students. It was just a matter of getting the books onto the store shelves. They weren't concerned about the quality of their products, just the profits.

Having read some of their books before I started law school (and more, that have been published since I graduated), I completely agree the major publisher in question is only in it for the money. *PLS* was written largely as a rebuke to the mentality of that firm, and of others like it (and there are many). I hope you will agree that this new edition (as with the original) fully lives up to its title, including the subtitle. And I hope that, for once, future law students will get what they paid for when it comes to a book about how to succeed in law school.

"I attended the live program." But then, come to find out, they only skimmed the LEEWS manual afterwards (if that). None of these people worked old exams until shortly before their finals. Nor did they ever practice the 'Ugly But Effective' writing method, at all.

One woman wrote to say, "Every night for several nights, before law school, I'd start a LEEWS tape when I went to bed, and fell asleep listening to it. I went through all of them that way." That was it.

As a dear friend of mine says, such a person is "Too stupid to live"—or, at least, is too stupid to be worthy of law school in the first place. If she bought any of the primers, I'll bet she stuck a copy under her pillow every night, and then expected that her brain would somehow absorb the text as she slept.

There are those who say they've "read" the Aspen primers...but they did not work the examples. Their comments always go something like this: "I didn't want to waste time, so I just read the questions and then skipped ahead to the answers." Or, "I ignored the questions and answers completely, because I felt I'd gotten what I needed just from reading the text."

One guy complained about the difficulties he was having working an old exam. I urged him to get a copy of Delaney's examsmanship book, ASAP. He wrote back: "I already have that. But I haven't read it yet. I'll take a look at it this weekend." This was *two weeks* before his final exams were to start. "Take a *look* at it"??!!

This seems to be an example of a common American attitude, the opposite of the "cheapskate." This attitude, instead, says the solution to a problem is to throw money at it. Apparently, a huge number of law students somehow believe that if they have "paid good money" for the primers, or LEEWS, and gone through the material once, then that, all by itself, should be enough. It doesn't occur to them that they need to follow through—actually *work*—to make the most of their investment.

I worked in a bookstore for a summer while in high school. Several regular customers were obese. They'd buy a diet book...and a month or so later, another. I asked some of them what they thought of a diet book they'd bought earlier. The responses would always be something like this: "Oh, it says to eat a lot of fruits, but I got tired of eating so much fruit." "It says not to eat chocolate cake. But I just *love* chocolate cake!" "It says to take a vigorous walk for at least 15 minutes every day. But I don't have time for that." *Et cetera*.

Those people were not serious about losing weight. And they apparently fantasized, deep in their hearts, that just by *reading the book* (and maybe even just by *buying* it) *that alone should do*. They had enough diet books and diet cookbooks to fill shelves. But they'd wasted their money on all of them...not because the books weren't good, but because these people did not want to do the work necessary to effectively *use* what was *in* the books.*

Some of them were well-to-do enough that they then spent thousands of dollars on "fat camps" or liposuction as a relatively quick way of dealing with their obesity. —But, of course, they'd have to go through it again, eventually, because they had no self-discipline...which is to say, they were not *sincerely* motivated to do what needed to be done. (There are, of course, many whose medical or genetic condition makes the obesity inescapable, but the discussion here has nothing to do with that.)

—Which brings me to the fifth (and final) group of those who eschew the primers, etc...

BarBri's Law School Prep Program & Law Preview

Several then-future law students e-mailed to say, "Well, I had to decide between, on the one hand, going to Law Preview or BarBri's Law School Prep program, and, on the other hand, paying for the books and LEEWS as *PLS* recommended. I decided to go with the former. Sorry, Atticus." I'm sorry too...sorry for *them*.

Each of these so-called "law school before law school" programs can involve total expenses that can be as much as *four times* the cost of the "do-it-yourself" materials *PLS* recommends. So these people's preference makes no sense, even if these programs were good. I don't think they are.

Despite their claims, Law Preview and BarBri do not prepare you for law school. They're a week-long "feel-good" program where, at best, you get a mild taste of the Socratic/Case Method in mock law school classes. The professors are (usually) friendly, and (for obvious reasons) keep everything at a *really* rudimentary level. More important, there isn't sufficient time for them to cover substantive material, show students how to do a lawyerlike analysis, and then give a mock law school exam and do a detailed post-mortem on it.

---

* Reminds me of people who have shelves full of "pop psychology" "self-help" books, but who never change their ways...or people who think they're "preparing" for law school by getting and reading *every* "how to succeed in law school" book—but who then do nothing else.

And, of course, the law school profs BarBri and Law Preview bring in are not about to let the cat out of the bag. They adhere to the professoriat's Code of Silence. While these programs *appear* to be like law school, they have almost nothing in common with what law school is *really* all about. As said earlier in this book, what goes on in class is just a way to fill the time until finals.

Yes, they spend some time on how to do your own outline. But you can get that from reading Chapter 4 of this book, and even more from the chapter on outlining in Delaney's examsmanship book.

Yes, they have a day-long program in legal writing. (For BarBri, it's part of their five-day program. For Law Preview, it's an extra day after the five-day program, at additional cost.) But one day is not enough to master legal writing, or even to get a basic introduction to it.

That said: of the two, Law Preview is not as bad as BarBri's Law School Prep program. For one thing, with Law Preview students get Aspen's E&E primer on Civ Pro, and also some commercial Black Letter Law outlines. BarBri used to provide a full set of commercial Black Letter Law outlines, a law dictionary, and some other materials. But now their website no longer mentions these.

Further, Law Preview sends out their materials to reach you two weeks before the program begins. You are expected to read approximately 200 pages of that material in order to "hit the deck running" and to make the most of your investment. In contrast, the rep I spoke with at BarBri said that its Law School Prep program wants students to enter "feeling just like they do on the first day of law school: confused, and lost." So, what BarBri does is mail you a copy of an appellate judicial opinion. You're to read that opinion, and will then be called on to discuss it. (Of course, the program then teaches you how to "brief" that case...as though that will be any real help to you, especially considering that any Black Letter Law commercial outline that includes case briefs will do that for you.)

Also, the founders of Law Preview are on-site, sitting in on every class at every location. This helps keep the profs focused (for what little that's worth). And Law Preview tells which profs will be at each location. BarBri, in contrast, lists a faculty with big-name-school credentials. But only a handful of these professors will be at any given site. BarBri does not say (on its website or in its brochures) who will be at each program. When I spoke with the rep at BarBri home office, only a few weeks before its various programs were to begin, the rep could not tell me who would be where. It makes me wonder if perhaps some of its illustrious professors do not actually teach for BarBri at all in certain years, despite being listed as faculty every year.

More important, BarBri uses Charles Whitebread to teach examsmanship. Yet, as his book on the subject makes clear, he advocates only the IRAC method. Law Preview, in contrast, has Jeremy Paul on its faculty. He's a co-author of *Getting to Maybe,* the examsmanship book—which has a devastating and succinct critique of IRAC.

Most important of all, BarBri engages in misleading practices. The first edition of *PLS* had complained of the practices of what was then called NILE—the National Institute of Legal Education. BarBri later bought NILE. For a time, the program was called "BarBri/NILE." Now it is called only "The BarBri Law School Prep Program." The original edition of *PLS* had complained about two of NILE's practices. Of those two, one has changed, sort of. The other has not. (And there are more.)

PLS "1" noted that what was then just NILE had a blurb from "Professor M. Kaufman, Loyola Chicago School of Law." The blurb said, "I had several NILE students in my first-year classes and they clearly had a competitive edge from the very first day." Later in that same brochure, NILE said one of its teachers was "Professor Michael J. Kaufman...a Professor of Law at Loyola University of Chicago School of Law." So, the "Professor M. Kaufman," supposedly giving his objective opinion (or her—clever the way they tried to disguise him at first by not giving his full name the way they did later) was *on their payroll.* Maybe the reason why his students "had a competitive edge *from the very first day"* (emphasis added) is because Kaufman *recognized* them as being among those he'd "taught" just a few weeks previously. Shame on NILE. And shame on Michael Kaufman. (I hope he's not been teaching legal *ethics* at Chicago Loyola.)

I cannot claim that the censure in *PLS1* had anything to do with the change, but BarBri/NILE then used the same quotation and immediately identified Kaufman as one of its faculty. His statement was still misleading, though. I do not know how large his first-year classes at Chicago Loyola were, but on "the first day of class" he would not be calling on more than a handful of students. Perhaps he made it a point to get the names of his students who have completed BarBri/NILE, and then called on one or two of them in addition to one or two students who did not take BarBri/NILE. I doubt it, though.

If he was trying to establish a causal relationship between BarBri/NILE and its students' purported "competitive edge," he would know that his proof does not rise above the level of a scintilla of evidence. Kaufman apparently went straight into teaching from a judicial clerkship. So, apparently, he has never been a trial attorney, and has never had to provide "proof of facts." What he has provided as testimony here, as an "offer of proof," does not even pass "the giggle test." In a court of law, this witness would be "impeached for bias." Yet, he and BarBri/NILE presented it in support of the program. At the very least, his endorsement still does not pass "the smell test" of ethics.

Further, as he and all law school faculty members know, the only competitive edge that counts in the first year of law school is one that results in higher grades. BarBri (and Law Preview) present many testimonial blurbs from law students who've supposedly taken the program, but identifies none of them by their full name. Anyone who is seriously considering the program should wonder just how well BarBri's (and Law Preview's) participants did *on their exams,* as opposed to how confidently they (allegedly) performed in class discussions.

Another matter: BarBri/NILE listed, as one of its faculty, David Sokolow, and said he's a "professor" at the University of Texas law school—thus implying that he's a full professor. *PLS1* criticized what was then just NILE for this, because Sokolow's title was just "assistant adjunct instructor." (*PLS1* did not disclose his name, though.) As Chapter 9 notes, that's quite different from a full prof. But BarBri/NILE *continued* to list him as a "professor" at the University of Texas. Granted, the man had received a promotion in the meantime. But he's still not a professor, nor even tenure-track. His title now is "senior lecturer." There's nothing like misrepresenting the "goods" to potential customers, is there?

Granted, if the guy can teach, his title is irrelevant. But what bothers me is why BarBri/NILE apparently went *out of its way to mislead students.* It's almost as though they really enjoy being sneaky just for the sake of it. Yet, if the program were entirely "on the up-and-up," *why play their own version of hide-the-ball in order to get business?*

The web site for BarBri's Law School Prep Program claims that you will "Learn the legal concepts and terminology for each course in the first year law school curriculum". Given that the program lasts five days, with one day devoted to legal writing, that means the Big Six courses the program covers are dealt with in just four days. No doubt students learn *some* concepts and terminology. But they can hardly get more than a smattering. BarBri also claims that students will "take practice exams in every course." That's "exams," plural, "in *every* course." Even just two "exams" of a mere *30 minutes* each would take an entire day. So that means an average of, at most, half-a-day of substantive instruction per course.

Most ridiculously of all, BarBri's web site proclaims its students "Develop a national network of contacts with law professors and law students." *What* "network"? And of what *possible* value are these alleged "contacts"? BarBri apparently thinks that future law school students—its prospective customers—are astonishingly gullible.

The bottom line regarding Law Preview and BarBri's Law School Prep Program is: if you're heading for law school in the fall, don't go to either of these programs, until and unless they can prove (giving students' names) that participants in their programs did better on first-year exams, to a statistically significant degree, than those who did not participate. The tuition alone is about $900, for just five days. Lodging and meals (and possibly air fare) can easily bring the total cost up to $2,000. You have better things to do with your time, energy, and money. Usually, there really isn't much time left, after you take the program, before law school starts. And the materials they give you are too little, too late.

BUT, if you are still in college, or have long been out of law school, and are just *thinking* about going to law school, AND if you (or your parent/s) don't mind blowing two grand on your musing, then one of these programs (Law Preview) might not be a total waste for you. Even so, you'd do better just to take a week and visit a law school and sit in on every class in each course for that week. (If you're working full-time, maybe you can sit in on evening classes somewhere.) Talk with students *who've taken some exams and gotten their grades back*. See how you feel. It will cost you less, and will be more useful.

CLEO

As near as I can tell, the worst hokum in law school prep programs is CLEO. The acronym stands for "Council on Legal Education Opportunity." It's funded mostly (perhaps entirely) by the American Bar Association (and its offices are housed in the ABA building in Washington, D.C.). CLEO puts on summer programs at law schools around the country, supposedly to help minority students prep. The program lasts six weeks. The faculty varies from site to site, and appears to mostly come from the hosting school.

"Low income" students pay $200, which covers everything: tuition, room, board, and materials. Those who are not low income pay $2,000— which is still a good deal...if taken at face value. Further, low-income students who attend are *paid* to do so, receiving a stipend. And through various funds, their law school expenses are also paid, nearly in full. Now that certainly *is* a good deal...or is it?

I've now seen course materials from three CLEO programs. (The programs are site-unique, not standardized.) They are very, very bad. Quite often, the materials are from professors at the hosting law schools, and are mostly low-quality photocopies of materials the profs had obviously prepared for other uses, in some cases years earlier. They are certainly not effective teaching materials. My hunch is that the profs (and the hosting schools) get a bundle of money from the ABA for what they're doing. But what they're doing is leading students down the primrose path.

A black student who'd gone through the program sent me an e-mail that said, in part:

> *The program...sucked. I guess the only benefit*
> *I got out of it is the financial aid they give to us*
> *CLEO Fellows. This year, for example, [thanks to]*
> *their scholarship check, I have only about $1,000*
> *in debt for the first year of law school. However,*
> *the quality of the program was shoddy. In the end,*
> *even though I am not paying much for law school,*
> *the disadvantages are that CLEO started me off on*
> *the wrong foot. I would now rather have incurred*
> *the extra debt if it meant getting better grades first*
> *semester. And I think I could have gotten better*
> *grades if I had not participated in the CLEO program.*

—But only if she'd used "The *PLS* Approach." Those six weeks are too valuable to waste on CLEO, but you still have to put them to good use.

There are those who will say "You can't please everybody," and that this student is a disgruntled ingrate. But the same criticism that applies to BarBri's Law School Prep Program and Law Preview applies to CLEO: until and unless they can prove (giving students' names) that participants in their programs did better, to a statistically significant degree, on first-year exams than comparable students who did not participate in these programs, there is nothing to show CLEO is worthwhile.

I know there are those who've gone through the CLEO program and attained prominence. But I believe them to be merely the exceptions that prove the rule. As Chapter 14 said, just because someone goes far after doing the *wrong* thing, that is not proof of a causal relationship. I believe such people succeeded *in spite of,* not *because* of, their participation in CLEO.

The Texas Program (Mostly) for Hispanics

There's another program I'm aware of. It's mostly for Mexican-American students. It's put on by the University of Texas School of Law. The law school itself is in Austin, but the program is at the university's El Paso campus ("UTEP"). I don't know if it's open to students from around the country, or only to those in Texas.

It's in two parts of a month each. Students who want to go to law school take it one month at a time. They can do the whole program in one summer, or split it up, one month in each of two summers. I do not know what it costs, if anything. The first month is devoted to LSAT examsmanship. The second is a prep program for law school itself.

I've seen the law school prep materials. It does not surprise me that a law school would have these trusting kids prepare for law school by reading *Plato* and *Aristotle*.

***

I could understand white racists putting on a program that's actually a fraud, to supposedly "help" minority students. That's an old, old story in race relations. But when faculty who belong to the minority groups themselves sell out in order to feast aboard a gravy train such as the ABA's (and to perhaps get hired at prestigious law schools), it makes me sick. The newfound (and erroneous) sense of self-confidence most of their students will have after taking these programs will probably be shattered when they encounter the reality of law school.

In-House Programs

A handful of law schools now offer in-house "prep" programs. They charge for this, of course. I've received e-mails from several students who've been through such programs. A couple of them sent me copies of the materials the programs used. From what I've seen and heard, these programs run a close third behind CLEO and UTEP as to uselessness. But on a cost/benefit basis, they *might* be worth more than BarBri's Law Prep Program and Law Preview—*if* you're going to law school in the town where you already live and thus don't have to pay for room, board, and airfare, or if the program is given immediately before you'd start law school and you'd be in that town anyway.

How to Save Money

Having exhorted you to spend several hundred dollars on materials for independent study, here are some suggestions on how to offset that expense.

CASEBOOKS

As for casebooks, the simple truth is you don't need to buy any. Repeat: you do not need to buy any of the assigned casebooks.

No, that doesn't mean you should steal them, or mooch other students' copies. Just think it through: no matter how efficient your professors are, they'll never cover more than a *small* fraction of the material in the casebooks. And *once you've finished the course,* you'll never again have any use for the casebook, because a casebook is *worthless* as a reference tool. So you're paying a lot for very little.

The casebooks are *expensive.* I've received several reports now from students who had to pay $70 for the casebook—and then had to buy a paperback supplement...for *another* $20.

And many casebook authors do "trivially new" editions in order to "obsolete" the old. They change the pagination a bit, add a small amount of new text (always a new preface, of course), and that's about it. Then their fellow professors assign the *new* edition to students, instead of using the old edition—which students could then have bought second-hand for, at most, half the cost of the new.

Books for lawyers, in contrast, come with a slot in the back for "pocket parts." These are updates in the form of pamphlets, to keep the book current until the next edition. Casebook publishers could do likewise, instead of issuing required "supplements" that have to be bought separately. (True, books for lawyers cost much more than casebooks, and even the pocket parts are expensive. But if professors cared about holding students' costs down, it would be easy for them to insist on pocket parts. —And it would also be easy for them to insist that casebooks not have 1,300 pages in them when the profs know damned well they'll never cover more than a few hundred of those pages. The added pages, of course, help "justify" the exorbitant price of the casebook.)

(On my "To Do" list is a research project, to get copies of the current and most recent previous edition of all the major casebooks. Then I will compare the old and the new, and report on the changes, listing the casebooks by title, author, and publisher...and also, if possible, listing the law school professors who require their students to buy the new editions.)

Sure, you might be able to sell them back to the bookstore when the courses they were used for are over. (Maybe...but only if they aren't about to be replaced by newer editions. And even if they're still current, you get back—at most—only one-fourth of what you paid for them.)

And they're *heavy.* If you feel you just aren't a proper law student unless you're lugging around 40 pounds of nearly useless books, you have an unfortunate psychological condition *this* book cannot cure.

Granted, if you buy your casebooks on CDs and print out the assigned cases as you need them, you've solved the weight problem...but not the problem of cost. However, you might even be able to sell your CDs back to the bookstore (or to another student).

For those of you who are practical (and dare I say, "wise"?), your law school's library should have at least one copy of the edition of your casebook that your prof has assigned. Look at the cases there, for free. If you want to have the casebook's edited text with you when you go to class, make a photocopy in the library. Or make a deal with a fellow student to photocopy out of his or her book. (Commercial copy shops generally charge much less per copy than libraries do—especially law school libraries.)

Of course, you're not supposed to photocopy copyrighted material. And as an attorney, I absolutely must advise you not to engage in a no-no. I am just saying you *can* photocopy the pages, not that you *should.* And, as mentioned, you should not. Definitely not. But no matter what you spend on photocopying, it would be a lot less than the cost of the casebook.

If the prof calls on you in class, it's unlikely he or she will even notice that you don't have the casebook itself with you. It would be astonishing if a prof upbraided you for using photocopies—because, for all the prof knows, the pages might be print-outs from a CD sold by the casebook publisher. And you will probably be called on only once, anyway, from the first day through the last of your course (unless you volunteer—which, as Chapter 11 said, you should not). You will not be penalized on your final grade even if you get "caught" without a hardbound casebook.

Don't buy the casebooks. Of course, it is your right to spend your money as you see fit. And if you have money to burn, and want to burn through $250 or more *per semester* to buy casebooks for just a handful of courses, well, that's your choice.

At least consider using only photocopies during your first week of classes. If you decide to buy the casebooks after that, fine. (Of course, by then all the used copies will be gone; you'll have to pay full price.)

I know from experience that most readers will ignore the preceding advice. So here's a tip on how to save money on casebooks even while spending money on them: as soon as you know what courses you'll be in, and who your professors are, call the bookstore at your law school and get the titles and authors' names for the assigned casebooks. Be sure to find out what *edition* of each casebook is assigned. Then get to the nearest law school bookstore or website and buy *used* copies. In a bricks-and-mortar bookstore, the price will be perhaps as low as half the new price. You might also find good deals on the Net. (It's getting more difficult to do all this, however. The law schools, more and more, are not telling students what courses they'll be in, or who their profs will be, until sometimes just a few days before classes start. Casebooks you order through the Net won't reach you in time.)

True, if you buy a used copy of a casebook, there might be some markings in it. Big deal. You shouldn't pay full price to get a pristine copy of something that's a waste of money in the first place.

If you do buy hardbound copies of your casebooks, here's a tip e-mailed to me by a law student: take the casebooks to a copy shop or printing shop and have them strip the text from the binding. Then have the shop three-hole punch the entire text. After that, you can put it into a thick three-ring binder (or a pair of them). But that would still be too much to carry around. So, you also get a *thin* three-ring binder, and put tabs in it for each course. Every day, you put into the thin binder (behind the appropriate tab) the text from the casebook of the assignments for that class. When the prof moves on to other cases, you remove those pages from the thin binder, and put them back in the appropriate thick one. (But if you use this system, you obviously can't sell the severed text from the casebook back to the bookstore, even if they're still buying back that edition.)

Taking this a step further: you could get together with a group of fellow students, pool your money, and buy just *one* copy of each assigned casebook for all of you. Then make photocopies of all the *assigned* material, for all but one of you (who keeps the original, of course—and contributes his or her share of the copy costs).

One more thing about casebooks: a couple of students have inquired about not using the casebook text, period. Instead, they wanted to download, from Lexis® or Westlaw®, the *full* text of the assigned cases, and read *that* for class.

No-no-no! What's in the *edited* version of the case, in the casebook, is bad enough, and takes long enough to get through. You would be out of your mind to read the *entire* case. Granted, the edited text in the casebook quite possibly leaves out important information that was in the original. However, Black Letter Law outlines that include case briefs will supply that missing information. (This is yet another reason why profs typically tell students not to use commercial outlines.) —Then again, the headnotes (a.k.a. "squibs") *might* be helpful, as Chapter 4 discussed.

If you're one of those who's really intent on not reading the cases *at all,* please at least get a commercial outline that has briefs in it for all the cases your professor might assign. (To repeat: some vendors now do casebook-specific outlines that contain only "briefs-in-a-can.")

One more time: I am only saying you should not *buy* the casebooks *new.* I am *not* saying you should *not read* the edited cases that are assigned.

PRIMERS

Unfortunately, Aspen has apparently started to do what many of the casebook publishers do: it brings out a new edition (at a higher price) that contains only a few, trivial changes from the previous edition.

Therefore, if you can, buy the Aspen E&E books *used* rather than new. A used copy, even of a previous edition, will do you just fine. As you've seen, Black Letter Law is old and well-settled. You're just trying to learn the basic concepts and jargon here, not seeking a cutting-edge understanding for the state-specific portion of your bar exam (which often tests the most recent changes in statutory and case law).

Next, please do not buy directly from Aspen itself (i.e., from its website or by phone). Publishers sell their books to distributors at nearly a 60% discount. Distributors then sell to wholesalers, who sell to retailers. (Retailers get a discount of roughly 45%-50% off the cover price.) Publishers dare not sell directly to consumers at a big discount (as from a website), because that would alienate the distributor, the wholesalers, and all the retailers. So, publishers offer other deals such as free shipping (sometimes).

When you buy directly from Aspen, you are allowing Aspen to keep, and to put into its own pockets, the 60% discount that it would normally have to give up to the distributor, wholesalers, and retailers. On a primer that costs $35, that means an extra profit of $21 to Aspen. And when they charge for shipping on top of that, it is outrageous.

Given that Aspen has started playing the "trivially new edition" game, I think that—if you're going to buy their primers new instead of used—you ought not to *reward* Aspen's greed by putting the extra 60% into *Aspen's* pockets...which is what happens when you buy directly from their website or by phone.

COMMERCIAL OUTLINES

I don't recommend any particular vendor's Black Letter Law outlines or case briefs. Although commercial outlines are vital, I believe they're all pretty much alike. Besides, the primers are far more important, and it was important to me to call your attention to the *specific* materials that can make a huge difference to your academic success.

As mentioned, commercial outlines—while necessary—are not sufficient...especially in laying the foundation for your future as a lawyer, not just as a law student. They provide the brass tacks, the nitty-gritty of the Black Letter Law. The main outline with which you should be concerned is your own *personal* Master Outline that you *make yourself,* as discussed in Chapter 4. Commercial outlines are just a supplement, to *help* you prepare your personal Master Outlines. So, there's no point in spending any more money on them than you have to.

Some students who have extra money to spend have gotten two commercial outlines for the same course, from different publishers. They've reported that sometimes one is better on some points, and the other is better on others. Between the two, they figure they have all the bases covered pretty well. If you have the money to spare, and want to do that, fine.

Because Black Letter Law is stable, you do not need to buy the latest version of a commercial outline. And you certainly do not need to buy any of your outlines *new.* If you go to a bookstore that caters to law students, you will be able to find many used copies of several vendors' outlines. Many of these will be in excellent condition. The best time to find them is right after the school year has ended, when students are trying to sell as many things as possible back to the bookstore where they bought them.

Black Letter Law outlines on disk are okay if the cost is cheap compared to buying hard-copy commercial outlines (which is extremely unlikely). I do not see any point in buying Buck-a-Brief® case briefs, etc. There's no point in paying good money for something you really do not need at all.

LAW DICTIONARIES

The first edition of this book proclaimed, at one point, "What follows is heresy: [...] once you're in law school, you do not *need* to buy a law dictionary. When you encounter a term the meaning of which is unknown to you, you can go to the law library and consult a dictionary there." I hereby back-pedal.

I still think you don't need to buy a *hard-cover* law dictionary (at least, not until you've become an attorney). The primers and other materials *PLS* has recommended are all straightforward. Terms used in those books are defined for you. Yet, it does behoove you to have a law dictionary handy when reading your assigned cases. There are also on-line law dictionaries at http://dictionary.lp.findlaw.com and www.lawstudentparadise.com.

A couple of students have e-mailed me that it was very helpful to have a *pocket* (paperback) law dictionary with them in class. (Of course, because the new words you encounter in class will likely be spoken, not written, you'd better be a *very* good speller.)

And I am happy to report that, a couple of years after *PLS* came out, West retained Bryan Garner, The God of Legal Writing (see Chapter 17), as editor-in-chief of *Black's Law Dictionary*, which is THE law dictionary. Garner has seen to it that the most recent versions of *Black's* are better written and that they include some terms that were not in earlier editions (but which should have been). The original edition of *PLS* said that if you're going to buy a law dictionary, buy something other than *Black's*, because *Black's* was no longer living up to its reputation. Thanks to Bryan Garner, *Black's* is back...on top.

LEEWS

You've already seen that, by signing up as part of a group, you can bring each person's cost down. But you can bring it down even more. As mentioned, you can get the LEEWS program on audio cassette tapes. The set of tapes comes with one LEEWS manual. But you can get extra copies of the manual, at $30 each, to go with the one set of tapes. (As I said, the guy is not in it to get rich.) So, you and others can pool your money, then rotate the set of tapes among you. Each person has to finish with them by a certain date and then pass them on to the next person. Meanwhile, each of you has a manual to study.

This could work during the summer between college and law school, if you have several friends in town who are all going to law school (which is quite likely). It's irrelevant that you'd probably be going to different law schools. LEEWS works wherever "fruitcake" exam problems are used...which is virtually everywhere.

HORNBOOKS & TREATISES

I hope you will not be the only person in your first-year classes who's read *Planet Law School* (although if you are, then you'll really have an edge). But whether or not you even go to law school, you'll be one of the few people who knows the origin of the term "hornbook," because you're about to find out. (This information is useless academically. But I was always curious about it, and you might be too.)

First, though, a falsehood: there are those who say the hornbook got its name during the old circuit-riding days, when lawyers and judges rode horseback from courthouse to courthouse. Supposedly, the hornbook was a reference work that was slung around the horn of the lawyer's saddle. Nonsense. Any books went into saddlebags. (Anyone who's ridden a horse can explain why.) Further, even back then most lawyers and judges rode in buggies. (Lawyers—and courts—are found only where there's enough of an economic surplus to support them...and only after the initial surplus has gone into the infrastructure, such as roads, however primitive.) Also, the only book (if any) that most lawyers and judges usually had in those days was *Blackstone's Commentaries* in an abridged one-volume edition. It concerned only English law, anyway. It was called "Blackstone's," not "the hornbook."*

The original hornbook was the generic term of a primer for children in England. (See the *Encyclopedia Britannica's Micropedia,* under "hornbook.") It was not even a book, in the modern sense. It had no pages and no paper in it. Instead, it had one small sheet to it, of vellum. This was what people were using until rag paper became the norm (as it still is). On the vellum was printed the alphabet, some diphthongs, and the first ten numerals. The vellum was then stretched onto a wooden rack. The rack had a handle. The vellum was delicate and easily soiled, especially by the very young children. So, it was covered with a layer of cowhorn, pounded so thin as to be nearly transparent.

Thus, the origin of the "hornbook" does not flatter future attorneys.

Usually a hornbook is just called a hornbook. But occasionally someone refers to it as a "textbook." (Normally, the term "hornbook" is exclusively associated with West publishing.)

---

* And by the way, I'm told that the proper pronunciation of "Blackstone" is "Black-stun" (like Gladstone, a Prime Minister of the U.K. in the 19th century). And as long as I'm on the subject, Justice Coke's last name is pronounced "Cook." The English are something else, sometimes. —Then again, Roger B. Taney, Chief Justice of the U.S. Supreme Court, 1836-64, pronounced *his* last name "Tawny."

Supposedly, a hornbook is written just for students, and a treatise is written for courts and scholars. However, court opinions cite both—which makes no sense if hornbooks are just for law students. It appears that, in a treatise, a scholar is trying to bring order to a heretofore disparate body of material, or else to put an entirely new "spin" on it. A hornbook author, in contrast, apparently is providing more of a scholarly survey. I am told that treatise-writing has gone out of fashion, because the Great Ones of old already did all the heavy lifting. The hornbook industry is still going strong, though.

If you buy a hornbook or a treatise for law school, you're wasting your money. Granted, they're tempting. You hope that by reading the hornbook or treatise by the same person who wrote the casebook you're using that you'll have everything in the casebook all laid out for you. No way. When you see how thick a hornbook or treatise is, you'll see that you won't have time to read it during your first year. (However—having seen the movie *The Paper Chase*—I foolishly did read most of *Prosser & Keeton on Torts,* a hornbook, before *starting* law school. Alas, it proved to be an inefficient use of my time, because it provided far, far more than I needed to know as a beginning law student. —I was studying hard, but not *smart*.) There are better ways of getting comfortable with the subject matter, as the preceding chapters have shown. (Chapter 4 discussed the limited conditions under which you might need to consult a hornbook—without buying it.)

Save your money. If you feel you really must read a hornbook or treatise to be a dutiful first-year student, go to your law school's library and peruse it there, for free.

—Not surprisingly, the same profs who tell you "Don't get any study aids!" will sometimes then tell you to go out and spend $75 for a hornbook or treatise. *That* should *really* tell you something.

Other Stuff NOT to Get

The first edition of *PLS* discussed many more study aids, and recommended some. One of the things recommended was audio tapes on the first-year courses. I should not have advised that. And I now apologize for it. In the years since the first edition, I've become aware that playing with hypotheticals, and working old exams, is the best way to learn Black Letter Law and how to think like a lawyer. The primers, commercial outlines, and examsmanship materials recommended here show you how to do all that quite well. The audio tapes can add little, if anything, to that. And they contribute to a "memorize-and=regurgitate" approach. On a cost-benefit basis, the audio tapes are just not worth it.

PLS1 also discussed software, and flash cards, but without recommending anything. Five years later, I just don't see that any of it is worthwhile. Flash cards, in particular, lead you to continue the old "memorize-and-regurgitate" approach that worked so well for you in your previous schooling, but which will not work well for you in law school. And as for the software, I realize that in this new "dot.com" world, everything has to be high tech. But sometimes a good old-fashioned medium like a book is the best way to go. And so it is with the materials recommended here. There is simply nothing on any CD study aid, except the CALI "Library of Lessons," that can even remotely compare.

If you want to spend your money on audio tapes, software, flashcards, and anything else vendors can think of to try to get your money, have at it. But, I don't think they're worth it. And unlike the materials recommended here, they will be useless once the course in question is over.

Making the Best of a Bad Situation

It shouldn't be necessary for you to prepare for law school on your own, and to pay for all these materials in addition to what you pay for law school tuition and materials. After all, you're paying big bucks to get a *legal education,* not just a sheepskin that says "Juris Doctor" on it. It shouldn't even have been necessary for me to write *Planet Law School,* whether the original edition or this one. I look forward to the day when students get what they pay for. Then there will be no need for Delaney's books, the Aspen primers, *The ABCs of the UCC,* LEEWS— and *especially* not for another edition of *PLS.*

But as long as the law schools continue to practice their perverted pedagogy, if you care about getting more out of law school than just an admission ticket to "sit for the bar," you are going to have to educate yourself in the law, and to learn how to play the law school's twisted game and beat them at it.

I am not the one who created this madness of law school, and I wish it would end. But until it ends, you will have to make the best of a very, very bad situation. Gripe all you want about being asked to pay for other books, or to take time out to prepare for law school. But within about 24 hours of starting law school, you'll understand. And when they come face-to-face with their exams and the implications of all the hide-the-ball (and the forced curve), then even those who criticized *PLS* might realize what *should* be the target of their ire.

Disclaimer

I've been through ten semesters (five fall, five spring) with students since the first edition was published. Certain things have become obvious.

Far too many students read *PLS* and then get overconfident. They think that merely having read it is enough to do well on exams. Others get the "do-it-yourself" materials listed in this chapter, but then don't read them. Or they read them, but don't *study* them. Or they study them, but never work the exercises in them. Or they work the exercises, but only in their heads, as "quickie" answers, instead of as thoughtful written answers.

The biggest mistake, though, is that far too many students still rely on the old "memorize-and-regurgitate" mode. They do a *great* job of learning the *substantive* (Black Letter) law. But then they let it go at that, and never master the art of doing a lawyerlike analysis of a hypothetical fact pattern. They listen to the LEEWS tapes or take the course on-site, but don't study the LEEWS manual. Or they read Delaney's examsmanship book, but never practice its HATRI method (or Miller's UBE method) to *prepare themselves* to handle exam problems long before finals. Or they learn how to do that, but they never prepare summary outlines to quickly write down before each final exam begins. Or else they don't work old exams under *timed* conditions.

Every semester, there's a surge of e-mails to me shortly before exams begin, from students who claim to have used "The *PLS* Approach." Almost invariably, those same people will tell me that they merely read *PLS*, or "skimmed" a primer, or maybe sat in on the LEEWS on-site course, and did nothing more—nothing to follow through. (One even wrote me to say, "My Con Law final is tomorrow! What can you tell me about Con Law?") Almost invariably, such people end up getting poor grades, and then complain that "*PLS* is wrong."

Such students were never serious about law school to begin with, and should never have gone to law school. They were looking for the "magic bullet," the easy path to high grades and big bucks as lawyers.

If that is your attitude, it will become obvious soon enough...whether you admit it or not. Maybe the damage from the fall semester will not be too bad, and you can change your ways in the spring semester and start using "The *PLS* Approach" and end up with a decent average for the entire year. Then again, maybe not. But it often takes the shock of fall semester grades to get students to start "getting *real.*"

PLS does *not* say that you do *not* have to work hard. It says that working hard, all by itself, is not *enough*. You have to "work smart" *in addition* to working hard, to have the best chance of success.

Taking Charge of Your (Law School) Life

There are those who will say, "Wait a minute, Falcon. You decried the professoriat's practice of 'blaming the victim.' Yet, now, aren't you doing the same thing? (Or are you, instead, using a 'double standard'?)"

There is a superficial resemblance. But the underlying reality is vastly different. The law schools don't even tell you how to play the game, and they constantly hide the ball. *PLS* gives you the rulebook, and even a playbook to help you win this game. Or, to shift the metaphor, the law schools drop you in the middle of nowhere, and tell you to go find the Holy Grail—without giving you a clue as to how to find it. *PLS*, in contrast, gives you a map and a compass, tells you what gear you'll need for the journey, and warns you of the dangers *en route*.

The professors will tell you it's all a matter of natural talent. And you might end up consoling yourself by pretending that you just weren't smart enough to begin with. Well, that's your choice. But I see that as a real "cop-out." People who refuse to take meaningful initiative, and who refuse to accept responsibility for the results are indeed still victims. But they are victims of their *own indolence and foolishness*.

This new edition includes dozens of e-mails and web-site postings from law students, and three testimonials from those who used "The *PLS* Approach." I've tried everything I can think of to "get through to you." *But I cannot come out to your law school and hold your hand and walk you through first-year.* You're no longer a child, and can no longer screw around in school the way you did before. It's time to get serious...preferably before you even *start* law school.

Nor do I understand the fashionable phrase, "I am a 'survivor.'" BIG DEAL. Many people survive attempted murders, car crashes, cancer—potentially *fatal* experiences. But to brag about "suviving" something that was not even life-threatening to begin with is beyond my comprehension. In this age of "lowered expectations," and "downsizing," have our standards, our hopes, become so low that people think it's an accomplishment to merely *survive?* And after students have shelled out as much as $100,000 for tuition alone, and given up three academic years' worth of potential income for what was supposed to be a legal *education?* I am truly amazed that they've been so well indoctrinated that they're satisfied merely to have "survived" law school. (The reason why they "survived" law school is because the school wanted to get three years' worth of tuition money from them. "Follow the money.")

To lift some words from William Faulkner's acceptance speech for the 1949 Nobel Price in Literature, you should not merely "endure," you should *prevail*. Don't just survive—*thrive!*

Into—and through—the Labyrinth

Once upon a time in the ancient world of the eastern Mediterranean, the Minoans were the dominant sea power. They lived on the island of Crete. Their navy gave them a veto over the movements of the merchant ships of the cities along the shoreline of the mainlands. The Athenians of that era were a relatively unsophisticated and powerless people.

A Greek myth says that every year, Athens sent tribute to Crete: seven young men and seven young women, whom the Minoans would then use as sacrifices. The King of the Minoans was named Minos. He owned a monster, half-human (male), and half-bull. Its name was "the Minotaur" (from "Minos" plus "tauros"—"bull"). Its favorite diet was human flesh. The Minotaur dwelt in a huge maze. The captives were put inside it. They'd wander around, terrified, with no way out. The Minotaur would hunt them down, one by one.

In the ancient Greek myth, only 14 young men and women were sacrificed each year. In America today, over 45,000 men and women (young and not-so-young) enter the law school labyrinth each year. And as Chris Goodrich said in his book about Yale Law School, *Anarchy and Elegance*: "[O]ur professors wanted us to get lost in the legal wasteland, apparently..."

In the Greek myth, one year the son of the King of Athens volunteered to be one of the young men who's sent to Crete as a sacrifice. His name was Theseus. As sometimes happens in myths, the daughter of King Minos fell in love with him. Her name was Ariadne. She told Theseus about the labyrinth and the Minotaur, so he'd know what he'd be up against. Then she gave him a ball of string so that he (and the other intended victims) could find their way out of the maze after they'd been put in it. Somehow (as also happens in myths), Theseus found a way to kill the Minotaur. He and the others escaped, and the Athenians never again provided human sacrifices for the Minoans.

That act of self-assertion was the beginning of Athenian independence and self-respect—what today is sometimes called "self-empowerment."

You've now been told about the labyrinth and the Minotaur of law school. This book is your ball of string. It will not enable you to avoid the maze or to slay its monstrosity. But it will help you to make your way through it without wasting time going down dead-ends...to where the Minotaur awaits you.

1st Addendum to Chapter 16:
Timetables for Prepping

These timetables are based on the use of the following materials (which were discussed in Chapters 2-7):

The CALI "Library of Lessons"
Delaney, *Learning Legal Reasoning*
Delaney, *How to Do Your Best on Law School Exams*
Delaney *or* Singer & La Fond, for Crim Law
May & Ides, *Constitutional Law: National Power and Federalism*
Glannon, *The Law of Torts*, 2nd ed.
Glannon, *Civil Procedure*, 4th ed.
Burke & Snoe, *Property* (but Boyer, Hovenkamp, & Kurtz is a good alternative)
Blum, *Contracts*, 2nd ed.
Miller & Cilke, *The ABCs of the UCC — Article 1: General Provisions*
Gabriel & Rusch, *The ABCs of the UCC — Article 2: Sales*
Restatement (Second) of Contracts - STUDENT edition - "Pamphlets" 1-3
Restatement (Second) of Torts - STUDENT edition - "Pamphlets" 1-4
Miller, Wentworth, *LEEWS* (Legal Essay Exam Writing System) -

As mentioned in the chapter, it is *very* important that you take time to work the questions in the material, and to *write out* a thoughtful answer. You should then check your answer against the model answer. If necessary, you should go over the material in the chapter again, or consult some of the supplementary materials listed in Chapter 4 (and again in the body of *this* chapter).

Do not go by the amount of pages in assessing in advance how much "work" is involved. In some instances (such as *Learning Legal Reasoning*), the reading is lengthy, but not difficult. In other instances, the reading is short but *very* difficult. If need be, go over it again, until you've "got it down."

I have tried to group these assignments in what I believe is their order of greatest importance and the likely order in which professors will take up these subjects.

It is crucial that you not try to save time by skipping the Q&A sections, or by just working out answers in your head. By putting your understanding to a good test, you'll find out if you really mastered the material. Without that, it doesn't make any difference how quickly you can go through everything. So don't rush.

Feel free to alter the length or order of these recommendations.

One-Year Schedule

This 50-week timetable is for those who have presumably been out of school for some time, are working full-time, and presumably will not be starting law school for at least 12 months. For each book, you should read the entire book, except as noted. If you cannot read the entire book, see the other schedules for what should get top priority in each.

2 weeks: *Learning Legal Reasoning*
5 weeks: *Torts*
    Consult the *R2T* as you read along, and work its "illustrations."
10 weeks: *Contracts* - the Blum book and both UCC books
    Read the Blum primer before the UCC books.
    Consult the *R2K* as you read along, and work its "illustrations."
    Read the UCC book on Article 2 before the book on Article 1.
4 weeks: *Property* (other than Estates & Future Interests)
9 weeks: *Civil Procedure*
4 weeks: *Constitutional Law*
4 weeks: *Criminal Law*
8 weeks: *Property - Estates & Future Interests* ("E&FI")
    Chapters 9-15 in the Burke & Snoe property law primer—and I urge you to first read the Moynihan/Kurtz book, discussed in Chapter 4 of *this* book.
Throughout: the appropriate lessons from the CALI "Library of Lessons"
4 weeks: *Examsmanship*
    LEEWS tapes + manual
    Delaney's examsmanship book
In addition to working the practice exams in those materials, this would be an excellent time to review previous subjects by working the practice exams (if any) in those books, such as the one in Glannon's *Torts* (in which all of Part IX is on torts examsmanship).

8-Month Schedule

The following 33-week timetable is another one for those who have presumably been out of school for some time, and who are working full-time. However, it assumes that you are starting your preparation, say, January 2 and intend to begin law school on August 24. For each book, you should read the parts or sections or chapters listed. If no chapters are listed, you should read the entire book.

1 week (vs. 2 in the year-long schedule): *Learning Legal Reasoning*
3 weeks (vs. 5 weeks in the year-long schedule): *Torts*
    1 week: Part I - Intentional Torts (60 pages)
            Part II - Negligence (65 pages)
    1 week: Part III - Causation (65 pages)
            Part IV - Duty (69 pages)
            Part V - Damages for Personal Injury (68 pages)
    1 week: Part VI - Analyzing a Personal Injury Case (24 pages)
            Part VII - Multiple Defendants (61 pages)
            Part VIII - Plaintiff's Conduct (67 pages)
        Consult the *R2T* as you read along, and work its "illustrations"
6 weeks (vs. 10 weeks in the year-long schedule): *Contracts*
        (All references to chapters are to Blum's Aspen primer)
    1 week: Chapters 1, 4, & 7 (107 pages)
    1 week: Chapters 11, 12, 14, & 15 (127 pages)
    1 week: Chapters 16 & 17 (105 pages)
    1 week: Chapters 18 & 19 (120 pages)
        Consult the *R2K* as you read along, and work its "illustrations"
2 weeks: The UCC books (256 pages, total)
        Read the one on Article 2 first
4 weeks (vs. 4 weeks): *Property* (other than Estates & Future Interests)
    1 week: Chapters 1-6 (65 pages)
    1 week: Chapters 16-22 (91 pages)
    1 week: Chapters 7, 8, 26-28, and 36 (189 pages)
    1 week: Chapters 29-32 (81 pages)
7 weeks (vs. 9 weeks): *Civil Procedure*
    1 week: Chapters 1-3 (52 pages)
    1½ week: Chapters 4-6, & 15 (24 pages)
    1 week: Chapters 7-9 (47 pages)
    ½ week: Chapter 18 (16 pages)
    1½ weeks: Chapters 10-13 (67 pages)
    1½ weeks: Chapters 24-27 (71 pages)
3 weeks (vs. 4 weeks): *Constitutional Law*
3 weeks (vs. 4 weeks): *Criminal Law*
4 weeks (vs. 8 weeks): *Property - Estates & Future Interests* ("E&FI")
    Chapters 9-15 in Burke & Snoe (117 pages)
        And as before, I urge you to read the Moynihan/Kurtz book first.
2 weeks (vs. 4 weeks): *Examsmanship*
    1 week: LEEWS tapes & manual
    1 week: Delaney's examsmanship book.
Throughout: The relevant lessons from the CALI "Library of Lessons"

If you have time, read the chapters not listed here—but only after you've finished the entire program listed here. And do not read the extra chapters just because of some "macho" (or "macha") desire to have read everything. Quality here is more important than quantity. Understanding is paramount.

In addition to working the practice exams in the examsmanship materials at the end of this program, that would be an excellent time to review previous subjects by working the practice exams (if any) in those books, such as the one in Glannon's *Torts* (in which, to repeat, all of Part IX is on torts examsmanship).

3-Month Schedule

This 13-week timetable is for those who have presumably graduated from college or some other school in the spring and will be starting law school in the fall. It assumes you are not working in the summer. Please spend "full-time" on preparing.

For many of you, one or both of your parents are paying for all or part of law school. I have received e-mails from students who've said "My parent/s want me to work this summer and make money to help pay for law school." Explain to them how law school and the legal job market works: how, if you ace first-year at a "name" school, then—after *second* year—you will have a shot at a summer clerkship that will pay you perhaps as much as $3,000 *a week*. But if you do not ace first-year, you can probably kiss that clerkship goodbye. And law school profs make it as difficult as possible for you to do well at all.

Maybe you won't want to make such an extravagant prediction about your potential income (especially if you'll not be attending a big-name school). Regardless, if you ace first-year, you have a good shot at a nice, fat merit scholarship for Year Two—which would be a big help to your parent/s, right? (It also gives you a shot at transferring to a big-name school.) Prepping full-time in the summer before you even *start* law school gives you your best possible chance of grabbing the brass ring. (If necessary, show them relevant sections of this book, including the study schedule below—and feel free to e-mail me so I can set them straight.)

To repeat: it's crucial that you not try to save time by skipping the Q&A sections, or by just working out answers in your head. By putting your understanding to a good test, you'll find out if you really mastered the material. Without that, it doesn't make any difference how quickly you can go through everything. So don't rush.

Throughout: the relevant lessons from the CALI "Library of Lessons."
For (Common Law) Ks & Torts, add the relevant *Restatement* "illustrations."

Week 1
Learning Legal Reasoning (172 pp.)
Ks: Chapter 1 (16 pages)
Prop: Chapters 1 & 2 (27 pages)
Civ Pro: Chapter 1 (20 pages)

Week 2
Torts: Part I (60 pages)
Ks: Chapter 4 (52 pages)
Prop: Chapters 3 & 4 (26 pages)
Civ Pro: Chapters 2 & 3 (32 pages)

Week 3
Torts: Part II (65 pages)
Ks: Chapter 7 (39 pages)
Prop: Chapters 5 & 6 (12 pages)
Civ Pro: Chapter 4 (23 pages)

Week 4
Torts: Part III (65 pages)
Ks: Chapters 11 & 12 (67 pages)
Prop: Chapter 29 (25 pages)
Civ Pro: Chapter 5 (18 pages)

Week 5
Torts: Part IV (69 pages)
Ks: Chapters 14 & 15 (60 pages)
Prop: Chapter 30 (17 pages)
Civ Pro: Chapter 6 (12 pages)

Week 6
Torts: Part V (68 pages)
Ks: Chapter 16 (55 pages)
Prop: Chapter 31 (19 pages)
Civ Pro: Chapters 7 & 8 (34 pages)

Week 7
Torts: Part VI (24 pages)
Ks: Chapter 17 (53 pages)
Prop: Chapter 32 (17 pages)
Civ Pro: Chapter 9 (13 pages)

Week 8
Torts: Part VII (61 pages)
Ks: Chapter 18 (89 pages)
Prop (E&FI): Chapter 9 (25 pages)
Civ Pro: Ch. 10-13 (67 pp.) - start

Week 9
Torts: Part VIII (67 pages)
Ks: Chapter 19 (41 pages)
Prop (E&FI): Ch. 10 (21 pages)
Civ Pro: Chapters 10-13
    (67 pages) - finish

Week 10
Torts: Part IX (57 pages)
Ks: UCC book on Article 2
    (159 pages) - start
Prop (E&FI): Ch. 11 & 12 (24 pp.)
Civ Pro: Chapter 15 (21 pages)

Week 11
Torts: No Assignment
Ks: UCC book on Article 2
    (159 pages) - finish
Prop (E&FI): Ch. 13 (21 pages)
Civ Pro: Chapter 18 (16 pages)
Examsmanship: LEEWS Tapes
    (approx. 6 hrs.)

Week 12
Torts: No Assignment
Ks: UCC book on Article 1
    (97 pages) - start
Prop (E&FI): Ch. 14 & 15 (18 pp.)
Civ Pro: Ch. 24-27 (71 pp.) - start
Examsmanship: LEEWS manual
    (136 pages)

Week 13

Torts: No assignment
Ks: UCC book on Article 1 (97 pages) - finish
Prop: Chapters 16 & 17 (28 pages)
Civ Pro: Chapters 24-27 (71 pages) - finish
Examsmanship: Delaney's examsmanship book (200 pages)

Week-by-Week Summary of 3-month program

1 - 235 pages (approx. 37/day)
2 - 170 pages (approx. 27/day)
3 - 139 pages (approx. 20/day)
4 - 175 pages (25/day)
5 - 158 pages (approx. 22/day)
6 - 176 pages (approx. 27/day)
7 - 107 pages (approx. 15/day)
8 - 175 pages (25/day) + 67 pages for 2 weeks (start)
9 - 129 pages (approx. 17/day) + 67 pages for 2 weeks (finish)
10- 102 pages (approx. 15/day) + 159 pages for 2 weeks (start)
11- 37 pages (approx. 5/day) + 159 pages for 2 weeks (finish) + tapes
12- 154 pages (22/day) + 168 pages for 2 weeks (start)
13- 228 pages (approx. 33/day) + 168 pages for 2 weeks (finish)

To repeat: do not go by the amount of pages in assessing in advance how much "work" is involved with this 13-week schedule, you will have read all of *Torts*, 11 of the 19 chapters in *Contracts*; 19 of the 34 chapters in *Civil Procedure,* and 17 of the 36 chapters in *Property.* Further, you will have read all of *Learning Legal Reasoning,* and of *How to Do Your Best on Law School Exams.* You will have heard the LEEWS tapes and read the LEEWS manual.

Regarding Torts, Contracts, Civ Pro, and Prop, the only difference between this and the 8-month schedule is in Property. You are not assigned Chapters 7-8, 18-22, 26-28, and 36. (Chapters 16 and 17 are just the first two chapters of a 7-chapter Part Three, on landlord-tenant law. If your progress is satisfactory to you, you might go ahead and read the other 5 chapters.)

Constitutional Law and *Criminal Law* are conspicuous by their absence. You are already at least somewhat familiar with Con Law and Crim Law. That does not, of course, mean that you can walk into either of those courses "cold." But it does mean you will probably not feel *totally* lost, the way you would with the other Big Six courses if you walked in "cold."

Please get the Con Law book, and Delaney's (or the Singer & La Fond) book on substantive Criminal Law, and read through the entire book on each subject. So, even though there are no specific assignments as to what to read when, you should add them to the schedule in your own way. (As Chapter 1 mentioned, at some schools, Con Law is an elective. If you are sure you will not be taking it in first-year, then skip the Con Law primer...for now. —But you should certainly read it before you take the bar exam.)

The *Restatements (Second) of Torts* and *Contracts* also have no specific assignments in them. But as with the year-long and eight-month schedules, you should consult them as you read along in Torts and Contracts, respectively. As time permits, you should try your hand at some of the "illustrations."

Six-Week Schedule

Week 1: *Learning Legal Reasoning* - Chapters 1-3 (80 pages)
          Property - Chapters 1-6 (80 pages)

Week 2: *Torts* - Parts I-III (190 pages)

Week 3: *Contracts* - Chapters 1, 4, & 7 (107 pages)
                  UCC book on Article 2 (159 pages)

Weeks 4 & 5: *Civil Procedure* - Chapters 1-6, 10-12, 15, 18, 24, 26
                  (231 pages)

Week 6: LEEWS - Tapes (6 hours) & Manual
          Delaney's Examsmanship book

Throughout: the relevant lessons from the CALI "Library of Lessons." For Torts and (Common Law) Ks: add the relevant "illustrations" from the *Restatements*.

And again: the reading recommended here might not cover all that your profs will take up in class, or the order in which they will take these topics up. But the odds are in your favor that your profs will start their courses with the material in this abbreviated schedule.

If you have *more than a year* before you start law school, and are feeling particularly ambitious, then—after you've done everything else recommended in this Chapter—start working with the *first-year* subject materials from the Multistate Bar, as discussed in Chapter 24.

Pushing the Panic Button:
What to Do When You've Not Prepped at All

1. Follow the recommendations in Chapter 4 about consulting the syllabus or casebook table of contents and using that as your guide to what to read in the primer and the commercial outline for each course.

2. Use your weekend to prepare for each class the following week (which is a good idea anyway). Spend your time on the relevant sections of the primers, and especially on the Q&A sections. Don't use your time to read the casebook. Instead, read about the assigned cases in the Black Letter Law commercial outline for the course—or, if you wish, get another commercial outline that just contains canned briefs. You might end up not being as well-prepared for class as you like. But class doesn't count. Only the exam does. Remember that. Playing with hypos is what gives you the understanding you need. The "class discussions" are mostly just time-fillers.

3. If the LEEWS program is being taught on-site near where you're in law school, take it. But get the tapes too. Whether or not you take the program on-site, listen to the tapes during Thanksgiving break, read the primer carefully, and work the practice exams. Read Delaney's examsmanship book and work the practice exams. And even if you are not taking Torts in first-semester, read Chapter 24 in Glannon's primer on Torts, because it covers common mistakes students make on exams and is a good reinforcement to LEEWS and Delaney.

4. Work old exams. Play with hypos. If you are taking Contracts or Torts, get the STUDENT edition of the *Restatements* in those, as discussed earlier, and work the "illustrations" there. Consider working exams in some of the supplemental exam books listed above, too.

5. Go to church, synagogue, mosque, temple, regularly, and pray your tail off. (If it's a "New Age Center," *meditate* your tail off regularly.)

Even if You HAVE Prepared

1. Start your own personal Master Outline from *Day One.* (Even if only one topic has been "covered" in class, that's enough to start with.)

2. Play with hypos—making your own as soon as you're qualified, but work the E&Es and the *Restatement* "illustrations" first.

3. Work old exams, starting ASAP. Work them *again,* weeks later.

4. Practice the LEEWS "UBE" writing method as he recommends.

5. A few weeks before exams, create your own personal "Summary Outline" for each course. And for those exams that are "closed book," memorize that Summary Outline and be able to write it out PDQ.

2nd Addendum to Chapter 16 -
Possible Further Assistance

On-Line: Part One

The page facing the inside front cover gives the PLS website and my e-mail address. As of this writing, the website is scheduled to revive the advice column I had on the 'net in '01. The site will also have reviews of new study aids, etc.

Several students e-mail me each fall who say they would like the e-mail addresses of other new students at their school, so they can form a PLS Study Group. (Of course, at large schools, where new students are divided up into 100-member sections, it's not easy to find others who are interested in this, in the same section as you.)

It would also be nice if students who've finished first-year would be willing to serve as sources of information for students just starting at the school in question. If you're beyond first-year, and want to help, please e-mail me, including the name of your law school.

Further, I'd like to establish a database on law professors. It would have information from each professor's *curriculum vitae* as to his or her background and publications. The latter could be especially useful in trying to "get inside the prof's mind." However, ideally, the database would also include (anonymous) comments about each professor, by his or her present or former students. These would include evaluations of the prof's teaching ability, etc. But they would also include tips on the prof's likes and dislikes regarding how to handle an exam, etc.

—And speaking of exams, I would like to establish an exam database. Students could send in exams (including old ones on file) by e-fax. Ideally, the database would be professor-specific. You might, for example, have a prof who's a visiting professor from another school. Maybe he or she does not make old exams available while visiting at your school. It might be possible to look up exams the prof gave in the subject (or other subjects—just to get a feel for his or her approach) at the home school. (There could be a problem here with professors claiming copyright of their exams, and not allowing them to be posted. However, the way around that appears to be for me to rewrite the exams in such a way that there is no copyright infringement. The result would be identified as "the sort of exam Prof. So-and-so gives.")

On-Line: Part Two

The foregoing items would be available at no charge. Not so regarding the following items...

I've been thinking about doing on-line tutoring in the substantive law of the Big Six first-year courses and Evidence. It would work like this: students who'd signed up (and paid the fee) would get a password and could access a website for a subject at any time and remain there as long as they wished. I'd have copies on hand of all the major casebooks for each subject. Perhaps there could be a vote as to which case would be used as a starting point for a discussion of the relevant Black Letter Law and for playing with hypos. (See Chapter 5 for a rough idea of how this might operate.) The case (or perhaps we'd do it by topic) that got the most votes would be the starting point. The second most popular vote-getter would come next. And so forth.

Ideally, students could post questions regarding the case (or topic) and I would answer them on that subject's website, for all to see. I am not a computer person, let alone an internet person. But I'm looking into the possibility of setting up a "chat room" in conjunction with this, whereby students who wanted to play with a hypo, live and on-line, could do so.

Related to this would be a site for examsmanship. An exam would be posted. Students would be invited to e-mail their proposed answers. I would then choose at least one and critique it on the website (without disclosing the student's name or school, of course). And then I would post a model answer. (See Chapter 7 for an example of this.) Again, this would be a subject-specific website, fee-based, with a password issued to each subscriber for unlimited access during the subscription period.

One more, similar to the examsmanship: a website for legal writing. Instead of posting an exam, though, it would have selections from items sent in by students. The student's original would be posted (without disclosing the student's name or school). I would then critique the writing. It might take a couple of iterations, but the result would be an edited draft. Every subscriber would see the original and the finished product—and, more important, the critique, to help them in their own legal writing.

At this point, I have no idea what the subscription fee/s would be. But if there is sufficient interest in any of these ideas, I shall proceed with it on a trial basis...although I can't promise how soon.

Also, as Chapter 3 said, most of the assigned reading in law school is make-work. More and more students have gotten "clued in" to the fact that they should not be spending much time analyzing the cases themselves, and are using the facts of the cases as the starting point for generating their own hypotheticals. It appears to me that the professoriat has responded by forcing students to spend more time on make-work by assigning them a staggering load of additional reading of articles, papers, etc. The students end up panning for gold, in effect, sifting through many pounds of gravel to find the very rare nugget or two. It is not an efficient use of their time.

Seems to me that it ought to be possible to provide a law school equivalent of Monarch Notes® or CliffsNotes™. And I'm thinking about trying it. It would work this way: there would be an on-line archive of such Notes on readings that were commonly assigned. Students could access the archive, and download the set of Notes they need on these readings, for a fee. (Initially, of course, there would be a problem in that it would take time to create the archives. This would be no help to a student who was assigned 300 pages of non-casebook material on Friday, to be discussed in class on Monday...which happens. But if there's enough interest in having a go at this, I'll seriously consider it.)

On-Site: Summer Program

The program would be six weeks long, and rigorous—all day, six days a week, with optional activities on the afternoon of the seventh day each week. It would include:

- 60 hours of classes in first-year courses and evidence;
- 12 hours of classes in informal logic and deductive logic;
- 5 days of instruction in examsmanship techniques, including "post-mortems" on practice exams;
- 24 hours of practice exams;
- 2 days of workshops on legal writing;
- 12 hours of classes editing students' legal writing;
- 12 hours of classes in legal research;
- 10 hours of public speaking classes for Opening Statements in trials;
- 1½ days of instruction in deposition and cross-examination techniques;
- Optional sessions on trial advocacy—direct examination, cross-examination, and objections;
- Optional sessions to view and then discuss documentary videos or feature films on legal topics.

The program presupposes that students would have already read all the recommended primers. Additional materials would be supplied that would have to be read before attending the program. Thus, the most likely people to participate would be those who have been out of school for months or even years, and have had time to study all of it.

Students would have to arrive on the Friday before the Monday on which the program formally begins. To ensure high-quality participation, there would be an entrance exam, to be administered the next day, Saturday. Sample questions would be mailed out to those who'd signed up, well in advance of the program. The entrance exam would be graded by Sunday afternoon. Those who failed it would not be allowed to begin the program on Monday. (They'd get a refund of their tuition—and, to the extent allowed by the institution hosting the program, would also get a refund of their payment for room and board.)

One reason for the entrance exam and the requirement of preparation is that the bulk of class time on the first-year courses would be spent playing with hypotheticals and "scoping out" the higher levels of the "Josephson Pyramid." In other words, the classes would be a lot like an introduction to Shakespeare. Those who don't even know their legal ABCs would be wasting everyone's time, including their own.

Class attendance and performance on the practice exams would be closely monitored. Those whose participation or performance was consistently unsatisfactory would be asked to leave the program, and would receive a pro rata refund.

Ideally, this would run from the second week in July through the second week in August.

I'd do most of the instruction. However, I've been talking with several people who are experts in various areas. Three have already agreed to present one- or two-day programs, and I am hoping to get more such people. The public speaking program would be handled by someone who's a longtime teacher in that subject.

I of course do not know yet where this would be held, or what the hosting institution would charge. However, because this would be a non-academic program, no federally guaranteed student loans would be available. Nor would there be any needs-based scholarships. However, there would be retroactive scholarships in the form of rebates, based on students' exam performance during the program. (This is just like the way doing well on law school exams tends to open doors to high-paying jobs. The better your performance in the summer program, the higher your rebate.) At present, I do not know how large the rebates would be. In part this is because I am hoping to find some "fat cats" who will make contributions so that ample rebates will be available.

But for now, you'd better play it safe and assume rebates would be minimal.

I criticized BarBri Law Prep Program, Law Preview, and CLEO, for claiming that their programs provided benefits that I believe are of dubious value, at best. As was said, the only benefit that really counts is better grades on final exams. One reason for the rigorous nature of this program (including the entrance exam) is that I believe virtually every student who participates will Make Law Review at his or her school. For that reason,   I don't want to accept students just because they can afford to pay. If applicants are not motivated enough to prepare for the entrance exam, then they will not be motivated enough to do well in law school. I will not allow them to merely "throw money" at law school preparation.

And I intend to put "my" money where my mouth is. If people who participate then go to a law school that ranks students, and a student in this program does not end up in the top 10% of the class at the end of first-year, I will give a full refund of that student's summer program tuition, and perhaps also of the money he or she paid for room and board. (Of course, if the student already got a rebate, the amount rebated would be deducted from the refund.)

The purpose of this program is, in part, to provide "proof of facts." Law school students are smart. Yet, even the smart, highly-motivated students often do poorly, because they were not even told what the rules of the game were, let alone how to play it. If virtually every graduate of this program does well in law school, then I believe I'll have made my case regarding the pedagogical malpractice of law school.

Participants would have to sign a release in advance, giving me permission to get a certified copy of their law school transcript, and permission to disclose that student's name and the name of his or her school if the student aces first-year. (I'd wait until after they've graduated from law school, though—unless, as with those who provided the testimonial essays in the addendum to Chapter 15, they allowed earlier release.)

More information will be posted on the website. If you are interested, please e-mail me directly, or wait and contact me through the website. The earliest summer this could possibly occur would be 2005.

Note, though, that *I am not promising* to do this program even if there is considerable student interest. Nor can I guarantee that its form would be as envisioned here. Things happen. I'm just saying that, at this point, I am really hoping to do this. It would be an opportunity to practice what I preach, as to the way law school *should* be.

Part V:

Coda
to
Parts I-IV

The Joy of LEX:
Foxes, Fish, Whales…and a "Million"-Dollar Baseball

"Lex" is Latin. Latin nouns have declensions, and "lex" is the nominative singular. One of its meanings is "the law." Hence the name "Lexis," as in Lexis/Nexis, the on-line information source. (But I assume there's no connection between "lex" and the car named "Lexus".) The genitive singular of "lex" is "legis." That's where "legislate," *et cetera,* come from. ("Lex" also means "the word." Hence "lexicon." The connection with "the law" is obvious.) So, in case you were wondering, that's why this Coda is entitled "The Joy of LEX."

Nearly all the previous chapters spoke of preparing for law school, and putting in a lot of effort. So this Coda shows how what you *should* do for law school can carry over into the real world.

Also, it's become obvious that many law students care only about getting good *grades.* And they only care about getting good grades because they know it will help them get a high-paying job. Sometimes, I'm tempted to announce the following: "Here's a box of 14 pills. Take one a day, starting two weeks before your first final. You'll ace every one of your exams—but afterwards, you won't know anything about the law." If the pills worked, thousands of law students would use them…and never crack a book.

So, one purpose of this Coda is to try to inspire you to want to get good at lawyerlike analysis for its *own* sake. It's meant to show you how much *fun* the law can be…*when you know what you're doing,* instead of running around in sheer panic and constant ignorance the way most first-year law students do.

This Coda partly involves an exercise in what John Delaney calls "parsing the cases." You won't get much chance to do that on a law school exam. But it's quite possibly what you'll be doing as a lawyer. This Coda is also an introduction to trial law.

The illustrative case is a lawsuit over title to a baseball. Perhaps you're not a baseball fan. So, you might be tempted to "blow off" this Coda. Well, I'm not a baseball fan either. But I think this is the most fascinating *case* I've ever seen. And as a teaching/learning vehicle for future attorneys, it's priceless. So, even if you have no interest in the sport of baseball, I hope you've sufficient interest in the "sport" of "lawyerlike analysis" to read on. (And if you don't, please reconsider your interest in *law school.*)

What follows first is the complete text of an article from the July 29, 2002 issue of *Sports Illustrated*…

"The Ball
(An American Story)"
by Gary Smith

Inside a locked metal box. Inside a thick gray vault. Inside a yellow stucco building. In a town named Milpitas, Calif.

There lies a baseball.

No one may play with this ball. No one may touch it or see it. Mr. Hayashi and Mr. Popov are just too angry—each insists the ball is his—and there's simply too much riding on it. Mr. Hayashi's reputation is at stake, and his obligation to the spirit that steered the baseball into his hands. So are much of Mr. Popov's savings, a year of his life, and his self-esteem as an outfielder. So are $1.5 million. That's how much the baseball is said to be worth.

It looks like such a simple thing, the ball in the metal box. But if you were to begin to pull it apart to know it at its core, you'd have to unstitch 88 inches of waxed thread sewn in a factory on the slopes of a Costa Rican volcano, peel back two swaths of cowhide taken from a tannery in Tennessee, unravel 369 yards of Vermont wool and pare away a layer of rubber applied in Batesville, Miss.—and you still wouldn't have gotten to its heart. It's sort of like this story.

It's the tale of a record-setting baseball struck by a wooden stick swung by the descendant of slaves from Africa, smacked into the glove of the son of a Russian immigrant who'd been captured and forced into labor by the Nazis, popped into the fingers of the child of Japanese-Americans once locked away in internment camps, and finally landed in a safe-deposit box whose key is held by a San Francisco judge, the grandson of Mexican immigrants who fled Pancho Villa. That's Bonds to Popov to Hayashi to Garcia, if you're scoring at home. And now the lawyers—third-generation Japanese-, Chinese-, and Italian-Americans—are in feverish preparation for an October trial to settle the lawsuit over who will possess this ball. That's right. It's a genuine American story.

Ah, but this is the America that makes your stomach turn. The one in which pettiness and greed and lawyers chasing contingency fees can sully anything, even a thing so pure as a baseball sailing through the sky on a Sunday afternoon. You're forgetting already: Nothing's simple. Wait till the stitches come off and the yarns start unfolding. Wait till you see how far back, back, back Barry Bonds' maple bat made that baseball go.

Their eyes met, a few minutes before their fates did. Two strangers, on last season's final day, standing upon the loveliest piece of baseball real estate on earth, the rightfield arcade at Pac Bell Park—a brick reef poised between the glorious green of a ball field and blue of a bay. Two strangers gazing together upon the festival in McCovey Cove, frisbees and foam balls flying over a flotilla of canoes, kayaks, surfboards, rowboats and motorboats, over women in wet suits and guys in bull's-eye T-shirts and Batman and Robin suits and barking retrievers and fishing nets lashed to broomsticks, all waiting for treasure to drop from the sky.

Something else, that very moment, was dropping from the sky. The U.S. assault on Afghanistan had commenced just a few hours earlier. Knots of people were staring at TV monitors near the concession stands as F-16s and cruise missiles screamed through the clouds and Special Forces parachuted behind enemy lines. We were all in this together. We'd all just learned, the hard way, what really mattered. Just 25 days had passed since Sept. 11.

Looking down from the arcade at all their bobbing brothers, Alexander Nikolaivich Popov and Patrick Mizuho Hayashi exchanged a smile.

They shared things, the two strangers, that they never would have guessed. Both had graduated from Cal Poly-San Luis Obispo. Both had become fascinated by computers and had majored in electrical engineering. Both had gone on to market high-tech equipment in Silicon Valley. Both were passionate golfers and still bachelors in their mid-30s. Both had come to Pac Bell Park wearing baseball gloves and accompanied by brothers with whom they'd shared bedrooms and front-year ball games growing up.

It was time to be boys again. Alex Popov, waiting with a baseball outside the subway station outside the stadium, had tossed it to his brother, Michael, the moment he emerged, and the two of them had weaved through pedestrians, flinging fly balls to each other for a half-dozen blocks in preparation for the big one. As soon as they reached the ballpark, Alex traded his $40 lower box seat to a scalper in exchange for a ten-buck standing-room-only ticket, like the one his brother already held, so they'd both be able to stand in the rightfield arcade walkway.

Patrick Hayashi, picking up his brother Lane at the San Jose airport, had spoken excitedly about their chances as they drove to the ballpark. Patrick likened the SRO tickets they'd purchased on eBay to lottery tickets. Lane said no, their odds were much better than the lottery's—why, if Bonds pulled one to right, as was his habit, and *didn't* get quite enough of it to

blast it into San Francisco Bay, Lane and Patrick would be two of perhaps 1,500 people in the sweepstakes.

A few minutes before Bonds's first-inning at bat, both pairs of brothers split up. So they could cover more ground— that's what they told themselves. So brother wouldn't be clawing brother over a ball whose value, memorabilia marketing agent Michael Barnes estimated, was between $1 million and $2 million—that's what they didn't say.

By pure chance Michael Popov and Lane Hayashi ended up a few feet from each other, in dead right, while Patrick Hayashi and Alex Popov ended up likewise, just behind the 365-foot sign nearer to right center, where Alex's online research had told him the biggest number of Bonds's bombs had gone.

Bonds approached the plate. Two outs, nobody on. The brothers sized up their neighbors. Their *enemies.* Alex Popov, six feet and 200 pounds, decided he was taller than anyone within arm's reach, but just in case, he planted one foot on a box containing television cable so he could make himself even taller. He took no notice of the KNTV reporter beside him with a microphone stuffed inside his jacket, angling for the big story, nor of the reporter's camerman a dozen feet away. Kathryn Sorenson, a Xerox repairwoman in a cap, surveyed the eager mass of males in their 30s and 40s and noticed the 5'5" Patrick Hayashi. *How's that little guy gonna get the ball?* she thought. *He doesn't have a chance in hell. He's gonna get stomped.*

Three balls, two strikes to Bonds. Had the slugger mulled the ethical question staring him in the eye? He'd already smashed the alltime home run record held by Mark McGwire, hitting Nos. 71 and 72 two days earlier. The 72 ball ricocheted back onto the field and was presented to Bonds, which meant that all he had to do now, in a game that was meaningless in the standings, was to hit anything except a home run, and the 72 ball he possessed would be the million-dollar ball. What should he do?

Dodgers pitcher Dennis Springer coiled. The Hayashis and Popovs tensed. Springer slung a 3-and-2 knuckler. Bonds dropped his hands and lifted, a launching-pad lick, perhaps the most unselfish act of his life. The ball shot up, up and father up—could a ball hit that high travel far enough? Up over a city where the gold rushers had thronged a century and a half earlier in quest of instant wealth. Up over a town where the rush had just happened all over again, a dotcom boom in which websites and high-tech firms had sprouted and monetized, in the locals' lingo, over-night. Where everyone had babbled of click-through rates and vested stock options and rents tripling and condos that couldn't be built quickly enough to accommodate the wave of worldwide-webbers washing in. Up over the stadium at the epicenter of it all, the cyberbarons' playground where Yahoo.com, Schwab .com, Webvan, CNET, TicketWeb, TiVo, Blue Mountain and *Wired* magazine had hung their 10,000-watt shingles from the facades, and where every spiderwebbed warehouse within a 10-block radius had been converted into a dotcommer's office or his two-bedroom pad.

Up, up over a mob that had just seen the four-year bubble burst, the dot deto-nate, instant riches vaporizing and the lights blinking out on those ballpark bill-boards one by one as the city of San Francisco discovered, to its shock, that the world didn't need a dozen online pet-supply companies.

High above Hiyashi, one of 40,000 people laid off by Nortel Networks just a few months before, and Popov, whose online venture, Man.com, had gone up in smoke. High against a gray sky, one last dot worth a million bucks.

OH…MY…GOD. Slowly it dawned on Popov. That ball wasn't just high. That ball was deep. That ball was…monetized. And coming straight toward him.

As well it should. Who else in the entire ballpark had awakened that Sunday morning, pulled out a packet of flash cards and begun reciting a dozen statements crafted as neurolinguistic tools to play on his subconscious and improve his life?

Each and every morning I plan my day in an efficient and productive manner to maximize the hours.…

My lean waistline is an indication of my attitude toward life.…

Who else had awakened that morning and reminded himself of the 10 things he had pledged to do daily: plan his day, clean his one-bedroom San Francisco apart-ment, stretch, read, exercise, account for his expenditures, utter the 12 affirmations from the flash cards in the morning and then again at night, guess at something that might happen that day (to build anticipation) and practice his golf swing? Who else had awakened, and because it was the first weekend of a new month, checked a monthly review sheet to make sure he'd lived up to his vows during the previous month, that he'd bathed at least twice (baths are more contemplative than showers), read both a business and nonbusiness book, gotten his monthly massage, visited his parents at least twice, reviewed his file of photographs that elicited positive emotions, and graded himself from 1 to 200 on his relationships, health, nutrition, finances, career, educa-tion, spiritual life and golf game?

The beauty of it was, it worked! The baseball was flying, as if magnetized, straight toward the most enthusiastic, most determined, most optimistic American in the whole damn ballpark. Toward the one voted by high school classmates the likeliest to succeed, the who hadn't let the 20 intervening years wilt any of his wonder at the world or his belief in himself. The guy who'd spent 14 hours writing up a business plan for a start-up venture, hop in the car at 10 p.m., drive an hour and a half out of San Francisco to lay a sleeping bag on the hood and watch a meteor shower on a mountaintop until 3 a.m. and then decide, What better capper on a media shower than to watch the sunrise? The one who had called a pal on his cellphone just a few minutes earlier in the game to inform him that No. 73 was coming, baby, and he was going to snag it.

The headphones piping play-by-play into Alex's ears disconnected him from the world, cocooned him from everything except the ball soaring toward him. All sound ceased. The dot in the sky grew larger. Time became taffy tugged at both ends: 5.7 seconds became forever. He didn't have to move.

Clearly, he'd think later—for he believed in such things—the ball was meant for him. He lifted his glove, unaware of what was happening around him. Unaware of how many other human beings believed Barry's ball was just for them.

This was what Todd McFarlane had feared. This lust, this frenzy, this stampede was whaat he'd felt in his bones, the premonition he'd had the moment he'd purchased McGwire's 70th home run ball for $3 million two years before. That was 25 times the amount paid for the next-most-expensive baseball in history: Babe Ruth's first Yankee homer, auctioned off in 1998 for 120 grand. *I've just given people a false sense of just how much a baseball is worth,* he remembered thinking. *I've just turned people into lunatics.*

The ball struck the top of the webbing of a glove whose pliability Alex Popov so prized that he'd appropriated it from his girlfriend a year and a half earlier. There was an explosion of noise from 41,000 throats, then darkness as he fell to the cement floor beneath a wall of flesh and bone. All sounds—the crowd's roar, the blasting home run music, the shrieks of treasure-seekers entangled in the pile *(Help! Get off me!)*—grew muffled and distant, as if heard through water. Alex's headphones were ripped off, a lens of his glasses knocked out. Michael Popov, a surfer, felt as if he were being lifted and carried by a way, only the liquid below and above him was human, the man on his back was Lane Hayashi, and suddenly he couldn't breathe.

What was occurring in that heap? Each survivor tells a different tale.

KNTV reporter Ted Rowlands says his first flush of ecstasy at finding himself at the bottom, literally, of a big story was replaced by panic as he was crushed against Alex Popov, the air driven from his lungs.

Kathryn Sorenson, who played tackle football with boys while growing up, says it felt like the middle of a blitz with Alex Popov as the quarterback. She says she saw people raking at him and kneeing him to obtain the ball she's sure he caught and took to the ground. Says she saw Patrick Hayashi bite a teenage boy and thrust his hand underneath Popov's crotch to try to get the ball.

Jim Callahan, a piano-shop proprietor whom Kathryn Sorenson identified as one of the ball-rakers, says no, the experience was neither scary nor violent—that he, in fact, said, "Sorry, excuse me," as he foraged for the nugget beneath a man's buttocks. Besides, he says, he was looking right into Alex's glove one second after Alex hit the ground, and the ball he saw inside it wasn't the Bonds ball, but somehow another one, with black felt-tip lettering on it.

Doug Yarris, a dentist, says that's not possible, that he landed with his head two or three feet from Popov's glove as it lay tucked near Alex's torso, and that the ball inside the glove was the one Bonds hit.

Kevin Griffin, a plumbing contractor who agrees that the ball should be Popov's, reeled away with a new insight into his species: "I felt bad for Alex. I felt bad for humanity. It opened my eyes to how ruthless human beings can be."

Jeff Hacker and Paul Castro, who design display panels for military aircraft, insist that no theft or atrocity occurred and that Popov himself told them a half-hour later—which Popov denies—that he must have lost the ball after transferring it into his clothing in an attempt to protect the million-dollar one by pulling a switcheroo with a second ball.

Alex? He says he had the ball for at least 45 seconds but that no man could be expected with withstand such an assault, and that he can't recall transferring it from his glove to his clothing, but God knows, in that madness he might've considered it.

On and on went the scrum, new bodies joining in whooping celebration as if it were a mosh pit, some in hope that a TV eye was watching and making them immortal, others determined to keep scavenging because no one had yet stood and displayed ownership of the ball. Somehow the million-dollar nugget seemed to have vanished.

And where was security? Nearly half the security guards that the Giants had contracted to supervise the stands that day were no-shows. A half-minute eclipsed before a Major League Baseball security officer could reach the maelstrom, another half-minute before two reinforcements arrived, all in plain clothes. "Where's the ball? Cough it up!" they demanded, yanking bodies out by the scalp and scruff of the neck, but because they wore no uniforms the chaos multiplied, the treasure-seekers believing that three more bullies were bent on becoming rich by hook or crook.

At last Alex was excavated, gouged and dazed. All eyes fixed on him. The ball in his hand was a squishy imposter, one he'd just picked up as he'd felt around for the Bonds ball now missing from his glove. "This isn't it!" he cried. Ted Rowlands, still convinced Alex was the new millionaire, whipped his microphone out of his jacket to interview him. Kathryn Sorenson flinched—she thought the flash of metal was a gun. Alex's hands groped his jacket and pants pocket in bewilderment. "I caught it!" he cried. "It f——' hit my glove!"

Slowly, a few people began to notice a small Asian man behind Alex wearing a wide grin…and holding up a baseball. Who was he, the littlest guy in the bunch — and how could he possibly have come up with the treasure? "Who's got it?" Patrick Hayashi quietly asked. "I got it."

The security men's eyes flashed: Yes, it bore the markings of a big league ball. People blinked. People cheered. People began coming to their senses. An African-American man, blood running down his nose, hurried to his crying daughter. A wheelchair was summoned for an injured woman. An Asian woman sobbed.

Popov spluttered as the security men formed a wedge around Hayashi and the sacred ball, and swept them away.

The world needed to know who possessed the pearl. A Giants official placed a pen and notepad in Hayashi's hand. Patrick tried to write his name and gave up. His hand shook so much he couldn't grip the pen.

In the quiet of the Giants' ballpark operations office, he stared at the ball. What had he just done? He'd gone to the concrete amid the tangled heap. He'd seen the ball—just lying there on the cement, he says. Opportunity: the thing that his grandparents and mother had left war-decimated Japan in search of. He'd extended his hand....

Him. The boy who'd always been careful not to do anything that would make anyone look at him. Not to sing. Not to dance. Not to argue. Not to sign up for any extracurricular activity at school nor to raise his hand from his seat in the back of every classroom, even when he knew he knew the answer. The chunky second baseman who might've played more than just two years of Little League ball if not for the part where you had to step to the plate with everyone watching you.

Lane kept bopping him on the shoulder, crowing, "You got the ball! It's the biggest record in all of sports! You've got *history!*" Even Patrick, nowhere near the sports fan Lane was, felt its power. It was as if the ball had sailed through the century, from Babe Ruth to Roger Maris to Barry Bonds...to him. What should he do with it? Just walk out of here with it in his hand? The Giants suggested placing it in the vault of a local hotel, and he nodded. His lips and tongue couldn't form words.

Just once before in his life had he taken a risk, lit a match to a piece of paper when he was seven, and whoosh, the pine tree that stood a foot from the house next door had shot up in flames, and in another few seconds, if his father hadn't raced over with a hose....

His father. What else could explain how the ball had ended up, out of all those hungry hands, in Patrick's? Nothing else made sense. In almost all his memories of his dad—repairing dents and repainting cars in the driveway for friends, puttering around the house, taking walks with Patrick to feed the ducks at the pond—there was a Giants hat on his father's head and a Giants game on his transistor. There was that yelp and hand clap that jolted his wife every time Bonds jolted one. There was that easy thing to talk about whenever Patrick wished to feel close to him. Right up to the end, when the clot formed in his father's brain two years earlier and all but snuffed out that happy-go-lucky man, leaving him on life support while the family frantically tried to find Patrick, who was driving home from San Diego. Two days later Patrick walked through the front door, expecting the welcoming goody bag his father always prepared for his visits, and got the wallop of his life.

He spent his dad's last night watching and talking and crying over the near-lifeless body, and he spent the days leading up to the historic Giants game thinking, God, how much I wish Dad could be right there with us watching this guy, Barry, launch one into eternity.

Maybe...yes, he *must've.* Suddenly Patrick was filled with a certainty that it was his father who had guided the ball into his sight amid that snarl of fingers and elbows and knees. That Barry Bonds and a baseball had brought Patrick and Larry Hayashi together again. He pictured, at that very moment, his dad smiling down on him.

Now Patrick might meet his father's hero. A mob of media would be waiting to speak to Bonds and Patrick both at a press conference as soon as the game was over.

Patrick sagged into his chair as his brother left with a police escort to store the baseball. Two Giants employees were talking in the next room. Patrick couldn't help eavesdropping. "That guy's life's about to change forever," one said. "His neighbors will know who he is, people will recognize him where he goes."

Dread began to grow in some part of Patrick that wasn't numb. He was so simple and unadorned a man that he never hung anything on his apartment walls, so private a man that his personal life was a blank to his family. He hadn't thought of fame—of having all America's eyes on him—when he'd reached for the ball. Now he became aware of a stir outside the door. Someone else besides the media, he was told, was waiting out there. Some fan claiming that the sacred ball had been stolen from him.

No, Patrick told Giants officials. He didn't want to meet the media horde. He just wanted to go home and begin sorting through another tangled heap, the pile of emotions inside him. It had all seemed so simple, just reaching out and taking hold of the ball. Or had the ball taken hold of him?

So many people all across the Mediterranean once craved possession of John the Baptist's skull that soon there were John the Baptist skulls all across the Mediterranean basin. The Shroud of Turin, reported to be the burial cloth of Jesus, was supposedly stolen from Constantinople and taken to France during the Fourth Crusade. Jesus's crown of thorns is said to reside in the church of Sainte Chappelle in Paris—never mind that 25 cathedrals across Europe claim to own thorns from that crown. In the sixth century the bodies of saints were dug up and cut into pieces to be distributed or sold.

Ownership of objects once touched by or belonging to one who has attained immortality makes a man matter—and maybe immortal too. Such objects have always been worth lying, stealing and pillaging for.

Something deep and powerful began to stir inside Alex as it sunk in that his relic was gone. By the second inning, ushers and police were arriving to sort out the mushrooming controversy, and a few dozen people who had seen the ball enter his glove began chanting, "Do the right thing! Do the right thing!" By the fourth inning he'd collected a pocketfull of telephone numbers from witnesses. Dough Yarris had offered his because as a 12-year-old at a Stanford game, he had caught a football that had been kicked into the stands on an extra point, and it had been ripped from his arms by two kids. Sorenson had offered hers because, she says, "I'm tired of seeing injustice. I'm tired of seeing O.J. Simpson get away with murder."

By the fifth inning, Alex had received a shrug from Giants officials—they said he'd have to pursue his claim on his own—and the attention of four reporters intrigued by his story. By the eighth he'd received a business card from a lawyer who offered to represent him. And a question from the KNTV reporter: "Are you gonna sue?"

By 6 p.m. he was standing in his underwear as his girlfriend snapped photos of the abrasions on his elbows and knees and the welts on his head.

By 1:30 a.m. he was waiting outside the *San Francisco Chronicle's* offices to get the story hot off the presses, the first-edition headline hitting him like a shovel in the gut: MAN LOSES FORTUNE AT BOTTOM OF PILE.

By 6 a.m.—after a sleepless night spent combing the Internet for information about Bonds's 73rd—Alex was calling local sports talk radio host Gary Radnich to tell his tale.

By 9 a.m. his phone was jangling, one local and national reporter after another calling.

By 1 p.m. he was sitting in an office at KNTV, his mouth agape. There it all was on the video that camerman Josh Keppel had shot, the ball flying into Alex's glove, the glove quickly disappearing from view, the rabble toppling him, the long struggle before the ball was produced and—wait, what was that, when the video was played in slow motion? Why, you couldn't see teeth, but it appeared that Hayashi, on his hands and knees in the pile, was doing what witness Sorenson had claimed he'd done: bitten the leg of a teenager in a Dallas Cowboys hat!

By 4 p.m. Alex was visiting the first of two newsrooms, presenting the video and a list of witnesses to the *Chronicle* and then to KRON-TV.

The days blurred for Alex. There he was at San Francisco police headquarters, a 37-year-old man reporting that his base-ball had been stolen. There he was dialing Hayashi, asking if they could meet over a beer and sort this out. There he was hiring lawyer Marty Triano. There he was on BBC Radio and Radio New Zealand. There he was—having received no return call from Hayashi and having read that Patrick had talked with Michael Barnes, the sports marketing agent who'd brokered the sale of Big Mac's 70th home run ball—filing a lawsuit against Hayashi for damages and to take possession of the ball.

Sept. 11's ashes had barely cooled, but materialism was back in full blaze—that's what commentators and columnists howled. A San Francisco sports anchor called it perhaps the most ridiculous story the station had ever covered. An e-mailer to CNN sneered, "If you can't play nicely, you'll have to go to your rooms," and a CNN commentator called Alex's claim and his hiring of a lawyer "pathetic." How could an artifact from a ball game mean than much, people wondered. What's happening to us?

In the Middle Ages, so many splinters of Christ's cross were sold to or bestowed upon the reverent that if the splinters had been laid end to end, it is said, they'd have circled the globe.

Splinters of major league ballplayers' bats, along with threads from their jerseys, are being encased in plastic and sold today in a hobby shop near you.

Nineteen hours after he'd given the world the slip, Patrick Hayashi climbed into his car to go to work and glanced into his rearview mirror. A news van had penned him in. He refused to do an interview on air and, after the van backed away, hurried to work. He returned home at dusk. Two more reporters awaited him outside his door.

He turned on the TV. There was Popov's head, telling the world that a great injustice had been done and that Patrick had his ball.

He went out to eat. A stranger approached his table and asked him if he'd go say hello to a friend, as if Patrick were a celebrity.

He went to work at Cisco Systems, where he'd been on the job for only two weeks.

He wasn't just imagining it, was he? Everyone was staring at him. He could barely concentrate. His stomach was in knots.

At home he picked up the phone to check messages: more reporters. And Popov's lawyer, threatening legal action. He picked up the newspaper. The media were licking their chops over allegations that Patrick had been taking a chomp out of the leg of a teenage boy and participated in a mugging—both preposterous, he insisted. A *Los Angeles Times* columnist wrote that Patrick had "slithered into the pack like a snake after a rat."

Who was this Popov, what else might he spread, and why, Patrick kept wondering, couldn't the man admit that he'd dropped the ball? Everywhere Patrick turned—on radio, television, and in newspapers—there was Popov again, accusing him.

Patrick confided in no one, not even his relatives, for fear they would be subpoenaed and dragged into court. He couldn't sleep. He got headaches and chills. Somehow, without ever having chosen to make a journey, he'd stepped onto a train he couldn't get off, a train whose destination was unknowable.

Why not end this agony? Why not settle out of court with Popov, sell the ball in the metal box, split the bounty and melt back into his levelheaded life, marketing telecommunications devices?

Settle rather than confront, acquiesce rather than assert: That's what he'd been raised to do. But then...wasn't that what his parents and grandparents and 120,000 others of Japanese descent had done in America in 1942? Bowed their heads and complied when they were given 48 hours to gather whatever they could jam into two suitcases, climb onto a bus full of dazed and weeping people wearing name tags, and report to a camp surrounded by barbed wire, gun towers and armed soldiers who they had thought were their countrymen?

Not a whisper of it had been breathed in his house as he grew up, but in his 30s Patrick had become fascinated by TV documentaries on the subject and had begun piecing together the story through relatives. His mother had been six years old, his dad 22 when they and their families were swept away to ease America's terror in the wake of the sneak attack at Pearl Harbor. Both families, who didn't know each other at the time, where transported by train at gunpoint from a camp in Fresno to a camp in the wastelands outside Jerome, Ark., where for two years they would sleep in cramped barracks on folding cots and hang blankets across rooms for a semblance of privacy.

Patrick's maternal grandfather, Jinkichi Fukui—sickened at the treatment of a people who had never committed an act of sabotage in America during the war—refused to vow allegiance to the U.S. government on a questionnaire. He was branded an enemy alien and banished to a camp in South Dakota for a half year, then was returned to his family and sent with it to yet   another internment camp, for those considered suspect or disloyal, at Tule Lake in northern California, surrounded by tanks and troops. For the third time in three years Patrick's mother carried her clothes and her doll to start over again amid strangers.

The Fukuis flushed the American dream and returned at war's end to Japan, where they lived, often racked by hunger, in a relative's barn, cold-shouldered as outcasts for all the years they'd spent in America. Twelve harsh years later Patrick's grandfather admitted that no soil grew opportunity like America's, even with its weeds, and so he brought the family back to California. After years of barbed wire, all that Patrick's mother wanted when she returned at age 22 was a white picket fence. She soon married a man who'd left his internment camp to work in a factory making ammunition for U.S. troops and had then been drafted into the U.S. Army and assigned to the Military Intelligence Service.

In a Sacramento house so small that a few family members had to sleep in a backyard camper, the Hayashis raised six children, sealing off their past so completely that their children knew nothing of their parents' internment, and so completely from each other that neither of them realized that they'd been locked up at the same time in the same camps, in Fresno and Jerome. They introduced none of the old rituals or language to Patrick and his siblings, so the children would have no accent and would blend in as swiftly and quietly as possible. So they would become like the people around them, quick to recognize opportunity and grab it: Americans.

Patrick scraped and sacrificed, working his way through college, and when he moved into his own apartment, he began watching documentaries on TV that showed all those impounded people staring from train windows, standing in food lines, wasting away lives they no longer recognized, never screaming no. He came to realize that he was staring at his parents, and maybe even himself. What would he do when his turn came, when someone tried to take what he felt was his and cast suspicion on him when he felt he'd done nothing wrong? What would he do?

"In Japanese culture you just go along with things, you don't create controversy," Patrick says. "But to give up now and give away what's mine would feel like what my grandparents and parents went through. I know that my parents had to buckle. I decided, no more."

Patrick hired Don Tamaki, a Japanese-American lawyer who in 1983 helped overturn the 40-year-old conviction of Fred Korematsu, one of three Japanese-Americans jailed for refusing internment. Patrick decided not to settle with Popov. He'd swallow his dread, step outside the shadows, outside his culture, outside himself, and fight this to the end. He'd scream no. For a baseball.

Here's a valuable object hit right to you, Alex, and then taken from your grasp. How are you going to react? What are you made of?

These are Alex's words. This is Alex's view of his war with Hayashi: A test, contrived by the cosmos, of Alex's character and will. What are you going to do? Here's what:

Wake up most days in darkness, on four to six hours' sleep, lift weights, do aerobics, shower, recite his 12 affirmations, and report for duty on the 25th floor of the Shell Building early enough to greet his attorneys and their office assistants by first name as they file in. Plug in his laptop in the office assigned to him for the year, sip from a deep cup of green tea, slip on his headphones and cue up one of the 96 Kruder & Dorfmeister he'd downloaded— why not *Deep S---, Parts 1 & 2?* Dig into one of the 300 computer files he'd compiled on the case or the 250 hard-copy files he'd jammed into four carboard boxes.

Speed-dial the fast-food health-food restaurant he opened in Berkeley six years ago after quitting his job as a marketing engineer. Make sure the veggie burgers and air-baked fries are still sizzling across the counter and that his girlfriend, Stephanie Dodson, is still vertical after months of managing the operation so he can keep chasing that baseball and keep paying the $120,000 in lawyer's fees, phone bills, airfare and miscellaneous costs—likely to reach nearly a quarter-million dollars by the end of the trial—of preparing for his cosmic exam.

Risk. Big. Bet that he'll win, retaining his attorneys' services at $200 per hour rather than the contingency fee of less than 33% that Hayashi will likely pay his.

It feels sometimes like my head is about to explode. The ball has become my life.

Cram for the eight-hour deposition that his opponent's lawyers would put him through—a duel of words in which one misspoken phrase could impeach him and cost him the million-dollar ball—and walk away deciding that he would play this game. That he would compose the line of questioning for every witness his lawyers would depose: 40 pages' worth of questions, 40 hours of work, for Hayashi's deposition alone. How else could he afford his gamble, keep the $200-an-hour meter from running wild?

I'm not afraid to want something. Show me your fear, and I'll show you who you are.

Learn a whole new language and spend hours on the Internet studying case law so he can fling *ex partes* and *pursuants* and *motions to compel* right back in his foes' faces. Analyze each word of each deposition for new leads, impeachable testimony, cross-referencing it with dozens of other witnesses' statements, with law journal notes and with media interviews he records and transcribes and can flash on his laptop screen with a blur of his fingers. Work all day at the law offices, then go home and work some more.

Don't be afraid that you don't know. Just learn as you go and trust that you'll overcome the problems as they come up.

You don't know where you're going to go and what obstacles you'll face—but that's the excitement of it!

Pay a videographer to enlarge and enhance critical images during the 4½-minute Keppel tape. Break the video down into individual images, each last one 30th of a second, then burn those images onto a CD and into his brain. Watch it in slow motion so many hundreds of times—with sound run through his stereo system and headphones so he can hear every utterance, or with no sound so he can focus on the most minute movements, with an erasable marker poised to scrawl lines and circles on the screen and compose a color-coded aerial map of witnesses—that he can tell you the names of a couple dozen people in the tangled heap and exactly what each will do next: *Watch! My brother's about to get his hair pulled! Did you see that? That was me calling for help. That sliver of black jacket you see there? That's the Asian girl. Look at her face—it's like the the fall of Saigon!*

Dart to Wal-Mart to purchase 60 blank tapes. Record the Keppel tape on each one while you're showering or sleeping, and mail them to media outlets across America.

Start a website, of course: www.bonds73rd.com, with the pie charts and quotes from witnesses and a pop-up box with a photo of the unidentified, allegedly bitten teenager over a caption reading, "Do you know this person?"

Create a Christmas card, a three-photo strip showing him and his brother at the ballpark, Bonds's 73rd home run swing and Alex making the snag, along with the greeting, "Happy Holidays! May your New Year be filled with unexpected opportunities!" Invite strangers he has met to the "touching party" he will throw if he wins the case and the ball. Why not have some fun?

They want to see how much I can en-dure. Their strategy is to break me. They won't. Show me the size of the problem that bugs the man, and I'll show you the size of the man.

Look over, as his eyelids sag, at the photograph on his bookshelf: the blond boy in the Little League uniform and blue cap. The kid people expected to bash balls off fences because he was taller and thicker than his peers, the one with asthma whose dad had that funny accent and no idea how to teach his son the game. The 12-year-old who found himself on second base with two outs in the last inning of a playoff game, his team trailing by one.

"Two outs, Alex!" cried the third base coach. "Run on anything! You're moving with the crack of the bat!" Crack! Alex obediently dashed toward third. The ball rolled to the one place those instructions didn't apply—third base!—and the third baseman gratefully slapped the season-ending tag on Alex. *Incompetent!* That's what everyone was thinking. He could see it in their eyes.

People can pile on and take the ball, but they can't take away that I caught it. I executed. They can't take that away from me.

He walked off the field in shame, his family about to depart for a summer on his grandfather's farm in Bethel, N.Y. He would never play organized sports again.

That boy in the picture. That's who was robbed.

Is there precedent in this case? Yes. The baseball is like the whale that Swift and Gifford were chasing in 1872 and the fox that Pierson and Post were pursuing seven decades earlier: an unowned moving object whose posssession came in dispute between two parties. That much, the lawyers of Mr. Popov and Mr. Hayashi agree on.

The whale was awarded to Gifford because his harpoon entered it first, and the fox to Pierson because his bullet mortally wounded it—each man thus exerting dominion over the contested object.

Surprise! Popov's and Hayashi's lawyers disagree dramatically over what constitutes dominion when the wild animal is Barry Bonds's 73rd.

Hayashi's lawyer, Tamaki—along with Cal law professor John Dwyer, his legal consultant—contend that dominion is exerted over a baseball in the stands, by common practice established over decades, when a customer holds up a ball to display ownership, as Patrick was first to do. "It's not enough to throw a harpoon that grazes the whale or to shoot a bullet that hits the fox's ear," declares Dwyer. The harpoon's got to stick in the whale. The bullet's got to *kill* the fox. You have to successfully assert ownership in the rule of capture." The moral of their story: A fan should be able to pursue a ball in the stands without fear of being sued.

Popov's attorney, Triano—along with Tulsa law professor Paul Finkelman, his expert witness—believe that Alex achieved dominion by spearing the ball from the sky with his glove. Any other interpretation, they say, rewards the violent behavior of those who separated him from the ball. "The rule of capture is designed to prevent the melee over the whale or the fox," says Finkelman. "[Tamaki's] interpretation of it encourages the melee. If the San Francisco police were doing their job, they'd go through the video and arrest everyone who can be identified and charge him with assault." The moral of their story: A fan should be able to pursue a ball in the stands without fear of being mugged.

"If Hayashi wins, would you bring your children into the bleachers when A-Rod's going for No. 756?" adds Todd McFarlane, the comic-book and toy tycoon who watched the value of his McGwire No. 70 ball plummet an estimated 75% thanks to Barry Bonds. "How do you know some 250-pound guy won't do a belly flop for the ball and permanently compress your child into the bleachers? Whoever catches it first should be the guy who gets it. But we'll probably wait until an eight-year-old gets his ribcage crushed."

"Mr. Popov's crying over spilt milk," the agent who helped broker the sale of the ball to McFarlane. "He had a *glove* on and couldn't hang on to it. Popov has nothing to blame except his own lack of baseball skill!"

If Solomon were deciding the case, he'd no doubt award the ball to both men and have them split the proceeds from its sale —or award it to neither and use the million bucks to buy baseballs for kids who can't afford one. But Solomon wouldn't have a prayer in an American civil courtroom, where it's all or nothing and one party or the other must win the lawsuit and get the ball.

A 12-person jury will decide the case, which is scheduled to begin on Oct. 7— by sheer chance, one year to the day after the event—and Popov will have to convince at least nine of the jurors in order to win. Jury selection will be critical because informal polls have shown that blue-collar males tend to favor Hayashi and the last man standing rule in bleacher baseball ethics, while females tend to side with Popov.

Clearly, the thick vault that contains the baseball under Judge David Garcia's temporary dominion hasn't diminished the ball's power over human beings. It lured Mike Wranovics, a young filmmaker from Stanford, to begin filming a documentary entitled *Up for Grabs*. It led a fan, who mistakenly believed he'd photographed the Bonds ball in Popov's hand, to try to sell the picture to him for $100,000. It made witness Yarris take out an extra million dollars' worth of life insurance, in case his testimony somehow leads to his elimination, and it haunted his sleep. He kept dreaming that in the chaos he couldn't find his way back to the son he left behind to pursue the relic that day.

It filled one gay witness with the fear of being outed by the trial and attendant publicity. It set off a security alert for Bonds's 600th home run, coming soon. It reduced Giants employees and Bonds himself to silence—none would comment on the case. It made the father of cameraman Josh Keppel wish his son's lens had never caught the ball's flight, for without the video there would probably never have been a lawsuit. It drove Patrick to move to a new apartment and change his phone number. It flushed him out of the woodwork and onto the network morning shows so the world would hear more than Popov's claims.

Still, eight months after the event each visit to the mailbox churns Patrick's dread, for he knows another letter full of bewildering legalese and mysterious ramifications likely awaits him. Still he broods over questions Popov's lawyer during the deposition that his own attorney angrily terminated. Why did the lawyer ask for Patrick's driver's license number? Why did he want to know how much memory and RAM Patrick's home computer has? Patrick doesn't know when or if he'll ever go to a ball game at Pac Bell Park again.

"It's a curse, getting that ball," says Ray Scarbosio, a friend of Popov's. "Look what Alex is going through. Look at Hayashi!— how'd you like to be him? And what do you do with the ball, anyway? You can't wear it around your neck. You can't leave it at your apartment. Someone could steal it, or the dog could eat it. It's no fun leaving it in a safe. So you sell it, and people call you a greedy son of a bitch. Or you don't sell it—and you're a fool. I'm telling you, it's a curse."

One Saturday in April, Alex Popov took his glove and his 72-year-old father, Nikolai, to the spot where he'd caught and lost that lovely curse. Picture the old Russian, who had never been to a big league game before, listening with furrowed brow as his son excitedly demonstrated everything that had happened there.

Picture Alex breathlessly explaining the loss of a cowhide-covered sphere to a man whose family had its 125-acre farm in Ukraine confiscated by the Soviet government and collectivized in 1929. Picture Alex describing his trauma to a man who, when he was 12 years old, was on his way to visit his uncle, grandfather, stepgrandmother and stepuncle when they were executed by the German army that had swept in and taken over their valleys and towns. Who hid with his father for a week beneath an overturned manure-covered hay wagon so the counterattacking Soviet army wouldn't find them and force them into service. And who finally fled the horror with his parents, a 700-mile migration that ended when German soldiers rounded them up on the Hungarian border and shipped them off to forced labor in Poland.

Picture Alex, with his wide-eyed fervor, decrying the injustice he'd suffered to a man whose own dad was not only in forced labor camp but also later locked away in a German concentration camp. To a man who, when the war ended, spent three years in a refugee camp in Germany with his family, hungering to emigrate to America, to freedom and opportunity, but unable to get the necessary documents. Who moved with his parents to Venezuela for nine years instead and finally, at 26, got the visa that put him on a freighter to Philadelphia in 1957 with a dozen words of English. Who helped his father establish his 170-acre farm in Bethel, then went cross-country with his Scottish bride to start on his own as a machinist for Hewlett Packard in Silicon Valley.

Barry Bonds? Nikolai didn't even know who the fellow was that day last autumn when his son called, babbling something about having just caught Bonds's 73rd. So imagine what the old man said a few weeks later when his son explained to him that he needed to file a restraining order to prevent a Japanese-American man from selling a baseball before Alex had a chance of proving that the baseball belonged to him, and that because the worth of the ball could plummet while it was locked away in a Bank of America vault awaiting trial— see, this Barry Bonds or someone else might hit 75 and knock a couple of zeroes right off the price tag—Alex needed, uh…well…he needed his father to pledge $100,000 worth of his property as collateral against the potential devaluation of this, uh…baseball.

Yes. That's what Nikolai said. Yes, because who knew better how it felt to have everything taken away, uncles and grandfathers, land and bread, in a place where there was nowhere to appeal? Yes, because if his son didn't fight to the end for justice when he felt he'd been wronged, then why had Nikolai trudged through Moldavia and Romania, through blizzards and mountains?

Yes, because of that Saturday when he'd sat in the car with Alex for hours in stoic vigilance outside the home of the boy who'd stolen Alex's skateboard, until at last he caught the boy on it and got it back.

Yes, because when one more horde overtook Nikolai's father's land in Bethel, in 1969—hippies trashing his farm as they overflowed the Woodstock Festival on Max Yasgur's place next door— Grandpa Popov, who could barely speak English, had a voice, had a lawyer, had a five-figure compensation that helped pay off the mortgage on the farm. And so he called Nikolai to come from California and walk the land with him. At last, said the old man in trembling Russian, he was back on his feet. At last he had what was taken from him nearly a half-century before. He said he felt like an American.

At the core of the ball in the metal box is a pellet of cork that once was bark on a tree that grew on the Iberian Peninsula. It was shipped to Maryland, ground into granules and transported to a plant in Batesville, Miss., where it was mixed with tiny flecks of rubber and cooked in molds to form the tiny ball inside the ball, giving it the pop, when struck properly with a bat, to rise toward a fence, toward a horizon, toward all those hands reaching for the sky.

Reprinted courtesy of SPORTS ILLUSTRATED. "The Ball" by Gary Smith. *SPORTS ILLUSTRATED*, July 29, 2002, Copyright © 2002. Time Inc. All rights reserved.

I've included this article because it lets you "play lawyer" in a way that even working on hypos and old exams does not. Pretend you're already a lawyer. Pretend that it's still the first few days after October 7, 2001 (when Bonds set the new season's home-run record). Pretend neither Alex Popov (whose surname is pronounced "Po-POVE") nor Patrick Hayashi has hired a lawyer yet. Pretend that both Popov and Hayashi want to hire *you*. And pretend that Gary Smith's article has already been published. So far, all you have to go on is that article (which is the most complete item that appeared in the national media). So you already know both Popov's *and* Hayashi's stories without having met with either of them, let alone having been hired and having started work on the case.

The rules of ethics forbid meeting with one if you've met with the other, even if the first one didn't hire you. But you *want* this case, and thus you have to make your choice (here) without meeting *either* party. So, based on what's in the article (and some preliminary legal research), *which* party do you want to represent? —More likely the one with the better chance of winning, of course. But which one is that?

Law v. Facts

Part I of this book spoke of the "chicken & egg" problem regarding the law and the facts. Sometimes what first strikes your mind is the way the facts clearly seem to evoke certain Black Letter Law. At other times, you wonder if certain Black Letter Law can be "made to fit" the facts. It's like a song. If the song does not have words, sometimes what strikes you first about it is the melody, or maybe the rhythm. Perhaps it's the arrangement, or the harmony. And if the song does have lyrics, maybe you first notice those most of all. But from one song to another, different things might be more important to you. The same is true from one case to another. No matter what you start with, you're eventually aware of everything—as long as you're paying sufficient attention.

There has never been a reported case involving a dispute like this over title to a baseball. So this is a **"case of first impression."** You have to look at the *existing* BLACK LETTER LAW, on topics that *might* be *related.* And then you have to figure out a way to argue, by analogy, that *that* Black Letter Law applies to *these* facts. Yet, at the same time, you have to read the facts carefully, to decide *what* Black Letter Law these facts *might* "trigger" in the first place. As always, the two are inextricably interwoven.

So now I hope you see (for yet another reason) why it is not only snobbish, but idiotic, for certain law students (and law professors, who actually know better, of course) to tell you "Black Letter Law is just so much verbal mechanics, and it's easy to memorize it all." And then they say, "What you really need to think about is 'policy.'" Policy arguments will indeed come into play here, but Black Letter Law, as always, dominates the discussion.

(As mentioned in Part I, "case law" and "Black Letter Law" are not two terms for the same thing. But they overlap, a lot. *Most* case law is "Black Letter Law, *applied.*")

First Run through the Facts

Earlier chapters spoke of the need to weigh the facts: irrelevant v. relevant, immaterial v. material, and "outcome-determinative" (a.k.a. "dispositive"). So pretend that you have *all* the facts, and they're as stated in Smith's article. (Later, we'll see other facts, not in his article.)

As a lawyer, your prospective or present clients will always be claiming that certain facts are important. But often those facts are important only to *them.* In the eyes of the Law, they're either irrelevant or, at best, immaterial. So, your first task is to look over the facts in

Popov's and Hayashi's stories. Just as when you look at the fact pattern in an exam problem, and start figuring out the legal angles, you should not be in the "advocacy mode." You're still trying to dispassionately evaluate both sides' stories.

It's irrelevant that Patrick Mitsuo Hayashi is of Japanese ancestry, and that people of Japanese ancestry (including Hayashi's parents and other relatives) suffered at the hands of "White America." It's irrelevant that Alexander Nikolaivich Popov is of Ukrainian/Russian ancestry, and that the Slavic people (including Popov's father and, no doubt, other relatives) suffered at the hands of Nazi Germany—and at the hands of communists in their own lands. These facts in their respective family histories are very important to them, and provide much of the emotional impetus to fighting this lawsuit out. But to you as a lawyer, this is of no concern. You would not try to argue to a court that your client is "owed" victory as a way for the American civil justice system to "make amends" for the suffering "his people" had suffered in the past.

It's also irrelevant that Alexander Popov had started a dot.com firm that had gone bust. It's irrelevant that Patrick Hayashi had been laid off from his job months ago and had only recently found employment and been working again for just two weeks before October 7, 2001. What each man did in the hours before going to the game is also irrelevant (with one possible exception, to be discussed later). Popov's "power of positive thinking" preparations are irrelevant...or are they? (We'll consider that.) So is the fact that Hayashi wished his deceased father, a big Giants/Bonds fan, were still alive to see the events of that day. And everything that either of them did after *leaving* the stadium that day is irrelevant.

In sum, from *your* perspective, 90% of what's in Smith's excellent article in *Sports Illustrated* is *useless*. And it will be the same when your future (for real) clients start pouring out their tales of woe and outrage when you meet with them for the first time.

First Run through the Law: Parsing the Cases

The Smith article says that the lawyers on both sides agree the case *Pierson v. Post* is "on point." Of course, each says the case favors *him*. *Pierson v. Post* is an 1805 New York state court case. It's in most first-year Property casebooks.

Post, with his hounds, had been chasing a fox. He apparently had just about run it ragged: the fox took to an open beach, with no protective cover, in its effort to escape. Unfortunately for the fox (and Post), another hunter—Pierson—was in the right place at the right time, with his own gun. Even more unfortunately for Post, Pierson was no gentleman. Despite the fact that he could *see* Post in pursuit of the fox, he shot it and kept it for himself. Post sued...and lost. The court said being merely "in pursuit" of the fox was not enough. Post had not brought it under his control, and thus it was not "his," regardless of whether Pierson had shot it. Had Post already *wounded* the fox, especially had the wound been *mortal,* he could claim the fox even though *Pierson* delivered the *coup de gràce* to it. But all Post had done was tire the animal out, and cause it to leave protective cover—thus creating the opportunity for Pierson. Pierson had engaged in highly unsportsmanlike conduct, but nothing "actionable" at law. "Capture" is key—but as a term of legal art, it has its own elements (i.e., definition: "looks/sounds/walks like a duck"?).

You might think it odd that lawyers would invoke an "animal case" in connection with a baseball. However, animal cases and the "rule of capture" were applied to the *oil and gas industry* throughout much of the 20th century. (In some jurisdictions, they perhaps still are, although in most states ownership of oil and gas is now defined by statutory allocation.) And the "rule of capture" is also applied, to some extent, in admiralty "prize" cases involving derelict or sunken ships.

Popov said that, under *Pierson v. Post,* he wins because he'd "captured" the ball when it hit his glove. He was then wrongfully deprived of the ball by others, through acts of battery. But Hayashi said that, under *Pierson v. Post, he* wins, as Popov was still "in pursuit" of the ball because it only momentarily had contact with his glove.

I'll discuss the arguments, shortly. For now, though, I want to note that I never would have dreamed, sitting in my first-year Property law class, that years later I'd be reading about a million-dollar lawsuit where the legal outcome largely hangs on the application of a case decided before the game of baseball had even been invented. In law school, *Pierson v. Post* seemed trivial. The only reason I even remembered it upon reading the article was because there were some beautiful women in my class, and other guys and I would speculate about "capturing" this or that "fox." Just goes to show: ya' never know.

Smith's article mentioned another case the two lawyers agree is "on point," *Swift v. Gifford.* I'd never had that one in law school. It's an 1872 federal case out of Massachusetts. The *Sports Illustrated* article somewhat misstates the facts and the issue. (Smith almost certainly had not read the cases himself.)

The crew of the whaling ship Rainbow had harpooned a whale and thought it nearly dead. So they secured it to their longboats and began towing it back to the mother vessel. The whale revived, however. It broke the lines securing it to the longboats, and escaped. The Rainbow gave chase, but could not keep up with the beast.

Later, the whaling ship Hercules sighted the creature. Its crew took to their longboats and went after it. They too harpooned it. This time it did not revive. They secured it to their longboats and hauled it to the mother vessel. But before they began to butcher it, the Rainbow showed up. Its Master said the whale belonged to *his* ship, as his crew had harpooned it first and had been trying to catch up with it. The Master of the Hercules honored the claim.

But when the Hercules returned to port, the ship's *owners* filed suit against the owners of the Rainbow, for the value of the whale. They lost, for reasons to be discussed shortly.

First, though, here are two other cases the magazine did not mention. They've not been cited by either side in this case, but they help in understanding *Swift v. Gifford*—and thus also *Popov v. Hayashi.*

Shaw v. Shaw is an Ohio state court case from 1902. The defendant had removed live fish from an unattended "holding" net. The net's owner brought *criminal* charges. The defense was that, because the sides of the net went far down into the water but did not stick up above the surface of the water, it was possible that *all* of the fish would have *escaped,* merely by swimming up to near the surface of the water and then moving outward past the net's perimeter. Because the fish were not held in "absolute security," it was not wrongful for the defendant to *help* them "escape"—into his own boat.

The court did not buy that argument. The court compared fish in a net that was open only at the surface to bees in a hive. It would be possible to steal the bees without stealing the hive, even though the bees were free to "escape" from the hive's owner on their own. (No mention of the fact that a hive is the bees' *home,* whereas a net is an offensive intrusion into the fish's environment...to the fish, anyway.) The act of physically *removing* fish from *within* the net gave rise to criminal liability, *even though the fish were free to leave the net on their own* (if they could figure out how or just got lucky).

Contrast that with another fish-in-the-net case, *Young v. Hichens,* an English civil suit from 1844. The plaintiff had set out a net, nearly in a circle, but with a gap in it. Fish could move in and out of the gap. But, being fish (and not very bright), most were apparently unaware they were even within the net or, if they were aware, did not try to get out. Defendant's boat had pulled up outside the gap...and proceeded to lay down its own net at the gap in plaintiff's net. The boat's crew then agitated the waters, so as to stir up the fish inside the plaintiff's net. As the fish sought to move swiftly from the area of the agitation (i.e., from within the perimeter of plaintiff's net) they swam through the gap in plaintiff's net—right into the defendant's net. Defendant then closed the gap in his own net, hauled it up, and left.

The court did *not* say that because the defendant had *not* physically *removed* the fish from *within* the net, the defendant was therefore not liable. But the court ruled the defendant was not liable anyway. Because of the gap in the net's perimeter, the fish within the net did not *belong to* the plaintiff. "An act of appropriation is effectual to vest the property only when complete." (However, the usual summaries of this case omit something potentially important: the court, in *dicta,* said that, although the plaintiff could not recover for the value of the fish on the basis that he allegedly *owned* the fish, he "might" have a cause of action for the value of the fish on the basis that, *but for* defendant's *interference,* nearly all the fish *would have* become plaintiff's. Today that's the "tort of interference with prospective economic advantage." Popov did not use that language, but that's what his case largely was.)

Now back to *Swift v. Gifford*...

Maritime law said (and still says) that ownership goes to whomever "completes" the act of "appropriation" of the fish. This, of course, is almost identical to *Pierson v. Post's* emphasis on "capture." The owners of the Hercules said, in effect, that the Master of their ship had been a fool to turn the whale over to the Rainbow. A harpooned whale that escapes belongs to whomever subsequently harpoons it and (in the language of *Young v. Hichens*) "completes the appropriation."

But there was a crucial difference between whaling and fishing. *Industry custom* among New England *whalers* said that if a whale had been harpooned by one ship's crew but escaped, and was subsequently harpooned and killed by another ship's crew, the first ship could still claim the whale for itself—but *only if two conditions were met:* (1) the crew of the second ship had not yet "cut into" (i.e., begun butchering) the whale, and (2) there was a harpoon from the first ship still in the whale. (The harpooners were the elite among the skilled-labor workforce of whaling. They often had custom harpoons, similar to a Medieval knight's beloved sword. But even generic harpoons still bore the name of the ship they came from.)

When the Rainbow showed up, the crew of the Hercules had not begun to cut into the whale. Inspection of the carcass revealed it had a Rainbow harpoon in it. So, the Master of the Hercules had honored the New England whaling industry's custom and relinquished his prize.

However, in filing suit, the owners of the Hercules said: (1) general maritime *common law* should trump mere industry custom, (2) even if industry custom could trump the common law, the custom here was *unique* to the New England whaling industry, and therefore was not widespread enough to be a binding custom, and (3) regardless, the custom was "unreasonable."

The court rejected all these arguments. The common law in question had developed within the fishing industry, and the custom here did not represent an attempt to reject the common law of the *fishing* industry. (Whales are mammals, remember, and they behave quite differently from a school of fish.) Further, *both* ships hailed from New Bedford (the capital of the American whaling industry). It might have been a problem if only one ship (especially were it the Rainbow) was a New England vessel but the home port of the other was, say, Charleston—whose whalers did not have such a custom. But that point was moot, given the *facts* of this case. So, the New England whaling industry's custom trumps the general common law about fish.

Popov argued, in effect, that when the ball hit his glove, that was the equivalent of his "harpooning" it. And although he of course had no harpoon in the ball, the video clip showing the ball hitting *his* glove served the same purpose. Hayashi said Swift favors *him* because (1) there is *no* industry custom in Major League Baseball that the ball belongs to whoever *first* grasps it, (2) there *is* an industry custom in Major League Baseball that the ball belongs to "the last man standing"—i.e., to whoever gains ultimate possession of the ball through means neither criminal nor tortious, and (3) the industry custom is *consistent* with the general common law rather than a departure from it, whereas Popov's "custom" *rejects* the general common law. (Popov, of course, would argue that it's the other way around on #3.)

One more, not mentioned in the article (another fox case, in fact)…

E.A. Stephens & Co. v. Albers is a Colorado state court case from 1927. Stephens & Co. raised silver foxes, whose pelts were especially valuable, for slaughter. And like cattle ranchers branding their cattle, Stephens & Co. placed a mark on each fox. One of its silver foxes escaped. Albers encountered it later and shot it. Stephens & Co. heard of this and sued Albers for the pelt's value. The company prevailed, for two reasons: (1) it was in the business of fox ranching, and that fox's very existence was the result of part of the "work-in-process" as commercial "production" on the ranch, and (2) the firm's marking could apparently still be seen on the pelt from the fox Albers killed, so the pelt was an identifiable item from Stephens & Company's inventory—which it had neither abandoned nor given away.

That case is not relevant to the Bonds ball case. Popov and Hayashi were not distinguishable on the basis that Popov was "in the business" of catching invaluable home-run balls while Hayashi was just a passerby. Although Popov might have argued that the fox ranch's marking was similar to the Rainbow's harpoon—and both to the video clip—the marking clearly required more control than harpooning did, which is more control than Popov believed to be necessary to establish his title to the Bonds ball.

(By the way: I got the cases that weren't mentioned in Gary Smith's article just by looking at the relevant sections in the Burke & Snoe property primer from Aspen and in the Boyer-Hovenkamp-Kurtz property primer from West. The only other "research" I did was to then "pull" those cases and read the full text of each.)

Chapter 3 spoke of "Case Briefing as Rabbit Trail," and I stand by that. However, it also mentioned that it can be well worth your while to look up the "note cases" and then "parse" them against the assigned case. (But, as mentioned, it takes time to look the note cases up, and takes money to copy them. Even so, if you can do it, it makes another excellent stepping-stone after the Aspen examples, and the *Restatement* "illustrations," before you create your *own* hypotheticals.)

Framing the Issue/s

In *Learning Legal Reasoning*, Delaney talks of the importance of "framing" the issue/s at the outset, i.e., of "setting the terms of the debate." What that means is: determining *which* Black Letter Law *controls*. This is *crucial*. From reading an appellate court case, for example, you can almost always tell, just by seeing how that court framed the issue/s, which side won if for some reason you hadn't already seen the word "Affirmed" or "Reversed" or "Remanded" at the start of the text. (That's because you already know the higher court has to accept the facts as found in the lower court. The facts are stated before the legal discussion is presented. Once you know the facts-as-found, it's usually child's play to figure out the result just from having seen what Black Letter Law the higher court says is applicable.)

In *Popov v. Hayashi*, here's the way each side framed the issue*:

---

* In civil law, shorthand for "plaintiff" is "Π" (the Greek letter "pi"). In both civil and criminal law, shorthand for "defendant" is "Δ" (the Greek letter "delta").

Π: Under Common Law ("C/L"), Popov acquired title to the ball when it remained in his possession and under his control for a sufficient time. The subsequent deprivation of his possession of the ball was wrongful, so he remains its true owner as against all the world.

Δ: Under C/L and industry custom (the Major League Baseball industry), Hayashi acquired title to the ball when he became its ultimate possessor, via means that were not wrongful, after Popov failed to bring it under Popov's control.

Case *THEME*

Related to framing the issue/s is the theme. (It's a term of art, in litigation.) A courtroom is a *moral arena*. Even in a bench trial (trial to a judge, without a jury), it's advisable to try to stake out a position on the high ground. Here's each party's theme in this suit, and a tag line expressing that theme:

> Π— Theme: "Fairness."
> One-Liner: "Hayashi robbed me!"
>
> Δ— Theme: "Play by the Rules."
> One-Liner: "Popov's a sore loser!"

Notice that "fairness" and "play by the rules" are just two ways of saying the same thing.

The theme should strike a chord with the trier of fact, and should resonate within the trier's psyche as the trial unfolds. Everything presented by way of framing the issue/s and the theory of the case should connect to that. Even though the trier of fact will be *consciously* "objective" when evaluating the evidence, having a good theme will get the trier *subconsciously* "leaning" one way or the other. *That* can cause a "selective perception" of the evidence. The side with the better theme, all other things being equal (which they never are) gets the benefit of any doubts as to whose story to believe.

"*Theory of the Case*"

Each side also needs a theory of the case. (That's another term of art, in litigation.) It's different from framing the issue/s and the theme, although these all overlap one another. Framing the issue/s puts the case in layperson's language, but invokes Black Letter Law. Its main emphasis is on the *law*. In contrast, *emotion* is obviously the main emphasis of the theme. The theory of the case is *empirical and psychological*. It shows how the factual pieces fit together—the story of what happened, and why, as that side's story unfolds in light of the issue/s as framed (and the theme). Like a good theory in physics, or the master detective's explanation of the murder and its aftermath in a mystery novel, it's what "makes sense" of everything, step by step. But because each side has its own theory of the case, what makes sense to one side is utter nonsense to the other.

The framing of the issue/s, the theme, and the theory of the case should all be simple and coherent. They should make sense to a typical twelve-year-old. (Don't snicker. Try to name one *successful* political platform, ad campaign, religious dogma, or work of literature for which you *cannot* express, "in 25 words or less," how the issue was framed, and what its theme and theory of the case are—in a way that's intelligible to the typical twelve-year-old.)

As you've seen, Gary Smith's article was almost entirely about Popov's and Hayashi's respective theories of the case.

Making a Good Record

Because of the baseball's value, this case could easily have "gone up on appeal." You have to lay the groundwork to win on appeal. If you win at trial, you want the appellate court/s to affirm. If you lose at trial, you want a reversal (in which case, you've won the whole case), or at least a "remand." (In a remand, the higher court says, "Do it over, gang. Back to Square One.")

So you want to "make a good record." By that, it's meant that you want to make sure that you've "put on the record" your arguments as to what the "controlling law" is. And you also want to make sure you've "put into evidence" the material facts that bring the controlling law into play so the law, as applied to those facts, means your side wins. (This is where Schlichtmann and Nesson blew it in the toxic tort class-action suit discussed in Chapter 9.)

As Chapter 5 said, the facts are "found" at the trial court level (whether by the judge, if there is no jury, or by the jury), and *those* facts are "binding" on the higher court/s. So, you have to make sure the "finder of fact" finds facts in your favor. However, a jury doesn't decide what the controlling Black Letter *Law* is. Only the judge does. But the judges on *higher* court/s are free to tell the *trial* judge that he or she either chose the wrong law to apply, or applied the right law in the wrong way in light of the facts as "found." So, a trial lawyer has to make sure, early on, that the judge decides to apply the law *that* lawyer wants applied, and to then present facts that are material under that Black Letter Law. But the trial lawyer also has to keep in mind the possibility that a higher court will say the trial judge should have used some *other* body of law. So, the trial lawyer has to try to present evidence to support findings of fact that will enable that side to win on appeal even if the higher court says some other Black Letter Law controlled. But what's relevant, and especially material, under one set of law might be immaterial, or even irrelevant, under another. Further, the trial lawyer, of course, can't present other evidence that *contradicts* the facts the lawyer wants the trier of fact to find under that lawyer's preference as to what the controlling law is.

This is (one reason) why trial law is the most demanding area of the law, unless the lawyer in question merely handles routine cases. *Popov v. Hayashi,* in contrast, was not only a case of first impression, it was a trial lawyer's dream come true. Like the baseball itself, it was all up for grabs.

Standards/Burdens of Proof

Each side tries to present **"proof of facts."** ("POF" is yet another term of art, in litigation.) Everyone's heard of the burden of proof required in a criminal case: *"beyond a reasonable* doubt." It's the highest there is. There are other standards/burdens of proof. Each is applied to certain kinds of *civil* cases. The *lowest* is **"preponderance of the evidence."** And that's the standard in *Popov v. Hayashi.*

If you think of the balance of the evidence as being the scales of justice, then think of both sides being equally weighted...except that another item is then added to one side: an eyelash. And the weight of that one eyelash provides a preponderance of the evidence to that side. That's how low the standard called preponderance of the evidence is. What it comes down to, though, is convincing the fact-finder that one side's story is true merely "more *likely* than not." That's all it takes—under the preponderance of the evidence standard.

Another Possible "Theory of (THIS) Case"

Gary Smith's article includes this curious statement:

> Jim Callahan...[said] he was looking right into Alex's glove *one second* after Alex hit the ground, and the ball he saw inside it *wasn't the Bonds ball, but somehow another one, with black felt-tip lettering on it.* [Ellipsis and italics supplied.]

What's *this?*
Later in the article, referring to the aftermath of the melee, Smith says:

> The ball in [Popov's] hand was a squishy imposter *[sic]*, one he'd just picked up as he'd felt around for the Bonds ball now missing from his glove.

"Just picked up?" During the *melee?*
There's a contradiction here. According to Callahan, Popov had a ball, with "felt-tip lettering" on it, in his glove—no *later* than *one second* after Popov hit the ground. So, if his testimony is accurate, Popov had not had time to "feel around for the Bonds ball...missing from his glove." That ball was in Popov's glove *by the time he hit the ground.*

Further, even in normal circumstances, stray baseballs aren't lying around on a ballpark's arcade walkway the way stray golfballs can be found around the edges of any course. And in the commotion to get the Bonds ball (which was just an ordinary baseball, after all), fans would be scooping up *any* baseball they spotted, even if (for some strange reason) loose baseballs *were* lying on the arcade walkway at Pac Bell Park.

It strains credulity to think that *another* fan inserted a ball into Popov's glove before Popov hit the ground or within a split-second afterward. If the Bonds ball were still in Popov's glove before Popov hit the ground, it would have taken two hands for someone else to make the switch: one hand to reach into Popov's glove and grab the Bonds ball from it, and the other hand to insert the other ball. But as the article mentioned, *Hayashi* was wearing a baseball glove, too. —And why would someone go to the trouble of inserting the fake into Popov's glove once they'd grabbed the Bonds ball? And what sort of *planning* would have had to go into the whole thing (including hiding the fake ball from others not just during the substitution, but before)?

So, whodunnit?

> Jeff Hacker and Paul Castro...insist that no theft
> or atrocity occurred and that *Popov himself told
> them* a half-hour later—which Alex denied—*that
> he must have lost the ball after transferring it into
> his clothing in an effort to protect the million-
> dollar one by pulling a switcheroo with a second
> one.*   [Ellipsis and italics supplied.]

Now here's the very next paragraph in Smith's article:

> Alex? He says he had the ball for at least 45
> seconds but that no man could be expected to
> withstand such an assault, and that he can't recall
> transferring it from his glove to his clothing, but
> God knows, in the madness he might've consid-
> ered it.

"Considered" it? *"Might've"* considered it? Hmm.

Popov went down within, at most, a *very* few seconds after the ball
hit his glove—and the substitute ball was in his glove, according to the
eyewitness account/s, within not many more seconds after that, at most.
There is simply no way Popov could've had the Bonds ball in his glove
for 45 seconds.

> Who else in the entire ballpark had awakened
> that Sunday morning, pulled out a packet of flash
> cards, and began reciting a dozen statements
> crafted as neurolinguistic tools to play on his sub-
> conscious and improve his life?
>   *Each and every morning I plan my day in an
> efficient and productive manner.*
>   [Italics in the original.]

Other statements from Smith, showing scenes from Popov's life in
the weeks and months (even years) before the game—apparently as
told to Smith by Popov—establish Popov as *obsessive-compulsive* (if I
may play amateur shrink for a moment). Alex Popov apparently doesn't
do *anything* spontaneously. And his evasive statement to Smith about
how, during the "madness," he "might've considered" making a switch,
is worthy of Bill Clinton. Popov didn't consider it *during* the madness.
He'd *anticipated* the madness...and *planned* the switcheroo.

Recall, from Smith's article, that Alex Popov had brought a ball to the game with him. He and his brother Michael had played catch with it as they walked toward the stadium from the subway station. There's no further statement in Smith's article about *that* ball. But it stands to reason *that* ball was the ball that ended up in Popov's glove. Popov, planning everything out, intended to use it as a *decoy*. He suspected others would try to strip him of his glove, or strip the Bonds ball from the glove, if he caught it. Arguably, Popov (who's six-foot, 200 pounds) went down not because he was pushed or accidentally fell, but because he intentionally *dropped* to the ground to make the switch on the way down—while out of the line-of-sight of others, especially the TV camera he knew would be present.

Unfortunately for him, he did not *secure* the Bonds ball in his clothing. The ball came out either during Popov's fall, or—more likely— was jarred loose from his clothing by the impact when he "hit the deck"…by which time Popov had already transferred the decoy from inside his clothing to his glove.

You might think this theory of the case farfetched. But I also obtained many of the documents filed with the court.

In the brief Popov filed in support of his request for a preliminary injunction against Hayashi (which, as the article mentioned, was granted), Popov stated he "picked up" the fake ball while at the bottom of the pile-up. Quoting from his own deposition, he said:

> As Popov attempted to get up to breathe
> because of the massive weight on top of him, he
> lifted himself up on his right forearm, reached
> for the baseball and discovered it was missing.
> Popov reached around trying to find the ball.
> Popov grabbed the ball and placed it in his glove.

One of the photographs accompanying Gary Smith's article shows the ball hitting Popov's glove as Popov stood amid the crowd trying to catch it. The glove is on Popov's left hand. The glove remained on his hand after he went down. If Popov levered himself up on his *right* forearm, that means his right *forearm*—and therefore his right *hand*— was still *flush against the floor* of the arcade walkway. He thus would not have been able to "reach around" with his *right* hand to "try to find the ball." (And note, he apparently could not *see* a loose ball. So, despite the competition from others at the bottom of the pile-up, it was Popov, through sheer *happenstance,* who came up with a ball other than the one Bonds had hit?) Further, because he was using his right forearm to prop himself up (and thus to also push up the "massive weight on top of him," remember), his *right* hand would have been *immobilized*. This means he could only have been "reaching around" with his *left* hand. But his left hand was *gloved*.

This in turn means two things. First, it would have been the fingers of the *glove*, rather than his *own* (real) fingers, that came in contact with the (allegedly) loose ball. Thus he would not have had the nerve endings of his real fingers in touch with the loose ball to let him sense that he was touching a loose *ball*. Second, he would not have said he "*placed* [the ball] *in* his glove," were he grabbing around with the *gloved* hand—which, as we've seen, is the *only* hand he could possibly have had *free*. Rather, he would have said "I grabbed it *with* my *glove*."

Smith quoted Jim Callahan as to "black felt-tip lettering" on the ball in Popov's glove. Here are two excerpts from Callahan's deposition:

> I did not see anyone grabbing at or clawing at Alex Popov or his clothing or his glove while we were on the ground. My head was next to his glove the whole time, and I never saw the 73rd home run ball in Alex Popov's glove, and no one ever tried to take the ball in Alex Popov's glove away from him.
>
> ...
>
> I could see Popov's whole glove and a ball in it that I immediately knew was not the 73rd home run ball because it had large letters on it that looked like it came from a thick, black felt pen. I couldn't see what the letters spelled, because they were wrapped around the ball, but I thought I saw a "C" or an "O."

And here's an excerpt from Jeff Hacker's deposition:

> When I was finally able to get off him, and Popov opened up his glove, Popov was holding a ball on which I could see letters wrapped around the ball, and I could see the letters "SUC." It was obvious that this ball was not the real 73rd home run ball.

Another witness, Paul Castro, was in the pile-up. Here's an excerpt from his deposition:

Popov *started* to get up, my buddy Jeff was right next to him. *I saw Popov's glove on the ground with a ball in his glove...* My first thought was "there's the ball," but *Popov was patting himself down, searching his clothes, patting his waist, putting his hands inside his jacket, saying something like "I've got the ball right **here.**"* Looking at the ball in his **glove,** *I could see the letters "SUC" handwritten on the ball by a marking pen* of some sort. Since those letters were wrapped around the ball, I could only see the letters "SUC."

> [Ellipsis in the original, italics and bold-face supplied.]

Popov, at that point, had *not even looked at* the ball in his *glove*—because *he already knew* it was a switcheroo: *his* switcheroo. *That's* why he'd *immediately* started "patting himself down," and why he said "I've got the ball right *here*" (i.e., *not* in his *glove*).

From Castro's testimony, it appears Popov had *discarded* his glove with the fake in it at some point during the pile-up. Thus, his left hand would indeed have been free to reach around for the Bonds ball. Yet, he certainly would *not* have discarded the glove had he thought the *Bonds* ball was *in* it. But he did know *a* ball was in it. In his first filing, the "complaint" against Hayashi, he said this:

> Upon landing on the ground, POPOV felt THE BASEBALL in his mitt pressing against his ribcage. POPOV immediately began to scream "GET OFF!" and "HELP!"   [Capitalization in the original.]

Presumably, "my buddy Jeff" Castro referred to was Jeff Hacker. According to Smith's article, Popov made his statement about the switcheroo to both of them. A cynic might think that Castro and Hacker were involved in some sort of plot with Hayashi. Yet, there is corroborating testimony from at least one other witness—Callahan, as we've just seen—at least as to "lettering" on the ball. (As we shall see, the ball that was pitched to Bonds had *no* lettering on it.)

Unfortunately, the ball that was in Popov's glove has apparently long since disappeared.

However, in addition to concurring testimony from Callahan, Castro, and Hacker is that from Paul Padilla, Director of Security and Operations for Major League Baseball. MLB had sent Padilla and a team to Pac Bell Park in anticipation of at least one more home run from Barry Bonds into the stands. (More on that, later.) Padilla was probably the person Smith referred to only as "a Major League Baseball security officer" who arrived at the pile-up less than 30 seconds after Bonds had connected with the ball. (Padilla's deposition testimony confirms that Hayashi was wearing a baseball glove.)

According to Padilla's deposition testimony, he examined the ball Popov had in his glove immediately after Popov got up. There was a complete word written on it. That word was "SUCKER."

Although Smith's article did not mention it, there is a practice among fans in the arcade walkway to bring baseballs to the game and to toss them back and forth to people in boats in McCovey Cove who are hoping to retrieve a homerun ball knocked out of the stadium and into the water. But there is also a practice of trying to play a trick on people in the cove: when a ball is hit that appears to be on its way to becoming a home run, people in the arcade will throw a ball into the cove in such a way as to make it appear the ball in question is a homerun ball that's gone out of the stadium. Sometimes, the ball has the word SUCKER written on it.

Theoretically, the suckerball in Popov's glove had just been lying around when he allegedly took it into into his glove while he himself was lying on the walkway (despite the improbability, as discussed, that he miraculously scooped it up). But it's highly unlikely the ball was a lost or abandoned ball left over from a previous game. More likely, it was brought to the game that day. And theoretically, it was inserted into the pileup after the Bonds 73rd ball had hit Popov's glove.

But does that make sense? Anyone *in* the pile-up would surely be scrambling to find and grab the *real* homerun ball. And inserting the suckerball into the *pile-up,* knowing that it would be knocked about, would make it easy for the trickster himself to end up chasing that ball. And, to repeat, the suckerball was in Popov's *glove* by the time he hit the ground.

The logical conclusion is that this "Smart Alex" had outsmarted himself in his effort to outsmart others. Had he not made the switch, he quite likely would not have lost the ball. He was too clever by half, and ended up (in the words of Shakespeare's *Hamlet*) "hoist on his own petar'."

As the poet Robert Burns wrote in "To a Mouse":

> The best-laid plans o' mice and men,
> Gang aft agley,
> And lae us nought but grief and pain
> For promised joy.

I smell a *rat*.

The Double-Edged Sword

Neither side mentioned anything about this possible alternative theory of the case, whether in statements to writer Smith or in documents filed with the court. Why not?

At first, it might seem in Popov's interest to admit that he'd brought in a decoy and pulled a switcheroo, and that he did subsequently make the statement to Castro and Hacker. Were he to admit these things, it would have *strengthened* his argument that he had control of the Bonds ball for a sufficient time to have "captured" it. After all, he would've not only had the ball in his glove, he would've obviously had it sufficiently under control to be able to remove it from the gloved left hand and hold it in his right hand and then hide it in his clothing.

But were he to admit these things, it would create two major problems.

First, it would almost certainly mean the Bonds ball was *not* taken from him by means of a *wrongful* act. It would be obvious that he had *lost* the ball, "more likely than not" through happenstance. The "wrongful" act was a key part of Popov's *theory* of the case—and was at the heart of his case *theme*. That's why he stressed Hayashi's alleged biting of the teenage boy who was wearing the Dallas Cowboys hat. (However, I know of several people who would say that anyone who's a fan of the Dallas Cowboys *deserves* to have others' teeth sunk into his flesh.)

Second, it makes Popov look bad. Suddenly he's not on the moral high ground. Suddenly he's a sneaky, conniving, cunning S.O.B.—or so Hayashi would portray him.

Remember: a courtroom is a moral arena. Jurors want to "do the right thing." But a courtroom is also a *theater*. Theaters require *drama*. And drama requires *the clash of good and evil*. That's why it's so important for each side to turn it into a good-guy, bad-guy situation...just like a Hollywood movie.

But if Popov admits he's a not-so-good guy after all, his theme goes from one of Day v. Night to either Dawn or Dusk v. Night—or maybe enters the Twilight Zone®.

(There is a third problem, but it's minor: Popov would now be seen as a *liar* for previously denying that he'd made the statement to Callahan and Hacker. But Smith did not write his article until many months after the event. Popov could—after meeting with his lawyer—have chosen to acknowledge to Smith the statement Callahan and Hacker said he made to them.)

However, Hayashi also had *his* reasons for wanting to ignore what appears to have been a switch by Popov. Quite likely, the "outcome-determinative" factual question the jury would decide was, "How much control did Popov have over the Bonds ball?" Hayashi needed to argue that Popov *never* had *any* control, not even while Popov was still *standing*. To have argued that Popov did have control while standing but then lost the ball *after making the switch*, would be to considerably muddy the fact-question waters of *Hayashi's* theory of the case.

Thus, this was a can of worms that *neither* side wanted to open.

And so they kept it firmly closed. For different reasons, each side had something to hide with regard to the implications of the same (likely) fact...and so both kept it "out of sight, out of mind."

"The truth, the whole truth, and nothing but the truth" has a lovely ring to it. But sometimes, opponents find it's in their interest to tacitly collude in keeping the truth from judge and jury. (The jury, and not even the judge, can go on their own search for the truth. They must deal *only* with what the two sides put in front of them. However, as we shall see, the Court can *disallow* presentation not only of individual pieces of evidence or testimony, but of an entire line of argument.)

As you can guess, a big reason why this Coda is about *this* case is because, having spent hundreds of pages talking of how *law professors* "hide the ball," here's a suit where both sides' *lawyers* were playing hide-the-ball, metaphorically...and where one of the *parties* apparently hid the ball for *real*.

Further Developments: Pre-Trial Activites

Popov sued not only Hayashi, but 25 other people whose identities and whereabouts were unknown. His causes of action were "**conversion**" ("the unwarranted interference by) with A's dominion over A''s property"), for "**trespass to chattel**" ("the act of committing, without lawful justification, any act of direct physical interference with a chattel possessed by another" — "The act must amount to a direct forcible injury"), for **assault,** and for **battery.** (These last two were defined in Chapter 5.)

San Francisco County's state courts use a "rotating docket." Whichever judge is available is the judge who's assigned to preside over a proceeding. Judge David Garcia heard Popov's request for an injunction to keep Hayashi from selling the ball, and granted the injunction. Much later, the two sides filed Motions for Summary Judgment. (MSJs were discussed in Chapter 9.) A different judge, James McBride, presided over the hearing on those.

He denied both motions. However, he did give each side something. He dismissed Popov's causes of action for assault and battery against Hayashi; the evidence on those was not sufficient, as a matter of law, to justify presenting it to a trier of fact. And he set trial on only *one* issue: whether Popov had sufficient "dominion and control" of the ball.

These rulings helped Popov far more than they helped Hayashi. Popov's argument of "assault" and of "battery" was ridiculous to start with, but his attorney apparently felt that, to maintain consistency, he had to argue them. The court made Popov's case much more reasonable.

Without saying so, the court nearly converted this from a "capture" case to a "finders" case. The difference is subtle, but important. The law of finders applies only to abandonded or lost property If someone finds *lost* property, he or she becomes its owner as against everyone but its *true* owner. But the finder of *abandoned* property becomes its owner against *"all the world."* So, now, if Popov had sufficient control, he acquired title, and keeps it as true owner, despite having subsequently lost it himself. (That is why the court did *not* dismiss Popov's causes of action for conversion and trespass to chattel.)

This *new* framing of *the* issue by the *Court* made the situation much more "iffy" for Hayashi than it would otherwise have been.

Neither side requested a jury.

There is no way of knowing for sure what Judge McBride had in mind when he said the sole issue at trial would be Popov's control of the ball. Perhaps he suspected the evidence (especially Hayashi's expert witnesses) would establish that Popov did not have control. Or perhaps he thought the presence of the crowd, as Popov argued, was all that prevented Popov from "pulling it in."

But Judge McBride was not likely to preside at trial. There was no way of knowing in advance who would. So, it's a toss-up whether this "suckerball" strategy would have backfired had Hayashi used it. (I *loathe* rotating dockets, because the judge presiding over each new proceeding is coming in "cold," and is never willing to "get up to speed." —Please forgive the mixed metaphor.) At any rate, Hayashi's attorney—Donald Tamaki—chose to play it safe and stick with the issue as successfully framed by Popov's attorney, Martin Triano.

Tamaki has been practicing law almost 20 years longer than I, and is probably a far better trial attorney that I will ever be. Further, he was *on* the case, and knew the facts inside-out, whereas all I have to go on is the *Sports Illustrated* article and the court documents I've seen. So, I shall defer to his greater experience and knowledge of the facts, his skill...and what is perhaps his wisdom.

A Question of Ball Control

Had Popov made a good, "clean" catch, then Hayashi would likely lose. But Popov did not make such a catch.

Hayashi relied on expert testimony to establish whether or not there was a "catch" at all. One of his expert witnesses was Jim Evans, a former Major League Baseball umpire with 28 years's experience. In deposition, he said:

> I have reviewed a copy of the videotape of Barry Bonds' 73rd homerun ball...When last seen before Popov falls out of view of the camera, almost all of the ball's circumference is clearly visible in the outermost finger portion of the glove's pocket-side and the pocket has not been closed. It is very difficult for a person to get and maintain secure control of a ball in this position because there is little direct finger pressure on the ball since the leather finger tunnels of the ball are considerably longer than most fingers. *Balls are often dislodged and dropped by even the best players in the Major Leagues when they fall to the ground, collide with another player,* or crash into a wall...Additionally, maintaining possession of the ball when the open pocket of the glove is facing down is difficult and complicated even further when one is using only one hand as is the case in the Videotape.
>
> [Italics added.]

A second expert witness for Hayashi was Richard Garcia, also a former Major League Umpire, with 25 years' experience. Here is an excerpt from his deposition:

I reviewed the videotape in real time, in slow motion, and frame by frame....As the ball strikes the webbing of Mr. Popov's glove, the glove begins to turn so that its opening faces the cameraman and I can still see almost the entire perimeter of the ball. In the last frame before he disappears into the crowd, the outer edge of the ball remains clearly visible and the ball appears to be moving upward and out of the glove. The fact that I can see almost the entire ball tells me that Mr. Popov doesn't have complete control of the ball because his glove does not close completely around it....The definition of a "catch" on the baseball field is that the player must firmly secure possession of the ball and firmly hold it *long enough to prove he has complete control of the ball and that his release of the ball is voluntary and intentional.* Moreover, it is *not* a catch if simultaneously or immediately after such player has contact with the ball, *he collides with a player,* or with a wall, *or if he falls down, and as a result of such collision or falling, he drops the ball.*

[Italics added.]

In documents filed with the Court, Popov merely argued that whether a ball is caught or not is not subject to expert testimony." "Any parent who has ever played catch with their child knows when a catch is made, without ever making any reference to Major League Baseball rules."

Slipping Hayashi a Weenie

Although Popov portrayed himself as having made a "clean catch," he clearly did not. And on the basis of ball control, he loses, I believe.

However, Popov's lawyer, Marty Triano, coupled a second argument with the first. Again quoting court papers: "Had Popov been left free of the subsequent assault and battery following his catch of the ball, there is no doubt that the ball would have remained in his possession." This is the implicit claim of "tortious interference with prospective economic advantage, disussed in connection with the dicta in *Young v. Hichens.*

Major League Baseball was not a party to this suit. But Triano in effect brought MLB in as a "shadow defendant": what would be called, in criminal law, "an unindicted co-conspirator." He did this by saying that MLB tacitly encouraged "mob rule"—a "free-for-all" where only the law of the jungle existed. He claimed this meant that "anything goes" and that in fact some things did go on that were unconscionable. Thus, in a "reverse halo effect," he tainted Hayashi by lambasting Major League Baseball. Had this been a jury trial, it is possible the jury would have chosen to vote for Popov as a way of "sending a message" to Major League Baseball.

Hayashi was put in the position of not only defending himself, but of defending MLB's practice with regard to "allowing" fans to scramble for a ball (as though MLB could possibly prevent it).

He responded that the scramble was itself a "contest," and all the fans know the rules of that informal contest. The contest was an "industry custom," and the winner of the contest was determined by the "last man standing" rule. Popov, the six-footer, was a "big boy." He knew the contest might involve some rough-and-tumble. He'd chosen to join the contest anyway...and lost out to the 5'5" Hayashi.

However, the Court's ruling, as to what the sole issue was, meant that Hayashi's "contest" counter-argument was almost completely irrelevant. Instead, Popov's "but for" argument with respect to the "interference" of the crowd logically took priority, although the "but for" was no longer couched in the language of battery or assault. Thus, thanks to the judge, Popov got to play both ends against the middle.

Policy Arguments

In the cases cited (which perhaps became irrelevant when the Court has reframed the issue), there were only *two* human actors in each of them: the plaintiff, and the defendant. And in each one, the lone defendant took action that was a deliberate imposition of himself between the plaintiff and the plaintiff's prey. Here, however, there was a *crowd* of people, all after the same "prey"—and *no one* having a superior right to it.

But Popov was arguing, in effect, that once the Bonds ball had hit his glove, *the crowd had a duty to him to back off,* to let him complete his "capture."

However, as a practical matter, it is quite possible that the crowd was *incapable* of backing off. Everyone, including Popov, had surged toward where the ball would appear to come down. Quite likely, the momentum was irreversible.

Smith's article stated this, remember:

> Popov, six feet and 200 pounds, decided he
> was taller than anyone within arm's reach, but
> just in case, he planted one foot on a box
> containing television cable so he could make him-
> self even taller.

So there was Popov, only *one* foot planted on the box, which is an inherently unstable stance. Add to that the fact that the photo (and presumably, the video) shows him stretching out to make the catch— further destabilizing himself. Even if he did not deliberately drop to the ground, it's easy to see how he could have lost his balance without being *deliberately* knocked down by others.

Smith's article said others were in pile-ups too, and not on top of Alex Popov. For example, by coincidence, Alex's brother Michael had ended up at the bottom of another heap—with Patrick's brother Lane among those on top of *him*. So, Alex was not unique in this regard.

The larger question, though, is "What made *Popov* so special?" Returning to deposition testimony from Jim Evans:

> In my 28 years of umpiring Major League Base-
> ball, I would estimate approximately *30 to 40*
> balls entering the stands each game. The vast
> majority of these balls are *not* finally secured by
> the person who initially touches it. In other words,
> it is not the fan that first has contact with the ball
> who is entitled to keep it.   [Emphais added.]

Yet, Popov was implicitly trying to replace the "last man standing" rule with a new "initial contact" rule. In papers filed with the court, he said, "Once the baseball entered Popov's glove, the fate of the baseball was sealed." —Popov had title to it.

But what if the person who first made contact with the ball did so by *stepping or reaching in front of* someone who was clearly in the best position to make a catch? The six-foot Popov, for example, could easily have blocked the 5'5" Hayashi's chances in such a situation.

And suppose the ball had *popped out of* Popov's glove while he was still standing, and into the hands of another fan. What then?

It's easy to foresee what might be called the "stopwatch problem." Say the ball popped out, into the hands of another fan, but then that fan, while still standing, also lost control of it. Assuming the event was on video, is ownership decided by who had contact with the ball for the longest time? And what if the video does not clearly show who had contact with it after it popped out of the first person's glove?

This becomes especially problematic with a bare-handed catch. It *hurts* to catch a baseball moving with the speed and force of the Bonds ball. It is conceivable the person who "caught" it would have to quickly transfer it back and forth from one hand to the other because of the pain. And, of course, it would be easy to lose possession then.

Would a new, "initial contact" rule make ownership more certain than the present "last man standing" rule?

Further, although the "last man standing" rule is obviously an invitation to a melee, would an "initial contact" rule really change things?

One more: what happens if the dispute is over a *routine* home-run ball, where no TV camera recorded the scramble in the stands? Say, for example, that someone who's a huge fan of the guy who homered really, really, wanted that ball—and made the intial contact with it—but another guy also really, really, wanted that ball...and ended up with it after the first guy fails to "pull it in"? Who would "run the stopwatch"? If the loser wanted that ball badly enough, he might sue to get it. And there would be a swearing match among witnesses, of course. Does a court want to invite that?

Baseball umpires must often deal with catches by *players* in the stands, as when a player tries to catch a foul ball hit out of play. (For non-baseball fans: if the player succeeds, it's an "out" for the other team.) Here's more of Jim Evans's deposition testimony:

> The videotape depicts the ball entering Popov's glove and almost instantaneously he drops out of sight among the fans scrambling for the ball. When a player attempts a catch in the stands and goes out of the umpire's sight, the umpire bases his ultimate decision on the legality of the catch on the following facts: (a) Did the player have reasonable control of the ball before he and the ball went out of the umpire's sight? (b) While out of the umpire's sight, did the umpire see any evidence that the player did not maintain firm and secure possession? (c) Did the player return to the umpire's sight [apparently with the ball in his glove—AF] in a reasonable amount of time?
>
> [Continued—]

It is my opinion Popov did not have reasonable control of the ball before he and the ball went out of sight as indicated by the precarious position of the ball near the fingertips of his glove as stated above, the fact that he was falling backwards, the fact that the open portion of the glove is facing down as he is falling, the fact that he is attempting a one-handed catch, and the fact that he collides with other fans and the ground.

Due Process of Law

"Industry custom" was first mentioned in Chapter 10, regarding a line of cases where the defendant pleaded that the industry custom provided the standard of care—which the court in each case rejected as inadequate. So you might think the court here is free to do likewise.

However, in each of those cases, the defendant was a *member* of the industry. Here, neither "Major League Baseball" (the corporate entity) nor the San Francisco Giants ball "club" was a party. So, neither would have been defending the industry custom of the last man standing rule.

Arguably, if the judge had expressly overturned that custom, he would likely have been reversed on appeal, for denying MLB and the Giants due process of law.

Different Strokes for Different "Fokes"

As you've seen, I believe Hayashi had by far the better case, even without the "suckerball" theory.

BUT, for the sake of using this case as a teaching tool regarding a "lawyerlike analysis," I'll further explore the "suckerball" theory.

I do not believe that either *Pierson v. Post* OR *Swift v. Gifford* was on point. At the least, I believe they should have been "distinguished" from the "instant case."

Both involved people who were actively chasing specific, identified prey. True, both Popov and Hayashi (and many others) were also actively trying to capture specific, identified "prey"—i.e., the Bonds ball. But the similarity almost ends there.

It seems to me that the more relevant capture cases are the two fish cases discussed earlier. Popov's glove functioned like a net. As did the fishermen ("fisherpersons"?), he set his net out where he hoped the prey would enter it. And indeed it did. But as the court held in *Young*

v. Hichens, a net with fish in it has to be *closed up* to acquire ownership of those fish. Popov didn't close his "net." (This part of the alternative approach, of course, tracks the one Hayashi used. But Hayashi did
not cite the fish-net cases. I believe such citation would have helped
his case.)

With regard to the presence of a net (as opposed to the presence of
a predator *fish*), fish have no awareness of their situation. In that sense,
they're a lot more like the Bonds ball than any whale or fox could be.
Popov's initial contact with the ball made no difference to the ball's
physical condition, in the same way that a net that almost completely
surrounds a school of fish makes no difference to their physical condition.

But as the court pointed out in *Young,* had the defendant not interfered with the fish in the net by agitating them, arguably most of them
would have become the plaintiff's property. Popov would argue that's
the situation here, too. But it is not.

And that's where the "suckerball" comes in. Popov, in effect,
agitated the "fish" *himself,* and, in effect, *drove* "them" from his own
"net," through his switcheroo.

By shifting the emphasis to *Popov's own self-defeating (and fraudulent) actions,* Hayashi could have *avoided* the risks inherent in the
"factual loose ball" of "Did Popov have control?" It would have injected
a powerful moral component, quite similar to contributory or comparative negligence in a torts case. It would have framed the issue/s in a
way more favorable to Hayashi. —And that's the *purpose* of choosing
the "right" way to frame the issue/s.

(Had Hayashi used *this,* he could have questioned Popov for
contradicting himself as to how long he had the ball, as discussed
earlier. Hayashi could then have severely undermined Popov's credibility
as to veracity. And Hayashi could also perhaps have nailed Popov for
perjury. After all, Popov, according to Hacker and Castro, *did* tell them
he'd pulled a switcheroo. Popov might have later made the same denial
under oath. Juries, and sometimes even judges, "turn off" to a witness
real fast if that witness has clearly committed perjury. —I would also
have called Gary Smith, the writer, as a witness.)

But the fishing cases mentioned were *commercial* fishing cases.
A more apt analogy would be to sport fishing—specifically, fishing
from a boat in a lake for a 15-20 pound freshwater *game*fish such as a
large-mouth bass, lake trout, Northern Pike, Walleye, or Muskelunge.

Many people go fishing in a small open boat such as a rowboat or
bass boat that has a small outboard motor at the stern. And many have

hooked a fish and reeled it in. But many have also hooked a fish that puts up a fight; and the hook works loose, or the line breaks. The fish escapes (sometimes with the hook still in its mouth and trailing many feet of fishing line). Many have even reeled a fish in close to the boat, put a small net into the water under the fish to scoop the fish up in it—even going so far as to start lifting the fish up out of the water—only to have the fish suddenly put forth a mighty, final effort...and escape.

There is a world of difference between a deadly harpoon embedded in a whale's side, or a bullet embedded in a fox's flesh, and a mere hook or torn tissue in the mouth of the big one that got away. Popov's initial contact with the Bonds ball is, at best, a mere hook, not a harpoon or bullet.

The fox and whale cases were quite simplistic. There was really only one act involved: a harpoon thrown, a bullet fired. Either the animal died, or was mortally wounded—or it didn't or wasn't, respectively. With sport fishing, in contrast, there's "many a slip 'twixt cup and lip."

So, say two guys are fly-fishing from a boat and one of them, using his favorite lure, hooks a big one. But the big one gets away after the line snaps. Say later the second guy hooks a big one, and lands it—and lo and behold, the other guy's favorite lure is still hooked in that fish's mouth. There's no way the first guy would claim that he's entitled to the fish, not even by arguing that the fish's previous struggle to escape *him* had weakened it and made it easier for the second guy to haul it in. At best, Popov's contact with the Bonds ball was comparable to that first guy's lure. A lot more was required than in any of the fox, whale, or *commercial* fishing cases. And once the first guy lost the fish, that's all she wrote, for him.

To play with this further: many a sport fisherman has lost a fish through his own screw-ups. The most common one is not letting the line play out when the fish is determined to run. The fish is streaking off in one direction, the fisherman is reeling it in—and the line snaps or the hook tears loose. Or maybe the fisherman had not kept his rod and reel or flyrod in good working order, and it fouls at a critical moment. Or maybe he went fishing for a 15-20 pound fish with only "8-pound test" line, and the line broke from having more stress put on it than it was made to handle. The fact that he'd managed to *hook* a fish is irrelevant, if the fish gets away.

In all these situations, it doesn't make any difference if the sport fisherman struggled with the fish for half an hour or more. The big one got away, and that's that.

And that was Popov's situation.

Popov argued that, but for the interference of the *crowd,* he would have *landed* the big one, thus trying to bring his case under the *dicta* in *Young.*

But pursuing this new analogy: many fishermen have gone out in a rowboat or bass boat loaded with fishermen—an *overcrowded* boat, where everyone's cheek-by-jowl. In a situation like that, trying to land a fish can be quite difficult. For those who do not do any fresh-water fishing in lakes: a hooked fish trying to get free goes all over the place underwater. If the fisherman is on one side of the boat, and the fish goes under the boat and comes out on the other side (and thus is now behind the fisherman's back) and streaks away from the boat, the fisherman has to swivel around and move to the other side of the boat, *fast,* to try to *keep* control of the situation. *But in an overcrowded boat, that is almost impossible—and can even be physically risky.*

Popov was like a fisherman in an overcrowded boat who hooked one. He in effect was saying that, had he been the *only* person in the boat, he would have landed the fish. That might well be true. And let's even grant that the fish would not have been able to break the line or work the hook loose. *But there were a lot of other people in the same boat as Popov* (as it were). Yes, but for their *presence,* Popov would have been able to keep the ball all to himself. But just because he lost the ball due to their *presence,* that does not mean he lost the ball due to their *interference.* (Again, this is a line of reasoning Hayashi did use—though he put it a different way.)

Per former MLB umpire Jim Evans's testimony, *players* on the *field* sometimes are ruled not to have made a catch, because they collided with a teammate going after the same ball. Clearly, *those* two guys are not working at cross-purposes. But if the ball comes out, that's that. This argument should apply with even more force to Popov's "catch."

Granted, in this analogy, only one fisherman has hooked the fish in question. And, in a real situation, no other fishermen in the boat would be scrambling to somehow try to also hook that same fish and reel it in for themselves in competition with the one who'd already hooked it. (Although, as we know, sometimes two teammates do go after the same ball—though admittedly, only one of them makes the initial contact with it.) But just as many a fisherman has lost a fish while in a crowded boat, and has lost it because he could not successfully maneuver to keep control of the fish, so Popov's inability to keep control of the ball was due to the mere and *unavoidable* crush of the crowd, in the same way that the presence of too many others in a boat can destroy a fisherman's freedom of movement.

The hunters in *Pierson* and *Swift,* and the *commercial* fishermen in the other cases, in contrast, all had complete freedom of movement.

Getting away from the whale and fox and commercial fishing cases allows for much more freedom of thought—and, I believe, the creation of an *apt* analogy.

But this new analogy allows for one more argument that the others really don't. Picture several guys in the boat, as before. One of them lands a whopper. However, he fears that each of his fellows will try to grab it for himself. So he doesn't take firm hold of the fish, place it on a stringer, and then put it back into the water, attaching the stringer to the side of the boat. Instead, he hurriedly gives the fish a kick with the back of his shoe, trying to knock it under his seat where others can't get at it. But the kick puts new life into the fish. In fact, it helps the fish launch itself into the air...and over the side—to freedom.

Popov did not trust the integrity of his fellow fans, despite the fact that there was no record of fans mobbing someone whose glove a ball had initially struck during previous record-breaking home runs: not during Sosa's and McGwire's rivalrous slugfest in 1999, nor during Bonds's solo slugfest in 2001. In court papers, Popov himself said that when Bonds hit record-breaking homers No. 71 and 72 on October 5—just two days before No. 73—there had been no such action against any fan by others. (However, Popov apparently didn't know, or forgot, that No. 72 had bounced off the wall back onto the field, and was recovered by a ballplayer and given to Bonds himself.)

And Popov's *contempt* for his fellow fans is evidenced by his having written "SUCKER" on the decoy ball.

Remember in Chapter 2, under "Legal Maxims & Doctrines," the maxim "He who would seek equity must do equity"? —and the "Clean Hands Doctrine"? Well, this is a perfect case for them, to Hayashi's benefit.

Thus, I would modify Hayashi's framing of the issue/s as follows:

> Hayashi, playing by the rules of an informal "game"
> —scrambling for a loose baseball—won "fair and square"
> after Popov, through his own ineptness *and an attempted
> act of fraud that backfired,* failed to secure the ball himself.

Granted, that's not "25 words or less." It's 38. But it is succinct.

Theme—   "Justice has *already* been done."
One-Liner— "Popov brought it on himself: he had a
           fair chance, played *dirty,* and lost."

Smith's article mentioned that informal polls showed that prospective female jurors favored Popov, while prospective blue-collar male jurors favored Hayashi. Use of this new theme would have appealed to both groups. Forgive the gender stereotyping, but for the women, this theme would translate as "Popov is Not a Nice Man." For the men, it would translate as "He's a cheater—and a con artist." That way, Hayashi's attorney needn't be so concerned about ending up with a jury composed mostly of women. Either way, it would have pulled the "moral rug," on which Popov is standing, out from under him.

The dropped switcheroo would also have helped Hayashi overcome the skeptical response to his comment that he just found the Bonds ball, lying there. (Jumping ahead: Popov's attorney scornfully hammered at this during the trial and in closing argument.)

Best of all, perhaps, this approach would have taken the monkey off the judge's back. It would not have required the judge to reach the decision of whether or not Popov had sufficient control. The judge could have ruled that, by his own conduct, Popov forfeited any claim he had to the ball. Thus, the judge need not arrogate to himself or herself the power of overturning not one but two "industry customs" in Major League Baseball: (1) the "last man standing" rule, and (2) MLB's definition of what constitutes a "catch." (We'll return to the last man standing rule in the addendum to Chapter 29.)

However, you remember the discussion in Chapter 1, "Sometimes the liar wins"? The judge might have ruled that regardless of Popov's attempted fraud against his fellow fans, the question *remains* one of ball control—and the attempted fraud *proves* Popov *had* control.

"Rant No. 1"

As mentioned, San Francisco County uses a rotating docket. The judge ordered the parties into a final mediation the week before trial. The mediation failed. The Honorable Kevin McCarthy then presided at trial.

Judge James McBride had shaped the case by tossing out Popov's claims for battery and assault. Judge McCarthy, however, allowed Popov to present extensive testimony of alleged battery and assault, from more than a dozen witnesses. (That, in my opinion, is part of the problem with a rotating docket. Had McBride remained on the case, he quite likely would not have allowed Triano to tacitly ignore the court's previous rulings.) Thus, Triano was able to "slip another weenie" to Hayashi.

The earlier "weenie," as mentioned, concerned putting Major League Baseball on trial, in effect, for its policy regarding the "mob scene" in the stands. The new "weenie" involved, in part, putting the "mob" itself on trial, in effect. Judge McBride had dismissed the 25 "John Doe" defendants Popov had sued. But Judge McCarthy allowed testimony concerning them.

In short, Judge McCarthy followed in the tradition of Judge Lance Ito (who presided over the notorious O.J. Simpson murder trial), by exercising extremely poor control over the proceedings. A trial that should have lasted, at most, three days, ended up taking 15.

Given that this is a case of first impression, it's understandable that Judge McCarthy took an inclusive approach. However, it was overly inclusive.*

"Rant No. 2"

Gary Smith's excellent article included two statements that cannot go unchallenged. (In e-mail correspondence and phone conversation, he made it clear that he was not giving his own personal opinion in these two statements, but rather was reporting the consensus among fans and fellow sports writers as he understood it.) Here's the first:

> [T]his is the America that makes your stomach turn. The one in which pettiness and greed and lawyers chasing contingency fees can sully anything, even a thing so pure as a baseball sailing through the sky on a Sunday afternoon.

Was it "greed" for Popov and Hayashi—each of whom was convinced the ball is rightfully his—to not pass up the chance to make a million dollars by prevailing in court? Popov, who'd just had a dot.com business go belly up? Hayashi, who'd been out of work for months?

Was it "pettiness" to seek the *honor* of being adjudicated the fan who came up with Bonds's 73rd? When this was probably each man's once-in-a-lifetime shot at a small piece of "immortality"?

It's amazingly easy to sit in judgment and play "holier-than-thou" with regard to others' pursuit of the American Dream—even if they're pursuing it in the courts as well as in a stadium. How would *any* truly reasonable person react *in similar circumstances?* The loftiness of those who criticized Popov and Hayashi sounds spiteful to me.

---

* One effect of this was, almost certainly, to drive Popov's outlays for legal fees, the cost of experts, etc., to a quarter-of-a-million dollars.

As to "lawyers chasing contingency fees," the article says that Popov's attorney, Marty Triano, was working on an hourly basis (apparently by Popov's choice). Lawyers have to earn a living. And they have to go through four years of college and three years of law school, and spend hundreds of thousands of dollars, just to have a chance to ply their trade. Would the average person refer to medical doctors who treat accident victims as "doctors chasing after fees?" Popov and Hayashi each chose to fight it out in court. *They* were the ones chasing after a *lawyer,* not the other way around. (And Hayashi *had no choice* about getting a lawyer, once he'd been sued.)

Here's the next passage from the article:

> If Solomon were deciding the case, he'd no doubt award the ball to both men and have them split the proceeds from its sale—or award it to neither, and use the million bucks to buy baseballs for kids who can't afford them.

Solomon was faced by two women who each claimed an infant was hers. He tested them, saying he would kill it, cut it in half, and award half to each woman. One woman immediately said "Okay." The other said she would rather let her rival have the baby. This supposedly proved her the real mother (or at least proved her the one who really loved the child).

The story is apocryphal, of course, because Solomon would not have put the child to death, regardless. The situation here was not comparable, as it involved a mere baseball, not a helpless infant. ("Solomonic wisdom" in this case would have been a threat from the judge to *destroy* the ball—which, as Smith pointed out, the judge did not have the power to do.)

Imagine a situation where you've been told a long-lost relative had died and left you a million dollars. But then some other person with the same name as yours comes along and says *he* or *she* was the designated beneficiary. Would a reasonable person meekly offer to split the money? —Especially if he or she believed the other was a mere gold-digger?

People might refer to these litigants as having "sullied" the sport of baseball. But surely those people would acknowledge that professional baseball is a no-nonsense *business.* The owners and players continually fight over who gets what slice of the pie. Yet, the owners and players are already making money hand-over-fist off the "game."

Smith's article said nothing about what happened when Mike Piazza, of the New York Mets, hit is 300th home run on July 13, 2001. The Mets had a longstanding policy that any ball hit into the stands belonged to the fan who came up with it. Rafael Vasquez made a clean catch of that ball, and handed it to his six-year-old daughter, Denise, as a present. But father and child were almost immediately confronted by ten security guards. They told Vasquez he had to give them the ball—because Mike Piazza had said before the game that he wanted his 300th home-run ball, as a keepsake for his trophy case.

The guards, in effect, seized the ball, through an act of intimidation, in violation of the Mets' promise to fans. Despite the ball's considerable value, and despite Piazza's considerable income, Piazza gave nothing to the Vasquezes—and the Mets only handed over some virtually worthless items as "compensation."

Just who is it who "sullied" the noble sport of baseball there?

To say that Popov and Hayashi had "sullied" baseball is like saying two film actors quarrelling over the placement of their names in a movie's credits have "sullied" the Hollywood film industry. Pull-eeze.

Media such as *Sports Illustrated* serve largely to provide escapism, in much the same way as "fan magazines" do with regard to the movies, television, or popular singers. They posit a fantasy world of heroes, melodrama, and moral simplicity. But as Justice William Doubles said (dissenting) in *Flood v. Kuhn, et al,* 407 U.S. 258 (1972), "This is not a romantic business baseball enjoys as a history. It is a sordid business." And Andrew Zimbalist's 2003 book, *May the Best Team Win: Baseball Economics and Public Policy,* documents that the behind-the-scenes story of professional baseball is at least as sordid today as it ever was.

As will be seen, this book is very critical of what the legal profession has become. And the legal profession in turn has contributed to an American attitude of using the civil justice system as a lottery. However, the ultimate purpose of the legal system is to resolve disputes in a peaceful manner, with the goal that the truth will out and justice will be done. Those who were quick to condemn Popov and Hayashi would surely be the first who, when it's *their* ox that's being gored, to say, "I need a good lawyer!"

"Rant No. 3"

But I also have a bone to pick with both attorneys in this case.

As Smith's article mentioned, each attorney brought in a "legal expert." Each was a law professor. Paul Finkelman (Popov's) is at the University of Tulsa School of Law. Hayashi's, John Dwyer was at the University of California at Berkeley, "Boalt Hall," at the time.*

Trial lawyers use consulting experts to help them get "up to speed" on technical subjects. But the subject here is *law*. Both Triano and Tamaki are *lawyers,* damnit. What need have they to *hire* "experts" who, after all, are just fellow law school graduates? (In fact, Finkelman is not even a law school graduate, but a Ph.D. historian.)

Finkelman's specialties are "American legal history," "race and the law," and "First Amendment issues." He teaches American legal history and Constitutional Law at Tulsa. Dwyer's sole speciality is environmental law, and (at the time) he was the Director of the Environmental Law Program at Berkeley. What does either of these members of the professoriat bring to the table that any decent lawyer couldn't?

(However, Tamaki—Hayashi's lawyer—might have been playing a clever game here. Smith's article didn't mention it, but Dwyer had been the *dean* at Boalt Hall since 2000. He was thus especially well known and highly respected in California. And, of course, this case was in a California state court, and would have gone up on appeal in a state court. Dwyer's name just might have been on some of the papers filed with the court. Enough said.)

During the trial itself, Triano brought in two *more* professors on Popov's behalf. The first was Roger Bernhardt, of Golden Gate University's law school. He's an expert on property law in general and California's property law in particular. The second was an expert on sports law and torts, Jan Stiglitz, at Southwestern University's law school.

(Dwyer said he had a schedule conflict on the day he was to testify. Tamaki brought in Brian Gray, of U. Cal. - Hastings School of Law, in his stead.)**

---

* We met Dwyer in the addendum to Chapter 13.

** Perhaps the schedule conflict was due to the internal investigation at Boalt Hall that occurred during the trial, in connection with the event discussed in the addendum to Chapter 13.

It appears that both Triano and Tamaki failed to "think outside the box." Their arguments were based almost entirely on case citations—to a mind-numbing list of cases, in fact. But while cases can be valuable as precedents, they are not the be-all and end-all of legal reasoning. Law professors, by their very nature, tend to be unimaginative, and also to be slaves to law books. And both Triano and Tamaki were apparently well indoctrinated in law school, and are *still* in awe of the professoriat. Better for them to have shown their mettle as lawyers on their own, by dispensing with the services of the denizens of the ivory tower.

All these experts charged a pretty penny. (Examples: Bernhardt - $450/hr., Stiglitz - $300/hr.. I do not know what Finkelman or Gray charged.) And that money had to be paid by Popov and Hayashi, respectively. For Popov, it was cash-on-the-barrelhead. For Hayashi, it appears Tamaki was "fronting" expenses. Tamaki was working on contingency. If the typical rate applies, he was to get a third to 40% of the proceeds from the sale of the ball if he won Hayashi's case at trial or obtained a settlement. (If the case had gone up on appeal, his contract probably gave him an additional percentage, if he won the appeal.) But if Tamaki's attorney-client contract was typical, *his* share was to come off the top. That means the cost of the experts' "services," and all other expenses, were to come out of Hayashi's share. (This is why, in contingency cases sometimes, nothing's left for the client after a "victory.")

Do not get me wrong: As a plaintiff's counsel in civil suits, I'm a strong believer in contingency fees. But as the arrangement stands now, there's no incentive for the lawyer to try to hold down expenses, such as for consulting "legal experts." (Tamaki became even more extravagant, and brought in two experts to testify on the body mechanics involved in Popov's fall.)

So, I believe that, by *statute*, all *expenses* in a contingency fee case should come off the top—and the lawyer then takes his or her cut only from what remains.

"Rant No. 4"

Popov's lawyer, Marty Triano, apparently brought Finkelman in on the case after learning that Finkelman had presented a paper on "who has title to home-run balls" at a conference held at Cardozo Law School on April 30, 2001—more than five months before Bonds's 73rd.

Finkelman subsequently turned his paper into a law review article, published in May, 2002 (23 Cardozo L. Rev 1609).

In it, he discusses the Bonds lawsuit. Describing what happened in the stands on October 7, 2001, he says: "Popov was *thrown to the ground and pounced on by at least ten fans.* Popov *screamed for help, while the Giants security forces did nothing."* (Emphasis added.)

Finkelman was not even in San Francisco that day, let alone an eyewitness to the scrum. People who *were* there, and in the arcade walkway at the time, have testified that Popov was not "thrown to the ground." Although fans were on top of him, they could just as easily have *fallen* on top of him as "pounced" on him.

Finkelman insists that Popov clearly caught the ball, and that Hayashi obtained it only as the result of a "battery" on Popov. His article was so one-sided and polemical that Popov's *lawyer* could have written it. It reads more like a pleading, and is a miserable excuse for "scholarship." But not even Popov's lawyer maintained that the security guards "did nothing." In fact, the parties agreed that security "forces" arrived within seconds, to break up the melee.

Further, Finkelman somewhat *misrepresents* the holding in *Swift v. Gifford:* "The court ruled that the whale belonged to the ship which first put a harpoon in the whale." As we've seen, that is technically true, but it was *industry custom* that led to the court's holding. (You can read the case for yourself: 2 Low 110 Fish 3, 23 F. Cas. 558 (D Mass. 1872).)

Finkelman also says there has been a "common law" of baseball for generations now, that the fan who *"catches"* a home-run (or foul) ball gets to keep it. But perhaps because Finkelman is not even a law school graduate, he apparently does not know what the term "common law" *means.* As mentioned, this is a case of *first impression.* Thus, there is *no* "common" *law* on this question. Further, his statement also misrepresents what has been baseball's *industry custom* for generations now: *the last man standing rule.*

Finkelman does not disclose that he was a paid consultant for Popov. Instead, in *footnote 70,* he merely says this: "In the interest of full disclosure, I gave an affidavit on behalf of Mr. Popov in this litigation based on an earlier draft of this article."

I seriously doubt that...and I doubt Finkelman even knows what an **affidavit** is. It's a declaration of *facts,* based on *personal ("first-hand") knowledge,* sworn to by the declarant. *Opinions, especially* as to the interpretation of case law, *cannot* be the subject of an affidavit. There is simply no way Finkelman could have given an affidavit in this case.

But even if he provided a signed document of some sort, he certainly did far more than that. He knew, when he was writing his article (a rough draft of which was posted to the Internet in January,

2002), that he was a *paid consultant* for Popov. And he surely knew that his involvement in the case might continue—as indeed it did, for (as mentioned), Finkelman testified at the trial.

I would call this a "prostitution of scholarship." But that would be an insult to the integrity of "the world's oldest profession." I guess that old habit of hiding the ball really dies hard.

There was a conflict of interest between Finkelman's role as legal "scholar" and his role as a hired gun for one side in the case. This is not-so-uncommon within the law school professoriat—as is the effort to conceal it. (Unfortunately, the professoriat has no rules of ethics in this regard. Interesting. So, it's a matter of individual conscience...or lack of it, as the case may be.)

As Yale Law School professor Grant Gilmore noted parenthetically in his classic 1977 work, *The Ages of American Law*—

> (Consultation work at high fees plays the same
> role in academia that bribery and corruption play
> in the courts and, like bribery and corruption,
> occasionally becomes institutionalized.)

What was perhaps only "occasionally" institutionalized a quarter-century ago is now *de rigueur*.

Resolution of the Case

Judge McCarthy issued a written opinion on December 18, 2002. It's available at http//www.sftc.org/Docs/dec.400345.dec.

Bottom line: he ordered the ball sold, and the proceeds split 50/50.

He ruled that Popov had no cause of action for trespass to chattel, because Hayashi neither damaged the ball nor interfered with Popov's (continued) use and enjoyment of the ball. And he ruled that Popov's only possible cause of action was in conversion, for Hayashi's wrongful exercise of dominion over the ball—but *only if* the ball were Popov's personal property or if Popov had the *right to possession* of the ball.

The key question was indeed that of "whether [Popov] did enough to reduce the ball to his exclusive dominion and control. Were his acts suffcient to create a legally cognizable interest in the ball?"

McCarthy adopted the definition of "possession of a baseball" that he said was proposed by Prof. Brian Gray (an expert witness for Hayashi). But Gray's definition was identical to that of Major League Baseball set out in the testimony of former umpires Jim Evans and Richard Garcia (who were also expert witnesses for Hayashi).

As a finding of fact, McCarthy said Popov had not achieved possession of the ball. Nor could the court conclude that Popov *would* have achieved possession but for the interference of others.

However, the judge ruled that Popov *did* have a "pre-possessory interest" in the ball, because of his "significant but incomplete steps to achieve possession," which steps were "interrupted by the unlawful acts of others." This gave him a "qualified right to possession which can support a cause of action for conversion." Yet, Hayashi was not among those who'd engaged in an "unlawful" act. And Hayashi did meet the definition of possession of the ball. So Hayashi also had a rightful claim.

Popov had filed suit in equity, not just in law. A court "sitting in equity" has much more freedom to craft its ruling. McCarthy relied on a December, 1983 law review article on "the rules governing finders of lost and abandoned property" as to when there was a dispute between the finder of lost or abandoned personal property and the owner of the real property (i.e., land or building) on or in which that personal property was found.* Using that article, and cases from California and New Jersey, the court chose a remedy in equity rather than law.

Legal Analysis

Judge McCarthy's decision was a bad one.

First, the Court made a legal error in treating the ball as abandoned or lost property. But the ball was, as a matter of law, a gift—from Major League Baseball. As mentioned earlier, the distinction is crucial for this case. (The addendum to Chapter 28 discusses this distinction further, and why the ball was a gift.) By treating it as abandoned or lost property, the Court kept alive Popov's causes of action for trespass to chattel and conversion, and made possible its declaration of a "pre-possessory interest." I've done no legal research on "pre-possessory interest," but it appears to be something the judge pulled out of the air. Nothing wrong with judicial innovation, in general; but in this case, it was a mistake. It throws out centuries of Black Letter Law regarding "capture"—an ill-advised thing to have done.

Second, once the Court had tossed out Popov's causes of action for battery and assault against Hayashi, it was wrong to, in effect, punish Hayashi for the alleged actions of others. True, Hayashi benefited from those actions. But legally, because he was not acting in concert with them, it was no different than if he'd benefited from an Act of Nature.

---

* The citation—not included in the court's opinion—is R. H. Helmholz, "Equitable Division and the Law of Finders," 52 Fordham L. Rev. 313 (1983).

Third, industry custom should have controlled the outcome of this case. Granted, the "last man standing" rule is a bad one, and is what caused the pile-up. (More on this in the addendum to Chapter 28.) But it *is* the rule. Once again, the judge was punishing Hayashi for the acts of others—here, the act of Major League Baseball in perpetuating its industry custom.

The Court should have granted summary judgment to Hayashi.

Policy Analysis

Gary Smith, in his *Sports Illustrated* article, had called for the "Solomonic" solution the Court adopted. But it was not Solomonic, for reasons discussed earlier in this chapter. The Court resolved this particular dispute, and granted, that's all a trial court has to do. But the Court went beyond that, in crafting what it apparently meant to be a policy solution to the problem of free-for-alls in the stands. But its decision is *still* an invitation to identical disputes in the future and to a possible tragedy. (The addendum to Chapter 28 discusses a way to deal with that.)

The Court clearly had larger issues in mind, and took them into consideration—yet, only between the lines. It should have expressly addressed those issues (although, granted, it could only have properly done so in dicta). As it is, the Court took the easy way out.

Ramifications for the Parties

Popov and Hayahsi both accepted the judge's decision. They placed the ball with an agent who auctioned it off on ESPN.

It brought just $450,000—about 15% of what Mark McGwire's homerun ball had sold for. (And the buyer was again Todd McFarlane.) Assuming 15% total commissions for the agent and auctioneer—which total is a *low* estimate—each litigant's share was $191,250.

Both sides ended up losing. Popov lost more, though.

Popov (by his own choice) was paying legal fees and expenses up-front. So he lost the income he could have made by investing that money instead of using it for the lawsuit. Further, his suit was not that of a business, able to deduct the expenses and fees against general income. That means he was forking over *after*-tax dollars. I have no idea what tax bracket he's in. But it's easy to see that, even if his total outlay through trial was close to a quarter-million dollars, the *real* financial cost to him was far higher.

He did not recover even his out-of-pocket costs, and his only deductible expense was the auctioneer's commission.

Hayashi's lawyers, in contrast, were on contingency. So his outlay was zero. That means he had no "opportunity cost" of funds. But Hayashi's share passed through his lawyers, first. They reimbursed themselves for expenses, and deducted their contingency fee. If they were working at a 40% rate, they took $76,500 of the net after the auctioneer's commission. At one-third, they got $63,750. Either way, expenses—which probably came out of Hayashi's share, rather than off the top—probably ate up all the rest, and Hayashi himself got...*nothing*.

Both men paid the "opportunity cost" of having been out of work (by their own choice, though) for over a year while suit was pending.

I've included this analysis because this is something that all lawyers—and future lawyers—need to consider when evaluating potential outcomes, whether from settlement or judgment at trial. And it's something that, as far as the law school professoriat is concerned, is "out of sight, out of mind" with regard to educating future attorneys The lawyers and the expert witnesses from the law schools had a fun time running up their respective clients' bills. But this was almost a case where, in the alleged words of an American colonel during the Vietnam War, they thought that "It was necessary to destroy the village in order to save it.")

Mini-Addendum

If you enjoyed following the story of *Popov v. Hayashi,* here's another book you might like, about the ins-and-outs of a civil lawsuit. It's *Cape May Court House: A Death in the Night,* by Lawrence Schiller.

The case concerns a suit against Ford Motor by a man whose wife was allegedly killed by an airbag's deployment in their SUV during a very minor accident. Ford's defense was the man had *murdered* his wife, and then staged the "accident" as a cover-up.

To me, it read like a thriller. The ebb and flow of each side's case, as new facts or expert opinions came to light, was amazing.

I'd bought *Cape May Court House* one evening after having had only 3-4 hours' sleep the previous night. I couldn't put the book down, except to take bathroom breaks or to grab a quick snack. Despite the previous night's lack of sleep, I stayed up reading all night, just to see how the story ended. (The fun came from the play-by-play, so I resisted the temptation to jump to the final pages.)

Especially if you liked Jonathan Harr's wonderful non-fiction book *A Civil Action* (mentioned in Chapter 9), you'll love Lawrence Schiller's *Cape May Court House: A Death in the Night.*

Part VI:

One Down,
Two to Go

Chapter 17 - The 3 "Rs" of Lawyering:
Research, Reasoning, and '[R]iting

There are several skills critical to good lawyering. Yet, for the most part, law school either ignores them completely or else gives them only lip-service. This chapter covers three of the most important.

Chapter 1 briefly discussed them. As pointed out there, these "don't count" in first-year...yet they can make or break your career in the law.

Legal Research

Chapter 1 noted that legal research has two purposes: to bring yourself up to speed on a new subject, and to Find Authority to back up your arguments. Both of these are especially important in your first few years of practice.

The law is supposed to be predictable. That means it's supposed to apply in the same way to everyone in similar circumstances. People have invested a lot of money in various things, based on the existing law. They've organized their lives and planned their futures based on it.

Anytime the law changes, it upsets some applecarts. Maybe a particular applecart *should* be upset. Regardless, invevitably, many other changes will result—a ripple (or perhaps *tsunami)* effect, to mix metaphors. Legal change is disruptive, period. That's why judges usually try to make their rulings as narrow as possible. They fear the Law of Unintended Consequences. (That's also why, when judges do change the law, they sometimes pretend they *haven't*.)

Good legal research means you can put the monkey on the judge's back. You're trying to force that judge to go out on a limb if he or she doesn't rule in your favor on the point in question. As with most of us, judges are (usually) "risk averse." They don't like to take unnecessary chances. It goes like this: if you're a judge, you're already somewhere in the judicial hierarchy. However, unless you're already one of the Supremes (or *old*), you can aspire to a judgeship on a higher court. Maybe you'll get there by rocking the boat—but only if you rock the right boat in the right way at the right time. But this is something that's obvious only in hindsight...and by the time that occurs, your chances for promotion may already be sunk. The advocate, by Finding Authority, lets the judge play it safe. That's what judges like. And, in general, that's what society likes—for good reasons.

So, you'd better be able to find that existing law, including the exceptions, the exceptions to the exceptions, and all the nuances of every bit of it.

There are lawyers who lie to a court, even in writing. They cite cases having absolutely nothing to do with the point at issue. They completely misrepresent the holding of a case. They cite statutory law that has long since been repealed, or cases long since overruled, but then claim such law is still in force. They know better. Sadly, there are judges who know they're being lied to, but do nothing about it. Maybe this is because the deceitful attorney has a special relationship with that judge. Maybe it's because the judge is determined to make a case come out a certain way, no matter what the law is. However, in general, if you Find Authority that's *decisive,* then that authority is "controlling." The judge *has* to follow it (supposedly). You win.

In law school, you look for the Highest Authority, usually U.S. Supreme Court cases. But in practice, you will seldom find something from a High Authority that seems to fit your situation "on all fours." And if you do, you'll probably also find (or your opponent will find) other High Authority that also seems to fit your situation—but goes against you. However, the farther down the authority hierarchy you go, the more detailed the law becomes. There may have been only one *U.S.* Supreme Court case in history that seems to fit your situation, but chances are good there have been dozens of cases in your *state's* supreme court. With luck, you'll find one that is "on all fours"—and favorable (and, of course, is not inconsistent with the one U.S. Supreme Court case on the subject).

You usually want to find the *lowest* authority that appears to control your situation: a state statute, a regulatory agency's rule, etc. The "controlling" authority that's closest to your client is the *easiest* to deal with (assuming it's "still good law"). If you have a municipal ordinance that explicitly governs your client's situation, chances are pretty good that's the end of the matter. It's a safe bet you don't have to worry about trying to apply a U.S. Supreme Court ruling that concerned facts quite different from yours. You still check the higher authority, of course, to make sure it hasn't trumped the lower. But most of the time—unless there's a Constitutional issue involved—the controlling municipal ordinance allows you to wrap things up quickly. Clients (and bosses) like that...as long as you weren't hasty about it and thus overlooked something vital, a land mine that will eventually cause them to lose an arm and a leg.

IT AIN'T OVER 'TIL IT'S OVER

As Chapter 5 and the Coda discussed, a case won at trial is not necessarily a case won. A civil court trial judge can overturn a jury's verdict. (A criminal court judge can do this only if the verdict was "Guilty.") And an appellate court can overturn the result of the trial, even if the trial judge is with you. It isn't enough just to win at trial.

However, less than 10% of all civil cases ever go through trial. (There are even cases where the parties settle while the jury is deliberating.) Your skill as a negotiator plays a big part in determining the nature of the settlement. So do the facts. And so do things like how believable your witnesses are versus how believable the other side's witnesses are. But if the law is clearly on your side—and you know it, and can prove it—your position is a lot stronger than it might otherwise be. (By the way, only about two percent of cases that go through a verdict at trial ever go through an appeal. However, in civil cases, often one side will file an appeal. The two sides then negotiate a settlement—different from the outcome at trial. So again, your skill as a negotiator is important...as are the facts, and the law.)

Say you don't want to be a trial or appellate lawyer? Even if you never do any litigation, the documents you draft may someday be subject to litigation. And many lawyer-negotiators handle business deals. They try to make sure their clients get the long end of the stick. If you've done your homework, and can prove that things "have to" be done *your* client's way because the law says so, you will do very well indeed. An ounce of prevention is worth a pound of cure.

Part of what legal research involves is being aware of potential problems that have occurred in similar situations, and being aware of how those problems were resolved in court. You then draft your document or tailor the business deal in question in such a way that your client knows, up front, that if push comes to shove the law is on his or her side.

If a dispute arises, and goes through litigation, your client will probably have to spend a lot of money to prevail. Even if you're eventually proved right, your client will not appreciate the fact that it took a long and expensive court battle to achieve final success. To change the metaphor yet again, if you've done a good job on your legal research, you can at least make sure all your client's bases are covered. However, the best victory is the one that occurs without fighting.

TIME IS MONEY

Legal research takes time. Most lawyers bill by the hour. And most clients will get very annoyed when they get a big bill that includes a lot of legal research. After all, you're a lawyer, and most clients (wrongly) think lawyers are supposed to know the law, *all* of it, off the top of their heads. No way.

As a good lawyer—if you are a good lawyer—you have two major skills: (1) You know how to Think Like a Lawyer, which (by the time you've been in practice long enough) includes a good "feel" for any given situation; and (2) You "know what you *don't* know"—and *how to find out* what you *need* to know. Thinking Like a Lawyer, you will know *what* to look for and *where* to look for it, which involves Legal Research.

In contrast to the client, your supervising attorney knows that a lawyer can't provide all the answers off-the-cuff. He or she knows it takes research. However, you'd better be efficient at it. Otherwise, it might take you five hours to locate what a good researcher can find in fifteen minutes. Your boss may end up writing that time off as a loss...and you will be made aware of his or her displeasure.

It isn't just a matter of holding the client's legal bill down, either. Sometimes, you have to be able to find an answer *fast*—such as over-night, or even within a few hours. If you don't know where to look, or what to look for, your client's troubles (or your boss's) will get much, much worse very quickly...and *your* troubles will *begin*.

LEARNING HOW

If you Make Law Review you will learn how to Find Authority, *very* well. But even if you Make Law Review, you should still take more courses in legal research.

All students should take a course in administrative law research (or, if that's not available, then in administrative law itself). Administrative law is *hard* to research. And as more and more areas of the law are handed over to bureaucracies for conflict resolution, knowing how to Find Authority in administrative matters gets more important.)

Whether or not you Make Law Review, you should take all the legal research courses you can. Unfortunately, few law schools even *offer* courses in legal research after the perfunctory course that's required in first-year.

C.A.L.R.

In most law schools, as part of their first-year course, students get a quickie introduction to "Computer Assisted Legal Research." The two major companies with on-line CALR are Lexis and Westlaw. If you know what to look for, and where to look, you can find some answers mighty fast by using an on-line service. However, it tends to be expensive. It can easily run hundreds of dollars an hour. So you can't count on being able to use Westlaw or Lexis when you're a practicing attorney. For law school students, though, there's *no charge* for time spent on-line. (The law school pays a flat fee for this, covering the entire student body.)

These days, you'd better be good at both the Westlaw and Lexis systems. You don't know which one your future employer will have…and your future employer will definitely not be patient as you try to get the hang of it.

Legal Reasoning

After your first year of law school (and sometimes even before then), you almost never "brief a case" the way you did then. But once you're out of law school (and perhaps even sooner, such as during a summer clerkship) you'll very often be "briefing a point of law."

If you're going into a trial or a hearing, and anticipate a dispute will arise over a point of law, you do a "bench memo" for the judge. (If that dispute does arise during the judicial proceedings, you give a copy of your memo to the judge—and hand opposing counsel a copy too, of course.) If you're going into a negotiation, you might want to do a memo to enlighten the other side and get them to abandon some ridiculous position they're holding that's based on their incorrect understanding of the law.

Most often, though, you'll be doing a memo for a supervising attorney or a client. Here you discuss what the law is, and whether and how it applies to the problem at hand. (Sometimes, the problem will remind you of a "fruitcake" exam.)

Above, under "Legal Research," it was mentioned that judges are "risk averse," and like to stick to precedent. You need to be able to find all the existing law on a point, including the exceptions, the exceptions to the exceptions, and all the nuances of every bit of it. That way, no matter what you're trying to accomplish, you can argue that it's justified under *existing* law—or under a logical extension thereof. (An alternative is to argue that the specific "controlling authority" in question is actually an imprudent departure from the overall pattern of existing law. All you're trying to do, you say, is to get this court to make an *exception* to this controlling law...but this exception will actually be in line with the rule. Seriously. —It's like the joke about the lawyer who's asked, "What's 2+2?" The lawyer responds, "What do you *want* it to be?")

The only way to truly be on top of things is to know how to "parse the cases" *in light of the facts of your client's situation*. It is vital that you be able to grasp the *crucial* aspects of a given case. It is equally vital that you be able to grasp the *distinctions* among cases. Something that at first appears to be "on point" might turn out to be completely irrelevant. (To repeat: John Delaney's book, *Learning Legal Reasoning* is the very best on the subject.) The Coda provided an example of how "parsing the cases" works.

If you can't do a sophisticated briefing of a point of law, your analysis may fall short...in which case you may take a fall.

But "legal reasoning" involves more than just "parsing the cases." And this is where *logic* comes in.

Everyone uses logic in their everyday lives, without even thinking about any rules of logic. And some people are just naturally more logical than others.

In these days of "self-esteem" and "touchy-feely" discourse on problems, many people regard anyone who explicitly relies on logic as an unfeeling creature, similar to "Mr. Spock" in the original *Star Trek* series. And it is certainly true that many of those who pride themselves on their ruthless use of logic are indeed unfeeling.

However, logic and feeling are not at all incompatible. Those who insist that's so (whether logical people who hate the messiness of "feelings," or "feeling" people who hate the rigor of clear thinking) have posited a false dichotomy. The fact that *everyone* uses logic in some form in their everyday lives shows that the two are not mutually exclusive. (And everyone also acts on the basis of feelings, to some extent, in their everyday lives, too—even those who insist they're "unemotional.")

In fact, you should use one to "test" the other, constantly.

People who are "emotional" are actually *over*-emotional. They do not balance feeling with reason. But that's a poor excuse for not balancing reason with feeling. (And besides, it's impossible to shut out either completely.) Sometimes, our "gut feel" (an "emotional" response) to a situation is the surest measure of what the reality of that situation is. As Michael Maccoby said in his classic book on corporate management, *The Gamesman*, "The head can be smart, but not wise." Wisdom is a function of the heart, in conjunction with the head. So are "street smarts." (We've all had the feeling, "Something isn't 'right' with this 'picture.'")

As to logic itself, Judge Ruggero Aldisert of the Third Circuit U.S. Court of Appeals says:

> After many years as a judge and teacher, I can quickly recongize the illogical lawyer or student. This person wanders aimlessly. He or she shifts the topic without being aware of it, skips about at random, not only jumps to a conclusion, but fails to retrace steps to see whether the conclusion to which he or she has jumped is supported by evidence. The illogical person makes contradictory, inconsistent statements without being sensitive to what he or she is doing.

***

Logic is of two kinds: informal, and formal. When you took the LSAT, you got a (maddening) taste of *informal* logic, in the "logic games" section. But Chapter 14 discussed, in passing, another aspect of informal logic: informal fallacies (such as the *argumentum ad hominem* and the *argumentum ad verecundiam*). Another type of informal logic is the use of analogy. Analogy is the single most important tool lawyers use (in a Common Law system)—and is intimately intertwined with "parsing the cases." You saw that in the Coda.

And yet another type of informal logic is the "inductive method" when reasoning. It's the basis of all of science. It's also the *proper* basis for the development of Black Letter Law—rather than the pseudo-scientific, top-down approach of the Langdellians.

And the last type of informal logic worth noting here is the effort to define words. This is, of course, crucial in the Law. As Chapter 2 said, all of Black Letter Law is really a matter of definitions (composed of "elements").

If you're not good at *all* the aspects of informal logic, you will not be a good lawyer, period. And although everyone employs informal logic in their everyday lives, that does not mean everyone's good at it. In fact, as any politician or other person in power knows, using faulty informal logic is the best way to manipulate gullible people. I assume you do not want to be manipulated, whether in your private life or when working on behalf of clients as an attorney. So it behooves you to get an understanding of informal logic that's a whole lot better than the understanding you have now.

Then there's formal logic, also known as deductive logic. Unfortunately, deductive logic scares a lot of people. And it's what gives "logic" a bad name. That's because logic teachers always, immediately, barrage students with a slew of jargon and rules to memorize. Of course, as with getting good in the law itself, it's a good idea to memorize all the jargon and the rules. But deductive logic would sure be less off-putting if logic teachers and texts would make it much more "user-friendly."

Although judicial opinions seldom specifically mention the jargon or rules of logic, all judicial opinions are based on the use of deductive logic. Even the tools of informal logic (such as analogy) are subsumed under formal logic (deduction).

Here's how all the pieces fit together...

As the Coda noted, each side chooses its starting point, the basic value it wants the court to use as the guiding principle for deciding the case. (This, by the way, is a matter of *feeling,* not logic. So you see, not only does "feeling" have a place in the law, it has the most important place, ultimately, because the difference in feelings about a matter are what helps resolve the dispute at hand, by "framing the issue.")

The starting point is always the question, "What is this case *about?*" The court itself gets the last word on characterizing the case. No matter what the basic value is, there's a whole line of cases that reflects it.

For example, in the typical criminal case that has Constitutional implications, the (convicted) defendant appeals on the basis of an alleged violation of his or her 4th, or 5th, or 6th Amendment rights under the Bill of Rights. Of course, the State responds by saying that the defendant's rights were not violated.

If it were clear-cut either way, the higher court would "pour out" one side or the other in a heartbeat. (Or, when the court has the power to refuse to hear the appeal in the first place, it can do that, if the case is clear-cut against the appellant. —There are other reasons for refusing to hear an appeal, though.) But what causes the higher court to seriously consider the matter is when the fact situation at hand is in some "gray area" of the law. To strengthen its position in that "gray area," in this example, the State further alleges that whatever happened to the defendant was justified as a matter of public policy. And because the case *is* in a "gray area," the entire case ends up "turning" on whether or not, as a matter of public policy, the cops or prosecutors should have a free hand to continue doing whatever they did in this case. If the Court decides that they should *not,* they say the fact situation *does* meet the definition of situations covered by the 4th, or 5th, or 6th Amendment. And if the Court decides that the agents of the State *should* be allowed to continue doing whatever they did in this case, the Court says the fact-situation does *not* meet the definition of situations covered by whatever Amendment the defendant is citing.*

Sometimes, there's a hidden starting point, beyond the official one. (This relates to the "story-behind-the-story," discussed in Chapter 5.) For example, there might be a well-settled area of the law, but "everyone knows" it's time to change. (The classic example is *Brown v. Board of Education,* the Supreme Court case that ended three-quarters of a century of law saying that "separate but (allegedly) equal" was okay regarding racial segregation. Chapter 10 argued that it's time to change the law regarding pedagogical malpractice and educational "contracts," at least as to law schools.) But the court in question does not want to be the one to rock the boat. So the judge pretends the boat is still ship-shape.

Each side will "parse the cases," to prove that the facts in *this* case fall within the line of cases that reflects the value this side favors and which should cause that side to win.

However, as Supreme Court Justice William O. Douglas once said,

> There are usually plenty of precedents to go
> around; and with the accumulation of decisions,
> it is no problem for lawyers to find legal authority
> for most propositions.

So, as you can immediately see, the discussion in the section above on Legal Research exaggerated. Finding Authority is just your *starting point*. As Aldisert says, *"Often the art of advocacy resolves itself into convincing the court which facts in previous cases are indeed positive analogies and which are not."* (Emphasis added.) —Remember: "Looks / walks / quacks like a duck?" (Just think of Popov v. Hayashi.)

As mentioned, though, all the informal logical methods are subsumed under formal logic. (This is so much taken for granted that it's rarely acknowledged.)

A court's decision takes the form of a syllogism. A syllogism has three "propositions" in it. A proposition, in logic, is any statement that can be either asserted or denied and which is either true or false. The first two propositions in a syllogism are called "premises," and the third is the "conclusion." Every syllogism also has three terms (and only three terms). The most famous syllogism is this:

* The events of September 11, 2001, have caused a huge increase in Constitutional litigation that features civil liberties v. the suppression of terrorism.

All men are mortal.
Socrates is a man.
Therefore, Socrates is mortal.

The first line is the "major premise." The second line is the "minor premise." Here, the term "mortal" is the "major term" (because it appears in the major premise and not in the minor). Here, "Socrates" is the "minor term" (because it appears in the minor premise and not in the major). And "men/man" is the "middle term" (because it appears in both premises). The major and minor term both then appear again in the conclusion, but the middle term does not.

The middle term always has to include a larger "class" than the minor term, for the syllogism to be valid. The middle term, as used in at least one of the premises, has to include *all* the members of the "class" the middle term refers to. And that class has to be larger than the "universe" of the "class" the minor term refers to. The middle term is used to establish a relationship between the major term and the minor term. The syllogism's conclusion states that relationship.

In law, the major premise is the value each side uses to frame the issue. The minor premise is the case at hand. Not surprisingly, each side then says this case, logically, falls within the ambit of the line of cases it says is "controlling," i.e., the major premise. All the tools of *informal* logic, as mentioned, are then used to convince the court that the advocate's implicit use of *formal* logic is sound. The court typically then agrees with one side or the other. The opinion is then written as an implicit syllogism, and this is the court's "rationale" (a.k.a *"ratio decidendi"*). The syllogism's conclusion is the court's "holding."

Here are some examples:

In the landmark case of *MacPherson v. Buick Motor Co.,* 227 N.Y. 392, 11 N.E. 1050 (1916), Chief Judge Bartlett of New York's highest court set up this syllogism:

Major Premise: As a matter of law, whoever sells a vehicle or vehicle part is not liable for negligence to anyone but the person to whom he sold that vehicle or part.

Minor Premise: The plaintiff is not the person to whom the defendant sold the vehicle.

Conclusion: Therefore, the defendant is not liable to the plaintiff for negligence.

However, the Court's majority preferred the syllogism of Judge Cardozo:

> Major Premise: Any manufacturer who negligently constructs a vehicle or part that is inherently dangerous as constructed, ought to be held liable to *anyone* who is injured as the result of that negligently constructed vehicle or part.
> Minor Premise: A manufacturer that constructs a vehicle with defective wheels is such a manufacturer.
> Conclusion: Therefore, a manufacturer that constructs a vehicle with defective wheels is liable to anyone who is injured as the result of that negligently constructed wheel.

Bartlett's syllogism was based on the law—specifically, Black Letter Law. Cardozo's was based on the facts...and rocked the boat by *changing* the law.

If Patrick Hayashi had won sole title to Barry Bonds's 73rd homerun ball (discussed in the Coda), here's how the syllogism would have worked:

> Major Premise: Under the "industry custom" of Major League Baseball's "Last Man Standing" rule, the owner of the ball is the person who ended up with the ball, regardless of who first had contact with the ball.
> Minor Premise: Patrick Hayashi was the person who ended up with the ball.
> Conclusion: Therefore, Patrick Hayashi is the owner of the ball.
>
> Major Term: "owner of the ball"
> Middle Term: "person who ended up with the ball"
> Minor Term: "Patrick Hayashi"

But because the court ruled that Popov and Hayashi each had a half-interest in title to the ball, the syllogism is more complicated:

Major Premise: Equal ownership of the ball
goes to the person who had initial contact with the ball
and to the person who ended up with the ball.
Minor Premise: Popov had initial contact with the ball,
and Hayashi ended up with the ball.
Conclusion: Therefore, equal ownership of the ball
goes to Popov and Hayashi.

Major Term: "Equal ownership of the ball"
Middle Term: "the person who had initial contact with
the ball and the person who ended up with the ball"
Minor Term: "Popov and Hayashi"

As you see, a "term" can contain more than one word that normally would be thought of as a "term" all by itself.

Seems simplistic, doesn't it? And it is...but only in hindsight.

There are a lot of traps for the unwary, however. And the traps involve faulty logic, whether formal or informal. If you use faulty reasoning, and the other side (or the court) catches it, you probably lose. And if the other side uses faulty reasoning, and you (and the court) miss it, you might lose a case that you could have won if you'd caught the other side's faulty logic.

Here's an example of faulty reasoning, in a "hypothetical syllogism"—

By statute, if a testator was insane
at the time of making his or her will,
that will is invalid.
This testator was not insane
at the time of making her will.
Therefore, this will is valid.

Uh, no. This is "the fallacy of denying the antecedent." —There are other ways for a will to be invalid.

The following is a *valid* form of reasoning in a hypothetical syllogism:

If A, then B. ("If A is present, B will always be present too.")
Not B. ("But B is not present here.")
Therefore, not A. ("Therefore, A is not present here either.")

(This is the *"modus tollens"* hypothetical syllogism.) Contrast:

> If A, then B. ("If A is present, B will always be present too.")
> Not A. ("But A is not present here.")
> Therefore, not B. ("Therefore, B is not present here either.")

—Which is what we just had with the example of the testator's will. A syllogism that's *logically valid* is not necessarily *true*. Example:

> No woman is fit for the study of law.
> X is a woman.
> Therefore, X is not fit for the study of law.

That reasoning is *valid*. But the major premise is *false*. (Yet, there's a long line of cases saying it's true...which cases have long since been overruled, of course.)

Here's one where the *conclusion* is *true*, but the *reasoning* is *invalid*:

> All members of the U.S. Supreme Court know the law.
> All who are lawyers by training know the law.
> Therefore, all members of the U.S. Supreme Court
>   are lawyers by training.

This commits the "fallacy of the undistributed middle [term]." It's possible to know the law without having had training in the law. (Unlikely, but possible.) —And in fact, members of the Supreme Court are not *required* to be lawyers, or to have had training in the law. The conclusion is true here as a matter of happenstance. But it does not follow logically from the premises.

That one is especially interesting as to how it also involves *in*formal logic. What does it *mean* to say, "know the law," and "lawyers by training"? In the old days, anyone could "sit for the bar exam," with or without any legal training at all. Today, the meaning of "training in the law" is clear. But the meaning of "know the law" still is not.

A *"sound"* argument/syllogism is both *"valid"* under the rules of logic, and *true*. (As we've seen, though, beliefs as to what is and is not "true" can change.)

The moral is: **truth is greater than logic.** Please do not forget that. **But if you can't *prove* it as a matter of *logic,* you're asking for trouble.** This does not mean that the *only* way you can reason correctly is if you've mastered formal and informal logic. It does mean that the way to give yourself the best chance of reasoning correctly, and of catching your opponent in faulty reasoning, is to become adept at formal and informal logic.

Legal Writing

Most of the cases you'll read in your casebook are poorly written. They tend to use stilted, pompous language. Latin phrases are frequent. Even the English is convoluted. This is what the typical layperson associates with legal documents. Unfortunately, many law students get the idea that this is the way lawyers *should* write. They say it conveys the "majesty" and the "mystique" of the Law. Don't you believe it.

No lawyer should ever write legalese. Granted, there are times when a bit of legal jargon is the most CONcise and PREcise way to express something. But then, you're just using a term or a phrase as legal shorthand, to save time and avoid misunderstanding. (For example, you might refer to the "Equal Dignities Doctrine" in property law, or to *res ipsa loquitur* in torts. You *could* use plain English, and "spell out" what each of these is. But if you did, opposing counsel and the judge would think you're talking down to them. The effect would be counter-productive.)

However, I've met attorneys who say they *deliberately* use the most obscure legal bafflegab they can in their writings. They give two reasons why this is supposedly a good thing. First, they say it makes it very difficult for opposing counsel to follow the argument. This, in turn, makes it very difficult for opposing counsel to *respond* to the argument. Second, they say it makes it *impossible* for the *client* to understand it. This, in turn, supposedly confers two benefits to the lawyer: (1) the client is impressed by the attorney's mastery of the Magic Words of the Law—and is therefore inclined not to protest a large bill from the lawyer for writing such drivel; and (2) if the lawyer made a mistake, *the client won't catch it!*

To take these one at a time...

NEVER FORGET YOUR AUDIENCE

If *opposing counsel* has trouble following the argument, so will the *judge*. You want to have the judge on *your* side. So you want to start off on the right foot. If what you present is obscurantist garbage, you won't even get your foot in the door. This is especially so with trial courts. (Judges are very busy—and impatient.) Finding Authority is paramount. But that's just the start. It is necessary, but not sufficient. You next have to let the judge know what you found, and present it in a manner that's convincing. Hence the importance of *good* legal writing, to reflect your *sound* legal reasoning (using both formal and informal logic).

> Writing, after all, is nothing but speaking on paper, speaking is nothing but thinking out loud, and thinking is nothing but silent speech.
>
> Rudolf Flesch,
> *How to Write, Think, and Speak More Effectively*

Articulate writing should come as easily to students as articulate speech does—and most law students are capable of articulate speech. Unfortunately, generations of students, from grade school on, have been intimidated by teachers who are more interested in the technical perfection of writing under the rules of grammar, etc., than they are in the real quality of the writing. And so, most students think of writing assignments with dread. They often have a mental block against writing. But like the college freshman who was amazed to discover that he'd been speaking "prose" all his life, just think of writing as speaking on paper, and it will suddenly seem a whole lot easier.

As Chapter 1 said, advocacy takes two forms: oral and written. Of these, oral is—nearly always—the less important. (As Chapter 1 noted, that is heresy for a trial lawyer to say...but heresy is sometimes also the truth. And in this case, it is.)

Television and the movies make it appear that the most important part of a trial is what goes on in the courtroom—the testimony that's heard, the physical evidence and documents that are presented. Maybe; but even when that's true, it's often true only in a formal sense, especially in a civil trial. Long beforehand, opposing counsel will have tried to frame the issues in such a way as to favor the outcome they desire. They also try to get rulings in advance of trial as to what testimony and tangible evidence will (and will not) be allowed during the proceedings. In a (civil) jury trial, by the time the jury hears the case the issues have often been cut down in size, and cut down in number. Sometimes the courtroom appearance is just a wrap-up for the client's benefit. (Again, heresy for a trial lawyer to say, but—again—true.) Even though *all* trials are dicey, each side tries to narrow the unpredictable possibilities to as small a range as it can. That way, even if the worst comes to pass (i.e., you lose) you will already have succeeded insofar as you've exercised "damage control" even before the damage occurs.

Example: The Walt Disney Corporation developed several "small towns" from scratch, to appeal to those who long for what they imagine were The Good Old Days of small-town life. Disney hired contractors to do all the construction work, of course. But Disney chose the materials to be used and provided all the blueprints.

In one particular venture, the construction was horrid, as were the materials. The new homeowners sued the contractor and Disney. Plaintiffs' counsel wanted to show Disney's involvement in the project—and to argue that the image of integrity Disney enjoys was entirely a public relations contrivance. The lawyers hoped to "rile up" the jury and thus have a better chance of getting them to vote for the plaintiffs.

For reasons not worth going into here, the trial court judge ruled that Disney's involvement in the venture was *irrelevant*. The judge ordered that plaintiffs and their ocunsel could not even mention Disney in front of the jury, nor could they provide the jurors with any documents that showed Disney's involvement.

This pre-trial ruling was a threefold coup: (1) Plaintiff's counsel had to come up with a new, less effective "case theme," (2) Disney avoided a huge amount of what would have been very bad publicity, and (3) the jury would not be aware of the "deep pockets" if and when it voted for the plaintiffs and then assessed damages. (And no, I was not involved in that case, nor were any of my acquaintances.)

The written arguments an attorney submits, whether to a trial court or an appellate court, are (usually) read before the attorney gets a chance to utter a word in the courtroom. Occasionally, if what's written is bad enough, the judge won't even let the attorney come in to the courtroom to be heard. And even if he or she does, quite often all the lawyer gets to do is answer the judge's questions—and the questions are sometimes based on what the lawyer wrote. Granted, with two advocates evenly matched in legal research and legal writing skills, with equally strong cases, before open-minded judges, the better oral advocate will win. But that constellation of circumstances never happens in the real world. If you've won the battle on paper, the battle is probably already over—if not at the trial level, then on appeal.

Even though, as mentioned, nearly all civil suits are disposed of without trial (they're "settled out"), that doesn't mean a judge isn't involved. Quite the contrary. Sometimes a case gets *"poured* out"—by the judge, on "Summary Judgment." Your client doesn't even get his or her day in court. (Chapter 8 discussed an example of this, involving Prof. Charles Nesson of Harvard Law School on the losing side.)

If the judge rules against you on anything (including summary judgment), you can eventually take it up on appeal. However, appellate courts are reluctant to reverse or remand most rulings of trial judges. This is especially so if the record includes a well-researched and well-written argument from the attorney who prevailed on the point in question. (Besides, appeals are very expensive and take a long time. Most clients, for some reason, don't like that.)

All judges work amid mountains of paperwork. In truth, modern judges are really just glorified, bureaucratic paper-pushers. The other branches of government have not made sufficient resources available to the judiciary for most judges to be able to truly *deliberate* any more. They have to keep processing paper, as fast as they can, to dispose of cases and move these documents out the door...because more are coming in all the time. "Case management" is the name of the game, especially regarding the parties' pre-trial maneuverings.

However, even though any one case will perhaps not get the attention it deserves, that does not necessarily mean it will be dealt with quickly. Judges review dozens of documents, hundreds—perhaps thousands—of pages, every week. Most judges can take a long time, if they wish, to make a decision on something. (I read where one state appellate court took *four years*, from 1992 to 1996, to decide a case. I do not know why.) They don't have to decide matters in the order received. Nor do they even have to read documents in the order received. Say you turn in a piece of legal writing that's opaque. It goes into the hopper, along with dozens of other pieces of legal writing from other attorneys on other matters. When the judge is considering what to read next, he or she looks through the piles of documents. If the judge picks up *your* masterpiece of obfuscatory fecal matter and quickly scans the first few paragraphs before deciding whether to continue, it will quickly go back into the stack. Quite possibly it will deliberately be placed at the *bottom* of the heap...and will stay there for months, and months, and months. (Two judges—one state, one federal—have told me that's exactly what they do.)

I know of one federal judge who not only refuses to read legaldygook, he has his clerk return the material to the lawyer who submitted it. There's a form letter with it, bluntly telling the lawyer that the judge will not read crap. So the lawyer then re-writes it in plain English...if he or she wants that case to be heard. Even if the attorney then satisfactorily re-writes the document, that lawyer now has an uphill battle to win the judge to his or her side.

There's a certain state court judge who, when the document is written in legalese, automatically rules against that party (assuming that opposing counsel's brief is intelligible). Tough on the lawyer. Tougher on the client...who hasn't a clue about it. (The client's lawyer might not either; but even if he or she does, the client will never be told.)

—Then again, I know of at least one judge who never bothers to read *anything*...including the rules of evidence and civil procedure.

In the higher courts, more and more, the lawyers' briefs are read only by a judge's *law clerk*. Then the clerk prepares a "brief" (as it were) summary for his or her boss. Thus, as an attorney, you're writing only for the eyes of someone who's been out of law school even less time than *you*. And while judges' law clerks tend to be the cream of the academic crop, that doesn't mean they'll be any more patient than their bosses when it comes to trying to make sense of legal gibberish. (*They* have mountains of paperwork to process, too.) If you can't lay it all out, clearly and *concisely*, you're almost *asking* to lose.

MAKING YOUR CLIENT PART of the TEAM

We've now arrived at the second reason short-sighted lawyers give for writing in legal bafflegab.

Clients are often a pain in the neck, because they don't think like lawyers. (If they did, they probably wouldn't have gotten into a situation that called for a lawyer in the first place.) Being laypeople, clients often get all excited about things that are totally irrelevant from a legal perspective. Sometimes it's hard to get a client to accept this. So, it can make life easier for the lawyer if the client doesn't even know the attorney has omitted from a document something the client thinks is so important. Hence the legaldygook. But this can come back to haunt you.

As Chapter 3 said, Thinking Like a Lawyer involves selecting the relevant law to correctly apply to the facts at hand. And as the various discussions of hypotheticals showed, sometimes changing the facts only slightly will cause a change in the legal outcome. (That's a big part of what "parsing the cases" is all about.) The layperson client will never understand the law as well as the attorney does. But even if the attorney *understands* the *facts* better, from a legal perspective, the attorney will never *know* the facts as well as the client does. And the client will always know *more* facts about the case than the lawyer ever will.

Unless your client is somewhat dim-witted (which happens), by writing in plain English you ensure that the client can follow your argument. (You can always explain, orally, the meaning of the few terms and phrases of legal jargon that are unavoidable.) If you've made a mistake regarding the facts, the client can catch it and you can correct it.

By this, I don't mean simply that you've stated an incorrect date or something. Rather, by "making a mistake regarding the facts," I mean you might have overlooked something important, or included something that was not important. A client, reading the document, will then probably say, "Why mention this?" or "But what about ———?" Whatever it is, it might be something you hadn't thought about at all, or hadn't thought about correctly. (Or, let's hope, it's something you did consider, and dealt with correctly.) In this sense, then, your client's reaction to what you said serves as a reality check. That can be a priceless gift to you as an attorney—because, other than your client, there's no one else who can perform this service as well, if at all.

Now take it a step further: if what you've written is a pleading in connection with a lawsuit, but it doesn't make sense to your client, then it won't make sense to a jury. Granted, the pleading is only for the judge's eyes, not the jurors'. But the argument you make to the court is the same argument you'll make to the jury—only when you argue to the jury, you'll hardly be using any legal terms at all. So, if it isn't clear to the layperson who's your client, chances are it won't be clear to the laypeople who are your jurors, even when you cut out the legalese.

And what if the document *isn't* in connection with a lawsuit? Say it's a letter. Well, for all you know, the sender and recipient of that letter might have a dispute someday. That very document might be relevant. If what you drafted for your client (to send out over *his or her* signature) was clear (simple and direct), there will be no disagreement as to what it means. It may be that, according to what's in that letter, your client is wrong and the other party is right. If so, it's better for your client to give in now, at minimal cost, than to let the disagreement grow into a lawsuit. If your client goes to trial and loses, the total costs will be much, much higher. "Eating crow" is a lot cheaper.

It also might be that your client is clearly right, but the other party won't give in. In that case, the document is headed into court, eventually. It might end up in front of twelve jurors' eyes. Now, you tell me: if what you wrote is entirely in legalese, and the other side is complaining about that very legalese, who has the jurors' sympathy?

A client who is intelligent, and has common sense, is an extremely valuable asset. Unlike most writing (such as the drafts of the manuscript of this book), you can't show your work to other people and ask them to critique it. (True, if you work for a law firm, or a corporate law department, or a government agency, you can—and *must*—hand your work over to your supervising attorney before it leaves the office. But your supervisor will not have your client's or the jurors' frame of reference, and will be looking at it in an entirely different way.) You have to ensure that the work you do for a client will be held confidential—until and unless the final document (such as a will, or a pleading in a lawsuit) is made available to outsiders. So, use the client as a critic. The client will never be able to criticize your understanding of the *law*, anyway. You won't lose face because you misunderstood the implication of a fact or two. And the client will probably appreciate you all the more for having extended an opportunity to participate in a meaningful way. (That doesn't justify a large bill. But I'll bet it makes the client more willing to pay, because the client has a better understanding of what you did to deserve your fee. —And good client relations can nip many a potential problem in the bud.* They can also bring in referrals.)

MORE PEDAGOGICAL MALPRACTICE

Other than the perfunctory introduction to Legal Writing you get in first-year (discussed, in part, in the addendum to Chapter 9), there are almost no legal writing courses offered in law school, let alone required—even in the big schools with numerous faculty members and impressive library resources.

This is more pedagogical malpractice. Incompetent sole practitioners, especially, who are recent graduates often poorly brief a point of law or poorly draft a key document. And, by definition, they have no supervisor to catch their mistakes. Sometimes they later lose a malpractice suit, as a defendant, because of this.

If legal writing is a critical skill, why do law schools habitually ignore it? You probably already know. But just in case:

It is impossible to correct students' papers in a casual way. Remember Chapter 7's discussion of how easy it is for law professors to grade final exams? To properly grade a legal *writing* assignment, the instructor must *edit* it. This involves a lot more work than just making a "model answer" checklist and awarding points based on how well a student "spotted issues." Also, if *everyone* in the class were expected to learn to write at least reasonably well, then it would be extremely difficult to decide who gets the "A" and who gets the "A-." And it would be much more subjective than an issue-spotting checklist. (Legal writing courses are nearly always on a pass/fail basis—so students give it *bottom* priority.)

---

* For one thing, the client will be less inclined to sue you for malpractice if that client had a hand in what you did. Machiavellian? You bet. "Saint Nick" was no fool. And the client who worships the ground you walk on when you first take the case can turn into the client who wants to see you burn in Hell for eternity if you fail to work the miracles he or she was expecting.

And remember Chapter 9's discussion of how students don't get any meaningful feedback? The essence of learning how to do legal writing, involves extensive (and often intense) 1:1 feedback. (Correcting and instructing with regard to legal research is much easier, in comparison.)

Legal writing, properly taught, involves *many* homework assignments, not just a final exam. (The same is true of legal research, and of legal reasoning.) A proper legal writing program would have students draft letters and memos, contracts, deeds, wills, agreed divorce settlements, releases, pleadings, motions, responses to motions, proposed court orders and injunctions, bench memos, trial briefs, and appellate briefs. It would not be just a first-year Mickey Mouse course.

To teach legal research and legal writing *well* requires a substantial commitment of resources to do the job right. The student-faculty ratio for the class has to be low, or else each instructor has to put in far more hours than the average professor. (Again, see Chapter 9's addendum.)

—But you can't use just an ordinary writing teacher. You have to have teachers who are trained in the Law, who know how to Think Like a Lawyer. In general, such people are not available. There are few attorneys who are really good at legal writing (or legal research). It isn't worth their while to teach, given that doing the job right requires such a huge commitment of time and effort...and a huge pay cut, probably.

However, it *would* be worth their time if the law school itself valued it. The typical legal writing instructor is very low on the academic totem pole, below assistant professors, and is usually not tenure-track. Whether or not a licensed and experienced attorney, he or she is paid only chicken-feed. And if the school has a full-time "Director of Legal Writing," the chicken feed becomes chicken *shit* when you calculate it on an hourly basis. With few exceptions, the only attorneys who apply for such a job are those who probably can't write at all. (At my school, the attorney was the underling. The Director was a non-lawyer Ph.D. in English...who wrote some of the dullest and most obscure prose I have ever seen.) Meanwhile, as mentioned in Chapter 9, the regular (full) professors are pulling down $100,000-$150,000 a year in *base* salary, for 6-8 hours a week, max, of "teaching."

If a law school valued legal writing, it would allocate at least $175,000 to hire a director of legal writing for 30-40 hours a week...and the school would hear from many *qualified* applicants for the post.

The bottom line is the most important thing. As Chapter 9 (and its addendum) stated, the profits a university makes off its law school are important to it. On a cost-benefit basis, a good program in legal writing simply isn't worth it to the law school—no matter how disastrous its effect on future lawyers...and on those future lawyers' future clients.

Of INSECURITY—and SNOB APPEAL

However, I believe there's a second (and perhaps more important) reason why the law schools all but ignore these crucial skills: legal research and legal writing are too bound up with the *real* world.

Before the rise of the law school, future lawyers learned their skills by serving as apprentices to practicing attorneys. It was training-in-the-trenches, learning-by-doing (under the presumably watchful eye of the Master). After Christopher Langdell, however, law school went to the opposite extreme: the retreat from the real world into the ivory tower.

Law school professors know that they aren't engaged in a genuinely intellectual endeavor. (How "intellectual" is a subject such as "commercial paper"? —or "agency"? —or "real estate transactions"? —or "federal income tax"? Sure, they require intelligence. Reasoning, too. But so does auto mechanics, especially today.) And they seem to think there's something wrong with that. I don't. But what *is* wrong is that law professors like to *pretend* they're intellectuals. Because few of them really are, though, most apparently haven't any idea of what the life of the mind is all about. Yet, they want to be *thought of* as intellectuals, and they know that professors are *supposed* to be intellectuals. And so, they mistake form for substance. They believe that if they don't allow anything "practical" (such as a worthwhile legal clinic) then this somehow makes them more "intellectual."

For the same reason, they write in an "academic" style. (And it's the style of the Ph.D. Director of Legal Writing I just mentioned.) You know what I'm talking about. They apparently believe that verbal garbage is the mark of a real egghead. If you can use big words that ordinary people can't understand, and put them together in sentences that even well-educated people have trouble comprehending, you must be an intellectual...or, at least, a lawyer.

So, lawyers write legaldygook to impress their clients—and to maintain a superior position *vis-à-vis* mere laypeople. Law professors write in "academic" style, for similar reasons. It's all vanity (arising from insecurity, if I may play amateur shrink for a moment). Neither lawyers nor law professors have any interest in seeing law students learn how to write *well*.

The "only" people who do have an interest in seeing law students learn how to right well are *your* future clients, juries, and judges. —But in the *real* world of the law, *those are the ONLY people who COUNT.*

THE TRADITIONAL ARGUMENT

There are those who say that it's a waste of time to compose a legal document that's intelligible.

Unless you go solo, your supervising attorney will not allow you to create your own documents. Instead, you'll be pulling documents from the files. This "boilerplate" did the job for other lawyers in previous matters. And all you'll be doing, in effect, is cutting and pasting. You'll just be changing things here and there to adapt the "model" to your client's needs. Last, they point out that "form documents" (generic forms, where you just fill in the blanks) have, along with the model documents, been *tested* in court and have stood up to judicial scrutiny.

All true. However, in a larger sense, all false.

First, there are some documents for which there will be *nothing* in the files, and for which there is *no* generic form. The most complex example is a trial brief or an appellate brief; the simplest, a progress report to a client. If you can't write well, what you'll provide will not exactly make a favorable impression on the recipient/s.

Second, while it's (usually, but not always) true the model and form documents have been successfully tested in practice, that's not necessarily to their credit. Often, if the documents had been drafted better in the first place (i.e., been clear), no one would have challenged them. There should have been no need to put them to the test, at all. Further, even though *one* court interpreted a convoluted document *one* way, some day some *other* court might choose to emphasize a *different* part of the bafflegab—and interpret the document's meaning *another* way. Happens all the time. (Oil and gas leases are notorious for this.) If the document is simple and direct (relatively speaking, of course—considering that this is a legal document), it's hard for a court to contradict its "plain meaning." (However, that happens too, but rarely.)

Third, once you've created a *well-written* document for a specific situation, you can use *that* as your model, or turn it into a generic form and store it on a disk. So, your initial investment of time and effort will save you a lot of both in the future, and will yield a good return. Besides, you don't have to create your first document from scratch. In fact, it would be risky to do so. But you're almost never completely on your own, anyway. In addition to the documents in the files, you can turn to "form books." These contain hundreds of samples—a form for nearly every purpose. In any given state, probably at least one or two publishers prepare these. So, start with the model document or generic form. If all else fails, search the courthouse files (they're open to the public) for cases similar to yours. Make copies of what you can use. Then cut the unnecessary words, taking out as much of the legalese as possible. Turn it into plain English. Add what you need to.

Fourth—and related to the third—a document that's readily understandable lets you *think* about it more clearly when you want to use it as a model or form. Even though a lawyer understands legaldygook, no attorney in his or her right mind wants to go through such muck. There's a tendency to grab and use anything that seems relevant. Without the legalese, it's easier to spot what fits the new situation, what doesn't. You can more easily see what to add, delete, or alter. This saves time, without turning into a situation where haste makes waste.

If you also consider the advantages of making the client part of your team, the argument for legalese fails.

However, if you work someplace where you *must* use boilerplate legaldygook, so be it. But you still should avoid it any chance you get—such as in letters to clients.

CONTRACTS CRAFTSMANSHIP

I am unable to sufficiently emphasize the importance of being able to draft contracts well. Very few lawyers can do it. (Before I went to law school, I'd hired an attorney to write one for me in a business deal. It was so poorly written—even containing misspelled words!—that even I, as a complete layman, knew it was worthless. I refused to accept it— let alone pay for it—and sought out a new attorney.)

Here's an example of poor legal drafting that ended up costing a client a bunch of money. It involved an agreement between a builder and the intended householder. They made a deal whereby the householder would pay on a cost-plus basis: the cost of materials and labor, plus a 20% fee as the builder's profit. They also put a "cap" on the amount the householder would have to pay. This is the relevant passage from their contract:

```
    It is specifically agreed by and
between the parties that notwith-
standing the agreement hereinabove
the owners shall not be required,
under the terms of this agreement,
to pay the contractor any amount in
excess of the sum of Three Hundred
Fifty Thousand Dollars ($350,000.00),
which is the estimated cost of con-
struction, plus the fee provided
herein.
```

Do you see the problem? —Ambiguity. Was the $350,000 the cap? Or was that just the maximum total of *costs* (materials and labor)—on which the builder was then *also* entitled to a 20% *fee* ($70,000)? Because of *that one comma* after "which is the estimated cost of construction," the court ruled the agreement meant the latter. The house-holder had to pay $420,000, plus prejudgment interest, postjudgment interest, court costs—and his own attorneys' fees, which were substan-tial, because this case went up to that state's supreme court.

The contract was filled with crappy legalese. I'll bet whoever drafted it—probably working with boilerplate—lost sight of that vital comma amid the gibberish. (Sometimes, though, I wonder if this is part of some great make-work scheme on the part of the legal profession. Good drafting would probably cut the number of contracts lawsuits in half.)

SIX REWARDS YOU MIGHT NOT HAVE THOUGHT OF

If you've learned how to write fairly well, and you learn how to do *legal* writing—and legal research—quite well, you'll have the edge regarding other possibilities...

Exams test your skill at legal research, sort of (because you had to dig out the relevant Black Letter Law, and learn how to apply it to a fact pattern, entirely on your own). Exams also test your skill at legal writing, sort of (because you have to put your analysis to paper).

Legal writing out in the real world is different. For one thing, you'll have more time in which to do it. But the subjects you'll be writing about won't be as "simple" as your exams were (if only in hindsight).

The first point at which legal research and writing skills can make or break your career might be as early as your summer clerkship/s (see next chapter) while you're still in law school. Each firm will assume you have what it takes to do your job, because you're a law student. However, they might want to test your skills before making you an offer for after you graduate.

They'll do this by giving you tasks in "briefing a point of law." Often these will be quasi-make-work, simple projects. But how quickly you complete your assignments, and how, is important.

Second, it may be that when you return in the fall after Year One, you'll find that you did not Make Law Review on grades. (And at your school, there might not be a grade-on in the first place.) But you'll still have a good shot at Making Law Review in the *write-on* competition.(See the next chapter.)

Third, as a general rule, only those who've Made Law Review have a chance of getting a student Note or Commentary published. Even then, the only Law Review that would consider it is the one the author works for. So it's a long shot. But it sure Looks Good on the Résumé if you succeed, especially if you want to become a judicial clerk and maybe then a professor. (Judicial clerkships—as contrasted with judicial internships—are discussed in Chapter 22.) (And if you Made Law Review through the "write-on," and your paper is good enough, you might be able to turn it into a Note or Commentary.)

Fourth, every year there are dozens of legal essay contests. If you win, that achievement Looks Good on the Résumé, too. And typically, the prize includes a few hundred (or even a few thousand) dollars.

The next-to-last reason to learn to get good at legal research and legal writing, though certainly far from the least, is this: more and more, especially in the higher courts, judges ask their *clerks* to write the court's Opinion. Sometimes the judge asks the clerk to do just a first draft, and has told the clerk what he or she wants in it. But sometimes the judge asks the clerk to do even the final draft, which the judge then just touches up here and there. (Even U.S. Supreme Court opinions have been written by judicial clerks.)

Part of the reason for this is that at least some judges can't write worth a damn. But the bigger reason, especially today, is that the judges themselves don't have time for it. Yet, they want their Opinions to make them look good. So, they want to hire clerks who can write well—both as to style and as to logic, etc.

If you can do that, your writing samples to your prospective judicial employer, will give you the edge in getting the job—all other things being equal (which they seldom are). And once you're on the job, if it turns out you can write better than the judge's other clerk/s, guess who becomes the judge's favorite? (If you're clerking for a federal appellate judge who serves as a "feeder" to the U.S. Supreme Court, this can make all the difference in the world. And even if you aren't, it can have a big impact because of the favorable remarks he or she will make about you to other judges and attorneys—and to faculty members at prestigious law schools where you just might be hoping to get an offer to teach.)

The favorable remarks, most likely, won't emphasize your writing or research ability. Instead, they'll concern your skill at "lawyerlike analysis" of the facts and the law. But your acumen will have shown itself primarily in your formal legal research, case parsing, reasoning, and especially in your legal writing (which combines them).

The sixth and final reason for you to get good at legal writing and legal research is that, quite often, Very Important Lawyers like to have articles published with their names on them, on topics within the law, as a form of public relations. Naturally, such lawyers are too important to do the work themselves. So—as often happens with professors in law school—they turn everything but the final draft over to an underling. That could be you. Sometimes you even get "co-"authorship credit when it's published. Regardless, the boss knows who did the work. And as long as the work was well-received upon publication, the boss will continue to Take Good Care of You.

Case Investigation

This chapter has concerned the "3 Rs" of lawyering. But there's a fourth skill that's also critical: case investigation. Technically, though, it can be thought of as a division of research, in the same way that informal logic is one of the divisions of logic—the other main one being formal deductive logic.)

Cases turn on *facts*—especially in a *jury* trial. What the jurors relate to are facts, especially insofar as the facts help the jurors decide whom to blame. Even trivial facts can loom large in their deliberations. (The mini-addendum to the Coda touted the book, *Cape May Court House: A Death in the Night*, by Lawrence Schiller. There, as new facts came to light, the advantage kept shifting back and forth between the parties.)

Perhaps the name "Leona Helmsley" means something to you. She was sent to prison for income tax evasion, several years ago. (She's out, now.) Income tax evasion is hard to prove when the evader is sophisticated. I don't know how sophisticated Leona Helmsley was or is. But I'll bet I know the key fact that got the jurors to vote "Guilty": Ms. Helmsley's maid testified that while she was serving food and drink to Ms. Helmsley and a visitor, Helmsley said to the visitor, "Only the 'little people' pay taxes." Helmsley may have been pure as the driven snow, but I'm sure the jurors' minds were irrevocably poisoned against her when they heard what she'd said. Someone had discovered a bit of evidence that, objectively speaking, was almost irrelevant to whether or not the defendant had committed the crime. But it was probably enough almost by itself to put her away.

Most lawyers, sooner or later, have to rely on a private investigator —or, at least, they *should*. But forget the detective novels and movies. Rather, for once, *The Perry Mason Show* was (almost) accurate: Paul Drake was (nearly) a typical investigator. Yet, today, depending on what type of law you practice, you're also likely to be dealing with a large firm such as Kroll Associates, of New York City. Such firms, among their many services, perform "due diligence" before one corporation acquires another, for example.

However, most investigations involve a search of public records, especially courthouse records. America is an amazingly open society. Many public records are acquired by private information services, and are available on CD-ROM or on-line for a fee: marriage licenses, voter registration, drivers' licenses, mortgages, creditor filings for goods, etc.

It behooves you to learn how to do case investigating yourself. True, the CD-ROMs or on-line services will be beyond your budget. But the old-fashioned gumshoe approach is not. You need to learn how to search through courthouse records. —Granted, if you do well in law school, and then go to work for a big-bucks law factory, it will almost never be worth your time to do any of this yourself. But that's why you should learn how to do it well in advance of the need for it.

Four reasons why: One, if and when you do rely on an investigator, you'll be better at evaluating that person's competence—and in spotting padded bills. (There are nincompoops and charlatans in the business...just as there are in the law itself.) Two, sometimes you might not want to make someone else privy to what's up. Then you'd better be able to do it yourself. (Unfortunately, some investigators are quite indiscreet, either habitually or occasionally; just like lawyers. You're always taking a chance, even if you've worked with someone enough to think he or she is close-mouthed.) Three, your client might not be able to afford it, or is too cheap to authorize it. If you *need* the information, you can get it yourself—even if you do it on your own time, at no charge. (You certainly won't want to make a habit of that, but sometimes that's the only way to go.) Four, it will make you a better attorney. You'll be aware of sources of information others might not otherwise have thought about. You'll do a better job of sensing when "something's wrong with this picture." You'll have the edge.

For example, each side in a lawsuit conducts "discovery"—formal procedures to gain information *from* the other side *about* the other side. I'm sure it will come as no shock to you that adversaries (both lawyers and laypeople) *lie*. Or, they just keep the truth all to themselves.

That's unethical. There are rules against it. There are penalties for it, sometimes severe. But it happens all the time.

However, if *you* have *already* conducted *informal* discovery, without the other side's involvement, you will be much better prepared for the *formal* process—and will get a lot more out of it. It will help you catch the other side's deceptions. It will help you trap them at it. (This is especially delightful when you do it in front of a jury. Then it's called "impeaching the witness.") And once in a very great while, you might even find a judge who cares about such things, who will do something about it besides going "Tsk, tsk. Shame, shame."

Example: I handled a breach-of-contract lawsuit that involved fee-splitting. One of the key issues was how much the "bad guy" had charged for a service he provided in years past. My client's "damages" were his share of those fees. The bad guy's current rate was available, but of limited use. I foolishly did not do any informal discovery before taking his deposition. At the deposition, he lied, and it was obvious. Only then did I come to my senses and start digging. Come to find out he had, over the years, filed suit several times to collect fees owed him for the service in question. The case files contained ample documentation. Reviewing his own evidence, it was easy for me to establish what his standard rate had been. Although the suit settled before trial, I'd really been looking forward to nailing him on this point in front of the jury. (In hindsight, if I'd known the truth *before* the deposition, I would have kept it all to myself anyway. But I would have done a much better job of pinning him down in his lies. As it was, I'd done poorly, and had left him much wiggle room.)

And here's how it can work for you in a different way: Sometimes, your *own* client is the deceitful one. Or sometimes your client is afraid to tell you the *whole* truth, thinking you then won't be zealous. Or sometimes your client just has a bad memory, or doesn't recognize the vital importance of something you need to know. You can only get so far by asking questions and looking over documents you get from the client. Sometimes, if the case is important enough, you need to run an independent check. (As the *other* side well might.) And there are few pains worse than getting blindsided because of you own client's omissions...especially when it happens in front of a jury.

Today, as standard operating procedure, I search out (1) other litigation the opposing client has been involved in, (2) other litigation the opposing client's *attorney* has handled—to see how he or she operates, and (3) other litigation my *own* client has been involved in—just in case my client says something now that *contradicts* what's in the public record.

Okay. Say you don't want to be a trial lawyer, and you won't be involved in lawsuits. Even so, case investigation can come in handy. Example: your client who wants to sign an important contract with a firm that he or she has never done business with before. The client has checked out the firm's credit rating, bank statement, etc. The "due diligence" seems complete. However, you—being a conscientious attorney in the service of your client—decide to check the courthouse records. You already know the other guy moved into town five years ago, and started this company of his from scratch. But the guy's 50 years old. Curious, you check him out where he lived before. Lo and behold, he went through a bankruptcy eight years ago—and took his former company down with him, leaving *its* bills unpaid. You then discover that he'd lived in another city before that—where, gee, he'd started a new company. *That* company had signed a five-year lease for a warehouse...and was evicted and sued a year later for not paying rent. And so on. Yes, you wouldn't have done this case investigation without your client's agreement to pay for it. And the client certainly didn't need *you* to do it. But *you're* the one who thought of it. *You're* the one who knew what to look for. And even if someone else did the work, it was *you* who saved the client a bundle.

One more non-litigation example: normally, a real estate sale includes "tracing the chain of title." Specialized companies do that. But sometimes they goof. Or, more often, they do it "by the book," and fail to go beyond the routine. If there's an odd deed or easement "outside the chain of title," it can cause big problems later. If you hope to have a real estate practice, intimate knowledge of the way the system actually works will enable you to check the specialized company's diligence. (I know of one real estate attorney who regularly embarrasses the title insurance firms by finding *important* things they've *missed*. He's very successful.) An ounce of prevention is worth a pound of cure.

As a lawyer, it probably isn't worth your time to do any of this investigating yourself. But if you know how to do it before you get your license, it will stand you in good stead.

No law school in the entire country, that I know of, offers even one course on case investigation, not even on how to search court records on-site. And as a result, many lawyers are not even aware of the possibilities for information-gathering: information that can be crucial to a case. Instead, they usually only consider the immediate fact-pattern of the case at hand. That's *tunnel vision.*

But—as with legal research, sound reasoning, and good writing— case investigation is a skill that can make or break your career.

Addendum to Chapter 17:
FILLING in the HOLES After FIRST-YEAR

LEGAL RESEARCH

Because legal research doesn't count in first-year, you might think there's no point in getting a head start on it. However, if you already know how to do it right before you even set foot inside the law school, it'll save you time and perhaps even trouble. (Legal Research is usually just pass/fail. But that doesn't mean it's a snap.) —And don't forget how important it might be to the success of your summer clerkship/s.

If you follow the recommendations of Chapter 16, and visit law school bookstores before you enroll, you can pick up the assigned textbook then, perhaps even a used copy. (It's a real textbook, not a casebook.) However, if you're still in college (or high school), I don't have any favorite/s to recommend as to books on legal research. All the ones I've seen are in paperback, and are good. Here are a couple of them: *Legal Research: How to Find and Understand the Law,* by Stephen Elias and Susan Levinkind. It's $20, from Nolo Press. It contains a number of research exercises—and then, separately, tells you what you should have found and where you should have found it. The book also has information on how to do on-line legal research. You can find *Legal Research* in—or order it through—a regular bookstore. Another good book is the *Legal Research Guide: Patterns and Practice, 2d ed.,* by Bonita K. Roberts and Linda L. Schlueter. It's $18, from Michie.

MORE on CALR

Legal research in a three-dimensional library is very time-consuming. But legal research in an on-line (or CD-ROM) library is comparatively fast—if you know how to do it right. (And, of course, you can use the materials mentioned above to guide your CALR, too.) You can save a lot of time and tedium. The book you need is *always* on the "shelf." And the ability to import material on-line will, alone, be a big help, because you don't have to photocopy hard-copy materials and then type their contents into your computer.

In law school, you get minimal training in on-line legal research. (At my school, we got one session of about 90 minutes. That was it.) Even if you're a whiz with computers, it takes practice to master CALR. So, you will need to put in *much* more time on it beyond the perfunctory training session. As mentioned earlier, you can do this at no charge.

Take advantage of such a wonderful opportunity. After you've had your initial training, find out when the Westlaw and Lexis reps will be at your school other than when they're conducting more training sessions. Then try to get them to help you, so you can improve your skills beyond the rudimentary ones you acquired during your own training session. You don't have to rely solely on the visiting rep, though. The services have toll-free numbers to call for assistance in conducting your search. You can learn a lot from the person at the other end of the line—especially if you call during the graveyard shift. (That person is an attorney, by the way.)

Further, in some cities, they provide additional training for free, at their local office. (They're trying to get the paralegals to come in, so the paralegals will make greater use of the on-line services their law firms subscribe to.) But *these* training sessions allow you to work on *your* legal research tasks, not merely the made-up exercises you will have done as part of your training in law school. You might have to be persistent to find out where and when the sessions are held. The best time to take advantage of this, for you, is while you're on vacation from law school. (But if your law school is in a city that has these sessions, the Westlaw or Lexis people might let you in even during a semester.)

Once you're in practice, you should carefully weigh the costs of any on-line research against the benefits. (CD-ROMs, in contrast, are clearly cost-effective...unless you have to buy them yourself.) The best time to use the *on-line* research is when you want to see if anything's happened in the law since the date of the last hard-copy materials you have. (There's always a lag between the time a regulation, statute, or court decision is issued and the time it's available in hard-copy. (Your local or state newspaper for lawyers, or the bar association you abelong to, will alert you to these developments.) But the "computer research" services often have these texts available on-line within hours.)

If you're going to a hearing to discuss a crucial point of law you've been researching, it's worthwhile to do some quick on-line legal research a day or two before. You don't want your opponent to pull the legal rug out from under you, especially in front of the judge. (Sometimes, by the way, your opponent will pull a case out of thin air, claiming that it was just decided within the past few days or the past couple of weeks. Surprise, surprise, the case is supposedly "on all fours"...and goes against you. It's truly gratifying to be able to call this liar's bluff—and you can do that only if you've done some final checking of your own, and have a copy of the case or statute to show to the judge...after you've made sure it does not support your opponent.)

LEGAL REASONING

Having gone through first-year, the last thing you'll want to do in the summer before second-year is to spend more time learning how to reason well. This is especially so if you take the advice of this book and get primers for the courses you'll be taking in the fall and read and study those primers in the summer, and if you also devote time to learning how to do legal research and legal writing well during the summer after first-year. (I can picture you now, saying to yourself, "This guy wants me to study *logic,* too? *Forget it!*")

So I know that 99.9% of those who read this section will "blow off" what's in here. Over 42,000 people start law school each year. Perhaps as many as 10,000 a year will read this book. (In my dreams.) But even if 10,000 read these words, that still means that, at most, only ten students a year will take the words in this section to heart and follow through on them.

But it's important enough to include here. If you just want to "get by," skip to the next section. If, however, you want to get "good"...

Logic, both formal and informal, is important. And very few people starting law school (or finishing law school, or practicing law, or sitting on the bench) are good at it. I can't promise you that it will help you ace your second-year finals (although it should). But it will definitely make you a better lawyer (or judge, if you go that route).

The "Grand Old Man" of Logic is Irving Copi. If you want to get good at logic, and have never studied it before, it's best to start with informal logic. *Informal Logic, 3rd ed.,* is by Irving Copi and Keith Burgess-Jackson. Even though it's in paperback, it's a textbook, and so its price is outrageous: $76. So, don't buy it new. Check the on-line out-of-print book dealers (such as abebooks.com and alibris.com—and Barnes & Noble often carries used copies of it through their on-line outlet). *Informal Logic* covers such things as analogies and informal fallacies (such as the "argumentum ad hominem"). It's a relatively painless way to start improving your logic ability.

Next up is *Introduction to Logic, 10th ed.,* also by Copi, but this time with Carl Cohen as co-author. It's on formal logic (deductive reasoning), among other things. This one too has an outrageous price ($84), so, again, get a used copy.

There's a workbook that goes with it, by Richard W. Miller. It's called *Study Guide: Introduction to Logic,* and is a companion volume to the textbook. The price on this one is more reasonable: $22.

I've quoted the author of the next work recommended here, Ruggero Aldisert. His book is *Logic for Lawyers: A Guide to Clear Legal Thinking, 2d ed.* It's in paperback, but again, the price is steep: $45.

You'll be tempted to cut corners and go directly to Aldisert's book. Don't. True, *Logic for Lawyers* does not require previous study of logic. But it covers a lot of ground, quickly (albeit well). To make sure you have a through understanding of logic, you really should go thorough the steps of informal logic, deductive reasoning, and then "logic for lawyers." This is especially so because Aldisert's book will also be a review of what you learned from the Copi books.

LEGAL WRITING

As for legal writing, any law school bookstore will have a selection in this area. But most of them will be textbooks for that school's course. That means they'll probably be expensive.

Here are two books that, while not specifically for *legal* writing, are 1) invaluable, and 2) cheap. The first is *The Elements of Style,* by William Strunk, Jr., with additional material from E.B. White. It's just eight bucks, in paperback. The second is *Simple & Direct,* by Jacques Barzun, a $15 paperback.

Normally, in expository writing, the "KISS" rule applies: "Keep It Simply, Smarty." But in legal writing, the rule becomes "KISS-A-MIC." —"Keep It Simple, Smarty...and Make It Complete." That is, you must try to cover all the bases. The following books will help you do that...

There is at least one book written specifically for legal applications, which is not a textbook. This is Bryan A. Garner's *The Elements of Legal Style.* As you can see, it's modeled on the Strunk & White book for laypeople. It's $30, in hardcover. I have a copy, and recommend it. Garner also compiled the *Dictionary of Modern Legal Usage,* $27.

Another work is Richard C. Wydick's *Plain English for Lawyers, 3d ed.* This paperback from Carolina Academic Press costs $14.

For non-litigation compositions, there's *Scholarly Writing for Law Students: Seminar Papers, Law Review Notes, and Law Review Competition Papers,* by Elizabeth Fajans and Mary Falk. I have a copy, and can vouch for the fact that it is wonderful. However, Amazon lists it as out of print, if you do your search by title. It is *not* out-of-print, though; Barnes & Noble's on-line store lists it, at $25. Another book is one that I discovered only when making final changes to this addendum. Thus, I've not yet seen it and so cannot vouch for it. It's *Academic Legal Writing: Law Review Articles, Student Notes, and Seminar Papers.* It appears the author is Eugene Volokh, though I am not sure. As of this writing, it's soon be available through Barnes & Noble, for $19.

I haven't found a book exclusively on contract-drafting that's both excellent and cheap. However, again while making last-minute changes to this addendum, I was told of a book called *Writing Contracts: A*

Distinct Discipline, by Peter Siviglia. It's a paperback, $12.75, and Barnes & Noble carries it on-line. Because I've not seen it, I cannot vouch for it. But the price is right.

Scott J. Burnham, of the University of Montana Law School, has done a book called *Drafting Contracts, 2d ed.* (1993). The price is about $18, in paperback. It's published by the Michie Company. (*Drafting Contracts* is also available on disk, through Lexis, for the same price.) It provides lots of exercises—which is good. However, it's a textbook. Because it's a textbook, there are *no answers.* (The answers are all in the teacher's manual, which you can't get.) Unless your school has a course that uses the Burnham textbook, you're out of luck. Even so, it is very good. As part of learning how to draft better contracts, you will find yourself understanding contract law much better, too.

Michie does a second Burnham book, *The Contract-Drafting Guidebook.* This one's for attorneys. It contains additional material not found in the student book. But this one is $60, and hard-cover. If you can't spare the money in law school, let it go. But if you enter the private sector, especially as a solo, this book is a *must.* And even before you become a lawyer, it's good to have, because it's never too early to start practicing on the drafting of contracts. (Even if your school doesn't have a course in contract drafting, your legal writing instructor might be willing to critique your work. —Just try to make sure that your instructor knows his or her craft.)

As you will see in Chapter 22, you should subscribe to publications for lawyers, and should join organizations for lawyers and law students. Chapter 22 recommends this in connection with your job search. However, there's another reason, and it's relevant here. By joining organizations and subscribing to publications, you get on mailing lists. For most people, "junk mail" is a nuisance. But you should *welcome* direct mail advertisements that relate to the law.

Because the law school is not on your side, the law school will do little to help you become a good lawyer. But those who already *are* lawyers (sometimes) want to get good, or better, at what they do. And so, the lawyer publications have ads for workshops, books, CD-ROMs, etc. And by getting on mailing lists, you will receive direct mail solicitations. *Take advantage of these.* With student I.D., you can often get a discount.

Note: When I was in law school, I'd subscribed to a newspaper for lawyers, and that got me on mailing lists. One day I got a piece of "junk mail" announcing a two-day workshop by Bryan Garner, on contract drafting. (He gives them around the country.) I called, arranged for a student rate, signed up, went—and loved it. Later, I took another two-day workshop, at a student discount, on how to draft litigation documents—and loved that, too. If you subscribe to publications or join organizations, you will likely have similar opportunities, wherever you are, for either strictly local programs or for local presentations of national programs such as Garner's. (If you want to attend, though, do try to get a student discount, because these programs are for lawyers and thus are high-priced.)

I'm sure you do not want to hear advice to spend more money on books for law school, after you've blown a bundle on the nearly worthless casebooks you had to use in first-year. But as with virtually all of the books recommended here, you will (or should) turn to these again and again as you continue your life in the Law. (And that includes, for example, when you're doing your summer clerkship/s, or a judicial clerkship after graduation.)

They will stand you in good stead,
for the rest of your life.

Chapter 18 - Honing Your Skills— and Enhancing Your Future

Law Review "Drudgeships"

Law Review is the Holy Grail of Law School, as you will fast discover. Many schools also have other journals, but Law Review is the "flagship" publication. (At a few schools, it's called Law Journal. You'll quickly learn what it is at your school.) Those who Make Law Review see themselves—and are seen as—an elite. Those who end up in the top positions on their school's Law Review regard themselves (and are regarded as) minor deities. There is a mystique about it. Law Review imparts a cachet that never diminishes.*

Law school academic journals are unique in that they are the only academic periodicals edited solely by students. Mere students choose which proposed articles to accept and reject. Yet, the submitted manuscripts come mostly from law school professors. Often, they're from assistant professors trying to get tenure. (As Chapter 9 said, tenure requires publication—preferably in prestigious journals.) However, the prestigious journals also get submissions from professors who've long had tenure. These hope to use the journal as a forum for influencing the law itself or the legal profession—or to get a job at a more prominent school, or to add to one's credentials for getting hired as a legal consultant. Manuscripts also come in from attorneys, judges, and an occasional public official in the legislative or executive branches. And there are submissions from law school students. (But a student's published article is only called a "note," or a "comment.")

The editors do more than accept and reject articles, though. They also edit them. A 23-year-old kid can slash passages, or rewrite them, in a manuscript prepared by someone two or even three times his or her age. There's give-and-take when the writer objects (and *all* writers object to *any* changes by an editor). But the student editor has the final say-so...unless the author is a legal superstar. As you can see, the student editors of a prestigious Law Review have an awful lot of power. It's heady stuff.

---

* Because Making Law Review (usually) means high grades, this is a good place to mention the Order of the Coif. Coif is to Law School what Phi Beta Kappa is to college. As with PBK, it's nationwide, and you don't get in until you're about to graduate. Most law schools also have their own individual honor society, and there are some legal fraternities that require high grades to get in. However, as with Phi Beta Kappa, Coif is in a class by itself.

CITE-CHECKING & FINDING AUTHORITY

Everything in a Law Review article must contain a citation to authority, via footnotes. The second-year slave's job is to check each of these citations for accuracy. The process is called "cite-checking," for short.

Example: on page 42 in Chapter 2, there's a reference in a footnote. If this were a Law Review article, a staff member would check that citation for accuracy, to ensure

(1) the author's name was correctly stated—and correctly spelled,

(2) the title of the article was correctly stated,

(3) the quotation is accurately stated, word for word,

(4) the article appeared in a Vanderbilt academic legal periodical,

(5) the academic legal periodical is called Law Review, not Law Journal,

(6) the correct abbreviation for "Vanderbilt" is "Vand."

(7) it was in the 42nd volume of the Review,

(8) the article started on page 433,

(9) the quotation presented appears on page 459, and

(10) the article was published in 1989.

Second example: On page 346 in Chapter 13, there's a case citation. Were this in a Law Review article, a staff member would check to make sure

(1) the "style" of the case was as given—and would find that it is more accurately written as *Owen Equip. & Erection Co. v. Kroger,*

(2) the case is reported in the official U.S. Supreme Court reporter starting on page 365 of volume 437,

(3) the case is reported in West Publishing's Supreme Court Reporter—the one most people use—starting on page 2398 of volume 98,

(4) the case is reported in Lawyers Co-Operative Publishing's case reporter starting on page 274 of volume 57, and

(5) the decision was issued in 1978.

Are we having *fun* yet? Sometimes one sentence will have references to as many as half-a-dozen footnotes, or more. These are so extensive that sometimes they take up half the article's space. (To the best of my knowledge, the record is 4,824—in one article. The record for the longest footnote is said to be five complete pages, of *tiny* print.)

But that's not all. If the article says "The sky is blue," there has to be a footnote to some Authority regarding that alleged fact. Often, the manuscript includes an assertion without any such reference. Or worse, the reference is incorrect. Shame, shame, shame. Then the Law Review slave has to Find Authority. —That is, the staff member must do what the author (or the author's assistant/s) should have done: "prove it." (This doesn't actually mean "proving" it, though. It just means there's some authoritative evidence out there, to support the assertion.)

If there's an error, whether in cite-checking or Finding Authority, it's the legal journal's reputation, not just the author's, that suffers.

(Increasingly, authors of law review articles use footnotes to score points that they don't want to try to make in the main text. Perhaps they feel footnotes are not subject to the same critical scrutiny. At any rate, this practice is called "barking from the bottom of the page.")

THE BLUEBOOK

As part of your Legal Writing course, you will at least hear of something called the *Bluebook*. If you Make Law Review, you will have to become intimately acquainted with it.

Andrew J. McClurg explains, in *The Law School Trip:*

> The *Bluebook* is the most hypertechnical text
> ever written. It makes the maintenance manual
> for the Hubble Space Telescope read like a Golden
> Book. The nit-picking complexity of the
> *Bluebook* over minutiae such as spacing, type-
> face and punctuation seems intentionally designed
> to trip up even the most anal-retentive student.

The *Bluebook's* subtitle is *A Uniform System of Citation.* Its creators (and constant revisers) are editors of the flagship publications at the law schools of Columbia, Harvard, Pennsylvania, and Yale.

It's so difficult to use that there was *A User's Guide to the Bluebook,* by Alan L. Dworsky, to try to make sense of it. (Sadly, it is now out-of-print. But you can still find it in the used book market on the 'net.)

The *Bluebook* is so difficult to use that the editors at the University of Chicago launched a competing citation manual, the "maroon book." (Alas, it failed to dislodge the *Bluebook*.) The Association of Legal Writing Directors has created its own *ALWD Citation Manual: A Professional System of Citation.* (Its author is Darby Dickerson.) This new manual is longer than the *Bluebook,* but clearer and easier to use. Too early to tell if it has a chance of playing nemesis successfully. But if your school uses the *Bluebook,* you're stuck with that.

JOINING THE CLUB

At most schools, those who have a sufficient gpa after first-year are automatically invited to join the Law Review.

As Chapter 17 said, the other way to Make Law Review is through the "Write-On." Early in second-year, the Law Review announces the topic of a legal essay. Each Law Review wanna-be then researches the topic and writes a legal essay on it. The editors pick the winners, and the student authors get to join the ranks of the slaves. (At some schools, grades count even in the write-on. Your law school gpa is combined with your write-on score to produce an index score—just like for law school admissions. Different schools weight the grades and the write-on score in different ways.)

Automatic admittance is better than write-on, but the latter is far better than not Making Law Review at all. However, some schools do not allow students to "grade on" to Law Review. The *only* way is through the write-on.

—And the same thing is true for those who transfer from one school to another after first-year, even when their new school does have a grade-on system. For a transfer student, the grades from his or her old school do not count, period. So, if, as a first-year, you do intend to transfer, but want to Make Law Review, check to see if your target schools have a write-on competition. And be sure to find out *when* it is. At some schools, it's during the summer.)

If you have to go the write-on route, be sure to choose a "safe" topic...and keep your discussion of it "safe" too. If you instead choose something controversial, or you say something controversial about a "safe" topic, it's certain you'll offend someone's sensibilities. New insights into a safe topic are fine. Just don't go out on a limb. Those who choose the winners are only looking for competence, not brilliance or creativity. So stick to a conventional topic, and only say conventional things about it.

Note: Page 568 in Chapter 17 discussed good books for aspiring legal writers. To of particular relevance here are *Scholarly Writing for Law Students: Seminar Papers, Law Review Notes, and Law Review Competition Papers*, by Elizabeth Fajans and Mary Falk, and *Academic Legal Writing: Law Review Articles, Student Notes, and Seminar Papers*, by Eugene Volokh. But please get the others, too.

At some schools where you can neither "grade on" nor "write on." You apply—and the current powers-that-be choose who gets in. At other schools, you can just sign up, no matter how low your grades or how bad your skills at legal research and writing. But the more prestigious the school, the more likely first-year grades will count...heavily.

MOVING into the INNER CIRCLE in THIRD-YEAR

Second-year students spend all of their second year on Law Review working as "volunteer slave labor" for third-year students who occupy the top slots. It involves an enormous amount of work, all of it boring. This is because, for the second-year slave labor, *all* they do is Check Citations and Find Authority. You'll be required to fulfill a commitment of *x* hours per semester to Law Review. However, the hours are flexible, as long as you meet your quota. There's no academic credit for this, so it comes on top of studying for classes.

A volunteer slave who goofs too often (such as more than once) on Cite-Checking or Finding Authority will lose his or her chance to be promoted to an editorship in third-year.

It should be obvious that, to have a shot at an editorship, you should be good with legal citations. These books will help you do that: *Legal Research Exercises: Following the Bluebook,* by Nancy P. Johnson and Susan T. Phillips; and for those who are fortunate enough to be at a school using the *ALWD Citation Manual* instead of the *Bluebook,* Johnson and Phillips have another work, also with the same main title *Legal Research Exercises,* but with the subtitle *Following the ALWD Citation Manual.* To improve on the minimal skills you acquired as part of your first-year legal writing course, there's also *Legal Research and Citation: Legal Citation Exercises,* by Larry L. Teply.

If you impress your superiors, and make enough of the right friends, you can become an editor in your third year. (The outgoing editors choose their successors just before graduation, by voting on who gets the top slot, the #2 position, etc. The current editors also started out as second-year apprentices, doing the slave labor.) Those who don't become editors are generously allowed to remain as staff members in year three...as slave labor.

However, the *highest* positions usually go only to those who *automatically* Made Law Review because of their first-year grades. Regardless, while your social skills may well be what get you a top editorship, it's your legal skills that get you *considered* for a top editorship. The difference is crucial. Social skills are necessary, but not sufficient.

If you're selected to be an editor for third-year, you'll have to make a *full*-time commitment. You'll have neither time nor energy for anything else. (Recall how Chapter 9 said that, for law professors, time spent in class was really just "moonlighting" to them. The same is true of third-year Law Review editors—who, unlike the professors, don't get *paid* for showing up for class.) Quite often, the top editors appear only for the final exam. (You will shortly see how they can do this and still ace their courses.)

LONG-TERM REWARDS

In general, if you Make Law Review at a reputable school, and end up as one of its editors, your future is virtually assured. But even if you merely remain slave labor in Year Three, you will still have received an invaluable—albeit dismal—training, for you will have learned how to do legal research and citation *very* well...and how to be a good slave.

The reason why your future is almost "in the bag" is twofold. First, most law firm partners and important judges Made Law Review themselves. They know about the second-year slave labor. They know how much work it is, how boring it is, how hard it is to keep on with the "drudgeship" month after month. And they know that such people are the perfect employees: robots-at-law, disguised as human beings. But the second reason is also very important, even though it's related to the first. As you saw in Chapter 17, Finding Authority is crucial to legal advocacy. Those who've Made Law Review know how to Find Authority —*boy,* do they know how to Find Authority. And if someone goes on to an editorship in third-year, then the future employer knows that person must have performed satisfactorily in second-year. Thus, it's really the *second*-year participation in Law Review, not your eventual third-year title, that's crucial.

Here's an e-mail I received from a student who was still in first-year:

Atticus—

Today I found a packet that had been misplaced at the law school. The cover letter inside was a form letter, with the salutation "Dear Law Review Member at the [school's name deleted]." It was a solicitation for résumés for summer clerkships with a major local firm, stressing the possibility of employment with that firm after graduation.

Your readers can draw their own conclusions about how important our first year of study is.

Here are two e-mails from a student who used "The *PLS* Approach" and graded onto Law Review.

Atticus—

Everyone treats me as a demi-goddess on campus. It's sort of funny. One of my friends said that I must be a genius, and I told him I just knew which study aids to buy. LOL.

I think some people would like to slit my throat and are willing to sell their first born child to get an interview with some of the firms that want to talk with me.

Atticus—

My semester continues to be quite challenging—ie, 12 hour days at school. I must have spent 20 hours this week checking footnotes and collecting sources...insane. [Ellipsis in the original—AF.] *I was at school every day from 7:30AM until 7:30 PM just to do my citations, read for class, and outline.*

I've been managing my time really well so that I don't have to do any law review work on Friday, Saturday and Sunday. The weekend is normally dedicated exclusively to studying, outlining, and hypos. And, I still have more to do this weekend—research for my Comment.

Law Review really sucks. The only reason I'm doing it is for resume potential—and to get something published.

I guess a lot of people would die to trade places, though.

Yup.

If you don't Make Law Review, it isn't the end of your life in the Law. But it will seem that way at the time. This is partly so because law school (and the legal profession) is *very* status conscious. If you thought *high* school was bad, just you wait.

Most firms hire only a handful of new associates each year. The more prestigious the firm, the more likely it will hire only from the most prestigious schools, and only from the very top of the Law Review staff. These people are supposedly the "best and the brightest." (Yet, as David Halberstam's book of that title showed, it was the "best and the brightest" who got us into the War in Vietnam. Many law firms have had similar debâcles.)

As mentioned, most schools have academic legal periodicals besides Law Review. But those don't carry the prestige of the flagship publication. Often, *their* second-year slaves were admitted because of their performance in just one particular first-year course, rather than because of their overall first-year gpa. And sometimes, the journal in question is so highly specialized that future employers shun those who work on it, unless they're looking to hire people for that specialized area of the law. (Law Review, in contrast, has a general editorial content.) Sometimes these *secondary* journals at the *top* schools count more, however, with future employers than even Law Review at lesser schools. (And lower positions with the Law Review count more than all but the highest positions on other journals, at all schools.)

SHORT-TERM REWARDS

Besides the post-graduate benefits described above, Making Law Review confers advantages even while still in law school. The first benefit concerns registering for the next semester's classes. Normally, there's a deadline for students to submit their "dreamsheet" as to what they want to be enrolled in for the next semester. They usually have to list alternative choices, as well. Supposedly, the recorder's office then fills each course's slots in the order in which the staff goes through the dreamsheets—and that order is random. At larger schools, it's all done by computer, supposedly. But funny thing, the students who Made Law Review always seem to get whatever they wanted. Could it be that their dreamsheets are pulled out, set aside, and processed before the others'? No, impossible.

The second reason involves making life somewhat easier for you. Chapter 4 stressed the importance of creating your own outline, and not relying on the work of others. In first-year, that's absolutely true; but not in Years Two and Three. In first-year, it's true because your year-one grades are the *sine qua non* (Latin: "without which, [there is] nothing"). But as Chapter 4 said, once you understand your first-year subjects well, it's no longer vital that you do all the work yourself: the advanced courses, for the most part, are just variations on the themes you learned in Year One.

Even though Law Review is an enormous amount of work, on top of classes, you don't have to run yourself ragged. This is because the third-year editors (usually) have a collection of *excellent* outlines for virtually *every* second- and third-year course, specific to *each* professor. When a prof teaches an advanced course, he or she uses the same casebook and notes year after year. The Law Review outline collection reflects this. One of the best perquisites of Making Law Review is that you get access to a very good outline for almost any course you take— although sometimes only the third-year staff, or perhaps just the very top editors, get this. Because class itself is nearly a complete waste of time (just as in first-year), being able to study a *good* off-the-shelf outline as finals approach can make all the difference in the world.

So now you know the secret of how it's possible to work nearly full-time on Law Review while carrying a full credit load...and still ace your courses. (Assuming they're available even to second-years, once you Make Law Review, you might want to choose your advanced courses based on the availability of a Law Review outline for the course and professor in question.)

And just in case the outlines aren't enough to get you to the top, there's a third possible reason. Recall Chapter 13's discussion of "blind" grading, and surreptitious revisions to grades before they're recorded. Unlike most other revisions, for those who Made Law Review the change can *add* points. It isn't automatic, and in fact it's rare, but it does happen—especially for the top editors...and especially if one of the editor's parents is a VIP in the legal community, who channels big bucks to the alumni fund. Rank Hath Its Privileges. Just as in the real world.

Summer Clerkships

"Summer clerkship" can mean just a summer job in a law office. However, at the prestigious firms—which are usually large—it's a structured experience: "summer associates" rotate through all the firm's departments.

Typically, students interview for them in the first semester of their second year. First-year grades are the major criterion. This is unfair, of course. Because the summer clerkships usually don't occur until after students complete second-year, the interviews could easily be delayed until the second semester of Year Two. Then the firms would have three semesters' worth of grades to go on, not just two. This is yet another reason why the hide-the-ball, and the bait-and-switch, of first-year is so...*despicable*.

If even just the "Trinity" (Harvard-Yale-Stanford) announced that henceforth (1) students would not be allowed to interview for summer jobs until *spring,* and would not be allowed to accept any summer job offers until spring, and (2) no law firm would be allowed to interview until spring, nor make a summer job offer to a student at that school until spring—and would be banned from on-campus interviewing if it violated this new policy—then virtually all the other law schools in the country would quickly do likewise. But Harvard, especially, calls the shots in legal education. And Harvard apparently likes the cruelty of the *status quo* just fine. (There is a move underway to change this practice, though.)

However, some firms even interview students in the second semester of their *first* year. These are for summer clerkships after Year One, which are rare. In that case, mid-term scores in full-year courses, and final grades in one-semester courses from the previous fall, are the criteria—along with your *college* transcript, and the prestige of that college. Either way, the clerkship then occurs the following summer.

The typical summer clerkship lasts six weeks. The firms run two sets of them, one in the first half of the summer, one in the second. So, during the two summers you're in law school, you can have four clerkships, tops.* (Actually, two, probably, because—as mentioned—few firms have summer clerks who've only finished one year of law school.)

You get paid the same rate as an entry-level associate attorney. So, if the going rate is roughly $100,000 per annum for a new hire, you get roughly $2,000 a week: more than $12,000 for your month-and-a-half. Not bad. (However, first-year summer associates might not make the same as a second-year does. Life can be cruel.)

The summer clerk gets rotated through the major departments. The workload is moderate, and stress is almost non-existent. (Once you're a *real* associate, though, the workload and stress will be crushing—and commensurate to your starting salary.) As Chapter 17 noted, you will quite likely be put to the test regarding legal research and writing. If you get a summer clerkship after first-year, and then clerk for the same firm the following summer, the test will more likely occur during your second stint.

There's a lot of structured socializing with members of the firm. That's because (assuming you pass the informal tests of your skills) the people at the firm are mainly interested in evaluating your character and personality. They want to see how well you fit in to the firm's culture. Each person is asking him- or herself, "Do I want to deal with this guy, or gal, day-in and day-out? Do I really want to have this person around for *years?*" (Employers in other summer jobs in the law are thinking the same thing. But the difference is that they will evaluate you much more on the quality of your work than on your social skills.)

At the end of the summer after a second-year clerkship, you will probably be told whether or not there's a permanent job waiting for you when you graduate the following spring. Those who interviewed you for the summer position will have already decided you are at least

---

* However, some firms are quite possessive: they don't want you clerking anywhere else, ever, especially if you clerk for that firm after first-year and they ask you to return the following summer. They say this tests the sincerity of your desire to work for *them*, your loyalty, etc. B.S. What it means is that you've put all your eggs in one basket—so now you have no place else to go. ("Early admissions" is similar…and then you lose your negotiating leverage regarding student aid.) But if you Make Law Review, they'll probably want you, regardless. At some firms, though, the clerkship lasts the entire summer, not just six weeks. If you're a summer associate following your first-year, you might be asked to return to the same firm after second-year, of course.

worthy of being considered by their peers. That's why you got the summer job. However, in the fall of their third year, many a summer associate is anxiously searching for post-graduate employment, just like everyone else.

It's important that you carefully choose where you seek a position as a summer associate. It's *vital* that you try to get with firms where you and the firm will be a good "fit." And yes, there are differences, one law firm from another—despite my sardonic comments about pinheads, drudgeships, robots-at-law, and so forth. (Chapter 22 concerns finding a permanent job, but is just as relevant to finding a summer clerkship.)

There is at most barely a year between the start of law school and the start of your first interview season. As noted, you will probably have a summer clerkship with only one or two firms. So, you need to choose your target firms wisely. And that means you need to start looking at law firms and areas of practice long *before* you start interviewing—which could be as early as the second semester of *first*-year. (Besides, if things don't "click" for you in your summer clerkship/s after year two, you sure don't want to be starting your job search from scratch in the fall of year *three*.)

Most students wait until it's almost too late. Then they grab the first thing they can get that looks decent. "What we do in haste we regret at leisure" (or something like that).

The American Lawyer Magazine is published ten times a year. The subscription rate for students (last time I checked) is $99. Every year, in one of its fall issues, *The American Lawyer* runs the results of a survey it conducted among summer associates at the most prestigious firms. Although the responses for any given firm are not consistent from year to year, this information can be a big help to you in deciding where to interview—and which summer clerkship offers to accept. (Of course, your best source of information is friends from law school who are in third-year, who've clerked at the firms in question, and who "think like *you* do.")

Warning: a summer clerkship has almost nothing in common with what it's like to be a "permanent" employee at that same firm after graduation. But at least you get to know the people there, somewhat, and to see if the "chemistry" seems right.

Internships

Unlike a summer clerkship, an internship is also possible during the school year—and sometimes you can get academic credit for it.

For future litigators, a *court* internship (working for a judge) can be a terrific introduction as to how—and, more important, now *not*—to do trial law. You will be disgusted at what some attorneys submit for a judge to read...and you will hear what the judge thinks of it. You get to sit in on hearings and trials, from which you can learn much (especially if the judge later shares a private critique with you).

In some states, appellate courts also have internships. This can be quite valuable even for someone who plans to be a trial attorney and to leave the appellate work to others. Here's why: as this book has already discussed, it's important to "protect the record" for the appeal. Unfortunately, many brilliant trial lawyers, who are consistently able to wrap entire juries around their little fingers, are woefully inadequate at protecting the case for the appeal. Many a large jury award has been knocked down, or knocked *out,* on appeal, for this reason. (There can be other reasons, though.) Sometimes, the victory itself is reversed. If you learn to see a trial the way an *appellate* court sees it, it will stand you in good stead. This is true no matter which litigation path (trial, appellate) you pursue. —And even if you decide not to go the litigation route, it still Looks Good on the Résumé.

Don't go for an internship with a trial court, and probably not an appellate court, until and unless you understand trial law. This includes your state's rules of civil (or criminal) procedure, the rules of evidence, etc. (See the addendum to this chapter for self-help study materials.) You'd better be good at legal research, too, because your major responsibility will be looking up cases, statutes, etc., to see if they say what the attorneys say they do. —And to understand what the cases, statutes, etc., actually mean, you must also generally understand their context (the area of the law they're in)...or be able to find out, fast.

Litigation isn't the only form of conflict resolution. There's also mediation and arbitration. (See Chapter 29.) If you don't want to do trials or appeals, but *do* want to help resolve disputes, try to get an internship with a mediator or arbitrator. You can sit in on the sessions, just as with a court internship.

Some universities have one of their own attorneys just for the students' needs. Sometimes law students can work as interns for that person. The pay is low or none, but sometimes there's academic credit for it. It resembles a clinic (see next chapter). You get real-live cases with real-live clients. (Usually these concern disputes with landlords and merchants.) Unlike a clinic, though, it is not a structured experience and there are only one or two students in it.

Your intended internship, whatever it is, might be something new. Hence, no provision was previously made for academic credit for it. Talk with the dean's office and see if you can at least get "independent study" credit for what you'll be doing. (You'll have to pay "tuition" for the academic credits, of course.) You might have to get an official supervising faculty member, and you might have to write a paper on your experience. Big deal. Find a friendly—and lazy—prof who will let you get by with a short report. (That should be easy.)

Research Assistantships

Working as a research assistant for a professor is similar to working as second-year slave labor for Law Review. However, while the nature of the work is similar, there's less work (usually). And it's far less prestigious. Chapter 9 discussed how professors try to enhance their reputations and their outside income, and how publication is the main way they do this. Their student assistants are the ones who Find Authority to provide the proper footnotes for the article. Sometimes the student assistants are the ones who *draft* (i.e., write) the article.

Research assistants, unlike Law Review slaves, often get paid—by the school, as part of a work-study program. But they don't get paid much. And as with Law Review, there's no academic credit for it. The only reason to become a research assistant is to attach yourself to a Big Gun in the Law. This means you have to scout the faculty.

If you're interested in a particular subject area, go to the secretary of the professor who teaches that subject. Get the name of that prof's current student assistant. Contact the assistant and explain that you're interested in the subject. He or she will probably let you know whether or not the prof is a VIP. The assistant you talk with might be a second-year who's planning to keep the job in third-year, in which case you have a problem. Or, the assistant might be moving on soon, and there'll be an opening for you. But if the prof is *not* a Big Gun in the area you're interested in, think twice before seeking the assistantship.

Then again, you can always do it the way I did. In both cases, I was extremely lucky, so I don't recommend this; but here it is. In the first, I signed up for a seminar in an artsy-fartsy subject I dearly loved. Then I went to the professor and asked him if he needed a research assistant in the subject. I hit paydirt. Not only did he need a research assistant but, unbeknownst to me, he was one of the Biggest Guns in the field— as I soon discovered from working for him.

In the second case, I was taking a course in a subject unrelated to the one I ended up working on as a research assistant. The professor had office hours, and welcomed visitors. I sometimes dropped by to ask him about this and that. Apparently he took a liking to me (or else he was scraping the bottom of the barrel): one day, he casually mentioned his old research assistant was graduating and he needed someone new. I casually asked what it involved. It was exactly the area I wanted to practice in upon graduation. Better still, it turned out this guy was the heir apparent to one of the Biggest Guns in *that* field, who was long past retirement age and was about to hang it up. My guy was the one who'd be doing the next edition of the VIP's hornbook—and would get his name added as co-author. Dropping the pretense of nonchalance, I leapt at the chance.

THE LITIGATION ASSISTANTSHIP

If a professor at your school is also a big-name litigator (whether trial or appellate), being a research assistant for that prof is like being a first-year associate at a law firm where that lawyer is a senior partner. But unlike what would happen at a law firm, you get to work *directly* for and with that lawyer, rather than for and with some intermediary who's senior to you. This is a *fantastic* opportunity to learn from a Master—perhaps once-in-a-lifetime. (Maybe call it a "*battle*-ship"?)

(The mini-addendum to Chapter 12 briefly discussed the film *Legally Blonde*. As a first-year student, the heroine could not have worked on the Superstar Litigator's defense team. And her partipation at trial would have been utterly out of the question even if she had been on the team. Yet, the scenes involving the team's *meetings* were realistic.)

Usually, to have a shot at this, you had to have taken a course with that professor, and had to have done very well. As a general rule, you also have to know the relevant rules of procedure and evidence—which usually means you need to have taken courses in those subjects, too. (But see the addendum to Chapter 19 regarding do-it-yourself materials.)

Chapter 19 - Clinics,
Formal Competitions, and Trivial Pursuits

Clinics

THE GOOD NEWS

A clinic is a real-world program, under the auspices of your school, for which you get academic credit. It has much in common with an internship, discussed in the previous chapter. However, in a clinic you deal directly with clients and their legal problems. Typical clinics involve criminal defense, consumer protection, landlord-tenant law, elder law, and family law.

In years two and three of law school, you no longer have the fear factor of first-year. As any second- or third-year student will tell you, those years tend to be boring. A clinic can be a wonderful change of pace, a chance to get out of the classroom and into the real world during the academic year. Unlike most of the rest of what happens in law school, it can also be a great learning experience. Most clients of law school clinics are poor. Most law school students come from solid middle-class backgrounds. At the very least, a clinic can be a real eye-opener, an often-disturbing exposure to the lives of some extremely unfortunate people.

For those who intend to be something other than "transactions" attorneys (who generally only write documents such as contracts or wills, rather than resolving disputes), a clinic can be a priceless introduction to just how "messy" real-world problems often are—and how difficult it can be to resolve them, often because of the clients themselves. (Corporate clients are no different.) Everything else in legal education involves analyzing only appellate cases, or BS-ing about "public policy." A clinic will likely be the only time in law school you will get to find out, through *first-hand experience,* what it's like to practice law. Not even an internship can do that. With an internship, you are not the one who's dealing with the clients (if, indeed, your internship involves dealing with clients at all—and the same thing's true regarding summer clerkships).

Further, in general, the profs who run clinics are unique within the professoriat. Often, they care about you even if you're not a potential law professor. Often, they actually want you to *learn* something. And, often, they work their tails off to *help* you. In the language used in Chapter 1, they are not concerned with the survival of the fittest (within the ivory tower of the law). They're concerned with fitting as many as possible to survive (out in the real world of the Law).

THE BAD NEWS

Chapter 9 was, in part, about seeing law school "teaching" from the perspective of the professoriat, and how, to them, it's largely a matter of economics. The same is true regarding clinics.

As in first-year, it's not unusual for students to take 15 credits a semester. If tuition is $10,000 per semester, that's $666 per credit. After first-year, most courses are three credits each. That's nearly $2,000 per student per course. And it's not unusual for a second- or third-year law school class to have 50 students in it. So, the course generates $100,000 in gross revenues for the law school.

From that, you subtract the cost of the prof's salary. If the law school is paying the prof $75,000 per semester to teach two three-credit courses, then he or she is getting $12,500 for each credit taught. Thus, $37,500 of the prof's salary is for teaching the three-credit course.

Typically, profs don't each have their own secretary; they share secretaries. But the secretary's work in connection with the profs' teaching duties (as opposed to the profs' consulting work) is minimal.

So, the gross profit a law school makes from the course in question is around $62,500—i.e., over $416 per student-credit (50 students x 3 credits, divided into $62,500).

Contrast that with a clinic. It's typically around five credits. If the prof who's officially in charge of it is making $75,000 per semester for six credit hours, that means it costs the law school $60,000 each semester to have him or her run the clinic. But the costs don't end there. There has to be a secretary just for the clinic, to answer the phone calls from the public and to handle much of the paperwork. If the secretary is getting $2,500 a month, that adds roughly another $10,000 per semester to the cost. Clinics also generally bring in practitioners from the real world to help students handle the cases. These practitioners are paid very, very little. But, to adequately supervise the students requires several lawyers. It's not unusual for there to be three. If they're getting $2,500 apiece for their work per semester, that's another $7,500 in costs. Total outlay: a ballpark figure is $80,000 per semester.

With a five-credit clinic at $666 per credit, revenue per student is $3300. But a clinic generally takes no more than two dozen students per semester. So total revenues are about $80,000 total per semester—and the gross profit to the law school is zero.

Further, clinics take up room, such as for all the files on past and current cases and the small offices in which the student lawyers meet with their clients. Generally, clinic space is not used for anything else. Classrooms, in contrast, can be used many times a day, for many different classes. So the institutional overhead costs are higher, too.

Actually, the disparity is even wider. The higher the prestige of the law school, the more likely it is to have numerous "endowed chairs." It works like this: a law firm or lawyer gives, say, two million dollars to the law school for the purpose of establishing a professorship in the donor's name—"The [Vain Fat Cat] Chair." The law school invests the two million bucks. The income is what pays the salary of the prof who "holds the chair." So the law school gets something for nothing: another faculty member who's a full professor. (And it helps the faculty:student ratio in the *USN&WR* rankings, too.) And any income from the two million, beyond what goes to the prof's salary, either gets reinvested or goes into the law school's general fund, to be spent as the law school pleases. At the very top schools these endowed chairs are quite prestigious. But at any law school, any endowed chair is prestigious, period. In contrast, I have never heard of an endowed clinical program. Fat Cats do not like to fund programs for poor folk who might—using student lawyers from the clinic—sue clients the Fat Cats represent. And even when that is not a concern, clinical programs are "not on the radar" of the law school's "development" (i.e., fund-raising) office.

And clinics pose potential problems that normal classes don't. For example, in 1998, the Louisiana Supreme Court enacted new rules that came down hard on student lawyers. This was because, in 1996, the Environmental Law Clinic at Tulane's law school represented an organization that blocked a proposed petrochemical plant in the organization's community. Tulane's clinic is alive and supposedly still well. But it would not surprise me at all if alumni contributions to the law school have fallen off considerably, or if other, more subtle, internal forms of retaliation occurred against the clinic itself.

Also, sometimes, local attorneys complain that a law school clinic is taking business away from them. So, clinics have to be very careful to handle only those cases no lawyer finds worthwhile.

Law schools, especially public ones, are quite "risk-averse." They'd much rather be safe than sorry. And "safe" means trivializing any clinic, as much as possible. On a cost-benefit basis, from the law school's perspective, clinics are a bad deal, a losing proposition. So they put as little money into them as they can. And for that reason, they also limit the number of students who can participate.

As an example of how little respect law schools give clinical programs, in October, 2002, Yale Law School sought applicants for a two-year "fellowship in public interest law," to begin July 1, 2003. Presumably, one would obtain an LL.M. during those two years. But the real purpose of the fellowship was to secure a new faculty member cheaply—for Yale's clinical law program.

"The fellowship is designed for lawyers with *at least four years of practice* who are interested in preparing for a career in law school clinical teaching. Responsibilities include *representing clients, supervising students, teaching classes, and* working on one's own scholarshp...Connecticut Bar admission or willingness to take the July 2003 bar examinsation required." (Emphasis added.)

And for all this, they're offering a stipend of...$40,000 a year.

For any lawyer with four years' experience, who's halfway decent as an attorney, this is truly an insult. But apparently Yale is counting on some lawyers' desire to try to get another chance at the brass ring...by picking up a Yale LL.M. in return for two years of what's nearly slave labor.

But the University of Wisconsin is even worse. In the spring of 2002, it sought new clinical faculty for the '02-'03 academic year. The law school said *no experience as a lawyer was necessary.* All an applicant needed was a Wisconsin law license. And because Wisconsin has a "diploma privilege" for graduates of its law schools, applicants who graduated from a law school in Wisconsin need not even have taken a bar exam. By not requiring *any* experience as a lawyer, Wisconsin of course could refuse to pay much to the people it hired.

From the law school's point of view, "In the kingdom of the blind, the one-eyed man is king." And that's all it cared about. Yet, seems to me Wisconsin has exhibited the ultimate in contempt for its entire clinical program, and especially for its students, as a cynical "public relations" exercise to placate students with minimal concessions.

Personal Experience

Unfortunately for me, the clinic I signed up for in law school was nearly a sham. The tenured professor who was officially in charge had nothing to do with it, other than being listed as the professor in charge. (Thus, he had the ultimate sinecure. He got paid for doing absolutely nothing.) Instead, he brought in a buddy of his from the real world to run the program on a (very) part-time basis. His buddy got the title of "adjunct professor." He, in turn, brought in two of his own buddies (but they did not get the "adjunct prof" title). Once a week, the three of them conducted a panel discussion in front of all the students in the clinic. It consisted of one-upmanship games and trying to bust each other's chops, for their own (and presumably the students') amusement. Often, they'd tell war stories (which were part of the one-upmanship).

At no time did we students get any materials to instruct us in the applicable law, nor were there any lectures on the substantive law. Nor were we told anything about how all the pieces fit together, and what procedural steps were necessary and why. The only way to find anything out was to catch the adjunct prof or one of his buddies either before or after the weekly bull session. If we students had to file a document with the court, we were told that all possible documents were on the secretary's computer. We had to go to the secretary (who was actually a paralegal) and tell her what our situation was. She would know what document we needed. She'd print out a "form document." It had blanks in it. We filled in the blanks with the client's name, the court name and number, the case number, and particulars regarding the facts of the case. The secretary then typed that in to the computer and printed out a new copy of the completed document. We filed that with the court.

The guy who was my supervisor was the lawyer the "regular" prof had brought in to run the program for him as an adjunct. He was never available except when he showed up for the weekly bull sessions. At one point, I had to handle an appeal. There was a deadline for filing the brief, of course. My supervisor was not available to discuss the case with me, for weeks. I wrote the brief. After much nagging, he finally agreed to see me...the afternoon before the brief was due. The brief was something like 45 pages long—way too much, as I eventually realized. He flipped through it for about 30 seconds, said, "Looks fine. File it," and that was it.

That guy is still in charge of that clinic. Four years ago I heard him give a public lecture to trial lawyers. He bragged about all the things he did for his students, and all that his students did for their clients. It was all I could do to keep from standing up and denouncing him. But because of my law school's prestige, the state bar association has given him a large grant every year to run a three-day program for "baby lawyers" on how to conduct a trial in this particular subject area. The man is apparently a good trial lawyer. But as a teacher, he's a fraud.

* * *

However, it appears to me that the guy who ran the clinic I was in is the exception to the rule. In 2001, I attended a conference of law school clinical education professors. Although I've not seen any of those clinical profs in action, I do not doubt that they are almost completely unlike the rest of the professoriat, in that they really care about their students. And they certainly are not in it for the money. (I sat in on a "break-out" session for adjunct profs. The person presiding was a regular prof, *of course*. The various adjuncts told about what they did, how much time they put in on clinic work—which was in addition to their regular work as attorneys—and also told how much they got paid. No one received more than $4,500 for a semester. Several got barely $2,000. All worked at least 15 hours a week (on top of their regular law work). The presiding prof was astonished. He blurted out: "No regular prof would ever put in that much work on a course." However, several full-time profs who officially run clinics do in fact get heavily involved in those clinics, and love it. So, just because someone is a full-time "regular" prof, that doesn't mean he or she is a shirker. (And, as mentioned, the *adjunct* prof in charge of the clinic at my school was one of the biggest shirkers of all.)

Several of the regular faculty who officially preside over clinical programs told me that clinics are not allowed to directly solicit funding from outside sources. *Regular* profs can subtly advertise their availability for consulting work, and all the money from that goes into their own pockets. But if a *clinical education* prof even *subtly* tries to solicit outside funds for the exclusive use of the *clinic,* then the prof gets fired.

But it gets worse. Several clinical education profs told me, privately, that their law school deans actively solicit money from law firms, claiming that the funds will be used to beef up the clinical programs. Some law schools raise tens of thousands of dollars from this. Yet, very little money goes into the clinical programs. In other words, it's yet another form of the "bait and switch" that's endemic to law schools. Here, though, the donors, not law students, are the victims—although, of course, the students get victimized too, indirectly. (It would make an interesting case if one of those donors knew what was going on and then filed suit for fraud.) If the clinical ed prof alerts the donor, that prof is out of a job, "tenure or no tenure," I was told.

Ironically, the more reputable the law school, the more likely its clinics will be of low quality. Prestigious schools tend to think that anything having to do with the real world, as part of the curriculum, is beneath that school's dignity. "Regular" profs, especially at big-name schools, have built their reputations on what they call "scholarship." Many of them are not licensed to practice law, have never handled a case—and couldn't handle a case if their very lives depended on it. Rather than even tacitly acknowledge their incompetence as attorneys, they hold a subtle contempt for those on the faculty who take *pride* in their competence as *lawyers* and who, for some odd reason, like the idea of helping law school students to become *competent* lawyers. It's part of the rationalization by which regular law profs keep their consciences clear. It's similar to their attitude toward their students in general (though they might be quite friendly—for what that's worth— toward specific individuals).

590

Further, as a general rule, the only income the clinical profs make is from their salary as professors. (These are often tenured profs, full time. I am not referring here to the adjuncts.) And they put in far more time, on a per-credit-hour basis, than the "regular" faculty members do.

As Chapter 9 pointed out, "teaching" is the least important part of what most law school professors do...and to them, students are a nuisance. As Chapter 9 also discussed, the "scholarly" profs use their salary as just a *baseline* income. On top of that, they can often derive enormous fees from consultation work, casebook royalties, etc. They simply cannot comprehend the mentality of a faculty member who wants to *teach,* instead of merely using the title of "professor" as a drawing card for income with which to line his or her own pocket. And the idea of a teacher being *devoted* to the education of his or her students simply does not compute. (I found it interesting that even the full-time tenured profs who run clinics would refer to their non-clinic fellow faculty members as "regular" professors. The clinical profs were well aware of their second-class status within the law school. But, for the most part, theirs was a labor of love...or insanity, perhaps.)

From the point of view of the rest of the faculty, and of the law school deans, clinics are usually just a token gesture, to try to keep the "natives" from getting too restless...and to please alumni (and get more money out of them).

ON BALANCE

That said, a *good* clinic can be an invaluable experience. And I believe that participation in a clinic should be *required* of *all* law students...but only if the school is willing to ensure that its clinics are *good.* It's up to you to try to find a clinic that's worthwhile. Even at the same school, their quality can vary enormously. If you can find a good one, though, I say "Go for it." You'll be glad you did. Something is (usually) better than nothing.

—In fact, if you have no intention of going to work in a "law factory" when you graduate (and especially if you're an older student), take all the (good) clinics you can. They will stand you in good stead, especially if you become a sole practitioner.

Also, I've heard repeatedly that law firms—especially law firms where the new associates are expected to work on litigation—prefer to make offers to graduating students who've had clinical experience, even if the clinic is in an area of law the firm does not practice. If a graduate has actually attended a deposition (or better yet, conducted or defended one), or has been "first-chair" at a court hearing, that graduate is already miles ahead of the job applicants who spent all their law school time in the classroom or the library. Enough said about that.

I know of only two drawbacks to clinical programs. The first is the flip-side of dealing with real-world cases. Depending on what kind of clinic it is, your cases might easily continue beyond the semester (or two) that you spent working on them in law school. So, you do not get to see them through from start to finish. Often, in fact, you'll be picking up cases others started one or more semesters earlier. So, chances are, you'll only get a small piece of each case you work on. But a good clinic director will see to it that you'll be working on several cases that are in various stages of completion.

The second drawback is that, because the lawyers who get down in the trenches with you are probably in it for the love of justice, humanity, etc., they tend to be one-sided in their case discussions. By the time you get into a clinic, however, you'll be at least a second-year student. So you'll be able to figure out the other side's point of view on your own. The absence of balance on the part of the clinical profs is a small loss in your education. (Come to think of it, even if you intend to go to work in a law factory and become a Fat Cat yourself someday, you should still take at least one clinic. You will eventually end up working for those who take advantage of the type of people you'd represented in the clinic. But the memories of your law school clinic might give you a twinge—albeit fleeting—of conscience. Maybe someday you'll at least assuage your guilt by making a "restricted gift" to your old clinical program when you're looking for some nice tax deductions.)

Before you decide whether to sign up for a specific clinic, sound out the students already in it. Hang out around the clinic office, pick some students at random and quiz them about it—in private, one at a time. Get a good sample before you make your decision. And if possible, sit in on some of the clinic meetings where the students report on their work and get comments and instructions. These things will give you a good feel for the program's quality. (The best clinical programs I've heard of put materials on the applicable substantive law into students' hands, and then make sure the students become familiar with it before they're allowed to start working on cases. And the very best clinics first make students work on a mock case, just to practice going through the substantive analysis and the procedural steps.)

Even though the clinic I was in was of poor quality, if I had it to do over again, I would, just for the experience of dealing with real-world legal problems and the people who have them. It's law-in-the-trenches, not the ivory tower. And it can make all the difference in the world to your development as a future attorney.

Formal "Make Believe" Competitions

MOCK TRIAL

"Mock" means fake, pretend, as in the Mock Turtle Soup in *Alice in Wonderland,* or as in the term "mock-up." (There's probably also a connection with the verb "to mock," as in "to ridicule"—but I'll let that go.) These days, even many high schools have mock trials for would-be lawyers to participate in. And many bar associations encourage this. So, perhaps you are already know the first part of what follows...

You'll prepare a made-up case for trial. The made-up case is often based on a real-world case. Except in the final rounds, there is no jury present, but you pretend there is. (This is important in terms of what you can say. Certain things cannot be uttered—or rather, aren't *supposed* to be uttered—in the presence of the jury. Part of the competition is knowing the rules about this, and following them. Out in the real world, things are usually different, unless the judge knows the rules of evidence, which is rare, and makes the lawyers follow them, which is rarer still.) Normally, in law school, you don't dare sign up for Mock Trial until you've completed a course in the rules of evidence, at least.

Each side has two "attorneys," and you split up the work. As you quickly find out, little of what you've ever seen on TV or in a movie, or read about in a novel, is allowed in a real courtroom—or even a mock trial. To do it right, you must make a heavy time commitment. (The addendum to this chapter lists some materials to help you do well.)

Many law students who want to become trial attorneys sign up for trial advocacy courses and enter as many Mock Trial competitions as they can. That makes sense. Unfortunately, though, most litigators prefer to hire those who Made Law Review, not those who starred at Mock Trial. In part, this is probably because of the snobbery of the legal profession. Yet, it also might have something do with why "law factories" —very few of whose attorneys will ever be in court—also prefer those who've Made Law Review. As Chapter 18 mentioned, Law Review involves much drudgery. *So does litigation.* (Again, see *Cape May Court House.*) Would-be litigators at the major firms are often assigned to spend a week going through hundreds of cartons of documents in warehouses, searching for items that might prove useful in litigation. The would-be courtroom stallion first has to be a burro, out-of-sight, out-of-mind...in the Grand Canyon. Law Review people have clearly demonstrated their willingness and ability to function as burros.

However, there's another reason that's probably even more important: odd as it may sound, Mock Trial usually rewards behavior the real world *penalizes*. In a real jury trial, you *lose* points—with the jurors—every time you make an objection. (Jurors resent it when they think some lawyer is trying to hide something from them.) So, in actual practice, (good) trial lawyers make objections only when they absolutely have to. Further, there are some types of objections that a trial lawyer would *never* make, period. (These are objections that alert the other side to something you'd rather your opponent not be aware of—such as when he or she is inappropriately asking leading questions during direct examination.) But in Mock Trial, you *have* to make objections, to score—even though you run the risk of building a bad habit.

Also, in the real world, if the trial is to a jury, the most important part of the trial is quite often the so-called "jury selection" phase. Mock Trial doesn't include this. (As mentioned above, Mock Trial usually does not even include a jury. You just make believe that a jury is present. Even when real people are present as jurors, there is no jury selection. Whoever showed up for "jury duty" serves on the jury.) A good trial lawyer is like a good public speaker: you have to be attuned to your audience, and to tailor your presentation to the mood of the audience. A good trial lawyer is keeping an eye on every juror, and is alert for facial expressions and body language that tell the lawyer what to do (or not to do) next.

Where I practice, there's a law school whose students consistently win national championships in Mock Trial competitions. I believe there's a direct connection between that law school's success in Mock Trial competitions, and the surprising (relative) failure of its students to then become stars in *real* trials.

As with clinics, law schools are not willing to invest the resources in trial advocacy skills-training courses that a *good* program requires. Instead, they offer the Mock Trial competitions. The law schools know their students have stars in their eyes and that the students' minds are filled with trial scenes from movies and TV shows. The law schools also know the students are utterly ignorant of how they're harming their own potential as trial attorneys, and that the students, in their ignorance, will flock to these competitions and love it. It's sort of like the Wicked Queen giving Snow White the poisoned apple. And this poison is potentially just as long-lasting, and can put your career as a trial attorney to sleep from Day One. Yet, this betrayal of students' trust is just more business-as-usual.

MOOT COURT

The term "moot" means "having no significance," or "irrelevant," as in "The point is moot." So, Moot Court could just as easily be called "Mock Court." But that would obviously cause confusion with Mock Trial, so "Moot Court" it is. Moot Court concerns appellate court. No jury, real or pretend. No "Objection, Your Honor!" No direct examination, no cross. No exhibits or testimony. Instead, you're arguing a case on appeal. It's a fake case. That's perhaps because most appellate cases are in the Reporters, and—at least theoretically—it would be possible for law students to find out what the real case was and to look it up and see all the arguments used and how the court analyzed them.

However, unlike Mock Trial, a key part of Moot Court is your written brief. Skilled legal writing counts. And here's the one time legal research becomes relevant (brief-ly, as it were) in law school (other than for Law Review slave-labor). Then you get grilled by a panel of "appellate judges" (usually practicing attorneys who volunteer). Their grilling is a lot like your classroom experience with the Socratic Method.

As with Mock Trial, each side has two participants. Again you split up the work—the research and writing, and also the oral argument to the judges. During your first year, participation in Moot Court might be required. After that, it's optional. As with Mock Trial, Moot Court requires a heavy time commitment to do it right. (See the addendum to this chapter for suggested independent study materials.)

Forgive me for sounding like a broken record, but I have serious doubts about the value of Moot Court, too. For a while, I served as a judge on Moot Court panels. But what happens in Moot Court has little to do with what happens in the real world of appellate law. For one thing, in Moot Court, the "judges" have not even seen the briefs. So, to a large extent, they're initially in the dark as to where each side is coming from. That means they don't get much chance to think about what points they'll need to get clarified during the oral argument. They do get an "information packet" as to what the case is all about, and sometimes get summaries of leading cases on the topic. But they do not get each side's brief, because (1) it would supposedly be too much work for them to read the briefs *and* preside over the oral argument— and in most of the panels I served on, there was always at least one lawyer who admitted he or she had not even read the information packet, and (2) supposedly their evaluation of the briefs would color their opinion of the oral advocacy, and the people who run the Moot Courts want oral advocacy skills and written advocacy skills to be entirely separate variables when scoring each team.

Further, the same thing happens during the oral argument as happens during Mock Trial: the wrong skills are emphasized. Good oral argument is a *conversation* between the attorneys (one at a time) and the judicial panel. Based on their reading of the briefs (and perhaps of "the record" in the case), the judges are trying to clear up any concerns they have, or to further explore various points of law, fact, and public policy. In general, this does not happen during oral advocacy in Moot Court. Instead, it's often a matter of gamesmanship, with the judges interrupting the speaker, or coming up with off-the-wall questions just to see how good the speaker is on his or her feet. Granted, in the real world, sometimes appellate judges do that. But it's infrequent. And at least in the real world the judges have (usually) read the briefs and perused "the record" on appeal. ("The record" consists of the court reporter's transcript of the testimony at trial, the exhibits, and all trial memos, motions, etc. that each side filed that might be relevant to the appeal.)

So, as with Mock Trial, what tends to happen is that the advocates develop the wrong skills. The winners in the ivory tower competitions often become the losers in real courtrooms, because they developed too many bad habits. However, the brief-writing part of Moot Court can indeed be a valuable learning experience.

* * *

This is not to say that you should not do Mock Trial or Moot Court at all. (Besides, at many law schools, they're mandatory—in first-year.) I have received a few e-mails from students who said, "I wasn't interested in litigation at all...until I participated in Mock Trial" (or Moot Court). So, actually, I think you should try both, even if they're not required.

I do, however, recommend that you not get *heavily* involved in Mock Trial or Moot Court in law school. If you like either Mock Trial or Moot Court, start sitting in on sessions of the real thing. Go to a courthouse and watch some real hearings, trials, and appellate oral arguments. You'll see just how bad most "advocates" are. Or, watch Court TV sometimes. Either one of those activities, all by itself, should make you feel good. You'll say to yourself, "*I* can do better than *that.*" And indeed you can, fairly easily.

Warren Burger was the Chief Justice of the U.S. Supreme Court from 1969 to 1987. On November 26, 1973, he gave a speech at Fordham University's law school. In it, he said, in part, "No other profession is as casual or as heedless of reality as the Law." He particularly condemned the lack of training for attorneys who become courtroom advocates.

> Many judges in general jurisdiction trial courts
> have stated to me that fewer than 25 percent
> of the lawyers appearing before them are
> genuinely qualified; other judges go as high
> as 75 percent. I draw this from conversations
> extending over the past 12 to 15 years at
> judicial meetings and seminars, with literally
> hundreds of judges and experienced lawyers.

In a footnote to the published version* of the speech, he added that "One former colleague of mine on the Court of Appeals...puts the figure [of *competent* advocates] at two percent."

In October, 2001, I received the following e-mail from a student at a law school in the District of Columbia (students' names deleted):

Atticus—

We have an assignment for our criminal law class to visit a trial court here in the District. Here are some postings to our class's message board.

FIRST POSTING

Superior Court — God, I hope they're not all like this.

So a few of us visited DC Superior Court this afternoon to see an exciting criminal proceeding. Little did we know that over the course of the hour we would be subjected to some of the worst lawyering I have ever seen.

It took the prosecutor about half an hour to cover 30 seconds' worth of action because he didn't know how to phrase a question to save his life. The judge repeatedly had to clarify the prosecutor's questions and to ask questions of his own just to figure out what the hell was going on.

The worst part is, the prosecution was a hundred times better than the defense. Defense counsel was so unprepared that he had to borrow the prosecutor's papers because he couldn't find them in his own briefcase. He also didn't know what to do with the papers once he'd borrowed them. The judge just took them from him and read them to himself to try to discern what counsel was trying to argue.

My question is: are all lawyers in DC Superior Courts as bumbling as the ones we observed today? I hope not.

* 42 FORDHAM L. REV. 227 (1974)

SECOND POSTING

I had a similar experience at DC Superior Court on Wednesday. I was at a homicide trial. The U.S. Attorney trying the case mumbled the questions to the witness. The defense attorney had to restate a question to the witness FOUR times before he figured out that he had to have the specific date of the incident included in the question. I'm afraid that they may all be like this.

They're *nearly* all like that...and not just in the Superior Courts of the District of Columbia.

* * *

As for appellate advocacy, it's worth the trip to a state or federal appellate courthouse to sit in on oral arguments. Elsewhere, Burger commented that at least two-thirds of the lawyers who appeared before him in the U.S. Supreme Court were not good advocates. Now think about that: you'd expect attorneys who argue cases before the Supremes would be the very best in the entire country. Not so. (And if you watched any of the televised arguments before the Florida Supreme Court, during the aftermath of the 2000 Presidential election, you saw that the quality of the lawyers varied enormously—which again was shocking, given what was at stake and the fact that each side could afford to hire what should have been only the very best.)

With regard to the brief-writing, the books recommended in the addendum to Chapter 17 are invaluable. And some law schools have courses in the writing of appellate briefs. These courses are often taught by real-world appellate court judges, serving as adjunct profs.

Full Disclosure: Confession

Other than the required first-year exercise, I did not participate in Moot Court. However, I did take an appellate advocacy course in third-year. It was taught by a federal appellate court judge. It was the single most valuable course I had in law school...not because the judge actually taught us how to write a brief, but because the judge told us how to *think about* an appeal. The judge spent a fair amount of time telling us how *not* to go about preparing for, and conducting, oral argument, and noted that most lawyers who appeared in that judge's court were of poor quality. This echoed Chief Justice Burger's statement that few *trial* lawyers were competent

Because this judge served on a U.S. Court of Appeals, you'd think this judge (as with Chief Justice Burger) would have seen only the best advocates. Again, not so. (The judge played tapes of oral arguments, to prove the point.)

Because I pose as a know-it-all regarding law school, I shall share with you a humiliating experience I had in that appellate advocacy course. I made the mistake of treating the appeal as just a *re*trial of the case, on paper. The judge had warned us not to do that, but I was incapable of shifting from the trial lawyer's approach to that of the appellate lawyer. And to make matters worse, I turned in a *fifty-seven page* brief. This was far more than almost *any* appellate court would ever normally allow out in the real world. The judge returned our briefs to us in time to meet with us individually and give an oral critique, privately, before the semester ended. (I am not about to go into just how much the judge criticized my work, or what grade I got.)

The judge photocopied the best brief anyone had turned in. It got an A+. It was just ten pages long. The student who wrote it took less than two pages each for two key points of law that destroyed the other side's case. (The other six pages were the statement of facts, procedural history, etc.) It wasn't its brevity that made it good. It was its *succintness*.

I saved that fellow student's paper, and still have it. Years later, I managed to get one of my own appellate briefs down to…nine pages. (I knew it was a winner, and waived oral argument. And I did win that case, just with the brief.) One reason why that course was the single most valuable one I had in law school was the sting of the embarrassment before that judge who served as an adjunct prof—and the revelation of that fellow student's ten-page brief.

A Digression, FYI

Despite the myth, trial is not a truth-seeking process. Rather, each side is trying to get an *opinion* as to which side's story is more *likely* the truth. No court can afford to take the time to find out the whole truth, before making its decision (or before allowing the jurors to make theirs). In fact, despite the oath witnesses take, any witness who told the *whole* truth would have to be on the stand for weeks, probably. So, the attorneys on each side take bits and pieces of the truth as *they* see it, and try to convince the "fact-finder" that those bits and pieces are representative of the whole. In other words, it's almost a sampling process. Or, more accurately, it's like the rhetorical device of synecdoche (in which the part stands for the whole).

Trial law is actually a *storytelling contest*. (So is appellate law, but to a far lesser extent.) It's said that "there are two sides to every story." However, juries (usually) don't hear out both sides and then compose their own story that takes something from each. (In contrast, judges on appellate courts often do exactly that.) Rather, before the jurors go into their deliberations, the attorneys for each side have met with the judge and have drawn up "jury questions" as to what the facts are. These questions are put in terms of "yes/no," "either/or." There's no middle ground. The jurors have to go one way or the other with each one. (However, if they're not happy about deciding facts that clearly favor the plaintiff, they can make the victory a bittersweet one by voting only nominal "damages" to the plaintiff, even though the plaintiff wins. So there's a middle ground, of sorts. —But not if the jury is unhappy about deciding the facts to clearly favor the defendant. Then there's no way to say the defendant wins, yet the jury then sees to it that the victory is bittersweet. Instead, all they can say is the defendant wins, period. So, they sometimes instead say the defendant loses—but then try to soften the blow by awarding small damages to the plaintiff, as before.)

That's why trial work tends to be more emotional—or, as non-trial law attorneys say (among themselves), good trial attorneys are good bullshit artists. And sometimes they're right, because all good story-tellers are, to some extent, bullshit artists. Further, juries—like voters—have an unfortunate tendency to decide in favor of who they find more "believable." which is usually just another way of saying "likable." It's a matter of whom you feel more comfortable with (or less *un*comfortable with, as is usually the case—as with political elections). Often, they focus on the attorneys. However, a particularly likable or unlikable party or witness is sometimes the main determinant of "credibility." (Looks also play a role. In general, all other things being equal—which they almost never are—the side that's better-looking, physically, wins.* Unfortunately, some people regard skin color, or religious apparel, as part of a person's "looks," in deciding what's "better"-looking.)

---

* One of the cases you'll almost certainly have in Torts is *Katko v. Briney.* The farm-house of an Iowa couple had been repeatedly broken into and robbed. So the husband, Edward Briney, rigged a spring-gun in a closet, to go off and blast the intruder next time someone illegally entered the house while the Brineys were away. The next in-truder was Marvin Katko. He survived the blast. Then he *sued* the *Brineys* —and *won:* $30,000 in damages (in 1970s Iowa), including $20,000 in *punitives.* The Brineys had to auction off 80 acres of their farm to pay [continued on next page]

If this disillusions you, you have my sympathy. But better for you to know the reality now rather than learning it the hard way later. Bad as it may seem, given human nature it's far preferable to any alternative—including dispensing with the jury altogether and letting some supposedly objective judge decide the case alone. There is no such thing as an objective judge, because judges are human too—even though they often like to pretend otherwise. (However, judges are supposed to try to be objective—as are juries, for that matter. So, the fact that true objectivity is impossible does not justify dispensing with any effort whatsoever to be impartial. At least with a jury, because it has several people, the various prejudices and "ignorances" might cancel each other out. Not so when there's only the one judge.)

Juries are vital. They bring together almost a cross-section of the community, with a wide range of experience and a lot of common sense (though, as one wag said, "'Common sense' is the least common of the senses.") And even though I admit that good trial lawyers are good with the smoke-and-mirrors routine, juries tend to see through that, usually. They have a good feel for which side "rings true." So the trial lawyer who relies solely on smoke-and-mirrors to win his or her case is (usually) asking for trouble. If the facts aren't on your side, and you haven't thoroughly prepared your case, all the smoke and mirrors in the world probably won't save you and your client.

As a general rule the only cases that make it all the way to a jury verdict are those "deep in the gray" regarding the facts. (If it were a clear-cut situation, there either never would have been a suit in the first place, or else it would have long since settled. —However, some clients want to fight it out to the bitter end, even when they had almost no case to start with. This is especially common when a big corporation or rich individual is waging a war of attrition against a less-well-off company or individual, knowing that the other side cannot afford a protracted war.)

---

the judgment. (The result was a series of "Briney Bills" passed by legislatures around the country. They generally say a criminal cannot profit from his crime if he is injured as a result of self-defense or defense-of-property acts committed by the victim.)

Casebooks typically do not include photographs. Yet, many casebooks that include *Katko v. Briney* print a picture of Marvin Katko. The man definitely has "bedroom eyes." Is it a coincidence that the jury was *all-female?* (And is it a coincidence that the Brineys were, shall we say, less than "appealing" in appearance?)

For fascinating reading about this case and its implications, two articles: Geoffrey W. R. Palmer, *The Iowa Spring Gun Case: A Study in American Gothic,* 56 IOWA L. REV. 1219 (1971), and Andrew J. McClurg, *Poetry in Motion: Katko v. Briney and the Bards of First-Year Torts,* 74 OR. L. REV. 27 (1995).

A Possibility

Part of the problem with Mock Trial and Moot Court is that, because they're made-up cases, all the quirky little things that happen in the real world are missing. There's a paucity of detail, sometimes even on the major issues. (For example, because there is no "locus" of the events in question, it's impossible to visit the scene and use one's observations as a basis for an argument at trial.) Many times, in the real world, these details, these quirky little things, can have a major impact on the result. Also, those who serve as witnesses in Mock Trials usually do not really behave the way real witnesses do—with all the flaws and idiosyncrasies that real people, who are caught up in a dispute, exhibit.*

You've probably seen one or more "real court" TV shows:** "Judge Judy," Judge Brown, *Texas Justice*, etc. Those are not real courts. They're binding arbitration, a form of Alternative Dispute Resolution ("ADR"—see Chapter 29), disguised as real courts. One of the methods of ADR is called "rent-a-judge." In it, both sides chip in to hire a former judge to serve as an arbitrator. Lawyers then argue to the judge on behalf of their clients. Usually, they dispense with the rules of evidence. Typically, both sides waive their right to appeal. And there's never a court reporter taking down the testimony. In these TV shows, the people who put on the program pay the judge—a whole lot more than any "rent-a-judge" ever makes. (Also, as part of the deal with the parties, the people who put on these shows pay any money to the party, if either, that the "judge" orders be paid.)

---

* By the way, the words "testify" and "testimony" are from the ancient Greek word "testis," (plural, "testes"—and both words have been taken over in English and are still used in their original anatomical sense). When the ancient Romans used the Greek word "testis," it also meant "a witness." The connection is this: in ancient Greece, apparently only men could be witnesses at trials. As part of the ceremony in which a man swore to tell the truth in court, he had to clutch his testicles. Greek mythology says that this requirement was instituted by Aphrodite, the "goddess of love."

** Sad to say, for the most part, those TV "judges" act in ways that no judge should ever behave. Granted, they have to make it dramatic, to hold the audience's attention (and get the ratings). But I believe that—with the exception (so far) of Larry Doherty, on the nationally broadcast *Texas Justice*—their behavior is disgraceful.

In law school, to learn litigation skills, students have only two choices. In Mock Trial and Moot Court, they have a made-up case, in which they can represent either side. In a clinic, they get a real-world case, but they can only take one side. (Usually it's the plaintiff, but in criminal cases it's the defendant.) Yet, Mock Trial and Moot Court programs could be combined with Clinics, in law school, in a "real world" way, similar to the "real court" TV shows.

Most states have "small claims" courts, in which the parties act as their own lawyers. But I'll bet those litigants would love to have even a student lawyer working their cases for them. There'd be no threat to the local attorneys' business, because there's no money to be made. By using real-world disputes, the trial (or appeal) would be a *lot* closer to what the students will be dealing with if and when they become litigators after graduation. And a trial is a trial, and an appeal is an appeal, no matter how small the interest at stake.

Here's how it could work, using a landlord-tenant dispute as the example: the clinic director would assign one student to represent the tenant, and one to represent the landlord. (On a later case, the student lawyers would have to switch sides. This would effectively rebut critics who say law school students should not be representing poor people against business interests, etc.) There would be a trial, before a rent-a-judge: a real (retired) judge. The students would have to master and follow the rules of evidence. The parties would have to agree in advance that they were participating in a form of binding arbitration, and would waive their rights to go into a real court. (They would also have to waive the conflict of interest that occurs when student lawyers at the *same* "firm"—i.e., the clinic—are representing *each* side.) But one side or the other could then appeal to a "final" arbiter. (In fact, because an appeal is not a retrial, it might make no difference what either party wanted. The student lawyers could automatically do an "appeal" anyway, perhaps—even though it would be agreed that the outcome would *not* effect the outcome at the "trial" level, no matter what happened on "appeal.")

Yes, this would probably be more expensive. For example, for the trials, there'd have to be a court reporter, taking down the testimony. But most law schools are in areas where there are also schools for court reporters. It should be easy to work a deal between the two types of schools, whereby student court reporters would be provided free for depositions, hearings, and trials. Perhaps even the retired judges would be willing to donate their time. So, in practice, it might not cost much more at all. There would still be the problem of rounding up a jury at no cost. But perhaps fellow law students, who are in the clinic, would serve, as part of their participation in the Trial Clinic. They would certainly benefit, both from the postmortem critique of the student lawyers, and from finding out what it feels like to see a trial through the eyes of a juror. (The law school could also recruit college students, especially those who want to go to law school someday. Most law schools try to promote themselves to potential applicants for admission. What better—and cheaper—way to promote the school than by having college students see the school's students in action...and giving them a free guided tour of the law school in return for their jury service?)

***

Okay: back to what already exists...

NEGOTIATIONS COMPETITION

In the real world, even trial lawyers spend far more time in negotiations than they do in court. Few cases ever go to trial, so most litigators have just a "motion practice." Because most cases settle before trial, negotiating skill is very important. Yet, in law school, Negotiations Exercises are much less common than Mock Trial and Moot Court. Perhaps this is because it's harder for an academic exercise to successfully emulate the real world.

As its name implies, you and a partner negotiate as a team against another team. Each side is given a set of materials, but neither side gets exactly the same material as the other. This introduces uncertainty, just as in the real world. Although my law school experience with this was limited, I had the strong impression that, if the negotiations had "fallen through," both sides would have been penalized heavily. In a sense, this is like the real world. But it's also unfair. In the real world the threat of "walking"—and going to trial—is a good negotiating tool. (This is especially true if you have a reputation as a decent trial attorney and the lawyer on the other side does not.) So, the Negotiations Exercise is even less worthwhile than Mock Trial and Moot Court.

Obviously, out in the real world, skill at negotiating is crucial. But few law schools provide training that is at all worthwhile. And negotiations competitions provide no training at all.

(See Chapter 29 for some recommendations of books that can help you develop an *excellent* approach to negotiating.)

CLIENT COUNSELING COMPETITION

This is a session with a new "client" who has a problem. As always, you work with a partner. Through questioning the client, you have to find out what the problem is and try to understand all its facets. Then you have to lay out some alternatives for the client's consideration.

It seems the original purpose was to demonstrate good "people skills," similar to a physician's need to have a good "bedside manner." But in practice, at least at my school, it was just an oral version of a final exam with only one conflict-pairing. It might be different at your school.

In the real world, client counseling is one of the most important skills of all. Word-of-mouth advertising is the best kind you can have, and word-of-mouth advertising depends largely on good client counseling skills. Further, if things go wrong, one of the best ways to avoid getting sued for legal malpractice is to have had good relations with your clients. Good counseling is a big part of that.

Unfortunately, it's almost impossible to practice doing this within the constraints of a law school. So, Client Counseling Competition is rare.

Another Possibility

The possibility of bringing the real world into the law school, discussed above in connection with small-claims court, could be extended to Negotiating and Client Counseling. Instead of being make-believe competitions, they'd be real-world. The people whose cases get handled would love it, because at least *someone* in the legal system is taking them seriously. It might heighten their respect for the Rule of Law.

And now that many schools are offering courses in mediation training, student mediators could practice with the real-world cases that have come into the law school. That could lighten the load of tax-supported mediation services that handle small claims matters.

(A major defect of mediation training is that students role-play. There's a great temptation to "ham it up," and to sometimes play it for laughs. And as with using pretend witnesses in mock trials, the learning experience is thus of limited value.)

As for criminal law: many communities have established "Youth Courts" (a.k.a "Peer Courts" or "Teen Courts"). Teenagers who've been accused of a misdemeanor can plead guilty and then elect to have their sentence set by the Court. (However, the Youth Court cannot assess jail time, only community service, restitution, and so forth.) In a Youth Court, a fellow teen gets to act as prosecutor, and another acts as defense counsel.

This concept could be extended to law school, but with a difference: the defendant would not have had to plead guilty to be eligible for the court. Law school students would serve both as prosecutor and defense counsel. There could be a jury, as discussed above.

Of course, the local authorities would have to permit all this, and each defendant would have to agree to it. But a program like this could take a big load off the local DA's office and the misdemeanor courts. The program could even include adults, and not be limited to teens under the age of 18. There could be a provision for appeals, in the manner discussed above.

Presumably, prosecutors from the DA's office would be involved, as would real criminal defense attorneys. It would be a wonderful chance for those who want to become prosecutors to get to rub elbows with real-world prosecutors. It would greatly add to their education, and would also likely help them get a job with the local DA's office. The same is true for those representing defendants, of course. (And, in fact, student attorneys should not be allowed to represent only the State or defendants all the time. It helps to walk a mile in the other guy's shoes.)

LEGAL WRITING COMPETITIONS

One of the critical skills you need to master is that of legal writing. Chapter 17 addressed this.

As was said there, every year, there are umpteen legal writing competitions. Some will be just within your school, others will be statewide or nationwide. The best legal paper or two get money, sometimes as much as several thousand dollars. Need I say more?

—Well, I will (of course). If you've prepared for law school, you'll have a far more sophisticated understanding than most students. So you'll likely have a better chance of winning.

Winning a writing competition Looks Real Good on the Résumé, especially when you're applying for judicial clerkships for after graduation, but even when you're applying for jobs with law firms. And maybe, just maybe, you can make the necessary changes to the paper and get it published as a Note or Comment in your school's Law Review, which also Looks Good on the Résumé. (Even if you don't win the competition, by the way, you can still try to turn your paper into a Law Review piece, and get it published.)

Student Organizations

Your law school will have many clubs, along with student "government." Many of those who join try to become high officers in them because they think it will Look Good on the Résumé. Forget that. (For those with political aspirations—whether in real government or the bar association—a position as an officer in student government seems especially attractive. As near as I can tell, it's a pure ego thing, because it simply is of no help to you down the road.) Sometimes these groups bring in guest speakers—and then everyone hits the speaker up for a job. (That's one reason it's hard to get guest speakers for student organizations in law school.)

Many students join clubs because they're still thinking like college students. They want to have a "well-rounded résumé" to present to prospective employers. That is ridiculous. When you are applying for a job as a lawyer, it is different from applying for admission to a school. In the same way that you have to get rid of your old memorize-and-regurgitate approach to doing well before you've even entered law school, so you have to get rid of the old "well-rounded résumé" approach to getting a job before you leave law school. Prospective employers won't give a damn that you belonged to the "Health Care & Law Club," or the Law Students' Division of the American Bar Assocation.

You get an interview based on (1) good grades, and (2) the courses in which you got those grades. But getting the interview only gets your foot in the door. You still have to make the sale, and you do that based on the "personal chemistry" between you and the interviewer/s. Your previous membership in student clubs is used only as a "talking point," at best, to help break the ice or to revive a flagging conversation (in which case you're already in trouble). *"Well-rounded" is irrelevant.*

But there can be good reasons for joining student clubs. Members can share information and thoughts on the topic the club is for, and that can be helpful to you. (And for members of minority groups, Chapter 22 discusses the best reason of all.) Just do not seek to become an *officer* of the club/s.

Trivial Pursuits

As for talent shows, softball leagues, etc., for the most part they take up too much time. They can be a good way to release tension, or to boost your morale. But you have to make a major commitment. It's difficult to back out of that commitment. To release tension, better for you to engage in the rather impromptu activities discussed in Chapter 11. That way, you retain control over your time.

(Being on top of your courses is the best morale-booster of all.)

One of the biggest traps of all is the end-of-semester "skit" for each course. Its function is much like that of the original "April Fools' Day" in Medieval Europe. A town's commoners, for one day only, were allowed to mock their "betters" among the nobility and the Church. It was a very subtle social control mechanism. By allowing the "lower orders" to blow off steam and express their resentments and frustrations, it prevented a more serious expression of their legitimate grievances.

In law school, students get their "revenge" on the prof in each class by putting on a humorous skit that mocks the prof. The skit is presented during the very last session of class. Everyone has a good laugh, including the prof. With the tensions released, students put their legitimate grievances aside and go back to cramming for that prof's final. As with the Medieval April Fools' Day, it's an excellent control mechanism. (A similar function is served by profs who, earlier in the semester, host gatherings in their homes for their students, or go out drinking with them in bars.)

Students who have no common sense devote considerable time to creating a script for the skit and rehearsing the skit. Doing so especially appeals to those who fancy themselves creative writers or undiscovered actors/actresses or comedians/comediennes. Thus, *they* are the new "April" Fools, for they have far, far better things to do with their time and energy at that point in the semester. The profs know this. But, of course, the profs remain mum.

If, coming down to the wire in first-year, you put even a small fraction of your time into an end-of-semester skit, you are an idiot.

Addendum to Chapter 19:
Resources for Future Litigators

Evidence

Those who want to go into trial law—or at least who enter the Mock Trial competition—feel obliged to take a course in evidence. However, apparently, professors often make evidence every bit as complicated and as confusing as they do their first-year courses. As with everything else in law school, it shouldn't be that way. It certainly doesn't have to be that way for you, because you can learn it on your own. In fact, to learn it *well*, you *must* do it yourself.

The following items meet two criteria: (1) they're the best, and (2) they're easily accessible to, and affordable by, law school students.

Start with the written materials. Then, when you're familiar with the jargon and the concepts, consider moving on to the audio–and perhaps video–tapes.

UNDERSTANDING the RULES

Best, Arthur, *Evidence: Examples & Explanations*, 2d ed., 1997, Aspen Law & Business, paperback, roughly $35. —Another of the excellent primers from Aspen. Best really does live up to his name.

Fishman, Clifford S., *A Student's Guide to Hearsay*, 1990, Matthew Bender, paperback, about $25. (This one might be out-of-print. If so, check alibris.com or abebooks.com.) —Another of the excellent works in the Matthew Bender "Student's Guide" series.

These two are wonderful, whether for a law school course in evidence, for Mock Trial, or for the evidence portion of the bar exam. They're so good that I regularly re-read them and re-work the problems in them, just to keep from getting rusty in areas where there's been no need to stay up to speed for specific cases.

Surveys of trial lawyers regularly disclose that the rules of evidence are the most difficult part of their practice—and hearsay is the most difficult of all. (In my own first outing, my client and I got slaughtered—largely because I was not sufficiently conversant with *using* the rules of evidence. And I did not get a firm grasp on hearsay until I'd read the Fishman book and worked its exercises.) If you have mastered the rules of evidence in general, and hearsay in particular, you'll "wow" your Mock Trial judge. You'll also win the respect and confidence of many a real-world judge. (You'll be surprised at how many trial judges have never mastered the rules of evidence.)

Aspen, in addition to its "Examples & Explanations" series, has an "Essential Terms & Concepts" series. *Evidence: Essential Terms & Concepts,* by Mark Reutlinger, is a 1996 book, in paperback, for $26. What I especially like about it is the way Reutlinger puts the rules of evidence into context. He provides background as to how the rules came to be as they are, historically. You don't have to just memorize a seemingly-arbitrary rule. Instead, he gives you a grasp of what the alternatives were and why they were rejected. That "big picture" understanding can be very helpful—especially when you're trying to deal with a particularly strange situation for which there is no clearly applicable rule.

Mueller, Christopher B., & Kirkpatrick, Laird C., *Federal Rules of Evidence, with Advisory Committee Notes, Legislative History, and Cases,* 1995, another Aspen Law & Business book, is in paperback, for approximately $26. Most states' rules of evidence are modeled on the federal rules. Many *state* courts, by law, expressly look to rulings in *federal* courts on the *federal* rules of evidence to guide *them.* The federal courts, in turn, usually look to the Advisory Committee Notes and the legislative history of the federal rules of evidence to guide *them.* Yet, for some strange reason, few books on evidence—and few law school courses—go into this material. It will impress the trial judge, or appellate court, if you can produce a "bench memo," based on this material, as to why the judge should rule in your favor on an evidentiary point. (In law school, though, you won't be doing bench memos for Mock Trial.) Even without a bench memo, if you've mastered this material, you will be in the right when you make your objections— or respond to the other side's objections. (In the real world, this will help you on appeal.) And the Mueller & Kirkpatrick book is excellent material for bar exam review. Sometimes, you have to go with your gut feel when answering a question on the bar exam. The M&K work helps you to digest evidence quite well.

PRACTICE MAKES PERFECT

No discussion of becoming skilled in the courtroom is complete without mention of NITA (the National Institute for Trial Advocacy). It trains aspiring trial attorneys around the country. In Mock Trial or a class on "trial ad," your law school will likely use one of many fictitious case files developed for a jurisdiction called "The State of NITA."

The Institute has a 1993 book by Anthony J. Bocchino and David A. Sonenshein, *A Practical Guide to Federal Evidence: Objections, Responses, Rules, and Practice Commentary, 3d ed.,* a $29 paperback. (NITA also has state-specific volumes for California, Iowa, Oregon,

Texas, and Wisconsin.) Bocchino and Sonenshein are co-authors for each of them, and bring in an expert from the state in question as a third co-author.) For both Mock Trial and real trials, the *Practical Guide* is awesome. It tells you what to do, when to do it, how to do it—whether it's on your own or in response to what opposing counsel has done.

Bocchino and Sonenshein are joined by a third author, JoAnne A. Epps, for something else that's wonderful. This is *Trial Evidence—Making and Meeting Objections*. The book presents several dozen situations that sound quite real-world. (Most involve civil trials.) If the question or answer presented is improper, you have to explain why. If an objection is made, your job is to explain whether it should be sustained or overruled, and why. The book is $22. However, you have to get an *Instructor's Manual* to get the answers, and that costs another $9. (The material in the situations book is also available on cassette tape, as mentioned below. I recommend you get that instead of the hard copy.) The *Instructor's Manual* mentions things about the rules of evidence that I've never seen elsewhere—yet they're things every trial attorney needs to know.

One more book is crucial: Deanne C. Seamer's *Tangible Evidence: How to Use Exhibits at Depositions and Trials, 3d ed.* It's a 1996 paperback from NITA. It costs $50, and I know that's a lot. But it's worth much more. I've photocopied the charts in the back of her book and then fill them in with every exhibit I plan to present in court. That way, I can anticipate virtually any objection that might be raised, and be prepared for it. Likewise, if both sides have exchanged "exhibit lists," I use Seamer's charts as a checklist for finding ways to try to keep the other side's harmful evidence out. This is the very best book there is on its subject, and can "save" you even in Mock Trial. In fact, you *must* get this if you intend to be good.

However, just knowing the rules of evidence isn't enough. In fact, even just knowing what to object to, or how to respond to groundless objections, isn't enough. You must also know the step-by-step "mechanics" of getting things *admitted into evidence* by the court. For that, Edward J. Imwinkelreid's *Evidentiary Foundations, 3d. ed.*, is an absolute necessity. This 1995 book is a $26 paperback from the Michie (to repeat: it's pronounced "Mickey") Company. If you're planning to do Mock Trial, and especially if you intend to become a trial lawyer, you must get this book. (This is the generic edition. Imwinkelreid, with co-authors, also does specialized editions for California, Florida, Illinois, New York, and Texas, as of this writing. More might be on the way.)

Some vendors do tapes for advanced law school courses. One of these is evidence. Although I do not, in general, recommend that you get tapes, the ones on evidence are the exception to the rule. The Gilbert "Law School Legends" series on Evidence is a set of five, just under seven hours' running time, for $46. The Sum & Substance series on Evidence is also a set of five, under eight hours' running time, for $50. PMBR sells its bar review tape on evidence—six hours, $50. As with all the other materials on evidence, it will concern the federal rules.

Use tapes only to *check* your understanding: The rules of evidence are so demanding that you need to study written materials, over and over, to master them.

"Trial Ad"

BOOKS

It appears that everyone in law school trial advocacy classes or mock trial programs is told to read two works: Thomas A. Mauet's *Fundamentals of Trial Techniques,* and James W. Jeans, Sr.'s *Trial Advocacy.* With all due respect to these scholars (and a lot of respect *is* due), I do not recommend their books. They're textbooks.

Instead, here are what in my opinion are the four best books for aspiring trial attorneys:

In no particular order: the first two are West Nutshell™ paperbacks: Paul Bergman's *Trial Advocacy in a Nutshell,* 2d ed., 1989, $25; and Kenney F. Hegland's *Trial and Practice Skills in a Nutshell,* 2d ed., 1994, also $25. The third is the best. It's also from West: Keith Evans's *The Common Sense Rules of Trial Advocacy,* 1994, paperback, $28. (However, amazingly, it is now out-of-print. I simply do not understand that. I urge you to track down a copy, for that book is *priceless.*)

The fourth is not from West. It's *Theater Tips and Strategies for Jury Trials,* rev. ed., by David Ball. This 1997 work is from NITA, $29 in paperback. Ball is a trial consultant, not a practicing attorney. His background is in theater. And he understands the nuts-and-bolts of what goes on in a courtroom far better than the vast majority of trial attorneys. The title of his book, however, is unfortunate. It sounds like it consists only of simple tricks to pick up for use "here and there" along the way. On the contrary: There's stuff in here you'll find nowhere else. *Jury Trials as Theater* would have been a more accurate title, and even that wouldn't do it justice. (All trial attorneys should have "Ball's," yes?)

I could rave about how great these are, but you can see for yourself, if you wish. For a "first book" on trial ad, go with either Bergman's or Evans's; ideally, both. In the interest of full disclosure, though, Hegland's book isn't *quite* as useful for law *students* as the other three are. However, it's still so good that I have to list it as one of the best on the market. Also, he touches on things that the other three "best works" mentioned here do not. So I still strongly recommend it. Just save it for last.

Actually, there's a third author whose works all law school students in trial advocacy classes or mock trial programs are told to read: James W. McElhaney. McElhaney's books are good. However, you shouldn't get them until you've become at least somewhat familiar with the federal rules of evidence and the federal rules of civil procedure, and have read the Bergman and Evans books. They're pricey—because they're published by the American Bar Association, which always charges too much. *McElhaney's Trial Notebook, 3d ed.,* is about $40 in paperback. *McElhaney's Litigation, 2d. ed.,* is roughly $35, paperback.

NITA has more materials, but these aren't in the same class as Ball, Bergman, Evans, and Hegland: *Modern Trial Advocacy: Analysis and Practice,* by Steven Lubet, is okay. But it's more of a textbook, really. It's a 1993 work, for $31. And there's *Closing Argument,* by Jim Seckinger, a $12 booklet published in 1992. It's very good, and well worth the twelve bucks.

COSTLIER ITEMS - AUDIO/VIDEO

The ABA publishes a *Litigation Manual, 2d ed.,* in paperback, for $85 (last time I checked). It also sells a decent book by Michael Tigar, a prominent trial lawyer (and law prof), called *Examining Witnesses.* The price on that one is *110* bucks. It's in hardcover. (For *that* price, it ought to be bound in leather, with gold foil trim.)

NITA's *Trial Evidence—Making and Meeting Objections* is available on audio cassette. The situaitons are presented using many different actors, in mock trial format. Whenever something occurs that (perhaps) calls for an objection, there's a pause. You have 1-2 seconds to make an objection or to respond to the other side's objection. (You can hit the "pause" button on your tape player, though, to give yourself more time.) When you get the tapes (or, if you wish, the video), NITA includes the Instructor's Manual, which has the answers.

Because I got this on audio tapes, I can't say for sure the tapes duplicate what's in the textbook. But on the tapes there are dozens of "vignettes," from both civil and criminal trials. No more than two or three are drawn from the same mock trial. The running time of the tapes is 2 hours, 40 minutes. But it takes many more hours than that to go through them, because you'll be pausing to consider your responses and to check your answers. The cost of the audio cassettes is $150. That's a lot. But it's worth it, if you can afford it. There's something about *voices,* as contrasted with just reading text, that makes a big difference. The cassettes are a much closer approximation of the real world. So they're much better as a practice tool. Because there are so many situations on the tape, there's no way you'd memorize them (and the appropriate response to each). That means you can work through them all again, from time to time.

When I was in law school, Court TV was just starting. So, we students had only videotapes of local attorneys doing *mock* trials. It was pretty bad stuff, but it was that or nothing. Now, however, Court TV has a Video Library Service. This includes tapes from real trials. Court TV has also established "The Art & Science of Litigation" series: videocassettes on basic skills, using clips from real trials. A moderator and a panel of attorneys then critique the lawyers' performances. There's one each on Opening Statement, Direct Examination, Cross Examination, Examination of Expert Witnesses, and Closing Argument. Each tape lasts about an hour. They cost me $100 a pop, but the price is probably higher now. If you can find some other students to split the cost with you, it might be worth getting some of these. Of course, you can also learn a lot from watching Court TV itself.

Irving Younger was a legend in his own time, as a teacher of the law. He had a gift for presenting detailed, difficult subjects in a way that was memorable, entertaining, and enlightening. He's the star of two sets of NITA materials.

The first is *Basic Concepts in the Law of Evidence with Irving Younger.* These 15 tapes run just over 12 hours. On audio, they cost me $100, but again, they might be more expensive now. With the tapes, you get a written outline of the subject.

The second is *Mastering the Art of Cross-Examination with Irving Younger.* This includes his famous "Ten Commandments of Cross-Examination." (However, be advised: his "commandments" have been criticized.) You get 11 tapes, running time nearly eight hours. You also get a *lot* of supporting material. This second set of tapes includes attorneys other than Younger. They also present "problem situations." The lawyers then attempt to deal with each problem. Then Younger discusses the attempted solutions—why they did what they did, and what others thought of it. The set is apparently meant to be used for teaching to a group. The audio tapes were $195 when I got them.

The Complete Advocate: Courtroom Speaking Skills is available only on video (to the best of my knowledge at this time). Brian Johnson is the presenter. The tapes last one hour, 15 minutes. It costs at least $130. I've not seen it, but I did attend a live lecture by Johnson. He was fantastic. I then spoke with him about the tape. He said it presents the same material as his lecture, but more of it. That being so, it's well worth getting.

NITA has many more programs on video. But they tend to be *very* expensive, intended only for purchase by (big) law firms.

Note: *No returns allowed.* But NITA has "preview tapes" for some of its videos. These tapes do "double duty" for the corresponding audio.

SOFTWARE

In a real trial, it isn't enough to say "Objection, Your Honor!" You must also state the grounds for the objection, unless they're unambiguously obvious. You must state those grounds—i.e., before the witness answers. (Otherwise, in a jury trial, the damage is done, even if the judge says "The jury is instructed to disregard the witness's answer." Yeah, sure.)

A company called TransMedia has developed four sets of software for trial advocacy. Its original program was called "Objection!" As the name implies, it tests your knowledge of the appropriate grounds for objecting to a question by opposing counsel. That program was for a criminal trial, with a complete cast of characters and a little bit of animation. I believe the current version is 3.0, but you can check.

They have an auto accident - negligence case for their "Civil Objection!" software program. And another program involves a "Slip & Fall" negligence case. Their final program deals with expert witnesses.

Three of these (all but the expert witness program) present an entire trial, with both direct and cross-ex and the presentation of documents. Last I checked, the expert witness program only had direct and cross. With each objection, there's a short tutorial discussion if you gave the wrong answer. Each program works like a game. You have to score *x* points at one level before you can proceed to the next level.

So far, while there is limited sound on each program, the questions asked of the witnesses appear only in text, on your computer screen. That is unfortunate, because it takes time to read the question. You lose points if you do not respond quickly enough, so the text puts you at an immediate disadvantage. (The folks at TransMedia have told me they're working on a CD that requires a sound card, so they can eliminate the on-screen text feature with respect to the questions asked.)

The only program I've bought so far is the auto negligence one, and I recommend it—although it might be worthwhile to wait for the spoken word version (as contrasted with questions-as-text).*

TransMedia also has a three-hour set of lectures on audio cassette, concerning trial strategies as they relate to evidence. I've not heard them, however, so cannot vouch for them.

Each program, and the lectures, are $100, and there's a "package deal" if you get the whole works.

You can download a demo segment from TransMedia's website, at http://www.objection.com. Their toll-free number is (800) 832-4980.

Resources for Moot Court

NITA has two books for appellate advocacy. Both are intended for use in the real world, not law school. However, they're useful even within the ivory tower.

The first is by Josephine R. Potuto, *Winning Appeals: Persuasive Argument and the Appellate Process.* This 1992 book is $23.

The second is *Winning on Appeal: Better Briefs and Oral Argument,* by Ruggero J. Aldisert. (As mentioned earlier in this book, he's a senior judge on the Third Circuit Court of Appeals, and the author of *Logic for Lawyers.*) *Winning on Appeal* is a 1996 paperback, for $35.

Then there's Bryan Garner's stuff. To repeat, I regard him as "The God of Legal Writing." If he wrote it, it's good. Oxford University Press has a hard-cover book of his, *The Winning Appeal,* for $50. That's steep, but worth it. Another you might consider is *A Dictionary of Modern Legal Usage* (mentioned in the addendum to Chapter 17). It's in paperback for $27.

As for tapes: Sum & Substance has a set of two, *Winning at Moot Court.* They run for three hours, and cost $40.

---

* Full disclosure: I have a "crush" on "Lisa Lamborghini," the star of the auto negligence program. This is the first time I've fallen in love with an animated cartoon character since...Pocahontas.)

Chapter 20 - What to Take in Years 2 and 3

It's no accident that the three chapters on improving your skills preceded this one. Just as *attending* class is the *least* important part of your first-year courses, so the very courses *themselves* are (almost) the least important part of years two and three. Law school could teach everything you need to know in just three semesters. Instead, it takes three years to teach far *less* than you need to know.*

Page 597 in Chapter 19 quoted a famous 1973 speech of then-Chief Justice Warren Burger. In that same speech, he said law school should be reduced to *two* years. Beyond that, law should somewhat imitate the medical profession. But instead of having an internship for all graduates, as medicine does, he said law should go directly to the equivalent of the medical residency: training in a specialty. Whether or not you agree with his proposal, the point here is that Burger was saying the "core curriculum" common to all future attorneys need last only two years, not three. This will not happen, of course. The reason for this is the prestige factor (and more money for the law schools and, often, through them, for their parent universities).

Law traditionally has been close to medicine in prestige.** Medical school lasts four years. Apparently med students need all four of those years to master the necessary skills. But if law school ran even one year less than it does, it would be difficult for lawyers to claim status comparable to doctors'. Instead, they'd be "down there" with mere MBAs. So, the curriculum gets padded with make-work courses, to ensure that a lawyer's formal education is comparable to that of doctors, if only as to duration.

---

* You perhaps think I'm engaging in rhetorical excess. Well, in Britain, roughly a third of all non-trial lawyers do not get a law degree (and in Britain it's an *undergraduate* degree). Instead, they get a year's intensive training in the law after finishing college. (And regardless of whether they have a law degree, future attorneys then take a year of courses in "lawyering.")

** Maybe that's because clients sometimes put their livelihoods—and perhaps even their lives—into a lawyer's hands, as patients occasionally put their very lives into a doctor's hands. That is power. Although you can make more money on Wall Street, Wall Street doesn't have the prestige. Bankers do—because bankers have power...though not nearly as much as they used to, in any given community.

In your second and third year of law school, you have two priorities: 1) activities related to getting a job, and 2) getting a job. As you plan your schedule, keep that in mind. (All of Chapter 22 concerns finding a job.) The first semester of your second and third year are the prime times for job-hunting.

If you do well in first year—and you probably will, if you conscientiously follow the recommendations in this book—you'll Make Law Review (if it's a school that has "grade-on"). Law Review will be your main concern for the rest of your days in school. You won't have to worry much about finding *a* job—just finding the *right* job.

Regardless, you should be looking for the maximum number of *credits*—and easy *high grades*—with the *minimum amount of effort*. You have better things—more important things—to spend your time on than make-work, to put it bluntly.

There are exceptions to this, of course. They are 1) more courses in Legal Research and Legal Writing. 2) courses that Look Good on the Résumé, 3) courses with a Big Gun professor whom you want to impress, 4) courses in a specialized area of law that requires an in-depth background, and 5) courses that prepare you for the state-specific portion of the bar examination you intend to take.

Note: If you want to have a career in corporate law (which includes a career with a prestigious law firm), there's a (small) list of courses that are virtually mandatory. (Examples: "Secured Transactions" and "Agency.") It will be easy to find out what they're called at your school.

After first-year, no course lasts more than one semester. However, some, in effect, actually *are* year-long. But (unlike what sometimes happens in first-year) there's a grade each semester. Better still, you don't have to take the second semester of the course immediately after the first—or ever, for that matter. Sometimes there's a different professor for part two than for part one. If the prof in part one was a dud, you can delay taking part two, in hope someone better comes along.

Other than in first-year, there are almost no mandatory courses in law school. If you had to take a one-semester course in Con Law during Year One, there's a good chance you'll have to take Con Law II later. (Chapter 1 explained the difference.) At some schools, first-year Con Law lasts all year: one semester each for what would otherwise be called Con Law I and II. (And for those of you who go where all of Con Law is just an elective, you should take a Con Law course, period. Who knows? —Someday you might be under consideration for a federal judgeship. Imagine how embarrassing it would be at your confirmation hearing if it were disclosed that you had not been interested enough in the Constitution to have even take one course on it in law school.)

Most schools also require a "Professional Responsibility" course. Chapter 23 discusses this.

Some courses have pre-requisites, just as in college. However, often the law school catalogue will not tell you what the sequence is, or else the courses it lists are no longer being offered under those names. In some cases, only one professor teaches a given subject, and only once a year—or once every two years. So, you have to take it at the right time, or you don't get to take it at all. (Usually, though, other professors offer comparable courses. One of them might even be better at it.) No matter what, though, don't trust the printed projection of future courses. Confirm everything you're seriously interested in, as to who, what, and when. (If your school has a club devoted to the area of the law you want to concentrate in, its members should be able to tell you what you need to know.)

You can only carry three to five courses a semester. Thus, in your final four semesters, you get to take maybe 15 to 20. That doesn't leave a lot of room for error. Further, at many law schools, after the semester has started you can't drop and add courses with anywhere near the freedom most colleges allow. If you're trying to pursue a specific program of study, fill those slots carefully.

REALLY *Planning Ahead*

Try to arrange your credit load in Years Two and Three so that by the time you reach your *last* semester you'll only need to take the *minimum* number of credits required to maintain full-time student status (and to graduate, of course). This is because, in your final semester, you should start studying for the bar exam. (Chapter 23 discusses the "barzam." Chapter 24 discusses how to prepare for it in a rational and cost-effective manner.)

"Majors"

Almost without exception, there are no "majors" in law school. You just get a law degree, period. However, it is possible to have a concentration of courses in one area, such as litigation (which I do not advise).

Yet, again, there are exceptions. To give its grads a competitive edge in the job market, Boalt Hall, for example, has a "Certificate Program" in "Intellectual Property," which requires several specific courses. Another example is Vermont's program in environmental law.

Some that Glitters is NOT "Gold"

Most first-year law students get their ideas of "growth" areas of the law from the general media. However, by the time the general media have learned of these, such areas have probably neared the saturation point. Worse, from your point of view, probably every other student looking for a job will tell the interviewer that he or she wants to go into one of those growth areas. The interviewer no doubt then thinks, "Another one who confuses the hype for the reality—and who's looking for the easy way to the top. Next!" So, be chary of what's "hot." (Chapter 22 tells how to find where the *truly* hot areas are.)

An example is "intellectual property." Used to be, all you had to do was take one course in it and you could probably find a job. As IP "took off," firms were desperate for warm bodies to handle the increased workload. That has all changed, because the firms have "staffed up." To get into biotech IP now, you almost have to have a Ph.D. in biotech— and several years' work experience in it before law school—to be seriously considered. (Yet, as of this writing, "toxic mold" litigation is still "hot," and *any* kind of biology background will at least get your foot in the door.)

However, my hunch is that bankruptcy, both personal and corporate, will be getting "hot" quite soon. It just might become a "seller's market." So, especially if you have a background in accounting or banking, or have an MBA, you might take a look at that area of the law. ("Water law," in the Western states, is another growth area, I believe.)

Then there's what's *cool*—courses such as "Entertainment and Sports Law," or "Art Law." These might sound wonderful, but only a handful of lawyers in this country can make their living at it. If you don't have the right connections for it, and are just hoping that a miracle will somehow happen to let you practice in that area, reconsider. Any serious firm looking at your résumé or transcript might conclude you're some kind of flake with stars in his or her eyes, unwilling to put nose-to-grindstone in the drab, drab world of the law. (If you Make Law Review, though, you can take at least one off-the-wall course without fear.)

However, if you're truly interested in an offbeat subject for its own sake, proceed. Although the odds against your ever being able to practice in this area are overwhelming, the course/s can still be a nice treat.

Just beware of "Law & a Banana" courses. (See Chapter 26.)

Neglected Niches

Several areas of the law are off-the-beaten-track. Few students even take a course in them, let alone using that course to give them an edge in job-seeking. One is Admiralty. Very few firms in the country do admiralty law. It is not and will never be a growth area. But the demand, while small, is steady—and there is not all that much competition for the few slots in it. Another example is Education Law. Far more firms do that. But relatively few students ever take a course in it. And a third is Administrative law, which involves state and federal regulatory agencies. This is an ever-growing area, for obvious reasons.

Options

Even if you go into law school absolutely certain what it is you want to do as a lawyer, please keep an open mind. For example, future visiting professors' courses aren't listed in the catalogue, for obvious reasons. So even if you know what you want to take and have confirmed its availability, there will be opportunities you'd not anticipated. Some of them will even come from the regular faculty, when a professor decides to offer something new, for the very first time.

Also, sometimes law students fall in love...with a subject. (I'll never forget one fellow student who raved about how surprised he was to find administrative law was the most wonderful thing there is. He is very happy now, practicing only within certain areas of administrative law.)

Even though, above, there was a warning about not wasting your slots, do consider exploring the Law. If you worked for a lawyer or law firm before going to law school, you might've already gained exposure to one area of the law—which you might or might not have liked. Regardless, the possibilities within the Law are far, far greater than anything anybody could possibly be aware of before starting law school.

Further, most attorneys concentrate their practice in areas they never expected to get into. For some, this means a broken heart. But often, it means he or she fell (or got pushed) into something and ended up staying in it by inertia, increasing returns on their investment—and maybe even by heartfelt choice. Come job-hunting time, unless you're set on practicing in just one narrow specialty, you might want to have had *some* diversity in your law studies.

—Just be sure that most of your courses are "respectable."

Checking Out the Profs

Throughout your first year, you want to meet as many second- and third-year students as you can. Learn from their experience as to who's who among the professoriat. They can tell you what to take, when to take it, what's easy, what's hard, who's good, who's boring, and who's a jerk. But keep in mind that just because several students have the same opinion, that doesn't mean they're right. If someone tells you Professor X is a great (or lousy), ask *why*. The more students you talk with, the better. You'll certainly have a better chance of getting a feel for what's right for *you*. (At the University of Texas School of Law, I'm told there's a prof named Dodge who's so boring and confusing that the mantra among the students is "*Dodge* Dodge.")

Do not rely on student surveys—unless they've thorough. They're usually almost worthless. At some schools, they consist merely of polls whereby professors are rated on a scale of 1-10 in various categories. Those don't tell you what you need to know.

If you actually want to learn something from your courses, look for the professors who can *teach*. There's an old jazz saying, "The singer, not the song." This means that a good jazz singer can take even a mediocre song and make it sound like something special—whereas a mediocre singer can take a wonderful song and turn it into musical mush. In law school, all other things being equal, go with the prof, not the course. The Law can be wonderful, but that's seldom so—especially in law school. The basic concepts stay the same. Choose the prof who has a reputation for helping students understand the ins and outs of those concepts. A lousy professor can ruin an otherwise-interesting subject. He or she can also reduce your drive to try to ace the course: you have to force yourself to do the work, and thus spend much more time and energy on it than you should. A professor who makes the subject interesting makes it easier for you to do the work on it. Your attitude toward a course makes a big difference in how much energy you have left over when you've finished the homework for it and have to move on. So, it *indirectly* affects your work on *other* tasks. (But beware also the prof who is merely "popular" because of his or her "compassion," or "sense of humor," but who does not *teach*.)

During your first year, the last thing on your mind will be what to take in years two and three—until the next fall's schedule is posted, that is. But *try to sit in on upper-level courses during your first year, even during your first semester*. Be sure to go to the professor beforehand to get his or her permission. Explain that you're a first-year, and the course is something that sounds interesting to you. Ask if you can sit in on it *once*. At the very least, by sitting in you get to see for yourself what kind of teacher this professor is.

Afterwards, ask if the professor will be offering that class in the next year's schedule, or the year after. (Of course, you will have started by expressing your appreciation for the opportunity to audit, and complimenting him or her for providing such a meaningful experience. Just don't overdo it.) If the class is already listed in the projected schedule, confirm it. If not, maybe some other professor teaches a similar course, and so it will still be available to you. Ask the professor what other courses he or she will be offering. And it never hurts to ask what you should take and in what order. This is particularly true if you—supposedly—might specialize in that professor's area of expertise. (Be sure to find out, beforehand, what it is. Your law school's library will have a copy of the *AALS Directory of Law Teachers*, listing all the full-time law profs in the country, and the upper-level courses they teach. But many profs have a sub-speciality not listed in the *Directory*.)

Do not make your after-class approach by going to the lectern immediately after the class. Instead, stand out from the crowd: catch the prof in his or her office later that day—certainly no more than a few days later. Handle all this carefully. As long as you don't act like a suck-up, the prof might be pleased. He or she will also be impressed by your thinking ahead (but don't expect a compliment). It always helps if a member of the faculty has a favorable opinion of you, especially if the prof in question is a Big Gun in some field. (Profs do talk among themselves about their students.)

Also, sometimes one of next semester's courses fills and "closes." Then you need to get special permission from the prof, waiving the class limit (just like college). If *you're* the one who expressed interest while still in first-year, and move fast, guess who gets the waiver?

Adjuncts

Chapter 19 discussed adjunct profs in connection with clinics. However, sometimes regular courses also have adjuncts. Practicing attorneys seek to become adjunct profs because it enhances their credentials. Unfortunately, that's often their only motivation. They're no more interested in actually teaching than the regular professors are. And, regardless, adjunct profs almost never have office hours (not that it makes much difference). If you don't catch them at the lectern after class, the chances of catching them outside of class at all are just about nil.

However, at least some adjunct profs are good teachers. And, more important, some of them have a motive for teaching other than enhancing their own credentials. They're actually scouts, looking for good recruits for their law firms. They know that student transcripts and the interviewing process is, at best, an "iffy" way to evaluate potential recruits. And they know that the summer clerkships are, for the most part, merely a test of how well a student's personality meshes with that of others at the firm. So, encountering students in the classroom can provide invaluable input to "what makes them tick." For that reason, taking a course from an adjunct prof just might provide you with an "in" that you would not otherwise have. Enough said.

Getting a Head Start—Again

The approach recommended in Chapter 2 is valid even beyond first-year. Chapter 2 listed sources of self-help materials for independent study of first-year subjects. Vendors have materials for advanced courses, too. So, you can again get the edge by prepping before the semester even begins. Whether you use it to get a head start—again— or to cut down on the time you have to spend on your courses, it works. Even though first-year grades are the ones that count the most, by far, you want to keep your average up in years two and three, also. (In fact, if you Make Law Review, getting high grades while working as a second-year slave will possibly enhance your chances of getting a top editorship in third-year. —But grades are less important than your "work product" for Law Review...and your social skills.)

Aspen, for example, has its series of books whose subtitle is always "Examples and Explanations," and another one subtitled "Problems and Answers." They also have a good book by Mark Reutlinger called *Wills, Trusts, and Estates: Essential Terms and Concepts.* (He also did *Evidence: Essential Terms & Concepts,* discussed in the addendum to Chapter 19.) Matthew Bender has its wonderful *Student's Guide to [Whatever]* series, with titles on the Uniform Commercial Code, the Internal Revenue Code, and evidence. West Publishing, of course, has titles on everything—the most useful of which (for you) are its *Nutshell*™ series. Law school bookstores carry the West books. The ones from Aspen and Matthew Bender are harder to find. You might need to call or these last two, or go on-line, and order direct.

If and when you call, ask for a copy of each publisher's *Law School* Catalogue. (However, West no longer publishes a catalogue in hardcopy format. Other publishers might drop theirs, too.) Look for titles that indicate their potential for independent study, as indicated above. However, the catalogues don't put these books in a separate section.

That's because these catalogues are for law *professors*, not students. With Aspen, for example, you have to carefully search for books with the subtitles mentioned—as well as for other self-help books that don't have *either* of the subtitles listed above, such as the Reutlinger book. With Matthew Bender, the only sure way to find them is to look at the end of the description of each book. There you will find *small* type in italics, saying if the work is a casebook, textbook, or part of the Student's Guide series. You do *not* want either of the *first* two. As with Aspen, some of Matthew Bender's independent study books aren't labeled as part of a self-help series, even though the book's description clearly indicates that's what the book can be used for. (Fortunately, both publishers have begun to print lists of other available self-help titles on or inside the covers of their independent study books. But for a complete list, you have to check the catalogue.)

Commercial outlines are published for advanced subjects, too.

By the end of each semester, you'll know what you'll be taking next semester. So, that's when to get the commercial outlines, the books. Then read them during the vacation before the next semester starts.

Even if you Make Law Review and then get access to the editors' outline collection, these books can help you. Use them to quickly get up to speed in the subject matter, which in turn will help you to *quickly* grasp what's in the outlines from the Law Review collection. That way, you won't lose any time getting yourself oriented once the course begins.

—And don't forget the ABA's series, *ABCs of the UCC*, discussed in Chapter 2. The series includes a volume on *each* Article of the UCC, some of which are the subject of an entire upper-level course.

Chapter 16 told how to contact all these vendors.

> If you're undecided as to what courses to take, you might even consider choosing some of them based on whether or not you can prepare for them before the semester begins. It'll certainly make it a lot easier to do well.

Killing Two Birds with One Stone

Much of the law is controlled by state courts and legislatures. This is especially true in family law. Wills, consumer protection law, real estate law, and landlord/tenant law are other examples. (True, federal law, and "uniform" laws are also applicable, but the generalization is still valid.) Many upper-level courses correspond to subjects that will be tested on the state-specific portion of your state's bar exam. And although the law schools do not like to admit this, often those courses are taught with reference only to the law of the state that law school is in. (This is expressly so in a course on that state's civil procedure.)

Students often take courses in subjects they know will be on the bar exam (such as family law, or trusts). And the materials mentioned on the preceding page are good for those. But they are obviously national in scope. So, they stick with the nationwide Black Letter Law. The bar prep materials, in contrast, go in to all the nitty-gritty.

You might be thinking you don't *want* to go into all the nitty-gritty. But you will be amazed at how well all the pieces suddenly fall into place when you are dealing with *specific* problems, to which you must apply *specific and discrete* rules of law. Hard to believe, but getting in to the nitty-gritty will quite likely help you understand "The Big Picture" a whole lot better than you otherwise would. This is another reason why those who denigrate Black Letter Law in favor of "policy discussions" are fools.

> So, if you anticipate taking the bar exam in the state where your law school is, you can get *bar review materials* for the subjects covered by upper-level courses you intend to take. You will then be further enhancing the odds that you'll do well in those upper-level courses, and you will already be preparing for the bar exam.

(Chapter 23 tells you how to get them long before you take a bar review course—and how to get them *cheap.)*

To Your Credit

If your law school is affiliated with a university (as nearly all are), you can often get credit in your law school for courses you take in another graduate program. Sometimes these are listed in your law school catalogue. The usual examples are from graduate schools in business or public policy—whatever these schools are called at your university. However, whether or not something's already been approved, you can still seek out other courses. You can even create your own. For example: You have a strong undergraduate background in economics. Find a sympathetic law professor and arrange for independent study credit in "law and economics."

If you're taking a course elsewhere in your university that's not already been approved for law school credit, or if you're creating your own unique project, you must get the approval of whoever handles such things in the dean's office at your law school. Usually, it isn't a problem—as long as your proposal is within reason.

Also, you'll probably find it's not as hard to get an "A" in some other school—and especially in an independent study project—as it is in a regular law school course. No guarantees, though.

Warning: Law firms don't like to see these on your transcript. So think carefully about it. Then have a good explanation as to why you took it. And also have plenty of typical courses—with top grades.

* * *

Through it all, your highest priority is having the freedom to *choose* the job after graduation that's right for *you*. Everything else is just a means to that end. *Once you have a job,* what's (probably) most important to your future is the ability to research well and to write well—even if you become a trial lawyer. That's why most of the particular *courses* you take in law school are of secondary importance—unless, as mentioned, you want to have a particular type of career in the Law.

The commercial outlines, Matthew Bender's "Understanding" series, West's "Nutshells," etc., will still be of value to you in practice. When you have to do something in a new area of practice, you might use one of these to get your bearings. Also, there are CLE (Continuing Legal Education) courses. These are put on by national organizations, by vendors of legal research materials, or by your state or local bar associations. Some of these are advanced courses, for those who've long been specialists in a particular area of the law. Others are for those who want to get into a new area, and thus are for beginners.

So, don't get the idea that if you don't study something in law school, you'll never again get the chance to study it. Quite the contrary. (For example, for aspiring trial attorneys, there are CLE programs in trial advocacy. Although these are generic, and not state-specific, they're better than most law school courses in trial ad and most mock trial programs. That's one reason why, when you're in law school, it's better to do the court internship if you must make a choice. There are also CLE programs in negotiating, and mediating.)

While you're in law school, *grades* count most—especially *first-*year grades. So you want high grades, regardless of subject, because:

With *very* few exceptions, *once you're out—and have a job—the subjects you took won't count.*

Chapter 21 - Foreign Studies/International Law

"International Law"

Students who want a legal career that's "glamorous" often announce that they want to go into "international law." Perhaps they visualize themselves jetting around the world, staying at fancy hotels, etc.

But the best comment on this came from the hiring partner at a firm who said, "When I interview a law student for a summer clerkship, and he or she says 'I want to practice international law,' it's as though that student just said to me "I want to be Peter Pan's attorney."'"

I agree. Granted, there are lawyers who want to glamorize themselves, and who say, "I practice international law." But all that means, usually, is that they have foreign clients, or that they advise their American clients as to foreign law. Big deal.

If you're interested in "international law," keep your mouth shut about it. (There are two exceptions to this. The first is if you are not an American. Then it will be obvious that you might be a good person to have in an American firm's office in your home country—or in the firm's American office that deals with clients from your home country. The second exception will be discussed below.)

Instead, take courses in one or more areas of the law that you know can involve multinational legal concerns. Then, when looking for a job, seek out firms that have offices in foreign countries. (More on this in Chapter 22.)

Foreign Studies

Even if you're hoping for a career that has nothing to do with foreign countries or international law, a foreign studies program can be worthwhile. Most law students have the equivalent of cabin fever by the time they're in third-year. At the very least, a foreign law study program is a nice—though expensive—change of pace and scenery.

If you've already travelled abroad, it was probably just as a tourist. But if you attended school abroad, you had opportunities denied the typical tourist. So it is with foreign legal studies, only more so.

And if you do want to practice "international law," it helps to put your money where your mouth is, and go. If you already speak a foreign language, then it can be invaluable for you to study law in a country that speaks that language, and to learn various legal terms in the local tongue, along with the rules of the business and legal systems there. (However, your instruction in class will be in English.)

Closing the Gap

I knew a guy who went on a summer law program in Japan after his first year of law school. He then took a leave of absence from his law school and spent the next academic year in Japan, studying the language full-time. Then he participated in another Japan summer law school program, and worked as a paid clerk for a Japanese law firm. He returned to his home school in the fall, and sought a clerkship for the following summer. Even though his first-year grades weren't great, he got some offers—including one that specifically stated he would be sent back to Japan, at the firm's expense, to do his clerkship there. It was a prestigious firm. He accepted that one. His entry-level starting salary was $70,000 a year. That was several years ago. He's still there, still with that firm, and doing quite well.

The moral is: even if you aren't in the top 10% of your class, foreign studies might help make up for the difference come hiring time. They might even give you the edge.

For example, consider the typical job interview with a law firm. Recruiters see the same person over and over, in effect: same appearance, same courses, same grades, etc. They get tired of talking about the same things again and again. When a job applicant comes in who has something unusual in his or her background, the interviewer will focus on that, just to have something new and different to discuss. If that "something unusual" is law-related, so much the better.

Granted, this doesn't justify the cost of a foreign program. Nor will it get you the job unless everything else looks reasonably good—and perhaps not even then. But it might help make you stand out from the crowd, to stick in the interviewer's mind. Every little bit helps.

Warning: if you talk about how exciting, glamorous, stimulating, etc., it was where you went, the interviewer will be worried that you expect to find your job to be likewise. No way. Virtually no job in the law (and especially not in the first few years) is like that. You might have just aced yourself out of an offer. So what you do instead is to emphasize all the negatives...but without sounding like a grouch. Talk about how much you just loved grinding away on the law books, to escape the temptations and delights of, say, Paris. Don't lay it on too thick, though. Lawyers tend to be pinheads, and pinheads definitely do not like to be mocked—especially by those hoping to join their ranks in the law factories.

At the other extreme, the interviewer might figure you have your heart set on a career in the country where you were. So, no matter where you were, stress how different it was from America, and how this resulted in all sorts of inconveniences. But again, don't sound like a pampered lout. Rather, emphasize how pleased you were to find the law school grind is the same, no matter where you are. And you found happiness in the sheer predictability of the drudgery, amid all the confusing cultural differences of the country.

In short, you—subtly—emphasize you are a legal robot who can steadily produce billable output under all kinds of conditions, pleasant or unpleasant. If you can say these things with a straight face, your interviewer might well make you an offer on the spot. (The foregoing assumes, of course, that you have not actually set your sights on a career in a specific country—unlike the Japan program student mentioned above. But even he did not take the attitude of "Tokyo or Bust" during his interviews. He let *them* spot the possibilities—which, of course, were staring them in the face.)

There's one other advantage to a foreign studies stint. Before you go, you find out all the American law firms that have offices where you're going to be. Then you write them before you go, and tell them that you'll be in their neighborhood on the foreign studies program. (You should write to the person in charge of that office, and maybe to one other person, just in case the head honcho or head honcha tosses your letter.) Enclose a copy of your transcript, and your résumé. Say you'd like to come in to find out what it's like to be working for that firm in that location. They'll know what you *really* want, and might chose to go along with the pretense that you just want to drop in for a friendly chat. It's called a "courtesy interview."

If you don't get a response, write to them again when you're over there, again enclosing a copy of your transcript, and résumé. It's unlikely you'll have an address there where they can respond by mail. So, you tell them you'll be calling. Pushy? Yes. But it can be effective.

If and when you get to meet with one or more people over there, he, she, or they just might like you, and want to have you working there when you graduate. Then the home office will be notified, and they'll set up a formal job interview for you.

I know of two lawyers who went this route, successfully. One of them got hired to work Stateside for a year. After he proved he was competent, they sent him to the foreign office where he'd first been interviewed while on the foreign studies program. The second was even more fortunate. He went straight to the foreign office as soon as he passed his bar exam. Both guys, to my knowledge, are still overseas —and quite happy about it.

If You Have the Yen for It

If you're interested in foreign study, be mindful it's expensive. Usually the programs are put on by American schools, in cooperation with a foreign institution. Each school gets a piece of the action. So, the tuition is higher than the normal tuition at the U.S. school—plus air fare, room and board, etc.

You can use federally guaranteed student loans, though. You don't have to get approval for your specific program. As long as you're going to get law school credit, you're eligible. Further, because these funds exist for "educational purposes," you should be able to use the proceeds to pay for room and board, as always...and for the air fare. (But don't forget, you have to repay those loans someday, with interest.)

The final consideration regarding money is that foreign law study programs are not a "now or never" thing. Even though most of them don't advertise the fact, nearly all are open to licensed attorneys, too. Sometimes, however, students get first priority; licensed attorneys get in only if there are unfilled slots at the time of the application deadline. Check this out. Sometimes it requires a phone call.

Other than cost, the main negative is that you're usually limited to a total of just a few credits. That's fine if you want to spend a lot of time sightseeing and carousing with the locals. But if you're paying a lot of money, and coming back with only a handful of credits compared to the time you were gone, you need to weigh the cost v. the benefit. And, of course, you might need to do something to make up the difference when you return (or before you go): take a heavier credit load than normal in one semester, or attend a summer session. So, be sure to find out the maximum number of credits you can get out of it, and plan your home credit load accordingly.

Shop around to find the best deals. Even more important, check with your law school before you even apply to one of these programs. Make sure you can transfer the credits home. Get it in writing. You have to move fast on this, because most foreign study program slots fill quickly. (And you usually have to pay a hefty, *non-refundable* deposit with your "application.") By the time you get confirmation from your school, it might be too late to get in.

When to Go

The other major thing to consider, besides the cost and transfering credits, is whether to go for a summer, semester, or an academic-year.

Nearly all the programs are summer-only: some for just two or three weeks, others eight to twelve. For the shorter ones, it's possible for you to work a summer job at home and still go.

If you Make Law Review, and you hope to become an editor in third-year, you should remain at your school throughout second-year. If you're chosen at the end of second-year to be a third-year *editor,* there goes year three (including the summer after second-year). The problem is that the deadline for most foreign studies programs is anywhere from late January to late March—long before year-end finals. Keep that in mind if you're in first-year and are interested in foreign study but hope you have a shot at Law Review.

In that case, if you think you can stand to immediately extend your studies, the best time to go on a summer program is probably after your *first* year. (The courses you'll take will be vastly different than the Big Six you will have just endured.) After either first- or second-year, you can do a summer clerkship *and* a foreign study program, if you wish: as mentioned in Chapter 18, clerkships are usually for just half the summer, either the first or the second. (Then again, as also mentioned, you might prefer to do two clerkships in one summer, back-to-back; or, your sole clerkship one year might be summer-long.)

As with all foreign studies programs, the semester and academic-year programs will likely be under the auspices of an American school other than your own. Again, be sure to check ahead of time with your own school about transferring credits.

Your own school might have semester and academic year programs with a foreign "sister school." Naturally, your school would prefer you to go on one of those, because then *they* get a piece of the financial pie. For that reason, they usually make it easier to get more credits than you would if you went elsewhere. Sometimes, they make their own funds available for this—as loans, with interest. (Less frequently, you can get an outright grant.)

The best time to go on a semester program is the *second* semester of either your second or third year—preferably the former. You will need the first semester to line up a job, whether it be just a summer job or a "permanent" one, to start after the academic year ends. However—as Chapter 18 said—most law firms that hire summer clerks as part of a formal program make their decisions about whether or not to extend permanent offers at the end of that summer, rather than in the fall. So, you might be one of the lucky few who starts third-year with a job already waiting for you at graduation. Also, perhaps you will *not* be chosen for a Law Review editorship for your third-year. Then, you might not want to stay on as a cite-checking slave. And perhaps you do *not* intend to apply for a judicial clerkship in lieu of going to work for the law firm that offered you the job. If all these conditions exist, you are then free to go where you wish in part or all of your third year.

While in law school, I participated in two programs, one in Europe, one in Asia. In Asia, classes were followed by an (unpaid) internship at a local law firm. Although each was very expensive, I would do both again. All of those in the Asian program were fellow law students, although one of them had been a practicing attorney who was then getting an LL.M. In the European program, again one of the participants was an attorney, but not a student. He was in a two-person firm that had recently won—and collected its fee in—a large personal injury case. The program was his treat to himself, a unique vacation.

The schools arranged for us to do the usual tourist things. However, many activities were unique to our status. We met with prominent attorneys, government officials, and judges. We got to sit in on a criminal trial (with translators for us). We visited with corporate counsel of local and American companies doing business in the country in question. In Asia, we toured a couple of factories. I found the American professors in foreign studies programs to be superior to those back home; very little hide-the-ball. Nearly all the foreign professors who participated (usually as guest lecturers) were excellent. (Then again, it's well known that even lousy wine always seems to taste better in a foreign locale. Your happiness with the local scenery, and the girls—or guys, as the case may be—clouds your judgment.) The assigned materials were wonderful—but voluminous. However, the assigned workload, though heavy, was not oppressive.

To learn what's available, check the December and January issues of *Young Lawyer* (published by the ABA Law Student Division) or *National Jurist,* an independent magazine for law school students.

If you can afford it, I recommend it. Also, except for the brief annual vacation or occasional business trip, convention, or conference, you're probably going to be spending nearly every day of the rest of your life in America. The USA's a great place. But it's also great to have a final fling before you settle down.

Chapter 22 - The Job Search

Disclaimer

This is a book on law school. Anything else is noted just in passing. That goes for a mere chapter on finding a job, when there are entire books on this one subject.

The purpose of this chapter is to share information and thoughts you perhaps won't encounter elsewhere.

Looking, Sounding, and Acting the Part

It's important for you to come across as a crisp (future) professional. This includes looking the part, as much as you possibly can. You'll need to look like a professional even during your Mock Trial, Moot Court, or other competitions, and at any official school functions where you mingle with faculty and deans in a formal setting. It's most important, of course, when you're around prospective employers—especially when you show up for your job interviews.

You're going to need professional clothing, so you might as well do it *right*. (I heard of one judge who, only half-jokingly, said, "In *my* court, the lawyer who wears *polyester* has the 'burden of proof.'")

John Malloy wrote two classics that are still in print. Both are now in paperback. His original book, for men, was *Dress for Success*. It's now in a revised edition. There's a companion volume, *The Woman's Dress for Success Book*. The men's book is $14; the women's, $11. Each is easily worth ten times its price. Get the Malloy book for your gender, and do what he says.

The words that follow I find distasteful. You will too, probably. However, the first part of the subtitle of this book is *What You Need to Know*. In the interest of telling you the truth, the whole truth, and nothing but the truth, I have to include this sub-section.

Discrimination on the basis of looks—appearance—is a fact of life. The movies and TV people understand this quite well. Villains nearly always have displeasing physical features. Heroes and heroines are nearly always good-looking. Studies have shown that mothers of newborns are less affectionate with their infant if the baby is ugly. And to get elected to public office these days, you'd better be photogenic.

The same sort of discrimination exists in the Law. Chapter 19 discussed how jurors favor the side whose attorney they like. More often than not, the one they like is the better-looking. Potential employers hire those they like. More often than not, the better-looking applicants are the ones they like, all other things being equal. The more prominent the law firm, the more likely its employees are winners in the genetic lottery. Keep that in mind. "Lookism" is especially important for rainmaking (bringing in new business).

This is not to say that you must have the face and physique of a model to be a success in the Law. But if your physical qualities are not within the parameters of a particular firm, chances are you won't get a summer clerkship, no matter how good your grades. Those with disfiguring birthmarks or scars are shunned, typically. Those with disabilities, especially something as salient as cerebral palsy, but even as relatively subtle as a gnarled left hand, are also subject to avoidance.

In one sense, this isn't the problem for men the way it is for women. The range of what's acceptable is greater for men. But there are limits. It's okay to be a large man. In fact, it's a plus: tall men, especially, are more admired, automatically—even by other men—than short men are. But large women have a problem. Fat people, of either gender, are discriminated against, but fat women moreso than fat men.

This is particularly important for two groups of lawyers. The first is trial lawyers, for reasons already stated.* The second group where appearance is particularly important consists of those who deal with highly successful people—corporate executives in the area of business law, and wealthy individuals in the area of estate planning. In either, "All-American good looks" count heavily. (In the latter, as an alternative, it helps to resemble the stereotypical, elegant aristocrat.)

---

* However, as elsewhere, there are exceptions to the rule. Too many male trial lawyers look too slick: the $1,000 suit, the Rolex watch, the silver hair and the $50 styling thereof. It apparently hasn't hurt them in court. But jurors resent the privileged status of attorneys. And so, often, they find the unpretentious lawyer more likable. One guy I know of wears decent but obviously inexpensive suits...and he has a very crooked set of teeth. He evidently came from a family that couldn't afford to pay for braces for him. Many jurors have a similar background, so they identify with him. (What they don't know is that this guy makes almost a million bucks a year, year in and year out.)

Gerry Spence, one of the most successful trial attorneys in America, constantly wears a silly fringe jacket in court—and keeps his hair long even today. (He's cultivating an image of rugged frontiersman, of course. If he could get it past the metal detectors, I'm sure he'd keep a Bowie knife in a buckskin sheath tied to his belt. And if he thought it would help, he'd probably wear a coonskin cap. By extension, this contrivance extends to his client's image. And it usually works with juries. —But then again, Spence is "ruggedly handsome" to begin with.)

However, while a handsome (but not *too* handsome) man has an advantage, a truly handsome woman has a number of disadvantages. I don't need to spell them out.

Next: If you come from a lower-middle-class (or downright poor) background, *you will need to learn how to act and sound like an upper-middle-class professional*. Although I have repeatedly condemned the portrayal of lawyers on TV and in the movies, I must admit that the "crispness" these actors (usually) exude in their attorney roles (when they're portraying the *good* guys—and gals) is exactly the sort of air you want to have. So, whatever your background, if you don't already come across this way, watch and learn from show business—*not* how the attorneys act in *trial,* but how they talk and carry themselves *outside* the courtroom. (*Big* exception: Ally McBeal.)

INTERVIEWING SKILLS

Related to this is learning how to handle an interview. If you have little or no experience dealing with upper-middle-class bosses when seeking a job, you'd better get some practice at it. Perhaps your school's placement office conducts "mock interview" sessions. If they don't, try to arrange it through a student association or a young lawyers' group. Obviously, if you blow the interview, you blow the job. Don't let poor *interviewing skills* cost you an opportunity for which you're genuinely qualified.

West's Sum & Substance division does an audio cassette called "Interviewing With Law Firms." It lasts an hour-and-a-half, and costs $20. Clifford Ennico has a book out, *The Legal Job Interview*. It's $18, and ought to be available through any bookstore.

But I've not heard the tapes, nor read the book, so can't vouch for either.

TIPS for WOMEN

Many young women (and even some older ones) talk with high-pitched "little girl" voices. Such voices carry little credibility as authority figures—and a lawyer is supposed to be an authority on the law. (A high-pitched voice in a man is also a problem. But it's much less of a problem, and obviously much less frequent.) If you have a voice like that, work on changing it. I mean it. It can be done.

At the opposite extreme: Far too many female attorneys seem to believe that the way to gain respect from men is by acting like jerks. They make a big show of macho toughness, maybe including off-color jokes. Perhaps they think that makes them one of the boys. It doesn't.

There's a difference between the no-nonsense approach and that of a pit bull. The women attorneys who are most respected are those who can be tough as nails when the occasion demands it, but who are always polite and even genteel. That's the way men should be, too. But unfortunately, it's still acceptable for men to be otherwise. It isn't for women. Instead of trying to descend to the level of a male jerk, women should be setting a better example. (So should those male attorneys who aren't jerks.) You don't have to be an asshole to gain respect as an attorney.

PONTIFICATION re. DISCRIMINATION

Two other groups merit special attention.

The first is racial minorities. Racial discrimination still exists, as you know. And, unfortunately, affirmative action all too often puts members of minority groups under a cloud of suspicion as to their competence. It used to be said that a *woman* had to be twice as good as a man to be regarded as an equal. I doubt that's true anymore. But it's probably still true for racial minorities.

Because of blind grading in law school, you can objectively prove your worth in the academic setting. But once you're out in practice, it's a whole new ballgame. And it starts when you're looking for a job. You *have to* look and act and sound like a professional...and *being professional is not a matter of race*—not in professional sports, not in the profession of arms, and not in the profession of the Law.

I've dealt with two blacks—one a man, one a woman—who are among the best examples of "crispness" I'll ever meet in my life. (One is a federal judge.) My hunch is that they're both involved in programs whereby they can serve as role models and mentors to aspiring black attorneys. If you're a member of a racial minority group, ask around: wherever you are, there should be at least one such person, and he or she might be willing to help *you.*

For the average man or woman, it's rough being a non-white person in American society, even now—and even if you come from a family that's upper middle class. (But this is hardly news to you.) Just be advised that the world of the Law is still overwhelmingly white, and part of the lingering racism of our society is that a non-white attorney will not get the benefit of the doubt the way the average white attorney will. (Recall the discussion on page 347 in Chapter 13 of the incident involving an overtly racist professor at my law school and a black student in one of his classes.)

ATTICUS FALCON, ESQ.

The other group that merits special attention is homosexuals. For homosexual women, there's not much of a problem. For homosexual men, there is. I will not urge you to stay in the closet. Just don't *flaunt* it. Your private life—including your sex life—is none of your employer's business, anyway. Please avoid an in-your-face attitude...unless you've found a law firm composed entirely of gays who cater to a gay clientele.

This really isn't a matter of sexual orientation, though: Straight males who are playboys will also find that it counts against them if they flaunt their sex lives at the office. The difference, as you know, is that many straights get up-tight just at the knowledge that a colleague is "gay."

Life is unfair. Life is cruel. And life is rough. So is a life in the Law. I can't do much to change it, and neither can you, although in our own small way, each of us can try. If you fit any of the descriptions here, perhaps my random comments will help you to evaluate your situation, and your prospects...and to plan accordingly.

I'm no expert in any of these matters. No doubt I'll get at least a few angry letters accusing me of being insensitive, at the very least, or bigoted, at worst. I'm not trying to pick a fight or to be condescending. I share these thoughts with you in the spirit of letting you know what you're up against. If, as a male WASP who's straight, *I'm* part of what you're up against, so be it. I apologize for whatever offense I've given.

Laying a Different Foundation for Your Success

Make Law Review.

Then Get a Judicial Clerkship. No matter what you want to do with your law degree in the long run, in the short run you should get a judicial clerkship. True, judicial clerkships pay only a fraction of what the big firms pay as starting salaries. But your short-term sacrifice will reap long-term rewards that just might astound you.

A judicial clerkship is similar to a court internship (discussed in Chapter 18). However, a judicial clerkship is a full-time job after graduation. If you did very well in law school, you have a shot at a clerking with a judge/justice on one of your state's higher courts, or with a federal judge/justice. And you should go for it. In fact, if you hope to become a professor, you *must*—with the highest court you can get.

But you don't just work for "the court." You apply for a post with a specific judge. (For a district court, there's only one judge per court. At higher levels, there are many. Either way, you have to choose whom to contact.) The higher courts also have "staff attorneys." That's a "career" job, and quite different from a judicial clerkship.

Usually, a graduating law school student who's good enough to get a prestigious clerkship has already lined up a job with a prestigious law firm. He or she joins the law firm after finishing the clerkship. (Sometimes, a graduate does more than one clerkship, in sequence. Usually, though, only future law school profs do more than one—especially if the second one is with a U.S. Supreme Court justice.)

However, even if you don't have a private-sector job lined up, you should still try for the clerkship. This is because your judicial boss can pull strings to get you an offer you'd otherwise completely miss. Not only does a clerkship Look Good on the Résumé; it can also provide a safety net if all else fails.

THREE TIPS re. (FEDERAL) JUDICIAL CLERKSHIPS

First, if you didn't use *O'Connor's Federal Rules—Civil Trials* (see the addendum to Chapter 16) to help you study first-year Civ Pro then you should get it and read it before you apply for any clerkship.

Second, be sure you know where your judge is…literally. A federal *district* court judge lives and works in the city where the district courthouse is. Such is not necessarily so with a federal *appellate* (circuit court) judge. (The district court is the trial court at the federal level. The circuit court is the first level of federal appeal.) Each federal circuit court covers several states. The judges on the court often continue to reside in the city where they were living before they were appointed to the court. They conduct most of their business by phone, including conference calls, and get together in person—in the city where the circuit courthouse is located—only when they're hearing oral argument in a case. So, if you're particular about where you want to live, find out where the circuit court judge you're interested in is *really* located.

The *Federal Judiciary Almanac* lists *every* federal judge in America: "Article I" judges as well as "Article III." (You'll learn the—crucial—difference, in Con Law.) It's published twice a year by Prentice-Hall's Law & Business Division. It should be in your law school's library.

Third: obviously, before you apply for a judicial clerkship (federal *or* state), you need to be prepared to discuss individual opinions the judge in question wrote. You read them in the case reporters. To find out what those cases are, you can use Westlaw or Lexis and do a search. (Any reference librarian at your law school can help you find all the opinions written by a specific judge.)

Your research should be nearly *complete* by the time you *start* third-year. The first semester of third-year is when judges will be recruiting judicial clerks to start the following summer. (It used to be they began hiring in the fall of students' second year. That has changed, although some judges still "jump the gun.")

General Tips

Your law school will have a Placement Office. It's primarily for graduating students who seek "permanent" employment, but probably also assists those who want to be summer associates. The Placement Office arranges for on-campus interviews with prospective employers. Make use of whatever help you can get from there.

The places where you apply for work know that you want a job. But they (quite rightly) suspect you really don't much care *where* you get work, as long as the money's good. You have to show them that you're after the *right* job, not just a "good" job—and that you've carefully selected this firm as your potential employer, whether summer or "permanent." The more you know about the legal industry, the particular law firm, and perhaps even individual senior attorneys there, the better.

Most of the major firms have promotional material. You should read this, of course. But anyone in his or her right mind will have read that material before the interview. So, it won't get you far in distinguishing yourself if all you know about that firm is what you read in its own literature.

During the typical job interview, the student talks about himself or herself, usually in response to questions from the interviewer. The interviewer talks about the student's answers, and about the firm. You want to turn that around, to gently *take charge*. *You* talk about the *firm*, and in such a way that you prove you know what you're talking about, instead of the usual nebulous nonsense. In passing, you show why *you're* right for *them*.

By carrying on a well-informed conversation during your job interview, you'll prove you selected this firm carefully. (And you certainly want to find a way to show off the extent of your knowledge. Just be sure to leave out any bad stuff you've discovered in your research.) This shows: 1) you're sincere, and 2) you did some real homework. (If you've read John Grisham's novel, *The Firm*, you perhaps recall how detailed the hero's knowledge was. He casually strutted his stuff in a pre-hiring encounter with the partners. They were impressed.)

LOOK BEFORE YOU LEAP

As Chapter 18 noted, even if you Make Law Review, that doesn't necessarily put you on the road to happiness. Most law students get caught up in the snobbery of the Law. They go for the status. As to a job after graduation, they go for the most prestigious firms. If they get an offer, they have bragging rights. But bragging rights are small consolation if and when they realize, too late, that they joined a firm that's wrong for them.

Chapter 20 noted that you only get to take another 15-20 courses in your second and third year of law school, so you need to fill those slots carefully. And Chapter 18 noted that even if you can do a summer clerkship with a law firm after first-year, you can only have, at most, four clerkships before you graduate. So you need to choose those *very* carefully. Doing your homework will not only help you get the job, it will help you get a job at the place that's most likely to be right for *you*.

Most job candidates come into an interview prepared only to talk about themselves. Other than grades and the résumé, there's not much for the firm to go on. Down the road, both parties are often disappointed. It's *your* responsibility to make an *informed* choice. In part this is because you will suffer more—*much* more—than your employer if the two of you were wrong about each other.

You need to know what's happening in the legal world. However, in the context of a job hunt, the "legal world" means what's happening in the "legal industry," the "law *market*."

Say you're looking at a particular law firm that's prestigious, high-paying, etc. However, unbeknownst to you, the firm is on the verge of dissolving; big egos are clashing. Naturally, as always happens in these matters, the firm's official spokesperson denies this, and no one at the firm will speak on the record. But it's common knowledge the firm's days are numbered. Meanwhile, to keep up the front, the firm continues to interview prospective associates. Do you really want to have one of your summer clerkships *there?*

Second example: Say you clerked at a firm, and have received a permanent job offer. You learned, while a summer associate, that the senior partners are big boosters of certain political causes and the candidates of a particular party. No problem for you, as it turns out, because you more or less believe in the same causes and candidates. But there were a couple of things you *weren't* told: 1) all employees are "encouraged" to contribute generously in money and effort to designated causes and campaigns, and 2) those who don't will receive assignments that are more and more thankless, tedious, etc., than otherwise. In short, you're expected to be more than an avid fan. You're expected to buy season's tickets, in expensive seats. If your prospects depend on this, do you want to make such a commitment to that firm?

On a much larger scale, here's a third and final example: It used to be the law factories hired new associates in the belief that all of them were "partnership material." Sure, they knew some of the new people would eventually leave or be asked to leave, but each new associate was expected to have a future with the firm. That's no longer true. For one thing, there's more lateral hiring—at *all* levels—than ever before.

Firms actively try to recruit one another's star performers, even entire departments. "Honor among thieves" has given way to back-stabbing and throat-slitting.

More and more, though, law firms engage in "bait and switch" regarding their new employees—the entry-level associates. I'm sure you've heard that many corporations replace mid-level (and middle-aged) managers with younger—*cheaper*—people; age discrimination laws to the contrary notwithstanding. The same thing now happens in law firms. An associate works at a "wholesale" salary, but his or her time is billed out at "retail." A $200,000 expense yields maybe $350,000-$500,000 a year in revenues to the firm. Once the associate makes Junior Partner (whatever it's called at that firm), or perhaps even just when he or she becomes a senior associate, the firm's profit margin shrinks. That person's salary has increased more, in percentage terms, than his or her billing rate has. So, at several firms, mass firings and replacements of nearly *all* associates who've been there awhile is nearly *routine* procedure. As you do your job search, find out if a firm you're looking at does this.

I've never gone through a job change in the law, but I've been told that the process of trying to go from one firm to another, even on your own initiative, can be pure Hell. Keep that in mind before you choose your initial employer...and before you (voluntarily) decide to seek a job with a new firm.

SCANNING the HORIZON CONSTANTLY

Chapter 19 said that special-interest clubs in law school, in practice areas that appeal to you, can be of use to you. (To repeat, though: You should not become an officer in any of them.) You might be able to pick up some good information about firms that hire summer associates for those areas of practice. (However, keep in mind that everyone in that club is your competitor *vis-à-vis* the job market; so don't expect much.)

Even before you start law school, you should consider getting a subscription to *The National Law Journal,* a weekly newspaper for lawyers. It normally costs $179 a year, but the student rate is half-price. *NLJ* will be a great source of information as to what the "hot" (and "cold") areas of the law are. It also runs articles on specific firms. This will help you pick up information as to a given firm's "culture." And *NLJ* runs a column on recent articles of interest that have appeared in academic law journals; these can help you in school, and out. (*NLJ* has also run reports on which federal judges get the most respect...and which ones serve as "feeders" of clerks to Justices of the U.S. Supreme Court.)

As Chapter 17 mentioned, *American Lawyer,* the national magazine, is another excellent source of information. (They run a survey of summer associates every year, and publish it in the fall. You can learn much from it.)

Depending on where you're located, there are state-specific publications. (Examples: *California Lawyer, New York Lawyer, Texas Lawyer, Chicago Lawyer,* and the *Lawyer's Weekly* for Massachusetts, Michigan, Virginia, and other states.) These are even more likely to have articles on law firms in the area. If you know where you intend to practice, you should perhaps subscribe to a legal newspaper for that jurisdiction, if one exists. Call or visit a law library in that jurisdiction to find out what's available. (Many times, practicing attorneys don't know.) Be sure to speak with a real librarian, instead of a student assistant. Many of these publications also have a student rate.

Official bar association publications usually are little help. They always play it safe. Even so, once in awhile you can learn something from them that will aid you in your job search. If you know where you intend to practice, join that state's bar association if you can while you're in law school. (Many state bar associations have something similar to the ABA's Law Student Division.) This should get you a subscription to that state's bar journal. Most major cities have their own bar association, too, with a "house organ."

If you can't afford all these dues and subscriptions, don't worry. You can read the various publications for free in a law library. Don't limit yourself to your law school's library, though. Depending on where you're attending law school, there will be other law libraries, and these are open to the public (though the public doesn't know that). If you're in a major city, the city or county or its bar association might have its own law library. If you're in a state capital, the state supreme court will have its own law library. (By the way, if you can't find what you need regarding *books* in your law school's library, you might check in these other places.)

Many of the law newspapers have columns on significant cases won by a given firm, or on big new clients a specific firm has obtained. Use this information to impress your interviewers. The same thing is true if a firm has opened a new department. Even if you have no desire to work in that department, it will please your interviewers that you're *aware* of it—especially if it's still a relatively new development not yet reflected in their own literature. (You can also avoid disaster. For example, you'd look pretty bad if you told them how much you wanted to join their securities law department...and the entire securities law department just defected to a rival law firm.)

Make a clipping file. (Save it even after you get a job following graduation. —It might come in handy some day, if things don't work out as you'd planned.) If you're reading these publications in the library, photocopy the relevant item, for your clipping file.

You should start your clipping file from Day One. Your prospective employer will not be impressed if the only "news" you know about that firm is what's in an article that had just recently been published. But if you have a clipping file, you can casually mention things about that firm that happened years before—things *not* mentioned recently. And if you can also discuss the firm's competitors on the basis of knowledge about those competitors (subtly indicating that you believe they're all inferior to the firm you're interviewing with at the moment, of course), your interviewer/s will be astounded at how savvy you are.

Read up on a firm in *Martindale-Hubbell,* the law directory. You can also do law firm research on-line. West's Legal Directory™, accessed through Westlaw, gives a profile of the firm you select. You can also access the National Association for Law Placement / *Directory of Legal Employers* database. Through this, you can get information on a specific office of a firm—for example, a large national firm with many locations. With Westlaw's access to the "Dow Jones - All Database," you can search out recent news media mentions of the firm or specific attorneys in it. Last, you can use Westlaw to obtain a list of litigation in which a particular firm or attorney was listed as counsel of record. Lexis has similar capabilities.

The "Selectivity Schedule"

Each major law firm has what I call a "selectivity schedule." It's based on that firm's opinion of applicants' law schools. The "schedule" is kept secret, for fear of giving offense. But it is very real.

So, Firm X will consider an interview for anyone who graduated in the top half of school A, the top third of school B, the top fourth of school C. and so on. The lower the firm's opinion of the law school in question, the higher the selectivity threshhold for getting an interview. And the firm will not consier grads of some schools, period.

The schedules differ from firm to firm, of course. Some of the ultra-prestigious firms in New York City *only* hire from, say, Harvard, Yale, Columbia, Pennsylvania—and *maybe* Cornell, NYU, Chicago, and Stanford. (I have not confirmed this, but I am told that at one snobbish firm, you can get an interview only if you Made Law Review at HLS or Yale—but if you went to Columbia or Penn you had to have been one of the top editors—and if you went to Cornell, you had to have been the Editor-in-Chief of the flagship journal. If you went to law school anywhere else, forget it.)

At a law firm located in only one city, of course, graduates of a "purely local" law school will get more respect than they do on the other side of the same state. And so on.

Exception: major firms that do a lot of trial work make it a point to hire at least some graduates of "lesser" schools.

Judges' salaries are typically lower than the starting salaries (even without the bonuses) that baby lawyers at the big-law firms get in their very first year on the job. So, in general, only three types of lawyers seek judgeships these days: 1) those who are incompetent either as attorneys or as business people, and just don't have what it takes to make a decent living as a lawyer, 2) those who are ambitious for prestige and money—so they "get their ticket punched" by serving just a few years in a judgeship...and then get hired away from the bench by a major law firm, after a decent interval has passed—to get a partnership and a lot more money because of their time as judges; and 3) those who are, in effect, "retiring"...onto the bench. (Don't get me wrong about this last one: judges have to work, a lot. But a judge—especially a trial court judge—is in control of his or her work in a way that almost no lawyer could ever be.) Yes, there are still some lawyers who become judges because they have great wisdom, integrity, etc. But they are a vanishing breed.

The major firms generally represent the vested interests against the "little guy" (or gal). That means the lawyer on the other side is likely to be a graduate of East Podunk U.'s law school. These days, more and more *judges* are graduates of lesser schools (especially in the state courts). So, to curry favor with the judges from lesser schools, the major law firms make it a point to hire at least a *sprinkling* of graduates from lesser schools. But as a general rule, they will hire these graduates only for the litigation department (or for departments whose clients end up in litigation quite often).

In fact, the *Martindale-Hubbell* will tell you where your best prospects are, especially if you are not at one of the most prestigious law schools in the country. Look at where the law firm has hired its most recent junior associates. And look at where the people higher up in the organization came from. The larger the percentage of their lawyers that came from *your* school, the better your chances—especially if they regularly hire many people each year from your school at the entry-level.

A DIGRESSION: LAW SCHOOL RANKINGS

This is as good a place as any to quickly discuss rankings. It's a safe bet that people who get into Harvard, Yale, Stanford, Chicago, etc., are smarter and more articulate than those who got accepted only by the Acme School of Law and Lawn Maintenance. But it's not what happens while they're *in* law school that's important.

The legal "education" students get at "The Trinity" is every bit as bad as that which students get anywhere else. But, for example, the Harvard Mystique is so strong that prospective (or current) clients will be impressed just because the firm hires "Harvard Law School graduates." So, you can graduate in *last place*, at the *very bottom* of your class at Harvard Law—and not only will you not have much difficulty finding a job, you will even find firms willing to outbid each other for your services. On the other hand, no matter how brilliant you are, if your J.D. is from East Podunk U., well, I needn't say more.

Yes, the "top" schools have big-name scholars, many of whom get appointed to high judgeships or executive branch positions. But virtually none of those scholars can teach, or even wants to. The students benefit enormously in the job market from the school's reputation—but not as to the *quality* of their *education*.

Yes, all other things being equal, the lawyer who went to one of the "Trinity" will be a better lawyer than the lawyer who went to East Podunk U. or the Acme School of Law & Lawn Maintenance. But if the two groups of students had been completely switched, somehow, I predict that those who would otherwise have gone *to* the Trinitiy would *still* be better lawyers than those who would otherwise have gone to those other schools. *That's because they had a lot more going for them to start with.* You've heard of the "bell curve"? The top schools take their students from the tip of the "right tail" of the distribution. As the book *Brush with the Law* showed, once you're *in* at Harvard (or Stanford), you can spend all three years merely carousing, and still do all right academically—*because of your natural cleverness and ability to B.S. your way through the system (which students who get in only at East Podunk and Acme typically do not have).*

As this book argues elsewhere, if the *Multistate Bar Exam* scores were released separately, and the *average* score of graduates of each *law school* were disclosed, we would see that the "top" schools' grads have only a small advantage, if any, over those at the low-ranked schools when it comes to mastery of the law and "how to think like a lawyer." But Harvard, Stanford, etc., will block any efforts that threaten their claim to providing the "best" legal education—versus merely providing the best "union card" with which to enter the guild.

Résumés

Do not rely on one all-purpose résumé. In these days of software and laser printers, there's no excuse for that. If you've done your research, prepare a *customized* résumé for almost every potential employer. Granted, most law firms look for the same things. But if you have a good feel for the distinguishing characteristics of a particular firm, you can put something special in the résumé for that firm. (The same thing goes for your cover letter.)

For example, if you're trying to get a job at a law factory known for its political connections with a major party, your résumé for that firm should list your own involvement with that party (assuming you have indeed been involved). If you notice that all the (male) senior partners at the firm belong to the Masonic Order, and you belonged to De Molay or Job's Daughters in high school, list it on the résumé you submit to *that* firm. (A good way to find out such things is to check publications such as *Who's Who* or the biographical index of the local paper.)

Do not list your membership in law-related organizations that might raise your prospective employer's eyebrows—unless you're *sure* your target firm will like it. Sometimes these are liberal organizations (The National Lawyers' Guild), sometimes conservative (The Federalist Society). In fact, don't list anything that *might* trip you up. Do your homework first.

Even if you can't customize your résumé for particular firms, you can do so for particular types of work. The résumé you prepare to try to get a job that involves work as a trial lawyer should be quite different from the résumé you prepare to try to get a job that involves work in the patenting and copyrighting of computer software.

Most of your competitors as applicants will present the same credentials as you: outstanding grades, Law Review, etc. You need to have something on your résumé that causes the firm to want to interview *you*.* If there's a way to make you stand out from the crowd, do so...as long as it isn't something weird. (Warning: It's very easy to be "weird," by lawyer standards.)

—Of course, if you've Made Law Review, they'll probably interview you without further ado. Then your task is to make sure *you're* among those they want to *hire*.

---

* I heard of a guy who won $67,000 on the TV show *Jeopardy* shortly before he started law school. He put that on his résumé. I doubt that's what *got* him interviews. However, *during* his interviews, *every one* of the firms asked him about it. In one or two cases, that's almost the *only* thing they wanted to talk about. (And don't forget the discussion of foreign legal studies, in Chapter 21.)

THE RÉSUMÉ WORKBOOK

Carolyn Nutter did a great book years ago that's still in print, *The Résumé Workbook: A Personal Career File for Job Applications*. It's not specifically for graduating law students or lawyers. However, I think it's the very *best* book of its kind. Nutter tells you how to create a résumé that gets you an interview. (If you don't get your foot in the door, you can't make the sale.) I used it myself, and *always* got called in. I was astounded to learn that this book is still just ten dollars, in paperback. As with Molloy's books on how to look like a professional, it's easily worth ten times its price. But it's hard to find in bookstores, and many won't even special order it. The publisher is Sulzburger & Graham. (If it goes out-of-print, you can get it through out-of-print dealers.)

A TIP for MINORITY GROUP MEMBERS re. YOUR RÉSUMÉ

Most firms—and *all* judges—choose whom to interview after screening applicants' résumés. Sometimes, they engage in affirmative action (or reverse discrimination, depending on your point of view). If you're Hispanic, and have an Hispanic surname, no problem. But if you're of Asian ancestry, with an "American" name such as Lee, your prospective employer won't have a clue. Same thing if you're black. So, the way you tip them off as to your minority status is to join your minority group's student association and then list it on your résumé. (You're probably welcome to join one of these clubs even if you're not a member of the minority group in question. But if that's the case, don't list it on your résumé: It will be assumed that you're trying to pull a fast one, and retribution will be swift.) If your school doesn't have an Asian-American Students Association, or a Black (or Afro-American) Students Association, start one—even if you're its only member. Then you get to list yourself as its president, too. (This is the sole exception to the rule that becoming an officer in a student organization is a waste of time for the purpose of Looking Good on the Résumé.)

——Also, if you're Jewish, with a "Gentile" name, and want to apply to a heavily Jewish firm, join (or start) a "Jewish Law Students Association." List that on your résumé for the target firm. (Or skip this, and just list your involvement with other Jewish activities, such as synagogue, UJA, and JCCA.)*

---

* The same thing works for a student who's Christian and wants to work for a firm heavy with those active in "Christian causes." Et cetera.

A TIP for WOMEN re. YOUR RÉSUMÉ

If you have a first name that could be that of either a man or a woman, clear up any possible confusion on the résumé itself, and in your cover letter. Example: Your first name is Sidney. Your name is at the top of your résumé. The assumption will be that you're male. If you're female, put "(Ms.)" in front of your name. Do the same thing where you type in your name below your signature on the cover letter. (But when you sign, leave off the "Ms.," of course.)

If you're a feminist, you might object to my statement about the presumption that you're a man. Maybe you think a man whose first name is Sidney should put "(Mr.)." Forget it. Besides, women have an advantage, although these days you seldom have an opportunity to use it. Example: You're married, and you want to get a job with an outfit you know is *very* conservative (traditional family values and all that). You signal your own conservativeness in part by putting "(Mrs.)" before your (married, not maiden) name—even if your given name is clearly that of a woman. (You should also belong to something like the Daughters of the American Revolution—and list that on your résumé for that firm.)

An alternative to this, regarding announcing your gender, is to just use your full name if it includes an obviously female name in it. "Sidney Jennifer Jones," for example. However, at some point, you'll have to let them know you go by "Sidney"; it would sound pretentious to seek to be informally addressed as "Sidney Jennifer."

Misc. Resources

USING YOUR CONNECTIONS

Sometimes the judge or professor or faculty litigator you worked for as a judicial intern, research assistant, etc., is asked to recommend someone. He or she just might recommend you. And sometimes, the judge or professor you worked for takes a more active role, and will pull strings to get you an offer—or at least a job interview—that you might never have been able to get on your own. So, always make sure these people respect you. (Just don't suck up too much.)

BOOKS for JOB-HUNTERS

Kimm Alayne Walton has three books out that might be useful—especially if you have less-than-stellar grades.

The first is *Guerrilla Tactics for Getting the Legal Job of Your Dreams*. It costs $25. The second is *The Best of the Job Goddess*, for $15. The last is *What Law School Doesn't Teach You but You Really*

Need to Know, which costs $25. (I do not know whether to feel complimented or offended by that third title, which is so clearly taken from the subtitle of *Planet Law School.* But as the man said, "Imitation is the sincerest form of *battery.*") You will have no trouble getting any of these through a bookstore.

I *hate* Walton's style. It is hard to believe she's more than 14 years old, let alone that she's a law school graduate. However, that said, if you can stand her style (and if you're desperate enough), you'll find some nuggets of gold in her work, things of substantive value.

Two books of general use are *The Official Guide to Legal Specialties,* by Lisa L. Abrams, for $20, and *Full Disclosure: The New Lawyer's Must-Read Career Guide,* by Christen Civiletto Carey, for $11. I've not seen either of these books, however, so cannot vouch for them.

As for a *judicial* clerkship, I repeat: no matter what you want to do in the law, you should try for a clerkship. And the book to get is *Behind the Bench: The Guide to Judicial Clerkships.* It's by Debra Strauss, and costs $22. I've not seen this one yet, either. But to the best of my knowledge, it's the only book on the subject. Even if it isn't great, it will surely be of value to you. (Strauss is a Yale Law grad, who did a clerkship. She's now back at Yale as its Director of Judicial Clerkship Counseling and Programs. So I assume she knows whereof she writes.)

Tips for When You're ON the (Summer) Job

"SURVIVAL SKILLS"

Here's something you should definitely read: *The Young Lawyer's Jungle Book: A Survival Guide,* by Thane Josef Messinger. It is truly wonderful, and now in its second edition. It was written mostly for entry-level associates at law factories. But no matter where you are, the ladder to the top gets narrower as you move up, and the rungs get farther apart. Messinger's book will be *invaluable* to you in avoiding a misstep. The lessons it contains apply to *anyone* who practices law, no matter whether you go to work for a law firm (big or small), a corporation, the government, the armed forces, a judge, or what have you—even solo.

Don't wait until you've been hired for a permanent job before you get *The Young Lawyer's Jungle Book,* though. On the contrary: it's important for you to know how to function smoothly even in a judicial internship, a judicial clerkship—and *especially* in a *summer* clerkship.

As with *Planet Law School, The Young Lawyer's Jungle Book* gives you the benefit of everything the author learned the *hard* way. Foresight is always better than hindsight. Messinger shows you how to be "professional" in fact as well as in job title. His book costs about $19—one of the best bargains you'll *ever* find in a book for lawyers.*

MAKING FRIENDS in THE RIGHT PLACES

If you work as a summer associate in a "law factory," and you like the firm, and you think you have a shot at getting a permanent offer, be sure to do the following during your clerkship: 1) become quite familiar with the library—especially the materials not available through CALR, 2) get on good terms with the librarian/s therein, 3) get on good terms with any and all secretaries and staff you deal with.

Your survival as an entry-level associate is officially in the hands of your supervising attorneys. (It goes without saying that you must also get on good terms with any and all attorneys you deal with...so I won't say it.) However, your skills re. #2-#3 can have a big impact on your job performance. This is true even when things are going smoothly. But it's especially true when you're in a crunch situation. This will happen—and usually when you least expected it. (The first one is important for its own sake. But it's also important because your firm's librarians will be more likely to help you if they know you've already familiarized yourself with the library—and thus don't have to be led around by the hand.) Members and veterans of the armed forces know that non-commissioned officers—the corporals, sergeants, petty officers—are sometimes in a position to make or break a commissioned officer's next promotion...or entire career. Be mindful of the Golden Rule.

Pro Bono & Public Initerest

PRO BONO

"Pro bono" is short for "Pro bono publico" ("for the public good"). It's where an attorney provides legal services free of charge, usually on a one-shot basis, for organizations or individuals who can't afford any attorney at all. This became quite fashionable during the '60s. There are still lawyers who do it.

---

* Yes, it's published by the same company (The Fine Print Press, Ltd.) that published *this* book. And yes, this second edition of *PLS* is *dedicated* to Messinger. But that's not why I'm recommending it. (In fact, I got the idea for doing *Planet Law School* while reading Messinger's.) If you take a look at his book, you'll see for yourself that it lives up to my praise for it.

During the past few decades, it's become standard procedure for big firms to talk about opportunities for new associates to do pro bono work. I urge you to forget it. You're not qualified to be practicing law on your own—which is usually what a pro bono case involves, in effect. Get good at what you're supposed to be doing for money, first. It's better to wait until you and your firm know if you're worth what they're paying you, before you start asking them to let you work for other people for free while you're on the firm's time.

Don't put the cart before the horse. There will always be plenty of pro bono opportunities. Show your sophistication by making this very argument if the subject comes up. (Your prospective employer doesn't like pro bono anyway—unless it's a high profile cause that adds to the firm's image. They talk about it because they think it's expected of them. But it's a trap. If you stress pro bono, you probably won't get a job offer. And even if you do get the offer, you'll never be allowed to do pro bono anyway—with the exception just noted.)*

Do not get me wrong: I think any attorney who graduated from a *public* law school (i.e., taxpayer-subsidized) ought to be *required* to do a minimum amount of pro bono every year. "Much is expected from those to whom much has been given." Everyone should do at least some pro bono. I urge you to, also...but only when you're experienced enough to be able to do it *right*. ("We are not the first who with best meaning have incurred the worst." —Cordelia, in Shakespeare's *King Lear*.)

PUBLIC INTEREST LAW

Technically, public interest law is sort of a full time pro bono publico. However, because those who do it are getting paid for it, "pro bono" does not include public interest law. (After all, those who successfully represent an employer who busts the workers' union will tell you, with a straight face, that *they're* acting for the public good, too—at $500 an hour.)

It used to be, a large majority of students in first-year said they wanted to go into public interest law when they graduated. But by the time they graduated, perhaps only one person in the entire class would actually have followed through. Today, hardly anyone even talks about it in first-year.

---

* Then again, there might still be some firms that take pro bono quite seriously. In fact, a handful have hired a full-time pro bono coördinator to try to match lawyers' desires to available opportunities. So, if you really are serious about doing pro bono, look for these.

For those who want to go into public interest law, be advised: the "selectivity schedule" is usually very exclusive, at least at the most prestigious outfits. I do not know why. Perhaps it's in part because most lawyers look down on those who go into public interest law, and assume that they did so only because they couldn't get a job anywhere else. The most prestigious public interest organizations, by usually hiring only top graduates of top schools, are perhaps trying to lay that myth to rest.

Hanging Out Your Own Shingle

I strongly advise you not to set up shop on your own, fresh out of law school. You should at least get some practice under the guidance of a more experienced attorney. However, for whatever reasons, there are people who hang out their own shingle before the ink is dry on their law license. If and when you go solo, here are two books that are the best. The first is *How to Start and Build Your Own Law Practice,* by Jay G. Foonberg. The American Bar Association publishes it—which naturally means its price is high: $40, in paperback. It is now in its 3d edition. Foonberg covers almost everything, but covers it rather quickly.

Another book, less costly, is *The Young Lawyer's Handbook.* This one's also in paperback, and costs $16. (It should not be confused with Thane Messinger's *Young Lawyer's Jungle Book: A Survival Guide.*) Its author is Polly McGlew. It's hard to find it in a regular bookstore or even to order it through one. You might have to get it through an out-of-print book dealer, on-line, if you really want it.

The McGlew book covers fewer topics than Foonberg's, but covers each of them more thoroughly, especially the nuts-and-bolts of setting up and running your own office. If you can afford to, get them both.

Many state bar associations also have their own books on going it alone. And approximately 20 states now have mandatory courses for new attorneys on "the basics of practicing law." So, although I still advise against going solo while you're still wet behind the ears, at least there are some good do-it-yourself guides out there.

If you're planning to be a trial lawyer (and maybe even if you're not), be sure to get Kenney F. Hegland's *Trial and Practice Skills in a Nutshell, 2d ed.,* first mentioned in the addendum to Chapter 19. Its chapters on interviewing clients, legal problem-solving, counseling clients, negotiating, legal argument, and legal writing are all magnificent. It's the best one-volume reference you can find on these topics. It's especially good for sole practitioners.

Of Dual Degrees

Many students wonder if they should get a second degree. Sometimes this takes the form of a combination degree. For example, you go four years straight, taking courses in business school and law school. You end up with an MBA and a JD—in one year less than it would take you if you got the one and then the other. Another option is to pick up a second law degree, such as an LL.M. in Taxation. That takes a year.

I advise against either.

For one thing, if you follow the recommendations of *Planet Law School,* you almost certainly will not have to worry about finding a good job. Unless you plan to eventually work as corporate counsel, I do believe the MBA is a waste of time and money. As for the LL.M., you should have a practice concentration *before* getting the Master's— in which case, why bother getting the Master's? Having the LL.M. might get you a job you wouldn't otherwise get, but I doubt it. Both options are great money-makers for the law schools, though—*which is why they promote them.*

Finally, it appears that many LL.M. candidates are those who went straight into the Master's program after getting their J.D.…because they couldn't find a job when they got out of law school. *The law firms know this.*

"Reality Check" #1

Nearly everyone who goes to law school assumes that he or she is going to be at or near the top of the class. And nearly everyone assumes that he or she will be able to choose among several job offers that each pay at least $120,000 a year fresh out of law school.

Okay, granted, with *PLS* you do have a much better than average chance of being at your near the top of your class. However, unless you go to one of the top schools, the chances are small that you will get an offer of even $60,000 a year. (That is not a typo. It's sixty thousand.)

This chapter spoke of reading bar publications and legal periodicals to gain information about "hot areas" of the law and specific firms, etc. Another reason is to do a "reality check." Take a look at the "Help Wanted" ads in these publications. You will see what's being offered and what qualifications are sought. (Even no-name rinky-dink firms in the middle of nowhere typically require that you have been in the top 20% of your graduating class…even if you graduated from a no-name school, and graduated more than a decade earlier.)

So before you set your sights too high, and start getting your ego too inflated, read those ads. It will be a sobering experience.

"Reality Check" #2

As of this writing (spring, 2003), *King of Torts* is John Grisham's latest lawyer novel. On page 234, "Oscar Mulrooney" is speaking:

> You have no idea what it's like to go to Yale, or a school like it, get wined and dined by the big firms, take a job, get married, then get tossed out onto the streets with nothing. Does something to the old ego, you know?

No kidding. It also does something to the old bank account.

Even if you do go to a top school, and get a starting salary (with bonuses) after graduation that hits $200,000 in your first year out of school, you should still play it safe, financially. *There is no tenure at law firms.*

Far too many recent law grads decide that, after years of living hand-to-mouth, it's time to "wail." They get married—and (if male) blow a small fortune on the engagement ring or (if female) the fancy wedding. They immediately buy a house—and take out a 30-year mortgage. And naturally, they want to fill the house with furniture and furnishings such as drapes, artwork, and so forth. They "start a family" right away. And, of course, they immediately buy the Porsche, or the Mercedes, or the "Beamer," or a Jag.

Even if the U.S. economy is strong for the next five years (which is unlikely), it is always possible that the firm you work for will fall upon hard times for reasons other than lack of business. Or you yourself might get canned for reasons that have nothing to do with your competence.

I urge you to save as much money as you can if and when you get the big-bucks job fresh out of law school (or *any* job, for that matter). Pay down your student loans as fast as possible, and minimize incurring other debt, especially long-term debt. You should live modestly enough to be able to set aside enough money so that you can survive for a year without further income if and when disaster strikes. Let others show off and blow their newfound wealth while scoffing at your frugality. Better to be safe than sorry.

Part VII:

Countdown to Lift-Off for the "Real" World of the Law

Chapter 23 - MBE, MPT, MPRE

The Multistate Bar Exam

In all but two states (Louisiana and Washington) and Washington, D.C., you must take the Multistate Bar Examination (MBE) as part of your bar exam. It lasts one day. It's given twice a year: the last Wednesday in February and July. It has two sets of 100 multiple-choice questions; one's in the morning, the other in the afternoon. Each session lasts three hours. That's an average of one question every minute and 45 seconds.

The MBE covers six subjects: Contracts, Torts, Property, Constitutional Law, Criminal Law, and Evidence. All except Evidence are *first-year* subjects. (Evidence replaces Civil Procedure, the other Big Six subject of year one.) Of the 200 questions, Contracts and Torts each has 40. All the others have 30 apiece.

The distribution of sub-topics is also known. For Con Law, six questions concern the separation of powers within the federal government; six concern federalism itself. In Torts, half the questions deal with negligence. In Crim Law, five cover what are called "inchoate" crimes; six, homicide. Seventeen of the Contracts questions ask about contract formation and consideration. Nine of Property's questions deal with Estates and Future Interests. Hearsay is the subject of one-third of the Evidence questions; five involve impeachment and rehabilitation of witnesses; two ask about writings as evidence. Et cetera.

There's no order in which they're presented. You might get a series of questions each of which is in a different subject from the one before. Or, you might get ten in a row on the same subject.

MBE questions range in difficulty from easy to hard. On a scale of 1-10, the easiest is probably about a two, the hardest, about an 11. The Multistate people analyze candidates' performances for consistency. Those who score, say, below 50% ought to have incorrectly answered a disproportionately large number of the hardest questions—and vice-versa. Sometimes, the Multistate people discover something's wrong: for example, what they thought was a question of medium difficulty turns out to have been very confusing; even the best candidates often got it wrong. Sometimes, they throw that question out. *Everyone* gets credit for it, regardless of his or her answer.

Each time the MBE is given, 30 questions are taken from each of the two preceding exams and repeated in the new one. These 60 questions vary in difficulty. For each of those sets of 30, there was a relationship between candidates' overall performance and their performance on those 30. (That's a big reason why they were selected for later use. No doubt, at least a few of the 60 questions taken from the preceding two exams were questions that appeared on *both* of them.)

Each exam mostly contains completely new questions, of course. The questions repeated from old exams function as a "control." The new questions are supposed to come out the same way as the control set: Those who do poorly on the overall exam should also do poorly on the new questions that are really hard, while doing better on the less difficult ones. Those who do quite well on the overall exam are expected to do quite well on the new questions, too. Sometimes it doesn't work out that way. Then, once again, these questions are tossed out and *everyone* gets credit for them.

The Multistate folks feed all of this into a computer and do some fancy statistical work for what they call "equating." It's supposed to equalize the overall difficulty of the MBE, from one exam to another, in measuring the results. (The matter is further complicated by the fact that the typical performance on the February bar exam is considerably lower than that on the typical July bar exam.) You get two scores: raw and scaled. The raw score is pre-equating. The scaled score is post-equating. It's the one that counts. So, if you get a 70% scaled score on your Multistate, this means you would have gotten a 70% if you'd graduated from law school five years earlier and taken it then. That's what they say—for what it's worth.

The average raw score is around 128. That's just 64%. "Equating" typically adds 10-20 points. However, because each point is just 0.5% (remember, *200* questions), the average scaled score in recent years has been between 136 and 145. Even *that's* just 68% - 72.5%.

PICKY, PICKY, PICKY—and TRICKY, TRICKY, TRICKY

The MBE has many, many trick questions. But even the straightforward questions usually aren't easy. They test *very* narrow applications of legal rules. Often, the correct answer is a very narrow *exception* to a legal rule. If you don't know "everything" backwards *and* forwards, you'll screw up. That's a big reason why the average score is so low. It's not that candidates are lazy about preparing for the bar exam, nor are they stupid. They're just overwhelmed by minutiae. (It's said that the Multistate examiners regard 10,000 points of law as fair game.)

The potential choices nearly always include at least one *incorrect* statement of the law. If you've mastered the material, the incorrect statement/s can be quickly eliminated from consideration. Quite often, however, at least one of the choices will be a *correct* statement of the law—but that correct statement is *irrelevant* to the question. Frequently, each potential answer states an element of a cause of action that's relevant to the question. Each of these elements is correctly stated. However, you have to spot the one element that's the *key* to the problem. Or, *all* the possible answers state the *same* proposition of law—just in different ways. You have to select the one that's *most* correct. This is the one statement of the law that most *exactly* fits the facts of the question, the statement that hits the nail right on the head. The "wrong" answers are the ones that are unnecessarily broad—or too narrow. Or, it's the other way around: All of the answers are *wrong*. You're told to pick the one that's *most* wrong. So, you have to *reverse* your normal way of thinking.

As if that isn't bad enough, the "fact patterns" are often *bizarre*. The MBE Examiners want to *disorient* you. So they sometimes present facts that defy common sense, that contradict anything that could be called reasonable. It's like Lewis Carroll's poem, "The Walrus and the Carpenter" (presented in full as an addendum to Chapter 8):

> "The time has come," the Walrus said,
> "to talk of many things: Of shoes, and ships,
> and sealing wax; of cabbages, and kings...
> and why the sea *is* boiling hot,
> and *whether* pigs have wings."*

That way, the only thing you can rely on to answer the question is your own knowledge of the legal point at issue.

—And all of this concerns the *"straightforward"* questions.

One type of *trick* question relies on candidates' proclivity to jump to conclusions. For example, there's a lawsuit. Two answers say the plaintiff wins, two say plaintiff loses. You know, from reading the facts, that plaintiff wins. Yet, both of the answers that say, flat out, that "plaintiff wins" are *wrong*. One of the answers that starts off by saying "plaintiff *loses*" is the correct choice. Here's why: the "plaintiff loses" answers include the word "unless," or "if," followed by some basis for plaintiff to *win*. One—and only one—of these two is the *right* answer. The examiners really like to play with your mind this way. Any candidate who's feeling rattled probably won't even have the presence of mind to catch the phrase that turns one of the "wrong" answers into the only *right* one.

---

* I have taken liberties with the punctuation, condensed the spacing, and supplied emphasis.

My favorite among the trick questions is when two choices are in legalese, two in plain English. *Both* of the legalese answers are made-up nonsense (usually in Latin). The first of the plain-English answers is nonsense, too—and sometimes it's the very first choice presented. You read that, immediately see it's nonsense—and perhaps subconsciously assume the other plain-English answer is also nonsense. To further throw you off the track, the second answer written in plain English is too broad, or too narrow, or otherwise just a little bit odd. *So, all four answers are bad answers.* The "right" answer is the only one that isn't *total* nonsense—even though it just barely makes sense itself. Thus, you're supposed to make the best of a bad situation, choose the least of evils. Obviously, unless you know the ins-and-outs of everything, *cold,* you'll blow that question. The right answer (in this example) is the second one in plain English. Most students concentrate on the legalese choices, trying to figure out which one is right. Not only do they lose a point whichever of the two they pick, they also waste valuable time.

Here's another one that's barrels of fun: You get a *long* fact pattern, taking up half or three-fourths of the page. Then you get a series of as many as eight questions based on that one fact pattern. Not only do you have to know the relevant law extremely well, you have to be able to keep that one set of facts in mind as you work through all the questions. But wait—it isn't just *one* set of facts: Instead, for the next question in this set, you'll get something like this— "FOR THIS QUESTION ONLY, assume that everything is the *opposite* of what we just told you." (Actually, it isn't quite that bad, but it feels that way during the exam.) Then, right after you've *un*-memorized everything because they changed the facts for one question, the very next question will be something like, "FOR *THIS* QUESTION ONLY, assume everything's back to the way it was at first—except that the *following* facts are different from *either* of the previous questions..." And so on.

Clever, these examiners. Only a twisted mentality could concoct many of these questions. (When I was a child, some of the neighbor kids were really sick, mentally: They'd take a cat to an abandoned building and place a heavy weight on its tail, right up to the point where the tail joined the body; or they'd rig a harness and hang the cat by its hind-quarters upside-down from a rafter. A week or so later they'd return. You know what they found. Sometimes I strongly suspect that as adults they're drafting questions for the Multistate Bar Exam. They're far more perverse even than law school professors.)

You have to be able to *very* quickly spot the key factor and the right answer. Above, it was mentioned that you have about a minute and 45 seconds for each question. However, with four possible choices per question, you're going through *400* possible answers in 10,800 seconds (three hours). That's one possible answer every *27 seconds*— including the time it takes to read the *fact pattern!* Worse, the MBE comes at you from every imaginable angle, to throw you off balance.

The Multistate people "release" (i.e., divulge) some of the MBE questions they use, every year. For each, they announce what the right answer was and explain it. However, the questions they release are nearly always just the easy ones. The non-official sample questions are just as good, often better—and always harder.

In recent years, there have been candidates who got only one question right of the 30 on Property, or three right of the 30 on Con Law or Evidence, or five of the 30 on Crim, or just six of the 40 on Contracts. There have also been candidates who correctly answered *all* the questions in a given subject area. (I assume those are people from the bar review organizations, who regularly take the MBE to memorize questions so they can include them as practice questions in their bar review materials.)

If the bar exam is supposed to measure competence, then its Multistate portion ought to measure competence. But it doesn't. Instead, the mental games the examiners play have subverted its substantive aspects. From law school to "barzam," the more things change the more they stay the same regarding lawyers-to-be.

Yes, it tests what it's supposed to: the things lawyers need to know and understand. Even "coming at you from every imaginable angle, to throw you off balance" also serves a purpose. —After all, in the real world of the Law, you'll encounter some amazing situations and arguments. And there are those who insist that the time pressure separates the men from the boys (or whatever the non-sexist phrase is that has replaced that one). But the gamesmanship of the examiners has long since overwhelmed the substantive aspect.

Each state chooses how much the MBE will count in computing the final score. The lowest weight appears to be 30%, the highest, one-half. (It's surely possible to determine this. However, based on the materials I obtained regarding various states' procedures and policies concerning their bar exams, it seems many states do not make these things clear—intentionally.) Irrespective of how the MBE and other portions of the bar exam are weighted, most states require a combined *scaled* score of 65% - 70%. (The lowest passing grade appears to be 55%; the highest appears to be 76%.)

The Multistate Performance Test

When the first edition of *PLS* was published (1998), only two states (California and Colorado) included what's called a "performance test" as part of their bar exam. Now, 29 states and Washington, D.C., do. It's called the Multistate Performance Test (MPT), and is a national exam. It's administered on either the day before or the day after the MBE. It consists of two questions. States use either or both. You have 90 minutes per question.

You're handed a "case file" and some legal reference materials. The latter include copies of cases, statutes, rules, and regulations. (But some of the reference materials are more important than others. Indeed, some might be irrelevant.) You also get a directive, telling you what to cover in your response. It's your job to apply "the (relevant) law" to the problem/s in the case file. So you have to Think Like a Lawyer in much the same way as on a fruitcake exam—except that this time you're told what the problem is and are handed all the law you need. And as with a fruitcake, there's a premium on your ability to organize your thoughts quickly and express them succinctly on paper.

The Coda (Part V) of this new edition of *PLS* is a performance test of sorts. The *Sports Illustrated* article functions as the "case file," with mention of several reported cases included. The rest of the Coda then discussed the relevance (or irrelevance) of those cases, of industry custom, and so on. Granted, it had far more analysis than you would ever give in answer to a performance test, but at least you get the idea.

I believe that *all* second- and third-year law school *final* exams should be performance tests. It's much, much closer to what you'll be doing as an attorney in the real world. (Then again, I was told that the performance test on Colorado's barzam, as of 1998, was a farce.)

But law school *profs* will *never* start giving performance tests. Two reasons. First, laziness. (Witness the shift to multiple-choice questions.) Second, nine out of ten are *incapable* of dealing with a real-world problem. If *they* had to take a performance test, they'd fail. (I am not exaggerating. Remember "Billion-Dollar Charlie," in Chapter 9. Also, I've attended programs for the professoriat where they were given *simple* real-world problems, such as critiquing a fictitious complaint filed in a federal court. They couldn't even catch that the complaint had been filed in a court that had no connection whatsoever to the cause of action or to either of the parties. Several dozen members of the professoriat just sat there, helpless,.every bit as lost as they make their first-year students. But at least their students have an excuse. The profs, in contrast, simply *made light* of their *own* incompetence.)

It Doesn't End with the Multistate/s

Most states have additional tests as part of their bar exam. These are given on the day/s before or after the MBE/MPT. At least one full day is devoted to essay exams. You're given a set of facts. You have to prove you can Think Like a Lawyer, state the relevant Black Letter Law, and apply it correctly. So far, sounds like a law school fruitcake exam. But on a bar exam state essay question, you're told who all the parties are and the nature of the problem/s. Your job is to figure out the solution/s and to explain why you're right. (If there is no solution, you also have to explain why.) That sounds like the MPT. But also unlike a law school essay exam, and *unlike* the MPT, either, you have to show you know the *fine points* of your *state's* statutory and case law on the subject. (But again like a fruitcake, but unlike the MPT, you have to do it from memory.) You have between ten minutes and one hour per question.

Virtually every state administers its own essay questions. In addition, roughly a dozen give the Multistate Essay Exam (MEE—but the term "Multistate" always refers only to the MBE, and not even to the MPT). As with the MBE, the MEE tests six subjects, but different from the MBE's: Business Organizations (the principal-agent relationship, corporations, and partnerships), Conflict of Laws, Commercial Transactions (commercial paper, sales of goods, and consumer goods credit), Family Law, Federal Civil Procedure, and Wills-Estates-Trusts. The states' essay exams cover a lot of the same ground, but—as mentioned—they test state-specific law in those areas. Typically, there are at least 12 subjects. New York's bar exam is said to be the hardest in the country. In part, it's because—so I am told—its essay portion tests *34* subjects. (Nebraska is the only state that administers just the MEE for the essay portion of its bar exam, without additional state-specific questions.)

Many states' bar exams continue into a third (or even a fourth) day (or half-a-day). This usually concerns that state's civil and criminal procedure, federal civil procedure, or various other matters. So, you've not bid adieu to your first-year civ pro course after all, even though it isn't on the Multistate. Instead, it's back—with a vengeance: because now you have to know that *and* your *state's* civ and crim pro rules…and often the subtle differences among them.

* * *

In several states, if you get a high enough score on the MBE, you automatically pass the entire bar exam, regardless of your performance on the essay portion, etc. In others, if you get a certain minimum score on the MBE, every point above that can be used to offset a low score on the state-specific portion of the barzam. (In these states, it does not work the other way around.) In still others, if you *don't* get a certain minimum score on the MBE, you fail the entire bar exam, no matter how well you do on the state-specific portion.

A high score on the bar exam doesn't bring you rewards the way high scores on first-year finals do. And no one ever asks how well you did. Their—and your—only concern is whether or not you *passed.*

* * *

By the time you've finished your first-year finals, you'll think you've seen the limits of stress. Just wait 'til you get to the bar exam. (One candidate, during the February '93 barzam in California, had a heart attack.*) Law school finals are often spread out over two weeks: two to four hours per final, usually with a day off in between. The "barzam" is six to eight hours a day, two to four days straight. It's grueling, a gauntlet. By the end of just the first day, the fatigue factor has already set in. That's part of the plan.

Even during a formal bar review course, the mood is often one of sheer desperation—and the mood can be contagious. Many employers provide time off for new graduates to study full-time for the exam. However, there never seems to be enough time to prepare. Sure, the passing grade is (usually) less than 70%, and that's the *scaled* score. And yes, roughly four out of five people do pass it on their first try (except in New York and California). But there is simply no way to master everything the bar exam can test. Everyone sweats it.

If the bar exam were a serious measure of one's knowledge of the law, the minimum passing score would be set much higher. And the pace would not be hectic. Reflection is one of the hallmarks of a good attorney. In the real world, there is usually ample time for reflection.

---

* Other candidates came to his assistance. Those who helped the victim *were not allowed extra time to finish,* to make up for the time they spent trying to *save his life.* —As I said, these bar exam people are sick. (It had a happy ending, though, at least in the short run: after getting a lot of bad publicity, higher officials decided to "review" the scores of those who'd helped the victim. *And the victim himself showed up the next day to continue taking the barzam.* —See what law school does to you?)

The bar exam, in contrast, forces "instant analysis"—as does the typical law school final. Based on what I've seen in practice, this instant analysis becomes habitual. Thus, the artificial time constraints might actually be *counter-productive* in the long run. Out in the real world, a client might suffer because his or her lawyer was content with instant analysis that was erroneous.

The bar exam is a hazing ritual. Instead of being forced to drink too much alcohol or to perform ridiculous physical acts of self-degradation, future lawyers are forced to "drink in" an endless stream of legal lore— and to endure a nerve-wracking and gut-wrenching gauntlet spread over several days.

The "Ethics" Exam

Once upon a time, there was a President of the United States named Richard Nixon. His nickname was "Tricky Dicky." In 1972, living up to his sobriquet, he assembled a group of (supposedly) former CIA agents who played "dirty tricks" on the Democratic Party. These dirty tricks were discovered and traced to the Oval Office. The Watergate Scandal resulted. (It was named for the building in which the Democratic Party's national headquarters were located: the target of the agents' repeated burglaries.) As the scandal unfolded, the American public was astonished to see that nearly all of the President's men who supervised the (ex-?) CIA agents were *lawyers*. This further besmirched the reputation of an exalted calling that had long been badly misunderstood by an ungrateful laity.

The noble profession responed by creating a test of future lawyers' knowledge of "legal ethics"—an oxymoron. Hence the Multistate Professional Responsibility Examination (MPRE), first administered in 1984. (The MBE was first administered in 1972.) Today, to get a law license in any one of 47 states (and, of course, the city in which the Watergate complex is located) you must take it. Thus, it is one of Richard Nixon's unintended gifts to all his future fellow attorneys (along with several Supreme Court cases limiting the use of executive privilege).

The MPRE tests a "Model Code" and a model set of "Rules" of lawyer ethics. It also tests the Model Code of Judicial Conduct. Many schools now require students to take a so-called "Professional Responsibility" course, the subject matter of which is the same as the MPRE's. ("Professional Responsibility" is abbreviated "P.R." "P.R." normally stands for "Public Relations," as in blowing smoke. The P.R. course is definitely part of the legal profession's P.R. —MDs take the Hippocratic

Oath; JDs take a "hypocritic" oath.) The MPRE is given thrice annually (March, August, November). Most students take it when they'rer still in law school, after completing the P.R. course. (As with the bar exam, you can take a preparatory course for it—whether in a formal setting or via home-study materials.)

You get two hours to answer the MPRE's 50 questions. Compared to the Multistate, the pace is leisurely. Instead of being asked whether something is right or wrong, you are usually required to state the correct degree of the relevant rule's application. As with the MBE, you have four choices. Here is a typical set of possible answers:

> A. The rule requires this.
> B. The rule encourages this.
> C. The rule discourages this.
> D. The rule forbids this.

As with the MBE, there's a raw score and a scaled score. The scaled score range is 50-150. The lowest passing mark, scaled, is 70; the highest is 85. Most states set their passing score from 75-80. Future lawyers sweat out the MBE; in contrast, for most, the MPRE is a breeze—and there's no stigma even if you fail it a time or two. But try to get it out of the way before you take the barzam.

Chapter 24 - Lookin' Toward the "Barzam"

As Chapter 23 said, the bar exam is in two parts, Multistate and state-specific, and each part is further sub-divided. You will have studied as many as five of the six MBE subjects in first-year. You should get a firm grip on these subjects *long before* you graduate. Because most states combine the MBE score with your score on the rest of that state's bar exam, a high Multistate grade can (sometimes) make up for falling short in other areas. (And remember, you pass in most states if your combined average, however weighted, totals just under 70%, scaled.)

Yet, most students pay no further attention to first-year subjects after Year One, except insofar as first-year concepts come up again in advanced courses. Then, nearly two years after saying "Good riddance!" to Torts, Criminal Law, Contracts, Property, and Civil Procedure—*especially* Civil Procedure—and (maybe) Con Law, they find themselves having to learn it all over again. But *this* time around, they're expected to "review" things they never *heard* of (but should have been taught) in first-year.

Bar Review Courses

Most law school graduates take a bar review course, to prepare for the exam. I know of two people from my law school—and one from another—who sat for my state's "barzam" without first taking any prep course. All were brilliant. (One was editor-in-chief of the Law Review.) All flunked. From reading Chapter 23, you can understand why.

The typical bar review course presents law school professors, either live or on video, who lecture—straight lecture, no Case/Socratic Method crap. There are also practice exams to work, both multiple-choice and essay. Usually there's a feedback mechanism, to find out where you're weak and need more review. The practice-exam sessions are usually all day Saturday.

There are two approaches. Both involve cramming. The first is part-time. A course that covers everything lasts five to six weeks. Lectures are held on weekday evenings during a three-hour time slot. Typically, it ends about ten days before the bar exam. Then candidates cram even *more* frantically than they did during the course itself.

The second approach is full-time, intensive. Students attend 6-8 hours a day, at least three days straight. Because this involves a smaller timeframe, intensive day programs are offered more often than the part-time evening ones.

Some courses are "deluxe." They offer MBE, MPT, and state essay review; you have to take it all. Others offer everything, but you can pick and choose. Still others offer only one or the other. Several have a "home study" option, and some are exclusively so.

BarBri, a subsidiary of Harcourt Brace, is to bar review what West is to legal publishing: Goliath. BarBri's market share is huge, perhaps 90%. Its sales tactics are *quite* aggressive.)* As of this writing, its full bar-cram course costs about $2200. (At the time of the original edition of *PLS,* it was $1100. Based on conversations I've had with those in the industry, my guess is that BarBri's gross profit is around $1,800 per student.) Others charge anywhere from $800 to $1800.

Inquiring Minds Want to Know - Part I

The cram-courses devote more than half their time to the first-year material the MBE covers. (Granted, Evidence is not a first-year subject, but the argument holds.) Seems to me that—at least regarding the MBE subjects—these aren't *review* courses at all: they're *remedial.* Astoundingly, the law school professors habitually *justify* their spotty coverage of the their first-year courses by saying "Oh, well, your bar review will go over all the omitted topics anyway."

Imagine the outcry if for-profit remedial programs were needed to teach *elementary* schoolkids how to read, write, and do arithmetic in the summer between 6th and 7th grades—because the nation's primary schools had not attempted to teach these things themselves. Picture the reaction if elementary schools habitually excused their negligence by saying, "Oh, well, the for-profit course will cover all this anyway."

Yet, for legal education, there's hardly a murmur in protest. Once you have your ticket, who cares? —Just the clients ill-served by attorneys who have a license to practice, yet who are almost as functionally illiterate in the law as many of America's high school graduates are with respect to the 3Rs. (However, unlike those who deal with people who are illiterate and innumerate, clients seldom can tell the difference.)

---

* Just as West owns nearly *all* the other publishers of all law books, so (I'm told) BarBri owns nearly *all* the other bar-prep companies. The only exceptions I know of are The Study Group and a new one, just now getting launched, called BarPlus. (Interestingly, West started its own bar-prep program in the early '90s—and quickly achieved a large minority share of the market, as is to be expected, considering it was West. But then West *shut down* its program...and, I am told, BarBri bought out West's then-*defunct* operation, *three years later.* It amazes me the way the anti-trust division of the U.S. Department of Justice has had such a consistently lenient attitude toward anything having to do with charging law students "monopoly rents.")

Professors say the essence of legal education is learning how to Think Like a Lawyer. So, they say, they don't need to cover the entire spectrum of substantive law in any given course. In fact, they continue, any one topic—almost any one case—can function as a prism; properly used, it creates a rainbow of legal enlightenment.

They're right, insofar as legal reasoning is concerned. But if that's the only important thing students are to acquire in law school, it raises some obvious questions: Why does law school last three years, if the essence of learning how to Think Like a Lawyer can be acquired during first-year? —And if it takes some students all three years to acquire this skill, why don't the law schools make *sure* that *everyone* has it before they graduate? (I doubt it would take three years.) If the substantive aspects of the law aren't important, why have the Big Six of first-year? Why have even more than one subject in the first place? Why not let *students* pick *all* their subjects?

The professoriat plays both ends against the middle...and guess who's in the middle? The typical new attorney's analytical skills are poor—and his or her substantive knowledge is almost zero. Yet, while it's seemingly only the new attorneys who suffer as a result, the real victims—the worst victims—are the clients.

The bar review's cram-course does indeed help you to get a law license. But its purpose is to provide jam-packed short-term memory. After the exam, students "pull the plug" on what they've studied...and nearly all of it quickly drains away.

The ABA's rules that govern law schools state that law schools can offer their own in-house bar "review" courses. (However, they're not allowed to give academic credit for them.) The law schools could make a lot of money doing this. So, instead of jacking up students' tuition 10% or more every year, why don't they offer cram-courses?

First, they think it's beneath their dignity to teach students anything having to do with being able to practice law after they get licensed. (Just imagine if medical schools took that attitude toward future doctors —or if schools of engineering, architecture, or business did toward *their* students.) Second, and far more important, it would become immediately apparent to students that they had received virtually nothing as a return on their investment of time and money on their first-year courses, despite having been taught by profs at the very same law school. After all, the MBE (for all its perversity) *does* test your ability to "Think Like a Lawyer." So do the law school's fruitcake exams. *Both* test Black Letter Law. (Remember: the Multistate does *not* test *state-specific* statutes and case law, only general principles, just as do the first-year courses.) But the pedagogical malpractice of the law school professoriat would then become painfully obvious to everyone.

The California Model

California has many law schools that are not accredited by the ABA. To punish them, the ABA's adherents there got the state to establish the "Baby Bar Exam." For many years, only students at the non-ABA schools were required to take it. (Now, though, only students with certain backgrounds have to, regardless of school.)

It tests only three subjects: Contracts, Crim Law, and Torts. It's based on general legal principles, not on the law specific to California. (So, for example, the UCC principles are generic, rather than from California's statutory version of the UCC.)

Students take it at the end of their *first* year of law school. If they don't pass, they don't get to "sit for the bar" two years later—the "general" bar exam for *all* who want to get licensed in California.

Chapter 11 noted that state bar organizations release only the pass *rate,* school by school, on the barzam. And the chapter then said it would be more meaningful to reveal the average *scores,* school by school, on *each* area of the barzam.

But there should be a *national* exam for *all* students who've finished first year...and it should be a *performance* test (or a performance test and a multiple-choice test), on *all* of the Big Six subjects. No forced curve, no profs grading their own students' work (and thus creating the impression that SOME students have "gotten it" when in fact they haven't). The average scores would be released on a school-by-school basis. It would be glaringly apparent which schools were helping their students lay the foundation in first-year, and which weren't.

There really are, in fact, students who don't have what it takes. At present, the law schools allow those students to continue their studies, because *then the law school gets two more years of tuition and fees from those students.* (I won't mention any names, but certain schools flunk out many students—though only in their *final* semester. The schools know these students will *fail* the bar exam. So they protect the schools' "bar pass" rate by flunking out their weakest students...but only after getting their money for all three years of law school.)

By *statute,* states should require a *high* score on this new nation-wide "baby bar" exam, as a pre-requisite for sitting for the real bar (as California does now, at least with regard to *some* students). To avoid a large number of drop-outs at the end of first-year (and thus, to *keep the money rolling in*), the law schools would have to *make sure* that their profs who teach the first-year courses are *competent* in the subject matter and that they try to *teach* (for a change).

Looks like a "win-win" situation to me.

> For those schools trying to boost their prestige,
> it would be far better for them to be able to point
> to a record of producing students who come out
> on top of the rankings for this national "baby bar
> exam." Firms that hire "summer associates" would
> surely take notice...as would prospective law
> school applicants.

Unfortunately, in general, the faculty at the no-name law schools and at the also-ran law schools are no more interested in *teaching* than are the faculty at the big-name law schools. Even though this proposed national baby bar exam could benefit these schools and their students enormously, it is too risky for the professors themselves. And so, it will not happen. A school's prestige will always rest solely on the "quality" of its faculty's "scholarship." And in *that* game, the no-name schools and the also-rans don't stand a chance. But they really do not care. After all, they've got theirs.

Inquiring Minds Want to Know - Part II

However, there's another effect of the bar-cram system. At $2,200, the course is beyond many students' ability to pay for it. (I cannot think of any good reason why BarBri's costs have increased in the past five years sufficient to justify a *doubling* in the price of their course.)

> Law schools are rated, in part, on how many of their
> graduates pass the state bar exam on their first attempt.
> But because the law schools themselves make it clear
> that they are not interested in preparing their students
> to pass the bar exam, what the passage rate *really*
> measures is how many students *took a bar review course.*

So, another interesting bit of information that the powers-that-be are not about to disclose is how many students took a bar-cram course,* I do believe the bar exam people do not want to risk finding *proof* that success on the barzam is directly related to having taken a cram course.

And the reason for that is that *the logical next step would be to abolish the requirement that students attend law school* before "sitting for the bar." If all law school does (by its own admission) is to (allegedly) teach students "how to think like a lawyer," at least some people could learn how to do that on their *own*. Then those people ought to be able to take a cram-course whenever they wish. They could then take the bar exam immediately thereafter...without having spent a day in (or a dollar on) law school.

But, as noted above, there's also a discriminatory effect based on socio-economic class. Students at high-ranked schools have the wherewithal to shell out more than two thousand bucks for a bar-cram course. (They either have their own resources, or scholarships, grants, and loans. And quite often, future employers of graduates of the "name" schools pick up the tab for the bar review course.) Very often, students who attend low-ranked schools do *not* have the wherewithal for this. (They make just enough money to disqualify them from federally guaranteed student loans, and their grades and scores aren't high enough to get the scholarships and grants. And future employers of graduates of the also-ran schools do *not* pick up the tab for the cram course.) If my suspicion is correct, then the low barzam pass rates at many low-ranked schools are not because of any alleged inferiority in the "quality" of legal "education" students get at those schools, but *merely the result of their inability to pay for a bar-cram course.*

Thus, the law school system is rigged against students from poor backgrounds, despite all the lip-service given to diversity, etc. *This in turn has a major effect on the supply of students from poor backgrounds who would be willing to provide legal services to the poor.* But if they can't afford the bar-cram course, and thus don't pass the barzam, they (and their potential clients) are out of luck.

---

* And whose course they took. It's just possible that BarBri's pass rate is no better than that of its (two?) competitors, even though BarBri charges far more. (This is not to suggest, of course, that the law schools or the Multistate people or the bar exam people in the individual states are "in bed with" the BarBri people.)

(It is *racist* to assume that someone "of color" who goes to law school does so with the intention of returning to a supposedly poor neighborhood to provide legal services for "his—or her—people" at low cost. In general, those who get into the "name" schools—regardless of those students' color—want to make *big* bucks. Yet, few graduates of no-name schools have even a prayer of making big bucks after graduation. So it's a shame that many of them cannot even get a law license merely because they can't afford to take a cram-course that would enable them to pass the bar exam. But *these* might be the very people most likely to be willing to make a relatively modest living as lawyers serving the legal needs of people who are not well-to-do.)

The Wisconsin Model

As Chapter 19 said, Wisconsin has a "diploma privilege." Anyone who graduates from either of Wisconsin's two law schools can be licensed to practice law there without taking the bar exam...but only *if* the graduate took certain prescribed courses and received a certain grade or better in each of them. (This is interesting, because Wisconsin requires its law schools to get ABA accreditation—and the ABA forbids giving academic credit for what would otherwise be called "bar prep" courses. So the ABA apparently "looks the other way," perhaps because Wisconsin exempts from the bar exam those students who took those courses and received satisfactory grades in them. Thus, those courses are not "bar prep" courses. A nice loophole...and creative "lawyering," too.)

I am suspicious of the quality of those courses—but not because they're taught for the purpose of helping students avoid the "barzam." Rather, my suspicion is because Wisconsin's law schools use the same abysmal teaching methods as all the other law schools in the country.

As already mentioned, neither a bar-cram course nor the bar exam itself prepares students to practice law. So, the fact that Wisconsin has this qualified diploma privilege is not a problem. Rather, I mention it because *other states could easily follow Wisconsin's example.*

If they did so, each law school student could save as much as $2,000 or more (by not having to take a cram course). Plus, students would avoid the "opportunity cost" of having to take off weeks to cram. Instead, they could be on the job, making money.

But the most important effect would be that of removing the dicriminatory factor against students who lack the wherewithal to pay for the bar-cram course. And, as argued above, this means more law school graduates from lower socio-economic groups could quickly get licensed to practice.

Getting a Head Start, Yet Again

An on-site bar-prep course is a business. They're in it for the money. Nothing wrong with that, in and of itself. They want to maximize their efficiency—which means they want to minimize their costs, to get the highest possible profits.* So, they schedule their courses accordingly. In almost any state, there are several law schools. The cram companies don't start their courses until *all* the schools have recessed. This means, for a summer course, it won't begin until the first week in June. Everything is scheduled for the *company's* convenience (i.e., profits), not *yours.* They hire temporary help to put these things on, and they want those people on the payroll for the shortest time possible. (For example, the materials are mailed out to everyone at the same time, but not until shortly before the course begins— even though many students finished their final exams in law school *several* weeks before. So, they end up making your bar review even more frenzied than it would otherwise be, unnecessarily.)

Do not wait until your bar review course to start preparing for the bar exam. You won't have time to learn all the law you should have learned long ago. This is especially true regarding such arcane topics as the Rule Against Perpetuities in property law. By the time you get into a bar-cram course, it just isn't worth your while to spend time and effort on topics that you didn't understand *at all* before. You're looking for the *maximum* return on your investment, not a *diminishing* returns situation. You need to make sure you *totally* understand things you *thought* you understood before. However, by starting on the MBE practice questions before your third—or even *second*—year of law school, you can do *both:* fill in the big gaps in your knowledge *and* nail down the stuff you'd only "sort of" understood before. If you've already *mastered* the five first-year topics the MBE covers (as opposed to merely having passed your first-year courses in them), you won't have to spend much time on them. Bar review will truly be a *review.*

---

* One way they maximize their profits is by getting students to pay a "course reservation fee" during first-year. In return, students get a "locked-in price" for the course two years hence, even though the company has raised the price in the meantime. This so-called "reservation fee" is, in effect, a two-year, interest-free loan to the company. —Without mentioning any names, let's say there's a bar-cram company that has 35,000 students a year taking its course. And every one of those students paid a deposit of $100 during the fall semester of their first year. That's $3,500,000. If the firm gets a 10% return on its investments (a realistic figure), then, during the 34 months it holds those deposits, that $3.5 million, all by itself, yields compounded profits of a million bucks. Not bad.

Here's how to do it:

- Re-read your Master Outline for the first-year subjects on the MBE from time to time in your remaining two years of law school. (Your Master Outline is just supposed to trigger your memory regarding the details. You need to keep this stuff fresh in your mind. This review might help you in some of your advanced classes, too, when basic principles from first-year subjects come up again.)

- Read the student edition of the *Restatements* on Contracts and Torts between the end of first-year and the start of your prep course. (Those two subject comprise 40% of the MBE.) And get and study the materials on Property listed in the addendum to Chapter 16.

- Whether or not you take a course in Evidence, get the independent study materials on it, discussed in Chapter 19's addendum. As with the other materials, study them while you're still in school.

STORE-BOUGHT MULTISTATE BAR MATERIALS

However, there's only so much effort you can put in to reviewing your old Master Outlines, etc. Besides, as is clear from Chapter 23's discussion of the tricky-picky nature of the MBE, "merely" knowing *everything* about the law *isn't* enough. You need to get comfortable with examsmanship, MBE-style. That means you have to work Multistate practice-questions, which are multiple-choice. This is the best way to *test* your knowledge—and to cope with the devious nature of the MBE. At some point, you'll find it far more worthwhile to work through the questions and then see why your wrong answers were wrong, than it will be for you to simply keep studying the same old outlines, etc. You'll pick up a lot of nitty-gritty—and it's the nitty-gritty that the MBE tests. Because you'll be proceeding at your own pace, you don't have to worry about brain-overload.

One of the really nice things about the Multistate subjects is that (as the name implies) they're nationwide in scope. Unlike the state-specific part of a bar exam, no state legislature can overhaul the law, or even make minor changes. (The only exception to this is Con Law, where the U.S. Supreme Court sometimes changes a rule or two, one year to the next. But the Con Law questions are only 15% of the Multistate, which itself is—at most—50% of your combined final score on your state's bar exam. Thus, each Con Law question counts, at most, a mere one-quarter of one percent of your overall barzam score—and there are only two or three Con Law questions whose answers will change because of a new Supreme Court decision.) So, you can safely work through "old" questions.

Today, you don't have to wait until your bar-cram vendor provides you with materials shortly before its course begins. You can get such material on your own, from other sources:

Blond's®, the Sulzburger & Graham subsidiary that does commercial outlines, has a book titled *Blond's Multistate Questions,* with 1,000 practice multiple-choice questions and answers in it. It costs about $30 in paperback, and is available on disk for $50. Emanuel, another commercial outline publisher, does a book called *The Finz Multistate Method.* Its price is around $34. It contains nearly 1,200 practice multiple-choice questions (with answers and explanations) for the MBE. Steven Finz does a 1-tape, 1-hour lecture on audio cassette as part of the "Outstanding Professor" series of Sum & Substance (a subsidiary of West Publishing). It's called "Mastering Multiple Choice (MBE)," and costs $25. The Siegel's commercial outline for each subject costs about $16 or so. Each includes multiple-choice questions with answers, as well as sample essay questions with model answers. Gilbert, the Harcourt Brace subsidiary, has a 210-page book titled *Gilbert Law Summaries: Multistate Bar Exam,* for $18. Richard Conviser is the author. It has 200 sample questions are in it—so it appears to be more of a "how to" book than a practice-questions book.

Law-in-a-Flash® has a volume called *Strategies and Tactics for the MBE,* by Kimm Alayne Walton. This includes 550 Multistate questions and answers. It costs $35. Walton gives *excellent* advice on "How to Attack the MBE," including a great discussion of all the traps the MBE examiners set for the unwary. Even though her book only has 550 questions in it, it would be worth the price even without *any* questions. As you've seen, there are thousands of questions available in other materials, but her examsmanship discussion is unique. *Her* questions, for example, tell what sub-area each of the possible answers is in. That's *enormously* helpful as you try to pinpoint your weaknesses and work on them. Further, she gives points for each possible answer, and tells you whether you scored a hit, a near-miss, were wide of the mark, or failed to aim in the right direction in the first place. This too is of enormous help. If you're trying to decide which of these books to get first, this is the one.

You should get *several* MBE Q&A books, and work through them one after the other during your remaining two years of law school. If you can't find them in a law school bookstore, check for web sites.

You can save money by making a deal with one or more fellow students—such as those who were in your first-year study group. Split the cost evenly. Then each of you takes one book. Part of the deal has

to be that you won't put *any* marks in these books: You will not under-
line or otherwise mark any portion of the fact patterns, nor will you X
out what you think is a wrong answer, or circle or put a checkmark
next to what you think is the right answer. That would destroy the clean
slate the next person should have. (Make your own answer sheet.)   Nor
should you mark anything in the section that discusses the answers. Set
a deadline. When the deadline arrives, you swap books. Repeat the
process until everyone's worked every book. Then *start over*.

BAR-PREP VENDOR MATERIALS

You can get books of practice questions from the bar-cram vendors
too, of course. Harcourt Brace is the parent company of both BarBri
and Gilbert. Candidates get two Multistate Q&A books, one from each
subsidiary. The BarBri book has over 1100 practice questions; the
Gilbert, slightly more than 1300. During a BarBri course, students make
use of both of them. You can too—on your own.

But you can also get *substantive* materials. These contain text-only.
They cover the law itself: torts, property, etc. The self-help materials
discussed in previous chapters *don't* cover *everything*. The *bar-
prep* materials *do*—but *their* goal for you is memorizing, not *understanding*.

You should've gotten the self-help materials long ago. Then, right
after first-year, you should get the bar-cram Q&A *and* substantive materials. *You get them from someone who took the most recent bar exam.*

When someone takes a prep course, he or she has to pay a "materials deposit" of, say, $125. The deposit is refunded when the materials
are returned to the bar-cram company. (Funny coincidence, though:
the deadline for at least one company for returning the materials is
before the date when students find out if they passed the barzam. Many
students play it safe and keep the materials...and thus forfeit the deposit,
and add to the company's profits.)

If you try to buy these items separately, without signing up for the
bar review course, they cost $100-$150 *per book*—and there are
several volumes. Students rightly decide it makes more sense to pay
the extra money and get the lectures as well as the materials.

Here's how to get those books cheap: Make a deal with a third-
year student who's about to graduate. If the materials deposit is $125,
you offer—say—$175 for them. The student forfeits his or her own
deposit, and makes a 40% profit off you ($50). If you don't know any
graduating third-year students, post notices on the bulletin boards at
your school, offering to buy the materials. (You aren't limited to seeking
only BarBri's stuff. There are several bar prep firms.)

Generally, these people don't get their hands on these materials until they've already graduated. That means they probably won't be around the law school anymore. So, you have to connect with them before they leave. Further, bar exam results aren't announced until months later. (For those who take it in February, the results are announced in late April, usually. But because most people sit for the July bar, it usually takes a month longer to grade all the tests; scores don't come out until late October.) As mentioned, most students will probably want to keep their bar review materials until they find out if they passed. Therefore, you have to plan on a lag between making your deal with someone and getting that person's stuff.

Do not pay in advance, not even a deposit. Also, have more than one prospective supplier lined up: Law students (and lawyers, for that matter) are notoriously unreliable about keeping their promises. (However, you should be up-front about the fact that you have more than one potential supplier.) First-come, first-served.

Make sure it's understood you will be getting *clean* materials, with *no* marks in them. (That's one reason why you offer a nice premium over the materials deposit.) Different people like to mark different passages, and usually mark things in different ways, too. As with preparing your own personal outline, you want to be able to do what works best for *you*. The person who had these books can mark them in pencil. There's no need for him or her to use ink, including highlighters. Then you erase the pencil markings before using these books—and marking them up—yourself.*

If possible, get the substantive texts and the Q&A materials from at least *one* bar-cram vendor *far* ahead of time. It's worth paying $175 or more to get these from a graduating student, even though you'll be taking a bar-prep course later and getting (updated) materials then.

If you're splitting the cost with one or more other students, the same rules apply to the substantive materials as to the Q&A materials: no marks. That means no highlightings, no underlinings. Instead, make your own notes, *extensive* ones. By getting the materials far ahead of the bar review course, you'll have plenty of time to do this. (During a bar-cram course, you won't.) Your note-taking will help you learn the law much better than you would otherwise. So, it's worthwhile to get the substantive materials as well as the Q&A materials—*early*.

---

* True, if someone circled or crossed out answers in pencil, you can still see the mark after you erase it. But the way to deal with that is to put the *same* mark by *every* answer. Then erase these, too. You (usually) won't be able to tell which was the original. As for the pencil-markings of passages in the text or the answer-explanations section, don't worry: you'll be doing your own markings, in ink, and you won't notice the traces of the pencil marks you've erased.

Consolidate Your Strengths,
Eradicate Your Weaknesses

By dealing with the Multistate's narrow questions, you will be amazed at how you'll see connections you would otherwise have missed. You will often find yourself simultaneously understanding *both* the big picture *and* the nitty-gritty, in a comprehensive way you would not have dreamed of. Eventually, everything will come together for you. Several times, I had a "Eureka!" experience: "So *that's* what that point in first-year was all about!" Despite commercial outlines, *Restatements*, independent study books, and even the lectures during my bar review course, it was only the discussion of the answers to the MBE practice questions that cleared up many of the *finer* points of the law for me. *That's why you should start on this as soon as possible.*

It's just like doing your personal outlines: it takes time for the material to sink in. The earlier you start, the longer you'll work with it; the greater the likelihood it'll become second nature to you. Then, during the real thing, you'll *immediately* spot the possible answers that contain incorrect statements of the law. That saves you some time. You use that time to go over the facts *again, carefully*. (Very often, the *correct* answer is based on some seemingly minor detail. If you miss that detail, you miss the question—just as in the practice of law.)

Another important consideration is "the *call* of the question"—what the question is really asking. Sometimes, what at first seems to be a property question turns out to be a torts question, for example. And quite often, many of the facts given are irrelevant to the correct answer. By understanding the call of the question, you can immediately separate the useful from the useless.

When you test yourself, don't *guess* at any of the answers. Save that for the real thing, where a question not answered at all counts the same as a question answered incorrectly, i.e., zero. (So, the MBE rewards good guessing, and doesn't penalize bad guessing any more than it does a thoughtful answer that's wrong.) When practicing, it's better to leave the answer blank—and fill in your knowledge later—than it is to guess correctly and then fail to review the answer at all because you got it right. You may have guessed wildly and correctly on the practice question—but you almost certainly won't get so lucky on the real thing.

On practice questions, separate those you missed because *you didn't read the facts carefully enough* from those where you honestly thought the wrong answer was the right one. The day of the MBE, your concentration will be much better—although you should try to improve it beforehand. However, missing questions because you didn't understand the *problem*, or didn't know the *law,* is more serious. (Yes, a wrong answer is a wrong answer, regardless of the reason why. But the ability to stay focused is something you'll either have or you won't. And if you've truly mastered the law—and the quirks of the MBE—you'll find your concentration has improved. One hand washes the other.)

Although the right answer to any given question will be the same regardless of which company prepared the materials you're using, the different vendors sometimes explain the answers in somewhat different ways. Sometimes, one book's way of explaining a point of the law just won't "get through" to you. But some other's might. At least, that's the way it was for me. (And, surprisingly and culpably, you'll sometimes see the explanation one company gives *contradicts* that of another. If you start preparing for the MBE far enough in advance, you can find out which one is right.)

Unfortunately, and hard to believe, you will unintentionally start to memorize answers if you work through the same set of questions too soon after your previous round with it. That's bad. But if you get Q&A materials from several vendors, not just one, it will be much harder for you to accidentally slip into rote. It's also a reason to do your first round shortly after you finish first-year...and to then set the materials aside for *months*. In your spare time between vacations after Year One, you should keep re-reading your first-year Master Outlines and the *Restatements* on torts and contracts. You should also review the do-it-yourself study materials on evidence and property—especially the really difficult areas (hearsay in evidence, Estates and Future Interests in property).

If you can stand it, begin working Multistate practice questions during the summer vacation after your *first year* of law school, while the first-year curriculum is still fresh in your mind. Start with sets of questions that are all in the same category (contracts, torts, etc.). Get the do-it-yourself evidence materials and study them during that same vacation. Before returning to law school in the fall, you should have worked practice MBE exams with 200 questions drawn from all six Multistate categories, just like the real thing. During your winter vacation in second-year, answer the same questions all over again (another reason not to mark your question books up).

Believe it or not, you will find this process *enjoyable*. To return to an analogy used in Part I: It's like the pleasure you'll feel when you find you're actually *thinking* in the *foreign* language instead of mentally *translating* all the time. You'll feel a truly deep sense of satisfaction from this sense of *mastery*. ("Good God, I'm *getting* there. I might have 'what it takes' after all!")

Because there are only 200 questions on the Multistate, there are only so many points of law *your* MBE *will* test. If you've been working multiple-choice questions *far* in advance of the barzam, you'll have tested yourself on virtually every conceivable point of law that might be on the real thing. You will have answered many, many questions in each area of the law. If you don't know a given point of law, the pattern will become painfully obvious. So, put some time in on it, to improve your understanding.

Take careful notes on what you missed.
Save your corrected answer sheets.

Then, assuming you started practicing far enough ahead, you'll be able to take each practice exam a *second* time. Check to see if you're still missing questions in the same sub-area, especially if you're giving the *same* wrong answer each time. If so, you'll know what to do.

D-Day, H-Hour

During the Real Thing, you'll want to write down the numbers of the questions where you're not sure what the right answer was. If you have time left over after going through all 200 questions, review the difficult ones. I set up two columns on the cover of the exam booklet. In the first, I wrote down the numbers of those questions where I didn't have the foggiest idea what the right answer was, the first time through. I had guessed at the answer. (*Completely* skipping questions is dangerous —because when you go back you can easily lose track, and then you fill in the blanks for the wrong questions. —And you might not even have time to go back. So, better to fill in anything the first time around, then go back and erase it if and when you have time and decide that some other answer is superior to the one you'd originally guessed.)

In the second column, I wrote down the numbers of the—many more—questions where I thought I knew the answer, but wasn't sure. I'd also filled in an answer to each of these, of course.

At the end of the first pass-through, I still had about 20 minutes left. So I went over all the questions in the first column. Time ran out before I'd finished reviewing my answers to the questions in the second column. (One attorney who read this book in manuscript said he'd done it the other way around: He put his extra time in on those questions where he thought he'd picked the right answer earlier, and now just wanted to make *sure*. On those questions where he'd just made a random guess, he left his answers as they were, without a second look. As he explained it to me, "Why waste time on complete unknowns?" I disagree with him—but to each his or her own.)

Develop a system *you* feel comfortable with. Then use it during your timed *practice* exams.

If you already know the points of law, and can concentrate on the facts and the call of the question, it will make a *big* difference to your state of mind during the exam. While you can't exactly lollygag, you're just naturally much calmer, and more clear-headed. It's hard for me to explain this, but perhaps you've already had the feeling yourself—in which case you already know what I'm talking about. It's the difference between approaching something in fear and trembling, and approaching something with a quiet confidence. Then, even if you have a bad day, you'll still do all right. It's the difference between anxiety as to whether or not you'll even pass it, on the one hand, and being curious as to whether you'll *ace* it, on the other. (Notice the similarity concerning first-year?)

State-Specific
Essay Exam Preparation

If you concentrate on Multistate materials and working MBE questions between the end of first-year and the end of the first semester of third-year, you'll be way ahead of the game. In your final semester, you should continue working MBE questions. However, in that final semester you should begin *studying* (not just reading) state-specific materials. Then, in the time between your graduation from law school and the barzam, you want to concentrate on the state-specific materials. These are the "advanced" subjects.

The biggest decision most law school students must make regarding the bar exam is whether to take courses that cover subjects the barzam tests. If you hope to have a career in estate planning, you should take wills, estates, and trusts anyway. If you plan to be a trial lawyer in the state where your law school is located, you should take courses in that state's civil procedure anyway, not just for the bar exam. And so on. The question is whether to take something just because it's on the barzam, even though you're not at all interested in that subject.

No matter what courses you take, however, you will still be hit with a lot of strange and completely new material as part of your bar review course. (Having read Part I of this book, you know why.) In that sense, it will almost be like first-year, all over again—at a *much* faster pace.

The more that's completely new to you, the worse it will be for you in trying to memorize all of it in time. Therefore, better something (a course in law school) than nothing.

After first-year, I took only one course in a subject on my state's bar exam. It made a big difference concerning bar review, and I wished I'd taken more such courses. However, when I was in law school, I was unaware of the do-it-yourself materials. My law school's bookstore did not stock them. Indeed, many of them did not even exist then. So, you do not have to make the difficult choice I did.

> Whether or not you take a course after first-year that will be included on your state's bar exam, you should *still* get a primer for each new subject, if you can. As with prepping for *any* course, getting a head start never hurts. Study these materials during the vacation before the semester in which you'll be taking that course.

If you do *not* take a particular law school course that covers a bar exam subject, but have the materials mentioned above, then you should begin studying them during the summer vacation before your third year. —And if you have summer (law-related) employment, these materials just might help you on the job, too. At the latest, you should begin studying them during the winter vacation in Year Three.

The generic materials are good preparation. However, they won't be enough, because they aren't state-specific. To my knowledge, though, the only people who do *state-specific* materials are the bar review organizations. You should get these materials at the same time you get their MBE materials mentioned above. They'll help you to do better in your upper-level courses. (The materials deposit covers *everything*. So, when you pay a premium over that deposit, *you* should get everything too. —To make sure you don't get cheated by the law school graduate who's your supplier, call the prep firm and ask them to list all the materials candidates get in return for the materials deposit.)

And in your last semester of law school, you should *begin working essay questions from past bar exams*.

Bar exam candidates are not allowed to walk out with the *MBE* exam question booklets when they leave each session. (This probably has something to do with the fact that some questions will be repeated in later exams.) But in most states, those who take the *essay* exam *are* allowed to keep the questions. The bar-cram courses have been collecting these for years. Their materials for the *essay* exam subjects include actual essay questions from dozens of previous bar exams, and a model answer for every one of them. There are only so many major points of law the essay questions can test. So, if you work old essay exams, and compare your answers to the model answers, you *will* be prepared for *anything* on your state's essay portion of the barzam. (Exception: when the state legislature overhauls the law. However, even there, the lead time for preparing the essay exam is at least six months. —The lead time for the next Multistate is a *year*. Those who prepare the exam questions know what areas of the law are in flux. They'll *avoid* asking questions in those areas.)

Tape, not Live

If you've done well in law school, you'll probably already have a good job lined up before you graduate. If so, your future employer will almost certainly pay for your bar-cram course. (However, note: fewer employers are directly picking up the tab. Instead, they give you, say, $5000, for expenses—renting an apartment, moving, and the bar-cram course. It's up to you to allocate the funds.) In that case, take a bar review course—the most thorough one you can get, even though you've already done the things recommended above. But get it on *tape*.

On-site courses are often *presented* on tape: videotape. But nearly *all* of them do *audio* cassettes. (For those whose lectures are also on video, the audio cassettes have identical content, other than the absence of the picture, of course. The audio is taken from the video. — And, by the way, there are no visual aids on the videotapes.)

Listening to bar review tapes confers two big advantages over attending on-site lectures:

1. *You save a lot of commuting time.* You can spend this time studying, instead. Why spend 1-2 hours five or six days a week going to and from lectures that last 3-4 hours? (Actually, they're even shorter than that, because of breaks.) For a five-week evening-weekend course, that could total *30-60 wasted hours*. (There are the "intensive" bar review courses, too. For these, the ratio of class to commute time is much more favorable.) If you're working full-time, you normally would not be able to leave early enough to make a 6:00 bar review lecture every night. So, if you're doing an evenings-weekends bar review course, you'll be cutting back on your job. With tapes, you minimize the amount of time you're spending away from your tasks at work.

2. *You can progress at your own rate.* You can stop a tape to look something up in your written materials. And you can *replay* any portion of any tape. Can't do *that* with on-site live lectures or videos. Best of all, perhaps, you can listen to the cassettes when you're in a receptive mood, at your convenience. (By now, you know how hard it is to absorb lecture materials when you're in no condition for it.*) So, you can start reviewing far ahead of time—such as during your final semester of law school.

True, the on-site courses offer "real world" test conditions for taking mock exams. But you can always time yourself, and limit yourself to three hours for a 100-question MBE set. And you'll already have been through several high-stress time-pressured exams: your first-year finals, for example. You'll have already been through a less stressful multiple-choice exam, the MPRE. However, as always, it's your call.

> You need to be *highly* self-motivated to get your bar review just from the tapes, without attending lectures. It's very easy to procrastinate when you're on your own. The best way to protect yourself against this is to have a study group. Each of you takes the cassettes for one or two subjects. Just as with the MBE Q&A books, set a deadline. Each of you listens to his or her cassettes before that deadline. Then you get together and exchange them. Repeat until everyone in your group has heard all the tapes. This externally-imposed discipline might make up for your own possible lack of self-discipline.

---

* If you're working full-time (or even part-time) while preparing for the bar exam, you can listen to the cassettes while commuting. However, I found it difficult to absorb the material while in traffic. For me, listening while behind the wheel was something reserved only for subjects I already knew pretty well...of which there were few. However, if you commute by bus, train, subway, or carpool where someone else is driving, you can listen (through headphones) without distractions.

MNEMONICS

Mnemonic. Here's one: "**MADAM**—*M*nemonic: *A*ny *D*evice *A*iding *M*emory." See? ("KISS-A-MIC," on page 568 in Chapter 17, is another.)

Mnemonics aren't much help on the Multistate. But they're vital for the essay exam. Like a Master Outline for first-year courses, you should be preparing them long before it's time to take the exam. But like the Summary Outlines for Year One, you should be able to regurgitate all of them, very fast, on scratch paper before you start to work the essay questions during the bar exam. (As mentioned above, you should have largely finished your study of the first-year Multistate subjects *before* your *final year* of law school, and you should spend most of your final *semester* of law school studying for your state's essay exam. This final semester is when you should be developing mnemonics.)

Before I sat for the bar, I *bought* a set of mnemonics from someone who'd developed hundreds of them...only to find out the hard way that what worked so well for him didn't work at all for me. So I then made up my own. Often, I just reworked the mnemonics of others— including the ones I'd just bought, plus a smaller set I got from the bar review course. Here are two of my own:

Q: What are the "general intent" crimes?
(Mnemonic: "The General Intended to BARF.")
A: *B*attery, *A*rson, *R*ape, and *F*alse (Imprisonment)

Q: Who can be excused from jury duty (petit or grand)?
(Mnemonic: "APES can be excused from Juries.")
A: The *A*ged (over 65), a single *P*arent with sole responsibility for a child under 10, any other *E*xcuse the court thinks okay, and full-time *S*tudents

One way to practice these is to do two sets of flash cards. The first set consists of 3x5 index cards cut up into 1x3. On one side, put an abbreviated form of the question. On the other, put just the acronym of the mnemonic, all by itself. Example: Front— "General Intent Crimes" Back— "BARF."

The second set consists of 3x5 cards, too, but full-size. On the front, write out the entire question. On the back, write the full mnemonic horizontally across the top. Then write the acronym vertically on the left side.

Example:

Front— "Who can be excused from jury duty, whether petit or grand?"

Back—

APES can be excused from Juries.
    A - <u>Aged</u>: over 65
    P - single <u>Parent</u> with sole responsibility for a child under 10
    E - any other <u>Excuse</u> the court thinks valid
    S - full-time <u>Student</u>: high school, college, grad school, etc..

From time to time, take a few minutes and check the 1x3 cards, to see if you can still remember the MADAM. Then, less frequently, use the 3x5 cards to test your detailed knowledge.

(I have my doubts as to how well mnemonics work for first-year courses, because the memorization required there consists of the elements of causes of action. Besides, you should know them so well that you don't need mnemonics, any more than you need them to recite the ABCs.)

More on Timing—and Priorities

As Chapter 20 said, after first-year, try to arrange your credit load so that by the time you reach your *last* semester you'll only need to take the *minimum* number of credits required to maintain full-time student status (and to graduate). During your final semester, you review all your first-year Master Outlines again, and anything else you need—the primers, for example. Then you re-work all the MBE practice questions you did before. You should also review all the tapes and written materials for the essay subjects that will be on your state's bar exam. If you'll be tested on federal and state civil and criminal procedure, you should be memorizing all those rules. And you should be working on your mnemonics. Then get *new* materials and start going over those. This includes answering the new MBE practice questions and past real-life essay exam questions.

If you do this, then by the time you start a formal bar review course after graduation, you will already be in excellent shape for your state's bar exam.

* * *

Based on your educational experiences so far, by now you're thinking this entire book sounds crazy. And it *does*: "Classes are the least important part of law school," "Making Law Review is the most important thing of all," and now, *"Start preparing for the bar exam as soon as you've finished first-year."* It's all topsy-turvy, and seems to stand common sense on its head.

Once you're in law school, you'll see and hear with your own eyes and ears, and you will know that's the way it has to be—if you want to *thrive,* not just *survive.* I did not design this crazy law-school set-up ...and if I were King of the Forest, I'd certainly do some clear-cutting and removal of deadwood. As it is, all I can do is show you the least difficult way through this thickest of all the groves of academe.

* * *

Perhaps you're thinking, "Hey, 'Atticus,' this is too much work." Fact is, you're going to have to work hard in law school, no matter what...if you hope to do well. But—to again quote the Opening Statement—the only question is whether you'll be working *smart,* too. Even though working smart is also hard work, it's actually *less* hard than *just* working hard. The choice is yours.

Come bar review time, even if your employer gives you a mini-sabbatical to study for the barzam, you won't get *much* time off. Regardless of whether or not you get a break, you don't want to get into a frenzy similar to what most students experience. —And if you do *not* get time off, or not *enough,* you will probably be a nervous wreck by the time of the bar exam. In the meantime, you will probably have neglected your duties at work. (And by the way, see if you can at least cut back to half-time during the six weeks before the barzam.)

Although most students pass the bar exam on the first try, a substantial minority fail. (Interestingly, most who fail it the first time fail it the second time, too. I met a law school grad who'd flunked the California bar *four* times.) The stigma of having failed the bar exam is severe. The late John F. Kennedy, Jr., could afford it (literally—and *twice*) but for the average person, flunking often leads to a pink slip at the office. (You'll have to wait roughly six months for the next exam; and don't forget the months afterward, before the results are announced. In the meantime, without a license, you can't perform some of the work you were hired to do. This includes signing off on documents as attorney of record, and making occasional court appearances.) It's *very* embarrassing for your employer to have a flunker around—and lawyers *hate* to feel embarrassed.

Even if you don't get fired, failure hinders your career prospects. Your dossier will always remind your supervisors that you flunked the bar the first time around. However, failure—even repeated failures— don't necessarily doom your career prospects: several prominent lawyer - politicians flunked it more than once. (Perhaps, though, that's why they went into politics; after being forced out of the firms they worked for.)

You ought to start on the bar exam early—much earlier than you would normally think prudent—because 1) you want to make sure you pass it the first time, and 2) when you're pouring it on in the home stretch of your bar review, you want to still be able to take it in stride. (Also, the chances are very good you're going to be quite bored in second- and third-year...especially third-year.)

There are even more good reasons to start early. They're discussed at the end of this chapter.

If You Have to Go It Alone

It's possible that, despite following the recommendations of *Planet Law School,* you will *not* be an exceptional law school student. (Maybe, for some reason, you will have put most of your energy into your love life. Or maybe you're one of those people who "freezes up" during an exam.) Or maybe, for whatever reason, you've decided not to practice law, but want to get the law license anyway, just in case whatever it is you *do* want to do doesn't work out; so you're sloughing off on grades. In any of these circumstances, you must either then pay for a bar-prep course yourself, or else forgo it. I recommend the former. A bar-cram course is a *structured* program. And it makes you work harder than you otherwise would.

Again, get it on tape—even though a program on tape costs more than the same program presented on-site. In addition to the advantages already stated, you can split the cost with fellow bar exam candidates. As mentioned, use the same rotation system as was recommended for sharing the Multistate Q&A books. (However, if you're *really* pinched for funds, consider getting only the *state* bar review tapes.)

Let's say you can get state-only materials for $600 (a realistic figure). If you can get just two other people to go in with you, that's $200 apiece. Each of you has saved $400 right there. (Each of you will also have to chip in for a refundable security deposit on the tapes.) Then share the tapes, as discussed above.

HOW to GET a FREE BAR REVIEW COURSE

Most of the bar-prep firms have on-site student representatives at each law school. In large schools, they have a rep in each section of the first-year class. The sales push begins in the very first semester of law school. If the student rep signs up X number of his or her fellow students, the rep gets a free bar-cram course.

So, as soon as you know you're going to a particular law school, call the bar review companies. Tell them you want to be a student rep at your school. (If you're going to a large school, maybe you should find out what section you're assigned to before you call.) —And when you call, don't refer to them as cram courses: They take offense at that. See if you can get the name and phone number of a current rep at your (future) school, and then talk with that person.

Try to get an exclusive agreement in *writing*—i.e., a contract saying you will be the only rep for your section, or the only rep for your entire first-year class, as the case may be. Make sure there's a clause concerning the grounds for getting fired, and what compensation you receive based on your performance to date. If you exceed the number of sign-ups you need to get a free course, you ought to get a cash commission for the extra ones. If so, be sure to find out *when* you get the money. You should also try to get a *free* set of Multistate Q&A (and substantive) materials at the end of *Year One*. Get your state essay review materials early, too. —And get the course on tape, during your final semester of law school.

Because BarBri is the biggest, start there. Then go down the list. But even if BarBri is receptive, don't stop there. You might be able to get a better deal from another firm. —Some of them might not presently be using campus reps. If so, the first test of your ability to make a sale is to sell the firm on the idea of making an exception for *your* school, using *you* as its rep. (This can work even with home-study courses, if you do it right.)

Another thing: Find out if any of the lecturers for a given bar-prep course are professors at *your* school. *That's* the firm you want to represent. (Chapter 13 said professors can be just as petty and vindictive as you or I. One way to find this out for yourself is to be in a course with a professor who's a lecturer for a bar review company that you don't represent. —Because of my law school's prominence, several of its faculty members do bar prep lectures. All work for the same bar-cram company. Their clout with the administration is such that for years the dean's office tacitly banned all other bar-prep firms from soliciting business within the walls of the law school. Then these professors used *class* time to urge students to sign up with the bar-cram company *they* lectured for.* No rival company's student rep dared speak up in protest. —This is a big-bucks business, and hardball tactics are the norm. The image of the law school as an ivory tower is deceiving. (And no, I was not a student rep for one of the shut-out firms.)

Also, as a rep, you'll have more occasion to talk with students than you otherwise would. This isn't a matter of mere socializing. As Chapter 11 mentioned, you'll be dealing with these people, lawyer-to-lawyer, someday. The better you know them, the better.

BAR REVIEW COURSES: VENDORS

I am aware of seven bar-prep firms that operate on a national scale: America's Bar Review (a.k.a. the Reed Law Group), BarBri, BarPlus, Micromash-Nord, PMBR (which stands for "Preliminary Multistate Bar Review," though they never spell it out), and The Study Group. There are others that operate only within one or several states. You will need to find these on your own, when the time comes.

Some are "deluxe," some aren't. Some are just on-site, others just on tape or via home study, and still others offer both. Some will give you practice essay exams and will then grade each answer individually and tell you where you're strong, where you're weak. Some give a money-back guarantee or a reduced rate for a re-run if you fail the bar exam. Be sure to ask. And if the answer is "Yes," get it in writing. (It should be part of the standard contract, though.)

> To repeat: assuming that you do take a full-scale bar-prep course, any bar-cram course stresses only the key points. These are the items that have repeatedly been tested on your state's bar exam (and the MBE). That's the nature of the beast, given the time constraints of the course. The odds are that those points of law *will* be tested again on *your* exam. But if you've been studying *well ahead of time,* you'll already know *all* the key points and a lot *more.* That way, if what your bar-prep course emphasizes gets slighted on *your* bar exam, you'll *still* be prepared— because you studied the "possible" *as well as* the "probable" exam material. That's called *insurance.*

---

* Things are not as they were in Dean Langdell's time at Harvard Law School. Today, in all university-affiliated law schools in America, the faculty—not the deans—are in charge. Deans are hired to do three things: [Cont'd on next page.[

(Again) Killing Two Birds with One Stone

Even if you take a *deluxe* bar exam preparatory course (MBE/MPT plus state-specific), whether free or not, try to follow the recommendations of this chapter. By doing so, you kill two birds with one stone.

The first is what's already been said: by starting early, you minimize the strain of studying for the bar exam—and maximize your chance to pass it the first time around.

The second involves a longer-run view. Low as the image of lawyers is, laypeople still *trust* lawyers to *know the law.* —They have *no choice,* at least in this regard...because that's what a layperson goes to an attorney for. There are many, many basic principles of the law that any lawyer *should* know. Even if you leave out specialized areas such as Estates and Future Interests, and Evidence, there are hundreds of basic principles of the law that *every* lawyer should know. But in fact, few do. (No attorney can know it *all,* however. In fact, no attorney can know more than a tiny percentage of the law. Even so, my statement still holds, regarding basic principles.)

People think students learned these basic principles in law school. But, as Part I showed, the reality is otherwise. Later, the (future) attorneys were supposed to have learned these things for the bar exam. And maybe they did. But that "learning" involved cramming thousands of points of law into their heads. They held them there just long enough to get a passing score. After that, they forget nearly all of them. And once they have their ticket (i.e., law license), there's little incentive to go over any of them again. They—maybe—look up what they need to know to do what they have to do; the rest is out of sight, out of mind.

So what's wrong with that?

For starters, people hit on attorneys for free legal advice. It's a real ego trip to have someone sucking up to you because of your (supposed) expertise—especially if it's someone who's a big-shot, or someone you find sexually attractive. It's just human nature to puff oneself up a bit when the opportunity arises. No reason why lawyers should be any different.

---

1) raise money, 2) deal with the university administration, and 3) run such mechanical operations as alumni affairs, student admissions, placement, and the hiring of non-faculty staff. The typical dean doesn't stay on the job very long—and even many of the top schools are having trouble getting the best people to accept an offer.

Few lawyers have the humility to say "I don't know" when asked a question—especially if the person asking the question is someone you want to impress. Regardless, few people want to appear ignorant—especially if they know the other person thinks it's something he or she *ought* to know, cold. Most laypeople will resent it if a lawyer says "That's not my area of the law" and then explains that it would take some legal research to find the answer. They'll think the lawyer's a "typical greedy bastard attorney," who doesn't want to give anything away he or she can charge for. They honestly believe there are some things *any* lawyer should know, just by virtue (ah, the irony) of being a lawyer.

And they're *right*.

So, the attorney gives an answer off the top of his or her head. Usually it's the *wrong* answer. It might not be *dead* wrong, but it's seldom *as* right an answer as it *should* be.

Okay, say you don't care about giving bad advice to freeloaders. Say you don't care one of them later finds out how wrong you were, and bad-mouths you to anyone who'll listen. Say you don't care you might lose some potential business as a result.

Okay. So here's the second thing wrong with not knowing basic legal principles. Here's something you *definitely* should care about:

If you work the Multistate questions regularly, and set aside ample time to truly master the state-specific material for the essay portion of your state's bar exam, *you'll gradually build up a general awareness, a sense of additional relevant points of law in any given situation.* And so, when you're working on a problem on behalf of a *paying* client, there will be things that will come to mind you might not otherwise have thought of. "Seems to me, I remember—somewhere in the back of my mind, something about…"

Your gut feel will alert you to the possibility of something "out there" that you might be able to use. If you check it out, you might get a pleasant surprise.

If you truly *know* the basic principles of the law, you will be constantly amazed at how ignorant so many of your fellow attorneys are regarding those same basic principles. The general level of ignorance of this "learned profession" is truly astonishing. *You* be the *exception* to the *rule*. This is where you can out-maneuver your opponent. This is where you can build a reputation as a *good lawyer*. (Having a reputation as a good lawyer will often get you the benefit of the doubt in a close-call situation.)

It may be hard for you to imagine it now, but being well-respected by other *attorneys* as a craftsman (crafts-person?) of the law might someday be important to you. After all, other lawyers (particularly in your specialty, if you have one) will know the law better than your clients will, by definition. The respect of your clients will be crucial, of course. But they're like the audience at a jazz nightclub: the musicians are there because the audience is willing to pay for the performance. And the musicians respond with tunes that are "crowd-pleasers." That's as it should be. However, the really *good* musicians are actually playing for *each other.* It's great for them to be making money, and to be popular. But what they *most* value is the *respect of their fellow musicians.*

You will find that what truly warms your heart as an attorney (other than a fat check that doesn't bounce) is the awareness that other *good* attorneys respect *you.*

And if you don't care about *that,* then please do the world a favor: Don't go to law school.

**There are far too many lawyers in this country as it is...
just far too few *good* ones.**

Part VIII:

Deeper Games

Chapter 25: The Games beyond the Games

The games that most concern law students in the short run are the hide-the-ball and the bait-and-switch. But the law school plays some deeper games, too—games beyond the games.

The "Haves" v. the "Have-Nots"

Law school has no labs, such as the graduate schools in the sciences do. It has no need for fancy equipment such as a physics department or medical school has. And the student-teacher ratio at all law schools is notoriously bad. So why do the schools charge so much?

Granted, as Chapter 9 noted, if the law school is affiliated with a university, the parent institution rakes off as much as 40% of the law students' tuition to subsidize its other schools that are more costly to operate. And granted, the law profs want to make big bucks for their 6–8 hours a week of "work."

There's another reason, however. Consider the ABA's effort to increase law school profs' salaries—which practice, as Chapter 9 stated, was (supposedly, but even so, only until 2006) ended by a settlement agreement in the federal government's antitrust suit against the ABA. Pushing profs' salaries up had the effect of *pushing students' tuition up*.

The ABA's effort on behalf of law professors was not a matter of the right hand (the parent organization) not knowing what the left hand (the accreditation committee and council) was doing. On the contrary. The ABA's president defended the practice. (Because the feds did not seek damages in their suit, it would have cost the ABA nothing had its president admitted its accreditation practices were corrupt.)

Something else that pushes students' tuition up is the ABA's requirement, still in effect, that law schools have ample libraries. Accreditation Standard 606 says a law school has to have a "core collection" in its law library. The list of what's required in that "core collection" is about what you'd expect: case reporters, statutes, regulations, and so forth. The library's collection must "meet the research needs of the law school's students, satisfy the demands of the law school curriculum, and facilitate the education of its students." But the accreditation committee (and eventually, the Council, as discussed in Chapter 9), gets to decide (in secret) whether a law school's library "meets" these needs.

In your first-year legal research course, you likely will be given some assignments that require you to know your way around the law library, and to look some things up in law books of various types. However, in your other first-year courses, or in any of your courses in second- and third-year, you will not likely need to look at even one book in the law library, and certainly not more than half-a-dozen. (Exception: if you take a seminar that requires you to write a paper based on legal research.) Yet, the ABA requires each law school to have a law library *vastly* larger than its students could ever possibly need. Why?

The ABA's Hypocrisy

If the ABA and the accreditation committee were sincere in their insistence that what might be called "library overkill" is essential to a good legal "education," how to explain their Interpretation 601-1 to Standard 601? It concerns law school libraries, and says "Standard 601 is *not* satisfied by arranging for the students and faculty to have access to *other* law libraries within the region." (Emphasis added.)

If what counts is ensuring *access*, what difference does it make who *owns* the books? Several law schools could pool their resources to establish one library for the students of all those schools—a library far better than what any one of those schools could fund. And the law libraries supported by taxes or bar associations would surely welcome an arrangement whereby a law school paid a fee so its students could have access to that library—at a fraction of what it would cost the law school to create its own library. *If* the ABA and its accreditation people from the law schools were *sincerely* concerned about providing good resources for law students, wouldn't it make sense to have rules that enable law schools to maximize *efficiency and productivity* with regard to law libraries?

The burden hits the *freestanding* law schools especially hard. Most of them are in big cities. And in most big cities there are ample law libraries open to the public: county and city bar association law libraries, etc. Most of the independent law schools' students are commuters. They have no problem commuting to the school—and would have no problem going to a library located off-premises. But nope, the ABA says the school itself has to shell out for the books.

Is it just a coincidence that Interpretation 601-1 was put in final form in August, 1996—just two months after the settlement agreement was made that banned the ABA from using faculty salaries as the basis for denying accreditation to a law school?

The Hidden Motive

As legal education was being tranformed after 1870, the "better law schools" did not want people from the "lower orders" as students. And so, the admissions requirements were skewed in the direction of rich kids. For example, for *years* after Langdell assumed its deanship, Harvard Law School required applicants to translate the following into English:

> Sacra Dionaeae matri divisque ferebam
> Auspicibus coeptorum operum, superoque nitentem
> Caelicolum regi mactabam in litore taurum.
> Forte fuit nixta tumulus, quo cornea summo
> Virgulta et densis hastilibus horrida myrtus.
> Accessi, virdidemque ab humo convellere silvam
> Conatus, ramis tegerem ut frontendibus aras,
> Horrendum et dictu video mirabile monstrum
> Nam, quae prima solo ruptis radicibus arbos
> Vellitur, huic atro linquuntur sanguine guttae
> Et terram tabo maculant.*

The "respectable" law schools also excluded those who were "undesirable" on the basis of their race or religion. (Roscoe Pound, who eventually became dean of Harvard Law School, once wrote about how ridiculous was the very idea that a "Chinaman" could be fit for the study of law.)

Even after many schools "lowered their standards," and began admitting non-WASPs (and women), the major law *firms* refused to hire them. For example, in his book *The Betrayed Profession: Lawyering at the End of the Twentieth Century*, Sol L. Linowitz (who overcame substantial prejudice against Jews to become a pillar of the legal Establishment) wrote:

---

* And you thought the *LSAT* was rough.

Until 1943, like most professional (and sports) associations, the American Bar Association explicitly banned Afro-Americans from membership; the first blacks were not admitted until 1954. In 1956...Mario Cuomo [a white, Italian-American Catholic who later became Governor of New York] on graduation from Saint John's Law School could not even get an interview with any of the eighty-four firms to which he applied...Women were not admitted to Harvard Law School until 1950...

Repression, Resistance, and Revised Repression

Mary Ann Glendon, a Harvard law professor, comments in her book, *A Nation Under Lawyers:*

> The distaste of the "better class" of lawyers for litigation, coupled with the large firms' lack of interest in plaintiffs' personal injury, criminal, and domestic relations work, left niches for others. This created opportunities that were especially welcome to the Irish, Italian, and Eastern European Jewish lawyers who appeared on the scene in the great wave of immigration between 1891 and 1920.

As she noted, one of the opportunities was in litigation: filing suits on behalf of "the little guy" against the huge corporations (especially the railroads, oil companies, and manufacturers) that were, in those years, achieving dominance of the American economy. (When the big corporations had disputes, they settled them behind closed doors—often with an important banker acting as the mediator, because the major banks owned a large percentage of the shares in many of these corporations. This was true until quite recently in American business. And it's the way things are done even today in Japan and Germany, where the banks still dominate the industrial companies. —The American "litigation explosion" of recent decades resulted from *corporations'* abandoning mediation in favor of going to court over their disputes.)

It wasn't necessary to go to a "respectable" law school to get the ticket to "sit for the bar" (exam). To provide legal education to non-WASPs, freestanding law schools sprang up. Nearly all were night schools, because their prospective students—unlike the well-to-do who attended "respectable" law schools—could not afford to give up their jobs to become full-time (day) students.

(Walter Reuther, the longtime leader of the United Automobile Workers in the 20th century, took night school law courses while working in a Ford Motor plant by day. Those courses perhaps aided his rise to union leadership and his ability to deal with the auto manufacturers.)

It didn't take long for America's legal Establishment to retaliate. One way was through the "minimum fee schedules" the ABA created and urged all bar associations to require. Attorneys who charged less than the minimum fee for a service were taken before a grievance committee and disciplined. These minimum fee schedules were struck down by the Supreme Court as a restraint of trade only after a *century* of use.

Most commentators say that the purpose of the MFS was to help lawyers feather their nests. But arguably, the real purpose was to deliberately price legal services beyond the reach of most people—the people who were being systematically victimized by the major corporations whose lawyers dominated, and still dominate, the ABA. Holding the prices high, across the board, reduced the demand (by those who lacked the wherewithal) for legal services. Reducing demand reduced the supply—the supply from non-WASP lawyers who would otherwise serve non-WASP clients—by reducing the supply of non-WASPs who were willing to invest in becoming lawyers.

Likewise, the ABA's "Model Rules" banned all advertising by lawyers. (Again, it took a century for this to be struck down by the U.S. Supreme Court.) As the ABA knew, the ban on attorney advertising worked a great hardship on the poor and less well-to-do, especially when seeking lawyers to represent them against the wealthy and powerful. The latter *already* had a transactions lawyer or law firm on annual retainer. They could easily get the name of an *excellent* trial attorney to defend them against lawsuits filed by the little guys, who did not know where to turn even for merely *competent* trial counsel.

But as long as there were schools where those from the "lower orders" could go with the intention of serving "their people" when they graduated, more was required than minimum fee schedules, bans on advertising, and keeping "undesirables" out of the "respectable" schools.

So the ABA tried to put the night schools out of business. This is where the claim of "maintaining standards" in legal education arose—and the ABA's role in accrediting law schools.

This is not the place to go into that story in detail (although I intend to in a forthcoming book). Suffice it to say, the effort was almost completely successful. Largely, this was because influential lawyers who belonged to the ABA convinced their states' supreme courts or legislatures to require all in-state law schools to be ABA-accredited. Today only a handful of independent law schools still exist as survivors from the ABA's campaign to destroy them. (Chicago's John Marshall Law School is one. Houston's South Texas College of Law is another.)

Eventually, of course, the ABA and the "respectable" law schools realized that they could not continue as just the enclave of upper-middle class male WASPs. So the racial and gender discrimination finally ended. But the ABA, on behalf of the corporate attorneys who controlled (and still control) the legal profession, continues its own version of *class warfare*. Even today, it seeks to destroy the freestanding night schools—or to price them beyond the reach of the "lower orders" (including male WASPs who are not well-to-do).*

For example: as part of the continuing effort to make it impossible to obtain low-cost legal education, the ABA's newest Standard (promulgated December 7, 2001) says that "distance education" credits will be available only to students who attend a *residential* law school" (that is, *only* to *full-time day students*).

No doubt, some readers will say this is nonsense. What about "affirmative action"? After all, many students from "underprivileged" (racial minority) backgrounds are not only admitted to big-name schools, they're given a free ride there.

But most of the members of racial minorities who benefit from affirmative action come from well-to-do backgrounds themselves. They already have far more in common with stereotypical white law students than with other people of color, at least socio-economically. Further, where do those students end up working? For their fellow "underprivileged"? For "public interest" groups? Of course not. They sell out—as do the WASPs from the "privileged" backgrounds. That's the American Dream (and indeed, the story of "humanity"). There's no reason to expect them to be any different. The result is that they kiss the old days goodbye, and move on to a new life among the Fat Cats…serving the interests of the Fat Cats, of course. And so the *class* war *continues*.

---

* True, Georgetown has a night program, and GULC is one of the top law schools in the country. But every rule has its exception. And Georgetown is a university.

Anatomy of the Murder of a Law School

Consider the experience of Atlanta's John Marshall Law School (not to be confused with Chicago's school of the same name). It was founded in 1933, as a night school. Its tuition has always been low. For decades, it met the accreditation requirements of the State of Georgia, and did not seek ABA accreditation. The school's brochure tells the story:

> In 1978, the Supreme Court of Georgia promulgated standards and procedures for the approval of law schools, and set forth an application process similar to the accreditation process of the American Bar Association (ABA). Under these new rules, law schools were required to submit to annual inspections until final approval was granted. After gaining its initial approval, John Marshall Law School had its approval renewed after each subsequent inspection between 1978 and 1987.
>
> In 1987, the Supreme Court of Georgia changed its 1978 promulgation to require that all law schools meet the standards set forth by the ABA. To meet the goal of ABA accreditation, the John Marshall Law School Board of Trustees endorsed an ambitious plan of adding approximately 50,000 volumes to the School's law library; increasing the number of faculty members fourfold; purchasing, renovating and furnishing a 60,000 square-foot building; and installing a state-of-the-art computer network.

Law books are *expensive*. I don't know what those 50,000 volumes cost, but $3,000,000 is a ballpark figure. Students' tuition was increased, of course, to help foot the bill.

Yet, the ABA refused to accredit the school, and still refuses, even though the school has existed for *70 years* now, and has graduated hundreds (perhaps thousands) of lawyers who had successful careers. Not surprisingly, enrollment has fallen off drastically. It's unlikely the school will survive. That's the *idea*. (And if the ABA's minions in Massachusetts can get that state's supreme court to do what Georgia's did, the days of the Massachusetts School of Law will be numbered, too.)

The HLS Umbrella

This raises another question: Why does Harvard Law School cost more than $25,000 a year? (And that's just for the tuition.)

Harvard University has an endowment, as of this writing, of nearly $20 *billion*—by far the largest in the entire world. So, the parent institution does not need to skim funds from the law school the way most universities do. Further, the law school has its *own* endowment—of nearly a *billion* dollars. (In 1995, the school sought to raise $130 million...and received *183* million. Six years later, it raised another *$203 million*. And in the spring of 2003, it began yet *another* fund-raising drive, seeking *$400* million...of which it had already raised $170 million even before the drive was publicly announced.)

HLS claims it needs this bloated endowment for the same reasons all other law schools give: professors' salaries, new buildings, scholarships for students, etc., etc., etc. Nonsense. HLS could easily drop its tuition to $3,000 a year. Then it wouldn't need to provide so much for scholarships. (Note: Scholarships provided by the law school don't take money out of the law school's pocket the way scholarships provided by a foundation take money out of the foundation's pocket. For the law school, it's just a bookkeeping entry. The scholarship just keeps the law school from getting as much money from the student as it otherwise would have. But the big advantage of charging high tuition, and then giving a big scholarship, is this: the student is *grateful* for the scholarship, naturally. So, when he or she is out making big bucks in the real world, the law school comes a' callin', to ask for a return on its "investment." And, of course, the student is nearly always happy to oblige. Harvard Law School has *perfected* this system, but virtually all law schools work the same way.)

By charging close to $30,000 a year for tuition alone, despite its stupendous wealth, HLS accomplishes two things:

1. HLS grads have virtually *no choice* but to seek jobs with the big law firms that serve the interests of the wealthy and powerful, because it's those firms that pay the big bucks the students need to pay off their student loans.

2. All other law schools in the country can base their tuition on Harvard's. (In business, this is called a "price umbrella." If the dominant firm is charging $X for a product, and that price is a high one, other firms can charge less than $X and still make a decent profit.) Thus, Michigan, despite being a public law school, can get away with charging more than $23,000 per year, as *in*-state tuition. And because it and so many other schools are charging high tuition, *their* graduates *also* have

almost no choice but to try to go to work for the big law firms that serve the interests of the wealthy and powerful.

Between Harvard Law School's "price umbrella," and the ABA's deliberate policies of needlessly inflating the cost of a law degree, would-be lawyers are caught between a rock and a hard place.

The Role of Pedagogical Malpractice - Part One

The curriculum that was established at Harvard Law School in the early 1870s is the standard curriculum at all law schools in the country. Those were also the years, as mentioned, of the rise of the big corporations in America, and the foundation of stupendous personal fortunes. The HLS curriculum sought to serve their interests.

For example, first-year Property courses cover Estates & Future Interests, including the notorious Rule Against Perpetuities. Yet, only perhaps one-tenth of one percent of all practicing attorneys will ever have anything to do with a situation that involves Estates & Future Interests—and the (C)RAP. Those topics belong only in an upper-level course...not the *basic* course in Wills, either, but a course in Estate Planning or Trusts.

But this first-year curriculum is still tacitly *mandated* by the ABA. A school that disregards it jeopardizes its accreditation. And the influence of the ABA is sufficient that, for example, Estates and Future Interests are an important part of the Property section of the Multistate Bar Exam...which is supposedly intended to test the *basic* legal principles that *all* attorneys *need* to know.

Two-thirds of all attorneys in private practice are *sole* practitioners. They provide legal services to the middle and lower classes, in family law, criminal law, simple real estate matters, employment law (sometimes), and consumer protection. What they need is simultaneously far less and far more than what's in the first-year curriculum.

True, the graduates of Harvard, Yale, Stanford, etc., are unlikely to become sole practitioners. But even if *all* the graduates of, say, the Top 20 law schools in the country, were to go to work on behalf of the rich and powerful, they total less than 6,000 new lawyers annually. This is less than 15% of all law graduates each year. Yet, *all* law schools in the country *require* courses that will make their graduates conversant with the subject matter of interest *only* to the wealthy and powerful.

True, too, graduates who become sole practitioners or small-firm attorneys can take Continuing Legal Education courses to "get up to speed" in a subject. But CLE courses are expensive. They're put on by law schools and bar associations to make a big profit. (The speakers at these programs do not get paid. They do it for free because it allows them to add it to their credentials as experts on the subject in question.) Further, most sole practitioners and small-firm attorneys cannot afford to take time away from the job to attend a CLE course. (With a sole practitioner, there obviously is no lawyer left in the office to "cover" for the absent attorney.)

But this bothers the ABA, the Association of American Law Schools, and the law schools themselves...not at all.

The Role of Pedagogical Malpractice - Part Two

Even in first-year courses that contain subject matter that all future attorneys (including solos and small-firm lawyers) need to know, the law schools practice hide-the-ball and bait-and-switch, as discussed in Part I and in Chapter 8. Thus, knowledge of the law and learning how to "think like a lawyer" is *denied* to all but those who are regarded as "natural-born geniuses of the law."

The wealthy and the powerful are represented by attorneys from the law factories, which only hire those at the top of the class. The wealthiest and most powerful of all, of course, are represented by attorneys from the wealthiest and *most* powerful of the law factories, which only hire those at the top of the class from the *top* schools. (While it's true that virtually *any* grad from the law school at Harvard, Yale, or Stanford can find "a" job, that certainly doesn't mean he or she will get a job with a *major* firm.)

The major law firms are aware that graduating students know next to nothing about the law—just enough to pass the bar exam, in fact...and even that thanks only to a bar "review" course. (New associates are referred to as "the children.") But they know that those who consistently did well on their finals in law school at least know something of the Black Letter Law and how to do a good lawyerlike analysis. The odds are, that of the 42,000 people who graduate from law school each year, only a few thousand have enough *basic* lawyerlike skills to be worth hiring—and the top law firms snap them up (and give them absurdly high pay).

The great bulk of the graduating class each year still hasn't mastered the basics of Black Letter Law, or how to think like a lawyer, well enough to ever be a potential threat to the lawyers at the major firms—which is to say, to the clients the major firms represent. *And that's the way the major firms want it.*

For would-be litigators, major firms don't let the "children" handle cases (except trivial ones, if any) until they're sure the neophytes are up to it. They require their new recruits to serve a long apprenticeship, to make up for the lack of worthwhile "trial ad" courses in law school. They send their potential litigators to programs such as the two-week training the National Institute for Trial Advocacy puts on once a year. And there are many other programs as well, shorter ones, that the major firms send their people to. (NITA is not the only source of these programs.) Sometimes, if the firm has enough associates to train, it pays NITA, etc., to present the course *at* the law firm. The cumulative effect makes a big difference. So, whereas all graduates start out equal in their ignorance as to how to be good trial lawyers, those who are hired by the top firms are the ones who get "brought up to speed."

(Digression: Big corporations and insurance companies have funded many successful "lawsuit abuse" campaigns. All that those corporations need to do to prevent lawsuits is to *clean up their act*. But they know it's in their interest *not* to clean up their act. We hear about "runaway jury verdicts." But what we don't hear about is (1) most of those verdicts are knocked down or wiped out by what's called a "remittitur," either by the trial judge or the appellate court, and those that aren't are often settled for a far lesser amount during the appellate process, to protect the victorious plaintiff from losing everything as a result of a reversal by the appellate court; and (2) even when a huge jury verdict is upheld, the corporate defendant is still making a ton of money from what it's done—and *continues* to do, because it knows that only one in a thousand potential plaintiffs will ever decide to sue...and of those few who do, only one in a hundred will find a lawyer willing to take the case. And most of those lawyers will either lose, because they were outclassed by the defendant's lawyer, or else will quickly settle the case for peanuts. On a cost-benefit basis, it *pays* to be a corporate tortfeasor, even *with* the large jury awards that are upheld. And the big manufacturers and insurance companies *know* that.)

Those who are the victims of the wealthy and the powerful, or who want to challenge the wealthy and the powerful, can seldom afford any attorney at all. Granted, if the stakes are high enough, a truly good trial lawyer who's an independent will take the case on a contingency fee basis. However, cases worth taking on contingency are rare, and the best plaintiff's attorneys carefully pick and choose among them. So, usually, it's David v. Goliath. But in a modern courtroom, unlike ancient Israel, there is no divine intervention. Goliath wins. (In part, this is because the big law firms are very good at currying the judges' favor behind the scenes, between trials.)

The Role of Pedagogical Malpractice - Part Three

The first year of law school is relevant here, too. If law schools *educated* students in the law, and made exams *fair* measures of students' abilities, the mystique would be gone—not just the profs', but that of the top students in the class.

Yet, as the Josephson Report made clear, the exams law students take are very poor measures of students' abilities. This is not the place to rehash that discussion. Yet, assuming the studies Josephson cited are valid, the question arises: why is the evaluation process not made *fair?* Why do the law schools persist in their ways?

—Because the *major* purpose of the forced curve is to create winners and losers, regardless of the performance measure. At any given law school, any given student is comparable to any other student in intelligence, drive, and so forth. *Every* student is capable of mastering Black Letter Law and learning "how to think like a lawyer." But the law schools don't help them do that. Instead, they try to keep the students ignorant and confused. As has already been discussed, that makes it easier to grade students' exam answers. But far more important, it creates clear "winners" and clear "losers." That is the ulterior motive for the forced curve...and, audacious as it sounds, producing *losers* is more important than producing winners.

The first edition of George J. Roth's book, *Slaying the Law School Dragon,* included this passage: "The big pitch is to get high grades so you can get a job in a good law firm when you graduate." It's too bad he cut that from the second edition. For what he was talking about was what lawyer-turned-psychotherapist Benjamin Sells, in his book *The Soul of the Law,* calls "developmental ideology."

> Before the law student has ever opened a book or read a case, the placement office, career consultants, job manuals, and the profession in general have already defined the proper path: good grades / law review / interviews / summer job / offer / associate / partner / corner office.

Everything is geared toward prestige—a job with a "name" firm and making big money at it. (This urge for prestige includes summer clerkships.)

The quotation from George Roth, above, continued as follows:

> The inordinate competition is engendered by a
> system of daily recitation which is designed to
> make you look stupid, cause traumatic embar-
> rassment, and make you feel like you were never
> cut out to be a lawyer in the first place.

Again, it's unfortunate that sentence too was cut from the second edition of his book. For what happens, to most law students—thanks to the forced curve—is that their feelings of inadequacy are *confirmed* when they get their grades.

So, students who had always been the "best and the brightest" in school before, but who don't do well in law school, are led to believe "Gee, I guess *I don't have what it takes.*" Thus a *permanent intimidation factor* is put in place, giving yet another advantage to the top students who are then hired by the major law firms.

And that is another reason why the law schools tell students not to engage in any meaningful preparation for law school (such as reading primers), and tell them not to take LEEWS. If students saw how relatively simple it is to master Black Letter Law and do a good lawyerlike analysis, they would immediately see the pedagogical fraud of the law schools. More important, students who use the primers and LEEWS to do well in law school are more likely not to feel awe toward their fellow high achievers (including their professors who hire out as paid consultants).

So, by making sure the vast majority of law school graduates are incompetent and *feel* inferior as to even the "baby stuff" of the law, the law schools serve the interests of the major firms, which have the resources to ensure that *their* new lawyers get a *remedial* education.

Not surprisingly, the bulk of any law school's endowment fund comes from...guess where?

The Role of Pedagogical Malpractice - Part Four: Fail-Safe Indoctrination

Hard to believe now, but the earliest modern scientists (in England, especially) were devout Christians. They sought to accomplish two things: (1) reveal the wonder's of God's Creation, by helping people gain a deeper understanding of it; and (2) reveal new aspects of the Mind of God. They believed that if people understood the laws of Nature (i.e., of Nature's God), that would deepen their faith.

Unfortunately, the Church responded that (1) the Mind of God and the wonders of Creation are not to be explored by mere laypeople, only by trained theologians, and (2) anything the scientists discovered that conflicted with religious dogma had to give way to the dogma.

And so a war broke out between Science and Religion, which continues to this day. (Witness fundamentalist Protestantism's insistence on so-called "creation science.")

The scientists sought to distance themselves from anything having to do with religion. Unfortunately, they included morality in their list. And so, science claimed morality was irrelevant to science. (Science is supposedly "value-free." But truth and objectivity are *values*.) By default, serious discussions of morality remained the province only of religion.

The Law pretends to be a science. And so, when legal education was tranformed from 1870 on, jurists downplayed morality as a source of legal principles. (Hence the great Oliver Wendell Holmes, Jr., uttered one of the few truly stupid things he ever said: "This is a court of Law, young man, not a court of Justice.")

And so, even today, the *main* goal of law school, especially what occurs in first-year, is *to destroy students' belief in morality*. Future lawyers are indoctrinated that there isn't *really* any such thing as "right" or "wrong." There are only legal maneuvers. Those who persist in a sincere belief in ethics are treated with the same disdain—or alarm—as a 16-year-old who still believes in Santa Clause or the Tooth Fairy. Students are left in no doubt that concepts such as "truth," "justice," "humanity," and "morality" are just emotionally charged words to use when trying to *manipulate others*. Anyone who takes them seriously is obviously a mental defective, unfit for a life in the Law.

The law school professors inculcate the attitude that rules have no *intrinsic* value, and that *no higher values exist*. Students leave school believing that the Law is just a game. The only thing that counts is winning. Winning, in turn, means prize money—and, of course, prestige. You help the client to "get his" (or hers), and thereby "get yours." Then take the money and run.

As Grant Gilmore observed, in his classic *The Ages of American Law* (1974.): "In Hell there will be nothing but law, and due process will be meticulously observed."

In 1991, Chris Goodrich's book, *Anarchy and Elegance: Confessions of a Journalist at Yale Law School*, was published. (Sadly, it is now out-of-print. But if you track it down through an out-of-print book dealer on the internet, it is well worth reading.) In it, he described the process. Speaking of a particular professor's use of the Socratic Method, he said:

His <u>inducement of mental vertigo</u> was so complete, so far beyond the necessary, that I had no difficulty believing that a deeper agenda lurked beneath the surface orientation. Many critics of legal education use the word *brainwashing* to describe the process, and I began to understand what they meant. By <u>eliminating all nonlegal points of reference,</u> [the professor] forced us to accept his word about the law; by implying that every assumption students had made prior to law school was presumptively wrong, <u>he made us doubt our self-worth.</u> And when he hinted at the existence of a legal framework that could encompass *all* thoughts and ideas, <u>accessible only to those who adopted the legal point of view—</u>courageously and altruistically, by implication—<u>he had us eating out of his hand.</u> In those early weeks, we were so relieved to be told that certainty existed somewhere in the legal world that <u>we didn't care whether it was valid.</u>

(Italics in the original; underlining supplied.)

I disagree only with Goodrich's statement that it's just in the "early weeks" of law school that this attitude exists among the students. On the contrary: one of the *major purposes* of law school is to ensure that this attitude is *permanent*—especially the part about not caring if the "legal point of view" *is* valid.

In passing, Goodrich again hit upon the truth when he said "Law had made me less human, asked that I *dismiss my moral center* as a dangerous, incomprehensible Pandora's box." (Emphasis added.)

Richard D. Kahlenberg, in *Broken Contract: A Memoir of Harvard Law School* (still in print) had this to say: "That phenomenon is unnatural. The human condition does not require that smart people, when they reach a certain age, must jettison their convictions (even as they mouth those abandoned beliefs with greater vigor)."

Goodrich put it in personal terms: "Law school hadn't turned me into a jerk, but it told me that if I felt the need to be a jerk, I should be a first-rate jerk, and not feel guilty about it."

Of course, if you're really *good* at being a jerk, and it gets you where you wanna go, then it's awful easy to feel the "need" to be a jerk. That includes what in effect involves cheating one's own clients (which is standard operating procedure).

Goodrich then provides the transition from the personal to the societal: "Legal training doesn't create selfish, aggressive people—but it does provide the intellectual equipment with which recipients can justify and give force to beliefs and actions most people would wholeheartedly condemn."

Anna Freud (Sigmund's daughter, and a psychiatrist herself) discovered and named what she called "identification with the aggressor." Her fellow shrink, George Vaillant, summarized it best, in his book, *Adaptation to Life*: "Through such an identification, an individual who hitherto has felt safe only by prostrating himself before a potential aggressor, now achieves mastery by *incorporating or identifying with the very traits in the aggressor that he used to fear.*" (Emphasis added.)

That, in a nutshell, is the source of the personality change that law students undergo because of the professoriat's twisted mind-games.

This ensures that those whose goals invol*ve wrongdoing* will have no difficulty in hiring the "best" and brightest law school graduates to work on their behalf.

> The *a*-morality of law *school* is what makes possible the *im*-moralities of the legal *profession*.

The result is best described by Stephen Crane's poem "In the Desert":

> In the desert
> I saw a creature, naked, bestial,
> Who, squatting upon the ground,
> Held his heart in his hands,
> And ate of it.
> I said, "Is it good, friend?"
> "It is bitter—bitter," he answered;
> "But I like it
> "Because it is bitter
> "And because it is my heart."

As you will see in Chapter 27, I am not beating the drum for a "return to religion." Quite the contrary. For, in a multi-religious society, it is impossible to obtain moral consensus when each religious group makes public policy proposals based solely on its own scripture, its own god. *Reasoning* provides the only possible common ground—reasoning based on logic, experience, and common sense.

Even in fundamentalist Christianity, many Biblical teachings have been discarded. So, if people of one religion decide to "pick and choose" with respect to their own scripture, surely they do so on the basis of logic, experience, and common sense. And even more surely, they should use logic, experience, and common sense when appealing to those *outside* that religion to adopt policies that, for the people *within* the advocates' religion, are regarded as divine commands.

In the May, 1989 issue of *The Washington Monthly*, an article by Garrett Epps was published. Epps was then a first-year at Duke University's law school. He said this:

> The function of law, as many have rightly argued, is to fashion a public morality—a way of resolving contentious issues like integration, executive power, abortion, womens' *[sic]* rights, and church-state relations without resorting to the naked ability of the powerful to impose their will.

But the powerful have *always* imposed their will. That's why they're called "powerful." That is not going to change. But what the Law can do, as Epps pointed out, is restrain their *naked* ability to impose their will. It's a question of social legitimacy, of maintaining the social fabric.

At the end of the epilogue to *Broken Contract*, Kahlenberg explains his book's title:

> You can blame the individuals for breaking their personal contracts—the agreements they had with themselves that they were pursuing law not for the money but to do good. You can blame the institution, Harvard Law School, for breaking its implicit contract, proclaimed on the walls of its buildings, that law is about justice, and then fostering an atmosphere where it is hard not to be a hypocrite. But no matter who is ultimately responsible, the sad truth is that every time an idealistic law student turns into a hardened attorney for the wealthy and powerful, she brings closer to the breaking point another agreement— the social contract—and that is simply unacceptable.

No disrespect to Kahlenberg, but it *is* acceptable, very much so—to those who benefit from it.

Alexander Pope, the English poet, came up with the words to describe this transition (in his *Essay on Man, Epistle II*):

> Vice is a monster of so frightful mien,
> As to be hated needs but to be seen;
> Yet seen too oft, familiar with her face;
> We first endure, then pity, then embrace.

By breaking a student's spirit, law professors needn't be much concerned that he or she will become a threat to the established order. With their idealism eradicated by law school, few lawyers have any interest in "fighting the good fight" for the sake of a worthwhile cause. If there's no money in it—or at least free publicity—they just don't care any more, no matter what the cost to society from their inaction.

> The law school professioriat has long since sold out to the ABA's hidden agenda. In return for the ABA's effort to perpetually inflate their salaries —and ample opportunities to make far more money on the side—they blithely remain wilfully ignorant of their pedagogical malpractice and its effect on future lawyers, on those future lawyers' future clients, and on society itself.
> They ought to feel *ashamed*. Instead, they're smug.

The Downward Spiral

Sells, the lawyer-turned-psychotherapist, talked about another problem with the legal profession, in *The Soul of the Law:*

> For a lawyer to admit ignorance is to admit weakness, and to admit weakness is to open oneself up to attack. People who are close to lawyers can attest to the depth of this training and often comment how rare it is to hear a lawyer admit to not knowing something. Lawyers are taught to bluff, expected to bluff. Lawyers must always give the impression of knowledge and confidence, must always know.

This leads to what Sells calls the "impostor syndrome."

> The roots of the impostor syndrome begin in law school, where lawyers are taught it is better to bluff than to admit ignorance....*At first,* the lawyer feels merely inadequate and dishonest. But the next step is *cynicism. The lawyer decides everyone else is faking it too,* and begins to relate with people on the assumption rhat everyone is lying and posturing.
>
> (Emphasis added.)

And in fact, with respect to other *attorneys,* that assumption is usually correct. The lawyer who is somewhat ignorant and incompetent rationalizes his or her inadequacy by saying that others are no better. Then he or she uses that as the excuse for *not trying* to get any better.

Some trial attorneys even take *delight* in *not knowing the substantive law.* They pride themselves on having "forgotten everything I learned for the bar exam." Although that's surely an exaggeration, it's as though they're belatedly rebelling against what law school put them through.

They rely on little more than hot air—and their ability to ingratiate themselves with juries. When involved in litigation, they often "throw everything against the wall, to see if something sticks"—including things that ought to have brought *sanctions* against that attorney. (Usually, such nonsense won't hold up on appeal. But most cases are not appealed. If a case has gone all the way to a judgment, the judgment stands.)

However, the failure of the law schools to properly educate students in the substantive law and skills has another effect: the rise of "Rambo tactics"—the vicious and petty practices of many attorneys. Perhaps I am generalizing too hastily, but it has been my experience that the lawyers who "play dirty" are those who do not know the law, and do not care to learn it. So they use underhanded methods to make up for their ignorance and indolence.

For several years now, commentators have deplored the rise of Rambo tactics. Many of these commentators are law school professors. They pretend to be "holier than thou." However, to understand the origin of the phenomenon, they need look no farther than the nearest mirror. And this includes the "teaching" techniques they use in the classroom.

To Thine Own (Better) Self, Be True

Forgive me for raising the subject, but someday—no matter how young you are now—you are going to die. (Yes, it's true. Trust me: I'm a lawyer.) If and when you know your time is almost up, you will no doubt look back on your life. When you do, what will you think of it? Will you feel smug because you made it to the top in some prestigious law firm? Will you take satisfaction that the net worth of your estate will perhaps be in the tens of millions? Will you be proud that your actions—and inactions—as a lawyer helped to make the world a *worse* place?

Here's the last piece of poetry I'll quote (in this chapter). It's from Robert Frost's "The Lawyers Know Too Much":

> Tell me why a hearse horse snickers,
> Hauling a lawyer's bones?

Or, as some guy from Nazareth said, nearly 2,000 years ago: "What is a man profited, if he shall gain the whole world, and lose his soul?" (This goes for women, too.)

Before you decide what path to pursue in the Law, you might want to read Leo *Tolstoy's The Death of Ivan Ilych.* (Ilych was a lawyer.)

There's a difference
between idealism and utopianism;
between skepticism and cynicism;
between objective detachment and amorality.
However, the law schools pretend
that these differences do not exist...
and the legal profession itself
gives them only "lip service."
If you want to make the effort
to retain your humanity in law school
and as an attorney,
please keep these distinctions in mind.

ATTICUS FALCON, ESQ.

This book is dedicated to Thane Josef Messinger, Esq.,
author of **The Young Lawyer's Jungle Book: A Survival Guide.**
He's a 1991 graduate of the University of Texas Law School
(where he Made Law Review and served on the editorial board).
Here are his thoughts on the humbuggery at his own school:

In 1991 and perhaps even now the graduation ceremony at
the University of Texas School of Law included the "Sunflower
Ceremony."

In explanation, the law school proclaimed in the official
announcement that "just as sunflowers turn to the light of day,
so too must our lawyers turn to the light of justice."

Aside from being rather bad poetry, it is offensive on
(at least) two counts:

Sufficiently saccharine as to induce immediate indigestion, it
is an insult, intended or not.

And it is clearly wrong: Many lawyers are simply not good
lawyers *or* good people. Many of those were not very nice law
students.

It is an insult in part because it makes a mockery of the *true*
nature of the law, of "justice," and of the importance of
impressing the weight soon to be borne by its newest members.
Justice is not so easily granted as to require turning one's face
toward her. If it were so easy, there'd be no meaning in the
word. No, she requires instead a series of trials, and often ones
that require perseverance *in spite of* one's pragmatic interests...or
the interests of one's client. Our society proclaims mightily these
precepts; it grows conspicuous by its silence when ethical push
comes to unethical shove. The law is especially susceptible to
this indolent sin. When *your* money's at stake, *then* you be the
one to speak so freely.

One point of the law—and more specifically, legal
education—is that of free will to use one's mind to craft a
legal course or response that fits one's obligations, interests, and ethical constraints. All too often we fail. This is,
or ought to be, entirely the point. Justice—*real* justice—is
rarely easy. If it were easy, there would be no *in*justice.

Legal educators' duty is to equip the law's newest
members to face this challenge. In this, I have come to
side with Mr. Falcon in his judgment that our legal education system is near-criminal in its negligence in this role.

Addendum to Chapter 25 -
The Accreditation Monopoly

As Edward de Bono puts it:

> It was Bernard Shaw who said that progress
> was always due to unreasonable people because
> reasonable people wanted to use the system as
> it was, not change it....
>
> The system will always be defended by those
> countless people who have enough intellect to
> defend but not quite enough to innovate. There
> are always those who believe that any change,
> by definition, will threaten the security of their
> position. Furthermore, since we cannot fully see
> the consequence of a change before it has
> happened, it is better to avoid the risk.

The Council on Accreditation is not going to change its ways.
Although it is now officially independent from the ABA, it is still housed
within the ABA's offices and is dependent on the ABA for its power.
The ABA it is an extremely powerful organization. (Until recent years,
no person could be confirmed for a federal judgeship until and unless
he or she received the formal approval of the ABA.)

The Council is the only national agency recognized by the U.S.
Secretary of Education for approving law schools so that those schools'
students will be eligible for federally guaranteed student loans. And the
Council insists that law schools have a curriculum, pedagogy, grading
system, and cost structure that serves the interests of the wealthy and
powerful. That's fine for "Fat Cat" schools such as Harvard, Yale, and
Stanford. It's not so good for most of the *other* 200 or so law schools.

Given that the present administration in Washington is allegedly
devoted to competition, perhaps now is the time to authorize one or
more alternative organizations to accredit law schools, nationally.

A different organization might promote a curriculum that serves the
needs of the vast majority of Americans rather than a tiny elite. It might
promote a pedagogy that ensures that *all* law students will be competent
upon graduation. And it might promote cost structures (such as distance
education or the sharing of law libraries by schools) that enable far
more people than now to afford a legal eduation without then having to
sell out in order to pay off massive student loans.

Just a thought.

Chapter 26 - The Chickens
Come Home to Roost

In the 1930s and '40s, a jurisprudential school of thought arose that, in the words of Daniel Farber and Suzanna Sherry, attacked "the formalist notion that law embodies neutral, general principles derived from cases." This "formalist notion" included the idea that law was a science and thus that the Law was also "value-free." The "Legal Realists" (as they were called) declared, in contrast, that it was a delusion to believe that law was based on logic and predictability as to the "proper" outcome of a given case. Instead, they maintained that the Law was both "indeterminate" and "incoherent" as a discipline. (The quotation on page 543, from Supreme Court Justice William O. Douglas, is an example. Douglas was one of the Legal Realists.)

The challengers, however, shared the formalists' faith in science, despite their own belief that the Law itself was not a science. And so, they sought to have the Law look to *real* science, or at least, to the "social sciences." They wanted to rely on scientific expertise and empirical data to decide individual cases and to resolve public policy issues. Their goal was "efficiency" in the legal process, in place of the randomness and messiness of the status quo.

The Legal Realism school included some of the giants of American jurisprudence: Karl Llewellyn and Jerome Frank among them. Robert Maynard Hutchins (professor and then dean of Yale's law school, who ended up as president of the University of Chicago) was a member.

The bastion of law-as-science was, of course, Harvard. Thus, Legal Realism was a challenge to the Langdellians' "scientific" approach to the Law. And it's been said that the battle was a disguised academic power struggle: Yale and Columbia v. HLS.

Harvard won. (Perhaps that's because it has always played the power game brilliantly. Langdell, early on, sought to place HLS grads as deans and professors in the new university-affiliated law schools that were springing up around the country during his tenure as dean. Northwestern, among others, was established as an HLS epigone. Further, the "Harvard Mafia" has always been assiduous in placing its people in high governmental and judicial posts. HLS has turned out more graduates each year than almost any other law school in the country—more than Columbia and Yale combined, for example—for nearly a century now. By sheer force of numbers, they habitually fill a sizeable number of prestigious slots that open up each year. Harvard had—and still has—a hammerlock on the power structure of legal education, the judiciary, and the legal profession. And the "Harvard Mystique" was and still is awesome. So, regardless of the intellectual merit of Legal Realism, the outcome of the challenge was virtually a foregone conclusion.)

As a result of Harvard's victory, jurisprudence in the 1950s and '60s focused its attention on legal processes rather than substantive law.

(Echoes of that distant struggle perhaps included the 1974 statement from Yale's Grant Gilmore, quoted on page 698, that Hell will have only Law in it—but due process will be meticulously observed.)

Legal Realism spawned two descendants—one on the right, one on the left. (The latter in turn spawned descendants of its own.)

The heir on the right is "Law and Economics" (mentioned in previous chapters). As their name implies, the L&E people also rely on social "science" (though just one: economics) as the oracle for resolving legal disputes. The law school at the University of Chicago is their Mecca...or perhaps we should say, their Delphi. When Ronald Reagan became president in 1981, they moved into his administration in droves. Their credentials of high government service then enabled L&E to go "big time" as a respected, even prestigious school of thought.

Whaddaya Got?

The left-wing heirs of Legal Realism arose in the late 1970s—ironically, at HLS. Their school of thought was called "Critical Legal Studies." The founding "Crits" (as they were called) included Duncan Kennedy, Mark Tushnet, and Roberto Unger.

They jettisoned the faith in science altogether, including the "science" of economics, as irrelevant to the Law. But they kept alive a central tenet of their forebears: the "indeterminacy thesis." This said that there's nearly always "good law" on both sides of an issue, so a judge can rationalize his or her own ruling by invoking whichever line of cases he or she has decided, purely because of personal (emotional) bias, to follow.

The Legal Realists were perhaps not interested in transforming society. The Crits were. (So are the L&E people.)

All of Critical Legal Studies was based on their great "discovery" that law and the legal system serve as tools of the Establishment. Gee, who'da thunk? (It brings to mind the sardonic definition of a management consultant: someone who uses your own watch to tell you what time it is...and then keeps the watch as his or her fee.) The fact that they trumpeted this great "new insight" shows just how isolated their ivory tower was from reality.

The Wild One, a 1953 film, made Marlon Brando a star. In it, he's a member of a motorcycle gang called the "Black Rebels." (The film was based on a true incident: Two motorcycle gangs battled in a small California town—and as a side effect, the town was subjected to pillage and rapine for two days.)

In one scene, Brando's character is asked, "What are you rebelling against?" He replies, "Whaddaya got?" That exchange expresses the relationship between the legal Establishment and the Crits.

For CLS, the purpose of the Law, paradoxically, was to destabilize society. They wanted to use the Law to smash up the established arrangements and procedures—and especially the established hierarchies. In this way, freedom would somehow be maximized, they said. Although they didn't admit it, *anarchy* would be "the best of all possible worlds," and the natural result of their forlorn hopes.

(They would have done well to ponder the nihilistic line in the song "Bobby McGee," about how "Freedom's just another word for nuthin' left to lose." This downward spiral into an inevitable world of dog-eat-dog was something else they had in common with the folks in L&E, their alleged arch-rivals.)

But the Crits did not want to smash up the cozy nest they'd made for themselves in the ivory tower (heavily subsidized by education's tax-exempt status and alumni contributions). One thing at a time, perhaps. Save the law schools for last. However, even before that final step, there would no longer be any law...nor would there be any society, or even civilization—other than the "families" of organized crime.

Unlike Law & Economics, CLS maintained that a "commonality" approach is just as valid as individualism. However, the Crits didn't promote it. Instead, they simply turned up their noses at the individual *and* communal approaches. They attempted to provide a new foundation for legal theory. We might call it "Zero-Based Jurisprudence," i.e., starting from scratch.

Ironically, though, despite their declarations to the contrary, the Crits started with the individual in their thinking. In this, they were far more the children of the American culture than they would've had people believe. They differed from the L&E school in refusing to accept, as "received tradition," the secular theology of Western capitalism. Yet, their own approach was quite theological.

Indeed, although it might not seem possible, they carried the dogma of individualism to an extreme that exceeded even that of Law & Economics. They hailed what might be called "person-as-process." For them, each of us could constantly re-make himself or herself, breaking free from the past, whether cultural or personal. However, this was an old (and romantic) notion in Western culture, and especially in American culture. As so often happens when radicals call for the "New Man" (or "Womyn"), the self-proclaimed revolutionaries were putting aged wine into new skins.

But the Crits fell victim to in-fighting. As with the Jacobins in France, the revolution devoured its own. With the rise of radical feminism and of "turnabout racism" among black law profs, the Crits were condemned as sexist and racist and were discarded. (They're still alive and well, though—on law school faculties. They'd made sure they'd obtained tenure before they started their failed "revolt.")

Their successors signal their CLS ancestry by using the word "Critical" in their name, and—as with the original Crits—they're far left of center. One is based on gender, the other on race.

The founders of Critical Feminism (or, sometimes, "Feminist Crits") were Mary Jo Frug and Clare Dalton. Members include Catharine MacKinnon, Andrea Dworkin, Patricia Cain, Pauline Caldwell, Robin West, Marie Ashe, Lucinda Finley, and Kathryn Abrams.

The other descendant of CLS is known as "Critical Race Theory." Its leading members include Derek Bell, Richard Delgado, Patricia Williams, Jerome Culp, Mari Matsuda, Kimberlé Crenshaw, and Paul Butler.

The two groups have three things in common. The third is an emphasis on what CLS called the "commonality" approach. The second is a contempt for white males. The first—we'll get to, shortly.

"Buffaloes" v. "Buffalo-Hunters"

Arthur Austin is a prof at Case Western University's law school. In his book, *The Empire Strikes Back: Outsiders and the Struggle over Legal Education,* he refers to himself and many of his fellow "fiftyish white male law profs" as "buffaloes." They "keep the faith" of New Deal liberalism, and are "traditionalists."

The heart of this tradition is "scholarship." It's exemplified by the "doctrinal [law review] article."

> It starts with the statement of a problem, followed by the identification and discussion of prevailing perspectives and solutions. *Objectivity rules; the existing positions have to be acknowledged and thoroughly explored.*
>
> (Emphasis added.)

Granted, Austin continues, the work of few law professors meets that standard—and once they've obtained tenure, most stop researching and writing altogether. But the *ideal* remains, even if it only receives "lip service." (It's routinely invoked when the professoriat claims that, because they're "scholars," they can't be *practical*.)

Unfortunately too, Austin adds, the typical doctrinal article includes what he says is called "The Harvard Stutter." It was invented by Derek Bok—HLS law prof, then HLS dean, then president of Harvard University —in a 1960 *Harvard Law Review* article. The "stutter" is a failure of nerve, a hedging by calling for further study of and thought on the topic.

In the piece Bok wrote (which was on antitrust law, even though Bok had specialized only in labor law), Austin says,

> Bok never boxes himself into a corner by endorsing a specific position or rule. He utilizes the "scholar's doubt" technique of using phraseology that, while exalting predictability, reflects a healthy suspicion of certainty.

Thus, a good doctrinal article is...wishy-washy. The author "plays it safe."

The Crits rebelled against this. They wanted *action*. But the *way* in which they rebelled is best described by Edward de Bono, without reference to the law or law professors:

> Youngsters have found that logic has little value because you can argue equally well on any side of a question provided you choose your values and perceptions. They also see their apparently "logical" elders behaving in unattractive ways. They know that emotions cannot be swayed by logic. So they turn away from logic toward raw emotions and feelings. Surely these are the only real and true guides for action?

This is what the adult, highly educated law profs who belong to the Fem & Race Crit schools of thought have done.

From Objectivity to the Ultimate Subjectivity

The New Crits expressly reject almost *every* concept on which the law is based. To them, what we call "objective" reality is just a sneaky construct by the wealthy and powerful to "maintain their hegemony." (It works sort of like *The Matrix*.) And because objective reality does not exist, there's no need to be concerned about facts, let alone about "truth." Thus, they feel free to misstate history, and even to misstate the holdings in U.S. Supreme Court cases, if it will serve their purpose. Logic? Forget it.

The New Crits invoke the latest pseudo-intellectual tool of nihilism: "deconstruction." Its creator was a Frenchman, Jacques Derrida.

(Digression: one of the puzzling things about American intellectual history is the frequent reluctance of American thinkers to accord respect to their own. In the 18th century, and into the 19th, Americans looked to the English for guidance. Perhaps that was understandable. But with the rise of the prestige of Teutonic scholarship, philosophy, and science in the 19th century, they turned to the Germans. This lasted until WWI. There was a hiatus in the interwar period. But since WWII, American intellectuals have looked largely to France for leadership. In recent decades, that "leadership" has come from Jacques Derrida and Michel Foucault—two of the most aberrant people who ever walked this planet. The consistent pattern is the *reverse* of the "Not Invented Here" Syndrome. If Americans created it, it can't be good. Thus, the philosophy of pragmatism, created and developed by Charles Peirce and John Dewey, is just a footnote in any college survey course on philosophy. —Interestingly, a similar pattern exists when hiring conductors for the most prestigious orchestras in America. With only the rarest of exceptions, No American Need Apply. Go figure.)

Back in the days of CLS, one Crit had denounced the idea of individual *rights*, because it "legitimizes the status quo." The Crits' heirs agree. Stanley Fish is a scholar of English poet John Milton's work who also teaches at Duke's law school. A "deconstructionist," he has declared that concepts such as "fairness," "free speech," "the marketplace of ideas," "individualism," "justice," and "merit" are devoid of intrinsic meaning. He even dismisses the Constitution as an empty document. Virtually all the Fem & Race Crits agree with him. They also dismiss reason, knowledge, and the concept of universal validity of truth as "belief systems" foisted on the gullible masses by the powerful.

It's interesting that the New Crits denounce concepts created by white males as frauds used to manipulate others, yet the New Crits embrace "deconstructionism"...a white male's creation.

Not surprisingly, they say that the only thing they believe in is *power*. And apparently they regard power as the *only* aspect of reality that *is* objective. Naturally, they want more of it...for themselves.

In their law review articles, the original Crits had used what they called the "intersubjectivity zap." Austin describes it as "writing in private code to fellow true believers while purposely obfuscating the message so that even they cannot respond."

The New Crits, whether feminist or reverse racists, have retained that. But they call it "storytelling." (Those who write the material are called "voice writers," however, not "storytellers.") The stories are either allegorical tales or first-person narratives. The purpose of the stories is to have an *emotional* impact on the reader. Hence, as with Hollywood, the writers feel free to ignore or misrepresent facts. And because they rightly recognize that emotion is more powerful than reason, they do not use logic. They rely instead on anecdotal evidence—more sympathetically referred to as "casual empiricism."

Ironically, this gives them something in common with Ronald Reagan, who habitually relied on anecdotes to make a point—and whose disregard for facts and reason was well-known. Rush Limbaugh does employ reason at times, to impress his readers, listeners, and viewers, but feels free to play fast and loose with the facts in a manner similar to that of the New Crits. Strange bedfellows.

Farber & Sherry are profs at the University of Minnesota's law school. In their book, *Beyond All Reason: The Radical Assault on Truth in American Law*, they note—

> [F]irst-person storytelling is fraught with exactly the kind of dangers that scholarship is designed to avoid: creating, through interpretations, a biased, misleading, and nonverifiable account of the world.

But, of course, to the New Crits, those concerns are just so many "hang-ups" and are beside the point. The purpose of storytelling is to express the writer's "voice." The writer is in touch with what might be called "deeper truth" (though they can't use the word "truth," remember). The writer, if female, is an initiate into a mystical understanding largely just because of her gender. But even males can have this mystical understanding, as long as they are "of color." This deeper understanding surpasses such mundane concerns as Farber & Sherry's.

Like the "new journalism" of the late '60s, this new "scholarship" is anything but.

Ironically, they have a fundamental likeness to the L&E crowd, which looks solely to economics. Contemporary "higher" economics consists of mathematical models of the economy. These in turn are based on abstract assumptions. (Thus the secular theology of economics approaches the trivial other-worldly nature of Medieval Scholasticism, satirized centuries later as being concerned with such questions as "How many angels can dance on the head of a pin?")

Austin described it as reliance on the "black box."

> Wassily Leontief, the Nobel prize winner for economics in 1973, surveyed the *[American Economic] Review* over a four-year period and concluded that the black-box equations had *no nexus with the real world* except for an article about the utility maximization of pigeons. "Page after page of professional economic journals are filled with mathematical formulas leading the reader from sets of more or less plausible but entirely arbitrary assumptions to precisely stated but irrelevant theoretical conclusions."
>
> (Emphasis added.)

And as Austin notes, "Model creation and tinkering always allows one to go on a power kick. 'You can't argue about what's inside my black box [i.e., the economic model] because I made it. The God's truth isn't in the black box. I am the God's truth.'" (Brackets in the original.)

Panhandling from the Ivory Tower

The stories from the New Crits are neither theological abstractions nor mathematical equations. The New Crits have rejected the intellect and everything associated with it (other than the English language and technology such as computers, copiers, and books). Instead, they want to *emote*. And that they do, *ad nauseum*.

Austin refers to their tales collectively as "a personal agony of experiences." Their theme is "woe is me, woe is us."

In 1977 a work from Ann Douglas, *The Feminization of American Culture,* was published. In it, she described how, as this country industrialized in the 19th century, women's important economic roles diminished, leading to a decline in respect for the distaff. In response, American women turned to "sentimentalism."

> [S]entimentalism might be defined as the political
> sense obfuscated or gone *rancid*....[U]nlike the
> modes of *genuine* sensibility, [it] never exists
> except in tandem with failed political conscious-
> ness ...*[It] seeks and offers the distraction of sheer
> publicity.* Sentimentalism is a cluster of ostensibly
> private feelings which always attain *public
> and conspicuous expression.* Privacy functions
> in the rituals of sentimentalism only for the sake
> of *titillation*...Involved as it is with the *exhibition
> and commercialization of the self,* sentimental-
> ism cannot exist without an audience. *It has no
> content but its own exposure, and it invests
> exposure with a kind of final significance.*
>
> (Emphasis added.)

The New Crits meet Douglas's definition of "sentimentalism"—the "political sense...gone rancid," a *failed* political consciousness.

From the mid-1940s until the mid-'50s, there was a radio show (and from the mid-'50s to mid-'60s a TV show) called *Queen for a Day*. In it, the host would present four women to the audience. Each would tell a tale of woe—of poverty and thus inability to buy durable consumer goods such as a washer and dryer or an oven. The women usually looked like hell. (I've seen episodes of the TV show, on tape.) They would always cry, of course. Had they not been on television, they would have been out panhandling. The audience, via an "applause meter," would then (allegedly) vote on who would be "Queen for a Day." The winner was adorned with a crown and a lavish robe, and handed a dozen roses. She would also get the goodies she wanted.

Reading the tales of the New Crits, I get the feeling I'm reading submissions for a storytelling contest similar to that of *Queen for a Day*.

And as with the women on that show, the New Crits want applause —and the goodies: the feminists, by manipulating "Sensitive New Age Guys;" the new racists, by manipulating white liberal guilt.

But there are two differences:

First, the stories are not about being poor. Instead, they concern alleged acts of sexism or racism, of a *trivial* nature—which the writer then invests with a *monumental* significance. (Example: two authors discuss at length how "demeaning" it is for a police officer to call out "Hey you!" to someone in the distance who's black, and whose name the cop doesn't know. They assume, but do not say, that the cop is white—and do not regard their assumption as racist. They also do not suggest what the cop *should* have yelled, or what someone *other* than a cop might have yelled in similar circumstances. But they also acknowledge that the example was entirely of their own creation. They never saw it happen, and thus never talked with the "victim" of this "racism" to see if he or she felt "demeaned" by it.)

Second, their *tone* is different. Instead of begging (which would be demeaning), the New Crits are strident in proclaiming the "outrages" to which they have supposedly been subjected. Their attitude is: "Just look at *this!* They *owe* us, because of what they put us through! "

(Their posturing brings to mind a line from a song, "On the Blank Generation," recorded by the musical ensemble "Little Jack Melody with His Young Turks": "Let's call this whimper here a shout.")

They see themselves as martyrs. But, as with all true believers, they also look forward to a Day of Judgment, when the unrighteous shall be smited, after which a (secular) Kingdom of God will prevail.

Getting "Sane"

Austin uses the term "Newspeak" several times, without attribution. It's from George Orwell's novel, *1984.* "Newspeak" was the term for the new vocabulary the Party had invented, comparable to our own "politically correct" terms such as "underprivileged" for "poor."

Although the term "politically correct" is new, "political correctness" has been with us for quite some time. In the past, however, it was most often imposed by the Right. One has only to think of the Cold War Era, during which any support for a governmental program such as national health insurance was labelled "socialist," and anyone who *opposed* supporting brutal right-wing dictatorships in the name of "fighting communism" was called "pinko." So pervasive and intimidating were the conservatives that few dared "speak truth to power" about what the conservatives had done and were doing.

Orwell's novel was published four years after WWII. At the time, liberals who reviewed it said that "the Party" it referred to was the Nazis. But Orwell had in mind the communists. After all, Nazism had been vanquished. Communism remained, however, and was spreading. (Orwell had first-hand experience with it in the Spanish Civil War.)

Winston Churchill had been Britain's prime minister through most of WWII, and had helped put some backbone into his countrymen, to get them to stand up to the Nazis after the appeasement policy of his predecessor. The first name of the protagonist in *1984* is "Winston," an obvious reference to Churchill. His last name is "Smith," an equally obvious reference to an "Everyman."

Winston Churchill, as the leader of his nation, triumphed over totalitarian Nazism (thanks to the USA and above all to the—totalitarian —USSR). Winston Smith, however, is an ordinary citizen...who is entrapped, then betrayed, tortured, and brainwashed, by a Party official named O'Brien. (And the name "O'Brien" appears to be an oblique reference to the Catholic Church's Inquisitions.)

Orwell describes the thought processes of the Party members.

> To tell deliberate lies while genuinely believing in them, to forget any fact that has become inconvenient, and then, when it becomes necessary again, to draw it back from oblivion for just so long as it is needed, to deny the existence of objective reality and all the while to take account of the reality which one denies—all this is indispensably necessary.

Near the novel's end, O'Brien says:

> "Only the disciplined mind can see reality, Winston. You believe that reality is something objective, external, existing in its own right.....Reality exists in the human mind, and nowhere else. Not in the individual mind, which can make mistakes, and in any case soon perishes; only in the mind of the Party, which is collective and immortal. Whatever the Party holds to be truth *is* truth. It is impossible to see reality except by looking through the eyes of the Party. This is the fact that you have got to relearn, Winston."

After a torture session, there's this exchange:

> "You are a slow learner, Winston," said O'Brien, gently.
> "How can I help it?" he blubbered. "How can I help seeing what is in front of my eyes? Two and two are four."
> "Sometimes, Winston. Sometimes they are five. Sometimes they are three. You must try harder. It is not easy to become sane."

It's an old, old story in the history of the world, or at least of the West. For example, in Christian theology, going at least as far back as the Middle Ages, the Church maintained (in the words of Saint Anselm in the 12th century) that "One must *believe,* to *understand.*" (The intellectual seeds of the Reformation—and perhaps the Enlightenment— were unwittingly first sown when Peter Abelard, a few decades after Anselm, instead said that "One must *understand,* to *believe."*) And to this day, the.guiding principle is "Outside the Church, there is no salva- tion." This is true of all Christian denominations...and of most other religions, *mutatis mutandis.*

Lessons from the Animals

Orwell's other most famous novel, *Animal Farm,* was published in 1946. In it, the animals—led by the pigs—rebel against their human master and take over. As part of the "priming" for the subsequent revolt, a boar named Major gives a speech to the assembled animals:

> "Never listen when they tell you that Man and
> the animals have a common interest, that the
> prosperity of the one is the prosperity of the
> others. It is all lies. Man serves the interest of
> no creature except himself. And among us
> animals let there be perfect unity, perfect
> comradeship in the struggle. All men are
> enemies. All animals are comrades."

What today is referred to as "solidarity" was the key. The animals had a slogan, "Four legs good! Two legs bad!"

They posted Ten Commandments. The seventh was "All animals are created equal." Yet, the pigs took all the leadership roles. The dogs, under the direction of the pigs, maintained "discipline" among the others. The pigs were the only ones who could read and write. One of the other animals eventually became literate, however—and noticed that the wording of the Seventh Commandment had been changed, with a new phrase added: "But some animals are more equal than others."

The Race Crits seek solidarity among "people of color." (This "Us v. Them" is another old story in the quest for power. Irish- and Italian- American Catholics, in particular, used it—rightly—to challenge the Protestant Establishments in the big cities of the North.)

But some people of color are more equal than others. This is not a matter of being of "pure blood." Rather, it concerns having the correct consciousness, of being "authentic."

Lani Guinier, an HLS prof, claims to discern who is "authentic" as a person of color and who is not. Coincidentally, those who endorse her views are indeed "authentic."

(The head pig in *Animal Farm* was named Napoleon. Because all the animals were "comrades," he was "Comrade Napoleon." Boxer, a workhorse, would quell any question about the leader's judgment by declaring either "If Comrade Napoleon says it, it must be right," or, "Napoleon is always right.")

Going 'Round the Bend

Guinier has co-authored, with Gerald Torres (of the University of Texas law school), *The Miner's Canary: Enlisting Race, Resisting Power, and Transforming Democracy*. (Torres was discussed on pages 179-180 in Chapter 6, regarding his indolence concerning final exam questions.)

Guinier and Torres have apparently concluded that the Critical Race Theorists have painted themselves into a corner in a manner similar to the original Crits. So, their book attempts to start a new school of thought, "*Political* Race Theory." They say that "political race" is "a new, twenty-first century way of talking." They also refer, on pages 112-113, to "the modern idea that power is domination by those with power over others."

Excuse me? "Modern"? Have they not heard of Plato? The Torah? Or the more than *4,000 years* of *Chinese* political thought?

"Political" race is a matter of individual consciousness, not genetics. (This is convenient for Guinier, whose mother is white—and Jewish.)

But despite saying that it's "all in the mind," Guinier and Torres constantly speak of "people of color," in contrast to "whites." As with the original Cris, they claim to be against *all* "hierarchies." But then they say that "people of color" must lead this new "movement." (They don't mention just who they have in mind as the supreme leaders, however.) They graciously say that whites can "support" the movement and even join it. But, they add, whites just don't have the proper background to have developed the appropriate "consciousness." (In *1984*, there's the "Inner Party," and the "Outer Party.") The message to whites is clear: "Know your place—and don't get 'uppity.'"

The most significant difference between the Critical Race Theorists and these "political race" theorists is that Guinier and Torres tacitly seek an alliance with black churches to create a power base. Presumably, this would not trouble people of color who are Buddhist, Hindu, Sikh, Jain, Moslem, Jewish (as with certain black African Jews), animistic, agnostic, or atheist. So, they would perhaps gladly join in the Christian prayer sessions G&T describe and endorse.

They also urge thinking in what they call "magical realism." (Honest. That's their term. —It's borrowed from Hispanic/Latino/Chicano writers of *fiction*.) "Magical realists infuse ordinary situations with an enchanted quality that distorts both physical and temporal reality." (Page 32.) "But unlike Freud, for whom the importance of dreams resided in their distinction from working reality, magical realists dissolve that boundary and narrate fantasies, myths, and quotidian life in the same frame." (Pages 32-33.)

In the mental health literature, this "dissolving" of the boundary and "distortiion of reality" is called "psychosis." Fortunately, Guinier and Torres say "we are not magical realists ourselves." *Whew.* (So, "magical realism" is something only their *followers* are to engage in?)

"Speaking Truth to (the New Crits') Power"

As Austin commented, each New Crit "invokes deconstructionism to attack the status quo of the dominant message, yet rejects deconstruction when it is directed at his own work."

Well, again, that's the idea. The goal is *power*. And because even truth does not exist, remember, apparently a "double standard" is "fair play."

Farber & Sherry comment,

> Besides being impervious to formal empirical evidence, [the New Crits'] views also resist counter-stories. Any story that is inconsistent with [their] views can be knocked out—either the storyteller is not an authentic member of the group, or his perceptions have been warped by the dominant culture.

(Obviously, Austin, Farber & Sherry are sexists—even though Sherry is female: they all wrote only "his" instead of "his or her.")

> Criticisms [of the New Crits themselves] are seen as pandering to the power structure if they come from women or minorities, or as sexist and racist if they come from white men.

ATTICUS FALCON, ESQ.

Thus, when Betty Friedan—one of the *founders* of contemporary feminism—and Adrienne Rich defended the Constitutional rights of pornographers and their customers to "free expression," Catharine MacKinnon denounced them for "flirting with male supremecy." (MacKinnon has also written that "existing standards of literature, art, science, and politics, examined in a feminist light, are remarkably consistent with pornography's mode, meaning, and message.") Like Senator Joe McCarthy in the 1950s, who claimed the federal government was honeycombed with commies, or 17th-century Massachusetts Puritans— or 21st-century Evangelicals—for whom the Devil is everywhere, MacKinnon *knows*.

(MacKinnon started out quite sensibly, by demonstrating how sexual harassment in the workplace had a negative effect on women's jobs and career prospects. But, as with Camille Paglia—her "opposite number" among women who are public intellectuals—she turned herself into a two-dimensional caricature, gaining attention and becoming a celebrity through shocking, absurd ravings.)

Likewise, when Randall Kennedy (not to be confused with Duncan Kennedy, his fellow HLS prof and one of the original Crits) *mildly* criticized the Race Crits, he was all but accused of being a card-carrying member of the Ku Klux Klan....even though he is black.

During the late 1960s and early '70s in America, a black who disagreed with the "Thought Police" (another term from *1984)* was called an "Uncle Tom." But that, technically, could be used only for males. So now there's a new abusive eptithet, for both men and women: an "oreo," who's "black on the outside, white on the inside."

(When the Crimean War was imminent, Prince Albert—husband of Britain's Queen Victoria—publicly opined that perhaps war could be averted "if we just sat down and talked with the Russians." For this, he was accused of being in the pay of the Tsar. The war's carnage was appalling, despite the best efforts of Florence Nightingale to save the lives of the wounded. —And it was the Crimean War that gave rise to Tennyson's antiwar poem, "The Charge of the Light Brigade." The key lines from that poem are "Theirs not to reason why / Theirs but to do and die." Fortunately or unfortunately, the New Crits who belong to this new—mental—"light*weight* brigade" have forsworn reason altogether.)

Farber & Sherry reached this conclusion:

> With no possibility of appeal to a standard of truth independent of politics, there is no way to mediate among truth claims except by recourse to authoritative fiat.

Thoughts from a Kindred Spirit

The Critical Race Theorists' and Political Race Theorists' thoughts are perhaps best expressed thus:

> [Society] must make up for what everyone else today has neglected in this field. *It must set race in the center of all life.*
>
> (Emphasis in the original.)

> ...I must evaluate peoples differently on the basis of the race they belong to, and the same applies to the individual men within a national community.

> [We must] attempt to *promote in the most exemplary way* those elements within the national community that have been recognized as *especially valuable from the racial viewpoint* and to *provide for their special increase.*
>
> (Emphasis added.)

This writer, too, favored the idea of "mind sets" (although without using this New Crits' term), and emphasized that story-telling was paramount. (He was a masterful storyteller—spellbinding, in fact.)

However, he referred to "storytelling" as "progaganda," which is what it was for him—and is for the New Crits, though they won't admit it publicly.

Analyzing the failure of others in a previous effort, he said this:

> What [they] least understood was the very first axiom of all propagandist activity, to wit, the basically *subjective and one-sided attitude toward every question it deals with.*
>
> (Emphasis added.)

Elsewhere, he said:

> As soon as our *own* propaganda *admits so much as a glimmer of right on the other side, the foundation for doubt in our own right has been laid.*
>
> (Emphasis added.)

> But the most brilliant propagandist technique will yield no success unless one fundamental principle is borne in mind constantly and with unflagging attention. It must confine itself to a few points and repeat them over and over. Here, as so often in this world, persistence is the first and most important requirement for success.

> When there is a change, it must not alter the content of what the propaganda is driving at, but in the end must always say the same thing.

He noted the importance of eschewing *reason*, "particularly for a people that suffers from the mania of objectivity as much as the Germans [do]." (This "mania for objectivity" had contributed to the stunning achievements of Teutonic science, including Einstein's theories.)

> Like the woman, whose psychic state is determined *less by grounds of abstract reason* than by an indefinable longing for a force which will complement her nature, and who, consequently, would rather bow to a strong man than dominate a weakling, likewise *the masses...* feel inwardly more satisfied by a *doctrine, tolerating no other* beside itself, *than by* the granting of *liberalistic freedom* with which, as a rule, they can do little, and *are prone to feel that they have been abandoned.*
> (Emphasis added.)

(One of the slogans in *1984* was "Freedom is slavery.")
Speaking of the eventual triumph of his own movement to "raise consciousness" (as we would say today), he made these comments:

> At first the claims of the propaganda were so impudent that people thought it insane; later it got on people's nerves; and in the end, it was believed.

Of course, while at the abstract level of procedure this fellow and the new American racists are indistinguishable, they did part ways as to the substantive details. For example, this lovely passage:

From time to time illustrated papers bring it to the attention of the German petty-bourgeois that some place or other a Negro has for the first time become a lawyer, teacher, even a pastor, in fact a heroic tenor, or something of that sort. While the idiotic bourgeoisie looks with amazement at such miracles of education, full of respect for this result of modern educational skill, the Jew shrewdly draws from it a new proof of the soundness of his theory about the *equality of men* that he is trying to funnel into the minds of nations. It doesn't dawn on this depraved bourgeois world that this is positively a sin against all reason; that it is criminal lunacy to keep on drilling a born half-ape until people think that they have made a lawyer out of him while millions of members of the highest culture-race must remain in entirely unworthy positions; that it is a sin against the will of the Eternal Creator if his most gifted beings by the hundreds and hundreds of thousands are allowed to degenerate in the present proletarian morass, while Hottentots and Zulu Kaffirs are trained for intellectual professions. For this is training exactly like that of the poodle, and not scientific "education." The same pains and care employed on intelligent races would a thousand times sooner make every single individual capable of the same achievements.

(Emphasis in the original.)

The title of his two-volume memoirs (from which these passages are taken) translates as "My Struggle." (The "Acknowledgment of Permissions" at the end of this book provides information as to the English edition excerpted here. E-mail me for volume, chapter, and page number of each quotation, if you wish.) He was the apotheosis of what the Feminist and Racial Crits celebrate as a "voice writer."

If the Critical Race Theorists and Political Race Theorists would like to perfect their strategy and tactics, they would do well to read the work of the Master of the "Master Race." They and he are kindred spirits, siblings under the skin.

ATTICUS FALCON, ESQ.

Of the Double Standard—
and "Being in Denial"

Anyone white (or male) who claims not to be a racist (or sexist, as the case may be) is said to be "in denial." And being "in denial" is further proof of that person's racism or sexism. It's a perfect Catch-22 for those accused. But it's nothing new—having started with the Catholic Inquisitions and being continued in the Protestants' own "witch hunts," as well as in the modern "Anti-Communist Crusade."

Guinier & Torres rightly note (page 103) that:

> When working-class and poor whites fail to get ahead, they often turn to racial stereotypes as a way of explaining their own powerless positions. "Other people," black people, have simply stolen the American Dream, by getting undeserved benefits such as welfare or quotas.

Yet, nearly all of *The Miner's Canary* (and of the works from the CRT writers) is a lament about how "other people"—racially-stereotyped white people, or perhaps just white males—have stolen the good life for themselves alone, at the expense of people of color.

Chapter 25 briefly quoted psychiatrist George Vaillant's book, *Adaptation to Life,* where he summarized Anna Freud's theory about "identification with the aggressor." In that book, he also said that:

> The low SES [socio-economic-stratum]...tends to accumulate people who have used...relatively maladaptive or impairing devices to relieve their stressful situation.

He refers to psychological "defenses." Their purpose is to "resolve conflict." And he ranks them, from psychotic to mature. "The immature defenses externalize responsibility; the intermediate and mature defenses internalize responsibility." Discussing this in another of his works, *The Wisdom of the Ego,* he states that the "immature" defenses include "Projecting, Acting Out, and Fantasy." These attitudes and behaviors fit the Critical Feminists and the Critical/Political Race Theorists.

The members of these groups are what Vaillant calls "grievance collectors." They seek out (and if necessary, fabricate) "chips" to put on their own shoulders, which they then proudly display to others as part of their (in Douglas's term) "sentimentalism."

But the New Crits are not in the low socio-economic stratum themselves. Quite the contrary. In their quest for power, however, they claim leadership of those who are far less well off than themselves. This too is an old story in the world. It goes at least as far back as ancient Athens. It's called demogoguery. And as the fellow from Austria, quoted earlier, proved to the world, the essence of demogoguery is a denial of objectivity and truth, of reason and accountability.

The New Rednecks

In the 1920s, long before the rise of the Civil Rights Movement, H.L. Mencken wrote an essay called "Sahara of the Bozart." ("Bozart" was a reference to the French words, "beaux arts"—literally, "good arts.") His essay was about the American South and how it was an intellectual wasteland. (Thus, its inhabitants would naturally and ignorantly *spell* "beaux arts" the way the French *pronounce* it: "bozart.")

> The Southerner who is chiefly heard from is apparently all toes; one cannot have commerce with him without stepping on them. Thus, he protests hysterically every time northern opinion is intruded into his consideration of his problems, and northern opinion...now prudently keeps out. The result is that the Southerner struggles alone, and that he goes steadily from bad to worse.

As Michael Graham noted in his recent book, *Redneck Nation*, "We [white Southerners] invented the idea that offended people have no duty to be rational." He also says:

> The insipid idea that southern whites fought for during the civil rights movement—that *it's okay to stay stupid*, that *it's easier to blame those who point out that you're wrong than it is to figure out how to do what's right*, and, of course, the right to treat people differently based on race—these ideas have overwhelmed by force the principles of merit, intelligence, self-criticism, and antiracism that the North once stood for. We are truly one nation, one giant redneck nation.
>
> (Emphasis added.)

In 1961, *Black Skin, White Mask* was published. Its author was a black African writer (and M.D.) named Franz Fanon. Its title referred to those who, in America, were later called "Uncle Toms"—or, now, "oreos."

The Critical/Political Race Theorists speak of "people of color." Red, too, is a color. And it appears that the Critical/Political Race Theorists could be said to have "black (or brown) *faces,* red *necks.*"

Here's another passage from Graham's book:

> During the Civil Rights Movement...[t]he rest
> of the country understood that Southern whites
> *felt* put upon and out of sorts, but Northerners
> rejected those feelings as delusional.

But self-proclaimed leaders who are "people of color" are taken at face value. They are America's "sacred cows," despite their "bull."

The American Dream as "Sham"

There's a crucial difference, though, between the old rednecks and the new "rednecks of color." The old Southern racists (and Northern, lest we forget) believed that the American Dream was only for whites. The new racists claim to reject the American Dream altogether— because it's based on the idea of color-blindness, merit, and personal effort, which they say are a white sham.

Guinier and Torres say (page 49 of their book), "[T]he entire enterprise of civil rights is limited to creating opportunities for individual advancement for those talented enough to take advantage of a new colorless order." (But if there's no such thing as "truth" or "objective reality," how can their statement have any *meaning?*)

They're the beneficiaries of the Civil Rights Movement, yet reject most of its underlying values. Even more ironic is that "civil disobedience" was modelled on Mohandas Ghandi's "Satyagraha," which means "truth force." Yet, they reject "truth," preferring only (political) force.

If "merit" and "individual effort" are a sham, then we can dismiss the accomplishments of, for example, Lani Guinier and Gerald Torres. (Her B.A. is from Radcliffe, her J.D. from Yale. His A.B. is from Stanford, his J.D. from Yale, and he has an LL.M. from Michigan.) By the terms of their own theory, their intelligence and perseverance (i.e., merit) had nothing to do with their academic success. No objective performance measures exist, to account for their achievements. We are left with the inescapable conclusion that they got their degrees from those schools solely through tokenism, or through sheer, random good luck.

And if merit and objective standards are meaningless, then we should choose all law students, and even all law professors, at random. In fact, we should hand out law licenses at random, and not require either a law degree, attendance at law school, or the passing of a bar exam. — Granted, though, the new racists would want a "set-aside" to ensure that "people of color" would be handed degrees and law licenses and law professorships in a percentage equal to those groups' percentage of the general population. (Or perhaps Guinier and other members of the "Party's" Central Committee will hand out these credentials on the basis of "authenticity.") —But then again, if race is "all in the mind" (as they insist it is), then savvy law school applicants, for example, would claim to be members of whatever "political race" (G&T's term) that was currently privileged. (Rutgers-Newark now says that its applicants can designate themselves as members of whatever race they choose. Were I to be applying to law school now, and to Rutgers-Newark, I'd declare myself one-quarter black, one-quarter Hispanic/Latino/Chicano, one-quarter Inuit, and one-quarter Ainu—the Ainu being a tiny minority of Caucasians, in Japan.)

Guinier and Torres focus exclusively on race, yet claim that their focus on race is economic, because a disproportionately large number of blacks and browns are poor. Yet, they also acknowledge (page 56) that, "In fact, there are many more poor white people in America than poor black people." But instead of widening their critique of society to an analysis of class (as, for example, Barbara Ehrenreich does in her book on working-class women, *Nickled and Dimed*), they provide (pages 102-103) this *astonishing* rationalization for their approach:

> Another answer to "Why not class?" is that we are working with categories that people understand. *There is simply no American vocabulary for class as a linked fate or as a basis for critique of systemic failure.*   [Emphasis added.]

Huh?

Apparently, G&T would have us believe that ordinary people, unlike professors at the law schools at Harvard and the University of Texas, cannot understand, and have never articulated, the concept of the exploitation of one economic class by another.

Can G&T's ignorance truly be *that* abysmal?

Or, like that guy from Linz, are they perhaps instead working with a different agenda?

History Repeats

Populism arose in America in the early 1890s. In fact, it started in Torres's own state of Texas (Lampasas County, to be specific). For its first few years, it emphasized the class struggle of poor and working-class whites *and people of color* against the banks and great business interests that were ruthlessly exploiting them. They were a serious threat to the powers-that-be.

The powers-that-be responded with a strategy of divide-and-conquer. They promoted new "leaders" who played the "race card," to set poor and working-class whites against poor and working-class blacks. They succeeded brilliantly. Populism became a house divided against itself and soon was marginalized.

Guinier and Torres denounce what they call "racial identity politics" as the tool of white conservatives. Yet, they then offer a racial identity politics of their own. (The first clause in the subtitle of their book, recall, is "Enlisting Race.") Thus, they talk out of both sides of their mouths. (Under the rules they set for themselves, however, this is fair. All that counts is the pursuit of power, remember? So, contradicting oneself is of no matter.) And by choosing to build their own personal power base (and celebrity) on racial animosity, they perform the same function as the old racist demogogues who perverted and destroyed populism at the end of the 19th century. In short, they're *frauds*.

The Critical/Political Race Theorists (and the Fem Crits) pose as "outsiders," allegedly challenging the citadels of white male power. America has a tradition of romanticism regarding the "outsider" (such as the "loners" of the old Westerns—and all "action-adventure" films). And Americans have a natural sympathy for the underdog. And so, clever politicians have repeatedly used these two themes to ride to power— Ronald Reagan being the best example.

Although the New Crits are vociferously political, their behavior is aptly described by what novelist Tom Wolfe, in his non-fiction book *The Painted Word,* called "The Boho Dance."

Wolfe told of young artists in New York who were "hot," and whose works had suddenly begun to sell for hundreds of thousands of dollars, making the artists rich. But artists are supposed to be bohemians ("bohos," for short—and never mind that Picasso had become a *billionaire* long before his death). They had an image to maintain as "outsiders." And this image was in conflict with their newfound wealth.

So, they did the Boho Dance: the more prosperous they became, the more they tried to look and sound like anti-Establishment bohemians.

(This is a common practice. Witness the "rock" singers who use sub-standard English in their lyrics, despite the fact that the singers in some instances were raised in a life of luxury, complete with attendance at private boarding schools, and have long since become multimillionaires. This is true even of some country-western singers. Something similar occurs with televangelists who accumulate great personal fortunes while presenting themselves as preachers of only modest means.)

But as long as the audience is willing to look only at the carefully contrived image, not the reality, the impostors get away with it.

Some Colors are More Equal than Others

The Critical/Political Race Theorists habitually use the term "people of color," and it is now politically correct to do so. However, their term is a false generalization. In practice, it refers only to those who are black African-Americans (as contrasted with North Africans who are Arabs or Berbers) or who are Hispanic/Latino/Chicano. It does not, in practice, refer to those whose ancestry is that of the Middle East, the Indian sub-continent, or any of the peoples of the Far East.

The reason for this is that those other peoples accept objective reality, truth, merit, intelligence, and the value of individual effort. The self-proclaimed spokespeople of the B&B group (blacks and certain browns) do not. They see "their" people as deserving of a privileged status and special treatment, as they revel in their sentimentalism and celebrate their role as "victims." They speak only for a subset of people of color, despite their propagandistic claim to speak for all.

By framing the discussion only as one of color, they ignore the group that has been most victimized in the history of the West: Jews.

Indeed, the history of hostility to Jews goes back to the ancient Greeks. Their warrior culture was hostile to the merchant culture of the Phoenicians—who were, for centuries, the dominant sea power in the Mediterranean. Before Christianity, the Romans, as intellectual heirs to the Greeks, institutionalized Greek anti-Semitism for two reasons. First, two traits of Judaism threatened the social cohesion of the Roman Empire: (1) Judaism was monotheistic and, unlike all other religions, refused to acknowledge the legitimacy of others' beliefs; and (2) it was the fastest-growing religion in the Roman world, actively seeking converts in the manner of the modern Church of Jesus Christ of the Latter Day Saints. Second, Judaea repeatedly rebelled against Rome, and set a bad example, in Rome's eyes. The New Testament (composed mostly after the failed Jewish Revolt of 67-70 A.D.), in an effort to distinguish Pauline Christianity from that of, for example, James—the brother of Jesus—made anti-Semitism an article of faith. Thus, the Holocaust was an inextricably *Christian* phenomenon, at least passively or indirectly supported by nearly *all* "good" Christians at the time. The Nazis were evil, but they had many, many fellow travellers...including Henry Ford and Charles Lindbergh. But all that is now "down the memory hole" (another term from *1984).* No people have done more than the Jews to triumph over pervasive, systematic victimization.

(However, because of the Holocaust, Christendom is now on a "guilt trip"...to the benefit of Israel. Anyone who dares "speak truth" to Israel's power is instantly labelled "anti-*Semitic.*" The role of *Jewish* terrorism against the British, in the *founding* of Israel—via the Stern Gang, the Irgun, and the Hagannah—has disappeared down the memory hole. al-Qaeda, Hezbollah, and Hamas are epigones. They vent their fury on those who took—or who support those who took—from the Palestinians the country now known as "Israel." The moral is: No one has "clean hands." The human race would have a better chance for improvement if each race would face up to its own ignobility.)

Chinese-Americans and Japanese-Americans, much more recently than American Jews, were subjected to cruel discriminatory practices. And consider the successes of Vietnamese-Americans, many of whom arrived as "boat people" refugees, often without knowing more than a handful of words in English. Many Korean-Americans likewise prevailed over adversity. (In fact, whereas there is now an informal "quota" to get *enough* blacks and browns admitted to law schools to ensure "diversity," there is also an informal quota at many schools to *limit* the enrollment of *Asians*—just as, after Jews were first allowed into prestigious law schools, there was a quota to limit *them.*)

But the Critical/Political Race Theorists will not hear of it. As Farber and Sherry explain, these new racists have developed an "internal logic" to account for these other groups' successes: "If Jews and Asians are better at playing the crooked card game than the dealer, Jews and Asians must be even more crooked than he is."

Instead of stereotyping all "Asians," though, the new racists should consider a few hundred years of Chinese and Japanese history...

For most of its history, China had the highest civilization in the world. As Galvin Menzies has shown in his recent book, *1421,* large fleets of huge Chinese ships circumnavigated the globe many decades before Magellan. But even as the fleets were at sea, a power struggle broke out within the Chinese bureaucracy, between the Mandarins and the eunuchs. Ironically, the eunuchs were the ones with the balls (metaphorically speaking). They were open to science, new technology, commerce, and exploration. The Mandarins wanted a closed, static society. They won. And so, early in the 15th century, China turned inward, and remained frozen in time. Resting on its laurels, it stagnated. The European powers soon surpassed it, and then mercilessly subjugated and plundered it—as they did nearly everyone else.

For centuries, Japan was left virtually untouched...because Japan had nothing the nations of the West desired. But in 1853, at the height of Western domination of China, the Americans forced their way into Japan and demanded a series of "unequal treaties" that left the Japanese largely at the mercy of the Americans (and British). The Japanese knew they would soon suffer the same fate as the Chinese.

The result was the Meiji "Restoration" of 1868. Initially, its purpose was to "expel the barbarians." They wanted to restore the static society (modelled on China) that had existed for the 250+ years of the Tokugawa Period, before the arrival of the Americans. But a couple of brief military encounters quickly convinced the Meiji leaders that they were doomed... unless they changed their ways. So, they changed their ways.

Their new guiding slogan transliterates as "Wa kon, yo-o sai." It loosely translates as "Japanese spirit, Western learning." The Japanese became students of Western science, technology, and commerce. And they built up great national wealth and power. In 1894, they tested themselves against the moribund Chinese. Ten years later, they were ready to take on a white power, the Russians. They triumphed.

(True, they overplayed their hand a few decades later. But by then, the leaders of the Meiji Era were long dead. The imperial throne was occupied by a young, overly ambitious, and foolish sovereign, and the military was dominated by a young, overly ambitious, and foolish officer corps. In the same way, Germany—united only in 1866—was, by 1914, in the hands of a sovereign who was young, overly ambitious, and foolish, and its military was dominated by a young, overly ambitious, and foolish officer corps. In each nation, they did not know when to leave well enough alone...a lesson that America is now perhaps about to learn. But after WWII, the Japanese and Germans redoubled their efforts, and again prospered. —A Japanese proverb says, "Knocked down three times, get up four." Historically, the Jews have had that same indomitable spirit. And for the past half-century, the Chinese have been making up for over half-a-*millennium* of lost time.)

The B&B crowd claim to be "multiculturalists." Yet, they're ignorant of any cultures, histories, law, philosophies, religions, and literatures other than their own (if even those). (One of the slogans in *1984* was "Ignorance is Strength.") They evince what *1984* referred to as "collective solipsism." They want only to continue their own newly closed-off system of sentimentalism and "Queen for a Day" sob-stories.

The Color of MONEY

The Critical/Political Race Theorists speak of "color" (though Guinier & Torres say it's "all in the mind"). Their discussion largely concerns wealth v. poverty. But by limiting their discussion to a subset of those who are not well-to-do among blacks or certain "browns"—in contrast to all "people of color" (or for that matter, to all people who are not well-to-do, regardless of color), they accomplish three things.

First, they carve out a racial constituency for themselves, for whom they claim to be spokespeople. They thus create a "pressure group" that is manageable, as opposed to, say, trying to claim leadership of *all* who are not well-to-do. Second, by insisting that "the American people" (versus, say, just the blacks and browns whom the C/PRT professoriat claims to represent) are *incapable* of understanding a discussion of economic exploitation, they divert attention from the fact that these law profs are *pseudo*-members of the group they claim to speak for.

Third, despite their rhetoric, their goal is merely to have more "seats at the table" for their followers—which in turn builds up the power base of these self-proclaimed leaders. In other words, what they seek is more *tokenism* (although the politically correct term for it is "affirmative action"), with themselves as "head tokens."

Thus, *they are no real threat to those whom they claim to be challenging*. A savvy "ruling class" is willing to reach an accommodation with those who demand a place at the table.

(Something else that's gone down the memory hole is that the *first* "affirmative action" program was started by *Richard Nixon*. After the Congressional Democrats pushed through Civil Rights legislation in 1965, racist whites in the South deserted the Democratic Party. First they went to George Wallace's racist independent party. But after the ghetto rioting that followed Martin Luther King's assassination, Nixon brought the white racists into the GOP with his code phrase rhetoric of "law and order." So, the fact that it was Nixon who began "affirmative action" ought to give its advocates pause. —And, also, Nixon was the only president who's ever proposed a *"negative* income tax," whereby everyone in America would be guaranteed sufficient "transfer payments" from the federal government to provide them with an annual income of x dollars.)

The "buffaloes" (in Austin's term) who control faculty appointments and admissions to law schools are quite happy to establish larger quotas for blacks and browns, at the expense of whites and of other people of color such as Asians. After all, the "buffaloes" have already been "grandfathered in." It costs *them* nothing to discriminate against Gentile whites, Jews, and Asians, even if that means exacerbating racial animosities between the favored and disfavored groups. The only way the "buffaloes" would themselves have to pay the price they impose on others would be if their law schools announced a lottery among the white (male) profs. Those whose names were drawn would be fired, and replaced by blacks and browns—preferably female.

By pretending that economic exploitation is of concern only to the B&B crowd, and by exhorting, for example, "magical realism," the C/PRT merely engage in a subtle form of *extortion,* the ultimate goal of which is their *own* aggrandizement. They condemn what they say is America's "political gridlock"—yet seek to exploit it.

But do the corporate executives who perpetrated frauds that wiped out the value of the pension funds of hundreds of thousands of people care what color those people were? Does it make any difference the color of the person who has worked hard all his or her life at an hourly wage, when he or she sees those who've been raised in privilege then rip off hundreds of millions of dollars and get away with it?

So-called economic "globalization" has meant the hollowing-out of the American manufacturing sector. Capital has become internationally mobile, but labor has not. In this age of "hyper-capitalism," the rich get richer, the poor get entitlements (so far)...and the *middle class,* the backbone of any democracy, is being *wiped out.* America is well on its way to becoming the world's largest "banana republic"—with all that implies for freedom and an "open society." With the trade deficit and federal budget deficit now both approaching half-a-*trillion* dollars *each year,* our economic house of cards is overdue for collapse.

Thanks largely to the demogogues of both Left and Right, the races will then be pitted against each other, fighting over mere scraps, instead of uniting to revise our economic policies and to revive the American Dream for all.

(But Guinier & Torres dismiss the American Dream in the first place. I wonder what they'll call for when push does come to shove.)

Deeds, not Words

If the Critical/Political Race Theorists were sincere about wanting to improve the lot of "their people," the natural place for them to start would be their own backyards: the law schools where they have tenure and full professorships.

On page 110 of *The Miner's Canary,* Guinier and Torres say:

> In short, *there are "winners": there is a bias in the rules that defines "winning" and there is a narrative that justifies both the winners and the rules by which they win....Those with control maintain control because they set the agenda.* With no voice in the process that distributes power, those out of power have a hard time wresting control. *And they become further isolated and alienated because the stories that the winners tell the losers make the losers feel as though they deserve their condition and do not have a legitimate right to complain.*
>
> (Emphasis added.)

That is a perfect description of *law school* (as discussed in Chapter 25).

Guinier, Torres, Derek Bell, Richard Delgado, Patricia Williams, Jerome Culp, Mari Matsuda, Kimberlé Crenshaw, Paul Butler, and their ilk, by being tenured professors, "maintain control and set the agenda." They give lip-service (following the original Crits) to "abolishing hierarchies." But they are deeply imbedded in, and benefit from, the perpetuation of the law schools' hierarchy, culture, and political and economic agenda. Thus, they too are "oppressors" in a system that continues to disadvantage not only the stereotypical "people of color," but *all* people who are not among the wealthy and powerful.

(Another quotation from *Animal Farm* is apt: "Somehow it seemed that the farm had become richer without making the animals richer—except, of course, for the pigs and dogs." And the very last words in *Animal Farm* are these: "The creatures outside looked from pig to man, and from man to pig, and from pig to man again, but it was already impossible to tell which was which." Power to the Pigs!)

Were they sincere, one of the first things they would do would be to try to *teach* their students both the substantive and procedural law, instead of playing hide-the-ball. They'd demand changes in the law school curriculum and the bar exam, to no longer require mastery of topics (such as Estates & Future Interests) that are of concern only to a tiny elite of the truly wealthy. It is said that any given case, or any given topic of the law, can be used to teach "The Law"—i.e., "how to think like a lawyer." So why not emphasize a curriculum that includes topics for "lawyerlike analysis" that will be of use to the vast majority of future lawyers? Topics such as consumer protection, family law, debtor-creditor law, and a *worthwhile* course in criminal law.

Granted, such changes would not be welcome at the elite law schools, where the new racists are comfortably ensconced. But that is further proof of the Race Crits' hypocrisy. Were they sincere, Guinier, Torres, Bell, Delgado, Williams, Culp, Crenshaw, and Butler would move to law schools where a *majority* of the students are "of color"—Howard, Southern, Texas Southern, UNC Central, UDC, or CUNY. (Texas Southern University and the University of the District of Columbia are currently "competing" for the title of "America's worst law school.") They would reform the curriculum and pedagogy so that it would be of *value* to students as future lawyers, beyond just being the gauntlet students have to run to get permission to sit for the bar. In place of the forced curve, they would *insist* on a minimal level of competence of *all* law students—a *high* minimal level. Thus, even the "worst" student at one of these schools would be better than even the best students at the "white" law schools. And the Race Crits would lobby truly wealthy blacks and browns in the worlds of commerce, show business, and sports, to contribute funds to enable these "minority" schools to *hold down tuition costs* and to turn out graduates who, as "people of color," would then habitually outclass and outmaneuver the stereotypical whites who allegedly are perpetuating a rigged system in favor of white folk.

And because these students would be graduates of low-ranked schools, there would not be the temptation for them to "sell out" the way people of color at the top schools now sell out—as do the white students. (As Chapter 25 explained, that's the whole idea, and students usually have no choice, because of their staggering debts.)

The pedagogy and curriculum of all law schools is now so bad that it would be fairly easy to start turning out large numbers of minority graduates who would quickly begin to have a major positive impact on their communities. Then, instead of thinking in polarized terms, of individual v. group, this would emulate other groups that have realized there's a third path: not the "survival of the fittest," but "the fitting of as many as possible to survive"—in the words of T.H. Huxley, first quoted on page 45 in Chapter 2. By making it possible for *many* individuals within the group to succeed, instead of only the chosen few who are favored by reverse discrimination quotas, the lot of the entire group would improve.

At the very least, the C/PRT professoriat should take charge of and overhaul the CLEO program (discussed on pages 446-47 in Chapter 16).

In short, these new rednecks should put up or shut up.

"Start with a Man"

Quite likely, the preceding jeremiad will generate a response that this is "blaming the victim."

But there are times when victims *deserve* blame; hence, sayings such as "A fool and his money are soon parted," "Those who live by the sword shall perish by the sword," "Lie down with dogs, get up with fleas," and "Fool me once, shame on you—fool me *twice,* shame on *me.*"

There are three possible explanations for the failure of blacks and certain browns to "get ahead" in academia, whether as students or faculty, in proportion to their numbers in the population.

The first possible reason is that they are incapable. They "just don't have what it takes" in the brains department. That, of course, is racist nonsense.

The second possible reason is related to the first, in that it too springs from racism (reversed): that blacks and browns are inherently capable, but are being held back by whites. Until quite recently in American history, blacks and certain browns were indeed held back, as were Jews and Asians. But now, the neo-racists insist that blacks and browns are still being discriminated against, despite the successes of Jews and Asians. Their argument is that white Gentiles were willing to allow Jews and Asians seats at the table, but still refuse to countenance the presence of blacks and browns.

But it's the third possible reason that seems to fit: that blacks and certain browns are *holding themselves back,* through a culture that rejects the values of the Life of the Mind in general, and academe in particular.

The proof for refuting the first two reasons given for the failure and blacks and browns in this regard has long been around. And it provides indirect proof for the validity of the third possible reason.

As soon as the barriers were dropped, blacks and browns began to succeed in large numbers in show business, professional sports, commerce, and the officer corps of the armed forces. Their successes required brains as well as raw talent, and perseverance—i.e., merit.

Marian Anderson, and more recently, Kathleen Battle, did not forgo opera as "white man's music." Oprah Winfrey, Bill Cosby, and the Wayans family did not dismiss television as "white man's technology." Arthur Ashe, and more recently, Venus and Serena Williams, did not belittle tennis as a "white man's sport." Tai Babilonia, Debi Thomas, Rudy Galindo, Randy Gardner, and Bobby Beauchamp did not reject figure skating as a "white man's sport." Nor has Tiger Woods denounced golf as "a white man's game." And the many black and brown athletes who've excelled in baseball, football, and basketball do not regard themselves as having "gone white." (As to professional football, there have now been several quite successful black quarterbacks, and black coaches. These two roles, perhaps more than any other in the NFL, require *brains*.) C.J. Walker, the first black businesswoman to become a millionaire (she died in 1919) did not eschew commerce as "only for white people." Nor did George F. Johnson, of Johnson Products; Don King, the impressario of heavyweight boxing; or Don Cornelius, producer and host of the old *Soul Train* television show (the first nationally syndicated "black" program). Oprah Winfrey, as an entrepreneuse, has parlayed her show business success into a business empire that now makes her one of the richest people, of any color, in the entire world. Blacks and browns in the armed forces do not disparage the arts and sciences of war as only suitable to "whites."

The Critical/Political Race Theorists write in English, and do not eschew it as a "white man's langauage" in favor of, say, "Ebonics." (Were the Hispanic/Latino/Chicano C/PRT writers to eschew English in favor of Spanish, they would have to acknowledge that Spanish is a "white man's language," derived from Latin. —And roughly one-third of the Latin vocabulary is derived from Greek...roughly a third of which, in turn, as Martin Bernal has shown in his brilliant *Black Athena* works, is derived from Semitic languages of the Ancient Near East.)

Success in show business, professional sports, commerce, and war are all based on objective reality, truth, individual effort, color-blindness, and merit. Yet, the New Crits deny these exist in *one* field—education—because, they say, those values are part of "the white man's" scam against "people of color" (i.e., blacks, certain browns, and even white women).

One of the films that stars Jack Nicholson is *As Good as It Gets*. In it, he plays a novelist. In one scene, he's visiting his publisher's office. The young female receptionist gushes about his work. Then she asks him, "How do you write your women characters so well?" He replies, "Start with a man." He pauses, then adds, "Take away reason and accountability."

The line is meant to get laughs, and it does. It's also meant to be an insult to women. But the radical feminists among the New Crits have expressly *chosen* that description as a badge of *honor*. So have the Critical/Political *Race* Theorists. (It brings to mind the animated cartoon character, Bart Simpson, who wears a T-shirt on which these words are printed: "Underachiever—and *Proud of It!*")

But what group is *best* characterized as lacking reason and accountability?

Small children.

And until relatively recently in America, what was the most common way that white men described white women and all "people of color"?

"They're like *children.*"

At their best, children are child-like—innocent, trusting, simple, honest (well, usually), compassionate, and inherently fair-minded. At their worst, they're child-*ish.* And the most common word for that is "brat."

Michael Jackson is the only adult I know of who remains child-like well into middle age. His hero is Peter Pan. But "Jocko" has a few hundred million dollars with which to fund his escape at will from the world of grown-ups.

The Fem Crits and Critical/Political Race Theorists, in contrast, are child*ish*—specifically, brats; more specifically, *spoiled* brats, well into middle age. (And even Jocko, when sales of his recordings declined, blamed it on his record company's "racism." Pull-eeze.) Thus, the quotation from Edward de Bono on page 725 about how "youngsters" turn away from logic to "raw emotions and feelings" was apt.

Contrast this with one of the founders of contemporary feminism, Kate Millet. Her influential bestseller, *Sexual Politics,* was originally her Ph.D. thesis at Columbia. Her dissertation advisor was a man, Steven Marcus. In the book's introduction, Millet says this about him (and about her editor, who was a woman):

> The book holds water thanks not only to his intellectual courage but to his *dogged insistence on proof and more proof, exhaustive reading, research, and analysis. He raised the argument above feminist rhetoric* into the kind of cultural criticism it aimed for and hoped to help invent. Betty Prashker was an editor who really worked on a text. *I was an angry young woman with a message....They taught me by being tough and patient and exacting;* the book owes them both a great debt. (Emphasis added.)

Of course, the Feminist Crits will have none of this. The same is true of the Critical/Political Race Theorists. They prefer exhibitionistic mental masturbation to procreation. They'd rather engage in psychological rapine than love-making.

(Despite the fact that there are scores of "Women's Studies" departments at major universities, I am told that Millet is now unemployed and living in poverty. Not by choice. Apparently, raising the argument above mere rhetoric is unacceptable to the extremists who've taken over in the ivory tower...and so is Kate Millet. And more than one black, who refused to "toe the party line" of the new racists, has been forced out of a Department of Black Studies.)

The New Crits say to white Gentiles, Jews, and "people of color" from North Africa, the Middle East, the Indian sub-continent, and the Far East: "We understand *you*. But *you* simply *cannot* understand *us*. For we are *sui generis* among the peoples of the Earth—and you have to *coddle* us, because *we are as little children*."

"Shall We (Ghost) Dance?"

Science fiction writer Kim Stanley Robinson, in his new novel *The Years of Rice and Salt*, has an appropriate line. As part of a fictional leader's efforts to unite and rally Native Americans against non-Indian invaders, he says, "[Y]ou can face them as one, resist their attacks, *take from them what is useful, and stand up to them as equals on this Earth*." (Emphasis added.)

Contrast that with a real-life Native American leader, whose name was Wovoka. He was born in the mid-1850s, and was a member of the Piute tribe. Around 1888-89, he had a mystical vision. In it, he was told that the American Indians were to recover all the lands the whites had taken, and to become prosperous. To help bring about that miracle, they were to do ritualistic "ghost" dances, while wearing a special white shirt. The "ghost shirts" had magical powers. In battle, the white man's bullets would bounce off them.

You know what happened. Many of those gunned down at Wounded Knee, for example, were wearing ghost shirts.

So much for a precursor to "magical realism." But just as Guinier and Torres say "but we are not magical realists ourselves," so Wovoka never put *himself* on the line. (He lived until 1932.)

Long after the gullible law students who become followers of the Critical/Political Race Theorists (and the Fem Crits) have had their futures shot down, and have joined the original Critical Legal Studies followers in the dustbin of American jurisprudential history, the founders of these schools—just as with the founders of CLS—will be living out their days in peace and prosperity as tenured faculty members at America's law schools. Yet, after their academic "pyramid scheme" has collapsed, they will blame the "white hegemonists" for their failure.

In the words attributed to philosopher George Santayana, "Those who do not learn from history are doomed to repeat it." But for the New Crits, there's no such thing as history, for there is no such thing as objective reality, truth, etc., etc.

Farber & Sherry, in *Beyond All Reason,* quote Salman Rushdie (who ran afoul of Iran's "Thought Police"): "[I]t matters, it always matters, to name rubbish as rubbish, to do otherwise is to letigimize it." Rushdie used a polite word, "rubbish," although a vulgar slang term is more appropriate. But I shall put it this way: the only "movement" Professor "Jive" Guinier and Professor "Pendejadas" Torres, for example, will be able to successfully bring about is that associated with the bowels.

None So Blind as Those Who WILL Not See

Here's another poem, "The Wayfarer," from Stephen Crane:

> The wayfarer,
> Perceiving the pathway to truth,
> Was struck with astonishment.
> It was thickly grown with weeds.
> "Ha," he said,
> I see that none has passed here
> In a long time."
> Later he saw that each weed
> Was a singular knife.
> "Well," he mumbled at last,
> "Doubtless there are other roads."

This fits the New Crits. Hence, for example, G&T's ridiculous statements about a "modern" understanding of power, and a "new 21st-century way of talking."

When speaking of the Bourbon Restoration in France after the years of Napoleon, Talleyrand said of the arrogant, reinstated royalty, "They have forgotten nothing...and have learned nothing." The New Crits, in contrast, forget whatever facts and truths are inconvenient to them. Like the Bourbons, however, they've learned nothing, nor do they wish to. They have no humility in the face of history, only hubris.

The New Crits aren't interested in teaching first-year students how to conduct a lawyerlike analysis, or in teaching worthwhile substantive courses to second- and third-year students. Instead, they offer courses that Austin rightly calls "Law & a Banana." They make their students keep diaries, which the New Crits call "journals." As with Ahab, there's a relentless quest, to harpoon the "Great White...Male." In these diaries, white students are to beat up on themselves for being white, and white *male* students have to *really* get masochistic. Students who are black and brown are to *celebrate* their alleged victimhood. If the prof is a *Fem* Crit, *female* students who are black and brown are also to beat up on their fellow black and brown students who are *male*. As for Jews, it brings to mind the old humorous, satirical song by Tom Lehrer— who was a (Jewish) professor at M.I.T.—"National Brotherhood Week": "All the Protestants hate the Catholics / All the Catholics hate the Protestants / All the Moslems hate the Hindus / And *everybody* hates the *Jews*."

I believe the unspoken reason why the New Crits do this is that they are *incapable* of teaching students how to do a lawyerlike analysis. (In this, of course, they're no different from virtually all white profs.)

Each of us is able to recognize quality in the performing arts, or athletics, even though few of us are capable of anything approaching that quality. So it is with law profs. They're able to *recognize* "thinking like a lawyer," but are not able to do it themselves. Hence, the emphasis on "policy discussions," which are just continuations of the "bull sessions" students are so familiar with from many college courses.

The New Crits do not admit the inadequacies they share with white professors. Rather than recognize them as inadequacies, they choose to *celebrate* them as their own "virtues." They're unable to reason, so they reject reason and logic. Evidence often goes against them, so they reject facts.

Rather than admit that times have changed since the days of Jim Crow, they—as with *white* rednecks—sing "Old Times there are not forgotten" and live in the long-ago past. They do not face the realities of the present and the needs of the future.

They're in the situation expressed by the words of the cartoon-strip character, Pogo, "We have met the enemy...and *they* are *us*."

For Those Who Believe in Learning from History

However, *The Miner's Canary* itself refers to someone who provided a real-life role model for what needs to be done: Septima Clark. Her name is but a footnote in the history of the Civil Rights Movement. (Interesting, that although G&T denigrate the Civil Rights Movement for its emphasis on individual effort, they make it a point to discuss Clark's program that demanded strenuous individual effort.)

Septima Clark was a black woman who set up "Citizenship Schools" for illiterate blacks in the South, to teach reading and writing. The "minority" law schools in America could be the *new* "citizenship schools," teaching future attorneys of color how to be good at their craft...not as "also-rans" against "Whitey," but *beating Whitey at his own game.*

Another role-model, still alive and well, is Wentworth Miller. Chapters 6 and 7 discussed his "Legal Essay Exam Writing System" (LEEWS). LEEWS is color-blind. And it's based, as were Clark's "Citizenship Schools," on all the things the C/PRT ideologues reject.

Miller's own "story" is particularly instructive. As with Guinier and Torres, he's a graduate of Yale's law school. (In fact, Guinier was a year ahead of him there, and the two were friends.) On his father's side, Miller is descended from black slaves in Jamaica; on his mother's side, from black slaves in Mississippi. Unlike all the black C/PRT folks, however, he spent several years in Africa (albeit while still a child).

Miller became a Rhodes Scholar. At the time, even though American blacks were eligible for that honor, blacks from South Africa (where Rhodes made his huge fortune) were barred. Miller began a three-year effort, ultimately successful, to get Britain's Parliament to end the Rhodes discrimination against South African blacks—which in turn led to another change that allowed *women* to become Rhodes Scholars.

In 1978, Miller did an article for blacks, on taking the bar exam. He was then hired by the Bar Association of the City of New York to tutor blacks for the barzam. LEEWS grew out of that effort.

He has told me that a disproportionately large number of attendees at his program are "the children of immigrants" from North Africa, the Middle East, the Indian sub-continent, and the Far East. (I have attended the live LEEWS presentation three times now—twice presented by Miller, once by his associate, JoAnne Page—and each time, a disproportionately small number of blacks and Hispanics/Latinos/Chicanos were present.) But LEEWS is something that all the C/PRT people (and the Fem Crits) should be *demanding* their law schools teach—*as part-and-parcel of students' basic instruction in the law,* in each course, as part of what they pay their *tuition* for. And certainly the six aforementioned "majority minority" schools should include LEEWS as part of their teaching. But of course, they do not. They would rather complain about "white male hegemony" than take effective measures to gain parity, let alone supremacy. When not angrily shaking their fists, they're passively sitting on their hands...or just playing with themselves.

However, that said, here are some words from Miller to me when I told him of my intention to cite him in this chapter. (These comments are reprinted with his permission):

"[I]t is evident to me that I live a very different life as the result of not being taken for black than if I had brown skin. [Miller is light-skinned.] I don't think I could show up at hotels [LEEWS is presented at hotels] and get people to do this and that, if I had first to deal with being perceived as black. So you have to be careful here in holding me up as an example....

"It certainly isn't as simple as saying, 'Well, here's Miller who's done this and that and isn't whining.' I'm not concerned with being perceived in some political light. You want to take on Guinier, *et al.*, as part of a critique of law school, etc., and interject me in some way...I might also note that Guinier, who is more obviously black than I, doubtless *has* experienced subtle and not-so-subtle racism as a steady diet in in her life....

"Of course, my philosophy has changed from when I was an angry black man (definitely was), wearing a black leather jacket, chanting 'Power to the People!' and supporting the Black Panthers. Even wrote a poem eulogizing the Symbionese Liberation Army....I am very much into ignoring racist stuff, which surely exists out there, and into working hard, not making excuses, etc....

"Be careful not to allow your central theme—confronting law school methodology—to be sidetracked or compromised by a diversion into race."

Points well made....and as you see, ignored. Please forgive my melodrama, but I believe that what's at stake, for the future of race relations, of legal education, the legal profession and the judiciary, and of this country itself, is just too important to let the New Crits go uncriticized, for I believe they are leading "naïve cynics" down the primrose path....to disaster.

When Miller sent me his comments, he'd not had the benefit of seeing a draft of this chapter in manuscript. I do not believe that this chapter is a *diversion* from a discussion of law school methodology into a discussion of race. Rather, the rise of the Critical/Political Race Theorists (and of the Critical Feminists) is inherently related to law school methodology. That's why this chapter is titled "The Chickens Come Home to Roost."

Excursus into the Legitimizing of the Totalitarian "Mind Set"

The Enlightenment and the rise of science came hand in hand, creating a "revolution of rising expectations." Optimistis proclaimed that "science" (especially the social sciences) would lead to the creation of the socially-engineered "New Man" (and Woman).

But with the horrors and utter irrationality of World War One, disillusionment set in. A reaction began against the Enlightenment's beliefs, and against science. Intellectuals moved from one extreme to the other. This soon took the form of an attack on the Life of the Mind itself. As Jacques Barzun (pronounced "BAR-zoon") describes it in his book, *The House of Intellect,* "In turning individual militant individualism into socially protective liberalism, they idealized all downtrodden minorities, including children, and instead of 'liquidating ignorance' hunted down Intellect as an ogre to be destroyed."

In America, though, intellectuals only reached the first part of that pattern, initially: the idealization of downtrodden minorities. And they put intellect in service to that idealization.

No matter how noble their intentions, however, this was a betrayal of intellect, for intellect must always be critical—not in the sense of being negative, but in the sense of questioning assumptions and being open to new ways of looking at old subjects.

American academics (following Europe's) exposed assumptions, and questioned them. But they did so only for the purpose of condemning them, as part of a *political agenda.* They were open to new ways of looking at subjects only if those new ways were politically correct.

And the intellectuals, as with virtually all self-conscious groups, never questioned *their* assumptions (pro or con) about the intellect itself. There's a saying, "When all you have is a hammer, every problem begins to look like a nail." Likewise, now that America is the world's only military superpower, every problem on earth seems to call for a military solution. And so with intellectuals. Although "feelings" took priority over rigorous thinking, the feelings were intellectualized.

Even in rejecting the Enlightenment and science, thinkers remained characteristically "intellectual." Barzun referred to what he called "intellectualism." Among its many characteristics was *a refusal to distinguish between abstractions based on facts and the facts on which the abstractions are based.* Having concocted a theory to explain reality, those afflicted with intellectualism then see reality through the eyes of the theory. (And with that, we're back to "One must believe, to understand.")

Those who fancied themselves intellectuals never lost their fascination with system-building. They wanted to maintain their identity as a group, as "intellectuals." They did so by continuing to create systems of abstractions. They would then regard as "anti-intellectual" those who criticized the sheer unreality of those systems. And having intentionally distanced themselves from the general public, they then bemoaned how the "philistines" did not appreciate them. (Example: Richard Hofstadter's *Anti-Intellectualism in American Life.*) Most artists, poets, makers of "art" films, and so forth, did likewise, in Europe as well as in America. As a result, Western culture is virtually "brain-dead."

But given the nonsense being preferred in the name of the life of the mind, small wonder that those with any sense became what was called anti-intellectual. (In the movie *Godfather II*, the Corleone family is at the dinner table around Christmas. This was just a few weeks after America's involvement in WWII had begun. Michael, the future godfather, has come in from college for the gathering. He announces that he has enlisted in the Marine Corps. His eldest brother looks at him incredulously, then says, "What—you went to college to get *stupid?*" Audiences burst out laughing at that line...because they knew that, to this very day, a college "education" *undermines* one's ability to develop one's intelligence, rather than enhancing it. But, with respect to legal educatoin, the process began much earlier.)

Both communism and fascism are theoretical systems based on abrstractions. And that is why communism and fascism had such appeal to intellectuals of the left and right, respectively, after the loss of faith in the Enlightenment.

The political system of communism was based on the system of abstractions that comprise Marxism. (Granted, though, Marx came up with many profound and penetrating insights.) And fascism (including its German manifestation as Nazism) was similarly based. But because intellectuals had lost faith in the intellect itself, they did not care that Marxism (or fascism) was really a religious dogma, expressed in secular language and concepts, rather than an expression of the Life of the Mind as that term had traditionally been understood. (Capitalist economic theory, after the passing of Smith, Ricardo, *et al.,* was largely developed as a response to the apparent sophistication of Marxist economics. That's why I spoke of it earlier, seriously, as "secular theology.") And echoing Saint Anselm, their attitude was "One must believe, to understand." What they believed in was the nobility of the downtrodden, as against the sheer idiocy and cupidity of the European (and American) ruling classes. ("Nazism" is just the contraction of the German words for "National - *Socialist* - *Democratic* - *Workers'* Party.")

One of the great tragedies of Western history is the sympathy so many intellectuals had for communism, in particular. And so, as the brutality of communism became apparent, they—for purely emotional reasons—either "looked away" or else tried to explain away those brutalities.

Conservatives, not wanting to acknowledge the legitimate grievances of the world's downtrodden, denounced all criticisms as "pinko." And in countries where popular movements arose against corrupt regimes, these movements were denounced as "communist." (It was true that often they received support from the old Soviet Union. But having been rejected by the Americans and Europeans, whose corporations were "in bed with" these exploitative regimes, the insurgents had little choice but to turn to the Russians for training, funds, and weapons. Such was the case, for example, with Vietnam's Ho Chi Minh, who—quoting our Declaration of Independence—had initially sought *American* support for his own independence movement, as early as the 1919 Paris peace conference after WWI. Likewise, Cuba's Castro turned to communism when it became obvious that the American government was more interested in promoting "capitalism"—i.e., the exploitation of Cuba—than in enabling those who were not part of the network of the Cuban elite to make a decent life for themselves.)

Had the intellectuals been willing to denounce communism for its theoretical absurdities and political brutalities, they would have had the moral leverage to challenge the conservatives who promoted right-wing dictatorships and brutalities in the name of "fighting communism." But they did not. Having lost faith in the Life of the Mind, they had abandoned their commitment to *intellectual* freedom—and to the *political* freedom necessary to protect it—and had willingly overlooked the communists' violations of both. Thus, they could not oppose the right-wing dictatorships on the basis of promoting either intellectual or political freedom. And so, unwittingly, they played into the hands of the far Right. The American people, presented with *only* the *two* alternatives, chose to back those who championed the dictators on the Right, not the Left.

Naturally, the new attitude among intellectuals became institutionalized and formed a hierarchy and orthodoxy of its own; hence the "speech codes" at nearly all American universities and colleges. The New Crits are now challenging it only by following through in the way the Europeans did three-quarters of a century ago, "hunting down intellect as an ogre to be destroyed." And as with most of the intellectuals in both Europe and America throughout most of the 20th century, they do not have a problem with "politically correct" totalitarian values—such as the "speech codes."

"As Ye Sow, So Shall Ye Reap."

With respect to the "scholarship" of the law school Establishment, the New Crits' attitude, as with the that of the original Crits, is "If *this* be *reason,* make the *least* of it."*

(The addendum to Chapter 9 discusses the AALS workshops for new law teachers. One of the speakers at the 2003 program, who'd been a law prof for decades, said that "Eighty percent of all law review articles are just *surveys*—of topics that have already been surveyed many times." In *The House of Intellect,* Barzun said, "It seems odd that a profession whose exercise requires the making of fine distinctions should fail to make one between significant knowledge and insignificant scribbling, while insisting pedantically on one restricted means of imparting new knowledge." Barzun was writing of academe in general, not legal education. But his comment applies *a fortiori* to the law school professoriat.)

As Chapter 25 discussed, law students are told that there is no such thing as morality, justice, or truth. There are only legal processes. Law is a science, and hence "value-free." All that counts is winning: a prestigious job that makes lots of money, or winning cases in court regardless of how—or the morality of the client's position.

It should come as no surprise that the New Crits are fixated only on winning, although they do not talk of "winning." Instead, they go straight to openly admitting their lust for power, which is just another way of saying the same thing.

Chapter 8 presented an analysis of articles by two tenured law professors, who talked of how Black Letter Law is supposedly so trivial that it's not worth class time—even though that's what's on the exams. Instead, all that counts is "policy discussions." And what is the New Crits' "storytelling" if not "policy discussion" in the guise of alleged autobiography and of allegory?

They strike a pose of "youthful" rebellion against their elders in the legal Establishment, but they are just chips off the old block(heads). They *themselves* are the *reductio ad absurdum* of a system that was already *far along* toward absurdity.

"By their fruits, ye shall know them." It's as though the trees in an orchard are diseased, and their fruits rot while hanging on the branches and never ripen. So the New Crits come along, see the diseased fruit ...and decide the solution is to cut down all the trees.

---

* My apologies to Patrick Henry.

There's a colloquial saying, "If it ain't broke, don't fix it." Langdell's system was an improvement over what preceded it. But that isn't saying much. The Langdellian pedagogy did not fix what was wrong with legal education—but it did make it more profitable for the law schools (and their parent universities). America's system of legal education has remained broken for more than a century now. But instead of trying to fix it, the New Crits want to smash it completely—and replace it with their own propaganda and power-grabbing.

In *The Empire Strikes Back: Outsiders and the Struggle Over Legal Education*, Arthur Austin, in particular, seems to regard it as a situation where "The barbarians are at the gates!" However, the barbarians are not only already *within* the gates, the gates were being *guarded* by barbarians all along. The only difference is that now the Vandals and the Huns want to displace the old Goths and Visigoths. The difference is one merely of degree, rather than kind.

It matters little who wins the present struggle, the "buffaloes" or the "buffalo-hunters." Law students, the legal profession, the judiciary, future clients of lawyers, and our society itself will continue to suffer from the pedagogical malpractice of law school regardless of whether the Establishment or the New Crits prevail.

We Americans invest enormously in refusing to face reality. As just one example: the huge "mood control" *prescription* drug industry, through which people can escape their reality (or force their children to escape reality) by remaining in a *chronic* state of "tranquillity." Yet, we put in prison those who choose to *occasionally* escape reality by having an *ecstatic* experience through drugs. Thus, the "War on (Illegal) Drugs" is ultimately just a way to avoid facing our own dependence on (legal) drugs. It's commendable to turn yourself (or your child) into an amiable near-zombie, more pliable in the hands of the powers-that-be. But it's deplorable to use drugs to "open the doors to perception."

During the "Motown Era" in soul music, a group known as The Temptations had a hit song called "Cloud 9," about escapism via illegal drugs. One of its lines referred to being "a million miles from reality."

The New Crits have escaped reality so utterly that they claim to deny the very existence of reality itself. As with others who pose as intellectuals, they fail to distinguish between abstractions based on facts and the facts themselves. But *they* (following the deconstructions and their totalitarian predecessors) declare that *facts* are abstractions.

Are their delusions and hallucinations any worse than the mind- (and soul-) dead mental gamesmanship of law school, which led them to seek escape?

An *"Allegorical Story"*

There's an old, old joke about a man who, at night, sees another man on his hands and knees searching for something under a streetlamp. The man searching is drunk. He tells the man on the sidewalk that he'd dropped his car keys in a nearby alley. "Then why are you searching *here?*" he's asked. "Because the light's better," he replies.

The law school Establishment lost the keys to legal education long, long ago. But they "lost" them under the *streetlamp*. The New Crits, though, now reject the idea that the keys even exist—let alone the metaphorical "car" in which the Life of the Mind could ride. And so, they hang out in the alley, avoiding anything that might illuminate their minds. They remain there, intoxicated with themselves and what they attempt to pass off as a school of "thought."

But the law school Establishment knows the car of the Life of the Mind *exists*, and that there are *keys* to it. They know that the keys were *tossed away* (not "dropped") long ago, and that the keys are right there under the streetlamp, in plain sight—for anyone who cares to look. But the members of the law school Establishment are drunk, too. And they care no more about the keys or the car than the New Crits do— although, in contrast to the New Crits, they like to *talk* about the keys and the car. They too stay put. They sit on the curb, passing around among themselves the intellectual equivalent of fifths of T-Bird, Mad Dog 20/20, and Night Train (the wines of choice of winos). But instead of the *belligerent, aggressive* intoxication of the New Crits, they have the mild manner of the chronically inebriated who are *always pleasant*. They have a mild "buzz" in their heads, as they babble to one another about "the importance of scholarship."

Farber and Sherry speak of the "radical" assault by the New Crits. They do not see that the New Crits are but the children of legal education's Establishment, despite the pose. In fact, what is *needed* is a radical assault—on law school pedagogy. But it must be a *wise* radicalism, in the tradition of the Founding Fathers of this country. Unlike virtually all of today's so-called "public intellectuals," the Founding Fathers were steeped in history, philosophy, jurisprudence, political theory—and, above all, in *practical experience* in the real world. Like good doctors, good generals and admirals, they knew that it's book-learning *in connection with practical experience* that gives rise to and *tests* the best theories. From their knowledge and experience, they were able to create "a new order for the ages," that preserved the best institutions and practices from the past, in part by adapting them to the needs of the present and the foreseeable future.

Part IX:

Rethinking "Thinking like a Lawyer"

Full Disclosure: I *"stole"* the title of this section—from Judith Wegner, former dean of the law school at the University of North Carolina - Chapel Hill, who's planning to use this phrase as the title of a section in a study of legal education she's currently doing for the Carnegie Foundation. (So, while I may be a "thief" of what might be called "intellectual property," at least I'm an "honest" thief—in part by having given Prof. Wegner notice of my "intent to steal.")

Chapter 27 -
Law and the Life of the Mind

The first edition of *PLS* quoted historian Richard Hofstadter's distinction (borrowed from Max Weber, the German philosopher–sociologist–jurisprude) between "true intellectuals" and "intellectual journeymen." The former "live *for* ideas," the latter "live *off* ideas" (the ideas of those who live *"for"* ideas). Lawyers typified the latter. But when writing the first edition, I'd not read Jacques Barzun's magnificent 1959 book, *The House of Intellect*. Barzun refutes Weber/Hofstadter: "The implication is false, like the distinction itself. Every mind *capable* of ideas must live *for* them as well as *by* them. Living exclusively *for* ideas does not describe an *intellectual* type but an *emotional* type." (Emphasis added.) The latter aptly describes those who live out their lives in the ivory tower, including that of legal education.

Describing what was going on in "higher" education in American even in 1959, Barzun also turned a wonderful phrase, when he referred to "the dampness factor which extinguishes any spark of intellect." Perhaps nowhere is this more true than in America's law schools.

Law professors *delight* in the accusation that they are "theoretical" and "too intellectual," because, by definition, the accusation assumes that they *are* intellectual. But the problem is not that law school is "too" intellectual. It's that law school is not intellectual at all. There's virtually nothing of the Life of the Mind there. Mental gamesmanship, yes; intellectual activity, no.

Most new ideas leading to changes in the Law come from practitioners, not law school professors. (Judges get the credit, because the changes occur only because the new ideas are adopted as judicial opinions by a sufficient number of courts. Yet, most judges' opinions merely reflect the winning side's arguments—including the new ideas. Granted, though, once in awhile judges come up with something new on their own. This is not meant to disparage judges. The fact is that most judges don't have time to deliberate. They're too busy trying to get through their dockets. So they have to go with what's in the advocates' briefs, and agree with one side or the other.)

Chapter 17 spoke of the importance of learning both formal and informal logic. Formal logic, especially, takes a binary ("either-or") approach to problems.

However, Edward de Bono, in his book, *I AM RIGHT — YOU ARE WRONG* (quoted in Chapter 26), says this about our methods of reasoning:

"We might summarize our existing methods as: 'the intelligent operation of traditional logic on existing information within a values frame." (p. 18)

You've heard the term "paradigm shift"? It's from Thomas Kuhn's classic, *The Structure of Scientific Revolutions*. The paradigm shift occurs in large part because the "values frame" (in de Bono's words) shifts.

De Bono is an M.D. He's best known as the creator of "lateral thinking." This provides a systematic approach to seeing a problem in a new perspective, a new "values frame," to gain new insights into the problem and to possible solutions to it. I shall quote extensively from *I AM RIGHT — YOU ARE WRONG* because it lays the groundwork and provides a justification for thinking about old subjects in new ways. His book has forewords by three Nobel Prize-winning physicists: Ivar Glaever, Brian Josephson, and Sheldon Lee Slashow. All three testify to the value of de Bono's methods.

On page 160 of his book, he says:

> A highly intelligent person usually grows up with a sense of...intellectual superiority and needs to be seen as 'right' and 'clever'. Such a person is less willing to risk creative and constructive ideas because such ideas may take a time to show their worth or to get accepted. *Highly intelligent people are often attached to the quick pay-off of negativity.* If you attack someone else's ideas or thinking there can be an immediate achievement together with a useful sense of superiority. In intellectual terms...attack is also cheap and easy because the attacker can always choose the frame of reference.
>
> *The intelligent mind works quickly, sometimes too quicky. The highly intelligent person may move from the first few signals to a conclusion that is not as good* as that reached by a slower mind which is forced to take in more signals before proceeding to a conclusion.
>
> (Ellipses and emphases supplied.)

Without even trying to, he has described *law students* and *lawyers, perfectly*. Future law students see themselves (and are seen by others) as "clever," Both the LSAT and "fruitcake" law exams place a premium on what has been called a "quick-draw intellectual contest." The goal is to *pounce* on something, like a cat leaping at a mouse and pinning it to the floor. But it's the negativity that is most prominent. And, of course, the essence of negativity is argument: "I am right, you are wrong." For most people, arguing is the *raison d'être* of the Law.

But earlier (page 7) in his book, de Bono said this:

> *Perhaps the greatest dangers are those of arro-gance, complacency and the ability to defend that arrogance and complacency.* A defence of arrogance is a denial of any need to change. If we believe our thinking habits to be perfect— as many people do—we shall never see the need to supplement them with further thinking habits (creative, constructive, design, etc.). We can always defend our existing thinking culture because, fundamentally, it is a peculiar belief system based on concepts of truth and logic. Every belief system sets up a framework of perception *within which it cannot be attacked.* The arrogance of logic means that if we have a logically impeccable argument then we must be right — "I am right — you are wrong."
>
> (Emphasis added.)

On page 209, there was this zinger:

> The unkindest thing about argument is that it occupies a great deal of time and gives to moderately intelligent people a sense of useful intellectual activity.

And earlier (page 19), he'd said:

> I believe these methods to be inadequate. Intelligence is certainly not enough. There are many highly intelligent people who are poor thinkers. For example, an intelligent person may use his or her thinking simply to defend a point of view. The more skilled the defence the less does that person ever see a need to explore the subject, listen to others or generate alternatives. This is poor thinking.

Virtually all of "higher" education in America (other than in the sciences) "sold out" a long time ago. (This started with the "G.I. Bill" after WWII.) People don't go to college or beyond to get an education. They go to get a job credential, a union card for a particular line of work. College graduates today are less literate, numerate, or cultured than were high school graduates of a century ago. There has been a staggering misappropriation of resources in this country to "higher" ecucation, for the sake of inflated job credentials. These funds should have gone to elementary and secondary education instead. (Indeed, were *all* students in these lower-level schools to get a truly decent education, the problems associated with reverse discrimination would probably vanish. But the people who call the shots on where the money goes are all university-affiliated, with advanced degrees. They want to keep the money flowing into their *own* gravy trains.)

The purpose of *education* is not that of providing a mere job credential. Nor is that of providing rote instruction in the state-of-the-art. Rather, its purpose was best expressed by T.S. Eliot, in *The Four Quartets*, "Little Gidding":

> We shall not cease from exploration
> And the end of all our exploring
> Will be to arrive where we started
> And know the place for the first time.

Law as The "Queen of the Liberal Arts"

Law school ought to be the *Queen* of the Liberal Arts. For it's only the law school that has, *as part of its "mission,"* the pulling together of all the other liberal arts: philosophy, history, political theory, economics, anthropology, psychology, sociology, literature, drama, poetry, you name it. Yet, instead, law professors (and even practitioners and judges) quote with misplaced pride the statement attributed to Edmund Burke: "The Law sharpens the mind, by *narrowing* it." (Emphasis added.)

True, a good legal mind can cut away all that is irrelevant and immaterial and get right to the heart of a matter. So, this "narrowing" is an important skill to have. But Burke himself was quite the humanist, and filled with worldly wisdom. His statement needs to be taken in context, for which Gestalt psychology provides the best model: the "figure" of thinking about a particular case (the "narrowing") is isolated only as an intellectual exercise within the (back-) "ground." (In the broadest sense, the background is civilization itself and all the wisdom that all the liberal arts—and the sciences—can bring to bear on a particular problem.)

Chapter 6, in Part I, spoke of Wentworth Miller's description of having a "toolbox" to use when doing a lawyerlike analysis. In the same way, law students and lawyers ought to have a toolbox of wider knowledge than just the current Black Letter Law and the elements thereof and the policy reasons for the current Black Letter Law. Rsepcially when trying to come up with a creative solution to a problem, it would help to know much more. The way the Law is now in America is not necessarily the way it "had to" be. As discussed in Chapter 1, the Law is no set of Platonic Ideas, floating around in the universe, waiting to be "discovered" and incorporated into our jurisprudence. The Law is really just a set of rules of thumb. Other nations, both past and present, have adopted different rules of thumb. It behooves law students (and lawyers, and judges) to be aware of the alternatives that existed in the past and of those that exist in the present. Thus we add to our intellectual "toolbox" when trying to solve a new problem, especially in a "case of first impression."

True, many law schools have brought in Ph.Ds from other graduate schools. The idea was to create "cross-fertilization" between the Law and the other discipline. But with very few exceptions, these have become merely what Arthur Austin (quoted in Chapter 26) referred to as "Law & a Banana" courses. There is only cross-*sterilization*.

Chapter 29 presents a new model for legal education. For now, here are examples of how law school could provide truly intellectual stimuli to future attorneys in three specific subjects, and then an example of a larger issue that legal education (and the legal profession) needs to address...

CRIMINAL LAW

We humans, perhaps because of our "descent" (or, more favorably, "ascent") from the apes, have always preferred enhancing our physical wellbeing to advancing our liberty and culture. Political liberty, for the most part, was (and still is) seen only as the servant of the individual's quest for material advancement. (Even in the Declaration of Independence, the immortal words "life, liberty, and the pursuit of happiness," as they'd originally come from Jefferson's pen, were "life, liberty, and the pursuit of *property*." Those who understood the nuances of propaganda even better than did the Sage of Monticello changed the wording—thus giving the future United States of America an everlasting claim to an allegedly higher national purpose.) And so, in the 17th and 18th centuries, while the great minds of Jurisprudence devoted themselves to property law (and later, contractual relations), criminal law—at the *heart* of what freedom is all about—was ignored.

Throughout most of history, there was no criminal law as we know it. Such as existed was mostly a tool of the Ruler to punish those who threatened his or her power. Crimes against ordinary individuals were seen as a strictly private matter, to be dealt with through private revenge. (As mentioned earlier in this book, the process was actually a part of tort law.) Hence the importance of the (extended) family and the "clan" throughout most of history (and in much of the world, even now).

But the rise of urbanization brought with it (for ordinary people) a decline in the role of the extended family and the clan, in favor of the individual. This, however, usually left ordinary individuals powerless in the face of crimes against them. With urbanization came a staggering increase in what moderns call "street crime." The State could look after itself. The individual man (unless able-bodied and skilled with a knife or sword) could not. (A woman, in contrast, was utterly vulnerable. Contemporary feminists decry "male patriarchy." But in large part, male "patriarchy" was a device by which the men of one family or clan *protected* their womenfolk—from exploitation and depredations by the men of *other* clans. And even then, the protections existed only for those reasonably well-off, economically. The poor, as always—both male and female—were subjected to the Law of the Jungle.)

And with urbanization also came increasing immiserization. Then, as now, most street crime was perpetrated by the poor. But because crime against indivivduals was dealt with as a species of tort, "justice" had often meant payment of money to the individual who'd been harmed. (We see this as far back as the Torah, for example.) But the diminished role of the family and clan as a result of urbanization meant that a solitary individual found it almost impossible to compel payment for the wrong. And even if he or she could, the poor, by definition, don't have money. So, you either had to be able to protect yourself against the attempted crime in the first place...or you were out of luck.

The males raised in reasonably prosperous families were well-fed, and thus more likely to be able-bodied. They could afford a sword and training in its use for self-defense. So, as street crime increased, they were largely able to look after themselves. (One reason for the proliferation of country homes, and the country estates of the truly wealthy, was to escape urban crime—just as, after WWII, Americans fled the cities for the suburbs.) And with the rise of the middle class in England, they also had increasing political power...which they used to *prevent* the creation of a police force. (A police force costs money, and that means taxes.) Only with the rise of firearms, and thus the utter irrelevance of a sword and skill at using it, did the middle classes "bite the bullet" (as it were) and support the creation of a police force (note, "force") as we know it (versus the "secret police" that had existed at least since the Middle Ages—first in the Church, and later in the State).

But the purpose of the criminal law was to *dispose of* alleged criminals. So, the accused had no right to counsel. Even in England, which required an indictment before putting a defendant to trial, the accused was not allowed to see the indictment—and was not even *told* of the charge against him until *trial.* Most offenses were capital. (Executions were cheaper than prisons. The distinction between "felony" and "misdemeanor" originally was that the former was punished by death.) Such prisons as did exist were horrid. Worst of all (and hard to believe), there was still no criminal *law* to speak of. Nor were there any prosecutors as we know them. Rather, the police brought the defendant to court and told the judge what the defendant was accused of. And of course there was no need to prove criminal *intent* (the *"mens rea"* of modern criminal law). The outcome was up to the judge and jury, as now. But if the accused was convicted, the judge would usually sentence him to death (or perhaps prison). And because the judges came from "the higher orders" of society, they had little interest in the consequences of injustice. (Things are very different now, *of course.*)

With the Enlightenment, however, there arose the view that Man was the product of his environment. That view is still ours. More important was the belief that people are rational creatures, who calculate the costs and benefits of every action.

It was just a matter of time before someone applied the principles of the Enlightenment to criminal law. And in 1763, Cesare Bonesana, Marchese of Beccaria, did exactly that—anonymously, in a book called *Crimes and Punishments.* (The work became well known among the intelligentsia throughout Europe. Fyodor Dostoyevski's 1865 novel, *Crime and Punishment,* is largely a rebuke to Beccaria's theories.)

Beccaria stated a proposition that, in hindsight, seems obvious: "No crime, no punishment, without a law." Yet, it was nearly another *half-century* before any nation in Europe (France) adopted this principle.

But Beccaria also assumed that anyone who committed a crime had thought things over, first. And he said the potential criminal would consider the punishment for that crime (perhaps by consulting a book of criminal statutes?), and would also calculate the risk of being caught in the first place. And he certainly would calculate the prospective benefit from the crime (money, material goods, emotional satisfaction). As you can see, these cogitations are a precursor to the theories of the British utilitarians. Beccaria had an enormous influence on them (an influence not acknowledged by economists). The most obvious result of this influence was Jeremy Bentham's "Hedonistic Calculus."

The major purpose of the criminal law, then, was to provide sufficient deterrence to would-be criminals, rather than to *punish* criminals. (In this, it is almost identical with the great Learned Hand's famous formula for assessing liability in tort, in light of the foreseeability of the following on the part of the "reasonable person": (1) What is the *magnitude*—or, if you prefer, the "cost"—of the *harm* that might occur if the proposed precautionary measure is not taken? (2) What is the *probability* of a harm occurring if a proposed precautionary measure is not taken? (3) What would be the *cost* of the precautionary measure itself? But Hand was looking at all this only in hindsight, in light of the facts of each tort case in his court. Before Hand, Beccaria, in contrast, was sincerely saying that a potential criminal takes these considerations into account *beforehand*.)

Beccaria then came up with the idea that is expressed today as "Make the punishment fit the crime." But in doing so, Beccaria also treated all instances of a given type of crime as equal to all other instances of the same crime. And he treated each crime as distinct, in a hierarchy of offensiveness. (Thus, for example, today, an executive at Enron, Tyco, or Worldcom who participated in a fraud which, when discovered, forced his company into bankruptcy—thus ruining the lives of untold thousands upon thousands of people—is less culpable than a stick-up artist who *points a gun* at a convenience store clerk during an armed robbery but never pulls the trigger.) The "reasonable person" rule applied, and all persons are assumed to be equally reasonable, despite their circumstances. (Therefore, the executive who, with a net worth of a hundred million dollars, decides to loot another hundred million from his company and its shareholders, is judged no more harshly than the man who breaks into a house and steals a television to "fence" it because he has just been released from prison—with nowhere to go, no money, no relatives or friends waiting to help him get back into the "real world," and no job prospects.)

Thus, even though Beccaria shared the Enlightenment's assumption that people are the product of their environment, he also subsumed that under the Enlightenment's "reasonable person" theory. The problem, as he saw it, was that people just weren't well enough informed of the alternatives, nor were they well enough trained in making their calculations. Knowledge of the criminal law would reduce people's criminal proclivities. The penalties could be adjusted upward or downward, in a manner similar to the economists' "law" of supply and demand, to hold down the level of crime. Seriously.

Futher, it's quite likely that Beccaria was inspired in part by the Church's "penitentials." (During confession, people were to report to their priests all the sins they had committed. The penitentials were books listing every sin the Church knew of or could think of, and provided the penitence—a.k.a. "penance"—for each sin. The word "penitentiary" is obviously related, and perhaps *Crimes and Punishments* provided the link between the one and the other.)

A quarter-*millennium* later, Beccaria's thinking is still the basis of all criminal law. (Example: "three strikes" statutes—get convicted of three crimes, and you're "out," permanently, with a life sentence.)

The only signficant change is that the "psychiatric model" has tacitly assumed that when an individual commits a crime, it's because his or her mental functions are "impaired." With proper psychiatric treatment (including mood-control drugs, such as so-called "chemical castration"), those with criminal tendencies would "come to their right minds" as "reasonable persons," and would not want to commit crimes. (Thus, the difference is one of degree, rather than kind, between the American practice and that under the old Soviet Union, wherein those convicted of "crimes against the State" were assumed to be "insane," because no *sane* person would ever commit a crime against the State— and in a communist society, *all* crimes are crimes against the State. Yet, even in America, all criminal indictments end with a phrase such as this: *"against the Peace and Dignity of the STATE."* In other words, by committing a crime, a criminal has disturbed the *State*. He or she has made the State "look bad," because the State is thus shown to have failed to make itself crime-free. This loss of "face," of course, the State finds more offensive than what the criminal did to the victim.)

Don't know about you, but I find all of that fascinating. I learned about these things only by happenstance, and only long after graduating from law school. It seems a shame that only a handful of criminal law professors are even *aware* of any of this intellectual background.

CONTRACTS

Contract damages are "compensatory." They "make the plaintiff whole," by "putting the plaintiff in the position he or she would have been in had the breaching party fulfilled its contractual obligations." There are no "punitive" (a.k.a. "exemplary") damages as a "remedy."

Why is that?

Torts also has compensatory damages (sometimes called "actual" damages) to make the plaintiff whole. But it's sometimes also possible to get punitive damages, for the breach of the duty of care the defendant owed the plaintiff. These damages are awarded when the defendant showed "gross" negligence. But there is no comparable concept for *gross* breach of duty under the terms of a contract.

Why not?

The chances are you will never get an explanation of this if you read a hornbook or ask your contracts prof. (I recently asked a law school dean if he knew why this distinction existed. All he could come up with was "Because that's the way the Common Law works.")

For those who prefer discussions of "policy," instead of "merely" discussing Black Letter Law, wouldn't it be nice to know the *policy* behind the refusal of punitive damages in breach-of-contract cases?

Well, here it is: contract law arose quite late in legal history—barely a century-and-a-half ago. Contracts as a distinct branch of law was the result of England's Industrial Revolution of the early 19th century. Speaking in the interests of all society, the British courts decided to give priority to economic development and industrialization. To allow punitive damages in breach-of-contract cases would put each business firm under the threat of a huge damage award that could put it *out* of business. (This, of course, is exactly the same excuse that the "tort reform" advocates are using today to try to abolish more than token punitive damages in gross negligence torts cases, even though—unlike in centuries past—*insurance* is available.) The courts figured that the breaching firms most likely had the ability to pay what they would have owed under the contract (usually just the other side's lost profits). Allowing only compensatory damages protected both firms' interests, and served society's interests.

The reasoning is sound. But times have changed. True, there are still many entrepreneurs, and many small firms. But the economic landscape of the 21st century is dominated by gigantic multinational corporations whose annual sales are higher than the entire Gross National Product of all but a handful of *nations*.

You've heard the saying "The big fish eat the little fish"? In business, one way they do this is by gobbling up smaller firms. And *one* way they do *that* is through a carefully-crafted *pre*-contractual breach of what under a contract is called the duty of good faith and fair dealing.

Here's an example of how it works: Megabucks Corporation tells Small Fry Enterprises that it's "considering" using Small Fry as a supplier for a whopping number of components in a potential Megabucks Corporation product. "However," Megabucks continues, "we can't seriously consider you unless you greatly expand your factory and also tailor your product to our specifications. *If* and when we determine that you have successfully done that, *then* we'll enter into contract negotiations with you." Small Fry borrows the money to make the investments, and meets Megabucks Corporation's criteria. But then Megabucks says, "Oh, gee, we've changed our minds and decided not to make that product after all. Sorry." Small Fry has gone way out on a limb, chasing the Megabucks deal. Megabucks then saws the limb off behind Small Fry...which (to mix metaphors) has put all its eggs into one basket. Small Fry goes belly up (to mix metaphors yet again). Megabucks buys its assets for a tiny fraction of their value. Megabucks then brings back all the factory workers who'd been laid off when Small Fry went bust (though Megabucks pays them a lower wage—but the workers are just happy to have their old jobs back, and so do not grumble too much about the pay cut). Further, because Megabucks is now making the components in-house, its costs do not include what would have been Small Fry's profit. Thus, Megabucks is now more competitive against other multinational firms. As for Small Fry...too bad.

This sort of thing, and many other dirty tricks, happen all the time. And under present law, there is nothing the Small Frys of the world can do about it. (Do not say to yourself, "Well, they shouldn't have trusted Megabucks and invested all that money without having already made a contract." The world of business is often dog-eat-dog. The Small Frys do not have the bargaining leverage to protect themselves in pre-contractual matters. They have no choice but to take their chances.)

In this instance, there was no way to make Small Fry "whole." They'd bet the future of the company on getting the Megabucks contract. Even if there had been a contract, the potential profits they would have made off the contract were "purely speculative," because the Megabucks product was a new one, and its potential sales were unknown. And even if Small Fry could prove that Megabucks had "set them up" for a fall, the best Small Fry could hope for would be to recover as "damages" the amount it had invested in the factory upgrade. There would be *no* damages awarded for all the profits on sales of its *other* products that Small Fry could have obtained if it had not diverted its attention to the Megabucks components.

As the terms "punitive" and "exemplary" damages imply, they're meant to *punish* the wrongdoer, to *make an example* of the wrongdoer. Yet, despite the increasing depredations by the Megabucks of this world against the Small Fry firms, there is no way under contract law to try to discourage the Megabucks Corporations from continuing (and even increasing) these depredations. (Although there is Black Letter Law on fraudulent *inducement into* a contract, and also on "reliance," there is virtually nothing on situations such as the one just discussed.)

Big businesses tend to stifle innovation. They have huge investments in their assets. They need to ensure a return on those investments. Those assets, and the organization built around them, are dedicated to one set of products or services, and to one way of providing them. With the exception of the high-tech firms, it's not in their interest to find a way to build a better mousetrap. (See, for example, *The Innovator's Dilemma,* by Clayton M. Christensen.) But it definitely is in their interest to find a way to destroy those who *are* trying to build a better mousetrap. (The Standard Oil Trust remains the most blatant example.)

A good policy argument can be made for a major change in the Black Letter Law regarding Contracts: to allow for punitive damages in breach of contract cases—and to expand the definition of "contractual" to include pre-contractual discussions such as those described above. It is now in America's interest to foster entrepreneurship and innovation perhaps more than ever before. This means that we should "level the playing field" for the Small Fry businesses *vis-à-vis* the Megabucks firms' predatory, bad-faith, *pre*-contractual and contractual practices.

Yet, none of this ever enters into a contracts course. In fact, the matter has gotten far worse: the "Law & Economics" school touts what it calls the "efficient breach-of-contract." —If you can make more money by betraying the firm that trusted your company enough to enter into a contract with you, you *should* "go for it." Take the money and run. After all, your firm's lawyer might be better than their firm's lawyer, or might have a cozy relationship with the judge who hears the case, or might have enough money to wage a "war of attrition" and win. You might end up not having to pay *anything* (except legal fees). No need to give a damn if your betrayal wreaks havoc on the victimized firm's workforce and shareholders. So, *screw 'em.*

Somehow, it never seems to occur to the L&E folks that they are advocating a *tearing up of the social fabric with respect to business.* They only need look at certain countries (which shall remain nameless here) where contracts are worth less than the laser printer from which they were spat out. And it's only a very small step from contempt for contracts to contempt for fiduciary duty to one's *own* shareholders and employees. The frauds at Enron, Tyco, Worldcom, and so many other American Megabucks firms are, in part, the natural outgrowth of a basic policy of Black Letter Law that has not only long since ceased to serve its purpose, but which is now even counter-productive.

The "policy wonks" might munch on *that* food for thought awhile.

CON LAW: CHURCH & STATE

America has been wracked in recent years by controversies involving the "separation of Church and State" under the First Amendment in the Bill of Rights. But law students have no grounding in the discussion, especially as to two crucial intellectual matters.

The first involves the *reason* for the "Establishment clause." Hardly any law student has even heard of the Thirty Years' War, which tore northern Europe apart from 1618-1648. It was a religious war, after the Protestant Reformation. And it had all the cruelties and atrocities that are systematically committed even today only by religious fanatics (in which I include ersatz religionists such as communists, especially the Khmer Rouge). The Treaty of Westphalia (1648) ended the War. Under it, the residents of a limited number of principates in what is now Germany gained religious freedom for the first time in European history since the advent of Christianity. The purpose of that freedom was to let people get on with more important things, i.e., making money, instead of wasting time and energy on religious strife.

Further, it's part of the American mythos that the "Pilgrims" (a highly complimentary term in its own right) emigrated from England to the New World to establish religious "freedom." But in fact they'd *had* religious freedom in England. They came here to establish their own religious *totalitarianism,* a theocracy. And just as many reclusive religious communities in America even today try to "shut out" the rest of the world, the Puritans wanted to shut themselves off from the cosmopolitan, intellectual freedom of England. And so, naturally, it did not take long before they were executing "witches" as "agents of Satan." That too was a reason for the freedom of religion clause in the First Amendment, which includes freedom *from* organized religion.

Lately we've seen an erosion of the idea of non-involvement of the State in religious matters. And as always happens when one group claims to have the ultimate truth, there has been a recrudescence of intolerance. Examples: (1) in 1980, H. Bailey Smith—then the president of the Southern Baptist Convention—declared that "God does not hear the prayer of a Jew"; (2) Louis Farrakhan, leader of the Nation of Islam, declares Judaism to be a "gutter religion"; (3) James G. Merritt, then the chairman of the executive committee of the Southern Baptist Convention, declared in 1998 that Mormonism is "counterfeit Christianity"; (4) after "9/11," the Missouri Synod of the Lutheran Church suspended one of its ministers for joining with "infidels" (a rabbi and a mullah) in public prayer for the terrorists' victims.

This leads to the second crucial bit of relevant intellectual history. It's illustrated by the words of Parson Thwackum, a character in Henry Fielding's novel, *Tom Jones*: "When I mention religion, I mean the Christian religion; and not only the Christian religion, but the Protestant religion; and not only the Protestant religion but the Church of England."

Today, in America, "religion" also tacitly means only "Christianity." True, Judaism has been accommodated, in so-called "non-sectarian prayers," etc. But, of course, the creator god of Judaism is the same as that of Christianity (and of Islam, for that matter—although, so far, the accommodation of Islam has largely been merely a matter of "lip service"). To say that the entanglement of the State with "non-denominational" religion is acceptable ignores the implicit "Thwackumism."

You don't need to invoke the Decalogue to criminalize murder. Banning murder is a matter of common sense. But by claiming that social order depends on obedience to a tacitly Judeo-Christian *religious* code, we also tacitly dismiss the legitimacy of all religions that are outside the Judeo-Christian (and -Islamic) tradition: Hinduism, Buddhism (in which, unlike the Western religions, there is no "god" as we understand the term), Jainism, Taoism, Shinto, animism, the Yezidi religion, Gnosticism, shamanism, and, of course, classical "paganism."

And because the U.S. Supreme Court discreetly follows Parson Thwackum's definition of "religion," it easily rejects Native Americans' claims to the free exercise of their own religion based on peyote, on the grounds that those claims fail in the face of society's "need" to criminalize all consciousness-expanding (versus mood-controlling and thus consciousness-"contracting") drugs. Likewise, with a straight face, the Supreme Court has rejected nearly all claims to the free exercise of what might be called "the varieties of sexual experience," including polygamy and prostitution, even as to mentally competent adults who give informed consent to the activity in question. (True, *Lawrence v. Texas* has recently overturned the 1986 *Bowers v. Hardwick* decision that approved the criminalization of sexual acts between homosexuals. However, the new ruling appears motivated by the social acceptance— and growing political power—of gays, rather than Constitutional rights.)

It's only through the myopic ethnocentrism of the Law that the courts pretend they aren't using religious dogma in deciding such cases.

(**Note:** *I am not necessarily advocating any of the practices mentioned above.* I'm only noting that, for the sake of the life of the mind in law school, shouldn't this hidden presumption of American law at least be a topic for discussion?)*

---

* However, I *would* like to have my own *harem*. :-)

PROPERTY LAW

A "bill of exchange" is a written order from one person or entity to another, to pay a stated sum of money to a third person or entity or "to the order" of that third person or entity. Personal or business checks are the best example. Pretty hum-drum.

However, none other than Charles de Secondat Montesquieu—a giant of Western political thought—saw the seemingly humble bill of exchange as *a turning point in world history.*

The reason? Before the rise of the bill of exchange, those witih wealth kept it close at hand, to protect it. Most wealth, of course, was tangible: land, buildings, materials goods, gold, etc. It was very easy for the State to determine who owned what and how much of it...and to tax it. As Montesquieu argued in *The Spirit of the Laws*, the bill of exchange allowed the wealthy to locate their wealth out-of-sight (and out-of-reach) of the State, yet to maintain their ownership and control of that wealth. Thus, the State's taxation and practices regarding wealth had to become rational rather than arbitrary.

I don't know enough about the subject to agree or disagree. But it's interesting food for thought in the development of the Life of the Mind in law school.

However, this raises a larger issue: the intellectual pretensions of capitalism. Virtually *all* of basic "capitalism"—the law of supply & demand, marginal utility, elasticities, etc.—existed long *before* capitalism. (Even the "bill of exchange" and a banking system had existed in the Arab world long before it arose in modern Europe.) There are just two features that distinguish capitalism from its predecessors: first, the use of capital "pooled" by strangers (rather than only rulers or family members) to finance (and share in the hoped-for profits from) a proposed enterprise; and second, a system of business laws, *and courts to impartialy enforce those laws,* so that *strangers* could trust one another without even so much as knowing the other's names.

Most of these business laws were taken copied by the State from "private law" (the "law merchant"). But the law merchant had operated almost entirely only within certain exclusive leagues of merchants, such as the Hanse. Those outside the league had no protections. Thus, it was the *State,* through the *courts,* that *made possible capitalism as we know it.* (See, for example, Michael Tigar's *Law and the Rise of Capitalism* —although, alas, it is now out-of-print.)

This is something the Law & Economics crowd apparently "doesn't get," as they seek to make the Law itself merely the "flunky" of the "science" of economics.

The Legal "Bed of Procrustes"

Chapter 25 quoted Benamin Sells's book, *The Soul of the Law.* In it, he also said this:

> Here we come to another reading of Justice's blindfold. It isn't only passion or prejudice that the blindfold obscures, but perception itself. Justice can no longer look out upon the world, can no longer appreciate its subtle variations and delicate distinctions. Instead, the blindfold turns vision inward so that Justice's struggle to comprehend reality becomes necessarily solipsistic. Of course Justice *must* "see" things in its *own* terms—*that's all that is left it.* Memories of how things looked before the blindfold begin to fade as the out of sight becomes out of mind. Abstractions, idealized systems, and coldly objectified facts replace sensory awareness, and *gone from view are all chances for shared vision.* With blinders in place, *"I don't see your point" comes to mean "I cannot look through your eyes."*   (Emphasis added.)

Elsewhere in his book, he said "Because non-legal experiences cannot help but remind the lawyer of his or her broader connections to the world beyond the Law, such experiences, like bad recruits, must be drummed out."

The Law is a haughty discipline. It assumes that anything and everything *worth* discussing can somehow be understood and discussed within the framework of the Law, using legal concepts and legal analysis. In *Anarchy and Elegance* (quoted in Chapter 25), Chris Goodrich expands on that insight. "[In] law...what one said was largely dictated by what the limited forms of the law allowed one to say, anything left out automatically being considered second-rate or useless." Like the Bed of Procrustes in the ancient Greek myth, whatever doesn't fit within it is cut off—or, at the very least, held in contempt as being unworthy of serious consideration.

Why is this important? As Goodrich put it, "[L]egal education has a way of replacing everyday human values with what I can only call 'legal' values—values that sustain the system of law *rather than the people that system was created to serve."*   (Emphasis added.)

Elsewhere, this: "Lawyers resolve conflicts by placing them in a hermetically sealed, self-referential loop that *ignores* precisely what it should *encompass*—the views of the millions of *nonlawyers whose lives their decisions affect.*" (Emphasis added.)

The Leviathan of the Law

Ironically, with their contempt for basic concepts such as truth, justice, humanity, and morality, America's law schools and its legal Establishment are gradually reducing us to the primitive state of nature described in Thomas Hobbes's *Leviathan*: "No arts, no letters, no society, and, which is worst of all, continual fear and danger of violent death, and the life of man solitary, poor, nasty, brutish, and short. To counteract this, Hobbes called for "a common power" to keep the people "in awe." Without it, he said, "they are in that condition which is called war: and such a war is of every man against every man."

Hobbes wrote in the 16th century. By the 18th, when Alis de Toqueville wrote his *Democracy in America*, the *Law* had largely taken upon itself the role of Leviathan. We have now reached the point where virtually the entire legal system in America is not just of the lawyers and by the lawyers, but *for* the lawyers. Its legitimacy has been severely compromised. This is because of the law schools and the legal Establishment.

"You don't know what you've got 'til it's gone." And if America's lawyers, law professors, and law students don't neither know nor care about what we have (as long as they can continue to "get theirs"), then they will easily switch their allegiance to a new regime and system of values that will make a mockery of freedom and dignity. As always, of course, they will do it in the *name* of freedom and dignity—subordinated to "national security." Their slogan will be "without safety, there is no liberty."

Learned Hand once said:

> I often wonder if we do not rest our hopes upon constitutions, upon laws and courts. These are false hopes, believe me, they are false hopes. Liberty lives in the hearts of men, and when it dies there, no constitution, no law, no court can save it; no constitution, no law, no court can even do much to help it.

We have more to fear from fascism than terrorism.

Chapter 28 - Lawyers as *Peacemakers*

As Chapter 28 noted, most who think about becoming lawyers like to argue. And nearly everything you see about lawyers in the movies or on television (including in the news media) involves lawyers-as-arguers. Yet, only a small percentage of lawyers become advocates before tribunals. (I say "advocates before tribunals" because that includes lawyers who represent people in administrative proceedings such as Medicaid claims or bankruptcy courts, as well as those who handle lawsuits and criminal cases.) The vast majority of attorneys do "transactions"—handling real estate matters, or drawing up wills, contracts, policy regulations, etc. Yet, even these are often advocates, too—trying to get the best deal for their clients, often through the way a document is written and without being in contact with anyone but the client.

One of the things litigation attorneys and transactions attorneys have in common is that they deal with disputes. Obviously, a litigation attorney usually enters the picture only after a dispute has arisen and has become quite serious. But also, obviously, even transactional matters give rise to disputes. And one of the tasks of a good transactions attorney is to structure a deal, or to craft a document, so that there will *not* be disputes about the terms of the deal or the document. This includes noting those points on which disputes might arise, and "heading them off at the pass." (As Chapter 17 mentioned, I believe at least half of all contract disputes could be prevented if the lawyers who drew up the contracts had done their jobs right. The same is true of at least some "will challenges.")

Whether the dispute has already arisen, or merely might arise, however, the vast majority of most lawyers' work (even of trial lawyers) involves resolving disputes (or potential disputes) without fighting it out in a tribunal. For example, the rule of thumb among trial attorneys is that 90% of all lawsuits are resolved through a settlement agreement. (In fact, some civil cases are settled *during* trial—sometimes even while the jury is deliberating.) And as also mentioned, often a case that's "up on appeal" is resolved through a settlement agreement and thus is withdrawn from the appellate docket. (Litigation attorneys need to be good at structuring deals and crafting documents too, i.e., settlement agreements and court orders. There are few things more embarrassing than to think a lawsuit has been resolved through a settlement agreement or court order, only to find out that there was ambiguity on a key point, or something important was left out entirely that should have been included, thus giving rise to new litigation.)

As you can see, one of the key skills a lawyer needs to have is that of negotiating. But unfortunately, as with legal writing, negotiating is one of the key skills that law school slights most. It does this because to properly help students learn how to negotiate well would require an enormous commitment of resources—far more than for legal writing or even for clinical programs.

Instead, the law schools typically offer a single course on what's called "Alternative Dispute Resolution." As its name implies, it presents a way to resolve a dispute without fighting it out in a tribunal (or, at least, without fighting it out to the bitter end). And typically, these courses are really bad.

Partly, this is because all of law school education is built on the case method, which deals only with disputes. But there's a huge diffeence between what's involved "when push comes to shove," on the one hand, and what might be called "prodding," on the other. Nearly everthing in law school is devoted only to pushing—even shoving—someone else around as a way of resolving a dispute.

Chapter 28 quoted Edward de Bono's *I AM RIGHT — YOU ARE WRONG*. Here's another passage from it (page 7):

> The most powerful case for the value of argument as a thinking method is that it encourages the motivated exploration of a subject. Without the personal gratification of argument (win/lose, aggression, cleverness, point-scoring), there might be little motivation to explore a subject. There is merit in this justification, except that *beyond a certain level of motivation the actual exploration of the subject starts to suffer. argument becomes case-making, point-scoring, and ego-strutting.* No person is going to bring to attention matters which would benefit the opposing side of the argument, even when such matters *might greatly extend the exploration of the subject.*
>
> (Emphasis added.)

Law school education is based *solely* on "case-making, point-scoring, and ego-strutting." Thus, even those who want to explore "kinder and gentler" methods of resolving disputes have great difficulty even *thinking* in ways that would "extend the exploration of the subject." And so, all too often, negotiating and "alternative dispute resolution" just turns into a toned-down version of the adversarial approach.

As de Bono also commented: "Critical thinking lacks the productive, generative, creative and design elements that are so needed to tackle problems and find our way forward."

But before recommending some materials to help you cope with the destructive "mind-set" you will learn in (or have brought with you to) law school, here's a quick tour of the varieties of ADR.

Mediation

A mediation is a "facilitated negotiation." A third party (the mediator) is the facilitator. It's an informal proceeding. So, no rules of evidence or civil procedure. And the sessions are in an informal setting and scheduled at the convenience of the parties (unlike those of tribunals).

The mediator tries to keep the parties talking to one another in a civil manner, and to get them to deal with their dispute in a cooperative spirit of solving a mutual problem rather than (as with a trial) in a spirit of confrontation and attempted mutual destruction. A mediator does *not* "play judge." While he or she might make suggestions to one or both sides to help resolve the problem, the mediator does not even advise one side or the other as to what's right or wrong, good or bad; that's up to the parties to decide for themselves. A mediator is truly a "lawyer as peacemaker." And the mediator does not "rule" on the dispute, saying who should "win"—or even who has the better case.

Arbitration

This is more like a hearing or trial. The arbitrator does "play judge," although again the proceedings are usually informal. Often, however, the arbitrator will first play mediator, to try to get the parties to resolve as many points as possible between themselves. Then the arbitrator rules on the remaining, unresolved, issues.

Arbitration can be either "binding" or "non-binding." The difference is obvious...though not ironclad. If the arbitration resulted from a court order, the court will review the arbitrator's decisions to make sure they were not abitrary (ironic word in this context, isn't it?). And if the arbitration occurred as a result of a clause in a contract ("all disputes will be referred to arbitratration by..." etc.), then it is still possible to take the matter to a court—although this is *very* difficult, and thus rare. (After all, the real main purpose of the rise of ADR was to lighten courts' dockets. So the last thing they want to see is a dispute that's already been through ADR, especially an arbitration that was "binding.")

Collaborative Law

This one's my favorite. It's something new in the Law. It was invented by one person: a lawyer in Minneapolis named Stu Webb, sometime around 1990.

To understand how wonderful Collaborative Law is, you first need to remind yourself of how litigation usually proceeds...

In a normal lawsuit, the two sides are already at each other's throats. The lawsuit just lets them bring out the knives and start slashing away at each other's jugular veins. The lawyers on each side love it, of course, because it often involves getting a blank check from the client. So the lawyer has a great time running up the client's bill for discovery procedures, hearings, lots and lots of documents—and perhaps even a trial (and one or more appeals). A well-heeled client who wants to file a lawsuit is like mannah from Heaven.

But many "trial" lawyers chicken out as trial approaches. They start advising their clients to settle, rather than risk losing at trial. Often it's because the lawyer knows he or she is not a good trial attorney, and fears the client's wrath after all the months or years of hearing the lawyer say what a great case the client has. "If it was so great, how come you *lost* it?!" So, the lawyer who has bled the client suddenly says, "Uh, something just turned up in discovery, and your case isn't so good after all. You need to settle." —Of course, it's quite possible that something *did* turn up in discovery, something the client either hid or forgot or just didn't appreciate the significance of, and then the client *does* need to settle. (Been there, done that.) However, it's almost impossible for a client to determine if his or her lawyer is giving an objective opinion as to either the merits of fighting it out *or* the merits of settling (and the terms for settling).

But in Collaborative Law, the two parties, and their respective lawyers, sign a four-way agreement that says if they cannot resolve their differences without resort to court, the two lawyers will *withdraw*. They *cannot* then turn over the case to other lawyers at their own firms.

This means that the lawyers do not have a vested interest in turning the case into a "war." And it also means the *clients* have to behave themselves. If they don't, each party has to hire a new lawyer and then pay that new lawyer to "get up to speed" on the case to pick up where the previous lawyer left off.

Collaborative law is not suited to many clients, for obvious reasons. But for those who are suited to it, it's a Godsend. So far, it has caught on only in family law. That is unfortunate, but it's a start.

Caveat: Three Dangers of ADR

As was said at the outset of this chapter, lawyers tend to be argu-mentative (even combative), confrontational people. Jerks, really. Even so, at least some people who want to become lawyers are not like that, and do not want to become like that. The problem is that they some-times tend to go too far in the other direction: "nice-nice."

The prof for my ADR course in law school was like that. No matter how outrageous the demands one side was making in a negotiation, he would always just say, "Split the difference."

So, at least one side would always act in bad faith, asking for the moon. Out in the real world, unfortunately, many negotiators and especially mediators are this way. That's *bad*.

Related to this is the second danger: the attitude that the other side is *always* entitled to respect, and their basic position should *always* be taken seriously. (This is especially so in a course for lawyers at HLS, which I took, on mediation. It was and still is taught by Frank—"Dead-wood"—Sander.)

At the risk of being accused of sexism...although law is still far too "macho," that does not mean we should go to the opposite extreme, to a wholesale "feminizing" of it. In *The Decline of Males*, anthropologist Lionel Tiger put his finger on the problem, in gender terms:

> [A woman] may well be correct in her culturally satisfying conclusion that females are better at negotiation than males...But this embraces a moral value that *accommodation is better than assertion*. It implies that a network of sensitive conversation is preferable to a hierarchy of clear authority which may well be correct, certainly for females and possibly for communi-ties at large. But it is a preference, not a fact.
>
> (Emphasis added.)

And as Ann Douglas said in *The Feminization of American Culture* (quoted in Chapter 16):

> I have a respect for so-called "toughness," not as good in itself, not as isolated and reified as it so often is in male-dominated cultures, but as the necessary preservative for all virtues, even those of gentleness and generosity.

"There's a time to kill, and a time to heal," according to the Book of Ecclesiastes. A good lawyer ought to be able to do both—and ought to know when to try the one or the other. At the very least, a lawyer who is really good only in *one* mode ought to know when his or her own "style" is not the appropriate one, and should advise the client that someone else should handle the matter. Even in a negotiation or mediation, "nice-nice" isn't always the right way to go.

The third danger of ADR relates to gullibility.

You've heard of Rodney King? He became a global celebrity several years ago when some L.A. cops beat the hell out of him after a high-speed chase. (Rodney King was black. The cops were white.) The beating was caught on videotape, and ultimately led to two trials of the officers involved—and to yet another round of massive rioting in L.A.'s riot-torn history.

Rodney King made a statement that will live in the quotation books: "Can't we all just get along?" He thus presented himself as an apostle of peace and goodwill. However, come to find out, he had a long record of criminal violence himself, which included habitually beating the hell out of at least one girlfriend or wife of his. So, Rodney King was a hypocrite. (But that, of course, does not excuse what several of L.A.'s "finest" did to him. After all, they were supposed to act like the trained *professionals* they claimed to be, not like the thugs they became when stressed out.)

Some of the dirtiest lawyers I have ever dealt with in negotiations were those who pretended to believe in openness and cooperation. One of the skills you have to acquire as an attorney is the ability to spot a fraud, and to then take appropriate measures.

Good Books

Regardless of your interest in formal ADR—and especiallu at its negotiating aspect—here are some excellent books that will help you get good at it. (These are in addition to Edward de Bono's *I AM RIGHT — YOU ARE WRONG,* which is available in paperback for $13.) All of these are in paperback, and listed here in their logical order.

Getting to Yes: Negotiating Agreement without Giving In, 2nd ed., by Roger Fisher and William Ury ("with Bruce Patton"), $14.

Getting Past No: Negotiating Your Way from Confrontation to Cooperation, by William Ury, $15.

Difficult Conversations: How to Discuss what Matters Most, by Douglas Stone, Sheila Heen, and Bruce Patton, $14.

Getting Ready to Negotiate: The Getting to Yes Workbook, by Roger Fisher and Danny Ertel, $15.

Getting it Done: How to Lead when You're Not in Charge, by Roger Fisher, John Richardson, and Alan Sharp, $13.

All these folks are part of Harvard Law School's "Negotiations Project." Roger Fisher is the Grand Old Man of *non-confrontational* negotating. Until recently, he taught a basic negotiating course at HLS for licensed attorneys (which I took). Fisher is one tough, no-nonsense negotiator. But he does not let his ego get caught up in the process, and always tries to keep the peace. In fact, he's the epitome of "gentle—but firm.")

There are many books on negotiating. You probably think I'm too quick to recommend (and even *urge* you to get) all of the above. But they're wonderful. (Much as I criticize HLS, I have to admit that at least *some* people there manage to do something *right.*)

There's one other book, but it's only for those *deeply* committed to the idea of lawyers-as-peacemakers. It's *Practicing Therapeutic Jurisprudence,* by Dennis P. Stolle, David B. Wexler, and Bruce J. Winick. Although it's in paperback, it's expensive. Even the "student price" (if you buy directly from the publisher, Carolina Academic Press) is $40. And it's a *long* book (though not nearly as long as *PLSII*).

I'll close the main body of this chapter by recommending *The Gentle Art of Verbal Self-Defense,* by Suzette Haden Elgin.

No need to repeat how abrasive, etc., lawyers are. But even those lawyers (and law students) who want to change their ways have enormous difficulty, thanks to the pressure-cooker atmospher of law school itself. The Harvard Negotiations people never mention *The Gentle Art of Verbal Self-Defense,* alas—probably because Elgin is not an HLS prof. (In fact, she is not a law prof anywhere, and not even a lawyer.) Astoundingly, her book is only $7.95. (That's seven dollars, ninety-five cents.) It's worth $50, even $100. The publisher is Barnes & Noble Books. Thus, it might be available *only* through B&N. Elgin's book is a gift from the gods. It shows you how to gently deflect personal attacks and criticisms, without self-abasement. It can save you from many a difficult situation, where your "gut instinct" would be to lash out in response to a cutting remark. Thus, it's useful not just for those who want to go into ADR. but for all lawyers.

Addendum to Chapter 29 -
More on the Baseball Brouhaha

The Coda (Part V) concerned the dispute of Popov v. Hayashi. It provides a case study in what *could* have been an example of "preventive lawyering," both with regard to the litigants, and with regard to Major League Baseball and its teams.

Many have the idea that ADR, discussed in the main body of this chapter, is all about being "touchy-feely." This addendum shows how a good ADR approach to the case can involve a detailed knowledge of the law—and a willingness to "press the point" when necessary.

The Litigants

The trial began only at the very end of the season *after* Barry Bonds hit his 73rd. Had that 73rd been available for quick sale, it would likely have fetched the full two million of its estimated value. Hayashi was apparently interested in selling that ball. It's unclear what Popov intended to do with it had he been the one declared its owner at the end of the melee on October 7, 2001.

Each lawyer should have said to his client: "You know McGwire's record-breaking 70th home-run ball sold for three million dollars right after it was hit, in 2000. And you know that now, thanks to Bonds's 71st and 72nd homers of October 5, the McGwire ball has lost three-fourths of its value. Please consider agreeing with the other side to *sell* that ball *now*. Strike while the iron is hot. Get yours while the gettin's good, and so forth. Then, the money goes into the 'court registry'—a bank account in the court's name, to be held there in trust—until we can sort out who the ball belonged to and thus who is entitled to that money."

Granted, Bonds's record was not broken in the 2002 season. But it could have been...such as by Bonds himself. I do not know why the ball was not sold. Maybe Hayashi was not really interested in selling it after all. (That's unlikely, though: his lawyer was working on contingency, had "fronted" the expenses in the case, and surely wanted to get paid and reimbursed.) Maybe Popov would not have wanted to sell the ball, period. (Again, unlikely. As the article in *Sports Illustrated* said, his lawyer was billing by the hour for his work and Popov was also having to pay cash on the barrelhead for expenses; the total as of the time of the article was $120,000. My estimate is that, through trial, the total reached $250,000.) Maybe the judge said he wouldn't let it be sold, even if the money were held in a trust account.

But I do hope the disputants' lawyers thought about this and talked it over with their respective clients.

As mentioned in the Coda, neither side appealed. But had there been an appeal, the ball would have remained "frozen" until *all* appeals were concluded. There might even have been a remand for a new trial, and everything would have started over. At least one more baseball season would have passed before the matter was finally resolved. If either party had appealed, both parties and their lawyers should have considered making an agreement to sell the ball and put the proceeds in escrow, during the appeal/s.

Major League Baseball—and the Teams

ABANDONED Property—or GIFT?

In documents filed with the court, Popov called the home-run ball "abandoned property." The trial judge agreed with that characterization. But arguably, that's incorrect.

In property law, "abandonment" is a term of art, with two elements:

(1) *intent* to relinquish all claim to title, possession, and control of the property, and

(2) an *act, failure to act, or "performative utterance"* which manifests that intent.*

Professional baseball teams normally seek to prevent the loss of baseballs. When a ball, even a foul, lands anywhere on the playing field, the team that owns that ball retrieves it. But as we know, when a foul ball goes "out of play," or when a home run goes into the stands (or out of the entire ballpark), the team does not try to retrieve it. Although a team prefers to keep its baseballs, if a ball goes into the stands (or out of the entire ballpark), that's the end of the matter. (In Japan, so I am told, if a ball goes into the stands, whoever gets it tosses it back to someone on the field, even if it's a home-run ball.)

So, both elements of "abandonment" appear to be met in the latter situation. But the *"intent* to abandon" the property could be said to arise *only at the instant* when the ball *crosses the imaginary plane* that extends vertically from the playing-field's perimeter. (This would be another example of a "legal fiction.")

Is that important? Maybe—though not in connection with abandonment.

---

* This definition, and the next one, are my creation. There are other ways of putting it. I just prefer mine. Of course, when handling a case for real, I'd use the elements and wording the highest court in my jurisdiction uses.

Now here are the elements of the legal term of art, *"gift"*:

(1) *intent* to voluntarily transfer to another the title to the property in question,

(2) *absence of consideration* provided from the recipient to the donor,

(3) an *act or "performative utterance"* which manifests the donor's intent, and

(4) *acceptance by the recipient* of the transfer of title to the property.

As before, the *"intent* to make the gift" could be said to arise only at the instant when the ball crosses the imaginary plane that extends vertically from the playing-field's perimeter. Thus, it's a gift only in hindsight: a "constructive gift."

So why make a big deal about this, when "abandonment" and "gift" appear to be identical?

Here's why: neither the teams playing the game in question, nor Major League Baseball (MLB) ever bothers to "authenticate" a *routine* home-run ball (or a ball that's been "fouled out of play"). Yet, it was anticipated that Barry Bonds might whack at least one or more *record-breaking* homers in that last game of the season on October 7, 2001. Normally, the balls used in a game are provided by the teams themselves. But the balls that were pitched to Barry Bonds as he was setting new records were all owned and provided by Major League Baseball itself (on October 5—when Bonds hit homers No. 71 and 72—as well as October 7, when he hit homer No. 73).

Each ball was carefully marked, two ways. The first was with ink visible to the naked eye: dots at points near the seams. But to ensure against forgery, the other markings were with ink that could only be seen under ultraviolet light.

MLB had also sent three officials from corporate headquarters to attend each of those final Giants games of the season. They maintained custody of the "Bonds baseballs" between games. A room was set up for authentication, with an ultraviolet lamp in it. All security personnel had been told to bring to that room whoever claimed to have a Bonds homer. As soon as Bonds hit that 73rd home-run, one of the three MLB officials went to that room. The other two went toward the place where it appeared the ball would come down: the arcade walkway. (One of those two officials was Paul Padilla, mentioned in the Coda.) The two escorted Hayashi to the room. All three officials then authenticated the ball he had.

The point here is that this is not consistent with abandonment. But it is consistent with a gift.

Many people who provide gifts have continuing contact both with the recipient of the gift and with the property they gave away. Of course, sometimes that happens as to abandoned property as well. But with abandoned property, the former owner is utterly unconcerned about the disposition or care of the property. With a gift, however, the former owner is often quite concerned about its future. And in this case, Major League Baseball was *very* concerned. That's why MLB went to the expense and effort to ensure the identity and security of the ball alleged to be Bonds's 73rd. That ball is a valuable artifact in the history of the sport, regardless of its monetary value. (Although Babe Ruth's record-setting 60th home-run ball from 1927 is still in a collector's hands, Roger Maris's 61st record-breaking/setting home-run ball from 1961—"61 in '61"—is now in the Baseball Hall of Fame.)

But again, you're wondering: *so what?* Hang on, we're getting there.

Recall that Gary Smith's article (reproduced in full in the Coda) referred to a man who got his nose bloodied in the scramble for Bonds's 73rd, to a woman who required a wheelchair because she'd been caught up in the melee and temporarily disabled, and of course to the injuries that Popov received. And recall Smith's rhetorical question, "And where was security? Nearly half the security guards that the Giants had contracted to supervise the stands that day were no-shows." (Actually, I'll bet that they did show up at the stadium, and went in, but then did not report for duty. They probably *were* at the game—but not to work. It's extremely unlikely they would have missed a chance to watch *that* game, at the stadium, for free.) Smith continues: "A half-minute elapsed before a Major League Baseball security officer could reach the maelstrom, another half-minute before two reinforcements arrived, all in plain clothes."

The Giants and MLB could respond that it's *impossible* to provide enough security, especially if a batter has no pattern as to where his home-runs go. But that's irrelevant here. Bonds *did* have a pattern.

Yet, Smith has put his finger on the larger issue. It's an issue that does not properly concern either Popov or Hayashi, but is one that will concern every court that deals with a case similar to this one.

Smith's article quoted Todd McFarlane, who'd paid the $3.1 million dollars for Mark McGwire's record-breaking 70th home-run ball the year before: "If Hayashi wins, would you bring your children into the bleachers when A-Rod's going for No. 756?" "How do you know some 250-pound guy won't do a belly flop for the ball and permanently compress your child into the bleachers? Whoever catches it first should be the guy who gets it. But we'll probably wait until an eight-year-old gets his ribcage crushed."

McFarlane (who ended up buying the Bonds ball, too) was wrong in saying Popov should get the ball just because of this "policy argument." No court can (or, at least, most likely would) overturn the written policies of the Giants ballclub and Major League Baseball, especially given that no one was seriously injured on October 7, 2001, and given that neither the Giants nor MLB were parties to the litigation. Besides, Popov did *not* "catch" the ball.

But McFarlane's also right: sooner or later, someone *will* be seriously injured in a scramble for another record-breaking home-run ball. On August 8, 2002, for example, Bonds hit his 600th career home run. No one made a clean catch of it, so there was again a scramble in the stands. The fan who came up with it had a "lot of" blood on him, I was told (but did not confirm). Bonds, who will surely be playing for at least a few more years (he's 38 as of this writing) is now chasing Hank Aaaron's 755 career home runs total—although there are three other players (long gone) who are still ahead of Bonds in the record books. And, of course, in any given year, it's possible that Sammy Sosa or some other player will surge again and break Bonds's current one-season record of 73. (Mark McGwire retired after setting the record of 70.)

Sooner or later, disaster will strike some fan...and it will be arguable that Major League Baseball and the team whose stadium the game is in are at least partly responsible.

But Major League Baseball is not concerned. Pat Courtney, an official spokesman, said, "We don't want people fighting and all that stuff, but that's just reality. They want the ball." Jeff Nelson, a major league umpire, was also unsympathetic: "You go to catch a ball like that, you pretty much know it's every man for himself until the cops come."

But the teams and MLB are ignoring two crucial things.

The first is the issue McFarlane raised, of the child who's in the wrong place at the wrong time. Sure, in response, one could say "A potentially dangerous scramble will happen only on the rare occasion when another potential record-breaker is in the offing. As with Bonds's 71st-73rd homers, and his 600th career homer the following season, this exists only within certain games, known in advance. So, play it safe. At such games, kids and old folks should get seats behind home plate or along the baselines running to first and third, where the only balls that go into the stands will be foul balls."

However, even though Bonds's 73rd fetched less than half-a-million dollars, there's still incentive for *considerable* mayhem, even against able-bodied adults. Further, if there's a pattern of a player hitting home-runs into a certain area of the stands (as is the case with Bonds), there's incentive for a *gang* of unscrupulous people to coordinate their efforts so as to wrongfully gain possession of a record-breaking home-run ball...but without it being possible to determine that they acted in concert. And, of course, if one of their number ended up getting arrested, the others would pretend to be disinterested eyewitnesses and would all testify their secret co-conspirator did nothing wrong.

The second crucial thing the teams and MLB ignore is that the San Francisco Giants, in the final home games of the 2001 season, were trying to *create a frenzy* among fans to become the person who would end up with a new record-breaking Bonds home-run ball. And when he was going for his 500th career home run in 2000, the Giants' website even had a page devoted to tips on how to be the one who ends up with that ball. That page stayed up when Bonds was breaking McGwire's season home run record. And Major League Baseball had tacitly *encouraged* that frenzy, through its official policy of relinquishing its claim to the baseballs *it* had provided *solely* for pitches to Bonds.

In other words, if and when someone is badly injured (or perhaps even killed) in a scramble for a home-run ball that breaks the current record, there are solid grounds for a heavy-duty lawsuit against the home team and Major League Baseball itself. And a successful suit for negligence opens up the possibility of *punitive* damages.

This is where the distinction between abandoned property and a gift (finally) is relevant. When a person abandons property, he or she has no thought of even getting goodwill from whoever (if anyone) then lays claim to that property. (Often, the person who abandoned the property has no idea who got it, if anyone.) But the San Francisco Giants and Major League Baseball were using the gift of the Bonds 73rd as a way to generate goodwill for themselves—and, in the case of the Giants, to pack the stadium (i.e., to make more money). They clearly wanted to authenticate the ball and to identify who had it. So, like many "gifts" from merchants and other businesses, *any* home-run ball is a *promotional* giveaway. Both the Giants and MLB expect something in return. It is not "consideration," as in a contractual exchange, but something of great value nevertheless.

Further, they *entice* the fans into the stadium on a potentially special occasion such as October 7, 2001 was. And they *incite* the fans to join a free-for-all for the Bonds ball. So, the Giants (or other teams) and Major League Baseball would have a difficult time playing innocent victims of "lawsuit abuse" if and when they get sued by an injured fan.

AN OPPORTUNITY for PREVENTIVE LAWYERING

But still, you wonder, how is this important to you as a law student?

—Well, remember the top two levels of the Josephson Pyramid? ("Judgment" and "Synthesis.") Someday you might be an assistant counsel to Major League Baseball, or to a Major League team. Or perhaps you'll be the lawyer an injured fan consults, inquiring about the possibility of filing suit against MLB and the team (whose stadium it is) instead of just suing the person who caused the victim's injuries. (Remember: *deep pockets.*) Or, you might get a question like this on an exam in law school...or maybe on the state-specific portion of your bar exam, or on the Multistate Performance Test (see Chapter 22).

So what should Major League Baseball and the teams do to avoid such litigation altogether, let alone avoiding liability?

For *routine* home-run balls, and clearly for foul balls, there is no need for a change in policy. But on those rare occasions when a record-breaking home run is in the offing, MLB and local stadium officials should publicize a policy with respect to the balls in question, *asserting MLB's ownership of them.* This means any scramble for the record-breaking ball would be more like that for a *routine* home run. Because there would be no potential claim by a fan to ownership of that ball, there would be little incentive for wrongful acts to obtain it. The scrambling fans would primarily be seeking just the celebrity status that (as with Hayashi) would come from ending up with the ball.

However, cynics would say MLB wanted to keep the ball for itself to sell it and pocket the proceeds. MLB is indeed a profit-seeking organization. But MLB could immediately place the ball in the Hall of Fame. More likely, MLB would announce that the ball would be auctioned off—but only the right to *possession* of it, not *ownership*. It would be understood that, after *x* years, MLB could reclaim the ball from its then-current possessor, but only for the purpose of putting it into the Hall of Fame. Or, there could be a clause in the auction agreement saying that the successful bidder would have the option of taking title to the ball if the record represented by that ball were broken in the meantime. As a fourth alternative, MLB might have discretion to relinquish title to the ball of its own accord (although it's extremely unlikely it would do that).

The money from the auction (if there were an auction) would be donated to an appropriate charity such as a drug rehabilitation program for major league ballplayers or summer "baseball camps" for "underprivileged" children.

The fan who "captured" the ball when it first came down in the stands would receive a relatively modest reward—say, no more than $1,000—in return for promptly handing it over to MLB. (The fan could perhaps also get something like 12 pairs of season's tickets annually, for life, to games of the team of his choice.)

Seems to me this would be a "winning" solution all the way around, and would nip some serious potential problems in the bud.

Just a thought.

AND ANOTHER ONE

As mentioned, on August 8, 2002, Bonds got his 600th homer. That too became a legal dispute. However, whereas the 73rd was a Property case, the 600th was a Contracts case: it wasn't about who owned the ball but about who would get the proceeds from its sale.

The plaintiffs said they provided tickets to two fellow employees at work, because the fellow employees wanted to attend the game where Bonds might hit his 600th. In return, the plaintiffs continued, the second pair made an oral promise to each of the first pair that, if Bonds did hit his 600th at that game and either of them caught it, he would share the proceeds of the sale of the ball with the two guys who provided the tickets. Sure enough, Bonds homered, and one of the guys caught it—and then denied having ever made any such deal. (Later, the recalcitrant catcher decided it was better to switch than fight. He withdrew his claim of exclusivity, and agreed to split the money when the ball was sold.)

Again, the above proposal for Major League Baseball might prevent such quarrels. I do not know what the Bonds 600th ball fetched. But I'll bet if the fan who'd come up with that ball had known in advance that he would "only" get celebrity status, a reward of, at most, $1,000, and several sets of free season's tickets annually for life, he would have been much less inclined to deny having made the bargain (if, indeed, he did "enter into" the contract). Likewise, had this policy existed on October 7, 2001, there would likely not have been a *Popov v. Hayashi*.

(As of this writing, I'm told that MLB's general counsel is Ethan Orlinsky. I am sending him this addendum, and getting proof of delivery, and will highlight this last paragraph for him. That way, if disaster occurs, MLB cannot disclaim having received notice of a suggestion that might have prevented a tragedy. Remember: reasonable person, punitive damages, and *deep pockets*.)

An ounce of prevention is worth a pound of cure.

Chapter 29 - Thinking "Outside the Box":
A New Paradigm for Legal Education

> America's system of legal education is a sham and shame. It has been so for a century. It is now time to "Think Outside the Box"—because the box of legal education is a *coffin*, for the Life of the Mind and the soul of the Law.

With the "dumbing down" of American education in general, there are now a handful of high schools in this country that provide a better education than all but a handful of colleges. New York's famous Bronx High School of Science and the famous Boston Latin are two examples. But now there are many other specialized high schools, particularly in the performing and visual arts. American legal education is so bad that it would be possible to produce graduates of a specialized *high* school of legal studies who could outperform the graduates of even the top law schools: on finals, the Multistate bar exam, the MPRE, and even the MPT (discussed in Chapter 22).

Long ago, law school was often an *alternative* to *college*. That's why, even now, some call themselves a *"College* of Law." But to get into law school today, you must first have a college degree. It used to be argued that what students learned in college comprised a necessary background to the study of law. Today, though, the *content* of one's college studies is irrelevant to law school admission. Even if the applicant took courses only in basket-weaving, interpretive dance, and so forth, no matter. All that counts is one's GPA and LSAT score (and, to a lesser extent, where the applicant attended college). So the requirement of a college degree is now but a subtle part of the "class war" discussed in Chapter 25.

Excursus into Cyberspace

As Chapter 25 noted, one aspect of the "class war" nature of legal education is the new ABA requirement that "distance learning" credits be available only to students who attend residential law schools. There is no sound pedagogical reason for that requirement. (At one point, Harvard Law School's Arthur Miller moonlighted as a member of the faculty of one of the on-line law schools—and no doubt was being paid extremely well for it.)

There are those who say that a "cyberspace law school" would lack the pedagogical value of the present method. Yet, the pedagogical value of the present method is nil. Even if on-line law schools were no better than those of the status quo, they could be no worse.

(The denunciation of on-line education is similar to the denunciation, 2,500 years ago, of the use of *writing* in education, when widespread literacy was new to the Greeks. Old Fogies, including Socrates, said that if students could consult written materials and take notes during "classes," they'd be less likely to pay close attention during class, to think—during class—about what they were hearing in class, and less likely to memorize what they'd learned. Socrates was right, of course. But the past two-and-a-half millennia have shown that the gains from the use of written notes and written texts outweighed the pedagogical losses. "Distance learning" is "same song, different verse.")

Other than the class warfare motive for opposition to on-line education, the other main motive, I believe, is that of self-preservation. If students are paying, say, $2000 for a one-semester, three-credit course, then each 50-minute session costs them approximately $50. Why should students pay a dollar a minute for the abysmal "teaching" they now get when, for a fraction of that amount, they could get an on-line presentation by a Master Teacher? The handwriting is on the wall, just as surely as it was for Vaudeville when movies with sound were created. (But at least the presenters in Vaudeville were talented. Most law school profs, in contrast, have no talent as teachers.) Nearly all of America's 10,000+ full-time law profs are obsolete. They know it. Hence the rear-guard action to save their jobs—with the full backing of the American Bar Association and the U.S. Department of Justice.

However, this is not to say that legal education should take place on-line. It does mean, though, that what *now* occurs in law school—which has almost nothing to do with legal *education*—could be presented more easily, effectively, and cheaply on-line.

The Role of SKILLS

This book has repeatedly objected to the professoriat's devaluation of the teaching of skills. If teaching "skills" makes a law school a mere trade school, then so be it, for law schools would then be in the same category as schools of medicine, engineering, and architecture, among others. The law school professoriat denigrates skills because the law school professoriat generally lacks those skills themselves; they certainly are unable to teach them. They say that what counts instead is "scholarship," as though the two are mutually exclusive. Yet their own "scholarship" makes a mockery of the term. And as Chapter 10 argued, those who want to be "scholars" instead of teachers should be moved to a "think tank" (more formally known as a "research institute").

As with students of medicine, engineering, etc., what law students *most* need is training in *skills*.

The "3 Rs" of legal education (discussed in Chapter 17) are a vital part of this.

Legal research should involve far more than the perfunctory first-year Mickey Mouse course. For example, *all* students should have to do at least one "cite check" for a law school periodical. (This does not mean checking just one citation. Rather, the term "cite check," in connection with a law school periodical, means checking *all* the citations in an article.) Legal research in administrative law is also a "must."

Legal reasoning (the second of the "3 Rs") is discussed below.

Legal 'Riting should be bifurcated. All law students should spend *at least* a year in a *serious* course of legal writing. In it, they would learn how to draft *contracts* (including *settlement agreements*), *wills,* and *legislation*. This category can loosely be called "transactional" writing. The second category would concern "advocacy." This would include bench memos, pleadings, motions, and appellate briefs. However, most of the "advocacy" writing would be part of a separate program discussed below.

The second set of skills (after the "3 Rs") concerns dispute resolution. This too should be bifurcated.

All future lawyers should be skilled at negotating, whether in person or in writing. And because mediation is just a facilitated negotiation, all future lawyers should be skilled in the role of mediator. Chapter 19 discussed how *real*-world disputes could be integrated into clinical programs in law school. No more need be said here.

Chapter 19 discussed trial advocacy courses in law school. Most are very poor in quality. They focus solely on the trial itself, whereas any decent trial lawyer knows that the trial is just the tip of the iceberg, or the capstone of the pyramid (whichever metaphor you prefer). *Depositions* can easily be far more important, and can make or break success at trial. Much the same is true of *pre-trial* motions and hearings on them. And it is also true of *jury selection*. Law schools ignore all that.

A good advocacy program would thoroughly integrate written advocacy with oral. And, as Chapter 19 proposed, it would also thoroughly integrate the real-world, via real-life disputes. (A good advocacy program would also demand detailed knowledge of the rules of civil procedure, criminal procedure, and evidence.)

There are those who say trial lawyering should become a new specialty and should require a fourth year of law school, or even an LL.M. That's hardly necessary. However, within law school itself, anyone who intends to become an oral advocate should be required to complete a prescribed program before being admitted to practice in any administrative law proceeding or civil or criminal hearing or trial. (This would be comparable to the federal courts' requirement that even a licensed attorney apply for and be "admitted into practice" in the federal courts. In at least some jurisdictions, the applicant must complete a training program on the federal courts, the federal rules of evidence, and the federal rules of procedure.)

In law school, those who intended not to become advocates in tribunals would not enroll in the certificate program. However, after getting their law licenses, they would not be allowed to become advocates in tribunals until and unless they completed such a training program despite having graduated from law school and having passed a bar exam. (Another implication of this proposal is that Evidence would be dropped from the Multistate Bar Exam.)

In connection with the advocacy program, students should be required to take a course in "judging." This would include reading various books by judges, and books about the "art and science" of judging cases. But it would also include writing well-crafted opinions... and *being* a judge.

Chapter 19 spoke of bringing in judges (most likely retired) from the real world to serve in cases heard as part of law school clinics. Law schools could somewhat imitate European courts that have three-judge panels hearing cases at the trial level. Often, in Europe, a jurist is the "head judge" and the other two panel members are laypeople. In the law schools, the other two panel members would be students in the advocacy program. They could not out-vote the judge, but they would hear the case along with the judge and would discuss the case in chambers with the judge. From time to time, the judge would let one or the other student "preside" in the courtroom—ruling on evidentiary matters and motions and on argument during one or more hearings in the case. (Appellate cases in the U.S. typically have three-judge panels, so this arrangement would also work for appeals in the clinics.)

At present, far too many judges are incompetent. The reason is that judges are woefully underpaid. So, typically, they come from one of two groups. The first is young lawyers who want to "get their ticket punched" as benchwarmers before moving on to greener pastures in private practice. A stint as a judge can bring calls from recruiters for big-name law firms that would otherwise never have hired that person.

The second group is political hacks—lawyers who are not doing well in private practice, but who have worked hard in the service of one political party or the other and who get the relatively easier life of the judiciary as their reward.

The young judges are still too "green" to be good at judging, and the older ones (who've put in the years as workhorses for a political party) were never that good to begin with, as lawyers, and will never be that good as judges. (But those who've gone onto the bench from the ivory tower are probably the worst.)

Are there exceptions? Of course—in fact, a surprisingly large number of them. But the rule still holds.

Ideally, the judiciary should almost be a career path in itself. Young judges, with only a few years' previous practice as attorneys, could preside over such minor tribunals as traffic court or small claims court. Gradually, they would move up the judicial ladder—although, of course, political appointments would still be required for, say, federal district judges. But if a given law school had a reputation for turning out graduates who were excellent judges, it stands to reason that the graduates of that law school would have an edge (all other things being equal, which they almost never are) in filling vacancies in the upper reaches of the judiciary.

This brings us back to legal reasoning. Chapter 17 stressed the importance of logic. However, Chapter 28 spoke of the limitations of logic and of our current methods of thinking. Logic is but a tool. Sometimes it is the most appropriate tool. Sometimes not.

In *I AM RIGHT — YOU ARE WRONG*, Edward de Bono noted this (page 27) about our present "binary" method of analyzing problems:

> The direct dangers include *crude perceptions, polarizations, misleading effects of language, unnecessary confrontations, righteousness, and aggressive beliefs...*   [Emphasis added.]

Instead of *starting* legal education with disputes that have already been shaped into a binary form, legal education should start with "preventive lawyering," to try to resolve disputes (and potential disputes) in a non-confrontational manner. (The proposal at the end of the addendum to Chapter 28 was intended as an example.) Instead of seeing problems as disputes to resolve by fighting it out, with one winner and one loser, law school should encourage attorneys to try to resolve a potential problem before it grows into a thorn bush.

De Bono has created a five-day workshop on his systematic approach to coming up with new insights and potential solutions to problems. This includes his famous brainchild, "lateral thinking," and others such as "parallel thinking." Dr. de Bono's course, in an expanded form, should be a major part of any future lawyer's legal education.

The same is true for Suzette Haden Elgin's programs on "the gentle art of verbal self-defense," discussed on page 791 in Chapter 28. It's common knowledge that lawyers tend to be abrasive and arrogant. Often this includes the way they treat their own clients. This "mind-set" is one reason why the legal profession has such a bad reputation. Often, as mentioned earlier in this book, students who are *already* obnoxious decide to go to law school because they rightly believe that the Law is a career that will give them a license to be assholes. That is bad. And legal education needs to do something about it. Spending considerable time in an expanded version of Dr. Elgin's program on verbal self-defense could make a big difference.

An LL.M. in LEGAL EDUCATION

Some people aspire to a career in a certain line of work, but don't have sufficient talent to be good at it (even though, unfortunately, they can often make a living at it). The same is true of teaching, especially law school teaching—which requires no training or *ability* whatsoever.

As mentioned, those who do not wish to teach law students could go straight into a "think tank" affiliated with a law school. But those who want to *teach* should have to get some training in teaching law—a one-year LL.M. in legal education after their J.D. This would at least test their sincerity. But it would also enable them to acquire teaching skills...and if it turns out that they don't have what it takes to teach the law, off to the research institute they go.

Such an LL.M. program in legal education would require study of books such as the Hess-Friedland volume, *Techniques for Teaching Law;* of the Munro volume, *Outcome Assessments for Law School* (both of which works were first mentioned on page 268 in Chapter 9); and, of course, of the "Josephson Report." It would require *practice in teaching* students who were willing to serve as "guinea pigs" (and who would help evaluate the would-be teacher's skill). And it would include auditing by experienced, excellent teachers who would evaluate the candidate's skill. Videotaping, such as the Institute for Law School Teaching now provides at its summer program (as an option), or which the Massachusetts School of Law *requires,* would be part of the evaluation process.

Substantive Courses

As you can see, substantive courses have a *minor* place in this new paradigm for legal education. That's because skills are far more important. Further, substantive knowledge can be acquired very quickly after first-year. CLE (Continuing Legal Education) providers present a semester's worth (and more) of material to practicing attorneys in as little as three days of classes (albeit, six hours a day). The same could be done in law school. There is no legitimate excuse for the time-filling make-work of the Case Method.

Instead of having semester-long courses in a topic, it could work like this: students would pick up the assigned reading materials on a Friday, and read them over the weekend. Classes would start the following Monday: three or four hours a day, through Friday. Students would review everything on their own on Saturday. The course exam would be Sunday afternoon. These week-long "mini-courses" could be scheduled at regular intervals during the school year, allowing students to take many of them during their final two years of law school.

Almost without exception, students cannot *know* what area/s of the law they'll be practicing in. With this system, they would not have to worry about putting too many eggs in too few baskets. Nor would they have to continue paying far too much for far too little.

Further, it would be possible to establish a system similar to that of the Achievement Tests used in conjunction with the Graduate Record Exam. (The GRE is what would-be grad students in the arts and sciences must take. It's analogous to the LSAT, GMAT, and MCAT.) Each Achievement Test is on one subject, and lasts around three hours. Tests could be developed for substantive legal topics, whether national or state-only, depending on the topic. Examples: secured transactions, bankruptcy law, admiralty, wills-trusts-estates, family law, real estate law, consumer law, business organizations, environmental law, trademarks, copyright, patents, immigration law, business transactions, international business transactions, and payment systems.

Each Achievement Test would be given at regular intervals, such as is now done for the MPRE.

In the alternative, law schools could skip the on-site "mini-courses." Instead, students wanting to take a given Achievement Test would study a standard package of materials (including CDs, perhaps) for each, on their own time (such as during summer vacation).

Students could present to prospective employers their scores on the Achievement Test/s they took. Regardless of whether the student first took an on-site "mini-course" at the law school or only did independent study before taking an Achievement Test, prospective employers would have an objective means of evaluating job applicants.

Thus, a graduate of East Podunk U's law school who aced the Achievement Test/s would have a fighting chance of leveling the playing field in the hiring competition against a graduate of a "big name" school (whose scores were lower).

PRE-Law Matters

Far too many students are in law school only because they couldn't come up with anything else to do after college. They are not sincerely interested in the Law—and, with few exceptions, when they do become lawyers, their lack of interest continues (with respect to everything connected with the law other than making money, that is). These people comprise another large group who give the profession a bad name.

At present, if a student's college grades are good enough, and his or her LSAT score is good enough for the school in question, *anyone* can get into law school. The law schools like it that way, because it enormously increases the pool of potential applicants, which in turn enormously increases the potential enrollment of law schools and the potential revenues to the law schools and to their parent universities. This is further proof that the law schools do not take the Law seriously, and have no respect for law students, lawyers, or society.

However, anyone who's *sincere* about possibly becoming a lawyer will have thought about it before college, and surely no later than the end of his or her first year of college.

There used to be "pre-law" programs, similar in purpose to the "pre-med" programs. The pre-law programs weren't very good. But they at least tested a student's sincerity and dedication. That, all by itself, "pre-selected *out*" many who would otherwise have applied to law school but who would have had no legitimate reason for doing so.

Then, at some point, the law schools stopped giving preference to those who'd been in pre-law programs. Their alleged purpose was to "enhance diversity." But although the law schools achieved more diversity as to their students' academic backgrounds, those students' backgrounds were irrelevant to what was demanded of them in law school. Benjamin Sells (quoted in previous chapters) speaks, for example, of the "Life-begins-in-law-school Syndrome." Sadly, he's right: that is indeed the attitude of the professoriat.

Imagine if schools of engineering or architecture did something similar. But, for the Law, however, the inescapable conclusion is that *any* background is good enough preparation. (Business schools are similar. However, they require students, if necessary, to take courses in economics and accounting, for example, to *make up for* the deficiencies in the their undergraduate preparation.)

As Chapter 1 noted, in law school itself, students get no courses in "The Western Legal Tradition" or "The Basic Principles of Anglo-American Law." Nor are they required to have such knowledge as part of their pre-law education. So, they get almost no understanding whatsoever of the foundations of the Law, no acquaintance with the alternative value systems that have existed through history—and which now exist in various other countries. They have little appreciation for why the Rule of Law is so *wonderful*—a *magnificent* achievement of the human race. (Thus, they have no meaningful introduction to its *flaws*, either.) Shouldn't this be an *inherent* part of a lawyer's knowledge?

(Interestingly, ABA Standard 302(b) states, in part that, "A law school shall require all students in the J.D. program to receive instruction in the history, goals, structure, duties, values, and responsibilities of the legal profession and its members..." Yet, there is probably not one ABA-accredited law school in the entire country that offers a course that includes "instruction" in the history or structure of the legal profession. —The "professional responsibility" course, discussed in Chapter 22, only discusses the Model Rules of Professional Responsibility, which have little to do with the values of the profession and its members. Even most lawyers who've been in practice for decades have never *heard* of *any* of the great figures of the law other than, say, Chief Justice John Marshall. And they certainly know nothing of the history of the profession—including how the legal Establishment and the legal education Establishment have subtly worked hand-in-hand to protect the interests of the wealthy and the powerful for generations now.)

The Law, as Chapter 27 argued, ought to be the Queen of the Liberal Arts. It ought to also be an honorable *calling*, not something anyone can just *fall into* because, at the last minute, he or she decided that going from college into the real world was too scary and so began searching for a place to merely "hang out" for a few more years.

Law schools should require that all their applicants have completed a pre-law program, similar to the pre-med program. That means, of course, that pre-law programs must be revived, as there are virtually no such programs around any more. (With the encouragement of the law schools, nearly all colleges have scrapped their pre-law programs.) And they would have to be worthwhile, unlike the old ones.

Such a program would include (but not necessarily be limited to) English comp, statistics, the basics of economics, ethics, Western political theory, American political theory, non-Western political theory, Western legal history (from Hammurabi through Justinian to modern Civil and Common Law), Anglo-American legal history, the basics of business (corporate governance, corporate securities, marketing), accounting, introduction to the scientific method and philosophy of science, and courses in psychology.

Further, students should not be admitted to law school unless they've had some time out in the real-world first. More respectable business schools, for example, require two or three years of work experience. Law is just too important to allow 24-year-olds (or 30-year-olds whose entire lives have been spent only in the ivory tower) to be in a position to give advice on "life and death" matters (as discussed in Chapter 8).

Granted, older applicants might have decided to consider law school only long after completing their previous schooling. But with them, too, it would be possible to establish something comparable to the GRE and its Achievement Tests.

And the instruction for all these pre-law courses could be done on-line, on CD, or on DVD. Thus, even college students would not *have* to take, even if they were *intending* to apply to law school in the *near* future.

End the LSAT Monopoly

In fact, **such an examination (including pre-law Achievement Tests) should *replace* the LSAT, or at least be an alternative to it.**

(The "A" in "LSAT," unlike the "A" in "SAT," stands only for "Admissionm" not "Aptitude." Granted, the organization that makes its money from the LSAT says that it does test aptitude. But all the studies that purport to bear out that conclusion were done *in-house*.)

To get or keep ABA accreditation, *all* law schools are *required to require all their applicants to take the LSAT.* The ABA says that a law school *can* require a test *other* than the LSAT—but only if the test is "acceptable" to the ABA. Care to guess how that plays out? Thus the ABA has, in effect, mandated an LSAT monopoly. Given that the LSAT is a high-pressure, intense experience that *has little to do* with aptitude for being a good lawyer, **the ABA should not have absolute power to tell law schools what indicia they should demand of students' potential in the Law. This is yet another reason to end the *ABA's* monopoly as the national accrediting body for law schools.**

Chapter 30 - Of Gravity—and Levity

It's easy—*very* easy—to get caught up in the madness Chapter 12 discussed. And you do need to be wary of the dangers discussed in Chapter 13 (and elsewhere). You need to take law school seriously.

But if you take it *too* seriously, it will probably interfere with your ability to learn. It will certainly interfere with your humanity.

The ancient Greeks had an ideal as to how a person should be. They sought to avoid the two extremes of personality. At the one end was the "funny man," always cutting up and horsing around. Their word for him was "bomolokos." You won't find many of that sort, if any, in law school. The other end of the continuum was the "agroikos," who seldom even smiled. "Pinheads" is a good modern word for them— and a lot of them are lawyers.

The Golden Mean was the "eutrapelos," a paradoxical combination and balance of gravity and levity. My favorite description of it is "one who kicks the world away, with the airy grace of a dancer—yet, at the same time, presses it to his or her heart." I am sure this is something like what Herman Hesse had in mind when he wrote the statement in *Magister Ludi,* quoted earlier "Although humble, he was completely at ease." To narrow the idea down to just one word, it's "grace"—not in the religious sense, but as in "grace under pressure." And boy are you ever under pressure in law school.

A naturally-gifted dancer has grace. However, natural talent is seldom enough to make a living. Even if you have a natural gift for the Law, it will take a lot of effort to acquire mastery of it. Don't let it get to you.

I'm sure you've seen the 1939 movie, *The Wizard of Oz,* starring Judy Garland. When Dorothy & Company first arrive in the Emerald City, they eventually enter into a great hall. The similarities between the Great Hall and Law School, and between the fraudulent "Wizard" and law professors, are amazing.

For example, when Dorothy and the others first enter the room, a curtain opens at the far end, revealing a huge screen surrounded by upward-shooting flames. Then there appears on the screen a frightening, awesome image: the disembodied head of what is supposedly the great Wizard himself. Remember?

"I AM *OZ*—THE GREAT AND POWERFUL!" his voice booms. He then arrogantly demands, "WHO ARE *YOU?*"

Dorothy identifies herself and her companions, then says, "We've come to ask—."

But the Wizard cuts her off: "*I'LL* ASK. THE GREAT AND POWERFUL WIZARD *KNOWS* WHY YOU'VE COME." He then insults the Scarecrow, the Tin Man, and the Lion. His visitors were terrified, and nearly lost their nerve—which is exactly what he wanted.

That is the ambiance of the Socratic/Case Method. If you really want to understand the Kingsfield Syndrome, discussed in Chapter 12, but without exposing yourself to the psychological virus of *The Paper Chase,* catch these scenes in *The Wizard of Oz* instead. (Okay, I'm exaggerating—but not by all that much, really.)

The band of heroes then leaves, as ordered. They eventually return with the broom of the Wicked Witch of the West. Again they appear before that awesome image. Recall that the Wiz then tries to renege on his pledge to grant their wishes if they brought him this trophy.

When Dorothy dares to take him to task for trying to break his promise, the Wizard warns her: "DO NOT AROUSE THE WRATH OF THE GREAT AND POWERFUL OZ!" "DO YOU PRESUME TO *CRITICIZE* THE GREAT OZ?!"

And when she again chastises him by saying, "You ought to be *ashamed* of yourself, when we came to you for *help,*" he peremptorily responds, "*SILENCE,* WHIPPERSNAPPER!"

Finally, the Wizard tries to dismiss her and her friends by announcing, "THE GREAT OZ HAS SPOKEN!"

However, Toto, Dorothy's mutt, pulls back a second curtain, on the side of the room, near where Dorothy and the others are standing. Turns out that the awesome image was just a projected picture of the altered face of a little old man who'd been a sideshow charlatan in the same world Dorothy came from. Exposed as a mountebank, he comes clean, and offers to do what little he can as a mere mortal to help the heroine get home.

Unfortunately, in real life, unlike the Wizard, the great and powerful law professors routinely are able to get away with breaking the law school's promise to educate students in the law. They feel no contrition whatsoever. Instead, as you've seen, they blame their *students.* (In law as in war, the best defense is a good offense.)

—And if you really want to understand *attorneys* (especially most trial attorneys), you can do no better than to contemplate those scenes near the end, when the "Wizard's" charlatanry has been exposed. He does not apologize for having sent Dorothy and the others to what he hoped would be their *deaths,* just so *he* would not have to *admit* his inability to honor his worthless commitment. Instead, the consummate con artist, he then persuades his "clients"—the Scarecrow, the Tin Man, and the Lion—to believe that he *has* done something for them, something *wonderful,* by giving them mere trinkets instead of fulfilling their needs as he'd promised. Then he takes his leave of the situation— appropriately enough, by means of a hot air balloon. *Unlike* attorneys, however, he did not collect a fee. (But then again, given the way some lawyers are, who knows but what he might have tried to get Dorothy to "take it out in trade" if she'd been able to go away with him after all.)

Like Toto, I've been yapping—and pulling back the curtain.*

---

* And as long as I'm grousing, I have a bone to pick with Glinda, the Good Witch of the North, too: She held herself out as a real know-it-all (that bit about how Dorothy could have used the ruby slippers to go home any time she wanted, for example). But if she was such a smartypants, how come she didn't know the guy she referred to as "The great and wonderful Wizard of Oz" was a *fraud?* Huh? That broad floating around in the bubble was a real bubble-head, as far as I can tell.

Seems to me, Dorothy had a cause of action in tort against Glinda: for the malpractice of witchcraft. *Dorothy Gayle, et al., v. Glinda, Good Witch of the North.* She'd need to file it in Kansas, though, to get the "home court" advantage—although Glinda would probably file for "forum non conveniens" to get it removed back to Oz.

—Nor does it stop there. Granted, the Wicked Witch of West was dead by movie's end. However, Dorothy, the Scarecrow, the Tin Man, and the Lion all had a cause of action against the Wicked Witch's estate for assault, battery, and intentional infliction of emotional distress—just for starters. Then there's the matter of the decedent's estate: the Wicked Witch had probably accumulated considerable assets (just look at that castle!), and I'll bet she died intestate (i.e., without a will). A probate attorney could get rich just from distributing the estate to her heirs—and could certainly run up a nice bill *looking* for those heirs, what with the sister of the Wicked Witch of West (i.e., the Wicked Witch of the East) having predeceased her.

—Come to think of it, there's even more legal work that needs doing in Oz: The Lollipop Guild probably could use a good labor lawyer—as long as they pay in cash rather than suckers. And the Lullaby League might need counsel, too. The Emerald City probably lacks a City Attorney, and the County of Oz probably has been doing without a County Attorney.

Then there's the matter of the Munchkins. Notice that *everyone* in Munchkin-Land is, well, a Munchkin? Birth defects on that scale must have a cause— groundwater contamination, perhaps. I can see it now: a class action on behalf of all the Munchkins for what is obviously some polluter's toxic tort.

Why, County Oz is a gold mine! "Yellow brick road," indeed: *paved* with gold for an enterprising lawyer.

However, as has been said, "If a town has only *one* lawyer, he or she will *starve;* but *two* will make their *fortune."* Anyone care to sign up? (Now you see what "Thinking Like a Lawyer" *really* means.)

Unfortunately, my bark is much worse than my bite...so far. And even if you are someday inclined to agree with me that law school is mostly smoke and mirrors, the *poseurs* who run the show will never admit their fraudulence. In short, unlike Dorothy when confronting the merely human "wizard," you will never be able to "call a spade a spade" in law school. You will have to play along. But at least, in your own mind, learn to see it for what it is, and to laugh at it...and at yourself.

Do not be in awe of the law. And *especially* do not be in awe of your law *professors*.

Chapter 25 spoke of how the "madness in the (Socratic/Case) Method" of law school is designed to disrupt your previous world-view, to thoroughly disorient you, and to get you to embrace amorality in place of morality. The process has been often described, aptly, as "brainwashing."

In his book *Taking Laughter Seriously,* John Morreall comments (page 107):

> [H]umor is one of the best defenses against the procedure known as "brainwashing." The person trying to brainwash another is essentially trying to take away that person's mental flexibility and capacity to think for himself, and implant in the person a single line of thought from which he will not deviate. But if the person can maintain his sense of humor, this will not happen.

And as you saw from many of the items presented from students in Chapter 15, hide-the-ball and subtle (or not-so-subtle) intimidation are tactics in this procedure. That's why Chapter 25 referred to the "deeper games" of law school: to destroy your sense of self-worth, to thus make you receptive to reforming your personality and character as a lawyer. ("Thinking Like a Lawyer" thus means far more than doing a lawyerlike analysis of a fact-pattern.)

Morreall had also noted (page 54)

> People who have a positive self-concept and a positive confident view of themselves as masters of their own fate laugh and enjoy humor more than those who do not feel in control.

Thus, humor is not something that's merely "for laughs."

As you can tell from this book, I am no *eutrapelos*—and I hope *you* prove better able than I to practice what I can only preach. *Planet Law School* has been a relentless jeremiad up to this point. In its own way, this book has taken law school too seriously.

So, heeding my own advice, I hereby present some tidbits to lighten the mood—and, more important, to help you acquire the frame of mind and mental resilience to help resist the depredations you'll be subjected to in law school.

The Truth, the Whole Truth, and Nothing but the Truth

Excerpts from transcripts of real-life Depositions, Hearings, and Trials, repeated verbatim...

LOVE THAT JURY DUTY

During jury selection, the following exchange occurred between the presiding judge and a prospective juror:

Female Panelist: Yes, your Honor. We were taken to a hotel while we were deliberating, and we were all seduced in the hotel.

Court: You were what?

Panelist: We were seduced in the hotel.

Court: Do you mean *"sequestered"*?

Panelist: That's the word.

YOU ASKED - PART I

Attorney: What were you convicted of?

Witness: Miscellaneous receiving.

Attorney: What did you receive?

Witness: I received one to five years.

GO FIGURE

Attorney: Do you have a middle name?

Witness: P.

Attorney: And what does it stand for?

Witness: For "Latimer," on my mother's side.

OF SAGES AND WAGES

Attorney: Were you paid by the hour?

Witness: No, on Saturdays.

YOU ASKED - PART II

Attorney: What did he do after that?

Witness: Well, he walked down the deck, as far as I remember.

Attorney: How did he walk?

Witness: With his two feet.

SO *THAT'S* HOW THE TERM ORIGINATED

Attorney: After the anesthesia, when you came out of it, what did you observe with respect to your scalp?

Witness: I didn't see my scalp the whole time I was in the hospital.

Attorney: It was covered?

Witness: Yes, bandaged.

Attorney: Then later on, when you first observed it, what did you see?

Witness: I had a skin graft. My whole buttocks and my leg were removed and put on top of my head.

From the Books

JUDICIAL NOTICE

"In protecting women, courts and juries should be careful to protect men, too, for men are not only useful to general society, but to women especially."

—Bleckley, J., *Humphrey v. Copeland,*
54 Ga. 543, 544 (1875)

ANOTHER ONE FROM THE IMMORTAL BLECKLEY

"[T]he venereal disease was not a partnership malady. That was individual property."

—Bleckley, J., *Gilbert v. Crystal Fountain Lodge,*
80 Ga. 284, 286, 4 S.E. 905, 906 (1887)

THE CASE NAME SAYS IT ALL

Swindle v. Poore, 59 Ga. 336 (1877)

They Call It "Thinking Like a Lawyer"

Questions that real lawyers asked at depositions, hearings, and trials (And for those who wish to become trial lawyers, these are at least as instructive as they are entertaining.)

THE THINGS THEY DON'T TEACH YOU IN LAW SCHOOL - PART I
Attorney: Mr. Josephson, you went on an extended honeymoon?
Witness: Yes, touring Europe.
Attorney: You took your wife with you?

WELL, HE DID LIKE TO "GROWL" AT SUSPECTS
Attorney: And how did you know the policeman wasn't a dog?

LOGIC 101
Attorney: What happened then?
Witness: He told me, he says, "I have to kill you because you can identify me."
Attorney: Did he kill you?

SUCH AS?
Attorney: Do you have any children or anything of that kind?

THINGS THEY DON'T TEACH YOU IN LAW SCHOOL – PART II
Attorney: Mr. Edwards, are you the father of Robert Edwards?
Witness: No.
Attorney: Do you know who the father is?
Witness: Yes. Bill Daniels is the father.
Attorney: Tell us how Bill Daniels happens to be the father of that child.

THE PRIVATE LIFE of a PROPER ENGLISH GENTLEWOMAN
In a British case, a woman sued a municipal bus company for personal injury. She said that as she exited from the back of the bus, the driver started to drive on, causing her to be thrown down, and her face struck the pavement. During his final argument, her lawyer made this statement:

"Through this most unfortunate accident, caused by the gross negligence of the servant of defendant Company, my unfortunate client suffered this most grievous injury to her jaw, with the dire result that she could not—for quite a long time after—bite her bottom with her top teeth."

DOCTOR'S REVENGE - PART I

Attorney: Dr. Browning, you conducted the autopsy on Mark Samuels?

Witness: I did.

Attorney: And he was dead at the time?

Witness: No, you stupid asshole. He was sitting up on the table, asking me what the hell I was doing.

DOCTOR'S REVENGE - PART II

Attorney: Dr. Gold, you say you're here to testify about the cause of Mr. Blake's death, correct?

Witness: That's right.

Attorney: But Dr. Gold, you did not, yourself, conduct the autopsy on Mr. Blake, did you?

Witness: That's right.

Attorney: Dr. Jeffries conducted the autopsy on Mr. Blake, didn't he?

Witness: That's right.

Attorney: You weren't present when Dr. Jeffries conducted the autopsy on Mr. Blake, were you?

Witness: That's right.

Attorney: In fact, you never even saw the body of Mr. Blake, did you?

Witness: That's right.

Attorney: And all you have are Dr. Jeffries's notes from that alleged autopsy, correct?

Witness: That's right.

Attorney: Then you cannot even say for certain that Mr. Blake is dead, can you?

Witness: That's right, counselor. I do have his brain sitting in a jar on a shelf in my office. But for all I know, the rest of him could be out practicing law somewhere.

Lawyer Jokes

The trial lawyer returned to court after lunch with the strong odor of an alcoholic beverage on his breath. As he approached the bench for a conference, the judge—a teetotaler—angrily said, "Counselor! You reek of whiskey!"

Proving that his potation had not impaired his powers of cerebration, the quick-thinking attorney replied, "If your Honor's sense of justice is as good as his sense of smell, my client will prevail in this case!"

Newspaper Reporter to Bragging Lawyer: How many court cases
have you lost?
Lawyer: None.
Reporter: None?!
Lawyer: None. *I* have *never* lost a case in court...but some of my
clients have.

The young attorney, fresh out of law school, had landed a very
wealthy client. She had some papers for the client to sign, but he was
leaving town. He told her to meet him at the VIP lounge at the airport,
and he'd sign the papers there.

The lawyer got there first. After awhile, she noticed none other
than Bill Gates also sitting in the lounge, with some of his aides. Thinking
fast, she approached him and stood silently until he noticed her and
indicated she could address him.

"Mr. Gates," she said, wringing her hands, her voice strained, "Please
forgive me for interrupting you like this. But...but...well, sir..."

"What is it?" Gates demanded.

"Well, sir, you see, I am a lawyer, a sole practitioner, fresh out of
law school. Through some sort of miracle, I have this one client who's
really wealthy. He's supposed to meet me here, to sign some papers. I
don't know how much he respects me as an attorney, because I'm
female and newly licensed. But what I was wondering was—well, Mr.
Gates, sir, if...later on...if you see me sitting with my client, and it
wouldn't be too much trouble, would you be willing to just say 'Hello'
to me, as though you know me? I am sure my client would we 'wowed.'"

Gates was delighted to hear such a simple request that would be
no trouble at all to grant.

"Why, sure," he replied, taking pity on the distraught young woman.
"What's your name?"

"Susan," she replied, nervously. "If you could just call me by my
first name, that would be *wonderful.*"

"Be happy to," Gates responded.

About five minutes later, the client showed up and joined the
lawyer. As he was looking over the papers to be signed, Bill Gates
walked over and stood by the two.

"Susan! My favorite attorney! How are you?" Gates asked, beaming.

"Bill," she replied coldly, glaring at him, "how many times do
I have to tell you? Don't interrupt me when I'm meeting with a client!
Now, *f— off!*"

Of Laughter and Lawyers

The following is an excerpt from an article in a long-defunct publication, *The Court Jester...*

According to Dr. William Fry, of Stanford University Medical School, there is a close relationship between laughter and mental and physical well-being. "We have a lot of evidence that shows that mirth and laughter affect most of the major physical systems of the body. You can get a really good work-out from it."

Dr. Fry is an authority on the physiology of laughter. He was interviewed at the sixth International Humor Conference, held at Arizona State University, where the topic was the subject of much—serious, scientific—discussion. He continued: "Laughter is an activity that has both physiological and psychological energy—like sex and exercise."

According to him, in less than 20 seconds, intense laughter can cause the rate of heartbeat to double, for three to five minutes. In contrast, strenuous exercise (such as rowing) must continue for three minutes before the change occurs. As for sex, the time it takes for the heartbeat to change, the rate achieved, and its duration all depend on psychological factors as much as physiological. For a some encounters, the rate can nearly triple—and stay that way for a long time. However, whereas the fatality rate during or shortly after these other activities is often remarked, people who've literally died laughing are virtually unheard of.

During intense laughter, the primary muscles involved are those in the abdomen, neck, face, scalp, shoulders, and chest. Fry also noted that the muscles not directly involved in laughter are more *relaxed* than usual during the paroxysm occurring elsewhere within the body.

And laughter clearly benefits the respiratory system. During normal breathing, much "tidal air"— a residuum of carbon dioxide-laden vapors—remains in the lungs. Fry says that laughing "makes you evacuate more of that 'tidal air,' so that you have an enlargement of 'air exchange.'" —More air is expelled with the next breath. But the new intake is oxygen-rich and interfaces with the lung tissue at sites where the carbon dioxide residuum had been. The improved "air exchange" can replace sluggishness with renewed mental snap.

What's more, says Fry, "During laughter, there is an increase in rapid [brain-] wave behavior which is indicative of greater alertness and greater cerebral functioning, such as occurs when a person is working on a mathematical problem..."

It isn't just the oxygen-for-carbon dioxide switch that does this, though. Laughter also stimulates the production of catecholamines. There are three, the best-known of which is adrenaline. These stimulate the nervous system and mental alertness.

Laughter has another benefit, for those whose days in the law are filled with clients and cases that are a pain in the neck (if not elsewhere). Laughing, says Fry, also stimulates the secretion of endorphins— the body's natural anesthetics. If an external problem is starting to have internal effects (such as a headache), a dose of humor is the prescription.

So, give your funny bone a regular workout, especially in first-year. (However, be careful about showing your sense of humor in class— at least until late in your first semester.) Although you certainly shouldn't spend much time watching television, do tune in your favorite comedy show—or, if you have a VCR or DVD player—rent a funny movie every so often. Go out to a comedy nightclub, read a Dave Barry book, whatever works. Assuming Dr. Fry is correct, you might even "seriously" consider doing at least one of these just before you go to take each final. —Get that rapid brain-wave pattern goin'. (But *never* display any humor in your answer to a final exam, even if the prof likes to have some jollies in class.)

Here's how that article from *The Court Jester* ended:

> As Samuel Richardson, the 18th-century English writer, put it: "I struggle and struggle, and try to buffet down my cruel reflections as they arise; and when I cannot, I am forced to try to make myself laugh that I may not cry; for one or other I must do; and is it not philosophy carried to the highest pitch for a man to conquer such tumults of soul as I am sometimes agitated by, and in the very height of the storm to quaver out a horse-laugh?"

Speaking of "Quavering out a Horse-laugh"...

The following addendum is world-famous, within legal circles. It's been reproduced in as many as 50 books since its original publication. It is the creation of two students who were then in their third year of law school at the University of Toronto.

Hart Pomerantz came up with the idea for it ("while cramming for his exams"!). Then he and Steve Breslin wrote it in 90 minutes flat after "brainstorming" about it for an hour.

It should come as no surprise that neither man entered the Law after graduating. Pomerantz went to California, where he became a writer for Woody Allen, then for the *Rowan & Martin's Laugh-In* TV show, then partnering with Lorne Michaels in writing and performing comedy. Breslin went to Switzerland, to go to work in the financial services industry.

Presumably, Breslin is still in Switzerland, and still in the financial services industry—though it's unclear whether his employment is in a legal capacity. Pomerantz eventually returned to Canada and became an attorney after all. He now practices employment law in Toronto...but also writes short stories and screenplays.

Acknowledgment: *Regina v. Ojibway* is reproduced from the Criminal Law Quarterly with the permission of Hart Pomerantz and Canada Law Book Inc. (1-800-263-2037, www.canadalawbook.ca).

Addendum to Chapter 30:

Regina v. Ojibway
In the Supreme Court of Canada[*]
8 Crim. L. Q. 137 (1965) (Canada)

Blue, J.—This is an appeal from the Crown by way of a stated case from the decision of the magistrate acquitting the accused of a charge under the Small Birds Act, R.S.O., 1960, c.724, s.2. The facts are not in dispute. Fred Ojibway, an Indian, was riding his pony through Queen's Park on January 2, 1965. Being impoverished, and having been forced to pledge his saddle, he substituted a downy pillow in lieu of the said saddle. On this particular day the accused's misfortune was further heightened by the circumstances of his pony breaking its right foreleg. In accord with the Indian custom, the accused then shot the pony to relieve it of its awkwardness.

The accused was then charged with having breached the Small Birds Act, s.2 of which states:

1. Anyone maiming, injuring, or killing small birds is guilty of an offence and subject to a fine not in excess of two hundred dollars.

The learned magistrate acquitted the accused holding, in fact, that he had killed his horse and not a small bird. With respect, I cannot agree.

In light of the definition section, my course is quite clear. Section 1 defines "bird" as "a two legged animal covered with feathers." There can be no doubt that this case is covered by this section.

Counsel for the accused made several ingenious arguments to which, in fairness, I must address myself. He submitted that the evidence of the expert clearly concluded that the animal in question was a pony and not a bird, but that is not the issue. We are not interested whether the animal in question is a bird or not in fact, but whether it is one in law. Statutory interpretation has forced many a horse to eat birdseed for the rest of its life.

Counsel also contended that the neighing noise emitted by the animal could not possibly be produced by a bird. With respect, the sounds emitted by an animal are irrelevant to its nature, for a bird is no less a bird because it is silent.

[* Canada was and still is a British Commonwealth country. So criminal cases are brought in the name of the Crown rather than the State. When the crown of the United Kingdom is worn by a queen, the case is styled "Regina v...." ("regina" being Latin for "queen"). Otherise, it's "Rex."]

Counsel for the accused also argued that since there was evidence to show the accused had ridden the animal, this pointed to the fact that it could not be a bird but was actually a pony. Obviously this avoids the issue. The issue is not whether the animal was ridden or not, but whether it was shot or not, for to ride a pony or a bird is of no offence at all. I believe counsel now sees his mistake.

Counsel contends that the iron shoes found on the animal decisively disqualify it from being a bird. I must inform counsel, however, that how an animal dresses is no concern to this court.

Counsel relied on the decision *In re. Chickadee*, where he contends that in similar circumstances, the accused was acquitted. However, this is a horse of a different colour. A close reading of that case indicates that the animal in question there was not a small bird, but in fact a midget of a much larger species. Therefore, that case is inapplicable to our facts.

Counsel finally submits that the word "small" in the title Small Birds Act refers not to "Birds" but to "Act", making it the Small Act relating to Birds. With respect, counsel did not do his homework very well, for the Large Birds Act, S.E.O. 1960, c.725 is just as small. If pressed, I need only refer to the Small Loans Act, S.R.O. 727 which is twice as large as the Large Birds Act.

It remains then to state my reason for judgment which, simply, is as follows: Different things may take on the same meaning for different purposes. For the purpose of the Small Birds Act, all two legged feather covered animals are birds. This, of course, does not imply that only two legged animals qualify, for the legislative intent is to make two legs merely the minimum requirement. The statute therefore contemplated multi-legged animals as well. Counsel submits that having regard to the purpose of the statute only small animals "naturally covered" with feathers could have been contemplated. However, had this been the intention of the legislature, I am certain that the phrase "naturally covered" would have been expressly inserted just as "Long" was inserted into the Longshoreman's Act.

Therefore, a horse with feathers on its back must be deemed for the purpose of this Act to be a bird, and, *a fortiori*, a pony with feathers on its back is a small bird.

Counsel posed the following rhetorical question: If the pillow had been removed prior to the shooting, would the animal still be a bird? For this let me answer rhetorically: Is a bird any less of a bird without its feathers?

Reported by H. Pomeranz and S. Breslin

Closing Argument

A Descent into the Maelström

Off the coast of Norway, near an island named Lofoden, there runs a strange current. It's called the Maelström. Under the right circumstances, cross-currents are set up. These in turn generate whirlpools in the ocean. Sometimes, the whirlpools created are sizable. Small boats—including boats made of steel, weighing many tons—have been capsized and sunk in these whirlpools. Small boats made of wood have been torn apart by the stress.

The Maelström became famous in America in the early 1800s, when Edgar Allan Poe (the Stephen King of the day) wrote a short story called "A Descent into the Maelström." In it, he said there was just *one* whirlpool—but he said it was *enormous*. And he said the *whirlpool's* name was the Maelström. (Old Hollywood saying: "Never let the facts get in the way of a good story." Hollywood learned from Poe.) Naturally, in Poe's story, a small wooden boat gets caught in the current near Lofoden Island at the wrong time. It gets swept toward and then into the Maelström. Two men are aboard; brothers. According to Poe, this oceanic maw was so huge that they could look far down into it as their boat was whirled around within it, circling on the surface of the Maelström's "walls."

As their vessel disintegrates, one of the brothers lashes himself to a mast. But the other has been more observant. As he'd looked about in terror, he'd retained sufficient presence of mind to notice that many objects caught in the Maelström had obviously gone all the way to its bottom and were now working their way back to the surface. All these objects were more or less short and cylindrical, almost round. Thinking fast, he decided his only hope for survival was to lash himself not to another mast, but to a *barrel*. He tried to shout to his brother, to explain his reasoning. But the roar within the Maelström was overwhelming. In desperation, he used gestures to try to communicate with his sibling. The other could not comprehend his meaning. There was but one survivor: he who saw what needed to be done, and did it.

Well, brother (or sister), the choice is yours. There is no background roar, and I have done what I could to warn you. The title of this book is *Planet Law School II*. But just as Jupiter has weather systems, and Mars apparently has water (albeit frozen), so this planet called Law School can have its own Maelström, of the Edgar Allan Poe variety. Poe's Maelström was a fiction. The Law School Maelström is real.

You're already caught in the current. That's why you've read this book. If and when you enter the Law School Maelström, you do so on your own: I've already been. Unlike the narrator of Poe's short story, I entered willingly, even eagerly. So will you, perhaps. But I hadn't a realistic understanding of what I was getting myself into. Like the survivor of Poe's short story, I have indeed lived to tell the tale—but not because I was smart and quick-witted, as he was; rather, I was merely lucky.

More than 40,000 people start law school every year. Three years later, nearly all have survived. Were they lucky, as was I? Yes, but only in the sense that they too survived. For good or ill, they will never be the same. —And for many of them, the experience has permanently warped their soul. It may twist yours as well, for all time. (As for mine: the jury's still out.)

You shouldn't have to run such a risk. It shouldn't be that way. Nor should it have been that way for me—nor for the hundreds of thousands of others. I have now given you the benefit of my experience, in a way that no other book does. It is too late for me. It is not too late for you.

You cannot use what's in this book to *overcome* the Maelström of Law School. Such an effort would be quixotic, even suicidal. But by knowing in advance the nature of the phenomenon, you can keep it from overwhelming *you*. You can not only survive it, you can even *thrive* in it as you plunge deep and then gradually come to the surface again.

This is how the tale of Poe's narrator ends:

> A boat pulled me up—exhausted from fatigue— and (now that the danger was removed) speechless from the memory of its horror. Those who drew me on board were my old mates and daily companions— but they knew me no more than they would have known a traveller from the spirit-land. My hair, which had been raven-black the day before, was as white as you see it now. They say too that the whole expression of my countenance had changed. I told them my story—they did not believe it. I now tell it to *you*—and I scarcely expect you to put more faith in it than the merry fishermen of Lofoden.

"I told you so" is not what I want to be telling you years from now—at least, not under the circumstances in which that statement is usually made. But it's your call. (And by the way: my hair didn't turn white in law school—although my countenance definitely changed. And I did have to start wearing glasses.)

Whether or not you go to law school, I invite you to contact me at any time. If you have found particular advice especially worthwhile—or worthless—I'd be grateful if you'd let me know. Likewise if you wish I'd explained something more (or less) fully. The same thing goes for study aids or suggested reading. And if, on your own, you've discovered a new trick to the trade, or a new study aid, good book, etc., please share the news. This new edition of *Planet Law School* was prompted almost entirely by thousands of questions, criticisms, and suggestions from those who'd read the original edition and were willing to share their thoughts. There likely will be yet another edition someday. (Though I can promise that it won't be as long as this one. Instead, there will be separate books, on different topics, I think. This one almost killed me.) If so, your input can help others, later: pro bono publico.

I wish you the best, whatever you decide to do. And I hope this book will have been a help to you in your life, whether or not yours is a life in the Law.

I'd like to end by saying something like "Don't let the bastards get you down." But from experience, I can say for certain that they *will* get you down. Just don't let them *keep* you down too long. And when it's all over, let's both hope you come up a winner.

Good luck, and good-bye.

"Atticus Falcon"
Member of the Bar
State of the Art

INDEX

A

"A" and "B" students 157
"a man's home is his castle" 16
a-morality of law school 714
AALS - see Association of American
     Law Schools
AALS Directory of Law Teachers
     (book) 256, 623
AALS workshops 762
ABA - see American Bar Association
abandoned property 794
ABCs of the UCC (books) 60, 367,
     432
Abelard, Peter 732
Abrams, Kathryn 724
Abrams, Lisa L. 651
academic freedom 310
Academic Legal Writing (book)
     568, 574
Accreditation Standards, ABA - see
     American Bar Association
Achievement Tests (GRE, and
     proposed) 807
"Acting Out" (immature psychologi-
     cal defense mechanism) 739
"actionable" 17, 50
Adams, Sam 379
Adaptation to Life (book) 714, 739
adjunct professors 623
administrative law 621
admiralty law 621
ADR - see Alternative Dispute
     Resolution
adverse possession (in property law)
     203
Advisory Committee Notes (Federal
     Rules of Evidence) 610
"advocacy mode" 69, 199
affidavit - defined 528
affirmative action 347, 638, 747
"affirmative defenses". 51
Afro-American Students Association
     649

Ages of American Law, The (book)
     36, 529, 712
aggravated rape 78
"agroikos," 811
Ainu 742
al-Qaeda, 745
Alabama 291
Alda, Alan 134
Aldisert, Ruggero 69, 567, 616
Alice in Wonderland (novel) 593
"All animals are created equal." 732
Ally McBeal (TV show) 637
Alternative Dispute Resolution 602,
     786 ff.
ALWD Citation Manual (book) 573
ambiguity doctrine 56
American Bar Association
     60, 249, 269, 279, 281, 702, 802
     Accreditation Standards
          No. 302(b) - page 809
          No. 303 - page 304, 316
          No. 303 - page 179
          No. 601 - page 700
          No. 606 - page 699
          No. 801 - page 289
     ABA's website URL 290
     Section Committee on ABA
          Standards for Appraisal 289
     Section of Legal Education and
          Admissions to the Bar 289
American Council on Education. 308
American Economic Review
     (academic periodical) 728
American Law Institute 102
American Law Reports. (legal
     encyclopedia) 28
American Lawyer magazine 252, 481
America's Bar Review (vendor) 693
Ames, James Barr 261
analogy, argument by 542
Anarchy and Elegance (book) 460,
     712, 782
Anderson, Marian 751
Andre v. Pace Univ. (case) 306
anecdotal evidence 727
Animal Farm (novel) 732, 749
animism 780

C

"C" students 157
Cain, Patricia 724, 749
Cal Tech 421
Caldwell, Pauline 724
CALI (Computer Assisted Learning
    Instruciton) 274
    CALI Library of Lessons 60, 432
California 291, 666
California, University of, at Berkeley
    351
California Lawyer (periodical) 644
"call of the question" 205, 207
CALR 539
canned briefs 87
Canon—i.e., Church—Law 258
Cape May Court House (book). 532,
    561, 593
capitalism 781
Capellanus, Andreas 382
Cardozo< Benjamin 545
Carey, Christen Civiletto 651
carnal knowledge 18
Carnegie Foundation 765
Carney, William J. 154
Carroll, Lewis 243
case brief, briefing 65, 79
"case file" 664
case investigation. informal 561
case law 47
Case Method 34, 66
case theme for trial 500, 550
Case Western University's law school
    724
Case/Socratic Method. 30
casebooks 28, 449
"cases and controversies" (in U.S.
    Constitution) 32
"casual empiricism" 727
Causation (as legal element) 48
    cause in fact. 48, 255
    see also "proximate cause"
"centrifuge" processing of exam
    problems 165
Certificate Program in Intellectual
    Property 619

chain of title (in property law) 564
changing a student's grade 296
Chaplin, Charlie 16
change of grade on final 342
Character & Fitness Committee 342ff
"Charge of the Light Brigade" (poem)
    332, 735
chastity 18
cheating 336
checking your work on exam
    answers 220
chess 29
Chicago Lawyer (periodical) 644
Chicago. 187
Chicago, University of 721, 722
"chicken-and-egg" situation 109
China 380
Chinese-Americans 745
Chirelstein, Marvin A. 100
choice of law 76
choses of action 62
Christensen, Clayton M. 778
Christian ministers 35
Chronicle of Higher Education, The
    (newspaper) 309
Church and State 779
Church of England 780
Churchill, Winston 374, 730
CIRI(P) 169, 174
Cilke, Kimberly J. 60
"Citizenship Schools" 757
Civil Action, A (book) 254, 532
"Civil Objection!" (software) 615
Civil Procedure (course) 19
Civil Procedure 59
civil rights 379
Civil Rights Movement 741
CJS 28
Clancy, Tom 370
Clark, Boardman, Callaghan (vendor)
    27
Clark, Septima 757
"class participation" points 297
"Classroom Assessment" 268
Clausewitz, Carl von 382
CLE (Continuing Legal Education)
    627, 628, 707, 807

difference between idealism and
utopianism; 718
Difficult Conversations (book) 790
Diotima 33
DiPippa, John M.A. 280
"diploma privilege" 588
Directory of Legal Employers (book)
645
"dirty professor tricks" 90 ff.
disabled, difficulties for the 349
"discovery" procedures (in civil
procedures - litigation) 287
discrimination - see also harassment,
racism
discrimination on the basis of looks
635
"dispositive" 106, 163
"distinguish" 25
Dittfurth, David A. 101
divorce 350
Doctor of Jurisprudence 13
Doctor of Juristic / 'Juridical Science
40
Doctor of Laws 40
"doctrinal [law review] article." 724
"doctrines," legal 56
Dodd, Victoria J. 308
Dodgson, Chas. Lutwidge, Rev. 243
Doherty, larry 602
Dolovich, Sharon 298
Donahue, Phil 134
Dostoyevski, Fyodor 773
"double standard" 734
Douglas, Ann 728, 789
Douglas, William O. 543, 721
"Dow Jones - All Database" 645
"downward spiral," the 716
Drafting Contracts (book) 569
Drake, Paul (character on *Perry
Mason* TV show) 562
drawing card, professorship as 252
Dress for Success (book) 635
"drudgeship" 260
dual degrees 655
"duckness" 46
due process of law. 22
Duke University - law school 726

duty as element in the law 48
duty - breach - harm - cause 254
Dworkin, Andrea 724
Dwyer, John 351 ff., 526
Dylan, Bob 17, 298
dynamic hypothetical 101

E

E&FI (Estates & Future Interests, in
property law) 99
easement (in property law) 99
easement by prescription 203
"Ebonics." 752
economics 728
economy, U.S. 656
ecosystem 109
Education, U.S. Dept. of 292, 293
education law 621
"Educational Malpractice: A Tort is
Born" (law review article) 307
Edwards, Linda Holdeman 98
"efficient breach-of-contract" 778
Eichmann, Adolf 380
Einstein, Albert 311
element/s (in law) 36, 46, 163
element-by-element, 163
Elements of Style (book) 568
elements. 163
Elgin, Suzette Haden 328, 370,
791, 806
Elias, Elias 565
Eliot, Charles W. 34, 35
Eliot, T.S. 770
Emanuel's "Crunch Time" (books)
434
Emory Law Journal 260n.
Emory University School of Law 154
"Emperor's New Clothes, The"
(fable) 370
Empire Strikes Back, The (book)
724, 763
employment, in law school, during
the academic year 319
Encyclopedia Britannica's Micropedia
455
"Engine Charlie" Wilson 281

English boarding schools 240
English cases - finding 94
Enlightenment, The 759, 775
Enron 281, 774
entertainment and sports law 620
entrustment 200
Environmental Law Clinic - Tulane
	University's law school 587
"equating" (of MBE scores) 660
"Equitable Division and the Law of
	Finders" (law review article) 530
equitable servitude (in property law)
	202
Ehrenreich, Barbara 742
Epps, Garrett 715
Epps, JoAnne A. 611
Ertel, Danny 791
Essay on Man, "Epistle II" (poetry)
	716
"Establishment clause." 779
Estates & Future Interests (in prop-
	erty law) 98
Estates and Future Interests (primer)
	98, 435
"ethics" exam 667
eunuchs (medieval Chgina) 745
"eutrapelos" 811
Evans, Keith 612
evidence, anecdotal 727
*Evidence: Essential Terms and
	Concepts* (primer) 610
Evidence: Examples & Explanations
	(primer) 609
Evidence, Federal Rules of - Advisory
	Committee Notes 610
Evidentiary Foundations (book) 611
Examining Witnesses (book) 613
"Examples & Explanations" series.
	58, 274
exams - fruitcake 162, 274, 768
	super-fruitcake exam 167
	multiple-choice 179
examsmanship 155 ff.
"executed" contract 76
exercise, physical 326
"express" vs. "implied" (contracts)
	75
Exxon 281

F

facilitated negotiation 787
fact pattern 70, 162
factual issue (on exams) 158
faculty law library 257
Fajans, Elizabeth 568, 574
Falk, Mary 568, 574
Fall of Rome 257
fallacy of the undistributed middle
	[term] 547
false 206
false dichotomy between "Black
	Letter Law" and "policy" 184
"false issues" (on exam problems)
	159
Fanon, Franz 741
Farber, Daniel 721, 727, 734, 735,
	755
Farrakhan, Louis 779
FDR (Franklin Delano Roosevelt)
	275
fear 225
Federal Judiciary Almanac (book)
	640
Federal Rules of Civil Procedure 19
Federal Rules of Evidence (book)
	610
Federal Rules of Evidence - Advisory
	Committee Notes 610
Federalist Papers, The (book) 378
Federalist Society 648
feedback mechanism 262
Feinman, Jay M. 261
Feldman, Marc 261
"fellow employee" affirmative
	defense of (in tort law) 19
"felony" v. "misdemeanor" 773
felony murder, defined 78
"Feminist Crits" 724
feminists 379
*Feminization of American Culture,
	The* (book) 728, 789
fetus 21
Feynman, Richard 421
Fielding, Henry 780
Fields, W.C. 377

K

Kabir 385
Kahlenberg, Richard D. 257, 713, 715
Kahneman, Daniel 120
Karr, Alphonse 294
Katko, Marvin 601
Katko v. Briney (case) 600
Kaufman, Michael J. 444
Kennan, George F. 378
Kennedy, Duncan 722, 735
Kennedy, John F. (President) - assassination of 281
Kennedy, John F., Jr., 690
Kennedy, Randall 735
Kerr, Irwin 280
"key point/s at issue" 71
"keys to legal education" 764
Khayyam, Omar 188
Kidman, Nicole 164
"KimChee" (internet posting) 387
King, Don 752
King, Martin Luther - assassination of 747
King, Rodney 790
King, Stephen 224, 384, 827
King of Torts (novel) 656
Kingsfield, Charles W. 330
    "Kingsfield Syndrome" 271, 812
Kirkpatrick, Laird C. 610
"KISS" rule 568
"KISS-A-MIC" 568
Kissam, Philip C. 42
knowledge (Josephson Pyramid) 56
knowledge of terminology 41
Knox, Doug 247n.
Korean-Americans 745
Krieger, Larry 280
Kroll Associates 562
"Ks" 72
Ku Klux Klan 735
Kuhn, Thomas 768
Kurtz, Sheldon F. 59, 98, 221

L

"L&E" - see Law and Economics
L&M 98
labyrinth, the 460
LaFond, John Q. 59
Lake, Peter F. 255, 263
Lamb, Cindi 378
"Lamborghini, Lisa" (animated character in software) 616
Langdell, Christopher C. 34, 261, 556, 693n., 701, 721
    Langdellian pedagogy 763
    Langdellians 38
    Langdell's casebook 67
Lapham, Lewis H. 9
Latin terms 202
Laurence, Robert 98
"Law & a Banana" courses 620, 755, 771
Law & Economics 40, 722, 723, 728, 778, 781
"law and order" (Nixon 1968 campaign rhetoric) 747
Law and the Rise of Capitalism (book) 781
"Law Day, USA" 9
law dictionaries 453
"law factory" 249
"law is 'a ass, the" 62
"law market" 642
"law merchant" (Medieval) 781
Law of Property, The: An Introductory Survey (primer) 59, 221
Law of Torts, The (primer) 59
Law Preview (vendor) 442
law review 383 ff., 571
law review article 251
Law School Confidential (book) 163, 164, 176
law school dean's duties 693n.
"Law School in the Nineties" (article in periodical) 294
"Law School Learning Pyramid" (Josephson's) 41
"Law School Legends" (audio tapes) 612

M

Marcus, Steven 753
M.A.S.H (movie) 131
Mauet, Thomas A. 612
M.I.T (Massachusetts Institute of
 Technology) 35
macho (or "macha") game 333
MacKinnon, Catharine 724, 735
MacPherson v. Buick Motor Co.
 (case) 544
MADD (organization) 379
Madison, James 378
"Maelström, The" (short story) 827
"magic" words 61
"magical realism" 734, 754
Magister Ludi (novel) 259, 321, 811
major elements in cause of action 48
major issues in exam problem 164
Major League Basebal 514, 793
"majors" in law school 619
Makdisi, John 98
"Making a Good Record" (in trial)
 501
"Making Docile Lawyers" (law review
 article) 298
"Male Chauvinist Pig" (on jury) 134
Malmédy 234
Malloy, John 635
Mandarins (China) 745
Mann, Gloria 154
Marine Corps, U.S. 329
Martin, Jeffrey C. 306
Martindale-Hubbell (Lawyer
 directory) 645, 646
Marx, Karl 40
Mason, Perry (TV show) 31
Masonic Order 648
Massachusetts 18, 291, 705
Massachusetts School of Law
 269, 284, 285, 293, 310, 705, 806
Master of Juridical (or Juristic)
 Science. 13
Master of Law 13
Master of the Game (novel) 259,
 811
master outline 112, 186, 335

Mastering Multiple Choice (MBE)
 (book) 678
*Mastering the Art of Cross-Examina-
 tion with Irving Younger* (audio
 cassettes and videotapes) 614
Mastering Torts (primer). 100, 436
Matasar, Richard A. 306
"material" facts 106
mathematical models (economics)
 728
Matrix, The (movie) 726
Matsuda, Mari 724, 749
May, Christopher N. 59
"May Day" parades 9
May the Best Team Win (book) 525
MBA degree 655
MBA candidates 248
MBE (Multistate Bar Exam) 99, 659
McBeal, Ally (TV character) 637
McBride, James 511, 522
McCann, Les 126
McCarthy, Joseph 529, 735
McCarthy, Kevin 522
McClurg, Andrew J. 573n, 601
McElhaney, James W.. 613
McElhaney's Litigation (book) 613
McElhaney's Trial Notebook (book)
 613
McFarlane, Todd 481, 796
McGlew, Polly 654
MCP ("Male Chauvinist Pig") 134
Maryland Law Review 306
meaningful changes to hypotheticals
 108
"mechanics with words" 266
mediation 787
medical school 44, 260, 617
Meiji "Restoration" 746
"memorize-and-regurgitate" mode
 80, 173
Mencken, H.L. 740
"Menexenus" (internet posting) 387
"mens rea" (in criminal law) 78, 123
MENSA (organization) 383
Mensheviks 380
Menzies, Galvin 745
Mercer University School of Law 269

N

"naïve cynics" 758
Napoleon 382
NASA 265
Nation of Islam 779
Nation Under Lawyers, A (book) 702
National Association for Law Place-
    ment 645
"National Brotherhood Week" 756
National Institute for Trial Advocacy
    610, 709
National Jurist (magazine) 634
National Law Journal (newspaper),
    643
National Lawyers' Guild 648
Native Americans 780
"natural-born genius of the law" 42
    and *passim*
"near-miss" issues 159, 164, 206
"negative income tax" 747
"negative" issue 206
negotiations competition 604
Nelson, Charles I. 98
Nesson, Charles 254, 550
    see also "Billion-Dollar Charlie"
New Crits 726
"new journalism" 727
"New Man" 759
"New Rednecks" 740
New Testament, The 744
New York 666
New York Lawyer (periodical) 644
New York Times 29, 176, 252
New York University's law school
    36, 37
"Newspeak" 730
"Nice-Nice" 271
Nicholas II (Tsar) 380
Nicholson, Jack 752
Nickled and Dimed (book) 742
night school 10
Nightline (TV shoe) 252
1984 (novel) 730, 735, 737
NITA 610, 709
Nixon, Richard 747
Nobel prize-winners 255

"Non-Contractual Nature of the
    Student-University Contract"
    (law review article) 308
non-confrontational negotating. 791
non-issues 156, 164, 274 - see also
    near-miss issues, negative issues
Normans, The (French) 17
North Carolina, University of, at
    Chapel Hill 765
"Not Invented Here" Syndrome 726
Nutshell™ series 28
Nutter, Carolyn 649
NYU - law school 26, 37

O

"obiter dicta" 66
"Objection!" (software) 615
O'Brien (character in *1984*) 731
O'Connor, Michol 100
O'Connor's Federal Rules - Civil Trials
    (book) 100, 435, 651
Ohio State U's law school 179
old exams as practice exams 174
Oliver Twist (novel). 63
Olympics, The 155
"on all fours" 25
"on point" 25
"On the Blank Generation" (song)
    730
On War (book) 382
On Writing (book) 224, 384, 385
On-Site: Summer Program 471
Once an Eagle (novel) 421
One L (book) 326, 329
"One must believe, to understand"
    732
"One must understand, to believe"
    732
one-upmanship 321
ones that count (now)- courses 15
ones that don't count (now) - courses
    15
operation of the law school accredita-
    tion process (in federal antitrust
    suit against ABA) 284

Opium Wars 380
opportunity cost 532
Order of the Coif 571
Organ, Jerome Michael 280
Orlinsky, Ethan 800
Orwell, George 730, 732
Osborn, John Jay, Jr. 329
Otto, Gordon 260
*Outcome Assessments for Law
    Schools* (book) 179, 268, 273,
    275, 299, 806
"outcome-determinative" 106
outcome-determinative facts 164
"outside materials" (during exams)
    112
"Outside the Church, there is no
    salvation" 732
*Owen Equip. & Erection Co. v.
    Kroger* (case) 346, 572

P

Pace University's law school 122,
    127
Page, JoAnne 165, 176, 757
Paglia, Camille 735
Paine, Thomas 379
Palm, Gary 290
Palmer, Geoffrey W. R. 601
Painted Word, The (book) 743
Pan, Peter 629
papal infallibility. 186
Paper Chase, The (novel) 39, 326,
    329, 456, 812
Parker, Dorothy 58
Parker, Johnny C. 307
Parson Thwackum (character in *Tom
    Jones*) 780
"parties and issues" (on exams) 70
"passive aggression" 89
Patton, Bruce 790
Patton, George S., Jr. 374
Paul 173, 383
Paul V (Pope) 376
Paul, Jeremy 171, 444
pedagogical "bait and switch" 234

pedagogical incompetence hidden
    from scrutiny 263
"Pedagogy and Politics" 261
"Peer Courts" 605
Peirce, Charles 726
"penumbra of the Constitution" 200
"people of color" 732 ff.
"per curiam" 309
"performance" (in contract law) 76
Perini (character in *One L*) 330
Perry Mason (TV show) 28, 561
"person-as-process" 723
personal outline 87 ff.
peyote 780
Ph.D. candidates 247
Phi Beta Kappa 571
Phillips, Susan T. 575
Phoenicians 744
physical disabilities, difficulty in law
    school for those with 349
Pierson v. Post (case) 494, 497, 521
"Pilgrims" 779
pinhead/s 343
placement office 641
plain English movement 62
planning your exam answer 207
Plato 31, 37, 733
Platonic Ideas 31, 38, 771
playing THE game v. playing A
    game 114
playing with hyptheticals 109, 115
plea of confession & avoidance 51
PMBR (vendor) 612, 693
Poe, Edgar Allan 827
POF (Proof of Facts) for trial 502
police force 773
policy discussions 52, 177
Pope, Alexander 716
"Political Race Theory" 733
"politically correct" 730
politically correct" prof 178
Polonius (character in *Hamlet*) 40
Pomerantz, Hart 822
Pomeroy, John Norton 36, 37
Popov, Alex 478 ff.
Populism 743

raw score on MBE 660
read the cases 80
Reagan, Ronald 722, 727
"real covenant" (in property law)
202 - and equitable servitudes"
(in property law). 99
"real issues" (on exams) 157 - see
aslo near-miss issues, non-issues,
negative issues
"Reality Check" re. potential salaries
655
"reasonable person," legal fiction/
standard of 48, 77, 132
Recent Developments Concerning
Accrediting Agencies 306
"recognized causes of action" 50
"red flags" (on exams) 206
"red herrings" (on exams) 159
Redneck Nation (book) 740
"rednecks of color" 741
Reed Law Group (vendor) 693
Regina v. Ojibway (case parody)
823
"relevant parties" (on exam) 205
religious freedom 779
"remand" (by appellate court) 501
remedial courses 670
"remote" (in tort law causation
element) 48
"removing" (in civil procedure) 20
"rent-a-judge" (in alternate dispute
resolution) 602
"Reporter's Notes" (in the *Restatements*) 104
"reporters" (law books) 27
"Reporters" (for *Restatements*) 102
research assistant 251, 583
research grants 253
Restatement (Second) of Contracts
72 - Section No. 47: 103
*Restatement (Second) of Contracts -
STUDENT Edition* 433
*Restatement (Second) of Torts -
STUDENT Edition* 433
*Restatement of the Law on Lawyer-
ing* 103
Restatement of Torts 123

Restatement "Reporters" 102
Restatements of the Law 102, 274,
677
Résumé Workbook, The 649
résumé tips 648
Reuther, Walter 703
Reutlinger, Mark 610, 624
reworking your personal outline 110
rhetoric 258
Rhodes, Cecil 757
Rhodes Scholarship - eligibility
change 757
Rich, Adrienne 735
Richardson, Samuel 822
Richter, Sviatoslav 370
RICO statute 305
Roberts, Bonita K. 565
Robinson, Kim Stanley 754
Roman law 258
Roosevelt, Franklin Delano 275
rotating docket 511
Roth, George J. 710
Rubenstein, Arthur 370
Rubaiyat, The (poetry) 188
Rudolf Flesch 549
Rule Against Perpetuities 99, 707
rule/s of law 66
rules and principles 41
Ruesch, Linda J. 60
Rushdie, Salman 755
Rutgers-Newark (law school) 742

S

sado-masochistic environment 240
"Sahara of the Bozart" (essay) 740
Saint Anselm 732, 760
Santa Clause 712
"Satyagraha" 741
Saul (Saint Paul) 382
save as much money as you can after
graduation 656
scaled score on MBE 660
Schiller, Lawrence 532, 561
Schlichtmann, Jan 254
Scholarly Writing for Law Students
(book) 568, 574

scholarships 706
Schlueter, Linda L. 565
Schuwerk, Robert P. 280
Schwartz, Frederic S. 99
Schwartz, Robert 430
Science, Law as a 35
science v. religion 712
Science magazine 120
Scriabin, Alexander 370
Seamer, Deanne C. 611
Seattle University School of Law 269
Seckinger, Jim 613
second-order lie 177
secret police 773
Section Committee on ABA
    Standards for Appraisal 289
Section of Legal Education and
    Admissions to the Bar 289
Secured Transactions in a Nutshell
    (book). 28
*Selections of Cases in the Law of
    Contracts* (Langdell's casebook).
    36
"selectivity schedules" used by law
    firms in hiring 645
"self esteem" movement 229
Sells, Benjamin 182, 710, 716, 717,
    782, 808
"Sensitive New Age Guys;" 729
"sentimentalism." 728, 739
service of process (in civiil procedure
    - litigation) 20
"Seven Principles for Good Practice
    in Legal Education" (ILST) 269
sex 326, 826
sexual harassment 339, 345
sexual orientation 639
Sexual Politics (book) 753
Shadow, Sheldon Lee 768
Shakespeare, William 40, 241, 369,
    508
shamanism 780
*Sharick v. Southeastern Univ. of the
    Health Scienc* (case) 308
Shaw v. Shaw (case) 496
Sheehy, Richard 280
Sherman Act 281

Sherry, Suzanna 721, 727, 734, 735,
    755
Shinto religion 780
Siegel, Stephen A. 100, 222
Silechia, Luria Ann 280
Silver, Marjorie A. 280
Singer, Richard G. 59
Simple negligence (in tort law) 89
Simpson, Bart (animated cartoon
    character) 752
Simpson, O.J. 21, 523
Siviglia, Peter. 569
S.J.M. degree 13
skills, legal 802
skits. at end of semester 608
"slander per se" 18
Slaying the Law School Dragon
    (book) 710
"Slipping [the other side] a Weenie"
    137, 513
"small claims" court, and law school
    603
Small Group Instructional Diagnosis
    268
Smith, Gary 492, 523, 531
Smith, H. Bailey 779
Smith, Winston (character in *1984*)
    731
Snoe, Joseph A. 59
Social Darwinism 45
Socrates 31, 802
Socratic Method 31, 34, 297, 712
Sokolow, David 445
Solomon 524
Sonenshein, David A. 610
Soul of the Law, The (book) 182,
    710, 716, 782
Soul Train (TV show) 752
"Sources of Soviet Conduct, The"
    (article in periodical) 378
South Texas College of Law 704
Southern University's law school 750
Southern Baptist Convention 779
Sowell, Thomas 291
space law 53

Special Commission [to review the antitrust settlement agreement between the ABA aqnd the federal government] 285

speech codes 761

Spence, Gerry 225, 636

"Spider and the Fly, The" (poem, reprinted herein) 276

Spirit of the Laws (book) 781

Sports Illustrated (magazine) 477, 525, 531

Sports Illustrated article (reprinted herein) 664 ff.

Sputnik 376

staff attorneys 639

Standard Oil Trust 778

Stanford University's law school 325

Stanford University 311

"Start with a man" 752

Washington, State 123

state-specific materials for bar review. 684

static 101

Stephens & Co. v. Albers (case) 498

Stern Gang 745

Stetson U. College of Law 235, 236

Stevens, Laura 351

Stevenson, Robert Louis 275

Stiglitz, Jan 526, 527

Stolle, Dennis P. 791

Stone, Douglas 790

"storytelling" 727

Strange Case of Dr. Jekyll and Mr. Hyde (novel) 275

Strategies and Tactics for the MBE (book) 678

Strauss, Debra 651

Structure of Scientific Revolutions, The (book) 768

Strunk, William, Jr., 568

student editions of *Restatements* 106

student organizations, in law school 607

"Student-Right-to-Know provisions of the Higher Education Act" (law review article) 306

"Student versus University" (law review article) 306

Student's Guide to Easements, Real Covenants, and Equitable Servitudes, A (book) 100, 222, 435

Student's Guide to Hearsay, A (book) 609

Student's Guide to Estates and Future Interests, A (book) 98, 435

Student's Guide to the Rule Against Perpetuities, A (book) 99

Study and Practice of Law in a Nutshell (book) 405

Study Group 151, 670, 693

study group 336

study groups/partners (students) 116

Study Guide: Introduction to Logic, A (book) 567

Study Partner 174

Study Partner - Exam Series (books) 434

"style" of the case (for briefing) 65

"SU2L" (internet postings) 399, 400

"substantial factor" test (in torts) 48

substantive law 22

Success in Law School (book) 171

Sullivan, Thomas 289

Sum & Substance (vendor) 616

summary judgment 254, 550

summary outline 112, 163, 186, 207

summer clerkship 579

Suni, Ellen Yankiver 280

super-fruitcake exam 167

Supreme Court of Georgia 705

Supreme Court of the State of Washington 123

"survival of the fittest" 45

Swift v. Gifford. (case) 495

Swindle v. Poore (case) 816

Swiss Movement (music album) 126

syllogism, in logic 543

synthesis, in Josephson Pyramid 83, 119

T

ACKNOWLEDGMENT of PERMISSIONS

Permission, where required, to reproduce passages from copyrighted material is gratefullly acknowledged for the following:

From *Learning & Evaluation in Law School* (2 vols.), submitted to the Association of American Law Schools Annual Meeting, January, 1984, Teaching Methods Section, by Michael Josephson, Copyright 1984 by Michael Josephson, reprinted by permission of the author.

From I AM RIGHT, YOU ARE WRONG by Edward de Bono, copyright (c) 1991 by The McQuaig Group, Inc. Used by permission of Viking Penguin, a division of Penguin Group (USA) Inc.

Excerpts from MEIN KAMPF by Adolf Hitler, translated by Ralph Manheim, Copyright (c) 1943, renewed 1971 by Houghton Mifflin Company. Reprinted by permission of Houghton Mifflin Company. All rights reserved.

* * *

Additional required permissions appear adjacent to the excerpted copyrighted material within the text of this book.

A Dissenting Opinion
re. the Original (1998) Edition

"Planet Law School is absolutely the worst, most destructive book about the law school experience in the past 20 years. It's beneath contempt, and I urge all of you strenuously to save your money. The book turns law students into sniveling, pathetic dweebs who turn law school into a gladiator contest. The philosophy of the book is that law school is simply a grade factory in which your job is to tear down other students, intimidate them, and treat law school like a bare-knuckled contest.

"PLS makes you a bad law student, a bad person, and a terrible lawyer. Seriously."*

"Professor" Joseph W. Rand

J.D., Georgetown, 1992
(Where he Made Law Review...after taking LEEWS)

Judicial Clerk, 1992 -1994,
  to the Hon. Frank X. Altimari,
  Second U.S. Circuit Court of Appeals (NYC)

Junior Associate, Debevoise & Plimpton, 1994-1996
  ("Frankly, I worked for two years at Debevoise & Plimpton in NY with Yale [grads] who *[sic]* I wouldn't hire to be a fuckup, excuse my language.")**

Teaching Fellow, Stanford Law School, 1996-1998

J.S.M., Stanford, 1998

Currently (2003) employed as a part-time
  (non-tenure track) legal writing / "legal process" instructor,
  with the title Assistant Adjunct Professor,
  *at The Brooklyn Law School****

---

* His posting to the public domain on the internet, at
  http://clubs.yahoo.com/clubs/guidetolawschool,
  in Message 297, on June 15, 2000

** His posting to the same public message board, in Message 331, on July 10, 2000.

*** **This Joseph W. Rand of the Brooklyn Law School should not be confused with the Joseph Rand who is a full professor at Fordham's law school.**